Fodor's

ESSENTIAL
CHILE

WELCOME TO CHILE

A long sliver of land wedged between the Andes and the Pacific, Chile packs a wealth of diverse landscapes in its narrow borders. In the north, the Atacama Desert enthralls with the world's highest geyser field and alpine salt flats dotted with flamingos. Vibrant beaches, first-rate vineyards, and bustling cities like Santiago and Valparaíso make it easy to tap into the good life in central Chile. In Patagonia, outdoor enthusiasts revel in exciting adventures, from climbing snow-capped volcanoes to trekking through the majestic Torres del Paine National Park.

TOP REASONS TO GO

★ **Stunning Scenery:** Postcard-perfect backdrops from Chiloé to San Pedro de Atacama.

★ **Wine:** Full-bodied reds and crisp whites flourish in wineries on the Andes foothills.

★ **Patagonia:** Immense blue glaciers, dramatic mountain peaks, and crystalline lakes.

★ **Outdoor Activities:** Hiking and spotting unique wildlife are just a few top options.

★ **Easter Island:** Mesmerizing stone moai loom large on this isolated island.

★ **The Central Coast:** Alluring beaches, fresh seafood, and Valparaíso's colorful hills.

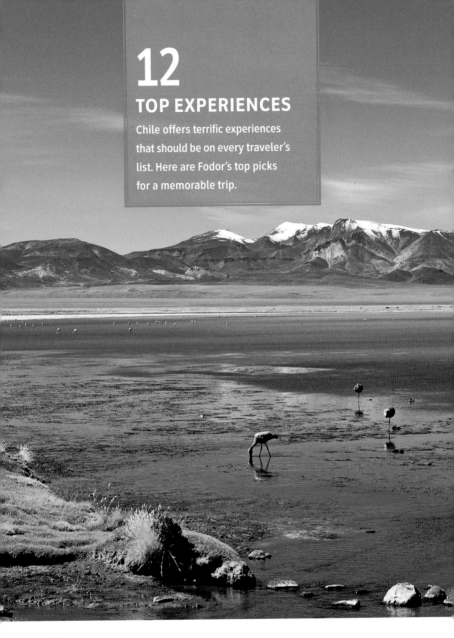

12
TOP EXPERIENCES

Chile offers terrific experiences that should be on every traveler's list. Here are Fodor's top picks for a memorable trip.

1 San Pedro de Atacama

In the heart of the Atacama Desert, San Pedro is renowned for its breathtaking scenery. Explore erupting geyser fields and blue alpine lakes, and watch multihued sunsets across lunar-like landscapes. *(Ch. 5)*

2 Chiloé's Churches

More than 150 wooden chapels dot Chiloé's rugged, misty landscapes. These historic chapels are elegant reminders of the island's missionary past. *(Ch. 8)*

3 Valparaíso

A UNESCO World Heritage Site, the port town of Valparaíso charms with its candy-color metal houses, dramatic hills overlooking the Pacific, and wooden funiculars. *(Ch. 3)*

4 Santiago

Surrounded by the Andes, Chile's vibrant capital is filled with top-notch museums, colorful crafts markets, colonial buildings, and trendy restaurants. *(Ch. 2)*

5 Wineries

Sample flavorful reds and crisp whites at the vineyards that line Chile's Central Valley. The often-stunning settings and generous tasting sessions are added bonuses. *(Ch. 2, 3, 6)*

6 Wildlife Spotting

Chile's ecosystems support a variety of wildlife. Expect to see penguins and guanacos (above) in Patagonia and alpacas and flamingos in the Atacama Desert. *(Ch. 5, 10)*

7 Seafood

You're never far from the ocean in Chile. Local restaurants serve delicious seafood throughout the country, from Patagonian king crab to mouthwatering stews. *(Ch. 1)*

8 Pablo Neruda's Houses

Even those unfamiliar with Neruda's poetry will be captivated by the whimsical objects and unusual architecture at his houses in Santiago, Valparaíso, and Isla Negra (below). *(Ch. 2, 3)*

9 Torres del Paine

This national park is Chile's premier destination for hikers and nature lovers. Its aquamarine lakes, abundant wildlife, and jagged peaks are spectacular. *(Ch. 10)*

10 Lakes and Volcanoes

Whether you prefer fishing, hiking, kayaking, climbing, or horseback riding, Chile's snow-capped volcanoes and glistening lakes offer outdoor activities for everyone. *(Ch. 7)*

11 Easter Island

Wandering among the mysterious moai, the colossal stone statues that keep watch over the most isolated island in the world, is truly awe-inspiring. *(Ch. 11)*

12 Beaches

Take your pick of gorgeous beaches—from the glamorous strands along the Central Coast to windswept beauties in the south—on the long Pacific coastline. *(Ch. 3, 4, 5)*

CONTENTS

CONTENTS

ABOUT THIS GUIDE

Fodor's Recommendations

Everything in this guide is worth doing—we don't cover what isn't—but exceptional sights, hotels, and restaurants are recognized with additional accolades. **Fodor's Choice★** indicates our top recommendations. Care to nominate a new place? Visit Fodors.com/contact-us.

Trip Costs

We list prices wherever possible to help you budget well. Hotel and restaurant price categories from **$** to **$$$$** are noted alongside each recommendation. For hotels, we include the lowest cost of a standard double room in high season. For restaurants, we cite the average price of a main course at dinner or, if dinner isn't served, at lunch. For attractions, we always list adult admission fees; discounts are usually available for children, students, and senior citizens.

Hotels

Our local writers vet every hotel to recommend the best overnights in each price category, from budget to expensive. Unless otherwise specified, you can expect private bath, phone, and TV in your room. For expanded hotel reviews.

Top Picks	Hotels &
★ **Fodor's**Choice	**Restaurants**
	⊡ Hotel
Listings	⬎ Number of
✉ Address	rooms
✉ Branch address	⍾⃝⍾ Meal plans
☎ Telephone	✕ Restaurant
🖷 Fax	⛝ Reservations
⊕ Website	⛼ Dress code
✉ E-mail	▭ No credit cards
🎫 Admission fee	$ Price
⊘ Open/closed	
times	**Other**
Ⓜ Subway	⇨ See also
⊹ Directions or	☞ Take note
Map coordinates	⚐ Golf facilities

Restaurants

Unless we state otherwise, restaurants are open for lunch and dinner daily. We mention dress code only when there's a specific requirement and reservations only when they're essential or not accepted.

Credit Cards

The hotels and restaurants in this guide typically accept credit cards. If not, we'll say so.

EUGENE FODOR

Hungarian-born Eugene Fodor (1905–91) began his travel career as an interpreter on a French cruise ship. The experience inspired him to write *On the Continent* (1936), the first guidebook to receive annual updates and discuss a country's way of life as well as its sights. Fodor later joined the U.S. Army and worked for the OSS in World War II. After the war, he kept up his intelligence work while expanding his guidebook series. During the Cold War, many guides were written by fellow agents who understood the value of insider information. Today's guides continue Fodor's legacy by providing travelers with timely coverage, insider tips, and cultural context.

EXPERIENCE CHILE

WHAT'S
WHERE

1 Santiago. Although it doesn't get the same press as Rio or Buenos Aires, this metropolis is just as cosmopolitan as its flashier South American neighbors. Ancient and modern stand side by side, and the Andes are ever present to the east.

2 The Central Coast. Anchoring the coast west of Santiago, port city Valparaíso has stunning views from the promenades atop its more than 40 hills. Next door, Viña del Mar has nonstop nightlife and the country's most popular stretch of shoreline.

3 El Norte Chico. A land of dusty brown hills, the "little north" stretches for some 700 km (435 miles) north of Santiago. The lush Elqui Valley grows the grapes used to make *pisco*, Chile's national drink. Astronomers flock here for the clear night skies.

4 El Norte Grande. Stark epitomizes Chile's great north, a region bordering Peru and Bolivia. This is the driest place on Earth, site of the stunning landscapes of San Pedro de Atacama.

5 The Central Valley. Chile's wine country lies south of Santiago, from the Valle Maipo to the Valle Maule. Some of the world's best wines come from this fertile strip of land trapped between the Pacific and the Andes. A drive through the valley is beautiful any time of year.

PERÚ
Arica
Iquique
BOLIVIA
EL NORTE GRANDE
4
Calama
San Pedro de Atacama
Antofagasta
NORTHERN CHILE
PACIFIC OCEAN
N
Copiapó
TO ← EASTER ISLAND
←10
Vallenar
EL NORTE CHICO
3
ARGENTINA
La Serena
Elqui Valley
Ovalle
THE CENTRAL COAST
Zapallar
Viña del Mar
Valparaíso
2
SANTIAGO
1
Maipo Valley
Rancagua
Curicó
Talca
Maule Valley
THE CENTRAL VALLEY
Chillán
5
Concepción
Pan American Hwy

0   100 mi
0   100 km

6 The Lake District. The austral summer doesn't get more glorious than in this compact stretch of land between Temuco and Puerto Montt. It has fast become vacation central, with resorts such as Pucón, Villarrica, and Puerto Varas beckoning visitors.

7 Chiloé. More than 40 islands sprinkled across the Golfo de Ancud make up the archipelago of Chiloé. Dozens of wooden churches, constructed by Jesuit missionaries during the colonial era, dot the landscape.

8 The Southern Coast. This stretch of coastline between the Lake District and Patagonia is one of the Earth's most remote regions. Anchoring its spine is the Carretera Austral, an amazing road trip.

9 Southern Chilean Patagonia. Look up "end of the world" in the dictionary and you might see a picture of Chile's southernmost region. It's home to some of the most stunning landscapes on the planet, including the majestic Torres del Paine.

10 Easter Island. The world's most remote island astounds with archaeology, trekking, and diving. Learn the mysterious history of the Rapa Nui and the iconic volcanic rock statues, but be prepared to leave with more questions than answers.

NEED TO KNOW

Pacific Ocean

Santiago

CHILE

Atlantic Ocean

AT A GLANCE

Capital: Santiago

Population: 17,650,114

Currency: Peso

Money: ATMs common; cash more common than credit

Language: Spanish

Country Code: 56

Emergencies: ☎ 133 for police

Driving: On the right

Electricity: 220v/50 cycles; plugs are U.K. standard three-prong or Chilean standard with three round prongs

Time: Same as New York during daylight savings time; two hours ahead otherwise

Documents: Up to 90 days with valid U.S. passport; visa on arrival required

Mobile Phones: GSM (850 and 1900 bands)

Major Mobile Companies: Movistar, Entel, Claro

WEBSITES

Chile: ⊕ us.franceguide.com

Pro Chile: ⊕ www.paris.fr/english

GETTING AROUND

✈ **Air Travel:** Santiago's Arturo Merino Benitez International Airport is the largest; others include Punta Arenas, Calama, Easter Island, and Puerto Montt.

🚢 **Boat Travel:** Boats and ferries are the best way to reach many places in Chile, such as Chiloé and the Southern Coast.

🚌 **Bus Travel:** Long-distance buses are safe and affordable. The biggest drawback is the time to cover the distances involved.

🚗 **Car Travel:** Rent a car outside of Santiago. Some regions, such as parts of the Atacama Desert, are impossible to explore without your own wheels.

PLAN YOUR BUDGET

	HOTEL ROOM	MEAL	ATTRACTIONS
Low Budget	42,000 pesos	4,000 pesos	Museum of Pre-Colombian Art, 3,500 pesos
Mid Budget	83,000 pesos	7,000 pesos	Flight of wine at a vineyard, 20,000 pesos
High Budget	139,000 pesos	11,000 pesos	Half-day trip to see Atacama Saltlake, 45,000 pesos

WAYS TO SAVE

Eat Chilean fast food. Stop at a fuente de soda (mom-and-pop shop) to feast on the ubiquitous empanada or a churrasco sandwich (thin strips of beef) for a low price.

Take a tax holiday. Hotels in Chile do not charge taxes (known as IVA) to foreign tourists. When checking the price, make sure to ask for the precio extranjero, sin impuestos (foreign rate, without taxes).

Take the fancy bus. Luxury bus travel between cities costs about one-third of what plane travel costs and is more comfortable, with reclining seats, movies, and snacks.

Hassle Factor	Medium. Flights to Santiago are frequent, and a wealth of domestic flights and luxury buses connect Santiago to Chile's far reaches.
3 days	Explore the neighborhoods of Santiago. Rent a car one day and head 90-minutes northwest from Santiago to Valparaíso or Viña del Mar.
1 week	Explore Santiago and overnight it in either Valparaíso or Viña del Mar. Fly north to spend several days in San Pedro de Atacama and the Atacama desert.
2 weeks	Spend your first week in Santiago and the north. Then head south to the Lake District and then farther south to the Patagonian city of Punta Arenas to explore Chilean Patagonia in depth.

WHEN TO GO

High Season: Across Chile, high season runs from December to March, peaking during January and February, except in Santiago, which tends to empty as most Santiaguinos take their summer holiday.

Low Season: May to September is considered the low season. The wettest months are June and July. During this time, places like Chiloé and Easter Island can feel forlorn and El Norte Grande and the desert can be cold and rainy.

Value Season: The high season tapers off in March, and April is an excellent time to visit for more tranquility. November is also quiet, but colorful. Expect vast north-to-south climatic differences because Chile's distances span the equivalent of Cancún to Hudson Bay.

BIG EVENTS

February: Chile's equivalent of Eurovision, the annual Festival Internacional de la Canción in Viña del Mar is Chile's best music festival.

February: The annual Tapati Rapa Nui festival is a two-week celebration of Easter Island's Polynesian heritage.

July: The town of La Tirana in Chile's northern Tarapac region hosts the country's most important folklore festival, Fiesta de La Tirana.

September: On September 18, Chileans all over the country celebrate their independence day with traditional activities and food.

READ THIS

■ *Residence on Earth,* Pablo Neruda. Breakthrough work by the Nobel laureate and arguably Chile's most famous literary figure.

■ *The House of Spirits,* Isabel Allende. The spiritual story of four generations of a Chilean family, filled with magic, history, and drama.

■ *Distant Star,* Roberto Bolaño. A searing short novel that takes place in the first years of Pinochet's military dictatorship.

WATCH THIS

■ *Los 33.* Hollywood blockbuster depicting the real-life rescue of 33 trapped Chilean miners.

■ *No.* A Chilean film about the creative advertising tactics that helped defeat the Pinochet dictatorship.

■ *Machuca.* Socially conscious film about the lives of two youths right before the military coup.

EAT THIS

■ *Empanada de pino*: savory pastry stuffed with meat, onions, olives, egg

■ *Paila marina*: a seafood stew served in an earthenware bowl

■ *Curanto*: a fish stew from Chiloé prepared in a pit with shellfish, meat, and potatoes

■ *Manjar*: milk caramel made from boiled condensed milk

CHILE TODAY

Politics

While the Chile of today is a democratic and peaceful country, it wasn't always that way. A military dictatorship led by General Augusto Pinochet shaped the country for 17 years, from 1973 until a return to democracy in 1990. Since then, this isolated nation at the end of the world has made great strides on several fronts. The World Bank classifies Chile's national economy as upper-middle income with only moderate debt, a drastic change from 30 years ago. Corruption is lower here than anywhere else in South America, one of the factors contributing to the country's political stability and economic development. On the political front, Chileans have democratically elected six presidents since 1990, including Chile's first female president, Michelle Bachelet, who was elected twice, and the more conservative billionaire Sebastián Piñera, who governed Chile from 2010 to 2014, and was elected again in 2017. Though income inequality is a significant concern, the number of people living below the poverty line in Chile was reduced by 18.1% (from 26% to 7.9%) from 2000 to 2017.

As for confronting Chile's recent torrid past, humans rights abusers from the dictatorship continue to be prosecuted, though the Chilean Supreme Court often reduces their sentences. These lenient decisions on ensuring punishments do not fit the crime continues to divide Chileans today.

The Environment

Unfortunately, Chile faces an array of environmental issues ranging from deforestation to intense mining, while air pollution is a serious problem in capital city Santiago. Between 1985 and 1995, some 2 million hectares of forest were lost to the pulping industry, causing high levels of soil erosion while mining aftercare is given far less attention than the actual extraction of natural resources such as copper and silver. Booming industries close to Santiago ensure the country's smog levels rank among the world's highest. Measures taken by the government to combat these issues include a carbon tax and district energy strategies. Chileans are now taking a more serious attitude toward climate change after joining the Paris Agreement in 2017 and setting two emissions reduction targets for 2023, though with just 10% of the nation's trash recycled, there's still plenty of work to be done.

Things are looking up for the country's national parks though. Via their Land Conservation Trust, North Americans and former CEOs of the outdoor clothing company Patagonia Inc., Douglas and Kristine Tompkins purchased vast swathes of land and recuperated them to create—then gift to the government—national parks. Yendegaia in the Magallanes region and Corcovado in the Lakes region are two such projects donated to Chile respectively in 2014 and 2005. A third national park, Parque Pumalín, an 988,000-acre private nature reserve near Puerto Montt, is currently in the pipeline.

Women and the Family

Over the past decade, women in Chile have become increasingly influential in both the government and the private sector. When the country's first female President, Michelle Bachelet, began her first term in 2006, she launched a campaign to promote gender equality in Chile and named women to a number of influential posts in her cabinet. During her second

term between 2013 to 2017, she proposed legislation on women's sexual reproductive rights and same-sex marriage, which is considered groundbreaking for this predominantly Catholic nation. Despite many advances, salaries for men and women remain unequal in Chile, and men typically occupy the most influential positions, particularly in the private sector.

Chilean Identity

Due in part to its overall economic success, Chilean identity is in flux. While Chileans are proud of their nationality and celebrate the *fiestas patrias* (independence-day holidays) with fervor, they also increasingly value cultural and material imports from abroad. Many Chileans flock to malls to buy the latest technological toys, and SUVs are common, despite high gas prices. Many members of the expanding middle class are moving to the suburbs and sending their children to private, bilingual schools; incorporating English words into conversations and having coffee at Starbucks have become status symbols.

Other sectors of the Chilean population, however, resist these influences, including members of the political left and indigenous groups. A number of popular Chilean artists have also commented on Chile's increasingly materialistic and outward-looking culture, including writer Alberto Fuguet and musicians Los Chancho en Piedra and Joe Vasconcellos.

An interesting example of these tensions in Chilean identity is the annual pre-Christmas charity event, the Teletón. Modeled on telethons in the United States, the Teletón is billed as "27 hours of love" and presided over by Chilean TV personality Don Francisco. Despite its growing commercialization—companies showing off with big donations to strengthen their branding—the event is remarkable not only because it raises large sums of money for children with disabilities, but also because almost all Chileans watch it and contribute funds, despite class, ethnicity, or geographic differences. The Teletón is truly an expression of modern *chilenidad* (Chileanism).

Healthy Eating

Facing an ever-growing obesity epidemic (nearly three-quarters of adult Chileans are considered obese or overweight), the Chilean goverment has decided to step in to regulate the packaging, marketing, and labeling of food sold in Chile, particularly junk food and sugary cereals. A bill was introduced in the Chilean legislature in 2007, requiring the removal of cartoon characters from food boxes and the addition of black warning labels for foods that are high in fat, sugar, salt, and calories. Due to intense opposition from major corporations, it took nearly a decade for the rules to finally be enacted (they became law in 2016), but now Chile is on the forefront of the push against the obesity epidemic. The sale of junk food is also prohibited in schools, and advertising for candy and junk food is banned during television programs aimed at young viewers. Obesity rates have yet to fall (and many think the new president will push back on these regulations), but a visit to a Chilean grocery store can be quite the experience for those used to the colors and logos (and lack of black warning labels) found in most Western grocery stores.

FLAVORS OF CHILE

Not to be outdone by neighboring Peru and Argentina, whose culinary traditions are famous throughout South America and beyond, Chilean cooking is currently undergoing a culinary renaissance with several pioneering chefs taking traditional dishes and giving them a modern touch.

Highlights of Chilean cuisine include a bounty of regional seafood, like salmon, sea bass (*corvina*), and conger eel (*congrio*). Mussels and scallops are widely available, and *locos* (abalone) and *jaiba* (crab) are frequently prepared as *chupes* (stews) or *pasteles* (pies). In addition, due to the Central Valley's temperate climate, a wide variety of fresh fruit and vegetables are available.

Fish and Shellfish

Although there isn't much variety in the way it's prepared, Chilean fish is so tasty that you probably won't mind that your options are mostly limited to grilled, baked, or fried. A trip to Punta Arenas would not be complete without trying *centolla* (king crab), nor should you leave Easter Island without savoring a yellowfin tuna ceviche (made by marinating the fish in lemon juice and adding a selection of shellfish, as well as onions, bell peppers, chili, and cilantro).

Many coastal towns have a central fish market where you can buy fresh catch or enjoy a *paila marina* (a seafood stew that is a mouthwatering combination of white fish, plus shellfish such as mussels, scallops, and razor clams, and white wine and seafood broth).

Barbecues

Asados (barbecues) are a national pastime, and any excuse—from birthdays to baptisms to national holidays—is used to start up the grill. While the uninformed might liken the country's asados to their North American counterpart, the Chilean version starts with *choripan*, a spicy sausage served in a bun and topped with *pebre*, a mixture of tomatoes, cilantro, onions, and chilies, as well as mayonnaise. Women are generally relegated to making salads (with *ensalada a la chilena* being a firm favorite) and providing drinks, including the obligatory pisco sour, while men gather around the barbecue offering advice to the official *parrillero* (designated grill master).

Merkén

Although Chilean cuisine is not renowned for its spice, the indigenous Chilean seasoning, *merkén*, is added to many of the country's dishes, providing a flavorful touch. Hailing from the native Mapuche tribe in southern Chile's IX Region, merkén is a powdered mixture of *cacho de cabra* chili, toasted coriander seeds, and salt. It is used to season everything from peanuts (for a tasty snack) to meats, such as venison and duck.

Empanadas

You can order an empanada as a starter or a main course. These come most commonly as *empanadas de pino*—stuffed with meat, onions, olives, egg, and raisins, or with *queso* (cheese); occasionally they'll be stuffed with *mariscos* (shellfish).

Fast Food

Along with the ubiquitous empanada, some of the most popular fast foods in Chile are the *completo* (a large hotdog in a bun), *churrasco* sandwich (thin strips of beef on your choice of white sliced bread or in an oversized bun), and *lomito* (a pork sandwich). Since all of them are available with a mind-boggling array of toppings, you just can't go wrong.

An *italiano* will get you a mountain of avocado, diced tomato, and mayonnaise;

the *dinámico* version adds sauerkraut to the mix; and the *chacarero* has green beans and green chilies. A common accompaniment for all of these is *ají chileno*, a spicy local version of ketchup.

Curanto

Chiloé is famous not only for its churches but also for its unique dish called *curanto*. No trip to the south would be complete without trying it, especially because the ritual of cooking the dish usually becomes an event in itself.

The stew is prepared outdoors buried in a pit in the ground, which is lined with stones that have been heated to red-hot over an open fire. Layers of shellfish, sausage, smoked pork ribs, potatoes, and pulses are added, and then covered with sodden earth and damp sacks to create a kind of pressure cooker. Everything is left to cook for an hour or so. Curanto is usually served with *milcao,* a moist and delicious potato cake steamed above the curanto; don't let its rather unappetizing gray color put you off.

Traditional

Robust and comforting Chilean dishes such as Mapuche *charquicán* (a hearty beef stew with potatoes, squash, and other vegetables) and *cazuela* (a beef or chicken casserole) are popular to ward off the chill of winter. *Humitas* (a lightly seasoned corn paste wrapped in corn leaves, normally eaten plain or sprinkled with sugar as a main course) and *pastel de choclo* (a mixture of minced beef, chicken, olives, hard-boiled egg, and raisins, topped with a layer of creamy mashed corn and served in a heavy clay bowl) are more common in the summer, when their main ingredient, corn, is in season.

Fruit

Walk into one of the *ferias* (street markets) during summer months and you will be overwhelmed by the colors and smells of all the fresh fruit. Papayas are particularly plentiful in Easter Island and La Serena, where they are used to make liquor and sweets. A wide range of berries—strawberries, raspberries, and blueberries—are grown in the central and southern regions and used to make fresh juices and tasty *kuchen* (tarts).

Custard apples (*chirimoyas*), with their mottled green skin and creamy texture, are divine on their own or can be made into juices or to flavor ice cream. It is not unusual to see succulent football-size *sandías* (watermelons) being sold at the side of the road on the highways leading to Santiago. And given Chile's reputation as a major wine-producing nation, it goes without saying that succulent table grapes are widely available.

A popular summertime drink sold on vendor carts is the traditional *mote con huesillo,* made from peaches and husked wheat, and served in a tall, chilled glass with a spoon.

Manjar

Manjar (known as *dulce de leche* in other South American countries) is a national obsession. Made from boiled condensed milk, this caramel-like sweet substance is used as a filling for everything from *alfajores* (two cookies sandwiched together and covered in chocolate) and *cuchuflís* (thin wafers rolled into cylinders) to crepes and *brazo de reina* (the Chilean equivalent of the Swiss roll).

Manjar is also sold in bar form and can be found at almost every street kiosk. It's commonly used as an ice-cream flavor, often combined with nuts or banana.

WINES OF CHILE

History

For the 19th and much of the 20th century, most Chilean wine was cheap and consumed domestically. It had been initially brought to the country by the first European settlers to make sacramental wine. With the rise of cross-Atlantic trade in the 19th century, some Chileans made fortunes in the mining industry. They returned from Europe and many began building their own châteaux, particularly on the outskirts of Santiago. French varietals such as Cabernet Sauvignon, Malbec, and Carmenère thrived in the Central Valley's rich soils and near-perfect climate.

Chilean wineries stagnated through much of the 20th century. The introduction of modern equipment such as stainless steel tanks and national and international investment in the industry made Chilean wine a tasty and affordable option in the 1980s. Continued advances in growing techniques and wine-making methods throughout the 1990s and into the 21st century have resulted in the production of excellent wines.

What to Taste

Cabernet Sauvignon. The king of reds grows well almost anywhere it's planted, but Cabernets from the Alto Maipo are particularly well balanced, displaying elegance and structure with a distinctive freshness.

Carmenère. Chile's signature red wine grape arrived in Chile during the mid-19th century from France, where it was usually a blending grape in Bordeaux. At the time, it could be found throughout Europe, but became nearly extinct in the late 19th century due to a continent-wide infestation of phylloxera, aphidlike insects. Over time Chileans forgot about it, mistaking it for a cousin of the Merlot vine.

It wasn't until the Chilean boom times of the 1990s that they realized they had a unique grape hidden among the other vines in their vineyards. It had thrived thanks to the country's unique topography, which provides natural barriers to the aphids. Today, Chile is the world's largest exporter of Carmenère wine.

Malbec. True, this is Argentina's grape, but Chile produces award-winning bottles of this red wine that have appealing elegance and balance.

Sauvignon Blanc. Due to cooler coastal climates, the region of Valparaíso is most notable for its Sauvignon Blanc, Chile's second-biggest varietal after Cabernet Sauvignon. Vineyards from Elqui to Bío Bío also produce this exciting white with fresh green fruit, crisp acidity, and often an enticing mineral edge.

Syrah. Chile produces two distinct styles of this red variety. Be sure to try both: luscious and juicy from Colchagua or enticingly spicy from coastal areas, such as Elqui or San Antonio.

Where to Go

Chile's appellation system names its valleys from north to south, but today's winegrowers stress that the climatic and geological differences between east and west are more significant. The easternmost valleys closest to the Andes tend to have less fog, more hours of sunlight, and greater daily temperature variations, which help red grapes develop deep color and rich tannins while maintaining bright acidity and fresh fruit characteristics.

On the other hand, if you're after crisp whites and bright Pinots, head to the coast, where cool fog creeps inland from the sea each morning and Pacific breezes keep the vines cool all day. Interior areas

in the Central Valley are less prone to extremes and favor varieties that require more balanced conditions, such as Merlot and Carmenère. Syrah, a relatively new grape in Chile, does well in both cold and warm climates.

Casablanca Valley. The name of this cool-climate coastal region, located 75 km (47 miles) northwest of Santiago, translates appropriately to "white house." Unsurprisingly, it turns out excellent, crisp white wines, including aromatics such as Riesling and Gewürztraminer. Several wineries in this area can be visited as day-trips from either Santiago or Valparaíso.

Central Maipo and Alto Maipo. This is the cradle of Chile's Cabernets, with more than half of its 32,000 acres of vineyards dedicated to what many believe is the country's best grape. In part due to its proximity to the capital of Santiago, this region is the most productive and the easiest to visit for most visitors.

While Alto Maipo extends into the foothills, boasting a microclimate ideal for viticulture, Central Maipo borders the Maipo River and is much warmer with less rainfall, allowing for the growth of highly praised Carmenère wines as well as Cabernet.

Colchagua Valley. The wines of this well-known Chilean region are regular headliners on the world's top lists, including robust red varietals such as Malbec, Carmenère, Syrah, and Cabernet, but also white Chardonnay and Sauvignon Blanc varietals as well. The Colchagua Valley is roughly 180 km (110 miles) to the south of Santiago, and the vineyards stretch from the western Coastal Range to the eastern foothills of the Andes Mountains. The best town to stay when exploring this area is the picturesque Santa Cruz.

Curicó Wine Valley. Thanks to its varied climate and fertile, high-yielding soil, more than 30 varieties of grapes—more than anywhere else in the country—can be found in Curicó's vineyards. The dominant grapes are Cabernet Sauvignon and Sauvignon Blanc in this region, which is located approximately 200 km (124 miles) south of Santiago.

Maule Valley. Chile's largest wine-growing region is also one of its oldest and most diverse. Roughly 250 km (155 miles) south of Santiago, the Maule Valley is home to both traditional, family-run vineyards and innovative, modern wineries, with an increasing focus on sustainable, organic wine-making techniques.

Tips for Visiting Chilean Wineries

1. The number one wine travel rule in Chile? Make reservations. Unlike wineries in the United States, many wineries are not equipped to receive drop-in visitors.

2. Don't expect wineries to be open on Sunday or holidays.

3. The distances between wineries can be longer than they look on the map. Allot plenty of travel time, and plan on no more than three or four wineries per day.

4. Contact the wine route offices in the region you're visiting. They can be helpful in coordinating visits to wineries.

5. Hire a driver, or choose a designated driver.

6. Keep in mind there are not only many different types of wineries available to visit, from family-run small businesses to large, mechanized operations, but also different ways to see them. Some wineries offer everything from thrill-seeking zip line courses to leisurely bike tours.

HIGHLIGHTS OF PATAGONIA

Patagonia is a wild and rugged land filled with breathtaking landscapes and eye-catching wildlife. There are few other places in the world where you can feel such a great isolation and vast emptiness, and yet see waters teeming with wildlife; visit *huasos* (Chilean cowboys) living on windswept estancias; and get so close to ancient glaciers that you can actually walk inside these ice cathedrals. With an area that spans over a million square kilometers between Chile and Argentina, be prepared to gasp at the majesty of the Patagonian wild.

Glaciers

The Patagonia ice field covers much of the southern end of the Andean mountain range, straddling the Argentina–Chile border. The glaciers that spill off the high-altitude ice field are basically rivers of slow moving ice and snow that grind and push their way across the mountains, crushing soft rock and sculpting granite peaks.

Most of Patagonia's glaciers spill into lakes, rivers, or fjords. Chunks of ice calve off the face of the glacier into the water, a dramatic display of nature's power that you can view at several locations. There are multiple options for viewing these majestic icebergs, whether by strapping on a set of crampons for a trek, horseback riding over the pampas, boating, 4x4 driving, or kayaking through the fjords. Some are accessible only through boat tours or by helicopter, though the stunning rugged scenery makes the travel time more than worthwhile.

Glaciar Grey, Parque Nacional Torres del Paine, Chile. Perhaps the most stunning of the many glaciers in this must-see national park, Glaciar Grey, with its fragmented icebergs, is an easy and rewarding site to hike to here.

Glaciar Martial, Ushuaia, Argentina. In a mountain range just above Ushuaia, this glacier can be reached by a panoramic ski lift. There are lovely hikes all around the glacier with great views.

Glaciar Perito Moreno, El Calafate, Argentina. One of the continent's most awe-inspiring sights, this majestic glacier is renowned for its sparkling blue facade, accessibility, and the blocks of ice that spill dramatically off it into the nearby lake.

Upsala Glacier, El Calafate, Argentina. Part of the Los Glaciares National Park in Argentina, the Upsala Glacier is the largest glacier in South America, and one of the most visually impressive. It is accessible only by boat.

Mountain Trekking

In Patagonia, mountains mean the Andes, a relatively young range that stretches for more than 4,000 miles down South America. Some of the most breathtaking summits are in southern Patagonia. Glacial activity has played an important role in chiseling the most iconic Patagonian peaks. The spires that form the distinctive skylines of Torres del Paine and the Fitzroy range are solid columns that were created when rising glaciers ripped away weaker rock, leaving only hard granite skeletons that stand rigid at the edge of the ice fields. There is no shortage of paths in the region that will get you up close and personal with these impressive peaks, and provide you with unobstructed views of the spectacular scenery.

Mt. Fitzroy and Cerro Torre, El Chaltén, Argentina. More than a dozen well-marked routes are available here within the Parque Nacional Los Glaciares. Awe-inspiring views of this massive granite structure, the highest mountain in the park, are well worth getting up early for.

Osorno Volcano, Lake District, Chile. Visible from every point in Osorno, the volcano reaches a height of 2,661 meters (8,730 feet) above sea level and takes six hours to ascend, usually in an organized group with a local guide.

Parque Nacional Torres del Paine, Chile. This national park offers wild rock climbing and no shortage of wildlife-spotting, including condors and guanacos, a smaller cousin of the alpaca and llama.

Penguin Colonies

The best time to see penguins is from November through February, which coincides with the best weather in coastal Patagonia. Most of the penguins you'll see in Patagonia are Magellanic penguins, black-and-white color birds that gather in large breeding colonies on the beaches here in summer and retreat to warmer climes during winter. They're smaller than the Emperor penguins in Antarctica, standing about 30 inches tall and weighing between 15 and 20 pounds. Due to oil spills and the effects of climate change, Magellanic penguins have been classified as a threatened species.

Some of the most convenient and impressive penguin colonies to visit are:

Isla Magdalena, Chile. Home to 150,000 Magellanic penguins, this one-square-kilometer island is the site of one of the largest such colonies in southern Chile. It's an easy boat ride away from Punta Arenas.

Puñihuil, Chiloé, Chile. Southwest of Ancud in Chiloé, the three small islets of Puñihuil are home to an abundant colony of Humboldt and Magellanic penguins.

National Parks

There is no better place to experience the majesty of Patagonia than in a national park. The most spectacular national parks include:

Los Glaciares National Park, Argentina. A UNESCO World Heritage site, Los Glaciares National Park is home to stunning lakes and natural scenery. About 40% of it is covered by ice fields that contain nearly 50 glaciers.

Parque Nacional Tierra del Fuego, Argentina. Accessible by car or train, this is the southernmost national park in the world. There are breathtaking wildlife refuges, mountain-ringed lakes, strikingly green lagoons, peat bogs, and wild cherry forests.

Parque Nacional Torres del Paine, Chile. Chile's most popular national park offers classic hikes with spectacular views of waterfalls and glaciers, and unusual wildlife like the guanaco and the *ñandú* (rhea). Its most spectacular attractions are its lakes of turquoise and emerald waters; and the Cuernos del Paine ("Paine Horns"), the geological showpiece of the immense granite massif.

Wildlife Spotting

Other than Magellanic penguins, animals you might see in Patagonia include whales, Andean condors, pumas, Albatross, and sea lions. Be sure to pack a good pair of binoculars, sunglasses, and sunblock to protect yourself from the glare of the sun's rays.

Torres del Paine. The elusive puma isn't as shy as you'd think and can often be spotted in this Patagonian national park. Ask your hotel about specific puma tracking tours.

GREAT ITINERARIES

THE CITY, THE BEACH, AND THE DESERT IN 10 DAYS

Days 1–3: Santiago

No matter where you fly from, you'll likely arrive in Chile's capital early in the morning after an all-night flight. Unless you can sleep the entire night on a plane and arrive refreshed at your destination, reward yourself with a couple of hours' shut-eye at your hotel before setting out to explore the city.

The neighborhoods, small and large, that make up Santiago warrant at least a day and a half of exploration. A trip up one of the city's hills—like **Cerro San Cristóbal** in Parque Metropolitano or **Cerro Santa Lucía**—lets you survey the capital and its grid of streets. Any tour of a city begins with its historic center; the cathedral and commercial office towers on the **Plaza de Armas** reflect Santiago's old and new architecture, while the nearby bohemian quarter of **Bellavista,** with its bustling markets and colorful shops, was built for walking. But Santiago's zippy, efficient metro can also whisk you to most places in the city and lets you cover ground more quickly. Avoid taking the metro during the morning and evening rush hour.

Alas, if you're here in the winter, gloomy smog can hang over the city for days at a time. Your first instinct may be to flee, and one of the nearby wineries in the **Valle de Maipo** will welcome you heartily. If it's winter and you brought your skis, **Valle Nevado,** Chile's largest downhill resort area, lies a scant 65 km (40 miles) outside Santiago.

Days 4–6: Valparaíso and the Central Coast

A 90-minute drive west from Santiago takes you to the Central Coast and confronts you with one of Chilean tourism's classic choices: Valparaíso or Viña del Mar. If you fancy yourself one of the glitterati, go for Viña and its chic cafés and restaurants and miles of beach. But "Valpo" offers you the charm and allure of a port city, rolling hills, and cobblestone streets with better views of the sea.

Here's a solution: Why not do them both? Only 10 km (6 miles) separate the two cities, and it's easy to travel between them, whether by taxi or the metro system that connects them. Besides, they offer their own distinct charms.

Spend the first day in **Valparaíso,** where you can ride the funiculars up the city's many hills, wander through streets lined with brightly painted houses, and feast on some of the country's freshest seafood near the port. Don't miss a visit to **La Sebastiana,** one of Pablo Neruda's houses. From the poet's bedroom window is one of the best panoramic views of Valparaíso that you'll encounter.

The following day, make your way to **Viña del Mar** and prepare to soak in the rays. Some of the best and most glamorous beaches in the country can be found here. When you've had enough sun, you can stroll through the numerous shopping galleries in downtown Viña.

Round out your visit the following day with a trip to the charming coastal town of **Isla Negra,** 90 km (56 miles) south of Valparaíso. The unmistakable highlight is another of Pablo Neruda's houses, easily the best of his three residences. It's chock-full of artifacts and curios from his many travels and overlooks a rough part of the

Pacific Ocean. Head back to Santiago at night in preparation for the next leg of the journey.

Days 7–10: San Pedro de Atacama

You certainly *could* drive the nearly 1,500 km (900 miles) to Chile's vast El Norte Grande, but a flight from Santiago to **Calama,** then a quick overland drive to **San Pedro de Atacama** will take you no more than 3½ hours. This is one of the most-visited towns in Chile, and for good reason: it sits right in the middle of the Atacama Desert, with sights all around.

You'll need at least two days here to do justice to the alpine lakes, ancient fortresses, Chile's largest salt flat, and the surreal landscape of the **Valle de la Luna.** Your best bet is to find a reputable tour agency in San Pedro—and there are many—and make at least two day trips: one to the **Geysers del Tatio,** which requires a pick-up around 4 in the morning; and one to the **Reserva Nacional Los Flamencos,** where you can watch flamingos fly over jagged salt flats and cobalt lakes.

Just remember that you'll be in a high-altitude zone, so it's best to take it easy during your first day here, wandering through the charming town and popping into the numerous gift shops. Don't miss the stunning sunsets over the nearby Valle de la Luna.

Transportation

It's quite easy, and even preferable, to explore Santiago, Viña del Mar, and Valparaíso using public transportation, and a car is not needed in San Pedro de Atacama if you use tour agencies. Once in San Pedro de Atacama, you can hook up with various tour agencies to visit sights not accessible by bus. There are frequent flights from Santiago to Calama and back.

HIGHLIGHTS OF PATAGONIA IN 14 DAYS

Days 1 and 2: Santiago

Arrive in Santiago early the morning of your first day. After a brief rest, set out to explore the city's museums, shops, and green spaces using the power of your own two feet and the capital's efficient metro.

Days 3–6: The Lake District

Head south 675 km (420 miles) from Santiago on a fast toll highway to **Temuco,** the gateway to Chile's Lake District, or even better, take one of the frequent hour-long flights. Temuco and environs are one of the best places in the region to learn about the indigenous Mapuche culture.

About an hour south, and just 15 minutes apart on the shores of **Lago Villarrica,** lie the twin resort towns of flashy, glitzy

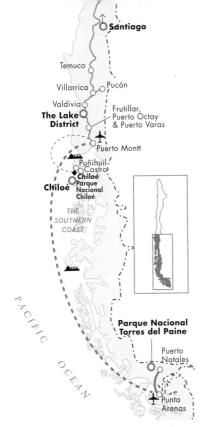

UNESCO World Heritage Site churches in surrounding towns as possible.

For those seeking to get away from it all, set out for a day-hike in **Parque Nacional Chiloé**, with its heavily forested trails and dramatic lookout points. Roughly 29 km (18 miles) southwest of the town of Ancud, you can visit **Puñihuil** and its colony of Humboldt and Magellanic penguins. Don't forget to dine on the island's famous curanto at night.

Days 10–14: Parque Nacional Torres del Paine

After taking a return ferry and bus ride back to Puerto Montt, take a spectacular morning flight over the Andes to the Patagonian city of **Punta Arenas**. On the next day take a bus north to **Puerto Natales**, gateway to the **Parque Nacional Torres del Paine**. You'll need at least two days to wander through the wonders of the park. On your final day, head back to Punta Arenas, stopping en route at one of the penguin sanctuaries, and catch an afternoon flight to Santiago.

THE ULTIMATE CHILEAN WINE TRIP IN 6 DAYS

Days 1 and 2: Santiago and the Maipo Valley

Start your oenophile adventure in the capital city of **Santiago**, from where some of Chile's best wineries are only a cork's throw away in the **Maipo Valley**. Look for bilingual tour availability and accessibility to public transit. The most fun time of year to visit is during the February to May harvest season, as many festivals and celebrations are held with unique opportunities to participate.

Book your winery tours at least 24 hours ahead to ensure the availability of an English-speaking guide. Private, personalized

Pucón and quiet, pleasant **Villarrica**. Base yourself in the latter if you're in peso-saving mode. Drive south through the region from the graceful old city of **Valdivia** to **Puerto Montt**, stopping at the various resort towns. Frutillar, Puerto Octay, and Puerto Varas still bear testament to the Lake District's German-Austrian-Swiss immigrant history. Be sure to make time for one of the region's many hot springs.

Days 7–9: Chiloé

From Puerto Montt, drive or take a bus 65 kilometers (40 miles) southeast toward Pargua and catch the ferry to Chiloé. Base yourself in **Castro**, the capital, which allows for easy side trips through the island. Take a full day to photograph the rows of multicolor homes on stilts, called *palafitos*, in Castro, and then visit as many of the

tours may be available depending on the establishment. Our top recommendations include **Viña Undurraga**, started and run by the same family since 1885; **Viña Concha y Toro**, Chile's largest wine producer and perhaps its most entertaining winery tour, with a visit to the Casillero del Diablo, the famed wine cellar where the devil supposedly dwells; and **Viña Santa Rita**, with an impressive on-site museum and Pompeiian-style manor.

Days 3 and 4: Casablanca Valley

From Santiago, it's a mere 45-minute drive to the **Casablanca Valley.** Just three decades ago, the land here was considered inhospitable for vineyards, but now winemakers have discovered that the valley's proximity to the sea is its main asset, because cooler temperatures give the grapes more time to develop flavor as they ripen.

The three can't-miss vineyards in this area are **Casas del Bosque,** which offers a vineyard tour in an old wagon; **Viña Matetic,** whose stunning bodega resembles a bunker worthy of a James Bond villain; and **House of Morande,** which is one of the valley's oldest wineries and a superb place to stop for lunch during your tours.

If you grow tired of vineyard-hopping, make your way to **Viña del Mar,** a mere 30 kilometers (18.6 miles) away from the heart of the valley. It's a great place to spend the night while exploring the Casablanca Valley. You can walk along the beach in the morning and then indulge in the vibrant nightlife when you've returned in the evening.

Days 5 and 6: Colchagua Valley

From Santiago, drive 90 minutes south to the **Colchagua Valley.** Stay overnight at an inn or B&B in **Santa Cruz,** the main town of the valley, with an attractive central square and several craft shops. There are numerous vineyards to visit throughout this valley, but one of the better ones to start with is **Viña Montes.** It's known for its deep reds, crisp whites, and feng shui design principles. Nearby, **Viña Lapostolle-Clos Apalta** is housed in one of the most handsome pieces of architecture in Chile: the barrel-stave-shape beams rising impressively above the vineyards create a wooden nest for the winery, which is built into a hillside to facilitate the gravity-flow process.

Be sure to make time to visit **Viña Santa Cruz,** which is really an entire wine complex. It features a cable car, astronomical center, and indigenous museum. Plan to spend several hours here.

Transportation

There are a variety of options available. If you prefer the independence of a self-guided tour, rent a vehicle in Santiago and pick up a map of the Chilean wine region, which is available at many bookstores and wine shops. From Santiago to Casablanca, you can take a public bus and then a taxi from the terminal to your wineries of choice.

Most organized tours are offered as either half- or full-day, and include guides as well as meals. There are alternatives to the tedium of bus tours; options can combine horseback riding, bicycling, and even zip-lining along with your wine tastings.

HISTORY OF CHILE

Precolonial Chile

The indigenous groups living in Chile before the arrival of the Spanish can be categorized as the pre-Incan cultures in the north, the Mapuche in the region between the Choapa River and Chiloé, and the Patagonian cultures in the extreme south. Although the Incan Empire extended into Chile, the Mapuche successfully resisted their incursions; there is a debate about how much of Chile the Incans conquered.

The **geoglyphs** constructed between AD 500 and 1400 in the mountains along ancient northern trade routes are some of the most important in the world. The **Chinchorro mummies**, relics of the Chinchorro people who lived along the northern coast, are the oldest in the world, dating from 6000 BC. They are visible at the Museo Arqueológico de San Miguel de Azapa near Arica. The **Museo Arqueológico Gustavo Le Paige** in San Pedro de Atacama has an impressive collection of precolonial and colonial objects.

In Temuco, the **Museo Regional de la Araucanía** provides a fairly good introduction to Mapuche art, culture, and history. Temuco and its environs also offer a sense of modern Mapuche life. Farther south, the **Museo Salesiano de Maggiorino Borgatello** in Punta Arenas has an interesting collection of artifacts from various Patagonian cultures. Finally, in Santiago, the **Museo Chileno de Arte Precolombino** has an excellent collection of indigenous artifacts from Mexico to Patagonia.

Colonial Chile

While Ferdinand Magellan and Diego de Almagro both traveled to Chile earlier, it was Pedro de Valdivia who founded Santiago in 1541. Before being killed in battle by a Mapuche chief, Valdivia established a number of other important towns in

Chile as well. Yet the Mapuche successfully resisted Spanish conquest and colonization, ruling south of the Bío Bío River until the 1880s.

The **Plaza de Armas** is where Pedro de Valdivia founded Santiago in 1541. The **Iglesia San Francisco** is Santiago's oldest structure dating from 1586, although it was partially rebuilt in 1698 and expanded in 1857. The **Casa Colorada** is a well-preserved example of colonial architecture. It was the home of Mateo de Toro y Zambrano, a Creole businessman and Spanish soldier, and now houses the Museo de Santiago. On Chiloé near Ancud, the **San Antonio Fort** constructed in 1786 is all that remains of Spain's last outpost in Chile.

Independence

September 18, 1810—Chilean Independence Day—is when a group of prominent citizens created a junta to replace the Spanish government. However, full independence was achieved several years later in 1818 with the victory of the Battle of Maipú by Bernardo O'Higgins and José de San Martín. Chiloé remained under Spanish control until 1826.

The **Temple of Maipú** on the outskirts of Santiago was constructed in honor of the Virgin of Carmen, patron saint of Santiago, after the Battle of Maipú. While the original temple was destroyed, its foundations still exist near the new structure built in the 1950s.

The **Palacio Cousiño** in Santiago, built by one of Chile's most important families in 1871, provides an excellent sense of how the elite lived in an independent, modernizing Chile. Note that the building suffered significant damage during the February 2010 earthquake and is currently closed until further notice.

Military Dictatorship

In 1973, Chile's first socialist president, Salvador Allende, was overthrown by a military coup by the Chilean Air Force. Some of the bullet holes from their bombardment of the **Palacio de La Moneda,** where Allende committed suicide after refusing to surrender, can still be seen today. Today, this building is the site of the country's presidential offices; construction first began on it in 1784.

A junta led in part by Augusto Pinochet, the commander-in-chief of the Chilean army, seized power and began to detain thousands of people whom they considered potential subversives, including political activists, journalists, professors, and trade unionists. The junta used the **Estadio Nacional** in Santiago as a prison camp and torture site for tens of thousands of detainees. The stadium is considered a national site and has since been renovated and expanded. First-division soccer matches and large concerts are now held in this stadium.

The most important site used by the Chilean secret police to torture and interrogate political prisoners during the Pinochet era is on the outskirts of Santiago. Once a spot where artists and progressives would meet up, **Villa Grimaldi** held more than 4,000 detainees in the mid-1970s. Today, it is a memorial site and peace park featuring a wall of names of its prisoners and a memory room containing personal items and mementos of the people who "disappeared" at Villa Grimaldi.

Two other prominent sites that the Pinochet regime used for torture and imprisonment are found in the Atacama Desert to the north of Santiago. In **Chacabuco,** a ghost town roughly 70 km (43 miles) north of Antofagasta in El Norte Grande,

the regime established a notorious prison camp, and the artwork of its former inhabitants still lines the walls. Farther north, around 168 km (100 miles) north of Iquique, **Pisagua** was where the Pinochet regime established a camp for missing persons and political prisoners. The camp still haunts the small town even now.

One of the largest cemeteries in Latin America, the **Cementerio General de Santiago,** is an important national monument that reveals a lot about traditional Chilean society. Most Chilean presidents are buried here, with the notable exception of Pinochet. Salvador Allende, who was originally buried in a makeshift grave outside of Viña del Mar, was transported here when democracy was restored to the country. His grave, along with the memorials for those disappeared during the Pinochet regime, make this cemetery an important pilgrimage site.

CHILE MADE EASY

How expensive is Chile?

Chile is among the most expensive countries in Latin America. Prices of hotels and transportation go up considerably from mid-December through mid-March and again in July and August.

What should I pack for a trip to Chile?

Many of Chile's attractions are outdoors, so packing sturdy, all-weather gear is a good idea. Sunglasses, a hat, and sunscreen are all musts because the ozone layer over Chile is particularly deteriorated. For your electronic gear, keep in mind that you will need a two-pronged plug adaptor and that voltage in Chile is 220 volts, 50 cycles (220V 50Hz).

Do I need to or should I rent a car? Is driving hectic?

You definitely don't need to rent a car in Santiago because you can take a combination of taxis, buses, and the metro to get around town. For day trips from Santiago to the coast or wine country, renting a car is probably the most convenient option, although buses to these destinations are also frequent and reasonably priced.

If you do rent a car, be aware of one-way streets and signs indicating right of way. You are not allowed to turn on red at a stoplight unless there is a specific sign indicating otherwise. To drive legally in Chile you need an international driver's license as well as your valid national license, although car rental companies and police do not often enforce this.

Can I drive between Chile and Argentina?

Yes, you can drive between Chile and Argentina, but there are a few things to keep in mind. First, because it is an international border, be sure to have your passport, along with your driver's license. Also, special insurance is required.

If you rent a car, the rental company will provide you with a permit to drive into Argentina (for an extra price, of course), which includes all the necessary paperwork to cross the border (including the insurance). The permit must be requested several days in advance of the day the rental begins. The rental car must be returned in Chile, and the permit is valid for one exit to Argentina and one entrance into Chile. Common border crossings include the route from Santiago to Mendoza and Valdivia to Bariloche.

Do U.S. citizens still have to pay a reciprocity fee upon entering Chile?

No. Until early 2014, all U.S. citizens entering Chile for the first time had to pay a reciprocity fee of US$161 before passing customs. Because the United States recently made Chile a country eligible for its U.S. Visa Waiver Program, Chile has dropped the reciprocity fee for U.S. citizens.

Do I need to speak Spanish?

It is always helpful to speak the language of the country where you are traveling, but it is less crucial in Chile. Particularly in Santiago, there is generally at least one person who can speak basic English in most restaurants, hotels, and shops. However, if you plan on traveling to less tourist-oriented destinations, fewer people will speak English, and you may need to resort to nonverbal means of communication or trying out those basic Spanish phrases you've learned.

SANTIAGO

WELCOME TO SANTIAGO

TOP REASONS TO GO

★ **The Andes:** Towering, jagged peaks over 4,572 meters (15,000 feet) high keep you oriented in Santiago, where "uptown" is always due east, toward the mountains.

★ **Great crafts markets:** Fine woolen items, lapis lazuli jewelry, carved wooden and terra-cotta bowls, and other handicrafts from the length of the country are bountiful in Santiago.

★ **Vibrant food scene:** Long considered a destination for the non-foodie, change is afoot in Santiago. Restaurants showcase some of Chile's finest agricultural products with innovative and traditional preparations, and many local ingredients are now given reputable "Denomination of Origin" status.

★ **World-class wineries:** Santiago is in the Maipo Valley, the country's oldest wine-growing area, home to some of Chile's largest and most traditional wineries. Concha y Toro and Santa Rita are within an hour's drive of the city, as is the lovely Casablanca Valley.

Pedro de Valdivia wasn't very creative when he mapped Santiago, sticking to the simple grid pattern typical of most colonial towns. The city didn't grow much larger before the meandering Río Mapocho impeded these plans, but you may be surprised at how orderly the city remains.

1 Santiago Centro. This area is undergoing a renaissance. The areas around La Moneda presidential palace and the Plaza de Armas are where you find most of the monuments and museums as well as innovative spaces such as Centro Cultural Palacio la Moneda.

2 La Alameda. Also known as Avenida Libertador Bernardo O'Higgins, La Alameda marks the southern boundary of Santiago Centro and is lined with sights that include San Francisco church, the Universidad de Chile, and Gabriela Mistral Cultural Center (GAM).

3 Bellas Artes and Lastarria. The Bellas Artes area houses a cluster of restaurants, stores, and two art museums. Lastarria, named after the area's famed cobblestoned street, has now become a focal point for foodies.

4 Parque Forestal. A leafy park along the banks of the Río Mapocho gives this tranquil district its name. It's been a prime spot for luxury and boutique hotels. Families and sporty types make the most of the green space on weekends.

5 Bellavista and Parque Metropolitano. On the north side of the Río Mapocho, Bellavista is Santiago's "left bank," a bohemian district of cafés, small restaurants, shops, and one of the homes of poet Pablo Neruda.

6 Parque Quinta Normal Area. Slightly off the beaten track in western Santiago, the Quinta Normal is one of the largest parks in the city and home to four museums, including one featuring old locomotives.

7 Vitacura. Well-heeled Vitacura is home to swanky restaurants, high rises, and posh boutiques.

8 Las Condes. This business area, specifically Isidora Goyenechea street, has upscale eateries, design and gift shops, and a few high-end hotels.

9 Providencia. This is where most tourists go out at night. It's slightly less urban and historical than the center and is divided into smaller neighborhoods linked by a metro station.

2

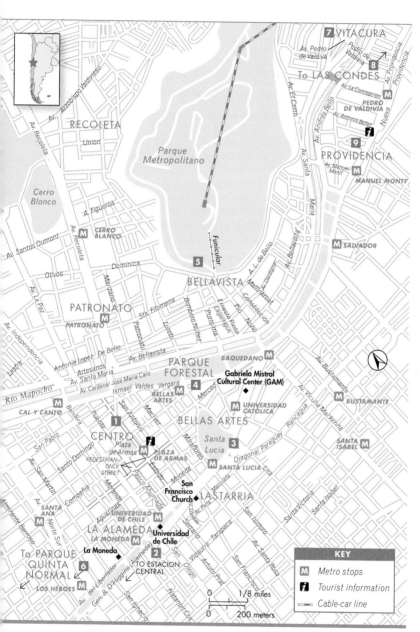

RECOLETA

Union

Cerro
Blanco

Av. Arzobispo Valdivirese

Av. Recoleta

Av. Santos Dumont

Av. La Paz

Av. Independencia

Lastra

CERRO
BLANCO

A. Figueroa

Olivos

Dominica

PATRONATO

PATRONATO

Parque
Metropolitano

Funicular

5

Av. El Cerro

VITACURA **7**

Av. Pedro
de Valdivia

Pedro de
Valdivia **8**

Av. Providencia

To LAS CONDES

Av. La Concepción

PEDRO
DE VALDIVIA

Av. Andrés Bello

Av. Antonio Bello

Nueva

i

9

PROVIDENCIA

Av. Manuel
Montt

MANUEL MONTT

Av. Santa

María

SALVADOR

Av. Bellavista

BELLAVISTA

Ernesto Pinto
Lagarrigue

Pío
Nono

Constitución

Purísima

A. L. de Bello

Mallinkrodt

Av. Dardignac

Av. Bustamante

Santa María

Marzano

Sta. Filomena

Bombero Núñez

Loreto

Antonia López De Bello

Río Mapocho

Artesanos

Av. Santa María

Av. Cardenal José María Caro

Ismael Valdés Vergara

Manuel

PARQUE
FORESTAL

BAQUEDANO M

Gabriela Mistral
Cultural Center (GAM)

4

Av. Vicuña Mackenna

BUSTAMANTE

CENTRO **1**

Plaza
de Armas

i

PLAZA
DE ARMAS

PEDESTRIAN-
ONLY
STREET

San Antonio

Puente

Bandera

Estado

BELLAS
ARTES

Merced

BELLAS ARTES

Santa
Lucía **3**

Diagonal Paraguay

UNIVERSIDAD
CATÓLICA M

SANTA LUCÍA M

Lira

Rancagua

SANTA
ISABEL M

CAL Y CANTO M

San Pablo

Santo Domingo

Compañía

Agustinas

Moneda

San
Francisco
Church

UNIVERSIDAD
DE CHILE M

LA ALAMEDA

LA MONEDA M

Universidad
de Chile

La Moneda

To PARQUE
QUINTA
NORMAL **6**

LOS HÉROES M

Av. del Libertador

Gen. B. O'Higgins (Alameda)

To ESTACIÓN
CENTRAL

Morandé

Teatinos

Miraflores

MacIver

San Diego

Arturo Prat

San Francisco

San Isidro

Santa Rosa

Santa Victoria

Santa Isabel

SANTA
ANA M

Av. San Martín

Norte Sur

ALMIRANTE BARROSO

Av. Brasil

Natanial Cox

San Ignacio

Paseo Ahumada

Serrano

Londres

Alonso Ovalle

Marcoleta

LASTARRIA

Tarapacá

Vidaurre

Copiapó

José Miguel de la Barra

Santa Lucía

San Isidro

Santa Rosa

0 ———— 1/8 miles

0 ———— 200 meters

Updated
by Sorrel
Moseley-
Williams

Plazas, parks, and fountains share space with street performers, urban photographers, and historical buildings in
downtown Santiago. Underneath it all, an ultramodern
metro system whisks residents to and from work and play. It
is this mix of old and new, neo-baroque architecture and
glass towers, and haute cuisine and streetside sopaipillas
(fried dough) that makes Santiago what it is today. All over,
the city's fairly bursting with restaurants, cafés, and hotels.

Santiago has come a long way from the triangular patch of land
hemmed in by the Río Mapocho (which has since been rerouted, and
has only one branch), when the city was founded by Pedro de Valdivia
in 1541. Today the area of the original municipality is known as Santiago Centro, and is just one of 32 *comunas* (districts)—each with its
own distinct personality—that make up the city.

In the city, the comuna names rule conversation, and can make or break
friendships. The most moneyed semi-central districts like Las Condes,
Vitacura, and to a lesser extent, Providencia and Ñuñoa are considered
part of the *barrio alto* (literally "high neighborhood, referring to both
topography and social strata). It's considered more bohemian to live
and spend time in Santiago Centro, particularly the neighborhoods of
Lastarria, Bellas Artes, near Parque Forestal, or even down in Barrio
Brasil, where some of the city's oldest architecture is found.

That is not to say that well-heeled Santiaguinos do not spend time
downtown. Santiago Centro is central to many businesses, and all the
bank branches and government architecture is here, including the stock
market (though trading is mostly done online now). It's also home to
several arts and performance spaces including the Universidad de Chile
Theater, Municipal Theater, and the Gabriela Mistral Cultural Center.

Parks are a major meeting point for friends and families in the city,
including Parque Quinta Normal (at the metro of the same name),
Parque O'Higgins, where the military parade is held every year for
Fiestas Patrias, Parque Forestal, and Parque Metropolitano, commonly
referred to as Cerro San Cristobal, the larger of the two hills that overlooks the city. Farther uptown in Vitacura, Parque Bicentenario, with its
waterfowl feeding ponds and dog park, attracts families with children.
In most city parks you can find people playing *fútbol*, riding bikes, or
just enjoying the green space as a retreat from what can be a busy city.

And it is busy. Santiago today is home to 6.5 million people—more than
a third of the country's total population. The city continues to spread
outward to the barrios altos east of the center, and all over the city there
are cranes, signaling the rise of new office and apartment buildings. The
tallest building in Santiago and in South America—making it a good
orientation landmark—is the nearly 1,000-foot-tall Costanera Center,

steps from the Tobalaba metro station and home to a flashy, upscale mall, which some consider a shrine to Chilean consumerism.

Yet, residents are just as likely to run into each other at the supermarket, Vega, weekend fruit and vegetable markets called *ferias*, or in the neighborhood plaza. When they do, they stop to greet each other and talk for at least a minute or two, because even though at times it's a hectic city, in many ways Santiago is just a giant small town at heart.

2

PLANNING

WHEN TO GO

Santiaguinos tend to abandon their city every summer during the school holidays that run from the end of December to early March. February is a particularly popular vacation time, when nearly everybody who's anybody is out of town. If you're not averse to the heat, this can be a good time for walking around the city; otherwise, spring and fall are better choices, as the weather is more comfortable. Santiago is at its prettiest in spring, when gentle breezes sweep in to clean the city's air of winter smog and when the violet-hued jacaranda and the yellow-blooming *aromo* (a type of acacia) begin to flower.

Spring and fall are also good times to drive up through the Cajón del Maipo, when the scenery is at its peak. In spring, the plum and cherry trees are in bloom, and in fall, you get some foliage change, and maybe an early snow. Also in fall, the vineyards around the city celebrate *vendimia*—the grape harvest—with colorful festivals that are an opportunity to try traditional Chilean cuisine as well as some of the country's renowned wines. Winters in the city aren't especially cold—temperatures rarely dip below freezing—but days can be gray and gloomy, and air pollution is at its worst, making it a good time to head to the coast or mountains.

PLANNING YOUR TIME

Santiago is a compact city, small enough to visit all the must-see sights in a few days. Consider the weather when planning your itinerary—on the first clear day your destination should be Parque Metropolitano, where you are treated to exquisite views from Cerro San Cristóbal. After a morning gazing at the Andes, head back down the hill and spend the afternoon wandering the bohemian streets of Bellavista, with a visit to Nobel laureate Pablo Neruda's Santiago residence, La Chascona. Check out one of the neighborhood's colorful eateries, or take a side trip down to Patronato for a falafel or some cheap clothes shopping.

The next day, head to Parque Forestal, a leafy park that runs along the Río Mapocho. Be sure to visit the lovely old train station, Estación Mapocho. After lunch at the Mercado Central, or across the river at Vega or Vega Chica, cover the city's colonial past in Santiago Centro. Requisite sights include the Plaza de Armas, where the cathedral and old post office are, and the nearby Museo Chileno de Arte Precolombino. Stop for coffee or tea in Lastarria or Bellas Artes and do some wandering in Plaza Mulato Gil de Castro and the connected Lastarria or Bellas Artes neighborhoods, ending at the culture and arts center GAM.

On your third day explore the sights along La Alameda, especially the presidential palace of La Moneda and the landmark church, Iglesia San Francisco. For a last look at the city, climb Cerro Santa Lucía. That night try dinner in trendy Las Condes or more upscale Vitacura.

GETTING HERE AND AROUND

AIR TRAVEL

Santiago's Comodoro Arturo Merino Benítez International Airport is about a 30-minute drive west of the city. An official taxi or private transfer from the airport to Centro is about 18,000 pesos (slightly more to Providencia and Las Condes); get tickets from the counters before entering the arrivals hall. A shared transfer (which departs when there are enough passengers) costs about 6,000 pesos; get this also from the counters. The cheapest option is to take one of two buses—Turbus or Centropuerto—that depart from the airport to Pajaritos and Los Héroes metro stations (Los Héroes is more centrally located), for about 1,800 pesos one way, per person, or 3,200 pesos round-trip. These buses leave from the departures terminal.

Airport Contact Comodoro Arturo Merino Benítez International Airport. ⊠ *Av., Armando Cortínez Norte, Pudahuel* ☎ *2/2690–1796* ⊕ *www.aeropuerto-santiago.cl.*

Airport Transfers CentroPuerto. ☎ *2/2601–9883* ⊕ *www.centropuerto.cl.* **Taxi Oficial.** ☎ *2/1601–9880.* **Transvip.** ☎ *2/2677–3000* ⊕ *www.transvip.cl.*

BUS TRAVEL

Buses are relatively efficient and clean, although very crowded at peak times. Fares on the subway and buses are paid using the same prepaid smart card (most easily acquired in subway stations), called a BIP (say: BEEP). The BIP card (*la tarjeta bip!*) itself costs 1,550 pesos. You can also buy single-use tickets for the metro, but not for the bus. Fares vary from 610 to 740 pesos, depending on the time of day, and transfers taken (one free transfer from bus to bus; one paid transfer from bus to metro within 120 minutes). At night, most tourists stick to the subway for simplicity's sake; however, if you do not have enough money on your BIP card, you can use the bus at night in an emergency by showing your BIP card.

Bus Depots Terminal Alameda. ⊠ *La Alameda 3750, Estación Central* ☎ *2/2822–7500.* **Terminal Los Héroes.** ⊠ *Tucapel Jiménez 21, Santiago Centro* ☎ *2/2420–0009.* **Terminal San Borja.** ⊠ *San Borja 184, Estación Central* ☎ *2/2776–0645* ⊕ *www.terminaldebuses.com/terminales-de-buses.* **Terminal Santiago.** ⊠ *La Alameda 3850, Estación Central* ☎ *2/2376–1750.*

Bus Lines Transantiago. ⊠ *Moneda 975, 4th fl., Santiago Centro* ☎ *800/730–073, 600/730-0073* ⊕ *www.transantiago.cl.* **Turbus.** ⊠ *Martínez 800, Estación Central, Estación Central* ☎ *600/660–6600, 2/2822–7500* ⊕ *www.turbus.cl.*

CAR TRAVEL

You don't need a car to explore Santiago if you're not going to venture outside the city limits, as most of the downtown sights are within walking distance of each other. A car is the best way to see the surrounding countryside, and the highways around Santiago are excellent. There is

an iPhone and Android app called Carretera that helps estimate cost of travel in Chile, calculating cost of gasoline and tolls.

SUBWAY TRAVEL

Santiago's subway system is the best way to get around town. The metro costs between 610 and 740 pesos per ride (depending on time of day and bus transfers). You can buy a single-use ticket or a BIP smart card (*la tarjeta bip!*). The metro is safe but gets very crowded at peak hours, and you should keep a hand on your valuables. The system operates weekdays 5:40 am–11:30 pm and weekends 8 am–11 pm, with some variation depending on the metro line. Metro opening and closing hours are listed at each station above the turnstiles.

TAXI TRAVEL

Taxis are plentiful, especially outside of bus stations and in touristy neighborhoods. The taxi service Uber has caught on, though some people prefer to use the app SaferTaxi to ensure that there is a record of their journey. If taking a taxi, be prepared with small bills, as some drivers may not have change. Tipping is not required, but it is customary to round to the closest 500 or 1,000 pesos.

Taxi Companies Andes Pacífico. ⊠ *José Pedro Alessandri 30, Ñuñoa* ☎ *2/2912–6000* ⊕ *www.andespacifico.cl.* **Apoquindo.** ⊠ *Bilbao 7202, Las Condes* ☎ *2/2210–6200* ⊕ *www.transportesapoquindo.cl.* **Italia.** ⊠ *Coquimbo 1469, Santiago Centro* ☎ *2/2591–8900* ⊕ *www.ritalia.cl.* **Neverías.** ⊠ *Apoquindo 4830, Office 22/23, Las Condes* ☎ *2/2207–0003* ⊕ *www.neverias. cl.* **Radio Taxi Las Condes.** ⊠ *Badajoz 12, Las Condes* ☎ *2/2211–4470* ⊕ *www. radiotaxilascondes.cl.*

SAFETY

Despite what Chileans claim, Santiago is no more dangerous than most other large cities and considerably less so than many other Latin American capitals. As a rule of thumb, watch out for your property, preferably keeping physical contact with it, but unless you venture into some of the city's outlying neighborhoods, your physical safety is unlikely to be at risk. Beware of pickpockets particularly in the Centro, near Los Leones metro, and on buses. Don't keep valuables in outside pockets, and exercise caution when using smartphones in very busy areas.

Visitors should be wary of parking attendants. During the day, they should charge only what's on their portable meters when you collect the car, but at night they ask for money—usually 1,000 pesos—in advance. This is a racket, but for your car's safety it's better to comply.

TOURS

Sernatur, the national tourism service, maintains a listing of experienced individual tour guides, who run half-day tours of Santiago and the surrounding area.

FoodyChile. The name of Colin Bennett's tour company is a play on words, meaning both "foodie Chile" and "food and Chile." Tours, booked online only, are always small, personalized, and focus on consumables, including wine, craft beer, and sweets. There are lunches and dinners hosted in private homes, as well as market tours. ⊠ *Providencia* ☎ *9/9538–4342* ⊕ *www.foodychile.com* 🍴 *From 60000 pesos.*

Fotoruta. Cat Allen, a photographer with lots of experience leading people around Santiago on foot, has a lovely way of encouraging you to take beautiful pictures, no matter the skill level. Check out the Streetscape or iPhoneography classes; also explore further afield on a Valparaíso tour. Some classes have a photo-sharing session at the end. ⊠ *Bellavista* ☎ *9/8766–6844* ⊕ *www.foto-ruta.com* ✉ *From US$32.*

Turismo Cocha. One of the biggest players in the Chilean tourism industry, Cocha books tours inside and outside of Chile, as well as hotels, airfare, and cruises. Single-day city tours are available, but the main focus is on multiday tours with lodging at three-, four-, and five-star hotels. The main office is in El Golf (Las Condes), but there are 13 offices around the city, including one at the airport that's open 24 hours. ⊠ *El Bosque Norte 0430, Las Condes* ☎ *2/2464–1000* ⊕ *www.cocha.com* ✉ *From 100,000 pesos.*

Upscape. This adventure tour company prides itself on running tours no one else does, such as heliskiing at Ski Arpa and thematic tours of Santiago, including Jewish culture, bicycling, and food. The company also organizes multiday trips inside and outside of Santiago, extending to the north and south of the country and beyond to Argentina and Uruguay. ⊠ *Tegualda 1352, Providencia* ☎ *2/2244–2750* ⊕ *www.upscapetravel.com* ✉ *From US$74.*

VISITOR INFORMATION

Visitor Information Sernatur. ⊠ *Av. Providencia 1550, Providencia* ☎ *2/2731–8310* ⊕ *www.sernatur.cl.*

EXPLORING

SANTIAGO CENTRO

Shiny new skyscrapers may be sprouting up in neighborhoods to the east, but Santiago Centro has its share of construction going on, too. During the past decade, the population downtown has nearly doubled, but that's for the whole comuna, not just the *casco histórico,* which is close to the Alameda and runs from La Moneda up to about Santa Lucía. Take the metro down here, not a taxi, for easy transportation, as the usual traffic headaches apply to downtown Santiago.

TIMING AND PRECAUTIONS

In this part of the city you can find interesting museums, performance spaces, galleries, imposing government buildings, and bustling commercial streets. Don't worry about getting lost in a sprawling area—it takes only about 15 minutes to walk from one edge of the historic center to the other.

TOP ATTRACTIONS

Fodor's Choice ★ **Gabriela Mistral Cultural Center (GAM).** This giant cultural center just steps from the Universidad Católica metro houses some of Santiago's most interesting indigenous arts exhibits and offers a packed cultural itinerary, as well as a nice wine store and theater. There is a large atrium between the two halves of the building with a colorful skylight, restaurant, and

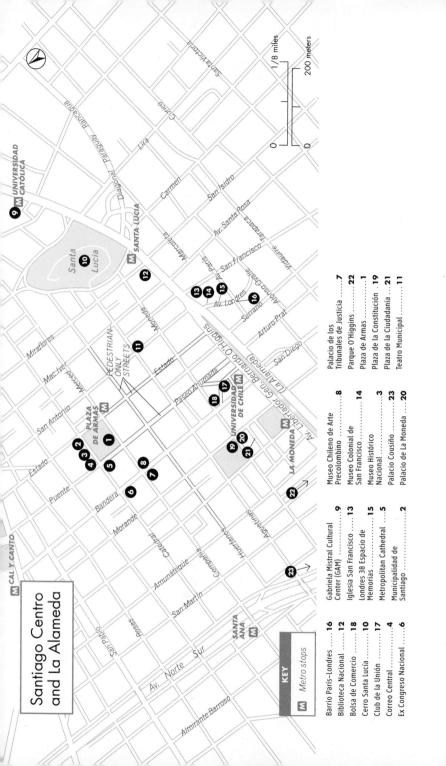

Santiago Centro and La Alameda

KEY

Ⓜ *Metro stops*

Barrio París–Londres **16**
Biblioteca Nacional **12**
Bolsa de Comercio **18**
Cerro Santa Lucía **10**
Club de la Unión **17**
Correo Central **4**
Ex Congreso Nacional **6**

Gabriela Mistral Cultural
Center (GAM) **9**
Iglesia San Francisco **13**
Londres 38 Espacio de
Memorias **15**
Metropolitan Cathedral **5**
Municipalidad de
Santiago **2**

Museo Chileno de Arte
Precolombino **8**
Museo Colonial de
San Francisco **14**
Museo Histórico
Nacional **3**
Palacio Cousiño **23**
Palacio de La Moneda **20**

Palacio de los
Tribunales de Justicia **7**
Parque O'Higgins **22**
Plaza de Armas **1**
Plaza de la Constitución **19**
Plaza de la Ciudadanía **21**
Teatro Municipal **11**

1/8 miles

200 meters

café. Outside the building, to the north side is an amphitheater that is occasionally used to host events. An antiques market takes place on the west side of the building Tuesday through Saturday, if it's not raining. **Tip:** A tourism office is located here. ⊠ *Alameda 227, Santiago Centro* ☎ *2/2566–5500* ⊕ *gam.cl* Ⓜ *Universidad Católica.*

Metropolitan Cathedral. Conquistador Pedro de Valdivia declared in 1541 that a house of worship would be constructed at this site bordering the Plaza de Armas. The first adobe building burned to the ground, and the structures that replaced it were destroyed by the earthquakes of 1647 and 1730. The finishing touches of the neoclassical cathedral standing today were added in 1789 by Italian architect Joaquín Toesca. Be sure to check out the baroque interior stained-glass-topped arched colonnade, and look out for the sparkling silver altar of a side chapel in the south nave. ⊠ *Plaza de Armas 444, Santiago Centro* ☎ *2/2671–8105* Ⓜ *Plaza de Armas.*

Museo Chileno de Arte Precolombino. This well-endowed collection of artifacts of the region's indigenous peoples, much of it donated by the collector Sergio Larraín García-Moreno, is displayed in the beautifully restored Royal Customs House that dates from 1807. The permanent collection, on the upper floor, showcases ceramics and textiles from Mexico to Patagonia. Unlike many of the city's museums, the displays here are well labeled in Spanish and English. Guided tours in English are available at no extra cost, but must be booked in advance. There is a shop with a good selection of on-topic books and an airy café as well. ⊠ *Bandera 361, at Av. Compañía, Santiago Centro* ☎ *2/2928–1500 general, 2/2929–1522 tours* ⊕ *www.museoprecolombino.cl* 💵 *4500 pesos; free 1st Sun. of every month* ⊗ *Closed Mon.* Ⓜ *Plaza de Armas.*

Museo Histórico Nacional. The colonial-era Palacio de la Real Audiencia served as the meeting place for Chile's first Congress in July 1811. The building then functioned as a telegraph office before the museum moved here in 1911. It's worth the small admission charge to see the interior of the 200-year-old structure, where exhibits tracing Chile's history from the preconquest period to the 20th century are arranged chronologically in rooms centered on a courtyard. Keep an eye out for Allende's eyeglasses. Ask for the English brochure and free audio guide, and if you are not heights-averse, take a tour up the tower for a bird's-eye view of the Plaza de Armas, cathedral, and downtown Santiago. ⊠ *Plaza de Armas 951, Santiago Centro* ☎ *2/2411–7010* ⊕ *www.museohistoriconacional.cl* ⊗ *Closed Mon.* Ⓜ *Plaza de Armas.*

> ## GOOD TO KNOW
>
> There are few public restrooms in Santiago. Ecobaños operates four public restrooms in El Centro that are clean and brightly lighted; the uniformed attendants even wish you a good day—all this for 500 pesos! They are located at Morandé and Huérfanos, Ahumada and Moneda, Ahumada between Compañía and Huérfanos, and Estado between Moneda and Agustinas. Sure-thing (free) bathrooms are also located in the basement at the Biblioteca Nacional and GAM.

Fodor's Choice **Plaza de Armas.** This square has been the symbolic heart of Chile—as
★ well as its political, social, religious, and commercial center—since
Pedro de Valdivia established the city on this spot in 1541. The Palacio
de los Gobernadores, the Palacio de la Real Audiencia, and the Municipalidad de Santiago front the square's northern edge. The dignified
cathedral graces the western side of the square. The plaza has historically been very lively, with chess players in a gazebo, street performers playing in the bandstand, and caricaturists. Recent improvements
have increased the number of trees and installed Wi-Fi. ⊠ *Compañía
at Estado, Santiago Centro* Ⓜ *Plaza de Armas.*

WORTH NOTING

Correo Central. Housed in what was once the ornate Palacio de los Gobernadores, this building dating from 1715 is one of the most beautiful post
offices you are likely to see. It was reconstructed by Ricardo Brown in
1882 after being ravaged by fire and is a fine example of neoclassical
architecture, with a glass-and-iron roof added in the early 20th century.
It has occasional exhibits in the main hall, plus an extensive collections
of stamps from around the world and other postal and telegraph memorabilia in the adjoining Postal and Telegraph Museum (free admission).
⊠ *Plaza de Armas 989, at Puente, Santiago Centro* ☎ *2/2956–5145*
⊕ *www.correos.cl* ☉ *Museum: weekends* Ⓜ *Plaza de Armas.*

Ex Congreso Nacional. Once the meeting place for the National Congress
(the legislature moved to Valparaíso in 1990), this palatial neoclassical
building became the Ministry of Foreign Affairs for a time but was
returned to the Senate for meetings after the Ministry moved to the
former Hotel Carrera in Plaza de la Constitución in December 2005.
The original structure on the site, the Iglesia de la Compañía de Jesús,
was destroyed by a fire in 1863 in which 2,000 people perished. Two
bells from that church now grace the elaborate gardens. To coordinate
a tour, email protocolostgo@senado.cl with at least two days' notice.
More formal attire is appreciated, and neither shorts nor baseball caps
are permitted. The tour is free and lasts approximately 30 minutes.
⊠ *Catedral 1158, entrance on Morande, Santiago Centro* ☉ *Closed
weekends* Ⓜ *Plaza de Armas.*

Londres 38 Espacio de Memorias. This lovely facade on Calle Londres
holds dark secrets: Londres 38 was a clandestine torture center for 98
people for one year during Chile's 27-year dictatorship, beginning in
1973. Rooms include a tiny bathroom, where multiple DNA was recovered that helped to identify victims; a video shows the work forensic
scientists undertook. Simple signs add to the sad and dignified ambience
that holds a torrid past and now plays its part as a space for memory.
⊠ *Londres 38, Santiago Centro* ☎ *2/2800–1898* ⊕ *www.londres38.cl*
☉ *Closed Sun. and Mon.* Ⓜ *Universidad de Chile.*

Municipalidad de Santiago. Today's city hall for central Santiago can be
found on the site of the colonial city hall and jail. The original structure, built in 1552, survived until a devastating earthquake in 1730.
Joaquín Toesca, the architect who also designed the presidential palace
and completed the cathedral, reconstructed the building in 1785, but
it was destroyed by fire a century later. In 1891, Eugenio Joannon,

who favored an Italian Renaissance style, erected the structure standing today. On the facade hangs an elaborate coat of arms presented by Spain. The interior now houses a tourist office as well as a small gallery and souvenir shop. The tourism office runs free tours on Monday, Wednesday, and Friday at 10 am with no previous registration required. ⊠ *Plaza de Armas, Santiago Centro* Ⓜ *Plaza de Armas.*

Palacio de los Tribunales de Justicia. During Augusto Pinochet's rule, countless human-rights demonstrations were held outside the Courts of Justice, which house the country's Supreme Court. The imposing neoclassical interior is worth a look, but the guards reserve the right to admission and prefer more formal attire (no shorts, flip-flops, tank tops). It is open for visits from 9 to 2. ⊠ *Av. Compañia 1140, Santiago Centro* Ⓜ *Plaza de Armas.*

OFF THE BEATEN PATH

Parque O'Higgins. Named for Chile's first president and national hero, whose troops were victorious against the Spanish, this park has plenty of open space for everything from ball games to military parades and a dedicated picnic area complete with barbecues. Street vendors sell *volantines* (kites) in the park year-round; breezy September and early October comprise prime kite-flying season, especially around September 18, Chile's national holiday. There are pedalcab and rollerblade rentals on weekends, a competitive rollerblade track, and a terrain park with a deep bowl for skateboarders and rollerbladers. The park has a beautiful covered pool, which costs 6,000 pesos for a day visit; goggles and bathing cap are required. Both the Movistar Arena and Cúpola Multiespacio theater are at this park as well. ⊠ *Autopista Central between Av. Blanco Encalada and Av. Rondizonni, Santiago Centro* ☎ 🖾 *Free* Ⓜ *Parque O'Higgins.*

LA ALAMEDA

Avenida Libertador Bernardo O'Higgins, more frequently called Alameda, is the city's principal thoroughfare. Along with the Pan-American Highway (Avenida Norte Sur) and the Río Mapocho, it forms the wedge that defines the city's historic district. Many of Santiago's most important buildings, including landmarks such as the Iglesia San Francisco, stand along the avenue. Others, like Teatro Municipal, are just steps away.

TIMING AND PRECAUTIONS

You could spend an hour alone at the Palacio de la Moneda—try to time your visit with the changing of the guard, which takes place every other day at 10 am on weekdays, and 11 on weekends. Under the Plaza de la Constitución, which is on the Alameda side of the Moneda, there's the Centro Cultural Palacio la Moneda—a culture, arts, and exhibition space with a few shops and cafés. Across the Alameda, take at least 1½ hours to explore Iglesia San Francisco, the adjacent museum, and the Barrio París-Londres. You could easily spend a bookish half hour perusing the stacks at the Biblioteca Nacional, where you can also take advantage of free Wi-Fi. Plan for an hour or more at Cerro Santa Lucía with its splendid view of the city and adjacent crafts markets.

TOP ATTRACTIONS

Fodor's Choice ★ **Cerro Santa Lucía.** The mazelike park of Santa Lucía is a hangout for park-bench smoochers and photo-snapping tourists. Walking uphill along the labyrinth of interconnected paths and plazas takes about 30 minutes, or you can take an elevator two blocks north of the park's main entrance (no fee). The uppermost lookout point affords an excellent 360-degree view of the entire city; two stairways lead up from the Plaza Caupolicán esplanade; those on the south side are newer and less slippery. Be careful near dusk as the park, although patrolled, attracts the occasional mugger. There is a tiny tourism office near the Alameda entrance, open weekdays, but closed for lunch from 2 until 3 pm, and a small indigenous crafts fair called the Centro de Exposición de Arte Indígena (or Gruta Welén) in a natural cavern carved out of the western flank of the hill. ⊠ *Santa Lucía at La Alameda, Santiago Centro* ☎ 2/2664–4206 Ⓜ *Santa Lucía.*

SOCCER IN CHILE

Chile's most popular spectator sport is soccer, but a close second is watching the endless bickering among owners, trainers, and players whenever a match isn't going well.

Estadio Nacional. First-division fútbol matches, featuring the city's handful of local teams, are held in the Estadio Nacional, southeast of the city center in Ñuñoa. Soccer (*fútbol*) is played year-round, with most matches taking place on weekends. The stadium is also a major concert venue. ⊠ *Av. Grecia 2001, Ñuñoa* ☎ 2/2238–8102.

Iglesia San Francisco. Santiago's oldest structure, greatest symbol, and principal landmark, the Church of San Francisco is the last trace of 16th-century colonial architecture in the city. Construction began in 1586, and although the church survived successive earthquakes, early tremors took their toll and portions had to be rebuilt several times. Today's neoclassical tower, which forms the city's most recognizable silhouette, was added in 1857 by architect Fermín Vivaceta. Inside are rough stone-and-brick walls and an ornate coffered wood ceiling. Visible on the main altar is the image of the Virgen del Socorro (Virgin of Perpetual Help) that conquistador Pedro de Valdivia carried for protection and guidance. ⊠ *La Alameda 834, Santiago Centro* ☎ 2/2638–3238 Ⓜ *Santa Lucía, Universidad de Chile.*

Palacio de La Moneda. Originally the royal mint, this sober neoclassical edifice designed by Joaquín Toesca in the 1780s and completed in 1805 became the presidential palace in 1846, serving that purpose for more than a century. It was bombarded by the military in the 1973 coup, when Salvador Allende defended his presidency against the assault of General Augusto Pinochet before he committed suicide there. Free tours can be arranged by email with at least two days' notice—tell them you want to see the Salón Blanco if you'd like to go upstairs. ⊠ *Plaza de la Constitución, Moneda between Teatinos and Morandé, Santiago Centro* ☎ 2/2690–4000 ✐ *visitas@presidencia.cl* ⊕ *www.gob.cl* Ⓜ *La Moneda.*

Fodor's Choice ★ **Plaza de la Constitución.** Palacio de la Moneda and other government buildings line Constitution Square, the country's most formal plaza. The changing of the guard takes place every other day at 10 am within

the triangle defined by 12 Chilean flags. Adorning the plaza are four monuments, each dedicated to a notable national figure: Diego Portales, founder of the Chilean republic; Jorge Alessandri, the country's leader from 1958 to 1964; Eduardo Frei Montalva, president from 1964 to 1970; and Salvador Allende (1970–73). ☒ *Moneda at Morandé, Santiago Centro* Ⓜ *La Moneda.*

WORTH NOTING

Barrio París-Londres. Many architects contributed to what is frequently referred to as Santiago's Little Europe, among them Alberto Cruz Montt, Jorge Elton Alamos, and Sergio Larraín. The string of small mansion houses lining the cobbled streets of Calles París and Londres sprang up in the mid-1920s on vegetable patches and gardens once belonging to the convent adjoining Iglesia San Francisco. The three- and four-story town houses are all unique; some have brick facades, while others are done in Palladian style. ☒ *Londres at París, Santiago Centro.*

Biblioteca Nacional (*National Library*). Near the foot of Cerro Santa Lucía is the block-long classical facade of the National Library. Moved to its present premises in 1925, this library, founded in 1813, has one of the oldest and most extensive collections in South America. The second-floor Sala José Toribio Medina (closed Saturday), which holds the most important collection of early Latin American print work, is well worth a look. The three levels of books, reached by curved-wood balconies, are lighted by massive chandeliers. The café on the ground floor is a quiet place to linger over a coffee. There is free Wi-Fi throughout the building. ☒ *La Alameda 651, Santiago Centro* ☎ *2/2360–5232* ⊕ *www.bibliotecanacional.cl* ☒ *Free* ⊘ *Closed Sat. afternoon, Sun.* Ⓜ *Santa Lucía.*

Bolsa de Comercio. Chile's stock exchange is housed in a 1917 French neoclassical structure with an elegant clock tower surmounted by an arched slate cupola. Business is now done electronically, but you can visit the old trading floor with its buying and selling circle called *rueda.* You must leave your ID at the door. ☒ *La Bolsa 64, Santiago Centro* ☎ *2/2399–3000* ⊕ *www.bolsadesantiago.com* ☒ *Free* Ⓜ *Universidad de Chile.*

Club de la Unión. The facade of this neoclassical building, dating to 1925, is one of the city's finest. The interior of this private club, whose roster has included numerous Chilean presidents, is open only to members and their guests, except for the last Sunday in May, when it is sometimes open for the Día del Patrimonio. ☒ *La Alameda 1091, Santiago Centro* ⊕ *www.clubdelaunion.cl* Ⓜ *Universidad de Chile.*

Museo Colonial de San Francisco. This monastery adjacent to Iglesia San Francisco houses the best collection of 17th-century colonial paintings on the continent. Contained in rooms that wrap around the courtyard are 54 large-scale canvases portraying the life of St. Francis, painted in Cusco, Peru, as well as a plethora of religious iconography and an impressive collection of silver artifacts. Most pieces are labeled in Spanish and English. Peacocks roam the central courtyard. ☒ *La Alameda 834, Santiago Centro* ☎ *2/2639–8737* ⊕ *www.museosanfrancisco.com* ☒ *1000 pesos* Ⓜ *Santa Lucía, Universidad de Chile.*

2

**OFF THE
BEATEN
PATH**

Palacio Cousiño. Dating from the early 1870s, this fabulous mansion was built by the wealthy Cousiño-Goyenechea family. All that mining money allowed them to build this palace with amenities such as one of the country's first elevators. The elegant furnishings were—of course—imported from France. The building suffered significant damage during the February 2010 earthquake; it reopened in May 2017 following extensive refurbishment to all four salons. Email ahead for 45-minute tours in English that take place daily. ✉ *Dieciocho 438, La Alameda* ☎ *2/2386–7448* ✆ *palaciocousino@gmail.com* ✉ *3000 pesos* Ⓜ *Toesca.*

Plaza de la Ciudadanía. On the south side of the Palacio de la Moneda, this plaza was inaugurated in December 2006 as part of a public works program in preparation for the celebration of the bicentenary of Chile's independence in 2010. Beneath the plaza is the Centro Cultural Palacio La Moneda, an arts center that puts on interesting exhibitions. The Artesanías de Chile crafts shop there has top-quality work, and the Tienda Centro Cultural is a good place to buy unusual souvenirs and jewelry. Also here are a restaurant, a café, a bookshop, and two movie theaters. ✉ *Plaza de la Ciudadanía 26, Santiago Centro* ☎ *2/2355–6500* ⊕ *www.ccplm.cl* ✉ *Building: free. Exhibition: Chileans and residents 3000 pesos, foreigners 5000, foreign students 2500. Free entry before noon weekdays* Ⓜ *La Moneda.*

Teatro Municipal. The opulent Municipal Theater is the city's cultural center, with performances of opera, ballet, and classical music. Designed by French architects, the theater opened in 1857, with major renovations in 1870 and 1906 following a fire and an earthquake. The Renaissance-style building is one of the city's most refined monuments with a lavish interior that deserves a visit. The cobblestoned walk around the building completes the picture. For greater insight, email ahead for a guided general tour in English. ✉ *Plaza Alcalde Mekis, Av. Agustinas 794, at Av. San Antonio, Santiago Centro* ☎ *2/2463–1000* ⊕ *www.municipal. cl* ✉ *General tour 6000 pesos; private tour 30000* Ⓜ *Universidad de Chile, Santa Lucía.*

LASTARRIA AND BELLAS ARTES

This contiguous area is really two neighborhoods, but elements of modern and artsy Bellas Artes and the more traditional and cobblestoned Lastarria flow in and out of each other. Bellas Artes has gone from seedy to universally popular within a decade. It is full of budget-friendly empanada joints, pizza places, ice-cream parlors, and all-natural food shops.

Mostly cobblestoned Lastarria starts at Merced, and extends south to the imposing new Gabriela Mistral Cultural Center. It's a better-heeled crowd in Lastarria, and the area has more upscale dining. Both areas have street-level commerce with clothing boutiques and art suppliers, and are popular among Chileans and foreigners.

TIMING AND PRECAUTIONS

You can't go wrong with a late afternoon in Bellas Artes, as restaurants and street-side cafés fill up with people off work early. In Plaza Mulato Gil de Castro, allot at least 30 minutes for the Museo de Artes Visuales

and adjoining Museo Arqueológico. Because both of these areas are busy and attract people who've come to spend money, simple precautions like keeping your purse in your lap, not on the back of your chair, are recommended. Consider coming down into Lastarria after a walk up Cerro Santa Lucía, the smaller of the two hills that overlooks the city.

Museo Arqueológico de Santiago. This archaeological museum, devoted specifically to the indigenous peoples of Chile, more than makes up for its small size with the quality of the exhibits, labeled in English and Spanish. Artifacts include an outstanding collection of the Andean headwear used to distinguish different ethnic groups, pottery, jewelry, and a collection of the woven bags used by Andean peoples to carry the coca leaves that sustained them during their long treks at high altitudes. It is located inside the Museo de Artes Visuales, and one entry fee pays for both visits. ⊠ *José Victorino Lastarria 307, 2nd fl., Lastarria* ☎ *2/2664–9337* ⊕ *www.mavi.cl* ✉ *Tues.–Sat. 1000 pesos (includes Museo de Artes Visuales), Sun. free* ⊙ *Closed Mon.* Ⓜ *Universidad Católica.*

Fodor'sChoice ★ **Museo de Artes Visuales.** This dazzling museum of contemporary art has one of Chile's finest collections of contemporary Chilean art and it displays the combined private holdings of Chilean industrial moguls Manuel Santa Cruz and Hugo Yaconi. The building itself is a masterpiece: six gallery levels float into each other in surprising ways. The wood floors and Plexiglas-sided stairways create an open and airy space where you might see—depending on what's on display when you visit—paintings and sculptures by Roberto Matta, Arturo Duclos, Gonzalo Cienfuegos, Roser Bru, José Balmes, and Eugenio Dittborn, among others. Pick up artsy souvenirs from Tienda Mulato or refuel at the café next to the entrance. ⊠ *José Victorino Lastarria 307, at Plaza Mulato Gil de Castro, Lastarria* ☎ *2/2664–9337* ⊕ *www.mavi.cl* ✉ *Tues.–Sat. 1000 pesos (includes Museo Arqueológico de Santiago), Sun. free* ⊙ *Closed Mon.* Ⓜ *Universidad Católica.*

PARQUE FORESTAL

You wouldn't think building-happy Santiago would let the prime real estate that is Parque Forestal go without construction, but the narrow strip of land was left over after a canal was built in 1891 to tame the unpredictable Río Mapocho. The area quickly filled with the city's refuse. A decade later, under the watchful eye of Enrique Cousiño, it was transformed into the leafy Parque Forestal. It was and still is enormously popular with Santiaguinos, and recent investments have cleaned it further, installed playgrounds for children, and created a bike path along the northern edge.

On weekends, the area near the Contemporary Art Museum fills with jugglers, people doing aerial silks, and those skilled in acrobatics. The eastern tip of the park, near Plaza Baquedano (also referred to as Plaza Italia, though that plaza is further north) is distinguished by the Wagnerian-scale *Fuente Alemana* (German Fountain), donated by the German community of Santiago. The bronze-and-stone monolith commemorates the centennial of Chilean independence.

TIMING AND PRECAUTIONS

You can have a pleasant, relaxing day strolling through the city's most popular park, losing yourself in the art museums and exploring the Mercado Central. You can easily spend an hour or two in the Museo Nacional de Bellas Artes and the Museo de Arte Contemporáneo. The Vega Chica, Tirso de Molina, and Vega Central are usually crowded, so keep an eye on your personal belongings. When the markets close around sunset, it's best to return to more lively neighborhoods south of the river.

TOP ATTRACTIONS

Mercado Central. At the Central Market you'll find a matchless selection of edible products from the sea. Depending on the season, you might see the delicate beaks of *picorocos,* the world's only edible barnacles; *erizos,* the prickly-shelled sea urchins; or heaps of giant mussels. If the seafood doesn't capture your interest, the architecture may: the lofty wrought-iron ceiling of the structure, reminiscent of a Victorian train station, was prefabricated in England and erected in Santiago between 1868 and 1872. Diners are regaled by minstrels in the middle of the market, where a few larger restaurants compete for customers. You can also find a cheap meal at the smaller restaurants around the edge of the market. ⊠ *Ismael Valdés Vergara 900, Parque Forestal* ☎ *2/2696–8327* ⊕ *www.mercadocentral.cl* Ⓜ *Puente Cal y Canto.*

Museo Nacional de Bellas Artes. Unfortunately, Chile's main fine arts museum now has only a small part of its excellent collection of Chilean painting on display, confining it to just six small rooms on the first floor. The rest of the museum is given over to temporary exhibitions of varying interest. The elegant, neoclassical building, which was originally intended to house the city's school of fine arts, has an impressive glass-domed ceiling, which illuminates the main hall. Guided tours are available in Spanish only, with reduced schedules in January and February. ■TIP➔ **Walk through to the Museo de Arte Contemporáneo, housed in the same building.** ⊠ *At José M. de la Barra and Ismael Valdés Vergara, Parque Forestal* ☎ *2/2499–1632* ⊕ *www.mnba.cl* ☉ *Mon.* ⌕ *Guided tours daily at noon and 4 pm (Jan. and Feb.), 10:30 am, 11:30 am, 12:30 pm, 3:30 pm, and 4:30 pm (rest of yr) in Spanish; reserve ahead to mediacion.educacion@mnba.cl* Ⓜ *Bellas Artes.*

WORTH NOTING

Centro Cultural Estación Mapocho. This mighty edifice, with its trio of two-story arches framed by intricate terra-cotta detailing, is as elegant as any train station in the world. The station was inaugurated in 1913 as a terminus for trains arriving from Valparaíso and points north, but after trains were diverted to Estación Central, the space was turned into one of the city's principal arts and conference centers. The Centro Cultural Estación Mapocho houses two restaurants, a café, a large exhibition hall, and arts space. The cavernous station that once sheltered steam engines now hosts musical performances and other events, such as the Cumbre Guachaca, a celebration of city-meets-down-home-country culture, usually held in April. ⊠ *Plaza de la Cultura, Independencia at Balmaceda, Parque Forestal* ☎ *2/2787–0000* ⊕ *www.estacionmapocho.cl* ◩ *Station free, exhibition fees vary* ☉ *Closed Mon.* Ⓜ *Puente Cal y Canto.*

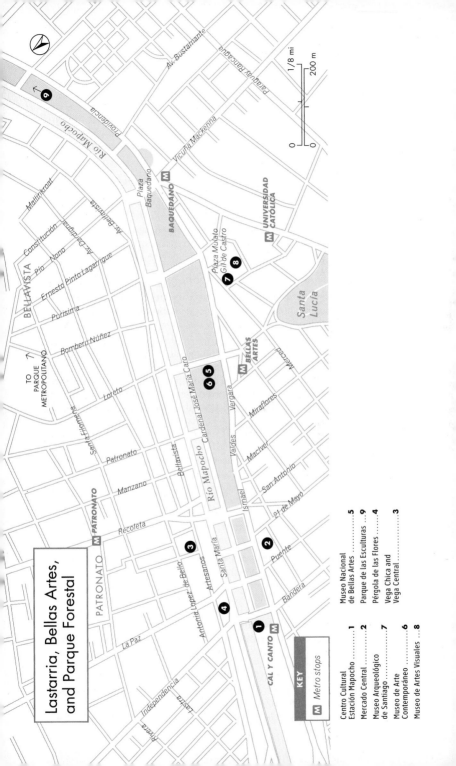

Lastarria, Bellas Artes, and Parque Forestal

Museo de Arte Contemporáneo. After two ambitious restorations—the first completed in 2008 and then another after the destructive 2010 earthquake—the elegant Museum of Contemporary Art has a sparkling new interior in this classic building. The museum showcases modern Latin American paintings, photography, and sculpture. The museum is run by the art school of Universidad de Chile and isn't afraid to take risks. Look for Fernando Botero's pudgy *Caballo (Horse)* sculpture out front, and drop in at its café serving gourmet coffee and homemade treats. There is a second location of this museum near Quinta Normal, and a bus-turned-café called *Central Placeres* or simply *La Micro* ("the bus," in Chilean slang) parked outside. ⊠ *At José M. de la Barra and Ismael Valdés Vergara, Parque Forestal* ☏ *2/2977–1741* ⊕ *www.mac.uchile.cl* ⊘ *Closed Mon.* Ⓜ *Bellas Artes.*

OFF THE
BEATEN
PATH

Parque de las Esculturas. Residents in Providencia know this as one of the city's most captivating—and least publicized—public parks. Its gardens are filled with sculptures by Chile's top artists and because of its pastoral atmosphere, the park is popular with joggers and cuddling couples. In the center is a wood pavilion that hosts art exhibitions. The park also hosts a jazz festival every January, and a little farther west of the entrance is one of the free exercise stations that dot the city. ⊠ *Pedro de Valdivia and Santa María, Providencia, Providencia* Ⓜ *Los Leones.*

Pérgola de las Flores. Santiaguinos come to the Pérgola de las Flores (literally: "gazebo of flowers") markets to buy wreaths and flower arrangements for decoration or to bring to the city's two nearby cemeteries. *La Pérgola de las Flores,* a famous Chilean musical and movie, is based on the conflict that arose in the 1930s when the mayor of Santiago wanted to shut down the market, which at that time was located near the Iglesia San Francisco on the Alameda; find a chatty florist at one of the two open-air markets—Pérgola San Francisco and Pérgola Santa María, each with about 40 vendors—and you may learn all about it. ⊠ *Av. La Paz at Artesanos, Recoleta* Ⓜ *Puente Cal y Canto.*

Vega Chica and Vega Central. From fruit to furniture, meat to machinery, these lively markets stock just about anything you can name. Alongside ordinary items you can find delicacies like *piñones,* giant pine nuts found on monkey puzzle trees. If you're undaunted by crowds, try a typical Chilean meal in a closet-size eatery, or *picada* in the Vega Central, chowing down on brothy *cazuela* (a typical meat and vegetable soup) or a plate of fried fish. For greater selection and a little more space, go to the second floor of the Vega Chica (now called Tirso de Molina) where Chilean, Colombian, Thai, Mexican, and Peruvian food is dished out in large portions at fair prices. As in any other crowded market, be extra careful with your belongings. ⊠ *Antonia López de Bello between Av. Salas and Nueva Rengifo, Recoleta* Ⓜ *Patronato or Puente Cal Y Canto.*

BELLAVISTA AND PARQUE METROPOLITANO

If you happen to be in Santiago on one of those lovely winter days when the sun comes out after rain has cleared the air, head straight for Parque Metropolitano. In the center is Cerro San Cristóbal, a hill reached via funicular railway, taxi, a 45-minute trail, or an hour-plus uphill walk

on the main road. Atop the hill are spectacular views of the city below the snow-covered Andes Mountains.

In the shadow of Cerro San Cristóbal is Bellavista. The neighborhood has but one sight—poet Pablo Neruda's hillside home of La Chascona— but it's perhaps the city's best place to wander. Strike out on your own, or start out in Patio Bellavista (an open-air mall/arcade); either way you're sure to find interesting shops, small art galleries, souvenirs, and food to suit most budgets and tastes.

TIMING AND PRECAUTIONS

Plan on devoting an entire day to visiting Parque Metropolitano's major attractions. During the week the park is almost empty, and you can enjoy the views in relative solitude. If you decide to walk up from the Bellavista side, take the road about 5 km (3 miles), or take a right at a sign about half a mile in that says Zorro Vidal and follow the path for a hike about 40 minutes to the top. This is best done on weekends. Avoid walking down the hill if you decide to watch the sunset from the lofty perch—the area is not well patrolled. Give yourself at least an hour to wander through Bellavista, and another hour for a tour of La Chascona.

TOP ATTRACTIONS

FAMILY **Cerro San Cristóbal.** This large, iconic hill within the centenary Parque
Fodor'sChoice Metropolitano is one of the most popular tourist attractions in Santiago.
★ From the western entrance at Plaza Caupolicán (Pio Nono) you can take a steep but enjoyable one-hour walk to the summit, or take the funicular, a historic monument that opened in 1925. After several years of disuse, the *teleférico* (cable car) reopened in 2016 and ascends from the eastern entrance, seven blocks north of Pedro de Valdivia metro stop. If you have a car, driving up costs 3,000 pesos per vehicle during the week and 4,000 on weekends. ⊠ *Cerro San Cristóbal, Bellavista* ☎ *2/2730–1331* ⊕ *www.parquemet.cl* 🖃 *Round-trip funicular: weekdays 2000 pesos, weekends and holidays 2600 pesos; Round-trip funicular: weekdays 2510 pesos, weekends and holidays 3010 pesos* ⊙ *Closed: park, after 9 pm; funicular, after 6:45 pm* Ⓜ *Baquedano, Pedro de Valdivia.*

Fodor'sChoice **La Chascona.** This house designed by Nobel Prize–winning poet Pablo
★ Neruda was dubbed the "Woman with the Tousled Hair" after Matilde Urrutia, his third wife. The two met while strolling in nearby Parque Forestal, and for years the house served as a romantic hideaway before they married. The pair's passionate relationship was recounted in the 1995 Italian film *Il Postino*. Audio guides are available in English, Spanish, French, Portuguese, and German, and the house is visually fascinating, with winding garden paths, stairs, and bridges leading to the house and its library, which is stuffed with books. There's Neruda's old bedroom in a tower, and a secret passageway. Scattered throughout are collections of butterflies, seashells, wineglasses, and other odd objects that inspired Neruda's tumultuous life and romantic poetry. Although not as magical as Neruda's house in Isla Negra, La Chascona still sets your imagination dancing. The house is on a little side street leading off Constitución. ⊠ *Fernando Márquez de la Plata 0192, Bellavista* ☎ *2/2777–8741* ⊕ *www.fundacionneruda.org* 🖃 *Audio guide 7000 pesos; students 2500 pesos* ⊙ *Closed Mon.* Ⓜ *Baquedano.*

WORTH NOTING

Jardín Botánico Mapulemu. Gravel paths lead you to restful nooks in the Mapulemu Botanical Garden, dedicated to native Chilean species. Every path and stairway seems to bring you to better views of Santiago and the Andes. On weekends, the Instituto Nacional de Deportes conducts classes starting at 9:30 am. These free municipality-run seminars may include yoga, Zumba, aerobics, aeroboxing, or *bicicleta estática*, a spinning-like activity. There are also paid yoga classes on Sundays from 10 to noon. The easiest access is from the Pedro de Valdivia side. ✉ *Cerro San Cristóbal, Bellavista* ☎ *2/2730–1331* 🎫 *Free* Ⓜ *Pedro de Valdivia.*

Patio Bellavista. This multilevel complex of bars, eateries, cafés, and souvenir shops is a Bellavista centerpoint. The patio houses a tourist office, free concerts or *cueca* (national dance) performance in the central plaza, a live music space, a theater, galleries, and restaurants dealing in Peruvian cuisine such as Tambo, as well as Italian, French, and Middle Eastern eateries. ✉ *Pío Nono 73, Bellavista* ☎ *2/2249–8700* ⊕ *www.patiobellavista.cl* Ⓜ *Baquedano.*

FAMILY **Plaza Tupahue.** The main attraction in summer of this area inside Parque Metropolitano is the delightful Piscina Tupahue, an 82-meter (269-foot) pool with a rocky crag running along one side. Beside the pool is the 1925 Torreón Victoria, a stone tower surrounded by a trellis of bougainvillea. If Piscina Tupahue is too crowded, try the nearby Piscina Antilén. From Plaza Tupahue you can follow a path below to Plaza de Juegos Infantiles Gabriela Mistral, a popular playground. ✉ *Cerro San Cristóbal, Bellavista* ☎ *2/2730–1300* 🎫 *Piscina Tupahue 6000 pesos; piscina Antilén 7500 pesos* ◷ *Pool closed Mon.* Ⓜ *Pedro de Valdivia.*

FAMILY **Zoológico Nacional.** The zoo is a good place to see Chilean animals, some nearly extinct, that you might not otherwise encounter. As is often the case with many older zoos, the animals aren't given much room. ✉ *Cerro San Cristóbal, Bellavista* ☎ *2/2730–1368* ⊕ *www.parquemet.cl/zoologico-nacional* 🎫 *3000 pesos* ◷ *Closed Mon.* Ⓜ *Baquedano.*

PARQUE QUINTA NORMAL AREA

Just west of downtown is shady Parque Quinta Normal, a 75-acre park with three museums within its borders, another just across the street, and two more down the block. This is an especially good place to take kids. The park was created in 1841 as a place to experiment with new agricultural techniques. It's great for quiet strolls, except on weekends, when you have to maneuver around noisy families. Pack a picnic or a soccer ball and fit right in. *The park is closed on Mondays.*

Near the park is the Museo de la Memoria, a museum in memory of the dictatorship, and the modern Biblioteca de Santiago. Closer to the Alameda is the arts and performing center Matucana 100 and the Quinta Normal branch of the Museo de Arte Contemporáneo, both of which have cafés outside.

TIMING AND PRECAUTIONS

Except on Monday, you can visit the museums in and around the park, stroll along a wooded path, take a pedal boat in the lagoon, rent a pedal car, or take the motorized pretend train around the park all within a couple of hours. Check out the dilapidated greenhouse midpark for photo ops.

TOP ATTRACTIONS

Estación Central. Inaugurated in 1897, Central Station is the city's last remaining train station, serving the south as far as Chillán. The greenish iron canopy of the station that once shielded the engines from the weather is flanked by two lovely beaux arts edifices. A lively market keeps this terminal buzzing with activity. The grand entrance has a colorful, illuminated carousel and a couple of cafés. As in any busy place, keep a close watch on valuables. ⊠ *Alameda 3170, Estación Central* ☎ *600/585–5000* ⊠ *Free* Ⓜ *Estación Central.*

OFF THE BEATEN PATH

Cementerio General. This cemetery in the northern part of the city reveals a lot about traditional Chilean society. Through the lofty stone arches of the main entrance are well-tended paths lined with marble mausoleums and squat mansions belonging to Chile's wealthy families. The 8- or 10-story "niches"—concrete shelves housing thousands of coffins—resemble middle-class apartment buildings. Their inhabitants lie here until the rent runs out and they are evicted. Look for former President Salvador Allende's final resting spot; a map at the main entrance to the cemetery can help you find it. Ninety-minute Historic Heritage Tours in Spanish run weekdays at 10 am and 3 pm. General tours are weekdays (except Wednesday) by prior arrangement and last 90 minutes. Three 75-minute night tours are available at 8 pm for kids and adults. All tours require reservations and cost 2,500 pesos. ⊠ *Av. Prof. Alberto Zañartu 951, Recoleta* ☎ *2/2637–7800* ⊕ *http://tour.cementeriogeneral. cl* ⊠ *Free* Ⓜ *Cementerios.*

FAMILY

Museo Artequín. The resplendent Pabellón París outside the Parque Quinta grounds houses this interactive museum that teaches the fundamentals of art to children, but the pavilion itself—with its glass domes, Pompeian-red walls, and blue-steel columns—is the real jewel. Designed by French architect Pierre-Henri Picq, it housed Chile's exhibition in the 1889 Paris International Exposition (where Gustave Eiffel's skyline-defining tower was unveiled); the structure was later shipped to Santiago. On weekdays, school groups explore the two floors of reproductions of famous artworks hung at kid-height as well as the virtual reality salon. There are occasional interactive exhibits and workshops, plus an on-site café. ⊠ *Av. Portales 3530, Parque Quinta Normal* ☎ *2/2681–8656* ⊕ *www.artequin.cl* ⊠ *1500 pesos; free Sun.* ⊙ *Mon. and Feb.* Ⓜ *Quinta Normal.*

Fodor'sChoice ★ **Museo de La Memoria y Los Derechos Humanos.** This museum is a powerful testimony to the coup that established the Chilean dictatorship of Augusto Pinochet; the resulting detention, torture, and murder of Chilean citizens; and the country's historic vote to return to democracy. There is a heavy audio-visual component, with moving letters by children about the events of the times. Some images and artifacts here might be challenging for children to process, but it's an important

part of Chilean history and arguably the country's best museum. It is just across the street from the Parque Quinta Normal, and there is also an entrance in Quinta Normal metro station. Audio guides in several languages are available for 2,000 pesos. ⊠ *Matucana 501, Parque Quinta Normal* ☎ *2/2597–9600* ⊕ *www.museodelamemoria. cl* ⊘ *Closed Mon.* Ⓜ *Quinta Normal.*

FAMILY **Museo Ferroviario.** Chile's once-mighty railroads have been relegated to
Fodor'sChoice history, but this acre of Parque Quinta Normal keeps the memory alive.
★ Sixteen steam locomotives and four passenger coaches are set within quiet gardens with placards in Spanish and English. You can board several of the trains. Among the collection is one of the locomotives used on the old cross-Andes railway to Argentina, which operated between Chile and Argentina from 1910 until 1971. Guided tours are available. ⊠ *Av. Las Palmeras, Parque Quinta Normal* ☎ *2/2681–4627* ⊕ *www. museoferroviario.cl* 🎫 *800 pesos* ⊘ *Closed Mon.* Ⓜ *Quinta Normal.*

WORTH NOTING

FAMILY **Museo de Ciencia y Tecnología.** Children can spend a happy half hour at this small science-and-technology museum's interactive exhibits, while adults can peruse its collection of old phonographs, calculators, and computers. A small part of the Museo Infantil's (Children's Museum) collection was also moved to this museum after the 2010 earthquake, and there are exhibits for ages three and up on astronomy and vision. ⊠ *Parque Quinta Normal, Parque Quinta Normal* ☎ *2/2689–8026* 🎫 *800 pesos* ⊘ *Closed Mon.* Ⓜ *Quinta Normal.*

FAMILY **Museo Nacional de Historia Natural.** The National Natural History Museum is the centerpiece of Parque Quinta Normal. French architect Paul Lathoud designed the building for Chile's first international exposition in 1875. Damaged by successive earthquakes, the neoclassical structure was rebuilt and enlarged. There are large dioramas of stuffed animals against painted backdrops, descriptions of wrongs committed against indigenous people, and occasionally, paleontologists working in glass-walled exhibits. The skeleton of an enormous blue whale hangs in the central hall, delighting children of all ages. Exhibits are labeled only in Spanish, but audio guides in English are available. ⊠ *Parque Quinta Normal* ☎ *2/2680–4600* ⊕ *www.mnhn. cl* ⊘ *Closed Mon.* Ⓜ *Quinta Normal.*

VITACURA

Vitacura is not only Santiago's top shopping spot, it is also—with its tree-shaded streets, gardens, and wide sidewalks—a great place for a stroll, especially on a Saturday morning when residents are out jogging, walking their dogs, or simply picking up a newspaper and some fresh *marraquetas,* Chile's favorite bread rolls. Parque Bicentenario is a great place for a run, or taking kids to feed the fish, geese, and other birds that live in the pond there (animal feed is sold on-site).

FAMILY **Museo de la Moda.** The Fashion Museum, opened in 2007 by a son of Jorge Yarur Banna, one of Chile's most successful textile barons, hosts small but choice exhibitions mostly featuring women's dresses that date to the 1600s. Housed in the Yarur family's former home, designed

by Chilean architects in the style of Frank Lloyd Wright in the early 1960s, the museum offers a fascinating insight into the lifestyle of the Chilean oligarchy in the run-up to the upheaval of Salvador Allende's socialist government and the ensuing military coup. The main rooms feature original furnishings, while the pink 1958 Ford Thunderbird driven by Yarur's wife is parked in a courtyard. ■TIP➜ **Call before visiting; the museum can close for up to two months between exhibitions.** El Garage café, open daily, serves light meals and snacks at reasonable prices. ⊠ *Av. Vitacura 4562, Vitacura* ☏ *2/2219–3623* ⊕ *www. museodelamoda.cl* ⊠ *3000 pesos* ⊘ *Closed Mon.* Ⓜ *No metro.*

LAS CONDES

One of Santiago's swankier residential neighborhoods and home to the banking district, Las Condes is home to a swath of stores, accommodations, and restaurants nestled among the high rises; it's also considered one of the capital's safer areas. Its northern location means it's a great base for easy access to the ski resorts.

PROVIDENCIA

A residential neighborhood, bustling Providencia lines two eponymous avenues and features a mixture of high rises and two-story buildings. There's plenty of accommodations to suit all budgets, plus a great selection of cafés and restaurants offering classic Chilean fare to creative paired tasting menus.

WHERE TO EAT

Menus cover the bases of international cuisines, but don't miss the local bounty—seafood delivered directly from the Pacific Ocean. One local favorite is *caldillo de congrio,* the hearty fish stew celebrated by poet Pablo Neruda in his "Oda al Caldillo de Congrio." (The lines of the poem are, in fact, the recipe.) A pisco sour—a cocktail of grape brandy, egg white, and lemon juice—is a great aperitif for any meal, especially when accompanied by a plate of *machas a la parmesana,* small razor clams served au gratin, baked in lemon juice or with white wine, butter, and grated cheese.

Tempted to try heartier Chilean fare? Pull up a stool at one of the counters at Vega Central and enjoy a traditional *pastel de choclo,* pie filled with ground beef, chicken, olives, and a boiled egg, topped with mashed corn. Craving seafood? Head to the Mercado Central, where fresh fish is brought in each morning. Want a memorable meal? Trendy restaurants are opening every day in neighborhoods like Bellavista, where hip Santiaguinos come to check out the latest hot spots.

In the neighborhood of Vitacura, a 20- to 30-minute taxi ride from the city center, a complex of restaurants called Borde Río attracts an upscale crowd, but other reservations-only restaurants worth a look are on Alonso de Córdova and Nueva Costanera. El Golf, an area including Avenida El Bosque Norte and Avenida Isidora Goyenechea

in Las Condes, has numerous restaurants and cafés. The emphasis is on creative cuisine, so familiar favorites are given a Chilean twist. This is one of the few neighborhoods where you can stroll between restaurants until you find exactly what you want.

Santiaguinos dine a little later than you might expect. Most fancy restaurants don't open for lunch until 1. (You may startle the cleaning staff if you rattle the doors at noon.) Dinner begins at 7:30 or 8, although most places don't get crowded until after 9. Many eateries close for a few hours before dinner and on Sunday night. People do dress smartly for dinner, but a coat and tie are rarely necessary. Avoid shorts, sneakers, and athletic gear, and you should be fine in most places. *Restaurant reviews have been shortened. For full information, visit Fodors.com.*

WHAT IT COSTS IN CHILEAN PESOS (IN THOUSANDS)			
	$	$$	$$$	$$$$
AT DINNER	Under 6	6–9	10–13	over 13

Restaurant prices are the average cost of a main course at dinner or, if dinner is not served, at lunch.

SANTIAGO CENTRO

$$$
CHILEAN
Fodor's Choice
★

✕ **Blue Jar.** Simple but creative dishes using the best and freshest Chilean ingredients appeal to local office workers and visitors alike at this popular downtown spot, where lunch patrons often enjoy a sandwich or soup–salad combo. The menu changes seasonally, with dishes like chicken cashew curry and venison with caponata sharing menu space with grilled bass and passionfruit mousse. **Known for:** great coffee; early dinners (closes at 9 pm except first Thursday of each month); reservations necessary for busy lunches. $ *Average main: 11000 pesos* ✉ *Almirante L. Gotuzzo 102 at Moneda, Santiago Centro* ☎ *2/2696–1890* ⊕ *www.bluejar.cl* ♢ *Closed weekends* Ⓜ *Moneda.*

$$$$
CHILEAN

✕ **Bristol.** This restaurant inside the sophisticated Hotel Plaza San Francisco serves creative seafood dishes like marinated scallops over octopus carpaccio and cold tomato-and-pepper sauce. Frequented by local businessmen, Bristol has won several awards and often makes it onto top lists in local media. **Known for:** seafood; efficient service; creative menu. $ *Average main: 15000 pesos* ✉ *Hotel Plaza San Francisco, Alameda 816, Santiago Centro* ☎ *2/2630–4454* ⊕ *www.plazasanfrancisco.cl* Ⓜ *Universidad de Chile.*

$$$
CHILEAN
Fodor's Choice
★

✕ **Confitería Torres.** Opening in 1879, this restaurant remains one of the city's most traditional dining rooms, with red-leather banquettes, mint-green ceramic floors, and huge chandeliers with tulip-shaped globes. Classic dishes such as *lomo al ajo arriero* (sirloin sautéed with peppers and garlic) are menu staples. **Known for:** quick bites; traditional decor; classic dishes. $ *Average main: 9400 pesos* ✉ *Alameda 1570, Santiago Centro* ☎ *2/2688–0751* ⊕ *www.confiteriatorres.cl* ♢ *Closed Sun. and holidays.* Ⓜ *Moneda.*

Restaurants	▼
Ambrosía Bistro	**30**
Anakena	**31**
Aquí Está Coco	**27**
Azul Profundo	**18**
Bandarián	**14**
Bocanariz	**10**
Blue Jar	**2**
Bristol	**6**
Café Clementina	**29**
Castillo Forestal	**12**
Colmado Coffee & Bakery	**9**
Como Agua Para Chocolate	**17**
Confitería Torres	**1**
Coquinaria	**32**
Divertimento Chileno	**22**
Dominó	**5**
El Cid	**34**
El Huerto	**28**
El Mesón Nerudiano	**21**
Eladio	**23**
Fuente Alemana	**13**
Galindo	**15**
Holm Ensaladería	**26**
La Bodeguilla	**20**
Les Assassins	**11**
Liguria	**25**
Majestic	**3**
Matsuri	**33**
Mercado Central	**7**
Normandie	**24**
Peumayén	**16**
Salvador Cocina y Café	**4**
Sur Patagónico	**8**
Uncle Fletch	**19**

Hotels	▼
The Aubrey	**13**
Carménère EcoHotel	**16**
Chilhotel	**17**
Director El Golf	**23**
El Castillo Rojo	**14**
Four Points by Sheraton	**31**
Happy House Hostel	**1**
Hotel Foresta	**8**
Hotel Fundador	**2**
Hotel Ismael 312	**10**
Hotel Magnolia	**7**
Hotel Orly	**20**
Hotel París 813	**4**
Hotel Plaza San Francisco	**6**
Hotel Vegas	**3**
Italia Suite Bed & Breakfast	**15**
Le Rêve	**19**
Loreto Hotel	**12**
Mandarin Oriental Santiago	**24**
Merdiano Sur Petit Hotel	**18**
Mercure Santiago Central	**5**
Neruda Express	**25**
NH Collection Plaza	**26**
The Ritz-Carlton	**27**
San Cristóbal Tower and Sheraton Santiago	**22**
Santiago InterContinental	**28**
Santiago Marriott Hotel	**29**
Santiago Park Plaza	**21**
The Singular	**9**
Su Merced	**11**
W Santiago	**30**

Where to Eat and Stay in Santiago

$ ✕ **Dominó.** A Chilean institution, this no-frills 50-year-old fast-food
CHILEAN chain is impeccably clean, and the service is fast and friendly. It's the
place to try an *Italiano* (a hot dog with tomatoes and avocado) or *chacarero* (hot dog or beef sandwich with green beans, tomato, and chili
pepper). **Known for:** fast food; cheap eats; no frills. $ *Average main:
5000 pesos* ⊠ *Ahumada 146, Santiago Centro* ☎ *2/2411–0600* ⊕ *www.
domino.cl* ⊘ *Closed Sun.*

$$ ✕ **Fuente Alemana.** Grab a vast, overflowing sandwich that Chileans
CHILEAN consider unique to their country. Try a *lomito completo* with thin
tender slices of pork with sauerkraut, mayonnaise, and tomato sauce,
or a *chacarero*, with slices of beef with tomatoes, green beans, and
chili pepper—get it "*sin ají*" if you don't like spicy food. **Known for:**
good prices; fast food; sandwiches. $ *Average main: 7000 pesos* ⊠ *La
Alameda 58, Santiago Centro* ☎ *2/2639–3231* ⊕ *www.falemana.cl*
⊘ *Closed Sun.* Ⓜ *Baquedano.*

$$$ ✕ **Majestic.** Santiago's first Indian restaurant, Majestic is considered by
INDIAN some to be the best. Whether you order a simple lentil dahl or sophis-
ticated curries, you're in for a good meal surrounded by tapestries and
shiny adornments. **Known for:** spicy food; Indian cuisine; reasonable
prices. $ *Average main: 10000 pesos* ⊠ *Santo Domingo 1526, Santiago
Centro* ☎ *2/2695–8366* ⊕ *www.majestic.cl* Ⓜ *Santa Ana.*

$$$ ✕ **Mercado Central.** Where better than to sample fresh Chilean seafood
SEAFOOD and eat where the locals eat than at Santiago's fish market? Bustling
and loud, the market has an ambience you'll want to soak up, whether
you visit Donde Augusto and La Joya del Pacífico in the center or at a
smaller, less touristy, and cheaper spot such as Marisol or Francisca.
Known for: fantastic seafood; casual dining; cash-only at smaller restau-
rants. $ *Average main: 12000 pesos* ⊠ *San Pablo 967, Santiago Centro*
☎ ⊕ *www.mercadocentral.cl* ⊘ *No dinner* Ⓜ *Cal y Canto.*

$$ ✕ **Salvador Cocina y Café.** This tucked-away two-story downtown lunch
CHILEAN spot offers unmissable weekday set menus with appetizer, main dish,
Fodor's Choice iced tea, and choice of coffee or dessert. Dishes adopt modern spins
★ on Chilean and international favorites, such as grain salad with *mote*
(hulled wheat kernels), beef carpaccio, kidneys in cream sauce, or
spinach-filled pasta. **Known for:** adventurous meat dishes; great lunch
options; reasonable prices. $ *Average main: 7000 pesos* ⊠ *Bombero
Ossa 1069, Santiago Centro* ☎ *2/2673–0619* ⊘ *Closed weekends. No
dinner* Ⓜ *Universidad de Chile.*

BELLAS ARTES AND LASTARRIA

$$$ ✕ **Bocanariz.** A haven with wine aficionados, trendy Bocanariz in Last-
CHILEAN arria has Chilean fare, but it's all about the wine and thus is a great
Fodor's Choice place to sample *vino chileno.* Waitstaff at this tastefully designed and
★ somewhat romantic venue are all sommeliers and they serve 300 wines
on any given evening, many by the glass or small pour. **Known for:**
wine by the glass; tapas; wine flights. $ *Average main: 12000 pesos*
⊠ *José Victorino Lastarria 276, Bellas Artes* ☎ *2/2638–9893* ⊕ *www.
bocanariz.cl* ⊘ *No lunch Sun.*

$$$ ✕**Castillo Forestal.** French fare is on the menu at this spacious national
FRENCH heritage converted castle with a turret room and gorgeous terrace. At
lunch, sample the set brasserie menu with onion soup and black angus
filet, or for something lighter and also less expensive, try a turkey club
or Mediterranean sandwich on focaccia with fresh Chilean mozzarella.
Known for: park views; French cuisine; great wine list. ⑤ *Average main:*
11500 pesos ⊠ *Cardenal José María Caro 390, across from Bellas Artes*
museum, Parque Forestal ☎ *2/2664–1544* ⊕ *www.castilloforestal.cl*
⊙ *Closed Mon.*

$ ✕**Colmado Coffee & Bakery.** One of Santiago's original quality coffee pur-
CHILEAN veyors, Colmado is where you order a Colombian Chemex teamed with
Fodor'sChoice gourmet bites such as Spanish sausage and cheeses, regular and gluten-
★ free sweets or tasty vegan sandwiches. Tucked inside a leafy courtyard,
Colmado attracts local caffeine addicts and visitors alike; brunch is
especially popular. **Known for:** great coffee; veggie sandwiches; bread
baked in-house. ⑤ *Average main: 5000 pesos* ⊠ *Merced 346, Location*
E2-Interior Patio, Bellas Artes Ⓜ *Bellas Artes.*

$$$ ✕**Les Assassins.** Although at first glance this appears to be a rather
FRENCH somber bistro, nothing could be further from the truth. The service is
friendly and the Provence-influenced food—such as the mouthwatering steak au poivre and beef Bourguignon—is first-rate. **Known for:**
exceptional French fare; great service; tasty meat dishes. ⑤ *Average*
main: 10000 pesos ⊠ *Merced 279B, Parque Forestal* ☎ *2/2638–4280*
⊙ *Closed Sun. No lunch Sat.* Ⓜ *Universidad Católica.*

$$$ ✕**Sur Patagónico.** Owned by an Argentine couple, this little restaurant,
CHILEAN with its black-and-white floor and bottle-lined wood-paneled walls,
serves up loads of atmosphere along with impressive homemade pasta,
seafood, and meats such as lamb and venison. Share a *tabla* (a charcute-
rie board), which might also come with seafood or mushrooms. **Known**
for: seafood; meats; bistro. ⑤ *Average main: 11000 pesos* ⊠ *José Vic-*
torino Lastarria 92, Lastarria ☎ *2/2638–6651.*

BELLAVISTA

$$$ ✕**Azul Profundo.** One of dozens of restaurants in trendy Bellavista, the
SEAFOOD two-level dining room—with walls painted bright shades of blue and
Fodor'sChoice yellow, and racks of wine stretching to the ceiling—stands out in the
★ crowd. Choose your fish from the extensive menu—swordfish, sea
bass, shark, salmon, and tuna are among the choices—and enjoy it *a la*
plancha (grilled) or *a la lata* (served on a sizzling plate with tomatoes
and onions). **Known for:** extensive and tasty seafood menu; trendy
vibe. ⑤ *Average main: 10000 pesos* ⊠ *Constitución 111, Bellavista*
☎ *2/2738–0288* Ⓜ *Baquedano.*

$$$ ✕**Barandiarián.** Originally founded by a chef to the Peruvian embassy,
PERUVIAN Barandiarián serves traditional favorites, like *ají de gallina* , a mild
creamy chicken stew, among other meat, fish, shellfish, and pasta
dishes. The restaurant has a cozy layout with bright red walls and
wood accents. **Known for:** Peruvian-inspired cuisine; casual ambience;
seafood. ⑤ *Average main: 10000 pesos* ⊠ *Constitución 38, Locale 52,*
Bellavista ☎ *2/2737–0725* ⊕ *www.barandiaran.cl.*

$$$
CHILEAN
Fodor's Choice
★

× **Como Agua Para Chocolate.** Originally inspired by Laura Esquivel's romantic 1989 novel *Like Water for Chocolate*, this Bellavista standout focuses on Chilean dishes made with "life, love, vigor, and passion" as per the book. Reserve the "bed table" if you want to be showy (it has a headboard but is not actually a bed). **Known for:** Chilean fare; romantic ambience; large crowds. $ *Average main: 13000 pesos* ✉ *Constitución 88, Bellavista* ☎ *2/2777–8740* ⊕ *www.comoaguaparachocolate.cl* ☉ *Closed Sun. lunch* Ⓜ *Baquedano.*

$$$
CHILEAN

× **El Mesón Nerudiano.** Evoking another time and place, El Mesón Nerudiano centers around traditional recipes, poetry, music, and live theater, all in homage to Chile's greatest poet, Pablo Neruda. A stone's throw from La Chascona, Neruda's house-turned-museum, this restaurant has a menu with Chilean favorites, including *caldillo de congrio*, a fish soup cooked from the recipe given in one of Neruda's poems. **Known for:** traditional ambience; popular with tourists; literary inspiration. $ *Average main: 12000 pesos* ✉ *Dominica 35, Bellavista* ☎ *2/2737–1542* ⊕ *www.elmesonnerudiano.cl* ☉ *Closed Sun.*

$$
CHILEAN

× **Galindo.** Starting life as a canteen for local workmen, Galindo today draws artists and the young Bellavista crowd, who come for traditional Chilean fare in an old adobe house. Although it gets crowded, it's a great place to try traditional dishes like *pastel de choclo* or a hearty *cazuela*, a typical meat and vegetable soup. **Known for:** Chilean dishes; reasonable prices; casual atmosphere. $ *Average main: 6000 pesos* ✉ *Dardignac 098, Bellavista* ☎ *2/2777–0116* ⊕ *www.galindo.cl* Ⓜ *Baquedano.*

$$$
SPANISH

× **La Bodeguilla.** Stop by this authentic Spanish restaurant after visiting Cerro San Cristóbal for tasty tapas like *chorizo riojano* (a piquant sausage), *pulpo a la gallega* (octopus with peppers and potatoes), and *queso manchego* (a mild white cheese) or for the house specialty—*cabrito al horno* (oven-roasted kid goat). Wine aficionados will appreciate the extensive list of *vino chileno*. **Known for:** Spanish cuisine; extensive wine list; casual vibe. $ *Average main: 12000 pesos* ✉ *Av. Dominíca 5, Bellavista* ☎ *2/2732–5215* ☉ *Closed Sun.* Ⓜ *Baquedano.*

$$
CHILEAN

× **Peumayén.** Traditional touches from all the regions of Chile along with a historical theme highlight Peumayén, where every meal starts with a colorful "bread basket," a slate plate with examples from the north to the south of Chile. Entrées designed for sharing include llama and horse meat, lamb, fish, and the much-celebrated potato, continuing the ancestral theme. **Known for:** Chilean cuisine; traditional decor; unique and tasty meat dishes. $ *Average main: 8000 pesos* ✉ *Constitución 136, Providencia* ☎ *2/2247–3060* ⊕ *www.peumayenchile.cl* ☉ *Closed Mon. No dinner Sun.* Ⓜ *Baquedano.*

$$
AMERICAN
FAMILY

× **Uncle Fletch.** Hereford beef burgers, onion rings, and three kinds of veggie burgers all share space at this American-style restaurant owned by a French expatriate. These are some of the best burgers in the city, with patties made from meat, mushroom, chickpea, quinoa, or shrimp. **Known for:** fast food; great burgers; casual dining. $ *Average main: 7500 pesos* ✉ *Dardignac 0192, Bellavista* ☎ *2/2777–6477* ⊕ *www.uncle-fletch.com* Ⓜ *Baquedano.*

VITACURA

$$$$
CHILEAN
Fodor's Choice
★

✕ **Boragó.** Concept meets Chilean products (which are foraged from the Andes and the length of the coast) at this minimalist space, where diners enjoy 6 or 16-step tasting menus. One of chef Rodolfo Guzmán's signature dishes is a spin on the *curanto* clambake from Chiloé, made with Patagonian rainwater and served in what looks like a small clearing in a tiny thicket. **Known for:** fine dining; tasting menu; eclectic decor and experience. ⑤ *Average main: 110000 pesos* ✉ *Nueva Costanera 3467* ☎ *2/2953–8893* ⊕ *www.borago.cl* ⊘ *No lunch; closed Sun.*

$$$$
SEAFOOD
Fodor's Choice
★

✕ **Europeo.** Seafood receives top billing at this trendy yet relaxed eatery on Santiago's swankiest shopping avenue. Try the shellfish risotto topped with a fish stock foam or wild game, such as venison ragout. **Known for:** seafood and wild game; efficient service; posh crowd. ⑤ *Average main: 17000 pesos* ✉ *Av. Alonso de Córdova 2417, Vitacura* ☎ *2/2208–3603* ⊕ *www.europeo.cl* ⊘ *Closed Sun. No lunch Sat. or Mon.*

$$$$
SEAFOOD
Fodor's Choice
★

✕ **La Mar.** Opened by Peruvian culinary legend Gastón Acurio, this restaurant with a busy road-site location is bright and airy, has turquoise chairs, and a white canvas roof over the terrace that mimics a boat's sails. For your palatable delight, tuck into Peru's emblematic ceviches—you're spoiled with choices due to the seven different varieties that you can eat at a special bar or at one of the tables. **Known for:** seafood; Peruvian cuisine; cocktails. ⑤ *Average main: 20000 pesos* ✉ *Nueva Costanera 4076, Vitacura* ☎ *2/2206–7839* ⊕ *www.lamarcebicheria.cl* ⊘ *No dinner Sun.*

$$$
FRENCH
FAMILY

✕ **Le Fournil.** This restaurant features Mediterranean fare and is a great place for a light lunch or supper of quiche and salad. Le Fournil also offers a unique version of pizza, known as *tartine*, which uses its own homemade bread as a base. **Known for:** on-site bakery providing homemade bread; unique Chilean speciality pizza; quick and easy dining. ⑤ *Average main: 11000 pesos* ✉ *Av. Vitacura 3841, Vitacura* ☎ *2/2228–0219* ⊕ *www.lefournil.cl.*

$$$
CHILEAN

✕ **Mestizo.** Sporting views over Parque Bicentenario, this is a great spot for a leisurely lunch or a generous pisco sour as the sun sets between the hills in summer. The eclectic menu brings together some of the best of Chilean and Peruvian cuisine, with an emphasis on fish, as well as *plateada*, a slow-cooked cut of beef on a bed of mashed potatoes and basil. **Known for:** outdoor seating; seafood; great views. ⑤ *Average main: 12000 pesos* ✉ *Av. Bicentenario 4050, Vitacura* ☎ *9/7477–6093* ⊕ *www.mestizorestaurant.cl.*

$$$$
ASIAN

✕ **Zanzíbar.** The decor here is a bit over the top though nonetheless fun. Tables are fanciful, with designs made from pistachio nuts, red peppers, and beans; and bright mosaic floors and dozens of silver lanterns create a sensual ambience and conjure up an exotic atmosphere for dishes taking origin from Africa and Asia, such as the flavorful Szechuan shrimp and Indonesian satay. **Known for:** buzzy atmosphere; pan-African and Asian cuisine. ⑤ *Average main: 14000 pesos* ✉ *Borde Río, Av. Monseñor Escrivá de Balaguer 6400, Vitacura* ☎ *2/2218–0118* ⊕ *www.zanzibar.cl* ⊘ *No dinner Sun.*

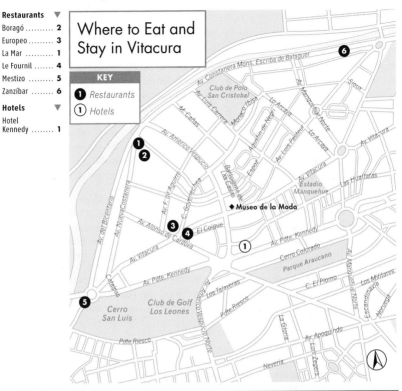

Where to Eat and
Stay in Vitacura

KEY
❶ *Restaurants*
① *Hotels*

LAS CONDES

$$$$ ✕**Anakena.** Thai favorites like pad thai curries are the mainstay at this
THAI Mandarin Oriental–located restaurant. Enjoy the elegant dining room
overlooking the garden. **Known for:** authentic Thai cuisine; sophisticated
ambience. ⑤ *Average main: 13000 pesos* ✉ *Mandarin Oriental Santiago,
Av. Kennedy 4601, Las Condes* ☎ *2/2950–3179* ⊕ *www.mandarinorien-
tal.com/santiago/las-condes/fine-dining/restaurants/thai-cuisine/anakena.*

$$$ ✕**Coquinaria.** Whether you want a full English breakfast, weekend
CAFÉ brunch or lunch on a shady terrace, or a good cup of tea to linger over,
this restaurant next to the W Hotel doesn't disappoint. It's also a gour-
met food shop, packed with temptations such as fresh pasta and cheeses
not easily found elsewhere in Santiago. **Known for:** breakfast; brunch;
gourmet food. ⑤ *Average main: 12000 pesos* ✉ *Isidora Goyenechea
3000, Las Condes* ☎ *2/2307–3000* ⊕ *www.coquinaria.cl* Ⓜ *El Golf.*

$$$$ ✕**Matsuri.** With a sleek design that calls to mind Los Angeles as much
JAPANESE as Tokyo, this Japanese restaurant in the Mandarin Oriental is one of
Santiago's most stylish eateries. Comprising a sushi bar and two tatami
rooms (no shoes allowed, but slippers are provided) with sliding screens
for privacy, Matsuri also has two grill tables. **Known for:** sushi; stylish
setting. ⑤ *Average main: 15000 pesos* ✉ *Mandarin Oriental Santiago,
Av. Kennedy 4601, Las Condes* ☎ *2/2950–3051* ⊙ *Closed Sat. lunch.*

PROVIDENCIA

$$ ✕**Ambrosía Bistro.** An intimate yet smart spot attracting foodies and
CHILEAN office workers, this sister restaurant to acclaimed Ambrosía in Vitacura
Fodor's Choice is setting palates on fire. Grab a comfy bar stool to watch chef Carolina
★ Bazán and team in action in the open kitchen, where they focus on
Chilean ingredients; the menu changes weekly, but if possible order
the citrus ceviche or steak from the dry-aged beef fridge. **Known for:**
seafood and dry-aged beef; extensive by-the-glass wine list curated by
top sommelier Rosario Onetto; large portions to share. ⑤ *Average main:
8500 pesos* ✉ *Nueva de Lyon 99, Providencia* ☎ *2/2233–4303* ⊕ *www.
ambrosiabistro.cl* ☉ *Closed Sun.* Ⓜ *Pedro de Valdivia.*

$$$ ✕**Aquí Está Coco.** Though a bit kooky, with a variety of themed dining
SEAFOOD rooms, such as one where diners eat at a boat-turned-table, this inti-
mate seafood spot pleases the eye. Traditional specialties, like grilled
corvina (sea bass) and the classic Chilean *machas a la parmesana* (razor
clams au gratin) are very popular dishes. **Known for:** seafood; buzzy
atmosphere; Chilean stews with swordfish and king crab. ⑤ *Average
main: 13000 pesos* ✉ *La Concepción 236, Providencia* ☎ *2/2410–6200*
⊕ *www.aquiestacoco.cl* ☉ *Closed Sun. and Feb.* Ⓜ *Pedro de Valdivia.*

$ ✕**Café Clementina.** Perfect for a quick coffee stop or a picnic, this tiny
ECLECTIC café-bakery makes sweet and savory treats. Have lunch on the grassy
Padre Letelier plaza—a tablecloth comes with your couscous salad,
chicken with mustard vinaigrette, or quiche—and don't miss dessert
(the brownies sell quickly). **Known for:** light bites; picnic lunch; sweet
treats. ⑤ *Average main: 5000 pesos* ✉ *Los Conquistadores 2242, cross
street Padre Letelier, Providencia* ☎ *2/2231–6832* ⊕ *www.cafeclemen-
tina.cl* ☉ *Closed Sun. and Feb. No dinner.*

$$$ ✕**Divertimento Chileno.** A favorite with Chilean politicians, journalists
CHILEAN and, on Sunday, local families, this restaurant serves both homemade
FAMILY pasta—the spinach and ricotta ravioli served with butter and sage is
excellent—and traditional Chilean fare such as *pastel de choclo* (beef
and corn casserole). For alfresco dining, book a table in the tranquil
tree-shaded setting at the base of San Cristóbal hill. **Known for:** Ital-
ian fare; child friendly; outdoor dining. ⑤ *Average main: 10000 pesos*
✉ *Av. El Cerro 722, Providencia* ✛ *at Av. Pedro de Valdivia Norte*
☎ *2/2975–4600* ⊕ *www.divertimento.cl* Ⓜ *Pedro de Valdivia.*

$$ ✕**Eladio.** A vast, rather retro space on the fifth floor of an office block,
CHILEAN Eladio invites you to enjoy a succulent *bife de chorizo* (sirloin), mouth-
FAMILY watering *costillas de cerdo* (pork ribs), or just about any other meat
with a good bottle of Chilean wine. Finish with a slice of *amapola*
(poppy-seed) sponge cake. **Known for:** traditonal Chilean meat dishes;
no-reservations policy; excellent wine list. ⑤ *Average main: 9000 pesos*
✉ *Providencia 2250, 5th fl., Providencia* ☎ *2/2231–4224* ⊕ *www.ela-
dio.cl* ☉ *Closed Sun.* Ⓜ *Los Leones.*

$$$$ ✕**El Cid.** Considered by critics to be one of the city's top restaurants,
CHILEAN this culinary centerpiece of the Sheraton Santiago has an excellent lunch
buffet, which includes unlimited wine. The dining room, which overlooks the pool, has crisp linens and simple place settings because all
the excitement here is provided by the famous grilled seafood—king
crab, prawns, squid, and scallops with a sweet, spicy sauce. **Known for:**

2

sophisticated ambience; seafood; great service. ⓈAverage main: 18000 pesos ⊠ Av. Santa María 1742, Providencia ☎ 2/2233–5000 ⊕ www. restaurantelcid.com Ⓜ No metro.

$$ ╳ **El Huerto.** One of Santiago's most established vegetarian restaurants, this wood-paneled eatery in the heart of Providencia serves both vegetarian- and vegan-friendly fare, including hearty soups and fresh-squeezed juices. The vegan set lunch is a good value, and the three-step menu that changes daily consists of an appetizer, main course, and dessert for 7,400 pesos. **Known for:** set menu lunch; vegetarian and vegan selections. ⓈAverage main: 6500 pesos ⊠ Orrego Luco 054, Providencia ☎ 2/2233–2690 ⊕ www.elhuerto.cl ⊘ No dinner Sun. Ⓜ Pedro de Valdivia.

VEGETARIAN

$ ╳ **Holm Ensaladería.** This salad bar is the brainchild of Victor Holm, a Danish entrepreneur who wakes up before the crack of dawn to source the fresh ingredients. Youngish patrons choose from a selection of predressed salads, such as pasta salad with pesto, bean salad, and chicken or fish (optional)—all served over a plate of mixed greens. **Known for:** amazing salads; vegetarian-friendly dishes; great brunch menu. ⓈAverage main: 4000 pesos ⊠ Padre Mariano 125, Providencia ☎ 2/9422–7400 ⊘ No dinner weekends.

EUROPEAN

$$ ╳ **Liguria.** This extremely popular restaurant and bar is always packed with a young crowd, so you might have to wait to be seated in the chandelier-lighted dining room or at one of the tables on the sidewalk. A large selection of Chilean wine accompanies such favorites as *cazuela* (a stew of beef or chicken and potatoes) and *mechada* sandwiches (thinly sliced beef). **Known for:** lively ambience; cocktails; Chilean fare. ⓈAverage main: 8000 pesos ⊠ Av. Providencia 1373, Providencia ☎ 2/2235–7914 ⊕ www.liguria.cl ⊘ Closed Sun. Ⓜ Manuel Montt.

CHILEAN
Fodor's Choice
★

$$ ╳ **Normandie.** This unassuming French restaurant with a slightly haphazard decor has service as friendly as the food is good. Join the regulars at the wooden bar for a steaming bowl of onion soup and beef Bourguignon with french fries (made from real potatoes) in winter, or a glass of wine at one of the pavement tables in summer. **Known for:** French cuisine; extensive Chilean wine list; alfresco dining. ⓈAverage main: 7900 pesos ⊠ Providencia 1234, Providencia ☎ 2/2236–3011 ⊕ www. normandie1234.cl ⊘ Closed Sun. Ⓜ Manuel Montt.

FRENCH

WHERE TO STAY

Santiago's accommodations range from luxurious *hoteles* to comfortable *residenciales*, which can be homey bed-and-breakfasts or simple hotel-style accommodations. All the construction in the past decade means competition between hotels is steep, but they still fill in the high summer season and when large trade fair or business conventions occur (March is a peak month). Outside these dates, you can often find a room for up to 20% less than the advertised rack rates, particularly if you stay for more than a couple of days. Call several hotels and ask for the best possible rate. It's a good idea to reserve in advance during the peak seasons (January, February, July, and August).

Some hotels, particularly more expensive ones, quote prices in U.S. dollars rather than pesos. Visitors from abroad are exempt from the 19% sales tax, provided they pay in foreign currency or with an overseas credit card. *Hotel reviews have been shortened. For full information, visit Fodors.com.*

WHAT IT COSTS IN CHILEAN PESOS (IN THOUSANDS)			
$	**$$**	**$$$**	**$$$$**
FOR TWO PEOPLE	Under 51	51–85	86–115	over 115

Hotel prices are the lowest cost of a standard double room in high season.

SANTIAGO CENTRO

$
HOTEL
Happy House Hostel. From the gorgeous baroque facade with balconies to the original ceiling medallion from which the chandelier in the giant salon and living room hangs, it's clear that Happy House Hostel is something special. **Pros:** historical architecture; a beautiful plaza; close to nightlife and Barrio Yungay. **Cons:** a bit farther afield from some sights; walls not thick to keep out noise; can be a little chilly in winter (but you'll be loaded up with comforters). $ *Rooms from: 40000 pesos* ✉ *Moneda 1829, Barrio Brasil* ☎ *2/2688–4849* ⊕ *www.happyhouse-hostel.com* ⇄ *25 rooms* ⑩ *Breakfast* Ⓜ *Los Héroes.*

$
HOTEL
Hotel Foresta. Staying in this seven-story hotel across the street from Cerro Santa Lucía is like visiting an elegant old home that has seen better days. **Pros:** great location near the quaint cafés and shops of Plaza Mulato Gil de Castro; rooftop restaurant and bar with a view; larger suites optional. **Cons:** rooms are small; no online booking; dated look. $ *Rooms from: 51000 pesos* ✉ *Victoria Subercaseaux 353, Santiago Centro* ☎ *2/2639–6261* ⇄ *35 rooms* ⑩ *Breakfast* Ⓜ *Bellas Artes.*

$$
HOTEL
Hotel Fundador. On the edge of the quaint Barrio París-Londres, this hotel has rooms that, although small, are airy and attractive. **Pros:** tucked away from downtown traffic noise; on the doorstep of a subway station; free Wi-Fi. **Cons:** not an area for a stroll at night; few restaurants or bars in the immediate vicinity; rooms a bit dated. $ *Rooms from: 69000 pesos* ✉ *Paseo Serrano 34, Santiago Centro* ☎ *2/2387–1200* ⊕ *www.fundador.cl* ⇄ *119 rooms, 28 suites* ⑩ *Breakfast* Ⓜ *Universidad de Chile.*

$
HOTEL
Hotel París 813. In the heart of Barrio París-Londres, this mansion-turned-hotel has old-fashioned, clean rooms with the basic furnishings; those in the more comfortable half, which you reach via a marble staircase, are more spacious and cost just a few thousand pesos more. **Pros:** excellent value for a modest price; friendly service; free Internet. **Cons:** breakfast room too small for hotel size; no elevator; no parking. $ *Rooms from: 30000 pesos* ✉ *París 813, La Alameda* ☎ *2/2664–0921, 2/2639–0437* ⊕ *www.hotelparis813.com* ⇄ *50 rooms* ⑩ *Breakfast* Ⓜ *Universidad de Chile, Santa Lucía.*

$$$ 🏨 **Hotel Plaza San Francisco.** Across from Iglesia San Francisco, this
HOTEL   sophisticated business hotel has everything traveling executives need:
Fodor'sChoice   spacious rooms with large beds and double-paned windows to keep
★   out the downtown noise, a sparkling indoor pool, a fitness club, and
even an art gallery. **Pros:** helpful English-speaking staff; on-site res-
taurant offers interesting cuisine; clean quiet rooms. **Cons:** nightlife
and other good restaurants are a metro or taxi ride away; on-site res-
taurant expensive; street-facing rooms can get noisy. ⑤ *Rooms from:
89000 pesos* ✉ *Av. Bernardo O'Higgins (Alameda) 816, Santiago
Centro* ☎ *2/2639-3832* ⊕ *www.plazasanfrancisco.cl* ⥱ *146 rooms*
❍ *Breakfast* Ⓜ *Universidad de Chile.*

$$ 🏨 **Hotel Vegas.** This colonial-style building, adorned with a bullet-
HOTEL   shaped turret, sits in the heart of the charming Barrio París-Londres.
Pros: good location for downtown sightseeing; free Wi-Fi; spacious
rooms. **Cons:** some rooms smell musty; cramped lobby, bar, and café;
no elevator or parking. ⑤ *Rooms from: 64000 pesos* ✉ *Londres 49,
Santiago Centro* ☎ *2/2632-2514* ⊕ *www.hotelvegas.net* ⥱ *20 rooms*
❍ *Breakfast* Ⓜ *Universidad de Chile.*

$$$ 🏨 **Mercure Santiago Central.** It's hard to beat the location of this busi-
HOTEL   ness traveler-minded hotel, which is close to Cerro Santa Lucía. **Pros:**
central location; within walking distance from many points of interest
downtown; clean and relatively quiet. **Cons:** a bit impersonal; some
rooms more outdated than others; lighting in some rooms not good.
⑤ *Rooms from: 95000 pesos* ✉ *La Alameda 632, Santiago Centro*
☎ *2/2595-6622* ⊕ *www.mercure.com* ⥱ *142 rooms* ❍ *Breakfast.*

BELLAS ARTES AND LASTARRIA

$$ 🏨 **Hotel Ismael 312.** This well-placed and well-run design hotel with a
HOTEL   personal touch has expansive views over Parque Forestal and a rooftop
Fodor'sChoice   pool from which to enjoy it. **Pros:** unbeatable location; high design ele-
★   ments; welcoming staff. **Cons:** the rooms can feel a bit sterile; rooms
overlooking the street (as opposed to the park) do not have much of a
view; no parking. ⑤ *Rooms from: 75000 pesos* ✉ *Ismael Valdes Vergara 312, Parque Forestal* ☎ *2/2616-7600* ⊕ *www.hotelismael312.com*
⥱ *45 rooms* ❍ *Breakfast.*

$$$$ 🏨 **Hotel Magnolia.** A welcome addition to the neighborhood, this beau-
HOTEL   tifully restored 1929 mansion is perfectly located on the cusp of both
Fodor'sChoice   Lastarria and Bellas Artes, a stone's throw from Santa Lucía hill. **Pros:**
★   great location; stylish and practical communal areas; abundant breakfast. **Cons:** some amenities lacking for what you expect of a higher-end
hotel (e.g., no slippers or free coffee in room); you have to ring the bell
to get in after midnight; some rooms are dark. ⑤ *Rooms from: 140000
pesos* ✉ *Huérfanos 539, Lastarria* ☎ *2/2664-4043* ⊕ *www.hotelmag-
nolia.cl* ⥱ *42 rooms* ❍ *Breakfast* Ⓜ *Bellas Artes.*

$$$$ 🏨 **The Singular.** This luxury lodging in Lastarria is a smart spot that's
HOTEL   well-furnished, with a modern, mainly European style. **Pros:** courtyard
Fodor'sChoice   for leisurely breakfasts; stylish and spacious rooms; spa with massages,
★   sauna, and steam room. **Cons:** exposed concrete of old buildings visible from rooftop deck; no daytime access to rooftop terrace; breakfast
can get crowded. ⑤ *Rooms from: 252000 pesos* ✉ *Merced 294, Bellas*

Artes ☎ *2/2306–8820* ⊕ *thesingular.com/hotel/santiago* ⇔ *62 rooms* ⦿ *Breakfast* Ⓜ *Bellas Artes.*

$$$$ Ⓣ **Su Merced.** This small boutique hotel in a historic building has a sleek
HOTEL   design and stunning views over Parque Forestal. **Pros:** design-focused;
family-owned; attentive staff. **Cons:** less expensive rooms have a view of
the street; breakfast portions a bit small; few extra amenities. $ *Rooms
from: 181000 pesos* ⊠ *Coronel Santiago Bueras 121, Parque Forestal*
☎ *2/2584–7230* ⊕ *www.sumercedhotel.com* ⇔ *11 rooms* ⦿ *Breakfast.*

BELLAVISTA

$$$$ Ⓣ **The Aubrey.** One of the city's favorite luxury boutique hotels, this
HOTEL   hotel was formed in 2009 when two 1920s mansions next to Cerro San
Fodor's Choice   Cristóbal were joined together, giving it ample outdoor space, including
★   a pool and an indoor–outdoor patio bar. **Pros:** well-lit; knowledgeable and friendly staff; 20% discount on rooms in winter. **Cons:** less expensive rooms lack hillside views and private terraces; aromas from the
nearby zoo can waft in; noise from nearby bars can make its way in.
$ *Rooms from: 158000 pesos* ⊠ *Constitución 317, Bellavista* ⊕ *www.
theaubrey.com* ⇔ *15 rooms* ⦿ *Breakfast.*

$$$$ Ⓣ **El Castillo Rojo.** This boutique hotel in a red castle just off the beaten
HOTEL   path in Bellavista is a step back in time, in all the right ways. **Pros:**
great location in Bellavista; attention to detail; superior customer
service. **Cons:** decoration feels fussy at times; main areas can be
dark; limited breakfast. $ *Rooms from: 120000 pesos* ⊠ *Consti-
tución 195, Bellavista* ☎ *2/2352–4500* ⊕ *www.castillorojohotel.com*
⇔ *19 rooms* ⦿ *Breakfast.*

$$ Ⓣ **Loreto Hotel.** This historic house nestled between Bellavista and
HOTEL   Recoleta neighborhoods has a great location and yet isn't close enough
Fodor's Choice   to hear any of the noise. **Pros:** great breakfast buffet; very helpful
★   staff; quiet. **Cons:** you need to take a taxi at night; no elevator; some
rooms are very small (ask for a larger one). $ *Rooms from: 67000
pesos* ⊠ *Loreto 170, Bellavista* ☎ *2/2777–1060* ⊕ *www.loretohotel.
cl* ⇔ *28 rooms* ⦿ *Breakfast.*

VITACURA

$$ Ⓣ **Hotel Kennedy.** Located on the main road out to the mountains, Hotel
HOTEL   Kennedy with its glass tower is popular with skiers who prefer to make
the 45-minute journey each day rather than pay higher hotel prices up
by the slopes. **Pros:** Aquarium restaurant, featuring good international
cuisine and a cellar full of excellent Chilean wines; free Wi-Fi; helpful
staff. **Cons:** now more than 20 years old, the hotel is showing its age;
Wi-Fi connection slow; not all staff speak English. $ *Rooms from:
76000 pesos* ⊠ *Av. Kennedy 4570, Vitacura* ☎ *2/2290–8100* ⊕ *www.
hotelkennedychile.com* ⇔ *133 rooms* ⦿ *Breakfast* Ⓜ *No metro.*

LAS CONDES

$$$$
HOTEL
Director El Golf. Aside from its location near the center of the El Golf entertainment district, this hotel has an important plus in that rooms—all spacious suites—have a kitchenette and small dining area. **Pros:** a good choice for longer-stay visitors who don't want to eat out every night; friendly staff; walking distance to the mall, coffee shops, and restaurants. **Cons:** decoration is a bit dated; limited breakfast options because of slow replenishment; some designated smoking areas. $ *Rooms from: 150000 pesos* ⊠ *Carmencita 45, Las Condes* ☎ *2/2498–3000* ⊕ *www.director.cl* ⤴ *49 rooms* ⑩ *Breakfast* Ⓜ *El Golf, Tobalaba.*

$$$$
HOTEL
Mandarin Oriental Santiago. The soaring spire of the Mandarin Oriental resembles a rocket, and you might feel like an astronaut when you're shooting up a glass elevator through a 24-story atrium. **Pros:** garden and swimming pool are particularly lovely; great views of Andes; three excellent restaurants. **Cons:** out of the way and not much else close by; fee for Internet; one of city's main shopping malls about a 15-minute walk away. $ *Rooms from: 203000 pesos* ⊠ *Av. Kennedy 4601, Las Condes* ☎ *2/2950–3088* ⊕ *www.mandarinoriental.com/santiago/las-condes/luxury-hotel* ⤴ *310 rooms* ⑩ *Breakfast* Ⓜ *No metro.*

$$
HOTEL
Neruda Express. This "express" version of the larger Hotel Neruda (on Avenida Pedro de Valdivia) lacks the space and other frills, but rooms are tastefully modern and bright (ask for one of the two suites on the second floor or one of the larger "superior" rooms on the 9th to 11th floors, which cost the same as standard rooms). **Pros:** convenient for fashionable Las Condes but priced lower; close to Costanera Center; free Wi-Fi. **Cons:** although all windows have double glass, rooms on Avenida Apoquindo still get traffic noise (those at the back are quieter); staff can be on the dry side; some rooms are very small. $ *Rooms from: 83000 pesos* ⊠ *Vecinal 40 at Av. Apoquindo, Las Condes* ☎ *2/2233–2747* ⊕ *www.hotelneruda.cl/hoteles/hotel-neruda-express* ⤴ *55 rooms* ⑩ *Breakfast* Ⓜ *El Golf, Tobalaba.*

$$$$
HOTEL
NH Collection Plaza. Santiago's World Trade Center is also home to the NH (until 2017, it was Radisson Plaza), a combination that makes sense to many corporate travelers. **Pros:** all the comfort and facilities of a top hotel (such as concierge service) at a more modest price; easy walk to the metro; spacious rooms. **Cons:** the presence of the nearby Costanera Center and an increase in car ownership snarls traffic during peak commuting hours; teething troubles with service following new (2017) ownership; rooms are gradually being overhauled so not all are the same standard. $ *Rooms from: 150000 pesos* ⊠ *Av. Vitacura 2610, Las Condes* ☎ *2/2433–9000,* ⊕ *www.nh-collection.com* ⤴ *159 rooms* ⑩ *Breakfast* Ⓜ *Tobalaba.*

$$$$
HOTEL
The Ritz-Carlton. The rather bland brick exterior of this 15-story hotel, the first Ritz-Carlton in South America, belies the luxurious appointments within, such as the mahogany-paneled walls, cream marble floors, and enormous windows characterizing the splendid two-story lobby. **Pros:** prime location on Avenida Apoquindo; close to the El Golf business and restaurant area; personalized service. **Cons:** some find the elaborate decoration fussy and oppressive; free

Wi-Fi only in lobby (there is a charge for in-room use); staff can be snooty. $ *Rooms from: 250000 pesos* ⊠ *El Alcalde 15, Las Condes* ☎ *2/2470–8500* ⊕ *www.ritzcarlton.com/en/hotels/santiago* ⤷ *205 rooms* ❘❂❘ *Breakfast* Ⓜ *El Golf.*

$$$$ 🏨 **Santiago InterContinental.** Attendants wearing top hats usher you
HOTEL into the two-story marble lobby of one of the city's top hotels. **Pros:** easy walking distance from the El Golf business and restaurant area; concierge; heated indoor pool. **Cons:** bad traffic congestion around the hotel; some rooms have not been renovated and are outdated, requiring regular maintenance; small breakfast salon for such a large hotel. $ *Rooms from: 252000 pesos* ⊠ *Av. Vitacura 2885, Las Condes* ☎ *2/2394–2000* ⊕ *www.intercontisantiago.com* ⤷ *296 rooms* ❘❂❘ *Breakfast* Ⓜ *Tobalaba.*

$$$$ 🏨 **Santiago Marriott Hotel.** The first 25 floors of this gleaming copper
HOTEL tower house the Marriott, which welcomes guests into its impressive two-story, cream marble lobby with full-grown palm trees in and around comfortable seating areas. **Pros:** excellent, friendly service; concierge; activities like wine tastings and live music. **Cons:** removed from the action in a suburban neighborhood; free Internet not included for all; some rooms could use an upgrade. $ *Rooms from: 222000 pesos* ⊠ *Av. Kennedy 5741, Las Condes* ☎ *2/2426–2000* ⊕ *www.santiago-marriott.com* ⤷ *280 rooms* ❘❂❘ *Breakfast* Ⓜ *No metro.*

$$$$ 🏨 **W Santiago.** Located in the heart of the fashionable El Golf business
HOTEL and restaurant district, South America's first W Hotel set a new standard of luxury and service in Santiago when it opened, and its smart, contemporary decoration still makes the city's other five-star hotels look staid. **Pros:** excellent location; heated outdoor pool; great shops inside the hotel (clothing, jewelry, crafts). **Cons:** expensive; not everyone is comfortable with the bath and shower integrated into the bedroom; Internet is free in lobby and some common areas, but there's a charge for in-room usage. $ *Rooms from: 254000 pesos* ⊠ *Isidora Goyenechea 3000, Las Condes* ☎ *2/2770–0000* ⊕ *www.wsantiagohotel.com* ⤷ *196 rooms* ❘❂❘ *Breakfast* Ⓜ *El Golf.*

PROVIDENCIA

$$ 🏨 **Chilhotel.** Good midrange hotels are few and far between in San-
HOTEL tiago, and this small, family-owned funky old house set on a quiet side street is one of them. **Pros:** excellent service closely supervised by owners; a 10-minute metro ride from downtown; free Wi-Fi. **Cons:** small rooms; no elevator; spartan. $ *Rooms from: 55000 pesos* ⊠ *Cirujano Guzmán 103, Providencia* ☎ *2/2235–0713* ⊕ *www.chilhotel.cl* ⤷ *17 rooms* ❘❂❘ *Breakfast* Ⓜ *Manuel Montt.*

$$$$ 🏨 **Carménère EcoHotel.** In an airy house on a quiet street, this eco-friendly
B&B/INN B&B evokes a country house in southern Chile. **Pros:** lots of care taken with decorations, plants, and food; personal touches include handmade chocolates on pillows; excellent breakfast. **Cons:** on occasion the whole property is rented out, leaving no rooms for other guests; some rooms are poky; Wi-Fi can be spotty. $ *Rooms from: 168000 pesos* ⊠ *María Luisa Santander 0292, Providencia* ☎ *2/2204–6372* ⊕ *www.hotelcarmenere.com* ⤷ *5 rooms* ❘❂❘ *Breakfast.*

$$$
HOTEL

⊞ **Four Points by Sheraton.** The heart of Providencia's shopping district is just steps away from this hotel, which is a favorite with savvy business visitors to the city. **Pros:** excellent value for money; a desk in each room; good, helpful staff. **Cons:** free Internet only in the lobby, hourly charge in rooms; restaurant just okay; sometimes it's noisy from the street or a/c. $ *Rooms from: 94000 pesos* ⊠ *Av. Santa Magdalena 111, Providencia* ☎ *2/2750–0300* ⊕ *www.fourpointssantiago.com* ↶ *128 rooms* ⦿ *Breakfast* Ⓜ *Los Leones.*

$$$
HOTEL
Fodor'sChoice
★

⊞ **Hotel Orly.** This sweet and economical treasure in such a convenient location in the middle of Providencia is a real find. **Pros:** free parking; excellent maintenance; free Wi-Fi. **Cons:** difficult to get a room on short notice; rooms are outdated; bathrooms are cramped. $ *Rooms from: 100000 pesos* ⊠ *Av. Pedro de Valdivia 027, Providencia* ☎ *2/2630–3000* ⊕ *www.orlyhotel.com* ↶ *28 rooms* ⦿ *Breakfast* Ⓜ *Pedro de Valdivia.*

$
B&B/INN

⊞ **Italia Suite Bed & Breakfast.** Stay in one of Santiago's most interesting design neighborhoods at this cozy B&B in Barrio Italia, a vibrant subsection of Providencia known for its design shops and antique stores. **Pros:** neighborhoody feeling; attentive hosts; free Wi-Fi. **Cons:** not on the main L1 metro line; breakfast is not very creative; owners speak little English. $ *Rooms from: 40000 pesos* ⊠ *Tegualda 1846, Providencia* ☎ *2/2505–9530* ⊕ *www.italiasuite. com* ↶ *9 rooms* ⦿ *Breakfast* Ⓜ *Irrarazaval.*

$$$$
HOTEL
Fodor'sChoice
★

⊞ **Le Rêve.** This classic 20th-century French house is a charming boutique hotel with comfortable rooms that all but guarantee a good night of sleep—after all, the name in French means "the dream." It's big enough not to feel closed in, and there are garden and street views from the spacious and stylish three floors. **Pros:** self-serve snacks in the kitchen until 1 am; great location close to restaurants; excellent buffet breakfast. **Cons:** some noise from nearby restaurants; street-facing rooms particularly susceptible to noise; breakfast time can be very busy. $ *Rooms from: 133000 pesos* ⊠ *Orrego Luco 023, Providencia* ☎ *2/2757–6000* ⊕ *www.lereve.cl* ↶ *31 rooms* ⦿ *Breakfast* Ⓜ *Los Leones or Pedro de Valdivia.*

$$
B&B/INN
Fodor'sChoice
★

⊞ **Meridiano Sur Petit Hotel.** In a conveniently located restored house, this small family-run hotel is a welcome addition to Santiago's limited range of midpriced lodgings. **Pros:** five-minute walk from metro; restful atmosphere; great collection of books about Chile to browse. **Cons:** rooms in basement have natural light but are very small, so it's worth the extra few thousand pesos per night for an upstairs room; no elevators; service can be hit and miss. $ *Rooms from: 87000 pesos* ⊠ *Santa Beatriz 256, Providencia* ☎ *2/2235–3659* ⊕ *www.meridianosur.cl* ↶ *8 rooms* ⦿ *Breakfast* Ⓜ *Manuel Montt.*

$$$$
HOTEL

⊞ **San Cristóbal Tower and Sheraton Santiago.** Two hotels sit side by side at this lovely property, almost functioning as a single entity, but they are distinct: the Sheraton Santiago is a midrange hotel, favored by tourists for it's more moderate prices, while the San Cristóbal Tower is pricier, more luxurious, and popular with business executives who value its efficiency, elegance, and impeccable service. **Pros:** excellent joint amenities; concierge service; free Wi-Fi in lobby. **Cons:** a taxi ride away from the nearest metro station and restaurant and shopping

areas; minimum three-hour charge in rooms for Wi-Fi; some rooms are outdated. $ *Rooms from: 186000 pesos* ✉ *Josefina Edwards de Ferrari 0100, Providencia* ☎ *2/2707–1000* ⊕ *www.sancristobaltowersantiago. com* ⇌ *139 rooms* ▯⃝ *Breakfast* Ⓜ *Pedro de Valdivia.*

$$ Ⓣ **Santiago Park Plaza.** Although this hotel bills itself as English in style, it's
HOTEL removed the formerly oppressive dark furnishings, making the lobby and restaurant larger and airier. **Pros:** in the heart of Providencia with a metro station at the doorstep; free Wi-Fi; close to Costanera Center mall. **Cons:** breakfast not impressive; room decor dated; hit-and-miss service. $ *Rooms from: 80000 pesos* ✉ *Av. Ricardo Lyon 207, Providencia* ☎ *2/2372–4058* ⊕ *www.parkplaza.cl* ⇌ *104 rooms* ▯⃝ *Breakfast* Ⓜ *Los Leones.*

NIGHTLIFE AND PERFORMING ARTS

Although it can't rival Buenos Aires or Rio de Janeiro, Santiago buzzes with increasingly sophisticated bars and clubs. Santiaguinos often meet for drinks during the week, usually after work when most bars have happy hour. Then they call it a night, as most people don't really cut loose until Friday and Saturday, unless it's before a long weekend, when Thursday is dubbed "*viernes chico.*" Weekends commence with dinner beginning at 9 or 10 and then a drink at a pub. (This doesn't refer to an English beer hall; a pub here is a bar with loud music and a lot of seating.) No one thinks of heading to the dance clubs until 1 am, and they stay until 4 or 5 am.

NIGHTLIFE

Bars and clubs are scattered all over Santiago, but a handful of streets have such a concentration of establishments that they resemble block parties on Friday and Saturday nights. Pub crawls along Avenida Pío Nono and neighboring streets in Bellavista yield venues aimed at a young crowd (the drinking age is 18). Across the river and further west, Lastarria hosts a busy bar scene. To the east in Providencia, the area around Manuel Montt and Tobalaba metro stations attract a slightly older and better-heeled crowd.

What you should wear depends on your destination. Bellavista has a mix of styles ranging from blue jeans to basic black and, in general, the dress gets smarter the farther east you move, but remains casual.

⚠ **Note that establishments referred to as "nightclubs" are almost always female strip shows. The signs in the windows usually make it quite clear what goes on inside. The same is true for certain cafés with blacked-out windows, called "cafés con piernas" (literally: coffee with legs).**

SANTIAGO CENTRO
BARS AND CLUBS
El Rincón de las Canallas. A secret meeting place during the Pinochet regime, El Rincón de las Canallas still requires a password to get in (it's *Chile libre,* meaning "free Chile"). The walls are painted with political statements such as "Somos todos inocentes" ("We are all innocent"). It's a two-story affair, with loads of graffiti and business cards on the walls and ceiling. ✉ *Tarapacá 810, Santiago Centro* ☎ *2/2632–5491* ⊕ *www.canallas.cl.*

CUECA CLUBS

El Huaso Enrique. This classic of Barrio Yungay predates the current immigration of hipsters and the revitalization of the neighborhood. For nearly 60 years, the kitchens have turned out Chilean specialties such as the heavy-hitting *chorrillana*, a plate of french fries covered in stewed onions and sausage, and topped with a fried egg. They also teach classes in the stompiest style of Chile's national dance, the *cueca brava*. Classes are Wednesday through Saturday at 7:30 pm and cost 3,000 pesos. Given the timing, it's best to dance first, then eat. ✉ *Maipú 462, Santiago Centro* ☎ *2/2681–5257* ⊕ *www.elhuasoenrique.cl* Ⓜ *Quinta Normal.*

Fodor'sChoice **La Chiminea.** Hidden on a side street downtown, you might be forgiven
★ for thinking that La Chiminea was just a hole in the wall. Besides towering plates of french fries and happy-hour specials, this place has an undying love of all things Chilean, especially cueca. Come here with nothing but a competitive spirit and a hanky, a dance essential. Classes run Monday and Thursday at 8 pm and cost 2,500 pesos. ✉ *Príncipe de Gales 90, Santiago Centro* ☎ *2/2697–0131* Ⓜ *La Moneda.*

SALSA CLUBS

Klub Mangosta. Live music accompanies dancers at Klub Mangosta. There are salsa and bachata classes Wednesday through Saturday nights from 9 to 11. Entry is 2,500 pesos. ✉ *Av. Vicuña Mackenna 1603, Ñuñoa* ☎ *2/2551–6879* ⊕ *www.klubmangosta.com* Ⓜ *Ñuble.*

BELLAS ARTES AND LASTARRIA

BARS AND CLUBS

El Diablito. Identifiable by the leering devil on the sign, El Diablito is one of the only divey places left in Lastarria/Bellas Artes, whose decor sports spurs, stirrups, and other metal items. If you want to see what this area felt like about 10 years ago, before gentrification, this is a good spot to try. It's popular for drinks after work or late at night. ✉ *Merced 336, Parque Forestal* ☎ *2/2638–3512.*

Fodor'sChoice **José Ramón 277.** A leader on the local craft beer scene, this friendly
★ *chopería* (pub) serves an array of brews on tap and classic Chilean sandwiches—the pulled pork and avocado is a delight—to soak up the alcohol. Hipsters and local Lastarria residents come together at wooden tables to enjoy a pint or two; early birds will appreciate the breakfast menu, from 8 am. ✉ *José Ramón Gutiérrez 277, Lastarria* ☎ *9/4258–1689* Ⓜ *Universidad Católica.*

PARQUE FORESTAL

BARS AND CLUBS

Catedrál. At the base of Cerro Santa Lucía, partially in a former convenience store, Catedrál is one of three establishments run by the same owners, all connected but with separate entrances. Live music and a heated-in-winter upstairs terrace make the Catedrál's bar popular among the 30-plus crowd (no happy hour). Upmarket Ópera restaurant serves dishes from far-flung places, such as trout wrapped in phyllo, veal, pork, and other nicely presented oven-cooked meats. Around the corner, on the street Mercéd is the café with Belgian sandwiches, large portions of cake, soup, and most importantly, the creamiest ice cream

in Santiago. ⊠ *José Miguel de la Barra 407, Parque Forestal* ☎ *2/2664–3048* ⊕ *www.operacatedral.cl* ⊙ *Catedrál and Ópera closed Sun.*

BELLAVISTA
BARS AND CLUBS

Bar Constitución. Following a relocation, Bar Constitución changed its remit from live music to full-on dance club (Thursday is reggaéton night) making it one of Bellavista's more popular venues. A twenties to thirties crowd hits the dance floor, fueled by *piscolas* (pisco and cola) and *limacuya* , a drink with vodka, lime juice, and passion fruit. ⊠ *Ernesto Pinto Lagarrigue 364, Bellavista* ☎ *2/4469–8275.*

El Toro. This gay resto-bar welcomes everyone. The cozy spot is packed every night except Sunday, and the tables are spaced close enough to eavesdrop on the conversations of models and other members of the *"farandula"* (Chilean celebrities) who frequent the place. Lunch is less expensive, with offers like eggplant lasagna or a Peruvian chicken stew. It functions as a bar-restaurant until 2 am, but may close earlier on quieter nights like Monday or Tuesday. ⊠ *Loreto 33, Bellavista* ☎ *2/2761–5954.*

Etniko. For a modern, minimalist fusion sushi bar, this is a good choice. The interior is mostly wood, enhanced by dramatic lighting, with long tables. Etniko also has good drinks and music ranging from electro house to lounge and techno, with local and international DJs. ⊠ *Constitución 172, Bellavista* ☎ *2/2732–0119* ⊕ *www.etniko.cl.*

La Casa en el Aire. Located within Patio Bellavista, La Casa en el Aire is a great place to catch live bands. There's also a larger venue at Antonia López de Bello 0125. If your Spanish is good, you can listen to storytelling and stand-up, too, or even perform. There's a happy hour daily from 4 to 9. ⊠ *Constitución 40, Bellavista* ☎ *2/2436–9002* ⊕ *www.lacasaenelaire.cl.*

SALSA CLUBS

Havana Salsa. If you're itching to dance salsa or merengue plus enjoy food and a show, come to this club Thursday, Friday, or Saturday night. It starts with an all-you-can-eat buffet of Cuban specialties, and at midnight, there's a 40-minute show with sensual professional dancers. Only after that does the dance floor open to the public. ⊠ *Domínica 142, Bellavista* ☎ *2/2737–1737* ⊕ *www.havanasalsa.cl* ☞ *13900 pesos with buffet; 6000 pesos without.* Ⓜ *Baquedano.*

Maestra Vida. This gay-friendly small club gets full quickly, but salsa dancers say it's the best in Santiago. Classes for beginners to advanced are 3,000 pesos and run Wednesday through Friday from 9 to 10:30, plus on Sunday from 8 to 10. Come alone or with a partner. ⊠ *Pío Nono 380, Bellavista* ☎ *2/2735–7416* ⊕ *www.maestravida.cl.*

LAS CONDES
BARS AND CLUBS

Flannery's. Flannery's, close to the main drag of Avenida El Bosque Norte, is an honest-to-goodness pub serving Irish food and beer. The upstairs, downstairs, and outside area often fill with expats and their friends. ⊠ *Encomenderos 83, Las Condes* ☎ *2/2233–6675* ⊕ *www.flannerys.cl.*

PERFORMING ARTS

From the dozens of museums scattered around the city, it's clear Santiaguinos also have a strong love of culture. Music, theater, and other artistic endeavors supplement weekends spent dancing the night away.

DANCE

Ballet Nacional Chileno. The venerable Ballet Nacional Chileno, founded in 1945, performs at CEAC U Chile (ex-Teatro Universidad de Chile) near Plaza Baquedano. ⊠ *Av. Providencia 043, Providencia* ☎ *2/2978–2480* ⊕ *www.ceacuchile.com/ballet-nacional-chileno*.

Ballet de Santiago. The Teatro Municipal has its own company, the Ballet de Santiago, which performs regularly, often with guest soloists. ⊠ *Plaza Alcalde Mekis, Agustinas 794, Santiago Centro* ☎ *2/2463–1000* ⊕ *www.balletdesantiago.com*.

FILM

Santiago's many cinemas screen movies in English with Spanish subtitles. Movie listings are posted in El Mercurio and other dailies. Admission is generally between 3,000 and 5,000 pesos, with reduced prices for matinees. The newest multiplexes—with mammoth screens, plush seating, and fresh popcorn—are in the city's malls, but don't overlook the offerings at the Centro Cultural Palacio La Moneda or el Biografo if you want more artsy or themed films.

Cine Hoyts Parque Arauco. Cine Hoyts Parque Arauco is the city's most modern cinema, with 3-D and deluxe seating. Be sure to check to see if movies are subtitled (*subtitulada*) or dubbed (*doblada*), especially for kids' movies. The website shows the current listings. ⊠ *Parque Arauco mall, Av. Kennedy 5413, Las Condes* ☎ *600/500–0400* ⊕ *www.cinehoyts.cl*.

Cinemark Alto Las Condes. Among the best theaters in town is the Cinemark Alto Las Condes. Its dozen screens, some of which are 3-D or XD, show the latest releases. The most expensive seats, in the premier class (for selected screenings), come with their own lounge, recline like spacious airline seats, and have a leg rest. ⊠ *Alto Las Condes mall, Av. Kennedy 9001, Las Condes* ☎ *600/586–0058* ⊕ *www.cinemark.cl/theatres/alto-las-condes*.

El Biógrafo. Most of the city's art cinemas tend to screen international favorites. The old standby is El Biógrafo, which shows foreign films on its single screen in the cute, cobblestoned neighborhood of Lastarria. There is a café upstairs with a nice rooftop deck, decent food, and good drinks for pre- and postscreening. ⊠ *José Victorino Lastarria 181, Santiago Centro* ☎ *2/2633–4435* ⊕ *www.elbiografo.cl* Ⓜ *Universidad Católica or Bellas Artes*.

MUSIC

CEAC U Chile. The Coro Sinfónico and the Orquesta Sinfónica, the city's highly regarded chorus and orchestra, perform near Plaza Baquedano at the Centro de Extensión Artistica y Cultura (CEAC) Universidad de Chile. Other functions such as ballet and quartets and solo vocal performances take place throughout the year. This venue is also home to the Ballet Nacional Chileno. ⊠ *Av. Providencia 043, Providencia* ☎ *2/2978–2480* ⊕ *www.ceacuchile.com*.

2

Club de Jazz de Santiago. This club has been in operation since 1943 and hosted jazz greats like Louis Armstrong and Herbie Hancock, as well as Chilean national performers. Performances take place Wednesday and Thursday at 9:30 for 5,000 pesos, and Friday and Saturday at 10:30 for 6,000 pesos. It's inside a restaurant called La Fábrica, which serves pizza, pasta, and other Italian dishes. ⊠ *Ossa 123, La Reina* ☎ *2/2830–6294* ⊕ *www.clubdejazz.cl* Ⓜ *Plaza Egaña.*

La Peña de Nano Parra. This brightly colored house in Bellavista is a great place to take in local music with a down-to-earth and generally young, local crowd. Peñas are traditional watering holes where *la nueva canción chilena,* a kind of Latin American resistance folk music, was first popularized. Due to their historically political nature, peñas became clandestine during the dictatorship. ⊠ *Ernesto Pinto Lagarrigue 80, Bellavista* ☎ *9/6586–6832.*

Movistar Arena. Movistar Arena, a covered stadium inside Parque O'Higgins, is a frequent venue for concerts by popular singers and groups, principally those on international tours. It seats 12,000, though seats to the side of the stage have poor acoustics. ⊠ *Av. Beaucheff 1204, Santiago Centro* ☎ *2/2770–2300* ⊕ *www.movistararena.cl.*

Parque de las Esculturas. This lovely little sculpture park is tucked in between the Mapocho River and Cerro San Cristóbal. Arrive there by walking over the bridge from Pedro de Valdivia, which also hosts several sculptures. In the park there is a map identifying dozens of trees and sculptures. It's a lovely place to spend an hour or two in the afternoon. The park hosts numerous open-air concerts in the early evenings in summer, including the Festival Internacional de Jazz de Providencia. ⊠ *Av. Santa María 2205 between Av. Pedro de Valdivia Norte and Padre Letelier, Providencia.*

Fodor's Choice ★ **Teatro Municipal.** The Teatro Municipal, Santiago's 19th-century theater, presents excellent classical concerts, opera, and ballet by internationally recognized artists from March to December. Opened in 1857, it was designed by French architects and has had several major renovations since. The Renaissance-style building hosts one of the city's most refined monuments with a lavish interior that deserves a visit. The cobblestone path around the building completes the picture. ⊠ *Plaza Alcalde Mekis, Agustinas 794 at San Antonio, Santiago Centro* ☎ *2/463–1000* ⊕ *www.municipal.cl.*

THEATER

Provided that you understand at least a little Spanish, you may want to take in a bit of Chilean theater. Performances take place all year, mainly from Thursday to Sunday around 8 pm.

Festival Internacional Teatro a Mil. In January, the year's best plays are performed at Estación Mapocho and other venues in a program called the Festival Internacional Teatro a Mil. The name refers to the admission price of 1,000 pesos (just under $2), though some spectacles, particularly the often large-scale opening and closing events near the Moneda Palace, are free. Some events, like those at theaters, cost considerably more. ⊠ *Santiago* ☎ *2/2925–0310* ⊕ *www.fundacionteatroamil.cl.*

Matucana 100. Over the past several years, Matucana 100, a converted train warehouse, has become one of the main anchors of the area surrounding Quinta Normal Park. On weekends there are outdoor dance events, and Matucana 100 frequently host fairs, art installations, and film festivals. New in 2014, Cafe 100—housed in a converted bus, continuing the public transport theme—sells specialty coffee and coconut water, a good complement to the nearby Soul Kitchen food truck, which serves a hearty Sunday brunch until 4 pm. ✉ *Matucana 100, Quinta Normal* ☎ *2/2964–9240* ⊕ *www.m100.cl* ☞ *Closed Mon. and Tues.* Ⓜ *Quinta Normal or Estación Central.*

Sala La Comedia. The well-respected theater company by the name of ICTUS performs in the Sala la Comedia, a theater just outside the Lastarria neighborhood. The company's been around for more than 50 years and is one of the most important independent groups in the country. ✉ *Merced 349, Santiago Centro* ☎ *2/2639–1523* ⊕ *www.teatroictus.cl.*

SHOPPING

Vitacura is, without a doubt, the destination for upscale shopping. Lined with designer boutiques with SUVs double-parked out front, Avenida Alonso de Córdova is Santiago's equivalent of Fifth Avenue in New York City or Rodeo Drive in Los Angeles. "Drive" is the important word here, as nobody strolls from place to place. Although buzzing with activity, the streets are strangely empty. Here you'll see names like Emporio Armani, Louis Vuitton, and Hermès. Other shops are found on nearby Avenidas Vitacura and Nueva Costanera.

Providencia, another popular shopping district, has rows of smaller, less luxurious boutiques. Avenida Providencia slices through the neighborhood, branching off for several blocks into the parallel Nueva Providencia. Shops continue east to Tobalaba metro, after which Avenida Providencia changes its name to Avenida Apoquindo and the neighborhood turns into Las Condes. To be on the cutting edge, head south to Avenida Italia (close to Salvador), where there are several blocks of shops stretching south from Bilbao. Converted row houses and workshops have been given over to (mostly) home design stores, cafés, and restaurants with courtyards in back. Girardi street also has several antiques dealers.

Bohemian Bellavista attracts those in search of the perfect thick woolen sweater or the right piece of lapis lazuli jewelry. Santiago Centro is more down to earth, while the Mercado Central just north of Parque Forestal sells ocean-related products, and nearby markets Vega Chica and Vega Central sell cheese, fruit, meat, eggs, vegetables, cleaning supplies, signs, and many other items. Shops are grouped together by type.

Shops in Santiago are generally open weekdays 10–7 and Saturday 10–2. Malls are open daily 10–10.

SANTIAGO CENTRO

ANTIQUES

Antiguedades Balmaceda. West of Estación Mapocho and at the end of Avenida Brasil, this complex also known as Anticuarios Parque de Los Reyes is filled with antiques dealers. They are used to foreigners coming and poking around, some of whom have been known to fill entire containers with jewelry, chandeliers, ceramics, and crystalware to bring back home. ■TIP→ **Take a quick peek across the street to the skate park at Parque de Los Reyes, where some of the best skateboarders in Chile practice on weekends.** ⊠ *Av. Brasil 157 at Balmaceda, Santiago Centro* ☎ *2/2688–1348.*

CLOTHING

Donde Golpea El Monito. In the countryside, men often wear *texanos* (cowboy hats), *paños* (formal hats), and *chupallas* (flat-brimmed hats). If you've ever wondered where to buy these proper toppers, head to Donde Golpea El Monito. At this downtown shop, in business for a century, the store's friendly staff shows customers the differences between each hat and how to wear it. Also for sale are spurs, ponchos, and other *huaso* (Chilean cowboy) essentials. ⊠ *21 de Mayo 707, Santiago Centro* ☎ *2/2638–7120* ☉ *Closed Sun.*

LA ALAMEDA

MARKETS

Centro Artesanal Santa Lucía. This souvenir market just across the Alameda from the base of Cerro Santa Lucía has some indigenous and locally made crafts, including some (not the finest quality) lapis lazuli items. Get your ears or navel pierced as well. It's open daily 11–7. As you should in all crowded and touristy areas, keep an eye on valuables. ⊠ *Alameda and Diagonal Paraguay, La Alameda.*

BELLAS ARTES AND LASTARRIA

BOOKS

La Tienda Nacional. For independent books from local authors, including kids' books and locally designed toys, head here. There are also postcards and posters with historical Chilean motifs, indie rock and folk bands from the '70s, and today's music, films, and documentaries for sale. ⊠ *Merced 369, Lastarria* ☎ *2/2638–4706* ⊕ *www.latiendanacional.cl* Ⓜ *Bellas Artes.*

WINE

Fodor's Choice **Santiago Wine Club.** Take your most finicky wine-loving friends to this ★ small storefront in Barrio Lastarria to try its highly rated, indie, terroir, and signatures wines, many of which are fairly hard to find elsewhere. The knowledgeable owners often have a bottle or two on the go to sample. ⊠ *Rosal 383, Lastarria* ☎ *2/2632–6596* ⊕ *www.santiagowineclub.cl* Ⓜ *Bellas Artes or Universidad Católica.*

BELLAVISTA

MARKETS

Feria Artesanal Pío Nono. Bellavista's colorful Feria Artesanal Pío Nono, held in the park at the start of Avenida Pío Nono, comes alive every night of the week. The area, particularly the south end of Pio Nono, is even busier on weekends, when vendors gather in Parque Domingo Gómez, in the shadow of the Universidad de San Sebastián Building to display handicrafts. It can be hit or miss for quality, but you can't beat it for convenience. ⊠ *At Pío Nono and Bellavista, Bellavista.*

VITACURA

ANTIQUES

Centro Comercial Lo Castillo. Some nice antiques shops are found in the basement of the Centro Comercial Lo Castillo, which is quite small and, apart from a cinema and the antique shops, sells mostly women's wear and jewelry. It's one block up from the corner of Avenida Alonso de Córdova. The indoor shopping arcade dates back to the '80s and *caracol-*, or snail-like, in its spiral layout. Le Fournil restaurant, just across Avenida Vitacura in Paseo Mañío on the fifth floor, is a good place for a coffee or light meal. ⊠ *Candelaria Goyenechea 3820, Vitacura* ☎ *2/2228–0432* ⊗ *Closed Sun.*

CLOTHING

Alfombras Wool. This shop sells a wide variety of wool carpets and other weavings designed and produced in Chile. ⊠ *Av. Luis Pasteur 6411, Store 115, 2nd fl., Vitacura* ☎ *2/4270–1611* ⊕ *alfombraswool. com* ⊗ *Closed Sun.*

Casimires Ingleses Matilde Medina. Yards and yards of cashmere fill the window of Casimires Ingleses Matilde Medina. The owner imports her beautiful scarves and sweaters from England and sells fine dress shirts, which are also imported. ⊠ *Av. Vitacura 3660, Vitacura* ☎ *2/220–7146* ⊕ *www.casimiresingleses.com* ⊗ *Closed Sun.*

Hermès. Looking a bit like a fortress, Hermès occupies some prime real estate on Alonso de Córdova, Santiago's main upscale international brand shopping drag. ⊠ *Av. Alonso de Córdova 2526, Vitacura* ☎ *2/2374–1576* ⊕ *www.hermes.com* ⊗ *Closed Sun.*

GALLERIES

Galleries are scattered around the city, and admission is usually free. The newspaper *El Mercurio* lists current exhibitions in its Saturday supplement *Vivienda y Decoración.*Bellavista, which is full of small galleries and where restaurants often put on exhibitions, is the place to scout the work of young artists, but Vitacura is the heart of the more consolidated gallery scene.

Galería Animal. See works by local artists at Galería Animal, a spacious, luminous gallery in Vitacura. The large-scale pieces include sculpture and other types of installations. ⊠ *Nueva Costanera 3731, Vitacura* ☎ *2/2371–9090* ⊕ *www.galeriaanimal.cl.*

Galería Isabel Aninat. Contemporary international artists hold exhibitions at this Vitacura gallery, which has two rooms and a sculpture garden. Just next door is Jorge Carrozo gallery, specializing in religious art. ⊠ *Espoz 3100, Vitacura* ☎ *2/2481–9870* ⊕ *http://galeriaisabelaninat.cl* ⊙ *Closed Sun.*

HANDICRAFTS

Pura. The staff at Pura has picked out the finest handicrafts from around the region. Here you can find expertly woven blankets and throws, colorful pottery, cushions, housewares, and fine leather goods. Most items are handmade. ⊠ *Parque Arauco Kennedy, Av. Kennedy 5413, 3rd fl., local 14, Las Condes* ☎ *2/2211–7875* ⊕ *www.purartesanos.cl.*

SHOPPING STREETS

Avenida Alonso de Córdova. In Vitacura, you can wrap yourself in style on and near Avenida Alonso de Córdova. This wide street, home to high-end chain stores, is where the well-heeled shop for more expensive items. Look sharp and ring the bell at these stores, as they usually keep their doors locked (not just anybody gets in). ⊠ *Santiago.*

WINE

La Vinoteca. Proudly proclaiming itself Santiago's first fine wine shop, La Vinoteca stocks vintages from all over Chile and abroad, as well as beer and liquor. There is an outlet at the airport for last-minute purchases and another shop 14 blocks down Manuel Montt from Providencia. ⊠ *Av. Nueva Costanera 3955, Vitacura* ☎ *2/2953–6290* ⊕ *www.lavinoteca.cl* ⊙ *Closed Sun.*

LAS CONDES

JEWELRY

Chantal Bernsau. For truly original jewelry using local materials, visit Chantal Bernsau's shop on the first floor of the W Hotel. She sells mainly chunky pendants with large beads made mostly of local stones (though she does not specialize in lapis lazuli). The items are pricey, but the work is top-quality. ⊠ *Inside W Hotel main lobby, Isidora Goyenechea 3000, shop 106-B, Las Condes* ☎ *2/2245–1984* ⊕ *www.chantalbernsau.cl/tiendas.*

MARKETS

Fodor's Choice
★ **Pueblito Los Dominicos.** This "village" inside a former cloister houses some 50 shops filled with crafts made of fine leather and wool, semiprecious stones (including lapis lazuli), and *greda* (Chile's version of terra cotta). There's also a wonderful display of cockatoos and other live birds. It's a nice place to visit, especially on weekends when traveling musicians entertain the crowds. It's open daily 10–8 in summer and 10–7 in winter, and there are two cafés serving traditional Chilean food. Next door is an attractive whitewashed church dating from the late 18th century. The complex is a bit far afield, but easily accessed by the metro of the same name. ■TIP→ **If you can find one of the old (paper, not plastic) 2,000 peso bills, the church is on it.** ⊠ *Av. Apoquindo 9085, Las Condes* ☎ *2/2289–69841* ⊙ *Closed Sun.* Ⓜ *Los Dominicos.*

SHOPPING MALLS

Fodor'sChoice ★ **Costanera Center.** This mall organizes stores by type and has 12 movie screens, free Wi-Fi, and a wide variety of food. You can't miss the building, which stands 62 stories (the mall is on the first six floors); it is the highest building on the continent. ■**TIP➜ Once you're done shopping, catch the sunset at Sky Costanera on the 62nd floor (10,000 pesos).** ⊠ *Andres Bello 2425, Las Condes* ☏ *2/2916–9226* ⊕ *www. costaneracenter.cl* Ⓜ *Tobalaba.*

WINE

Fodor'sChoice ★ **El Mundo del Vino.** This world-class store has an international wine selection, in-store tastings, classes, and books for oenophiles. In addition to this shop in the W Hotel, there are also branches in the Alto Las Condes, Parque Arauco, and Costanera Center shopping malls. ⊠ *Av. Isidora Goyenechea 3000, Las Condes* ☏ *2/2584–1173* ⊕ *www.elmundodelvino.cl.*

PROVIDENCIA

GIFTS

Manao. This leather goods shop sells colorful, bespoke purses, bags, and accessories with material sourced from Chile, Argentina, and Brazil. The craftsmanship is all Chilean though, with owner Paola Vidal behind all the designs and much of the handiwork. She can make custom items, though these will take a few days to stitch together. ⊠ *Condell 1447, Providencia* ☏ *9/9987–9984* ⊗ *Closed Mon.*

JEWELRY

Blue Stone. This is one of the top-end stores in which to buy lapis lazuli, the blue stone for which Chile is famous. Unlike other stores that have dozens of the same items, each piece of jewelry here is unique, as are decorative items for the table, including sets of cutlery inlaid with lapis lazuli and home furnishings such as copper vessels from replicas of original designs by indigenous peoples of Chile. ⊠ *Los Conquistadores 2020, at Los Araucanos, Providencia* ☏ *2/2232–2581* ⊗ *Closed Sun.*

SIDE TRIPS FROM SANTIAGO

For more than a few travelers, Santiago's main attraction is its proximity to the continent's best skiing. The snowcapped mountains to the east of Santiago have the largest number of runs, not just in Chile or South America, but in the entire Southern Hemisphere. The other attraction is that the season lasts from June to September and, in some places, October, so savvy skiers can take to the slopes in Chile when people back home are hitting the beach. It's no wonder that skiing aficionados and pros from around the world head to Chile.

The wineries around Santiago make for interesting day- or multiday trips. These winemakers provide the majority of the country's excellent exports, and you might find the source of your favorite Chilean *vino* back home just a short jaunt from the capital. The Casablanca Valley, west of Santiago, on the road to Valparaíso, is where some of the country's best white wines are produced.

The Cajón del Maipo in the Andes makes for a relaxing trip to soak in hot springs, take a hike, or wander through the crafts village of Pomaire, 70 km (43 miles) west of Santiago.

CENTRAL MAIPO

40 km (25 miles) southwest of Santiago.

The Central Maipo Valley is home to some of the most traditional wineries in Chile. In the lowest part of the valley, close to the coast, are the newcomers, producing lighter red wines from grapes cooled by sea breezes, as well as some Sauvignon Blancs.

GETTING HERE AND AROUND

The Autopista del Sol (Ruta 78) from Santiago to the port of San Antonio runs through the heart of the Maipo Valley, but vineyards are too far off the highway to be reached by public transport. Drive to these vineyards, take an organized tour, or combine local transportation with taxis or colectivos (shared taxis) to get to your destination.

WINERIES

Viña De Martino. The De Martino family has been making wine in Isla de Maipo since the 1930s and were the first in Chile to bottle Carménère, now Chile's signature grape. The winery is a strong proponent of organic viticulture. Its winemaking team has done groundbreaking work in seeking out the country's finest terroirs. Tours and tastings are run at a variety of price points and interest levels, and there's an elegant lunch for a minimum of seven people and buffet for less. Several vegetarian entreé options are available alongside meat and seafood. ⌧ *Manuel Rodríguez 229, Isla de Maipo* ☎ *2/2577–8837* ⊕ *www.demartino.cl* ⌧ *From 10000 pesos* ☉ *Closed Sun.* ⌧ *Reservations essential.*

Viña Undurraga. Don Francisco Undurraga Vicuña founded this traditional winery in 1885 in the town of Talagante, 34 km (21 miles) southwest of Santiago. Today you can tour the gardens—designed by Pierre Dubois, who planned Santiago's Parque Forestal—or take a look at the facilities and enjoy a tasting. Reserve ahead for a spot on a tour in English or Spanish. Viña Undurraga is along the way to Pomaire, so you might visit both in the same day. Private tours for a minimum of two participants begin weekdays at noon and must be reserved two days in advance at a cost of 28,000 pesos per person. ⌧ *Camino a Melipilla Km 34, Talagante* ☎ *2/2372–2950* ⊕ *www.undurraga.cl* ⌧ *8000 pesos for group tours; 28000 pesos for private* ☞ *Tours weekdays at 10:15, noon, 2, and 3:30; weekends at 10:15, noon, and 1:30 with 24-hr notice.*

ALTO MAIPO

39 km (24 miles) southeast of Santiago.

Some of Chile's finest red wines hail from the Alto Maipo, the eastern sector of the Casablanca Valley. There are a number of wineries—old and new, big and small—snuggled up into the foothills of the Andes Mountains.

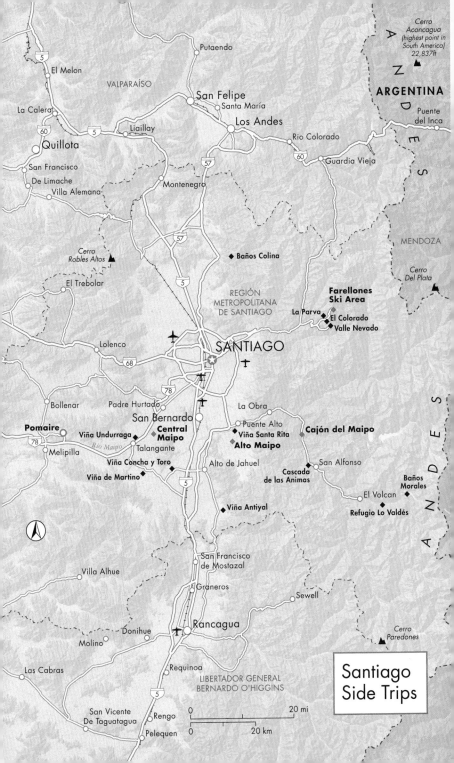

GETTING HERE AND AROUND

The only easy ways to reach the Antiyal and Santa Rita vineyards in the Alto Maipo are by car or on an organized wine tour. Pirque can be reached by taking Línea 4 of the metro to Puente Alto; from there, it is only a short taxi ride, and there are also frequent colectivos (shared taxis).

WINERIES

Fodor's Choice ★ **Viña Antiyal.** Chilean winemaker Alvaro Espinoza and his wife, Marina Ashton, harvested their first organically grown grapes from biodynamically managed vines in their own front yard in 1998 and Chile's first ultrapremium "garage wine" was born. They've grown since then and have more land higher in the mountains but still produce just 25,000 bottles (each numbered by hand) of their red-blend Antiyal. Tours are personalized, with emphasis on environmentally friendly and biodynamic winegrowing. Llamas, alpacas, geese, and the family dog wander the vineyards. Visits should be arranged at least a week in advance. Antiyal has also opened a small bed and breakfast on-site. Contact them through the winery to arrange a stay. ⊠ *Padre Hurtado 68, Buin* ☎ *2/2821–4224* ⊕ *www.antiyal.com* ⊠ *From 30000 pesos* ⌲ *Reservations essential.*

Fodor's Choice ★ **Viña Concha y Toro.** Chile's largest producer is consistently good in every price range, from inexpensive table wine to some of Chile's finest—and priciest—labels. Melchor de Concha y Toro, who once served as Chile's minister of finance, built the *casona,* or manor house, in 1875. He was among the first to import French vines, making this a cutting-edge winery since its foundation in 1883. The typical hour-long tour includes a stroll through the century-old gardens and vineyards, a look at the modern facilities, and a visit to the Casillero del Diablo, the famed cellar where Don Melchor kept his finest stock. There is a sound-and-light show in the dark here that appeals to lovers of kitsch. Tastings of three wines are included. Reserve a few days ahead for weekdays or a week ahead for popular weekend hours. Close to Puente Alto metro, the vineyard is easily reached by private or shared taxi (*colectivo*) from the end of the line, though the complimentary wine glass is unlikely to survive the way home. ⊠ *Av. Virginia Subercaseaux 210, Pirque* ☎ *2/2476–5269,* ⊕ *www.conchaytoro.com* ⊠ *Regular tour 14000 pesos; Marqués de Casa Concha tour 25000 pesos* ⌲ *Reservations essential* ⌲ *English general tours at 10:20, 11:30, 1, 2:30, 3:10, 3:40, and 4; Marqués de Casa Concha tour (includes more tastings with a sommelier) in English daily at 4.*

Fodor's Choice ★ **Viña Santa Rita.** Chile's third-largest winery, on a sprawling estate with an impressive museum, dates to 1880, when everything from vines to winemakers was brought from France. The Pompeiian-style manor now houses the pricey 16-room Casa Real Hotel, owned by, but operated separately from, the winery. The house, its neogothic chapel, and the park that surrounds them are strictly off limits to all but the hotel's guests, though on tours you get a good peek. The on-site Andean Museum, with its small collection of pre-Columbian artifacts

and textiles, is open to the public free of charge and highly recommended. Winery tours take you down into the musty fan vault cellars, now national monuments, which were built by French engineers in 1875 using a limestone-and-egg-white stone masonry technique called *cal y canto*. Stop in for a lunch at Doña Paula for a formal meal, or stick to the snack bar for lighter fare. There are six different types of tours including winemaker, picnic, bike, and wine. You must reserve a week ahead for tours. ☒ *Camino Padre Hurtado 0695, Alto de Jahuel* ☎ *2/2362–2594 weekdays or 2/362–2590 weekends* ⊕ *www.santarita. com* ☒ *Tour 12000 pesos; tours of grounds, but not wine cellars free with lunch at Casa de Doña Paula. Deluxe tour 75000 pesos, includes premium wines and cheese platter* ☾ *Closed Mon.*

POMAIRE

50 km (31 miles) west of Santiago.

You can easily spend a morning or afternoon wandering around the quaint village of Pomaire, a former settlement of indigenous people founded in 1771 comprising a few streets of single-story adobe dwellings. On weekends Pomaire teems with people wandering around, shopping, and having lunch in one of the rather touristy country-style restaurants with red-and-white checked tablecloths and clay ovens specializing in empanadas and other typical Chilean foods.

Pomaire is famous for its brown *greda,* or earthenware pottery, which is ubiquitous throughout Chile. Pastel de choclo is nearly always served in a round, simple clay dish—they're heavy and retain the heat, so the food arrives at the table piping hot.

The village bulges with bowls, pots, and plates of every shape and size, not to mention piggy banks, plant pots, vases, and the unmissable *"chanchito de la suerte,"* three-legged pigs that make great souvenirs. Most shops at the top of the main street sell the work of others; walk farther down or into the side streets and find the workshops they buy from (prices are cheaper there).

GETTING HERE AND AROUND

Pomaire is easy to find. It's clearly signposted to the right off the Autopista del Sol (Ruta 78). You can also take the Ruta Bus 78 buses, which depart frequently from Terminal San Borja in downtown Santiago and leave you at the turnoff to Pomaire, 2 km (1 mile) from the village. Once you get to the tiny village, it's small enough to get around on foot. To return to Santiago, simply walk back to the highway and hail the first bus, or in the late afternoon, wait at the church and take a bus back to Santiago (earlier in the day you have to make a connection in Melipilla).

EXPLORING

FAMILY **Granja Educativa Alfarera Greda.** Take a pottery-making course at this workshop, run by local artisans especially for visitors. Suitable for both children ages five and up and adults, the two-hour course starts with a video in English, followed by instruction in the use of a pottery wheel, and winds up with an insight into the techniques used by the area's indigenous

peoples. ✉ *Av. Bernardo O'Higgins 260* ☎ *9/9879–3533* ⊕ *www.greda.cl* 📶 *3600 pesos* ⚲ *4 classes weekdays, 6 classes on weekends.*

WHERE TO EAT

$$ ✕ **San Antonio.** The food is much the same here as elsewhere in Pomaire,
CHILEAN but San Antonio has a number of perks, particularly for families with
FAMILY children. There's a children's menu and, on weekends, everyone who
eats here can take the free pottery course at the Granja, just across
the road. **Known for:** kid-friendly atmosphere; classic Chilean cuisine;
nearby swimming pool for customer use (for a small fee). ⑤ *Average
main: 9000 pesos* ✉ *Roberto Bravo 320* ☎ *2/2831–9307.*

CAJÓN DEL MAIPO

60 km (37 miles) southeast of Santiago.

The Cajón del Maipo, a narrow valley deep in the Andes, is irresistible
for those who want to soak in natural hot springs; stroll through pictur-
esque mountain towns, where low adobe houses line the roads; or just
take in the stark but majestic landscape. In summertime, *humitas*, or
fresh corn (unfilled) tamales are a popular snack or meal. There are hot
springs at Baños Morales, just below the Refugio Lo Valdés, and higher
up the valley at Baños de Colina. The dirt road is rough (and impassable
in winter), but the pools of steaming water and the spectacular setting
are well worth the effort when the weather is in your favor.

GETTING HERE AND AROUND

To reach Cajón del Maipo, head south on Avenida José Alessandri until
you reach the Rotonda Departamental, a large traffic circle. There you
take Camino Las Vizcachas (aka Camino Cajón del Maipo), following
it south into the valley.

Expediciones Manzur sells round-trip tickets from Santiago to Lo
Valdés Mountain Center in Cajón del Maipo, Baños Morales, and
the Baños de Colina hot springs. Buses run Saturday, Sunday, and
Wednesday, with hotel pickups. A round-trip day ticket to Baños de
Colina and Embalse El Yeso is 33,000 pesos. Prior booking is essential
and you should sit on the right side of the van for a good view of the
river on the ascent.

ESSENTIALS

Bus Information Expediciones Manzur. ✉ *Sótero del Río 475, Suite 507,
Santiago Centro* ☎ *9/9335–7800.*

EXPLORING

Baños Colina. These hot springs high in the mountains are a series of
natural pools down which water drops, cooling gradually. The road is
rough and often impassable in winter and there is little infrastructure,
but the view is spectacular. Rustic lodging and camping is available.
Do not confuse these rustic springs with Termas de Colina, which are
similarly named but located north of the city. ✉ *Camino Cajón del
Maipo, 104 km (65 miles) from Santiago, Baños de Colina* ⊕ *www.
cajondelmaipo.com/banos_colina.php.*

Baños Morales. Two pools in the tiny village of Baños Morales, where the Morales and Volcán rivers meet, are pleasantly warm, not hot, and rich in iodine and other minerals. You can hike from this area as well. Be warned that surprise winter storms can trap you here. The village has some rustic lodging, but many people prefer to come for the day. ⊠ *Camino Cajón del Maipo, 92 km (57 miles) from Santiago, Baños Morales* ⊕ *www.cajondelmaipo.com/banos_morales.php.*

FAMILY **Cascada de las Animas.** This small tourist complex in the shadow of the mountains has a swimming pool and picnic area for short stays, as well as lodgings for longer sojourns. This is also a great base for exploring the Cajón. Accommodations come in several forms, including campsites, lodge suites, and free-standing cabins with rustic wood furniture. From here, multiday horseback-riding trips, guided hikes, and rafting excursions are available, as is transportation from Santiago. ⊠ *Camino al Volcán 31087, San Alfonso* ☎ *2/2861–1303* ⊕ *www.cascadadelas-animas.cl* 🖃 *14000 pesos for admission to swimming pool and picnic area in high season; 7000 in low season.*

Refugio Lo Valdés. The Lo Valdés Mountain Center, built in 1932, and also called the Refugio Alemán, provides basic, well-priced lodgings and organizes activities such as trekking and horse riding in the mountains. It is open year-round and has a restaurant that also serves day visitors until 8 pm; meals won't cost more than 9,000 pesos. If you'd prefer to do your own hike, the center can give you a map and instructions. ⊠ *Km 77, Camino Cajón del Maipo, Lo Valdés* ☎ *9/9230–5930* ⊕ *www.refugiolovaldes.com.*

FARELLONES SKI AREA

32 km (20 miles) east of Santiago.

Rub shoulders with pro skiers at three world-class ski resorts (El Colorado, La Parva, and Valle Nevado) that lie just outside Santiago near the village of Farellones. A total of 48 lifts carry you to the top of the 1,260 acres of groomed runs. Farellones, with some unremarkable shops, restaurants, and hotels, lies at the base of the Cerro Colorado mountain. Shorten your drive by parking at Curva 17 parking lot of Valle Nevado and taking the gondola up to midmountain from there. All ski areas rent equipment, for about 21,000 (basic) to 25,000 (professional) pesos per day.

GETTING HERE AND AROUND

It can take up to two hours to reach these ski resorts, which lie 48–56 km (30–35 miles) from Santiago. The road is narrow, winding, and full of Chileans racing to get to the top. If you decide to drive, make sure you have a four-wheel-drive vehicle or snow chains, which you can rent along the way or before you leave Santiago from international car rental agencies (such as Hertz or Avis). Chains are installed for about 10,000 pesos. Don't think you need them? There's a police checkpoint just before the road starts to climb into the Andes, and if the weather is rough they make you turn back.

To reach these areas by car, follow Avenida Kennedy or Avenida Las Condes eastward until you leave Santiago. Here, you begin an arduous journey up the Andes, making 40 consecutive hairpin turns. The road forks when you reach the top, with one road taking the relatively easy 16-km (10-mile) route east to Valle Nevado, and the other following a more difficult road north to Farellones and La Parva.

Several bus companies run regularly scheduled service to the Andes in winter. Skitotal buses depart from the company's office on Avenida Apoquindo and head to all the ski resorts. Buses depart as they fill, starting at 7:30 am; and the last trip up departs at 8:30. A round-trip ticket costs 16,000 pesos to Farellones, La Parva, and El Colorado, and 18,000 pesos to Valle Nevado. You can arrange for private transfer with them as well, which varies in price for round-trip from 130,000 for one to three passengers, to 180,000 for 6 to 10 passengers. Skitotal also offers hotel-to-slopes or airport-to-slopes service. Expediciones Manzur leaves daily at 8:30 from Ramon Carnicer 5 (near Plaza Baquedano) for 12,000 round-trip in a shared van, or 120,000 for up to 10 people in a private van.

ESSENTIALS

Bus Contacts Skitotal. ✉ *Apoquindo 4900, Las Condes* ☎ *2/2246–0156* ⊕ *www.skitotal.cl.*

WHERE TO STAY

$$$$
HOTEL
🏨 **La Cornisa.** This quaint old inn on the road to Farellones gives you easy access to the slopes with its free shuttle to and from the nearby ski areas. **Pros:** cozy, intimate ambience; outdoor hot tub; breakfast and dinner included. **Cons:** not as close to the slopes as the ski resorts themselves; some rooms are small and cramped; Wi-Fi can be very slow. $ *Rooms from: 178000 pesos* ✉ *Av. Los Cóndores 636, Farellones* ☎ *2/2321–1172* ⊕ *www.lacornisa.cl* ➫ *10 rooms* ⦿*Some meals.*

$$$$
RESORT
🏨 **Puerta del Sol.** The largest of the Valle Nevado hotels, Puerta del Sol can be identified by its signature sloped roof. **Pros:** only 160 feet from the ski slopes; interconnecting rooms good for families; giant Jacuzzi. **Cons:** rooms are quite small and basic; Jacuzzi packs out early in the evening; check-in and check-out are very busy. $ *Rooms from: 481000 pesos* ✉ *13 km (8 miles) beyond La Parva, Lo Barnechea* ☎ *2/2477–7000, 800/669–0554 toll-free in U.S.* ⊕ *www.vallenevado. com* ☉ *Closed Oct.–May* ➫ *124 rooms* ⦿*All-inclusive.*

$$$$
RESORT
🏨 **Tres Puntas.** It bills itself as a hotel for young people, though Tres Puntas may remind you of a college dormitory. **Pros:** slopes are a quick walk away; free Wi-Fi in lobby; friendly staff. **Cons:** rooms are very cramped; dated decor could use an overhaul; check-in and check-out is laborious. $ *Rooms from: 322000 pesos* ✉ *13 km (8 miles) beyond La Parva, Farrellones, La Parva* ☎ *2/2477–7000, 800/669–0554 toll-free in U.S.* ⊕ *www.vallenevado.com* ☉ *Closed Oct.–May* ➫ *82 rooms* ⦿*All-inclusive.*

$$$$
RESORT
🏨 **Valle Nevado.** The resort's most extravagantly priced lodge provides ski-in–ski-out convenience. **Pros:** ski in, ski out; free Wi-Fi; rooms have balconies. **Cons:** expensive, particularly if you plan to be out on the slopes all day; restaurants get very busy and require reservations;

slow Wi-Fi connection. $ *Rooms from: 194000 pesos* ⊠ *13 km (8 miles) beyond La Parva, Farellones* ☎ *2/2477–7000, 800/669–0554 toll-free in U.S.* ⊕ *www.vallenevado.com* ⊙ *Closed spring–fall* ⤳ *53 rooms* ⦶ *All-inclusive.*

SPORTS AND THE OUTDOORS
SKIING
El Colorado. The closest ski area to Santiago, El Colorado has 568 acres of groomed runs—the most in Chile. There are 19 ski lifts here and 101 runs for beginners through experts, as well as the best snowpark in South America, which has six jumps. The beginner runs are at the base of the mountain near the village of Farellones. Sled tracks and a few other activities for nonskiers opened in 2014. There are a few restaurants and pubs nearby, but most are down in the village of Farellones. The ski season runs from mid-June through September, depending on snowfall. ⊠ *On road between Farellones and La Parva, Lo Barnechea* ☎ *2/2889–9200* ⊕ *www.elcolorado.cl* ⊠ *Lift tickets 38000–45000 pesos.*

La Parva. This colorful conglomeration of private homes set along a handful of mountain roads with stunning views of Santiago is home to a resort with 16 ski lifts, most leading to runs for intermediate skiers. The more adventurous (and advanced) can take part in heliskiing on the resort's 1,800-plus acres. ⊠ *3 km (2 miles) up road from Farellones, La Parva* ☎ *2/2964–2100* ⊕ *www.laparva.cl* ⊠ *Day pass from 46000 pesos.*

Valle Nevado. Chile's largest ski region is a luxury resort area with 17 ski lifts that connect to 46 runs covering 7,000 acres. Intended for skiers who like a challenge, and attracting international ski teams, this resort has few beginner slopes. Two of the extremely difficult runs from the top of Cerro Tres Puntas are called Shake and Twist. If that doesn't intimidate you, then you might be ready for some heliskiing. The helicopter whisks you to otherwise inaccessible peaks where you can ride a vertical drop of up to 2,500 meters (8,200 feet). A ski school at Valle Nevado gives pointers to everyone from beginners to experts. Many visitors are European, as are the ski instructors, though Brazilians come to Chile for the skiing as well. ⊠ *13 km (8 miles) beyond La Parva, Lo Barnechea* ☎ *2/2477–7000* ⊕ *www.vallenevado.com* ⊠ *38000–43000 pesos* ⊙ *Closed Oct.–mid-June.*

THE CENTRAL COAST

WELCOME TO THE CENTRAL COAST

TOP REASONS TO GO

★ **Riding the ascensores:** Valparaíso's steep hills are smoothed out a bit by its 19th-century *ascensores*, or funiculars, that shuttle locals between their jobs near the port and their homes in the hills.

★ **Beautiful beaches:** Thousands of Santiaguinos flock to the Central Coast's beaches every summer, where hundreds of seafood restaurants of all types and sizes serve the masses.

★ **Superb shopping:** The streets of Cerro Alegre and Cerro Concepción in Valparaíso are lined with shops selling everything from finely wrought jewelry to hand-tooled leather, while Viña has everything from large department stores and outlet malls to trendy shops and boutiques.

★ **Seafood straight from the net:** Almost every town on the Central Coast has its own wharf where fishermen land with the day's catch. Bustling with shoppers, the *caleta* offers an excellent biology lesson on the diversity of sea life in addition to, of course, many a gastronomic treat.

The Central Coast lies two hours west of Santiago, across the Coastal Mountains. Dominated by the overlapping cities of Valparaíso and Viña del Mar, this is where stressed Santiaguinos come to sunbathe, party, and gorge on seafood every moment they can. In the summer, even the smallest resort can heave with visitors, but outside of January and February they can be quiet. Two of Neruda's three homes—La Sebastiana, nestled in the hills of Valparaíso, and his beach-side abode in small-town Isla Negra—are found along Chile's Central Coast. The sundry objects he collected in his vast travels around the globe inhabit his former residences and give each one a life of their own.

1 Valparaíso and Viña del Mar. The twin cities of Chile's Central Coast could not be more different. The winding streets of Valparaíso, a once great port, are filled with historic monuments recalling their 19th-century glory. Thanks to a tourism boom and UNESCO's naming of the city as a World Heritage Site, a cultural renaissance is underway. Neighboring Viña del Mar has one of the country's largest casinos, elegant hotels, and a sharp nightlife scene that make it an excellent place to blow off some steam.

2 The Southern Beaches. Isla Negra is where South America's most famous poet, Pablo Neruda, had his seaside retreat and has become the main attraction south of Valparaíso. Along the way, don't miss the relaxed charms of Algarrobo or Quintay, a forgotten former whaling station.

3 The Northern Beaches. The beaches north of Viña have something for every type of traveler, from the summer bustle of Concón to easygoing Maitencillo and stunning Zapallar, an exclusive seaside resort for Santiago's rich and powerful.

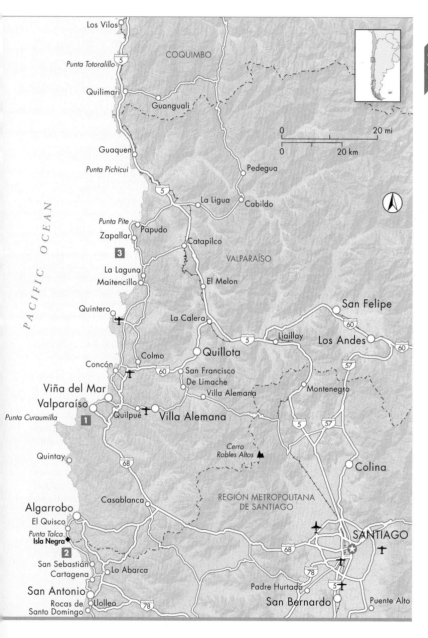

3

Los Vilos

COQUIMBO

Punta Totoralillo

5

Quilimarí

Guanguali

Guaquen

Punta Pichicui

Pedegua

0   20 mi

0   20 km

La Ligua   Cabildo

P A C I F I C   O C E A N

Punta Pite

Zapallar   Papudo

3

Catapilco

VALPARAÍSO

La Laguna

Maitencillo

El Melon

San Felipe

Quintero

La Calera

60

Liaillay   Los Andes

5

60

Colmo   Quillota

57

Concón

60   San Francisco

De Limache

Montenegro

Viña del Mar

Villa Alemana

Valparaíso

Quilpué   Villa Alemana

5   57

Punta Curaumilla

1

Quintay

68

Cerro

Robles Altos

Colina

Algarrobo

Casablanca

REGIÓN METROPOLITANA

DE SANTIAGO

El Quisco

Punta Talca

Isla Negra

2

SANTIAGO

San Sebastián

Cartagena   Lo Abarca

68

78

San Antonio

Padre Hurtado

5

Rocas de   Llolleo

Santo Domingo

78

San Bernardo   Puente Alto

Updated by
Margaret
Snook

Most people head to the Central Coast for a single reason: the beaches. And while yes, many are drawn here by the rough grandeur of the windswept coastline, with its rocky islets inhabited by sea lions and penguins, this stretch of coastline west of Santiago has much more than sun and surf. The biggest surprise is the charm of Valparaíso, Chile's second-largest city. It shares a bay with Viña del Mar, but the similarities end there. Valparaíso is a bustling port town with a jumble of colorful cottages nestled in the folds of its many hills. Viña del Mar has lush parks surrounding neoclassical mansions and a long beach lined with luxury highrises. Together they form an interesting contrast of working class and wealth at play.

The *balnearios* (small beach towns) to the north and south of the twin cities have their own character, often defined by coastal topography. You can take a long stroll along the stone path built between the mansions and rocks that jut out into the Pacific in Zapallar; watch or join the surfers in Maitencillo; indulge yourself in the culinary delights of Concón; gawk at the sculpted bodies that strut around Reñaca's hip beach; visit a former whaling station in quaint Quintay; discover Pablo Neruda's infatuation with the sea in Isla Negra; and take a dip in clear-blue and, yes, chilly water in Algarrobo's El Canelillo.

Proximity to Santiago has resulted in their development—and in some cases overdevelopment—as summer resorts. At the beginning of the 20th century, Santiago's elite started building vacation homes here. Soon after, when trains connected the capital to beaches, middle-class families started spending their summers at the shore. Improved highway access in recent decades has allowed Chileans of all economic levels to enjoy the occasional beach vacation.

Late December through mid-March, when schools let out for summer vacation and Santiago becomes torrid, the beaches are packed. Vacationers frolic in the chilly sea by day and pack the restaurants and bars at night. The rest of the year, the coast is relatively deserted and, though often cool and cloudy, a pleasantly tranquil place to explore. Local *caletas*—literally meaning "coves," where fishing boats gather to unload their catch, usually the site of local fishing cooperatives—are always colorful and lively.

PLANNER

WHEN TO GO

It seems that all of Chile heads to the coast in the summer months of January and February. This can be a great time to visit, with the weather at its warmest and the nightlife hopping. But it's also a tough time to find a room, especially on weekends. Make reservations as far in advance as possible. Spring (September, October, and November) and fall (March, April, and May) can be perfect times to visit, when the days are warm and breezy, and the nights cool. Consider visiting during the shoulder months of December and March too, which have decent weather but also provide relative solitude in which to explore.

FESTIVALS AND SEASONAL EVENTS

The annual Festival Internacional de la Canción (International Song Festival) takes place during a week in mid-February in Viña del Mar. The concerts are broadcast live on television. Most towns have colorful processions on Día de San Pedro (June 29). A statue of St. Peter, patron saint of fishermen, is typically hoisted onto a fishing boat and led along a coastal procession. When the clock strikes midnight on New Year's Eve, the bay that runs from Valparaíso to Concón plays host to one of the world's most spectacular fireworks shows.

PLANNING YOUR TIME

Plan to spend at least two days in Valparaíso, where you can ride a few funiculars and explore the cobbled streets. While you're there, a good day trip is an excursion to Pablo Neruda's waterfront home nearby in Isla Negra. You'll want to take a day or so to stroll around the bustling beach town of Viña del Mar. After that you can drive north along the coastal highway, stopping for lunch in either Concón or Maitencillo. From there you can return to Viña del Mar or continue on to spend a night in Zapallar.

GETTING HERE AND AROUND

AIR TRAVEL

The Central Coast is served by LAN Airlines, and a host of other carriers, via Santiago's Aeropuerto Comodoro Arturo Merino Benítez, a 1½-hour drive from either Viña del Mar or Valparaíso.

BUS TRAVEL

There is hourly bus service between Santiago and both Valparaíso and Viña del Mar. Turbus, Pullman, and other companies leave from Santiago's Terminal Alameda, or take buses from metro station Pajaritos and avoid most of the capital's traffic. Smaller companies serving the other beach resorts depart from Santiago's Terminal Santiago.

To get to nearby Concón you can take a *micro* or *liebre* (local bus) from Viña del Mar, or from Valparaíso to get to Laguna Verde. But your best bet for getting to the smaller beach towns farther north or south of the twin cities is from Valparaíso's bus terminal. Plan ahead, as the buses may fill up, especially in summer.

Bus Contacts Turbus. ☎ 022/822–7500 ⊕ *www.turbus.cl.* **Sol del Pacífico.** ☎ *32/221–3776, 022/276–2604* ⊕ *www.horariodebuses.cl/*

buses-sol-del-pacifico. **Pullman Bus.** ☎ *600/320-3200* ⊕ *www.ventapasajes.cl.*
Condor Bus. ☎ *No phone* ⊕ *www.condorbus.cl.*

CAR TRAVEL

Because it's so easy to get around in Valparaíso and Viña del Mar, there's no need to rent a car unless you want to travel to other towns on the coast.

Rental Cars Rosselot. ✉ *Victoria 2675, Valparaíso* ☎ *32/235-2365* ⊕ *www. rosselot.cl/rent-a-car.*

TRAIN TRAVEL

The bright, spacious Merval commuter train links Valparaíso with Viña del Mar. It runs every 12 minutes from 6 am to 11:30 pm on weekdays, and from 8 am to 10 pm on weekends and holidays. Check out the website to plan your trip: ⊕ *www.metro-valparaiso.cl.*

RESTAURANTS

Dining is one of the great pleasures of visiting the Central Coast. It's not rare to see fishermen bringing the day's catch straight to the restaurants that inevitably line the shore. Your server will be happy to share with you which fish were caught fresh that day. Try *corvina a la margarita* (sea bass in shellfish sauce) or *ostiones a la parmesana* (scallops served with melted Parmesan cheese). The more daring can also try a batch of raw shellfish bought direct from the fishermen's nets and served with a dash of lemon. With the exception of major holidays or fancier restaurants, reservations are almost never required here. Many restaurants still close between lunch and dinner: from 3 or 4 to 7 or 8. *Restaurant reviews have been shortened. For more information, visit Fodors.com.*

HOTELS

Because the central beach resorts were developed by and for the Santiago families who summer here, they are dominated by vacation homes and apartments, although new, often upmarket hotels have been built especially around Valparaíso, Viña del Mar, and Concón. *Cabañas,* somewhat rustic cabins with a kitchenette and one or more bedrooms, are designed to accommodate families on tighter budgets. An even more affordable option is a *residencial* (guesthouse), often just a few rooms for rent in a private home. *Hotel reviews have been shortened. For more information, visit Fodors.com.*

WHAT IT COSTS IN CHILEAN PESOS (IN THOUSANDS)				
	$	**$$**	**$$$**	**$$$$**
Restaurants	Under 6	6–8	9–11	over 11
Hotels	Under 46	46–75	76–105	over 105

Restaurant prices are the average cost of a main course at dinner or, if dinner is not served, at lunch. Hotel prices are the lowest cost of a standard double room in high season, excluding tax.

Beachgoing in Chile

To the vast majority of Chileans, summer holiday means one thing: heading to the beach. Whether on the banks of a southern lake, one of the north's deserted coves, or one of the pleasant towns of the Central Coast, beaches all over the country are packed from late December to early March. But this isn't your standard beach destination. Even where the water is safe enough to enter, the icy Humboldt Current, rushing up from the deep south only slightly north of Antarctica, means only the brave (and typically the local) can bear more than a few seconds up to their chests, and even then, many wear wetsuits.

Outside of the water, wandering vendors constantly appear, plying ice cream, drinks, *palmeras* (a heart-shape puff pastry), and other goodies. And watch out for the *promotoras*, scantily clad men and women promoting everything from batteries to beer. Where permitted, Chileans will set up a *parrilla* for one of their famous *asados* to grill meat and sausages over a charcoal fire. The athletic may go for a game of *paleta*, batting a tennis ball back and forth with a small wooden racket, or the occasional *pichanga* (pick-up soccer game). If you want to escape the crowds, try walking along to the next beach, which may be surprisingly empty though just a few hundred meters away. The southern end of Maitencillo or the north of Papudo are particularly suitable for exploration.

Strong sun protection in Chile is essential due to a hole in the ozone layer in this part of the world. Even if the day begins in a fog, the mist quickly burns off, leaving you vulnerable to the sun's rays. Be sure to pack a hat, strong sunblock, and something to cover you up. You might even consider a beach umbrella, often available to rent right on the beach. Once the sun goes down, temperatures can fall quickly as sea breezes pick up, so bring a light jacket or sweater as well.

VALPARAÍSO AND VIÑA DEL MAR

Viña del Mar and Valparaíso (Vineyard of the Sea and Paradise Valley, respectively) each maintain an aura that warrants their dreamy appellations. Only minutes apart, these two urban centers are nevertheless as different as sister cities can be. Valparaíso won the heart of poet Pablo Neruda, who praised its "cluster of crazy houses," and it continues to be a disorderly, gritty, bohemian, and charming town. It's still an active port and its lack of beaches keeps things more urban, if not urbane.

Viña del Mar, Valparaíso's glamorous sibling, is a clean, orderly, and elegant city with miles of beige beach, a glitzy casino, manicured parks, and shopping galore. Viña, together with nearby Reñaca, is synonymous with the best of life for vacationing Chileans. Its beaches gleam, its casino rolls, and its discos sizzle.

VALPARAÍSO

10 km (6 miles) south of Viña del Mar; 120 km (75 miles) west of Santiago.

Fodor'sChoice ★   Valparaíso's dramatic topography—45 *cerros*, or hills, overlooking the ocean—requires the use of winding pathways and wooden *ascensores* (funiculars) to get up many of the grades. The slopes are covered by candy-color houses—there are almost no apartments in the city—most of which have exteriors of corrugated metal peeled from shipping containers decades ago. Valparaíso has served as Santiago's port for centuries. Before the Panama Canal opened, Valparaíso was the busiest port in South America. Harsh realities—changing trade routes, industrial decline—have diminished its importance, but it remains one of Chile's principal ports.

Most shops, banks, restaurants, bars, and other businesses cluster along the handful of streets called *El Plan* (the flat area) that are closest to the shoreline. *Porteños* (which means "the residents of the port") live in the surrounding hills in an undulating array of colorful abodes. At the top of any of the dozens of stairways, the *paseos* (promenades) have spectacular views; many are named after prominent Yugoslavian, Basque, and German immigrants. Neighborhoods are named for the hills they cover.

With the jumble of power lines overhead and the hundreds of buses that slow down—but never completely stop—to pick up agile riders, it's hard to forget you're in a city. Still, walking is the best way to experience Valparaíso. Be careful where you step, though—locals aren't very conscientious about curbing their dogs.

GETTING HERE AND AROUND

By car from Santiago, take Ruta 68 west through the coastal mountains and the Casablanca Valley as far as you can go, until the road descends into Valparaíso's Avenida Argentina, on the city's eastern edge. If you don't have a car, Turbus, Pullman, and Condor buses leave several times an hour for Valparaíso and Viña del Mar from Santiago. Turbus and Pullman both leave from Terminal Alameda (the Universidad de Santiago Metro station), while Condor and Sol del Pacífico use Terminal Santiago (Estación Central station). Alternatively, you can save yourself a crawl through Santiago by catching a bus from the Pajaritos Metro station on the city's western edge.

If you're using Valparaíso as your hub, you can use Pullman Bus to get to most coastal towns south of the city. Turbus heads north to Cachagua, Zapallar, Papudo, and other towns. Sol del Pacífico also runs buses to the northern beaches. Valparaíso has two information booths: one at Muelle Prat that is supposedly open daily 10–2 and 3–6 (although in real life the hours vary wildly).

Bus Contacts Valparaíso Bus Terminal. ⊠ *Av. Pedro Montt 2860* ☎ *32/293–9669* ⊕ *www.horariodebuses.cl/terminal-de-valparaiso.*

TOURS

Fodor's Choice ★ **Tours 4 Tips.** Undoubtedly, the best way to explore Valparaíso's winding streets and steep hills is on foot. The Tours 4 Tips walking tour leaves from Plaza Sotomayor every day at 10 am and 3 pm. Just look for the guide in a striped, *Where's Waldo*–style shirt. This three-hour tour gives you an introduction to the port city's history, unique culture, culinary delights, and street art. There is no charge up front, but a generous tip is expected (5,000–10,000 pesos). ⊠ *Plaza Sotomayor* ☎ *22/570–9939* ⊕ *www.tours4tips.com* 🖃 *Free, but tips are expected.*

ESSENTIALS

Visitor Information Tourism Office. ⊠ *Condell 1490* ☎ *32/293–9262* ⊕ *www. ciudaddevalparaiso.cl.* **Valparaíso Municipal Tourism Kiosk at Muelle Prat.** ⊠ *Muelle Prat.*

EXPLORING

TOP ATTRACTIONS

Ascensor El Peral. In Valparaíso, riding one of the city's 14 *ascensors* (funiculars) is a must. El Peral, built in 1902 and now a national monument, is one of the six currently operating (another three are under repair). For just 100 pesos, it runs a very steep 52 meters (172 feet) from the Palacio de Justicia (court house) on the northeastern side of Plaza Sotomayor, up to the gorgeous Paseo Yugoslavo on Cerro Alegre, where the Palacio Baburizza houses a fine arts museum. ⊠ *Plaza Sotomayor, Cerro Alegre* ⊕ *www.ascensoresvalparaiso.org/taxonomy/term/2* 🖃 *100 pesos.*

FAMILY **Ascensor Reina Victoria.** This steep 40-meter (131-foot) funicular, built in 1902 and named for Queen Victoria of England who died a year earlier, connects Avenida Elías near Plaza Aníbal Pinto with the very popular Cerro Concepción. Once atop the hill, you'll come out to a small plaza where you can swoosh down a small metallic slide if your inner child so desires. ⊠ *Elías, Cerro Concepción* ⊕ *www.ascensoresvalparaiso.org/taxonomy/term/4* 🖃 *100 pesos.*

Fodor's Choice ★ **Cerro Concepción.** Either walk up from Plaza Aníbal Pinto or ride the Ascensor Concepción to one of the most popular of Valparaíso's famous *cerros* (hills). The greatest attraction is the view, which is best appreciated from Paseo Gervasoni, a wide promenade to the right when you exit the ascensor, and Paseo Atkinson, one block to the east. Over the balustrades that line the promenades are amazing vistas of the city and bay. Nearly as fascinating are the narrow streets above them, some of which are quite steep. Continue uphill to Cerro Alegre, which has a bit of a bohemian flair. ⊠ *Ascensor Concepción, Esmeralda 916.*

FAMILY Fodor's Choice ★ **La Sebastiana.** Tired of the frenetic pace of Santiago, poet Pablo Neruda longed for a calmer place overlooking the sea, and he found it here in the house that Spanish architect Sebastián Collado began building for himself but never finished. Neruda bought it with friends in 1959 and restored the upper floors in his own eclectic style, complete with curving walls, narrow winding stairways, and a tower. The view from the house is spectacular, but the real reason to visit is to see Neruda's extravagant collection of thousands of diverse objects. The house is a shrine to his many cherished belongings, including a beautiful orangish-pink stuffed

Valparaíso

Bahía de Valparaíso

Estación
Bellavista

Ascensor
Artillería

Plaza
Advana

Estación
Puerto

Ascensor
Concepción

Antonio Varas

Artillería

Av. Carampangue

Márquez

Valdivia

San Martín

Clavé

Cochí

Av. Errázuriz

Serrano

Blanco

Cochrane

Prat

Esmeralda

Papudo

Castillo

Tomás Ramos

Urriola

Templeman

Cumming

Monte Alegre

Av. Pedro Montt

Morrison

Hospital

Melgarejo

Beriberi

O'Higgins

Puerto

Av. Brasil

Salvador

Condell

Cementerio
Católico

Cementerio
de Disidentes

Cumming

Av. Ecuador

Plaza
Bismarck

Morín

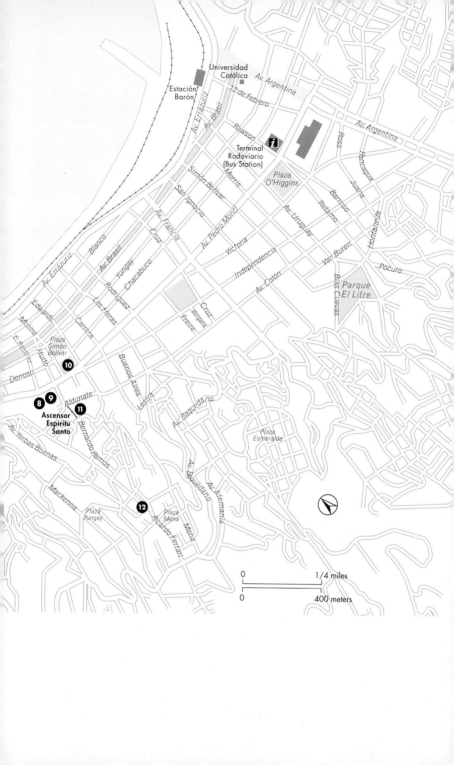

bird he brought back from Venezuela, a carousel horse, and the pink-and-yellow barroom stuffed with kitsch. ✉ *Ferrari 692* ☎ *32/225–6606* ⊕ *www.fundacionneruda.org* ☐ *7000 pesos* ⊘ *Closed Mon.*

FAMILY **Muelle Prat.** Valparaíso's main wharf, Muelle Prat, bustles with activity. Vendors hawk their offerings, from trinkets and snacks to face painting and temporary tattoos, and owners of the dozens of bobbing *lanchas* (small boats) dwarfed by enormous cargo ships call out departure times for the next tour of the bay. At 3,000 pesos, a half-hour tour is a great way to experience the activity in the port, see a spectacular view of the city, and even get a close-up view of a sea lion colony. Here you'll also find a tourist information office and a row of souvenir shops. ✉ *Av. Errázuriz at Plaza Sotomayor* Ⓜ *Estación Puerto.*

Museo a Cielo Abierto (*The Open Sky Museum*). This museum is a winding walk past 20 official murals (and a handful of unofficial ones) by some of Chile's best painters. There's even one by the country's most famous artist, Roberto Matta. The path is not marked—there's no real fixed route—as the point is to get lost in the city's history and culture. ✉ *Ascensor Espíritu Santo up to Cerro Buenavista* ⊕ *ucv.altavoz.net/prontus_unidacad/site/artic/20081030/pags/20081030165305.html.*

Fodor'sChoice **Museo de Bellas Artes.** The art nouveau Palacio Baburizza, built in 1916, ★ houses the city's fine-arts museum. Former owner Pascual Baburizza donated this large collection of European paintings to the city. The fanciful decorative exterior is reminiscent of the style of Spanish architect Antoni Gaudí—note the bronze children dancing around the portico. The paintings and the impressive mansion itself take you on a historical journey through Chile's past. ✉ *Ascensor El Peral to Paseo Yugoslavo, Paseo Yugoslavo 176, Cerro Alegre* ☎ *32/225–2332* ⊕ *www.museobaburizza.cl* ☐ *2000 pesos, 4000 pesos for foreigners with audio guide included* ⊘ *Closed Mon.*

Plaza Sotomayor. Valparaíso's impressive Plaza Sotomayor serves as a gateway to the bustling port. The **Comandancia en Jefe de la Armada,** headquarters of the Chilean navy, is a grand, gray building that rises to a turreted pinnacle over a mansard roof. At the northern end of the plaza the **Monumento de los Héroes de Iquique** honors Arturo Prat and other heroes of the War of the Pacific. In the middle of the square (beware of traffic—cars and buses come suddenly from all directions), the **Museo del Sitio** displays artifacts from the city's mid-19th-century port. A crafts and products fair also happens weekly during the warmer months. ✉ *Av. Errázuriz at Cochrane.*

WORTH NOTING

Galería Municipal de Arte. This crypt in the basement of the Palacio Lyon is the finest art space in the city. Temporary exhibits by top-caliber Chilean artists are displayed on stone walls under a series of brick arches. It's easy to miss the entrance, which is on Calle Condell just beyond the Museo de Historia Natural de Valparaíso. ✉ *Condell 1550* ☎ *32/293–9639* ⊕ *www.munivalpo.cl/cultura* ☐ *Free* ⊘ *Closed Sun.*

FAMILY **Museo de Historia Natural de Valparaíso.** Within the Palacio Lyon, one of the few buildings to survive the devastating 1906 earthquake is this small but interesting natural history museum. With a focus on land

and sea animals, it's a good place to take children. ⊠ *Condell 1546* ☎ *32/254–4840* ⊕ *www.mhnv.cl* ☜ *Free* ☾ *Closed Mon.*

Paseo 21 de Mayo. Ascensor Artillería pulls you uphill to Paseo 21 de Mayo, a wide promenade lined by a long row of booths selling crafts and souvenirs and surrounded by well-tended gardens and stately trees. From here you can survey the working port and much of the city through coin-operated binoculars. A gazebo—a good place to escape the sun—seems to be hanging in midair. Paseo 21 de Mayo is located in the middle of Cerro Playa Ancha, one of the city's more colorful and less touristy neighborhoods. ⊠ *Ascensor Artillería at Plaza Advana.*

FAMILY **Plaza Victoria.** Most Chilean cities have a Plaza de Armas that serves as the center of urban life, but Valparaíso has this, the "Victory Plaza," which dates back to the early 19th century. It was once the favored venue for bullfights and public executions, but today it's a lovely park graced by a large fountain. The fountain is bordered by four female figures representing the seasons and two black lions that look across the street to the neo-Gothic cathedral and its unusual freestanding bell tower. ⊠ *Condell at Molina.*

BEACHES

If it's beaches you're after, head to Viña del Mar or one of the other resort towns along the coast.

Laguna Verde. In a somewhat secluded cove 23 km (14 miles) southwest of Valparaíso, Laguna Verde is a stunning and largely uncrowded stretch of yellow-sand coastline that's worth the visit if you have some time to spend. You can get there via a 1½-hour local bus ride or can rent a car for the half-hour trip. Better yet, rent a four-wheel-drive vehicle to be able to explore the surrounding area. It's rustic, but there are now a few restaurants, food trucks during the summer months, basic services, and cabins ranging from very basic to utterly spectacular. **Amenities:** food and drink; parking. **Best for:** solitude; sunset; walking. ⊠ *47 Av. Principal.*

Playa Las Torpederas. Valparaíso's only true swim-worthy beach is set in a sheltered crescent of yellow sand east of the port. Although less attractive than other beaches up and down the coast, it's a fast and easy getaway from the busy port and does have very calm water. **Amenities:** food and drink; parking. **Best for:** sunset; swimming. ⊠ *Valparaíso.*

WHERE TO EAT

$$$$ **✕ Café Turri.** Near the top of Ascensor Concepción, this 19th-century
SEAFOOD mansion is one of the city's best-known restaurants. The traditional
Fodor's Choice menu has a French twist; onion soup with Gruyère and foie gras sit
★ alongside excellent seafood. **Known for:** an awesome view; excellent seafood; traditional fine dining. ⑤ *Average main: 12500 pesos* ⊠ *Templeman 147, at Paseo Gervasoni, Cerro Concepción* ☎ *32/225–2091, 32/236–5307* ⊕ *www.turri.cl.*

$$$ **✕ Café Vinilo.** Serving traditional Chilean cuisine with a contemporary
CHILEAN touch, Café Vinilo prides itself on making its own beer, bread, and desserts. They also work directly with their food suppliers, so you can rest assured the rock fish ceviche on your plate was likely caught that same morning by a diver in Quintero, an hour's drive north along the coast.

CLOSE UP

Chilean Coastal Cuisine

"In the turbulent sea of Chile lives the golden conger eel," wrote Chilean poet Pablo Neruda in a simple verse that leaves the real poetry for the dinner table. To many, dining is the principal pleasure of a trip to the Central Coast. Along with that succulent conger eel (*congrio* as it's known in these parts), menus here typically offer *corvina* (sea bass), a whitefish called *reineta*, and *lenguado* (sole). The appetizer selection, which is invariably extensive, usually includes *machas Parmesanas* (razor clams), *ostiones* (scallops), *camarones* (shrimp), and *jaiba* (crab).

Fish and meat dishes do not usually include *agregados* (side dishes), so if you want french fries, mashed potatoes, a salad, or *palta* (avocado), you have to order them separately. Bread, lemons, and a sauce called *pebre* (a mix of tomato, onion, coriander, parsley, and chili) are always brought to the table. Valparaíso is also known for a hearty, cheap meal called *chorillana*—a mountain of minced steak, onions, cheese, and eggs on a bed of french fries that is generally placed in the center of the table to be shared by the group.

Known for: youthful atmosphere; fresh seafood; jazz music ambience. ⑤ *Average main: 9500 pesos* ⊠ *Almirante Montt 448, Cerro Alegre* ☎ *32/223–0665.*

$$$ ✕**Casino Social J. Cruz M.** This eccentric restaurant is a Valparaíso institu-
CHILEAN tion, thanks to its legendary status for inventing the *chorillana* (thinly sliced beef with fried onions, and eggs served atop french fries), a dish that is meant to be eaten communally. There's no menu—choose either a plate of *chorillana* for two or three, or *carne mechada* (stewed beef) with a side of french fries, rice, or tomato salad. **Known for:** home of the Chilean classic chorillana; very casual dining; shared tables and dishes. ⑤ *Average main: 9000 pesos* ⊠ *Condell 1466, Casa 11* ☎ *32/221–1225* ⊕ *www.jcruz.cl* ▭ *No credit cards.*

$ ✕**El Desayunador.** Hearty breakfast foods are served up day and night
CHILEAN in this restaurant, whose name roughly translates to "the breakfast place." Located in the heart of one of Cerro Alegre's main drags, El Desayunador not only offers great coffee and eggs, but tasty sandwiches and salads as well. The cozy spot has quickly become a favorite among tourists. **Known for:** all-day breakfast; convivial atmosphere great for conversations; hearty sandwiches. ⑤ *Average main: 4000 pesos* ⊠ *Almirante Montt 399, Cerro Alegre* ⊕ *At confluence of Almirante Montt, Paseo Dimalow, and Av. Urriola* ☎ *32/236–5933.*

$$$$ ✕**Espíritu Santo Restaurant.** Clean, modern lines combine with warm
SEAFOOD touches of antique wood to create a light and inviting setting that
Fodor'sChoice puts full focus on the food. The specialty here is the freshly caught
★ rock fish that arrives daily. **Known for:** delicious rock fish; fine dining experience; nice steak and vegetarian options. ⑤ *Average main: 14000 pesos* ⊠ *Héctor Calvo 392, Cerro Bellavista* ☎ *32/327–0443* ⊕ *www. hosteriaespiritusanto.cl.*

\$\$ ✕**Hotel Brighton.** Seemingly dangling from the edge of Cerro Con-
ECLECTIC cepción, the bright yellow Brighton Hotel and its restaurant have an
amazing view from the black-and-white-tiled terrace. The limited menu
specializes in seafood, with such standards as *machas a la parmesana*
(razor clams with Parmesan) and ceviche, as well as several kinds of
crepes and hearty Chilean sandwiches. **Known for:** relaxed and inviting atmosphere; live music on weekends; wine list and cocktail menu.
⑤ *Average main: 8000 pesos* ⊠ *Paseo Atkinson 151, Cerro Concepción*
☎ *32/222–3513* ⊕ *www.brighton.cl.*

\$\$\$\$ ✕**La Caperucita y El Lobo.** This place is one of those delightful little res-
CONTEMPORARY taurants that seems to have it all—great food and an excellent view of
the bay in a warm and intimate setting. Seafood plays a key role here,
but the carefully constructed menu also features dishes like rabbit, lamb,
and steak along with some vegetarian options. **Known for:** excellent
seafood and other meat options; nice views; lots of local charm. ⑤ *Average main: 12000 pesos* ⊠ *Ferrari 75, Cerro Florida* ☎ *32/317–2798*
⊕ *www.lacaperucitayellobo.cl* ⊘ *Closed Mon.*

\$\$\$\$ ✕**La Colombina.** This restaurant is in an old home just steps from the
SEAFOOD Palacio Baburizza fine arts museum on Cerro Alegre, in one of the city's
most beautiful hilltop neighborhoods. The house specializes in Chilean
dishes, and seafood dominates the menu, but you'll also find a good
selection for meat lovers—served with flare. **Known for:** impressive bay
views from the top floor; cozy, eclectic decor; upscale Chilean cuisine.
⑤ *Average main: 13000 pesos* ⊠ *Paseo Apolo 91, off Paseo Yugoslavo,
Cerro Alegre, Cerro Alegre* ☎ *32/223–6254* ⊕ *www.lacolombina.cl.*

\$\$\$\$ ✕**Pasta e Vino Ristorante.** One of the hippest spots on fashionable Cerro
ITALIAN Concepción, Pasta e Vino is usually packed, and the hosts look like they
Fodor's Choice have escaped from a fashion magazine. The sophisticated and imagina-
★ tive Italian food is just as attractive. **Known for:** creative, sophisticated
pastas; elegant but cool atmosphere; impressive wine list. ⑤ *Average
main: 12000 pesos* ⊠ *Papudo 427, at Paseo Gervasoni and Pasaje
Galvez, Cerro Concepción* ☎ *32/249–6187* ⊕ *pastaevinoristorante.cl*
⊘ *Closed Mon.*

\$\$\$ ✕**Sabor Color.** Colorful inside and out, this trendy restaurant in a bright
CONTEMPORARY red turn-of-the-century home has a rotating collection of art (for sale)
hanging on its brightly colored walls, which is evocative of Valparaíso's
hills. And as the "sabor" in its name alludes, the menu is quite full of
flavor. **Known for:** creative and beautiful dishes; live music on weekends; interesting cocktails and local craft beers. ⑤ *Average main: 9500
pesos* ⊠ *Templeman 561, Cerro Concepción* ☎ *32/259–8472.*

WHERE TO STAY

\$\$\$\$ ⌂ **Casa Higueras.** The hills of Valparaíso have enjoyed a boom of bou-
B&B/INN tique hotels in the last decade, but this one is a cut above the rest. **Pros:** a
Fodor's Choice rare spot of luxury in Valparaíso; convenient location; pampering staff.
★ **Cons:** the rest of the street could benefit from a paint job; no parking
on-site; some rooms are a little noisy. ⑤ *Rooms from: 200000 pesos*
⊠ *Higueras 133, Cerro Alegre* ☎ *32/249–7900* ⊕ *www.casahigueras.cl*
⌁ *20 rooms* ❙⊘❙ *Breakfast.*

$$$
B&B/INN

Fauna Hotel. As the name suggests, Fauna stays true to its natural surroundings: the floors, stairs, and handrails are made from recycled native wood, adobe is used generously in the architecture, and the span of the hotel's interior street-side wall, extending some two floors, is actually the exposed containment wall originally constructed to keep Cerro Alegre standing. **Pros:** incredible views of the bay; centrally located; trendy. **Cons:** noisy; no access by vehicle; no elevator, so stairs could be a problem for some. $ *Rooms from: 100000 pesos* ⊠ *Pasaje Dimalow 166, Cerro Alegre* ☎ *32/327-0719* ⊕ *www.faunahotel.cl* ➪ *14 rooms* ⊙| *No meals.*

$$$
B&B/INN

Gran Hotel Gervasoni. Set in a sprawling Victorian mansion that spreads across five floors built in the 1870s, the Gervasoni is a chance to step back in time to Valparaíso's more elegant past. **Pros:** a chance to imagine life in Valparaíso's Victorian apogee; convenient location; attentive staff. **Cons:** very steep stairs; views are spoiled by a concrete office block; some of the rooms are a bit tired. $ *Rooms from: 80000 pesos* ⊠ *Paseo Gervasoni 1, Cerro Concepción, Cerro Concepción* ☎ *32/223-9236* ⊕ *www.hotelgervasoni.com* ➪ *9 rooms* ⊙| *Breakfast.*

$$$
B&B/INN
Fodor's Choice
★

Hotel Brighton B&B. This bright-yellow Victorian house enjoys an enviable location at the edge of tranquil Cerro Concepción. **Pros:** unmatched views across Valpo and the bay; nice restaurant and terrace below; convenient, peaceful location. **Cons:** some of the rooms are a bit noisy; no direct access from the street (requires a short walk); stairs may be difficult for some to manage. $ *Rooms from: 80000 pesos* ⊠ *At northern end of Paseo Atkinson, Paseo Atkinson 151, Cerro Concepción* ☎ *32/222-3513* ⊕ *www.brighton.cl* ➪ *9 rooms* ⊙| *Breakfast.*

$$$
B&B/INN

Hotel Manoir Atkinson. One of the first boutique hotels to spring up on fashionable Cerro Concepción and Cerro Alegre, this cozy house lies at the end of Paseo Atkinson, near many local attractions. **Pros:** many of Valparaíso's best restaurants are just a block or two away; peaceful location; friendly and attentive owner/hosts. **Cons:** despite location, many of the rooms lack sea views; parking is an issue; Wi-Fi can be spotty. $ *Rooms from: 80000 pesos* ⊠ *Paseo Atkinson 165, Cerro Concepción* ☎ *32/327-5425* ⊕ *www.hotelatkinson.cl* ➪ *7 rooms* ⊙| *Breakfast.*

$$
B&B/INN

Hotel Ultramar. Behind a staid-looking brick facade, there's an ultramodern yet simple interior in this early 20th-century building on Cerro Carcel. **Pros:** eye-popping views of the bay from terrace; friendly, helpful staff; free parking. **Cons:** location is a bit far from the action; not very kid-friendly; traffic noise at night. $ *Rooms from: 65000 pesos* ⊠ *Tomás Peréz 173, Cerro Cárcel* ☎ *32/221-0000* ⊕ *www.hotelultramar.com* ➪ *16 rooms.*

$$$$
B&B/INN

Palacio Astoreca Hotel. Complete with a piano bar, wine cellar, spa, massage room, indoor heated swimming pool, wood-fire heated hot tub, and indoor garden, this hotel aims to please. **Pros:** a beautiful setting in a renovated Victorian mansion; convenient, peaceful location; wonderful spa on-site. **Cons:** a bit pricey; spotty Wi-Fi; parking is limited and tricky. $ *Rooms from: 189000 pesos* ⊠ *Calle Montealegre 149, Cerro Alegre* ☎ *32/327-7700* ⊕ *www.hotelpalacioastoreca.com* ➪ *23 rooms* ⊙| *No meals.*

$$$ | **Somerscales Boutique Hotel.** Perched high atop Cerro Alegre, between
B&B/INN | ascensores El Peral and Reina Victoria, this palm-shaded mansion has
Fodor's Choice | an unobstructed view of the sea. **Pros:** light, bright rooms; in the heart
★ | of hip Valpo; beautiful garden. **Cons:** a steep climb back to your room
at night; no air-conditioning in rooms; breakfast is a little on the light
side. ⑤ *Rooms from: 100000 pesos* ⊠ *San Enrique 446, Cerro Alegre*
☎ *32/233–1006* ⊕ *www.hotelsomerscales.cl* ⟳ *8 rooms* ⑩ *Breakfast.*

$$ | **Wine Box Hotel.** This one-of-a-kind, brightly colored apart-hotel is
B&B/INN | one of the most creative lodgings in the country: in honor of the city's
Fodor's Choice | role as a working port, it was built from 25 recycled insulated shipping
★ | containers, and its rooftop terrace provides a 360-degree view of the
bay and entire city. **Pros:** all rooms include original artwork; wine bar/
restaurant and shop on-site; creative, container hotel design. **Cons:**
weekend terrace parties mean it can get noisy; not the best setting for
non-drinkers; no free breakfast. ⑤ *Rooms from: 65000 pesos* ⊠ *Av.
Baquedano 763, Cerro Mariposa* ☎ *9/424–5331* ⟳ *21 rooms* ⟳ *No
children allowed.*

$$$$ | **Zerohotel.** Set in one of the quieter corners of bustling Cerro Alegre,
B&B/INN | this former Dutch diplomat's residence dating to to the 1880s has been
transformed into a chic boutique hotel. **Pros:** a quiet, relaxing corner
on Cerro Alegre's normally bustling streets; lovely spa and wellness
area; very stylish. **Cons:** no restaurant; no on-site parking (paid parking is available nearby with reservations); presents some difficulty for
people with mobility problems. ⑤ *Rooms from: 190000 pesos* ⊠ *Lautaro Rosas 343, Cerro Alegre* ☎ *32/211–3113* ⊕ *www.zerohotel.com*
⟳ *9 rooms* ⑩ *Breakfast.*

NIGHTLIFE AND PERFORMING ARTS

Valparaíso has an inordinate number of late-night establishments,
which run the gamut from pubs to tango bars and salsa dance clubs.
Thursday through Saturday nights most places get crowded between
11 pm and midnight and young people stay out until dawn. The main
concentrations of bars and clubs are on Subida Ecuador, near Plaza Aníbal Pinto, and a block of Avenida Errázuriz nearby. Cerro Concepción,
Alegre, and Bellavista have quieter options, many with terraces perfect
for admiring the city lights.

Tango dancing is so popular in Valparaíso that you might think you
were in Buenos Aires. Then there's the *cueca brava,* a common Chilean song and dance (also called *cueca urbana* or *cueca chora* in these
parts); it's undergone a revival in recent years, taking on a much more
modern and urban slant.

BARS

Bar de Pisco. True to its name, this venue specializes in pisco, the national
drink distilled from muscat grapes. There are more than 30 different
available brands here. The bartenders in this cramped bar serve up
deliciously creative cocktails, such as *apiado* (a celery-based liquor) or
shots of *aguardiente* (distilled spirits) infused with vanilla, cinnamon,
or basil. ⊠ *Almirante Montt 484, Cerro Alegre* ☎ *32/319–2161.*

Bar Inglés. A short walk east of Plaza Sotomayor, Bar Inglés has dark
wood paneling and the longest bar in town. You can also order decent

food. More than a century old, this is one of the city's oldest and most traditional and best-loved bars. ⊠ *Cochrane 851* ☏ *32/221–4625.*

Bar La Playa. The huge antique mirrors of Bar La Playa, just west of Plaza Sotomayor, give it a historic feel. Open since 1908, it's Valparaíso's oldest bar. Go for lunch or for drinks in the evening—in Valpo, the later the better. Things tend to pick up around midnight on weekends in January and February. ⊠ *Serrano 567* ☏ *32/225–2838.*

LIVE MUSIC

Cinzano. Listen to live tango and other traditional Latin music Tuesday through Saturday here at Cinzano, an old-fashioned watering hole and restaurant facing Plaza Aníbal Pinto that's been open since 1896. The walls above the bar are decorated with scenes of old Valparaíso, including some notable shipwrecks. The restaurant serves traditional dishes for lunch and dinner daily. The dance floor—if you can call it that—is miniscule, but that doesn't stop people from dancing tango or *cueca urbana* in what little space there is between tables. ⊠ *Anibal Pinto 1182* ☏ *32/221–3043* ⊕ *www.barcinzano.cl.*

El Rincón de Las Guitarras (Casa de Cueca). Get a double shot of *porteño* (port city) nightlife at this classic restaurant with two rooms that feature two different acts simultaneously. Go ahead and try the traditional Chilean food, but the real reason to come is for the *cueca* , Chile's national dance, but forget everything you might know about the traditional folklore show. This is the gutsy, gritty, eye-to-eye, forehead-to-forehead *cueca chora*, which has undergone a revival in the past decade (much as *narco tango* has in Buenos Aires). If you want a table, you'll need to come early—and plan on staying into the wee hours. ⊠ *Freire 431* ☏ *32/223–4412.*

Fodor'sChoice
★   **La Piedra Feliz.** A favorite in this port city, music fans should check out La Piedra Feliz, which hosts performances by Chile's best bands Tuesday through Saturday. This multivenue locale has something for everyone, with different types of music or activities in various rooms. Plan on a very late night here—there won't be much going on until after 10 or 11 pm. ⊠ *Av. Errázuriz 1054* ☏ *32/225–6788, 9/8921–3389* ⊕ *www. lapiedrafeliz.cl.*

PERFORMING ARTS VENUES

Parque Cultural Valparaíso (Ex-Cárcel). In 1999, Valparaíso's prison population was moved to a new facility on the outskirts of town, and the old prison (Ex Cárcel), built in 1906, was basically abandoned until opened to the community as a museum and was occasionally used for plays and concerts. In 2011, it was renovated for use as a cultural park with excellent spaces for art exhibitions and for training in music, dance, and even circus arts. You'll find drumming groups practicing on the lawn and the occasional arts fair. ⊠ *Calle Cerro Carcel 471* ☏ *32/235–9400* ⊕ *www.parquecultural.cl.*

SPORTS AND THE OUTDOORS

BOATING

Muelle Prat Boat Tours. Boat operators at Muelle Prat offer 20- to 30-minute tours of the bay for 3,000 pesos. If you have several people, consider hiring your own boat for 30,000 pesos. ⊠ *Av. Errázuriz at Plaza Sotomayor* ⌨ *From 3000 pesos.*

SOCCER

Estadio Elías Figueroa Brander (formerly Estadio Municipal). Valparaíso's major sports stadium is known by many names, including most commonly as the Playa Ancha Stadium, but the city's first-division soccer team, the Santiago Wanderers, call it home. It was originally inaugurated in 1931; it was closed for renovations in 2012 and reopened in 2014. ⊠ *Av. Guillermo González de Hontaneda esquina Leopoldo Carvallo* ☎ *32/221–7210* ⊕ *www.santiagowanderers.cl.*

SHOPPING

Outside of Santiago, there are more shops in Valparaíso than anywhere else in Chile. If it's handicrafts you're looking for, head to the bohemian neighborhoods of Cerro Concepción and Cerro Alegre. There are dozens of workshops where you can watch artisans ply their crafts.

Feria de Antigüedades La Merced. The weekend antique and flea market has an excellent selection of antiques. ⊠ *Plaza O'Higgins.*

Ripley. One of the country's major department store chains, Ripley, is across from Plaza Victoria. The fifth floor has a food court. ⊠ *Plaza Victoria 1646* ☎ *02/2694–1000* ⊕ *www.ripley.cl.*

Víctor Hugo Art in Silver Workshop. Silversmith Víctor Hugo learned his trade in Brazil in the early 1980s and specializes in making a wide variety of silver jewelry with colored stones. His shop is open every day of the week, with a two-hour break for lunch. ⊠ *Lautaro Rosas 449A, Cerro Alegre* ☎ *9/315–0438* ⊕ *www.silverworkshop.cl.*

VIÑA DEL MAR

130 km (85 miles) northwest of Santiago.

Viña del Mar has high-rise apartment buildings that tower above its excellent shoreline, and the wide boulevards are lined with palms, lush parks, and mansions. Miles of beige sand are washed by heavy surf. The town has been known for years as Chile's tourist capital (a title currently being challenged by several other hot spots) and is currently in the midst of some minor refurbishment.

Viña, as it's popularly known, has the country's oldest casino, excellent hotels, and an extensive selection of restaurants. To some, all this means that Viña del Mar is modern and exciting; to others, it means the city is lacking in character. But there's no denying that Viña del Mar has a little of everything—trendy boutiques, beautiful homes, interesting museums, a casino, varied nightlife, and, of course, one of the best beaches in the country.

Viña del Mar

PACIFIC OCEAN

Valparaíso
Sporting Club

CHORRILLOS

FORESTAL

CASTILLO

RECRERO

Plaza Colombia

Casino Viña
del Mar ◆

Plaza
México

Estación
Viña del Mar

Plaza
Sucre

1/4 miles
400 meters

Av. Sporting
Av. Los Castaños
6 Oriente
5 Oriente
4 Oriente
3 Oriente
2 Oriente
1 Oriente
Quillota
Av. Libertad
1 Poniente
2 Poniente
3 Poniente
4 Poniente
5 Poniente
6 Poniente
7 Norte
6 Norte
5 Norte
4 Norte
3 Norte
2 Norte
1 Norte
Av. San Martín
Av. Perú

Peñablanca
Batuco
Quillota
Quinta
Echevers
Villanelo
Traslaviña
Ecuador
Von Schroeders
Berger
Callao
Iberia
Libertad
Balmaceda
Álamos
Av. Marina

Av. Marina
Av. Arlegui
Av. Valparaíso
Prieto Nieto
Montana
Errázuriz
Álvarez
Viana
Agua Santa
Bellavista
Av. Portales
Av. España

1 Norte
Av. Marina
Estero Marga-Marga
Limache
Álvarez

KEY

🛈 Tourist Information

Museo de Arqueológico e
Historia Francisco
Fonck **3**
Palacio Rioja **4**
Plaza José
Francisco Vergara **1**
Quinta Vergara **2**

GETTING HERE AND AROUND

From Santiago, take Ruta 68 west through the Coastal Mountains, turning off to Viña del Mar as the vineyards of the Casablanca Valley give way to eucalyptus forests. The spectacular twisting access road (Agua Santa), through hills dotted with Chilean palm trees, drops you on Avenida Alvarez, just a couple of blocks from downtown Viña del Mar. Turbus, Condor, Pullman, and Sol del Pacífico all run buses to Viña del Mar. Turbus leaves from its Alameda terminal. Viña del Mar has the best tourist office on the coast, offering fistfuls of helpful maps and brochures.

ESSENTIALS

Visitor Information Viña del Mar main office. ⊠ Arlegui 715 ✛ Beside Hotel O'Higgins across from park ☎ 32/218–4402 ⊕ www.visitevinadelmar.cl.

EXPLORING

FAMILY **Museo de Arqueológico e Historia Francisco Fonck.** A 500-year-old stone *moai* (a carved stone head) brought from Easter Island guards the entrance to this archaeological museum. The most interesting exhibits are the finds from Easter Island, which indigenous people call Rapa Nui, such as wood tablets displaying ancient hieroglyphics. The museum, named for groundbreaking archaeologist Francisco Fonck—a native of Viña del Mar—also has an extensive library of documents relating to the island. Other fun but freaky exhibits include shrunken heads, insects, and all sorts of stuffed birds and animals. ⊠ *4 Norte 784* ☎ *32/268–6753* ⊕ *www.museofonck.cl* 🎟 *2700 pesos.*

Palacio Rioja. This grand palace, now a national monument, was built by Spanish banker Francisco Rioja immediately after the earthquake that leveled much of the city in 1906. It contains a decorative-arts museum showcasing a large portion of Rioja's belongings and a conservatory, so there's often music in the air. Performances are held in the main ballroom. You'll find a nice café in the back with seating under the trees in beautifully landscaped grounds. ⊠ *Quillota 214* ☎ *32/218–4690* ⊕ *www.museopalaciorioja.cl* 🎟 *Free* ☉ *Closed Mon.*

Plaza José Francisco Vergara. Viña del Mar's central square, Plaza Vergara is lined with majestic palms. Presiding over the east end of the plaza is the patriarch of coastal accommodations, the venerable Hotel O'Higgins, which has seen better days. Opposite the hotel is the neoclassical Teatro Municipal de Viña del Mar, where you can watch a ballet, theater, or music performance. To the west on Avenida Valparaíso is the city's main shopping strip, a one-lane, seven-block stretch with extra-wide sidewalks and numerous stores and sidewalk cafés. You can hire a horse-drawn carriage to take you from the square past some of the city's stately mansions. ⊠ *Plaza Vergara, Arlegui 687.*

Quinta Vergara. Lose yourself on the paths that wind amid towering araucaria and other well-marked trees on the grounds that contain one of Chile's best botanical gardens. An amphitheater here holds an international music festival, Festival Internacional de la Canción de Viña del Mar, in February. ⊠ *Av. Errázuriz 563* ☎ *32/218–5720* ⊕ *www.quintavergara.cl* 🎟 *Free* ☉ *Closed Mon.*

BEACHES

FAMILY **Las Salinas.** Just north of town a white arch announces the tiny family-friendly Balneario Las Salinas beach area, a crescent of yellow sand that has the calmest water in the area. **Amenities:** food and drink; parking; toilets. **Best for:** sunset; swimming; walking. ⊠ *Jorge Montt 12021.*

FAMILY **Playa Caleta Abarca.** One of Viña's most popular beaches, smack in the center of town, Playa Caleta Abarca's golden sands are crowded with sun worshippers in midsummer, making it a great place for people-watching. **Amenities:** food and drink; lifeguards. **Best for:** swimming. ⊠ *Avenida España s/n* ✛ *Just south of Sheraton Hotel, across from Reloj de Flores.*

FAMILY
Fodor'sChoice
★
Playa El Sol. Just north of the rock wall along Avenida Peru and flanked by the old Muelle Vergara is a stretch of sand that draws crowds of people from December through March. Viña del Mar really has just this one main beach, bisected near its southern end by an old pier, though its parts have been given separate names: Playa El Sol and Playa Blanca. It's great for swimming and people-watching as well as for exploring the artisan fair nearby. **Amenities:** food and drink; parking; showers; toilets. **Best for:** sunset; walking. ⊠ *San Martín 1130.*

WHERE TO EAT

$$$$
STEAKHOUS-
ESTEAKHOUSE
✕ **Parrillada Armandita.** Meat-eaters need not despair in this city of seafood. This rustic restaurant half a block west of Avenida San Martín serves almost nothing but grilled meat, including various organ meats. **Known for:** Argentine-style grilled meats; excellent lomo a lo pobre (flank steak with fries and a fried egg); group dining. ⑤ *Average main: 14000 pesos* ⊠ *6 Norte 119* ☎ *32/268–1607* ⊕ *www.armanditaparrilla.cl.*

$$$$
ITALIAN
✕ **San Marco.** More than six decades after Edoardo Melotti emigrated here from northern Italy, his restaurant maintains a reputation for first-class food and service. The menu includes traditional gnocchi, as well as *pansotti del bosco* (spinach pasta filled with turkey and puréed chestnuts) and *bistecca alla toscana* (strip steak). **Known for:** traditional northern Italian cuisine; extensive wine list; elegant ambience. ⑤ *Average main: 15000 pesos* ⊠ *Av. San Martín 597* ☎ *32/297–5304* ⊕ *www.ristorantesanmarco.cl.*

$$
JAPANESE
✕ **Shitake.** With so much fresh fish available, it's a wonder that it took so long for sushi and sashimi to catch on with locals. Now that it has, it's hard to find a block downtown that lacks a Japanese restaurant, but a favorite with locals is Shitake, which occupies a few gold and beige rooms on Avenida San Martín. **Known for:** fresh sushi made for sharing; Ecuadorean shrimp tempura; local favorite. ⑤ *Average main: 8000 pesos* ⊠ *Av. San Martín 421* ☎ *32/290–1458* ⊕ *www.shitake.cl.*

WHERE TO STAY

$$
HOTEL
▦ **Cap Ducal.** A classic in Viña, this ship-shaped building on the waterfront is best known for its restaurant dating to 1936, but also offers fun, oddly shaped rooms inspired by a transatlantic ocean liner. **Pros:** unique architecture; breathtaking ocean views; excellent location. **Cons:** noise of traffic can spoil the great views; very dark, narrow hallways; decor is a bit tired. ⑤ *Rooms from: 71000 pesos* ⊠ *Av. Marina 51* ☎ *32/262–6655* ⊕ *www.capducal.cl* ⇄ *21 rooms* ❙◎❙ *Breakfast.*

$$$$ ⬚ **Hotel Del Mar.** A rounded facade, echoing the shape of the adjacent
RESORT Casino Viña del Mar, means that almost every room at this elegant
Fodor'sChoice oceanfront hotel has unmatched views. **Pros:** notable in-house restau-
★ rant; pure luxury in every direction; free access to the casino. **Cons:**
constant chiming of gaming machines may grate on your nerves; can
be a pretty busy place; no coffee or tea in the room means guests must
wait for restaurant to open. $ *Rooms from: 180000 pesos* ⊠ *Av. San
Martín 199* ☏ *32/284–6300* ⊕ *www.enjoy.cl* ⤴ *60 rooms* ¶○¶ *Breakfast.*

$$$$ ⬚ **Hotel Oceanic.** Built on the rocky coast between Viña and Reñaca,
B&B/INN this boutique hotel has luxurious rooms with gorgeous ocean views.
Pros: ocean views from hotel terraces; on-premise spa for massage and
pampering; great restaurant. **Cons:** beyond the city limits, making a
vehicle necessary for getting around town; standard rooms do not have
an ocean view; no air-conditioning in rooms. $ *Rooms from: 150000
pesos* ⊠ *Av. Borgoño 12925, north of town, Reñaca* ☏ *32/283–0006*
⊕ *www.hoteloceanic.cl* ⤴ *30 rooms* ¶○¶ *Breakfast.*

$$$$ ⬚ **Sheraton Miramar.** This sophisticated city hotel certainly earns it name,
RESORT as you can do almost everything here while you gaze at the sea. **Pros:**
Fodor'sChoice first-class city hotel with spectacular views; elegant and luxurious; the
★ beach is right next door. **Cons:** area around the hotel is partially blighted
by one of Viña's main access roads; a bit of a walk to main drag; access
to the hotel by car is tricky. $ *Rooms from: 200000 pesos* ⊠ *Av. Marina
15* ☏ *32/238–8600* ⊕ *www.sheraton.cl* ⤴ *142 rooms* ¶○¶ *Breakfast.*

$$ ⬚ **Tres Poniente.** Come for the personalized service and for many of the
B&B/INN same amenities you'll find at larger hotels at a fraction of the cost. **Pros:**
good value on a quiet backstreet; friendly, helpful staff; tasty breakfast.
Cons: a long walk from the beach or Viña's main attractions; plumb-
ing can be noisy in some rooms; no elevator. $ *Rooms from: 62000
pesos* ⊠ *3 Poniente 70, between 1 and 2 Norte* ☏ *32/247–8576* ⊕ *www.
hotel3poniente.com* ⤴ *11 rooms* ¶○¶ *Breakfast.*

NIGHTLIFE AND PERFORMING ARTS

Viña's nightlife varies considerably according to the season, with the
most glittering events concentrated in January and February. There are
nightly shows and concerts at the casino and frequent performances at
Quinta Vergara. During the rest of the year, things get going only on
weekends. Aside from the casino, late-night fun is concentrated in the
area around the intersection of Avenida San Martín and 4 Norte, the
shopping strip on Avenida Valparaíso, and the eastern end of the alley
called Paseo Cousiño. Viña residents tend to go to Valparaíso for live
music, since it has a much better selection.

BARS

Margarita. Margarita is a popular Tex-Mex-style watering hole late at
night, with live music and karaoke on weekends. The namesake cocktail
is a killer. ⊠ *Av. San Martín 5410* ☏ *32/268–9753.*

CASINO

Casino Viña del Mar. Built in 1930 in a neoclassical style that wouldn't
be out of place in a James Bond movie, Chile's oldest casino has a res-
taurant, bar, and cabaret, as well as roulette, blackjack, and 1,500 slot
machines. It's open nightly until the wee hours of the morning most

of the year. There's a 3,800-peso cover charge, and keep in mind that people dress up to play here, especially in the evening. ✉ *Av. San Martín 199* 🕾 *32/250–0600* ⊕ *www.enjoy.cl/enjoy-vina-del-mar.*

DANCE CLUBS

Club Divino. This gay club on the outskirts of town offers drag shows, along with one of the hottest dance floors in the area and some of the best DJs around. ✉ *Camino Internacional 537, Reñaca Alto* 🕾 *9/5708–4660* ⊕ *www.clubdivino.cl.*

SPORTS AND THE OUTDOORS

HORSE RACING

Valparaíso Sporting Club. Horse racing is hosted here every Wednesday. The Clásico del Derby, Chile's version of the Kentucky Derby, takes place the first Sunday in February. Rugby, polo, cricket, and other sports are also played here. The site is a favorite for other large scale events too. ✉ *Av. Los Castaños 404* 🕾 *32/265–5610* ⊕ *www.sporting.cl.*

SOCCER

Estadio Sausalito. Everton is Viña del Mar's soccer team. Matches are held at the 25,000-seat Estadio Sausalito, which hosted World Cup matches in 1962 and the Americas Cup in 1991 and 2015. ✉ *Laguna Sausalito* 🕾 *32/268–3718* ⊕ *sausalito.ciudaddeldeporte.com.*

SHOPPING

Avenida Valparaíso. Viña's main shopping strip is Avenida Valparaíso between Cerro Castillo and Plaza Vergara, where wide sidewalks accommodate throngs of mostly local shoppers. Stores here sell everything from shoes to cameras, and there are also sidewalk cafés, bars, and restaurants. ✉ *Viña del Mar.*

Centro Artesanal Calle Quinta. Local crafts are sold at the Centro Artesanal Calle Quinta. ✉ *Quinta 232, between Viana and Av. Valparaíso.*

Espacio Urbano. For one-stop shopping, locals head to the mall. Espacio Urbano, on the north end of town, is a longtime favorite. ✉ *Av. Benidorm 805 at 15 Norte* 🕾 *32/238–8200* ⊕ *www.espaciourbano.cl/15norte.*

Falabella. This popular department store is located south of Plaza Vergara. ✉ *Sucre 250* 🕾 *600/390–6500* ⊕ *www.falabella.com.*

Feria Artesanal Muelle Vergara. On the beach, near the pier at Muelle Vergara, the Feria Artesanal Muelle Vergara is a crafts fair open daily in summer and on weekends the rest of the year. ✉ *Viña del Mar.*

CASABLANCA WINE VALLEY

Don't miss the chance to stop at the many wineries along the road between Santiago and the coast. As you come out of the Zapata Tunnel (at Km 60 on Ruta 68), the importance of wine production to the local economy will be obvious. Vineyards carpet the floor of the Casablanca Valley for as far as the eye can see. Just 30 years ago most winemakers considered this area inhospitable for wine grapes, yet today it is at the forefront of the country's wine industry. Experts have come to recognize the valley's proximity to the sea as its main asset, because cooler temperatures give the grapes more time to develop flavor as they ripen.

Many of the wineries are open to visitors and offer activities such as tours, tastings, picnics on the grounds, or lunch at an on-premises restaurant, or even an overnight stay (all for a price, of course). Although most offer tours on a daily basis, call ahead to ensure someone is available to show you around.

GETTING HERE AND AROUND

Most of the vineyards are a bit of a trek from the main highway, so having a bus drop you off on the side of the road probably isn't the best way to go. If you drive there, plan to spend several hours touring and tasting the wines, and give yourself time for the alcohol to leave your system as Chile has a strict zero-tolerance policy on drinking and driving. Alternately, indulge freely and spend the night, or take one of many guided tours.

TOURS

If you want to visit more than one winery, the **Casablanca Valley Wine Producers Association** (☎ 32/274–3755 ⊕ www.casablancavalley.cl) offers a number of tour options.

WINERIES

Casas del Bosque. Nestled among rolling vine-covered hills just outside the town of Casablanca, Casas del Bosque offers tastings and tours as well as creative options that include bike riding through the vineyard, being a winemaker for a day, cooking classes, and more. During March and April, the main harvest months, you can learn even more about the production process with the chance to pick your grapes and take them for selection and pressing. Like many wineries in the valley, Casas del Bosque has its own restaurant, Tanino. ⊠ *Hijuelas No. 2, Centro Ex Fundo Santa Rosa, Casablanca* ☎ 2/2480–6940, 22/480–6941 ⊕ *www. casasdelbosque.cl.*

House of Morandé. Tour the House of Morandé and learn about winemaking, including the champenoise method for sparkling wine and the use of concrete eggs for aging red wines. But even if you don't have time to take a tour, at least make time to stop at the restaurant here, just off the highway as you hit the valley floor from the Zapata Tunnel. Pablo Morandé was one of the first to recognize Casablanca's cool-climate potential for producing wine grapes (mostly white) in the early 1980s and now uses his ultrastylish restaurant, which combines unusual local fare and modern techniques, to showcase the wines. ⊠ *Ruta 68, Km 61, Valparaíso* ✛ *Just past Viñedos Orgánicos Emiliana* ☎ 32/275–4701 ⊕ *www.morande.cl* ⊗ *Closed Mon.*

Viña Matetic. The biodynamic Viña Matetic straddles the border between the Casablanca Valley and the adjacent San Antonio Valley and may take the prize for having the region's most stunning bodega. Set into a ridge overlooking vines on both sides, it aims to harmonize with the gorgeous setting, with sloping passageways revealing glimpses into the barrels stored below. Just down the road, the winery's restaurant looks out over beautifully manicured gardens, in the middle of which is a restored guesthouse with seven elegantly decorated rooms. ⊠ *Fundo Rosario, Lagunillas, Casablanca* ☎ 2/2611–1501 ⊕ *www.matetic.com* ⊗ *Closed Mon.*

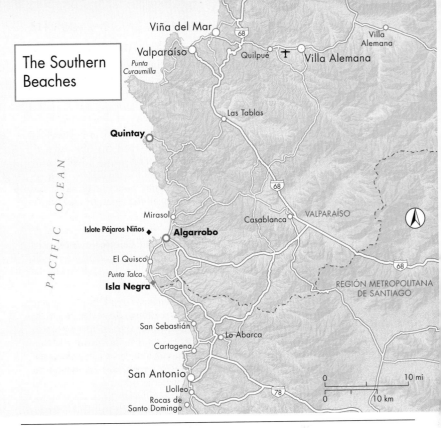

Viña del Mar
Villa
Alemana
Valparaíso
Quilpué
Villa Alemana
Punta
Curaumilla
Las Tablas
Quintay
Mirasol
Casablanca
VALPARAÍSO
Islote Pájaros Niños
Algarrobo
El Quisco
Punta Talca
Isla Negra
REGIÓN METROPOLITANA
DE SANTIAGO
San Sebastián
Lo Abarca
Cartagena
San Antonio
Llolleo
Rocas de
Santo Domingo

PACIFIC OCEAN

0   10 mi
0   10 km

THE SOUTHERN BEACHES

Once a dominion of solitude and sea, the stretch of coastline south of Valparaíso has seen much development, not all of it well planned, over the past few decades. A succession of towns here caters to the beach-bound hordes in January and February, and becomes a sleepy retreat for most of the rest of the year. Though none of the towns are terribly attractive, a few of the beaches are quite nice, and the towns, especially in the off-season, give you a good feel for rural life in this neck of the woods. The main reason to visit—and it's a great one—is to take a look at poet Pablo Neruda's hideaway in Isla Negra, where you can see the various treasures he collected during his lifetime.

Because large waves create dangerous undertows at some southern beaches, pay attention to warning flags: red means swimming is prohibited, whereas green, usually accompanied by a sign reading "*playa apta para nadir*" (beach suitable for swimming), is a go-ahead signal.

QUINTAY

30 km (19 miles) south of Valparaíso.

Not too long ago, migrating sperm whales could still be seen from the beaches at Quintay, although they were all but exterminated by the

whaling industry that sprang up in Quintay in 1942. Whaling was banned in 1967, and Quintay returned to being a quiet fishing village. If you wonder what the central coast was like before condos began springing up, head to this charming spot.

GETTING HERE AND AROUND

From Valparaíso, follow Ruta 68 toward Santiago and after 23 km (14 miles), turn onto Ruta F-800, which winds down through the hills to Quintay. From Santiago, follow Ruta 68, turn off at the Quintay-Tunquén exit and follow F-800 to the coast. Everything is located around the narrow bay except the museums, which are located in a school at the entrance to the village and next to the wharf.

EXPLORING

Quintay Whaling Factory. Fundación Quintay, a former whaling station that operated from 1943 to 1967, has been converted into a quaint museum that gives you a window into this coastal town's past. The museum, along with the skeletal remains of a whale, are just a stone's throw away from the handful of brightly colored fishing boats at the wharf. ⊠ *Caleta Quintay* ⊕ *www.fundacionquintay.cl* 🖹 *800 pesos.*

BEACHES

Playa Grande. Vacation apartments keep creeping closer to the beach, which gets its fair share of sun worshippers in summer. There are two ways to reach Playa Grande: through the town, following Avenida Teniente Merino, or through the gated community of Santa Augusta. **Amenities:** food; parking (fee); toilets. **Best for:** sunset; surfing; swimming; walking. ⊠ *Quintay.*

WHERE TO EAT

$$$ ✕ **Pezcadores.** Echoing the colors of the fishing boats below, this sea-
SEAFOOD   food restaurant is painted vivid shades of yellow, green, and red. The restaurant's proximity to the *caleta* (cove) means the fish on your plate was probably pulled from the water early that morning. **Known for:** fresh and tasty fish; nice wine list; bustling fishing pier atmosphere. ⑤ *Average main: 9000 pesos* ⊠ *Costanera s/n* ☎ *32/236–2068* ⊕ *www.pezcadores.cl.*

SPORTS AND THE OUTDOORS

DIVING

Chile's coastline has several interesting shipwrecks. Two are off the shores of Quintay, including *Indus IV,* a whaling ship that went down in 1947.

Austral Divers. Austral Divers offers diving courses for all levels, kayaking, and other water excursions from its beachside office. ⊠ *Caleta Quintay* ☎ *9/9885–5099, 9/9477–8409* ⊕ *www.australdivers.cl.*

ALGARROBO

35 km (22 miles) south of Quintay.

The largest town south of Valparaíso, Algarrobo has a winding coastline with several yellow-sand beaches and consequently attracts throngs

of sun worshippers. The pine forest behind two of its more popular beaches, El Canelo and Canelillo, is also worth exploring.

GETTING HERE AND AROUND

From Valparaíso, follow Ruta 68 toward Santiago and turn off onto Ruta F90 just after Casablanca. From there it is approximately 35 km (22 miles) to Algarrobo. Pullman and Turbus travel regularly to Algarrobo from the Alameda Terminal (Universidad de Santiago Metro station) in Santiago. Most of Algarrobo's main beaches lie within easy walking distance of the town. Regular buses run from here along the coast to El Quisco and Isla Negra farther south.

ESSENTIALS

Visitor Information Municipal Tourist Office. ⊠ Av. Peñablanca 250 ☏ 35/220–0100 ⊕ www.municipalidadalgarrobo.cl.

EXPLORING

Club de Yates Algarrobo. This private yacht club next to Playa San Pedro organizes and participates in numerous regatas throughout the year, including the Regata Mil Millas Náuticas. ⊠ Carlos Alessandri 2447 ☏ 35/248–3438 ⊕ www.cya.cl.

Islote Pájaros Niños. Just offshore from the Cofradía Náutica, this tiny island and penguin sanctuary shelters 20 species of marine birds, including some 350–500 Humboldt and Magellan penguins. The upper crags of the island are dotted with hundreds of little caves dug by the penguins using their legs and beaks. Though only members are allowed in the marina, a path leads to the top of a nearby hill from which you can watch the flightless birds through binoculars. ⊠ Algarrobo ⊕ www. vivealgarrobo.cl/html/m_5islotepajarosninos.htm.

BEACHES

El Quisco. South of Algarrobo, El Quisco is a long beach of pale sand guarded on either end by stone jetties. In the middle of the beach is a boulder with a 15-foot-high, six-pronged cactus sculpture perched atop it. South of the beach is the blue-and-yellow cove, where boats anchored offshore create a picturesque composition. Easily reached by all forms of transportation, the beach is packed on sunny summer days, when tourists outnumber *quisqueños* (locals) about 10 to 1. **Amenities:** food and drink. **Best for:** sunset; swimming; walking. ⊠ Algarrobo.

Fodor's Choice ★ **Playa El Canelo.** Algarrobo's prettiest beach is Playa El Canelo, located in a secluded cove south of town. It's actually two beaches in one, divided only by a small outcrop of rocks. The idyllic spot with fine yellow sand, calm blue-green water, and a backdrop of pines is blissfully quiet most of the year, but gets very crowded in January and February. From Algarrobo, follow Avenida Santa Teresita south to Avenida El Canelo and the pine forest of Parque Canelo, or from the main coastal road, take Bahía Mansa to Valle Verde. Because it's in a fairly tight cove, it's a great place for swimming, but other activities include boat rides, zip lines, body boarding, and walking the trails along the upper cliffs. **Amenities:** food and drink; parking (fee). **Best for:** sunset; surfing; swimming. ⊠ Algarrobo.

Playa Las Cadenas. Toward the northern end of town, where the promenade that runs between the beach and the long row of waterfront properties ends, Playa Las Cadenas is a popular, smaller spot to spread a beach towel. The calm and relatively shallow water makes it a good place for swimming. The name, translated to "Chain Beach," refers to the thick metal links lining the sidewalk, which were recovered from a shipwreck off Algarrobo Bay. **Amenities:** food and drink; toilets. **Best for:** sunset; swimming. ⊠ *Av. Carlos Alessandri 1928.*

Playa San Pedro. The most popular beach in town is tiny Playa San Pedro; a statue of Saint Peter in the sand next to the wharf marks the spot. It's small, but the waters are surrounded by a rocky barrier that keeps them calm and good for swimming. **Amenities:** food and drink. **Best for:** sunset; swimming; walking. ⊠ *Av. Carlos Alessandri* ⊹ *Just south of Club de Yates.*

WHERE TO EAT

$$$

SEAFOOD

✕ **A Toda Costa.** Head north of town to this hot spot right on the beach for the best seafood in town. The extensive menu includes the classics like razor clams Parmesan and crab gratin as well as more creative fare. **Known for:** creative and tasty seafood; great ocean view; vegetarian options. ⑤ *Average main: 9500* ⊠ *Av. Costanera s/n, Albarrobo Norte* ☎ *9/4424–5850* ⊕ *www.atodacosta.cl.*

WHERE TO STAY

$$

B&B/INN

▦ **Hotel Pacífico.** This older hotel in the heart of town, a block from Playa Las Cadenas, has bland but comfortable rooms. **Pros:** spacious rooms with views over the ocean; great location, close to everything; free parking. **Cons:** hotel is looking its age, with some rooms rather worn; can be noisy; some beds are small and uncomfortable. ⑤ *Rooms from: 73000 pesos* ⊠ *Av. Carlos Alessandri 1930* ☎ *35/248–2855* ⊕ *www. hotel-pacifico.cl* ⤸ *74 rooms* ❑| *Breakfast.*

$$

B&B/INN

▦ **Pao Pao.** The pine cabanas here range from cozy studios to two-bedroom apartments complete with wooden decks and hot tubs. **Pros:** rural setting makes it ideal for families; pool on-site; the perfect spot for rest and relaxation. **Cons:** the adjacent restaurant open only during January and February; pool could be a bit cleaner; gets noisy during peak season. ⑤ *Rooms from: 50000 pesos* ⊠ *Camino Mirasol 170* ☎ *9/3063–0898* ⊕ *www.turismopaopao.cl* ⤸ *22 cabins* ❑| *No meals.*

$$$

RENTAL

▦ **San Alfonso del Mar.** If you want to swim in the sea but aren't keen to brave the polar temperatures of Chilean waters, try this set of imposing apartment buildings on Algarrobo's northern edge with its eight-hectare, 1,000-meter, turquoise-blue seawater pool that stretches the length of the complex. **Pros:** avoid the chilly Humboldt Current in style; world's largest man-made pool; everything you need is close at hand. **Cons:** if you do feel the need to stray, it's a long walk to town; swimming is not allowed in the large pool; lack of coordination between management and owners make it difficult to resolve any problems. ⑤ *Rooms from: 100000 pesos* ⊠ *Camino Mirasol 866* ☎ *35/248–1636* ⊕ *www. sanalfonso.cl* ▭ *No credit cards* ⤸ *160 apartments* ❑| *No meals.*

Neruda's Inspiration

First, let's clear up one thing: Isla Negra may mean "Black Island," but this little stretch of rugged coastline is not black, and it's not an island. This irony must have appealed to Nobel Prize–winning poet Pablo Neruda, who made his home here for more than three decades.

Of his three houses, Pablo Neruda was most attached to Isla Negra. "Ancient night and the unruly salt beat at the walls of my house," he wrote in one of his many poems about his home in Isla Negra. It's easy to see how this house, perched high above the waves crashing on the purplish rocks, could inspire such reverie.

Neruda bought this house in 1938. Like La Sebastiana, his house in Valparaíso, it had been started by someone else and then abandoned. Starting with the cylindrical stone tower, which is topped by a whimsical weather vane shaped like a fish, he added touches that could only be described as poetic. There are odd angles, narrow hallways, and various nooks and crannies, all for their own sake.

What is most amazing about Isla Negra, however, is what Neruda chose to place inside. There's a tusk from a narwhal in one room, and figureheads from the fronts of sailing ships hanging overhead in another. There are huge collections ranging from seashells to bottles to butterflies. And yet it is also just a house, with a simple bedroom designed so he could gaze down at the sea when he needed inspiration.

SPORTS AND THE OUTDOORS
DIVING
Pablo Zavala. Pablo Zavala teaches diving and runs expeditions to half a dozen dive spots from the Club de Yates. ⊠ *Av. Carlos Alessandri 2447* ☎ *9/9435–4835.*

ISLA NEGRA

6 km (4 miles) south of El Quisco; 71 km (44 miles) south of Valparaíso.

"I needed a place to work," Chilean poet and Nobel laureate Pablo Neruda wrote in his memoirs. "I found a stone house facing the ocean, in a place nobody knew about, Isla Negra." Neruda, who bought the house in 1939, found much inspiration here. "Isla Negra's wild coastal strip, with its turbulent ocean, was the place to give myself passionately to the writing of my new song," he wrote.

GETTING HERE AND AROUND
From Algarrobo, head out as if returning to Santiago but turn southward at the crossroads on the road marked El Quisco. Follow the coastal road for about 9 km to the small village of Isla Negra. The path leading down to Neruda's house begins from the main road just after a row of stores selling handicrafts and souvenirs. Local buses run regularly along the coastal road between Algarrobo and San Antonio.

EXPLORING

Fodor's Choice **Casa-Museo Isla Negra.** Perched on a bluff overlooking the sea, the house
★ is a shrine to the life, work, and many passions of the Chilean poet
and Nobel laureate Pablo Neruda. Throughout the house, you'll find
displays of treasures—from bottles and maps to seashells and a narwhal
tusk—he collected over the course of his remarkable life. Although
he spent much time living and traveling abroad, Neruda made Isla
Negra his primary residence later in life. He wrote his memoirs from the
upstairs bedroom to the sound of the crashing waves and dictated the
final pages to his wife there before departing for the Santiago hospital
where he died of cancer. Neruda and his wife are buried in the prow-
shaped tomb area behind the house.

Just before Neruda's death in 1973, a military coup put Augusto Pinochet in command of Chile. He closed off Neruda's home and denied
all access, but Neruda devotees still chiseled their tributes into the
wooden gates surrounding the property. In 1989 the Neruda Foundation, started by his widow, restored the house and opened it as a
museum. Here his collections are displayed as they were while he lived.
The living room contains—among numerous other oddities—a lapis
lazuli and quartz fireplace and a number of figureheads from ships
hanging from the ceiling and walls.

You can visit the museum with an audio guide tour, available in
English, Spanish, French, German, and Portuguese (included in the
admission price) that describes Neruda's many obsessions, from the
positioning of guests at the dinner table to the east–west alignment of
his bed. Objects had a spiritual and symbolic life for the poet, which
the tour makes evident. Reservations are not required for the tour,
but space is filled on a first-come, first-served basis, so plan on coming
early and be prepared for a long wait during the busy summer months.
⊠ *Poeta Neruda s/n* ☎ *35/246–1284* ⊕ *www.fundacionneruda.org*
🎫 *7000 pesos* ⊗ *Closed Mon.*

WHERE TO EAT

$$$$ ✕ **El Rincón del Poeta.** Inside the entrance to the Neruda museum at Isla
SEAFOOD Negra, this small restaurant has a wonderful ocean view, with seating
both indoors and on a protected terrace. The name translates as the
Poet's Corner, a theme continued in the small but original menu filled
with classic Chilean dishes. **Known for:** another ode to the poetry of
Pablo Neruda; excellent seafood, including Neruda's favorite fried
conger eel; lovely views. ⑤ *Average main: 12000 pesos* ⊠ *Casa-Museo
Isla Negra, Poeta Neruda s/n* ☎ *35/246–1774* ⊕ *www.elrincondel-
poeta.cl* ⊗ *Closed Mon.*

THE NORTHERN BEACHES

To the north of Viña del Mar, the Pacific collides with the rocky offshore islands and a rugged coastline broken here and there by sandy
bays. The coastal highway runs from Viña del Mar to Papudo, passing
marvelous scenery along the way. Between Viña and Concón, it winds
along steep rock faces, turning inland north of Concón, where massive
sand dunes give way to expanses of undeveloped coastline, reminiscent

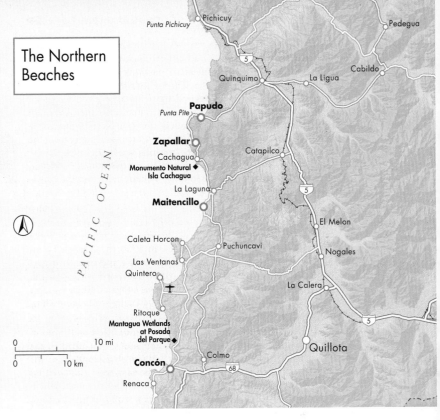

The Northern Beaches

Punta Pichicuy • Pichicuy • Pedegua
Quinquimo • La Ligua • Cabildo
Papudo
Punta Pite
Zapallar
Cachagua • Catapilco
Monumento Natural ◆
Isla Cachagua
La Laguna
Maitencillo
El Melon
Caleta Horcon • Puchuncaví
Nogales
Las Ventanas
Quintero
La Calera
Ritoque
Mantagua Wetlands
at Posada
del Parque ◆
Quillota
Colmo
Concón
Renaca

PACIFIC OCEAN

0 ——— 10 mi
0 ——— 10 km

of northern California's coast. The farther north you drive, the greater the distance between towns, each of which is on a significantly different beach. Whether as a day trip from Viña or on a series of overnights, this stretch of coast is well worth exploring.

CONCÓN

16 km (10 miles) north of Viña del Mar, along Avenida Borgoño.

How to explain the lovely name Concón? One theory is that in the language of the Changos, *co* meant "water," and the duplication of the sound alludes to the confluence of the Río Aconcagua and the Pacific. When the Spanish arrived in 1541, Pedro de Valdivia created an improvised shipyard here that was destroyed by natives, leading to one of the first known clashes between indigenous and Spanish cultures in central Chile.

Concón has been a seaside resort for Santiaguinos for a century, first with large stately homes surrounded by well-tended gardens or perched among the rocks just meters from the sea. Many of these still exist and jostle for space among a growing number of high-rise apartment buildings, all vying for a share of the impressive ocean views. Concón has also declared itself the Gastronomic Capital of Chile—a claim that

seems a bit of an exaggeration, although it may well have more restaurants per capita than any other Chilean town, many of which are great seafood restaurants. The other main attractions include its beaches as well as the rugged coastal scenery along the road that connects it to Reñaca, and the wetlands and sand dunes north of town.

GETTING HERE AND AROUND

Concón, occupying a long stretch of coast on the south bank of the mouth of the Aconcagua River, lies 16 km (19 miles) north of Viña del Mar along the spectacular Avenida Borgoño (check out the houses built into the cliffs), passing through Reñaca. If coming direct from Santiago, take Ruta 5 north until Km 109 and take the turn to Quillota all the way to the coast. Part of the route is called the Ruta Las Palmas, named for the giant smooth-trunked Chilean palm trees that produce tiny coconuts called *coquitos*. Buses from Viña del Mar leave regularly from Plaza Francisco Vergara and from Santiago's Terminal Alemada.

EXPLORING

Fodor'sChoice ★ **Mantagua Wetlands at Posada del Parque.** One of Chile's most important wetlands lies along the northern bank of the Aconcagua River, and a good place to explore it—especially for bird-watchers and photographers—is the Posada del Parque, 5 km (3 miles) north of Concón. This family-run lodge works hard to protect and educate visitors about the wetlands and offers guided or independent bird-watching, nature hikes, and kayaking, as well as simple but delicious home-cooked meals and a few very nice rooms to stay overnight. ✉ *Camino Concón-Quintero Km 5 (Ruta F30E)* ✛ *3 miles north of mouth of Aconcagua River* ☎ *32/281–1451* ⊕ *www.posadadelparque.cl.*

Roca Oceánico. This massive promontory covered with scrubby vegetation has footpaths winding throughout that afford excellent views of Viña del Mar, Valparaíso, and the sea churning against black volcanic rock below, as well as pelicans and other sea birds soaring and diving headlong into the sea. ✉ *Concón* ✛ *6.5 km (about 4 miles) north of Las Salinas in Viña del Mar* ▨ *Free.*

BEACHES

Playa Amarilla. One of Concón's most popular beaches, Playa Amarilla's yellow sand and relatively calm waters make it a favorite with families, many of whom own or rent apartments in the stair-stepped high rise buildings across the street. The street-level promenade makes for a nice stroll and a beautiful spot to sit and watch people, or the sunset. There are plenty of options for eating, ranging from kiosk snacks to formal dining. **Amenities:** food and drink; lifeguards; toilets. **Best for:** sunsets; swimming. ✉ *Av. Borgoño 175.*

Playa La Boca. At the northern end of town is the sprawling gray-sand Playa La Boca, named for the *boca* (mouth) of the Aconcagua River, which flows into the Pacific here and sometimes makes the water murky. The long, regular curl to the waves makes it a favorite spot for paddleboarding and beginning surfers (there are numerous places to take lessons along the beach). The southern end has a large parking lot with prices that vary throughout the year, and the northern end has a children's park and horse and kayak rentals. There's a very long stretch of

seafood restaurants in between. **Amenities:** food and drink; water sports. **Best for:** sunset; surfing' walking. ✉ *Av. Borgoño s/n.*

Fodor'sChoice
★

Playa Ritoque. Just north of the Mantagua *humedal* (wetlands), a long stretch of enormous sand dunes and golden sands hugs the coastline for 7 km (4 miles) to the southern edge of Quinteros, where it's called Playa *de* Ritoque. This beautiful long beach is too open for safe swimming, but ideal for strolling, sunbathing, fishing, and in some areas, surfing. Watch out for all-terrain vehicles and the occasional horse cruising along the more secluded sections of the beach. There are a few restaurants and kiosks on the beach proper, but nothing for the solitary miles along the dunes. **Amenities:** food and drink; parking. **Best for:** solitude; sunset; surfing; walking. ✉ *Concón.*

WHERE TO EAT

$$$
SEAFOOD
Fodor'sChoice
★

✕ **Aquí Jaime.** Owner Jaime Vegas is usually on hand here, seating customers and scrutinizing the preparation of such house specialties as *ensalada de mariscos Aquíjaime* (a seafood salad mix of abalone, crab meat, shrimp, scallops, fried calamari, and clams with melted Parmesan cheese), *arroz a la valenciana* (paella packed with seafood), and *ceviche de centolla* (king crab ceviche). Perhaps this is why the small restaurant perched on a rocky promontory next to Caleta Higuerillas has one of the best reputations in the region. **Known for:** fantastic seafood; ocean views; hands-on owner and chef. ⑤ *Average main: 11000 pesos* ✉ *Av. Borgoño 21303* ☎ *32/281–2042* ⊕ *www.aquijaime.cl* ⊗ *Closed Mon. No dinner Sun.*

WHERE TO STAY

$$$$
RENTAL

🏠 **Bahía Bonita.** Perched on a hilltop overlooking Concón, this all-suites hotel has rooms with flower-filled terraces—some more than one—overlooking the crashing waves. **Pros:** apartments have plenty of space to spread out; fantastic ocean views; excellent location. **Cons:** a steep climb from the beach; weak Wi-Fi; a little hard to find. ⑤ *Rooms from: 110000 pesos* ✉ *Av. Borgoño 22040, Subida San Fabián, Con-Con* ☎ *32/281–8757* ⊕ *www.aparthotelbahiabonita.cl* ⇨ *13 suites* ⑩ *Breakfast.*

$$$$
B&B/INN

🏠 **Radisson Acqua Hotel & Spa Concón.** Rising out of a craggy headland with spectacular views up and down the coast, this hotel blends almost seamlessly into its surroundings. **Pros:** escape the summer crowds of larger towns, while still just a walk from the beach; spectacular views; great spa on-site. **Cons:** hard floors and cool atmosphere not for everyone; parking is limited; indoor pool can be cold. ⑤ *Rooms from: 110000 pesos* ✉ *Av. Borgoño 23333, Concón* ☎ *32/254–6400* ⊕ *www.radisson.cl* ⇨ *66 rooms* ⑩ *Breakfast.*

SPORTS AND THE OUTDOORS

HORSEBACK RIDING

Punta Piedra. This long stretch of beach (not apt for swimming) begins about 5 km (3 miles) north of Concón and ends at Playa Ritoque in Quintero. It offers a wide assortment of entertainment, with horseback riding along the dunes a particularly popular activity. There is also paragliding, a go-kart course, four-wheeling, and more. ✉ *Concón.*

MAITENCILLO

20 km (12 miles) north of Quintero.

This town is a string of cabanas, houses, and eateries spread along the 4-km (3-mile) Avenida del Mar. Two long beaches are separated by an extended rocky coastline that holds the local caleta. To complement the abundant sand and surf, there's a decent selection of restaurants, bars, and accommodations. The windswept coast south of the town is almost completely undeveloped and a magnet for seabirds; it's also ideal for surfing, paddleboarding, and paragliding.

GETTING HERE AND AROUND

From Concón, follow Ruta F30 E north turning inland from the coast past Quintero until signs show the turnoff for Maitencillo and La Laguna. If coming from Santiago, take Ruta 5 Norte and exit at the turn for Catapilco (just after the El Melón Tunnel), and follow the road to the coast.

BEACHES

Playa Aguas Blancas. The light-gray sand of the long and narrow Playa Aguas Blancas lies to the south of a rock outcropping, protected from the swells, and consequently is good for swimming (and fishing). A constant stiff breeze and the cliffs leading down to the beach also make it ideal for paragliding. **Amenities:** food and drink. **Best for:** sunset; swimming; walking. ⊠ *Maitencillo.*

Playa El Abanico. This nice stretch of light-gray-sand beach on the northern end of town has the best of both worlds—the waves are big enough for light surfing, bodyboarding, and paddle boarding, but not big enough to be dangerous for swimmers. Life guards are on duty, beachgoers can rent lounge chairs and sun umbrellas, and beachside restaurants offer drinks and light meals. **Amenties:** food and drink; lifeguards; water sports. **Best for:** sunsets; surfing; swimming. ⊠ *Av. del Mar 1350.*

WHERE TO EAT

$$$

MEDITERRANEAN

✕ **La Canasta.** Serpentine bamboo tunnels connect rooms through La Canasta, and slabs of wood suspended by chains serve as tables, creating a scene that could be straight from *The Hobbit*. A small menu changes regularly but includes dishes such as *cordero a la ciruela* (lamb with plum sauce) and *corvina queso de cabra* (sea bass with goat cheese). Although it's across from the beach, there's no view. **Known for:** frequently changing menu featuring unique twists on Chilean classics; fun and charming decor; eclectic cocktail menu. $ *Average main: 11000 pesos* ⊠ *Av. del Mar 592* ☎ *32/277–1028* ⊕ *www.hermansen.cl.*

WHERE TO STAY

$$$

B&B/INN

🛏 **Cabañas Hermansen.** Set in an overgrown garden, these cabanas feel far away from everything, but in reality, they're just across from the beach. **Pros:** the best place to escape the crowds without leaving Maitencillo; friendly, helpful staff; cozy cabins perfect for families. **Cons:** you have to cross a busy road to reach the beach; sketchy Wi-Fi; heating can be an issue during cooler months. $ *Rooms from: 82000 pesos* ⊠ *Av. del Mar 592* ☎ *32/277–1028* ⊕ *www.hermansen. cl* 🛏 *16 cabins* ⦿ *No meals.*

$$$$
RESORT

☒ **Hotel Marbella.** Golf fairways, pine trees, and ocean vistas surround this four-story white-stucco resort building; the spacious, colorful rooms are decorated with original art and have large terraces with views of Maitencillo Bay. **Pros:** stunning setting; plenty to do; away from the crowds. **Cons:** distance from the beach—you need a car if you also want to explore the coast; unreliable Wi-Fi; could use some refurbishing. $ *Rooms from: 171000 pesos* ☒ *Carretera Concón–Zapallar, Km 35* ☎ *32/279–5900,* ⊕ *www.marbella.cl* ⤳ *72 rooms* ⧖ *Breakfast; All meals; Some meals.*

SPORTS AND THE OUTDOORS

HANG GLIDING
Parapente Aventura. *Parapente,* Spanish for paragliding, is a seated version of hang gliding and quite popular in many places along the Chilean coast. Parapente Aventura has classes and two-person trips for beginners. ☒ *Cerro Tacna, Calle Los Laureles 22-9* ☎ *9/7919–9292, 9/9547-5955* ⊕ *www.parapenteaventura.cl.*

HORSEBACK RIDING
Club Ecuestre Cachagua. In Cachagua, Club Ecuestre Cachagua runs horseback tours to scenic overlooks. ☒ *Costanera s/n, Cachagua* ☎ *9/9199–6194.*

ZAPALLAR

48 km (30 miles) north of Concón.

An aristocratic enclave for the past century, Zapallar doesn't promote itself as a vacation destination. In fact, it has traditionally been reluctant to receive outsiders. The resort is the brainchild of Olegario O'Valle, who owned property here. In 1893, following an extended stay in Europe, O'Valle decided to recreate the Riviera on the Chilean coast. He allotted plots of land to friends and family with the provision that they build European-style villas. Today the hills above the beach are dotted with these extravagant summer homes. Above them are the small, tightly packed adobes of a working-class village that has developed to service the mansions.

GETTING HERE AND AROUND
From Maitencillo, follow Ruta F30 E north over the clifftops until signs indicate the turn for Zapallar. If coming from Santiago, take Ruta 5 Norte, exit at the turnoff for Catapilco, and follow the road to the coast.

EXPLORING
Caleta de Zapallar. At the south end of Playa Zapallar is a rocky point that holds Caleta de Zapallar, where local fisherfolk unload their boats, sell their catch, and settle in for dominoes. The view of the beach from the caleta is simply gorgeous. On the other side of the point, a trail leads over the rocks to rugged but equally impressive views. ☒ *Zapallar.*

Monumento Natural Isla Cachagua. This 4.5-hectare protected island off the coast of Cachagua, a few miles south of Zapallar, is one of the world's most important Humboldt penguin breeding grounds. No one is allowed on the island, but you can see it from the beach below

Cachagua, though you need binoculars to watch the penguins wobble around. For a closer look, hire a boat at the Caleta de Zapallar. ⊠ *Zapallar* ⊕ *www.conaf.cl/parques/monumento-natural-isla-cachagua.*

FAMILY **Plaza del Mar Bravo.** Up the hill from Caleta de Zapallar is this plaza. Translated as the "Rough Sea Square," the park has a nice ocean view and a playground. In January and February, there are often mule rides for kids as well. ⊠ *Zapallar.*

BEACHES

Fodor'sChoice **Playa Zapallar.** Zapallar's raison d'être is a crescent of golden sand ★ kissed by blue-green waters, with a giant boulder plopped in the middle. Cropped at each end by rocky points and backed by large pines and rambling flower gardens, it's arguably the loveliest beach on the Central Coast. **Amenities:** food and drink. **Best for:** snorkeling; sunset; swimming. ⊠ *Zapallar.*

WHERE TO EAT

$$$$ ✕ **El Chiringuito.** Pelicans, gulls, and cormorants linger among the fishing
SEAFOOD boats anchored near this remarkable seafood restaurant. Because it's
Fodor'sChoice next door to the fishermen's cooperative, the seafood is always the fresh-
★ est in town. **Known for:** nice variety of fresh seafood; marine-inspired decor; beach views. ⑤ *Average main: 13000 pesos* ⊠ *Caleta de Zapallar s/n* ☎ *33/274–1024* ⊗ *No dinner weekdays Mar.–Nov.*

WHERE TO STAY

$$$$ ⚏ **Isla Seca.** Bougainvillea and cypress trees surround two identical
B&B/INN moss-green buildings with well-appointed, spacious rooms. **Pros:** quiet
Fodor'sChoice and rather secluded; gorgeous ocean views from many rooms; private
★ trail leading to the beach. **Cons:** not all rooms have ocean view; pricey; a bit far from the beach. ⑤ *Rooms from: 137000 pesos* ⊠ *Camino Costero Ruta F-30-E No. 31* ☎ *33/274–1224* ⊕ *www.hotelislaseca.cl* ⇦ *42 rooms* ⦿ *No meals.*

PAPUDO

11 km (7 miles) north of Zapallar.

In a letter dated October 8, 1545, Spanish conquistador Pedro Valdivia wrote: "Of all the lands of the New World, the port of Papudo has a goodness above any other land. It's like God's Paradise: it has a gentle temperate climate; large, resounding mountains; and fertile lands."

Today a jumble of apartment buildings and vacation homes detracts from the view Valdivia once admired, but the beaches and coast north of town remain clean and pleasant. You can still find bits of that history in the quiet resort town. Glorious old homes still appear interspersed among the smaller, newer houses. A palm tree–lined promenade runs through town between the beach and the main road, and is lined with vendors selling snacks, toys, and souvenirs. Up the hill in the town proper, a pleasant tree-lined plaza offers capriciously painted park benches as well as permanent chess tables.

GETTING HERE AND AROUND

From Zapallar, follow Ruta F30 E for 11 km (7 miles) north over the cliff tops until the road winds down into Papudo.

EXPLORING

Iglesia Parroquial de Papudo (Nuestra Señora de Las Mercedes). Near the south end of town, the lovely early 20th-century, neocolonial church seems out of place surrounded by modern buildings. It was once part of a convent that has since been replaced by vacation apartments. It was declared a national historic monument in 1995, but it's only open to visitors on weekends in January and February. ⊠ *Papudo* ☎ *33/279–1265* ☉ *Closed Mar.–Dec. and weekdays.*

Palacio Recart. Also known as the Chalet Recart, this Papudo icon and somewhat whimsical white house topped with a tall tower sits just a block from the beach in the center of town. It was built in 1910 and now holds municipal offices and hosts occasional art and history exhibitions. There's a small plaza just below with an outdoor café that's a great place to have a refreshing drink while relaxing and people-watching. ⊠ *Costanera s/n* ☎ *33/279–0080.*

BEACHES

No longer as popular as it once was, Papudo still attracts hoards of Santiaguinos during the summer and long holidays who come to play on its beaches.

Playa Chica. A small and attractive yellow-sand beach on the south end of town near where the fishermen bring in their daily catch, Playa Chica is well protected and safe for swimming. A promenade lined with tall palm trees runs between the beach and the road and provides a place for vendors to set up while strollers admire their goods as well as the beach. **Amenities:** food and drink. **Best for:** swimming. ⊠ *Costanera s/n.*

Playa Durazno. You'll have to do a bit of walking to reach the quiet Playa Durazno. It's an attractive, yellow-sand beach north of Playa Grande—past the condominiums—that's lined with pine trees and protected by a rocky barrier offshore. **Amenities:** none. **Best for:** solitude; sunset. ⊠ *Papudo.*

Playa Grande. Papudo's most popular beach is Playa Grande, a wide swath of yellow sand that stretches northward from the Barco Rojo for more than a mile. It's now lined with modern high-rise apartment buildings to house the Santiaguinos who flee the city for long weekends and vacations. **Amenities:** food and drink; parking. **Best for:** sunset; swimming; walking. ⊠ *Papudo.*

WHERE TO STAY

$$

B&B/INN

Hotel Carande. One of the few true hotels in a town with an abundance of cabins and apartments for rent, the Carande looks a bit worn, but it's just a short walk from the beach. **Pros:** great views down to the beach; convenient location; great restaurant on-site. **Cons:** lacks personality; a bit rundown; staff not very attentive. ⑤ *Rooms from: 48000 pesos* ⊠ *Chorillos 89* ☎ *33/279–1105* ⬋ *30 rooms* ⑩ *Breakfast.*

EL NORTE CHICO

WELCOME TO EL NORTE CHICO

TOP REASONS TO GO

★ **Sugar-sand beaches:** Soft sand and turquoise waters make El Norte Chico's beaches among Chile's best. In summer (January and February) you may have to fight for a place in the sun.

★ **Starry skies:** Thanks to some of the clearest skies in the world, Chile's northern desert is a top destination for international stargazers and scientists. A number of astronomical observatories in El Norte Chico arrange tours.

★ **Nature reserves:** Explore Parque Nacional Fray Jorge with its ghostlike fog, the petrified forest of Monumento Nacional Pichasca, and the barren desert landscape of the Parque Nacional Pan de Azúcar.

★ **Wine and pisco:** No trip to El Norte Chico is complete without sampling its most famous export, pisco. The liquor's muscat grapes flourish in this temperate climate, which is also ideal for wine-grape-growing (particularly pinot noir), making this an up-and-coming wine producing region.

El Norte Chico is a vast region spreading some 700 km (435 miles) between Río Aconcagua and Río Copiapó. Ideally, you need more than one base to explore the entire area. In the south, La Serena is a good place to start if you're going to the Elqui Valley. The Limarí Valley is where you want to be if your destination is Valle del Encanto. Copiapó, near the region's northern border, is a convenient stop if you're headed to Parque Nacional Pan de Azúcar.

1 The Elqui Valley. Hot sun, cool pisco sours, and a sky full of stars every night. Only an hour's drive from La Serena but a world apart from the bustling regional capital, the Elqui Valley is an inspirational place. It's easy to see where Chilean Nobel Prize–winning poet Gabriela Mistral, raised in the Valley, got her inspiration.

2 The Limarí Valley. This verdant valley is perfect for grape-growing and the source of some of Chile's newest and most exciting wines. It is also home to the only lapis lazuli mine in the country. The valley's main town, Ovalle is a good jumping-off point for nearby sites that feature ancient rock art and mysterious carvings cut into the rocks.

3 The Copiapó Valley. Copiapó itself is a hot, inland town where the mining industry's newly minted wealthy are building hotels and homes. Nevertheless, just 15 minutes outside of Copiapó is the desert, where quail and lizards scamper beneath the shadows of cacti.

4

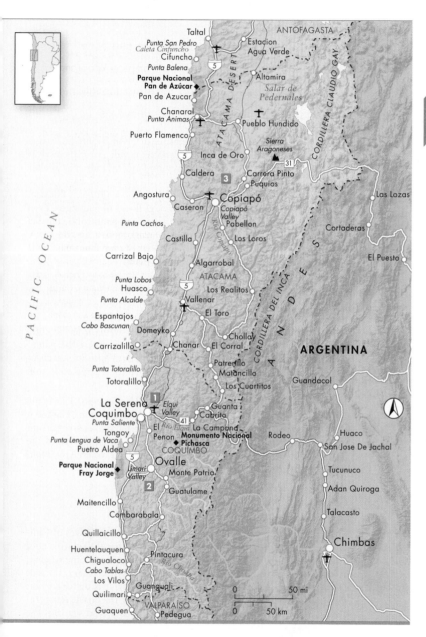

Taltal
Punta San Pedro
Caleta Cifuncho
Cifuncho
Punta Balena
**Parque Nacional
Pan de Azúcar** ◆
Pan de Azucar
Chanaral
Punta Animas
Puerto Flamenco

ANTOFAGASTA
Estación
Agua Verde
Altamira
Salar de
Pedernales
Pueblo Hundido
Sierra
Aragoneses

ATACAMA DESERT

CORDILLERA CLAUDIO GAY

Inca de Oro
Caldera
3
Carrera Pinto
Puquios
Angostura
Caseron
Copiapó
Copiapó
Valley
Pabellon
Castilla
Los Loros
Punta Cachos
Carrizal Bajo
Algarrobal
ATACAMA
Punta Lobos
Huasco
Los Realitos
Punta Alcalde
Vallenar
El Toro
Espantajos
Cabo Bascunan
Domeyko
Carrizalillo
Chanar
Chollay
El Corral
Punta Totoralillo
Totoralillo
Patrenllo
Matancillo
Los Cuartitos

Las Lozas
Cortaderas
El Puesto

CORDILLERA DEL INCA

A N D E S

ARGENTINA

Guandacol

PACIFIC OCEAN

La Serena
Coquimbo
Elqui
Valley
Guanta
Cabrita
Punta Saliente
Tongoy
El Peñon
41
La Campana
Rodeo
Huaco
San Jose De Jachal
Punta Lengua de Vaca
Puetro Aldea
Monumento Nacional
◆ Pichasca
COQUIMBO
Parque Nacional
Fray Jorge ◆
Limari
Valley
Ovalle
Monte Patria
2
Guatulame
Tucunuco
Adan Quiroga
Talacasto
Maitencillo
Combarabala
Quillaicillo
Huentelauquen
Chiqualoco
Pintacura
Cabo Tablas
Los Vilos
Quilimari
Guanguali
Guaquen
VALPARAÍSO
Pedegua

Chimbas

Rio Copiapó
Rio Huasco
Río Elqui
Río Choapa

0   50 mi
0   50 km

Updated by
Helen Cordery

Between the fertile central valley to the south and the vast expanse of the Atacama Desert to the north, El Norte Chico—or Chile's Little North—hosts a fantastically eclectic range of climates, landscapes, and activities in a compact area. Among the burnt hills, stargazers and wine buffs rub shoulders with adrenaline seekers in a region known equally for its white-sand beaches and towering mountains as its world-class research telescopes and vineyards.

These varied landscapes and ecosystems, unsurprisingly, are home to a diverse range of flora and fauna. Visitors with the will to tear themselves away from the beaches can tour rocky offshore islands that shelter colonies of penguins and sea lions or cruise the clear, cool waters of the marine reserves where sperm whales and bottlenose dolphins flourish. Shimmering mountain lakes are home to huge flocks of flamingos. Even the parched earth flourishes twice a decade in a phenomenon called *el desierto florido,* or the flowering desert. During these years, the bleak landscape gives way to a riot of colors—flowers of every hue imaginable burst from the normally infertile soil of the plain.

In a land where water is so precious, it's not surprising that the people who migrated here never strayed far from its rivers. In the south, La Serena sits at the mouth of the Elqui River. El Norte Chico's most important city, La Serena is the region's cultural center as well, with colonial architecture and a European flavor. Nearby, in the fertile Elqui Valley, farmers in tiny villages grow grapes to make pisco, the potent brandy that has become Chile's national drink. Those in search of archaeological wonders head to Valle del Encanto, a large collection of ancient petroglyphs.

On El Norte Chico's northern frontier is the Río Copiapó. This is the region that grew up and grew rich during the silver boom. The town of Copiapó, this area's most important trade center, makes an excellent jumping-off point for exploring the hinterland. Heading toward the ocean, you come to Parque Nacional Pan de Azúcar, where you'll find some of El Norte Chico's most stunning coastal scenery.

PLANNER

WHEN TO GO

During the summer months of January and February, droves of Chileans and Argentines flee their stifling hot cities for the relative cool of El Norte Chico's beaches. Although it is an exciting time to visit, prices go up and rooms are hard to find. Make your reservations at least a month in advance. For a little tranquility, it is better to visit when the high season tapers off in March. Near the coast, temperatures can be chilly due to the wind and famously cold sea, but the

weather inland is mild all year. The almost perpetually clear skies explain why the region has the largest concentration of observatories in the world, although the temperatures can drop quite a bit at night or when you head to the mountains.

PLANNING YOUR TIME

Five days should give you time for a quick road trip to see the best the region has to offer if you don't mind driving long distances at a stretch; if you have the time, allow yourself rest days to enjoy each place in more detail. Start by visiting the Valle del Encanto near Ovalle to see the petroglyphs, and then go to nearby Viña Tabalí vineyard, ending the day with a relaxing dip in the hot springs at the Termas de Socos. The next morning, head toward the coast to La Serena and spend the day exploring the whitewashed churches and lively markets of this quaint colonial town. On the third day, journey to the idyllic and mystical village of Pisco Elqui to relax with a massage and obligatory pisco sour, before spending the evening stargazing. The following morning, head north towards Bahía Inglesa to sunbathe on some of the region's most beautiful and deserted beaches, finishing on Day 5 in Copiapó after a visit to the Parque Nacional Pan de Azúcar.

GETTING HERE AND AROUND

AIR TRAVEL

While El Norte Chico lacks an international airport, both LAN and Sky operate several flights daily from Santiago to La Serena and Copiapó. Round-trip flights to El Norte Chico can be as cheap as 40,000 pesos if booked in advance but much more expensive in high season and for late availability.

Air Contacts La Florida Airport (LSC). ⊠ *Ruta 41* ☎ *51/227–0236.* **LAN.** ⊠ *Balmaceda 406, La Serena* ☎ *600/526–2000* ⊕ *www.lan.com.* **Sky.** ⊠ *Colipi 526, Copiapó* ☎ *600/600–2828* ⊕ *www.skyairline.cl.*

BUS TRAVEL

Every major city in El Norte Chico has a bus terminal, and there are frequent departures to other cities as well as smaller towns in the area. Keep in mind that there may be no direct bus service to the smallest villages or more remote national parks.

Bus Contacts Turbus. ☎ *600/660–6600* ⊕ *www.turbus.cl.*

CAR AND TAXI TRAVEL

Because of the distances between cities, a car is the best way to truly see El Norte Chico. Many national parks can be visited only by car, preferably a four-wheel-drive vehicle. Without one, metered taxis are the most efficient way to get around any city. A cheaper alternative is a *colectivo*, a shared taxi that picks up several people going in the same direction. Colectivos charge a fixed rate per person regardless of the number of passengers and run very regularly during business hours. Fares begin at around 800 pesos per person for inter-city trips, increasing up to around 3,500 for traveling longer distances between towns.

Taxi Contacts Pacífico. ⊠ *Los Carreras 572, La Serena* ☎ *51/221–8000, 51/221–8000.*

RESTAURANTS

Although El Norte Chico is not known for gastronomy, the food here is simple, unpretentious, and often quite good. Along the coast, you'll find abundant seafood. Don't pass up the *merluza con salsa margarita* (hake with a butter sauce featuring almost every kind of shellfish imaginable) or *choritos al vapor* (mussels steamed in white wine). Inland you come across country-style *cabrito* (goat), *conejo* (rabbit), and *pichones escabechados* (baby pigeons). Don't forget to order a pisco sour, the frothy concoction made with a grape-based brandy distilled in the Elqui or Limari Valley.

People in El Norte Chico generally eat a heavy lunch around 2 pm that can last two hours, followed by a light dinner around 9 pm. Reservations are seldom needed, except in the fanciest restaurants. A 10% tip is expected if you enjoyed the service, but check the bill before paying to see if it has already been included. *Restaurant reviews have been shortened. For full information, visit Fodors.com.*

HOTELS

The good news is that lodging in El Norte Chico is relatively inexpensive. Your best bet is often the beach resorts, which have everything from nice cabanas to high-rise hotels. Farther inland, the region is experiencing a boom in boutique hotels and innovative rental properties, meaning lodging in style in beautiful surroundings is more affordable than ever. Almost all lodging options listed offer breakfast included in the price. *Hotel reviews have been shortened. For full information, visit Fodors.com.*

WHAT IT COSTS IN CHILEAN PESOS (IN THOUSANDS)			
	$	$$	$$$	$$$$
Restaurants	Under 6	6–9	10–13	over 13
Hotels	Under 51	51–85	86–115	over 115

Restaurant prices are the average cost of a main course price at dinner or, if dinner is not served, at lunch. Hotel prices are the lowest cost of a standard double room in high season, excluding tax.

HEALTH AND SAFETY

Naturally, in the desert, drinking plenty of nonalcoholic fluids is crucial, as is protecting your face and body from the sun's powerful rays. Get a good pair of sunglasses for driving, as the glare can be intense. Keep in mind that pisco sours, though they may go down as smooth as lemonade, are a powerful drink, so a moderate intake is recommended.

TOURS

You're welcome to tour many of the region's pisco distilleries. Several of them are more than 100 years old, with the oldest distillery in Pisco Elqui in the Elqui Valley. The Solar de Pisco Elqui has been entirely renovated since it began operations, but you can still take a tour of the old plant and learn how pisco is made. This is where the famous Tres Erres brand is distilled. In Pisco Elqui you also find Los Nichos, a quaint

130-year-old distillery open to the public, whereas nearby Vicuña is home to Chile's most popular brand, Capel. To escape the crowds, head to the Pisquera Aba distillery near Vicuña or ask at your hotel about less frequently visited distilleries in the Limarí Valley.

THE ELQUI VALLEY

It's hard to believe that hidden by the dusty brown hills of El Norte Chico is a sliver of land as lush and green as the Elqui Valley. The people who live along the Río Elqui harvest everything from olives to avocados to papayas. The most famous crop is the grape variety distilled to make Chile's national drink—pisco. A village named after this lovely elixir, Pisco Elqui, sits high up in the valley.

The Elqui Valley is renowned not only for its grapes, but also for its unusually clear skies, which have brought scientists from around the world to peer through the telescopes of the area's many observatories. The stars also attract many new agers, who believe the planet's spiritual center has shifted from the Himalayas to the Elqui Valley. Many who came here to check out the vibes decided to stay. In tranquil Pisco Elqui, spa treatments and esoteric sessions like Reiki are commonplace on the list of hotels' additional services.

The Elqui Valley has been inhabited for thousands of years. First came the Diaguitas, whose intricate pottery is among the most beautiful of pre-Columbian ceramics, then the Molles. The Incas, who came here 500 years ago in search of gold, are relative newcomers. The clues these cultures left behind are part of what makes the Elqui Valley so fascinating.

LA SERENA

480 km (300 miles) north of Santiago.

Fodor's Choice ★ Steeped in history, Chile's second-oldest city, La Serena, wears two distinct faces today. On one hand, it charms visitors with its European-style old quarter. On the other, it dazzles with a dash of modern pomp and convenience through its upmarket beachfront—a great place to indulge in sunshine and luxurious hotels and restaurants. The city's location within easy striking distance of many top regional attractions makes it a good base to explore the budding astronomy, viticulture, and wildlife of El Norte Chico.

One of the most stunning features amid the pleasant streets and hidden plazas of La Serena is the number of churches: there are more than 30, and many date as far back as the late 16th century. Most have survived fires, earthquakes, and devastating pirate attacks, all common threats in the turbulent decades after conquistador Juan Bohón founded the city in 1544.

The preservation of colonial architecture, and its continuance, is thanks to Gabriel González Videla, who was president of Chile from 1946 to 1952. ■TIP➔ **Take care of banking or medical needs in La Serena, as there are fewer services in other towns in the area.**

GETTING HERE AND AROUND

La Serena is almost exactly 300 miles north of Santiago via Ruta 5, the Pan-American Highway. A direct bus trip takes about seven hours from the capital, and there are some that travel via Ovalle (from which it's an hour or less to La Serena). La Serena's bus terminal on Avenida Amunátegui is a 15-minute walk or a 5-minute ride from downtown (colectivos 21 and 44 make the trip for less than a dollar). Daily flights from Santiago take about an hour to reach La Serena's La Florida Airport, which is 20 to 30 minutes from downtown via car or taxi. The Pan-American Highway runs right through town if you follow Avenida Francisco de Aguirre toward the ocean. The Elqui Valley is just an hour to the east of La Serena via Route 41.

TOURS

From La Serena, tours can be arranged for regional highlights including the Elqui Valley, several observatories, and the Reserva Nacional Pingüino de Humboldt, a nature reserve where you can see the endangered Humboldt penguin as well as various types of birds, sea lions, dolphins, and the occasional whale. Historical tours of La Serena and the adjacent port city of Coquimbo are available from almost all local operators.

Elqui Valley Tour. This small but professional operator runs regular tours to the Reserva Nacional Pingüino de Humboldt, Mamalluca Observatory, the Elqui Valley, and La Serena. When there is sufficient demand, they also lead excursions to areas of Parque Nacional Fray Jorge and Valle de Encanto, as well as the nearby town of Andacollo. ⊠ *La Serena* ☎ *51/221–4846, 9/7374–2208* ⊕ *www.elquivalleytour.cl* ▦ *From 20000 pesos.*

Itravel. The holder of a national tourism service seal of quality, Itravel leads excursions to the Reserva Nacional Pingüino de Humboldt, the Elqui Valley, and Fray Jorge National Park. They also visit the Mamalluca Observatory as well as some of the more remote research observatories not serviced by public transport. Private tours to other destinations can also be arranged. ⊠ *Av. Bernardo O'Higgins 445, Office 44* ☎ *51/222–4350, 51/9–6190–7045* ⊕ *www.itravel.cl* ▦ *From 19000 pesos.*

Fodor's Choice ★ **Miles & Smiles Chile.** This small tour operator based in Santiago is known for their support of small and local businesses. They offer family-friendly private transfers from the capital to el Norte Chico with optional stops in Los Vilos, La Ligua, Fray Jorge National Park, and the Limari Valley, along with customized tours of the area. ☎ *9/8149–2832* ⊕ *www. milesandsmiles.cl* ▦ *Starting from 100000 pesos.*

ESSENTIALS

Visitor Information Sernatur. ⊠ *Matta 461, 1st fl.* ☎ *52/222-5199* ⊕ *www. sernatur.cl.*

EXPLORING

Iglesia Catedral. The largest church in La Serena, this imposing cathedral faces the beautiful Plaza de Armas and is open to the public. French architect Jean Herbage built this behemoth using stone from the Soldado mine in 1844 in the so-called Serena style of arches and columns, but it wasn't until the turn of the 20th century that the bell tower was added. ⊠ *Plaza de Armas, Cordovez and Balmaceda.*

Iglesia San Francisco. One of La Serena's oldest churches, Iglesia San Francisco has a baroque facade and thick stone walls. The exact date of the church's construction is not known, as the city archives were destroyed in 1680, but it's estimated that the structure was built sometime between 1585 and 1627. The church is open to the public. ⊠ *Balmaceda 640.*

Memorial en Homenaje a los Detenidos Desaparecidos y Ejecutados Políticos de la IV Región. A reminder of Chile's recent tragic past, this memorial is dedicated to the "disappeared" of the area, the prisoners and politicians who went missing during the Pinochet regime in the 1970s and '80s. More than 60 people, many of whom died in their early twenties, are listed on the large stone monument. ⊠ *Adjacent to Parque Japonés on steps leading up to Pedro Pablo Muñoz street.*

FodorsChoice ★ **Museo Arqueológico de La Serena.** Housing many fascinating artifacts and one of the world's best collections of precolonial ceramics, this museum is a must-see for anyone interested in the history of the region. It contains an impressive collection of Diaguita and Molle pottery, an Easter Island *moai* (carved stone head), and bones of the mysterious American Horse. ⊠ *Cordovez and Cienfuegos* ✛ *A short walk from Mercado La Recova* ☎ *51/267–2243 tickets, 51/267–2210 central desk* ⊕ *www.museoarqueologicolaserena.cl* 🎟 *Free* ☉ *Closed Mon.*

Museo Mineralógico. One of the most complete mineral collections in the world is on display here. Exhibits highlight fossils and minerals from the surrounding region. ⊠ *University of La Serena, Benavente 980, Faculty of Engineering* ☎ *51/220–4096* 🎟 *500 pesos* ☉ *Closed weekends.*

Museo Histórico Gabriel González Videla. Former president Gabriel González Videla is known for his vigorous renovation of La Serena, as well as for prompting the exile of senate member Pablo Neruda. The museum is housed in his former home and also contains works by Chilean artists. ⊠ *Matta 495* ☎ *51/221–7189* ⊕ *www.museohistorico-laserena.cl* 🎟 *Free* ☉ *Closed Sun.*

Parque Japonés. This park was a collaboration between a local mining company and its Japanese trading partners as a symbol of friendship between the two nations. Within it, you'll find Kokoro No Niwa, a Japanese garden filled with koi ponds, intricate bridges, and a network of walking paths. ⊠ *Eduardo de la Barra 25* ✛ *At bottom of hill inside Parque Pedro de Valdivia* ☎ *51/221–7013* 🎟 *1000 pesos* ☉ *Closed Mon.*

BEACHES

While vacationing Chileans often flock to La Serena for the beaches, it's usually just for sunbathing and water sports, and not for swimming. High winds and strong currents tend to make swimming quite dangerous here, so be sure to heed any warning signs that may be posted on the beach before venturing into the water.

La Herradura. Well-sheltered within a small cove, La Herradura—or The Horseshoe—is a small but attractive beach, which enjoys calm waters and lies within easy striking distance of Coquimbo. These days it is best known as a holiday destination or as a prime spot for diving and windsurfing, but the area's history as a fishing cove can still be seen in

the brightly colored boats tethered out in the calm waters of the bay. **Amenities:** food and drink; parking (fee). **Best for:** snorkeling; sunset; surfing; swimming; windsurfing. ⊠ *La Serena.*

Playa Peñuelas. Stretching along the city's coastline up until neighboring Coquimbo, this sandy city beach is La Serena's star attraction and a popular spot for families, surfers, and couples, who come to enjoy the great views over the bay at sunset. Like many city beaches, though, it suffers from mild trash problems in parts and is overrun with tourists during the summer high season. Be sure the beach is marked with a sign that says *Playa Apta* before swimming, as the high waves and fierce currents often make it a dangerous place for swimmers. **Amenities:** food and drink; lifeguards (summer only); parking (fee); toilets. **Best for:** sunset; surfing; walking. ⊠ *La Serena.*

Fodor'sChoice
★

Playa Totoralillo. Even though it's a bit of a trek, this stunning package of bleach-white sand, turquoise water, and rocky desert scenery is worth the trip. The 17-km (10-mile) journey south from Coquimbo is more than made up for by the natural advantages of the beach and the perfect conditions for swimming, diving, fishing, and snorkeling. **Amenities:** food and drink (summer only); parking (paid). **Best for:** snorkeling; sunset; surfing; swimming; walking. ⊠ *La Serena.*

WHERE TO EAT

$
VEGETARIAN
Fodor'sChoice
★

✕**Ayawasi.** Popular for its weekday set menu deal, this small vegetarian and vegan restaurant serves an eclectic mix of healthy salads, sandwiches, and pizzas. The outdoor seating is a lovely place to enjoy the delicious fresh juices and pad Thai. **Known for:** brunch made with "happy chicken" eggs; organic produce from restaurant's own garden; vegetarian and vegan dishes. ⑤ *Average main: 5000 pesos* ⊠ *Pedro Pablo Muñoz 566* ☎ *51/221–2026* ☾ *Closed Sun.*

$$
CHILEAN

✕**Donde el Guatón.** Popular with locals, this European-style steak house serves everything from shish kebab to steak with eggs. The early republic-themed decor and waiters clad in the traditional garb of the Chilean cowboy, or *huaso,* narrowly avoid coming off as contrived, but ultimately present a fitting backdrop for the plethora of hearty local fare. **Known for:** perfectly grilled meats; live music; romantic ambience. ⑤ *Average main: 7500 pesos* ⊠ *Brasil 750* ☎ *51/221–1519* ☾ *No dinner Sun.*

$$$
ITALIAN

✕**La Mía Pizza.** Just across the road from the beach and with great views across the bay, this restaurant serves a range of renditions of Italian classics appealing to holidaymakers and the business lunch crowd alike. The extensive menu includes locally sourced delights such as *cordero Sebastián* (lamb in a red wine and mushroom sauce, served with potatoes and polenta), as well as traditional Italian staples. **Known for:** family-friendly setting; outdoor terrace; beach views. ⑤ *Average main: 10000 pesos* ⊠ *Av. Del Mar 2100* ☎ *51/221–2891, 51/221–2232* ☾ *No dinner Sun. Mar.–Dec.*

WHERE TO STAY

$$$
HOTEL

▦**Costa Real.** Centrally located and replete with all the modern touches you might expect from an executive-class hotel—business center, meeting rooms, and Wi-Fi access throughout—Costa Real is an eminently

efficient, practical option for any visit to La Serena. **Pros:** modern and clean; good restaurant; big and comfortable beds. **Cons:** roadside rooms very noisy; slightly dated decor; no air-conditioning. ⑤ *Rooms from: 90000 pesos* ✉ *Av. Francisco de Aguirre 170* ☎ *51/222–1010* ⊕ *www. costareal.cl* ⮎ *51 rooms* ⑩ *Breakfast.*

$$$ 🏨 **Enjoy Coquimbo Hotel de la Bahía.** Every room has a sea view at this
HOTEL hotel that towers over the far end of the Avenida del Mar. Part of the exclusive Enjoy Casino & Resort chain, it also sits head and shoulders above its competition in every way, from its imposing modern lobby to five-star accommodations and service. **Pros:** a sea view from every room; top-tier facilities and service; excellent spa. **Cons:** can be noisy at night; out-of-the-way location (it's technically in Coquimbo); average restaurant. ⑤ *Rooms from: 100000 pesos* ✉ *Av. Peñuelas Norte 56* ☎ *51/242–3000* ⊕ *www.enjoy.cl* ⮎ *121 rooms* ⑩ *Breakfast.*

$$$ 🏨 **Hotel Club La Serena.** Defining itself in opposition to its more luxurious,
HOTEL high-end rivals, this hotel offers a professional but somewhat understated,
FAMILY four-star setting for business delegations in the off-season before letting its hair down for a few months each summer to cater to the die-hard beachcombers who descend on the conveniently located complex. **Pros:** across from the beach; amazing views; on-site restaurant. **Cons:** rooms are rather small; far from the main area of the beach; basic furnishings in rooms. ⑤ *Rooms from: 90000 pesos* ✉ *Av. del Mar 1000* ☎ *51/222–1262* ⊕ *www.clublaserena.com* ⮎ *98 rooms* ⑩ *Breakfast.*

$$ 🏨 **Hotel del Cid.** A good option for those keen to explore the history of
B&B/INN Chile's second oldest city, this welcoming B&B in a colonial-style build-ing provides personalized service and a homey atmosphere. **Pros:** family atmosphere; personalized service; tranquil courtyard. **Cons:** far from the beach; dated and basic decor; average breakfast. ⑤ *Rooms from: 65000 pesos* ✉ *Av. Bernardo O'Higgins 138* ☎ *51/221–2692* ⊕ *www. hoteldelcid.cl* ⮎ *25 rooms* ⑩ *Breakfast.*

NIGHTLIFE

Ovo Lounge. Vast, modern, and unashamedly generic, Ovo Lounge is a decent option for mainstream music until late every Thursday through Saturday. This chain club tends to attract a slightly more affluent crowd in the 25- to 35-age range. ✉ *Av. Peñuales Norte 56* ☎ *51/242–3000* ▱ *7000 pesos including cover.*

Rapsodia. A huge palm dominates the central courtyard at Rapsodia, a small coffee shop in the center of town that carries on late into the evening on Thursdays and Fridays. This is a great place to grab a snack and listen to live jazz and blues. ✉ *Arturo Prat 470, interior courtyard* ☎ *51/221–2695.*

SHOPPING

Fodor's Choice **Mercado La Recova.** On the corner of Cienfuegos and Cantournet, this
★ modern market housed in a pleasant neoclassical building sells dried fruits, handicrafts, and lapis lazuli jewelry. The Diaguita-style ceramics and the trinkets made from *combarbalita*, the locally mined marblelike rock, are particularly stunning. Don't forget to pick up some of the region's famous papayas, goat cheese, olive oil, and *copao* (a native fruit born from cacti). ✉ *Cantournet and Cienfuegos.*

VICUÑA

62 km (38 miles) east of La Serena via Ruta 41.

As you head into the Elqui Valley, the first town you come to is Vicuña, famous as the birthplace of one of Chile's most important literary figures, Gabriela Mistral. Her beautiful, haunting poetry often looks back on her early years in the Elqui Valley. Mistral's legacy is unmistakable as you wander through town. In the Plaza de Armas, for example, there is a chilling stone replica of the poet's death mask.

GETTING HERE AND AROUND

Vicuña is about an hour's drive or bus ride from La Serena, a straight shot on Route 41. Enjoy the views of the vineyards as you make the slight climb from the coast. The tiny bus terminal in Vicuña is serviced by a number of regular buses, vans, and colectivos.

Colectivos run 24 hours and can be flagged down at designated stops; they also have a large stand inside the Vicuña bus terminal. To take the colectivo from La Serena to Vicuña, go to the main office at Domeyko 565 or flag the colectivo from the corner of Cienfuegos and Cantournet, outside La Recova market.

ESSENTIALS

Visitor Information Vicuña Tourist Information. ⊠ *At bottom of Torre Bauer, opposite Plaza de Armas* ☏ *51/267-0308.*

EXPLORING

Fodor's Choice ★ **Alfa Aldea.** Although there are more established observatories in the area, Alfa Aldea has made its mark on the astronomy world due to the flawless attention to detail and excellent customer service. With a glass of wine in hand, embark on a journey to the beginning of time as the dome above you transforms into an interactive and 3-D exploration. While lounging among comfortable seating, carpeted floors, and blankets, a bilingual astronomer explains the inner workings of the universe. Afterwards, you pop outside beneath the stars to peep at constellations, nebulas, planets, and the moon with a real telescope before listening to light transformed into soundwaves by a radio telescope, one of the very few available to tourists in the area. You will need to book your visit here in advance. ⊠ *Parcela 17, La Vinita* ☏ *51/241-2441* ⊕ *www. alfaaldea.cl* ⊠ *10000 pesos.*

Centro Turístico Capel. Visiting a pisco vineyard is a great way to learn about the history of a product that has come to define the Elqui Valley, not to mention the perfect excuse to enjoy a relaxing glass of this tasty, fruity, aromatic drink in beautiful surroundings. At Centro Turístico Capel, just across the Elqui River from Vicuña, you can tour the bottling facility, well-groomed gardens, and artisan's gallery before tasting several piscos. ⊠ *Camino a Peralillo s/n* ☏ *51/255-4337* ⊕ *www. centroturisticocapel.cl* ⊠ *Standard tour 4000 pesos.*

Cerro de la Virgen. Devotees of the Virgen de Lourdes, the town's patron saint, consider this hill a place of pilgrimage. Overlooking the city, it affords a great view of Vicuña. It's a 2-km (1-mile) hike north of the city via a path on Baquedano between Independencia and Yungay.

STARGAZING IN EL NORTE CHICO

With some of the clearest skies in the Southern Hemisphere, El Norte Chico is home to observatories with many of the world's most powerful telescopes, several of which give guided tours by appointment. A boom in tourist-friendly observatories in the Elqui Valley means visitors have ample opportunity to peer into the depths of the universe for themselves.

Cerro Tololo Observatory. Perched at 2,200 meters (7,200 feet), Cerro Tololo Observatory runs free tours of its two principal telescopes on Saturdays. During January and February, priority is given to nonspecialist visitors—although high demand means it's worth reserving at least a month in advance—while the rest of the year the observatory tours cater principally to delegations. Tours should first be requested by phone or email; once the reservation has been made, permission certification can be picked up at the observatory's offices in Las Serena on the corner of avenidas Huanhalí and J. Cisternas. Tours may be canceled in bad weather. ⊠ *Rte. 41, 80 km (50 miles) east of La Serena, Colina El Pino, Vicuña* ☎ *51/220–5200* ⊕ *www.ctio.noao.edu* ☞ *Free.*

Gemini South Observatory. With one of the largest telescopes in the world, an 8.1-meter (26.5 feet) Cassegrain, this observatory 10 kilometers (6 miles) from Cerro Tololo is operated by a consortium of six nations. Tours are free of charge on Friday mornings and can be tailored to the interests of the group (usually between 10 and 25 people). Email at least a month in advance to request a place on the tour. Priority is given to student and scientific delegations. ⊠ *Rte. 41, 90 km (55 miles) east of La Serena, Cerro Pachón, Vicuña* ☎ *51/220–5600* ⊕ *www.gemini.edu* ☾ *Closed June–Aug.*

Las Campanas Observatory. This observatory of the Carnegie Institute of Washington, 100 km (62 miles) north of La Serena, has twin 6.5-meter Magellan telescopes (internationally recognized as the best natural imaging telescopes) as well as two others. Free tours of the facilities take place on Saturday between 10 and 2:30, but due to high demand visitors are advised to make reservations several weeks in advance. Preference is given to school groups and delegations. ⊠ *Rte. 41, 80 km (50 miles) east of La Serena, Colina El Pino, Vicuña* ☎ *51/220–7301* ⊕ *www.lco.cl.*

La Silla Observatory. Administered by the 15-member European Southern Observatory (ESO), La Silla Observatory is one of the largest and most important observatories in the Southern Hemisphere. Free tours are available of the three principal telescopes each Saturday at 2 pm, except during July and August, due to the risk of snowstorms in this period. Note that bookings are accepted only if made via the online visitor form. ⊠ *Pan-American Hwy., about 130 km (80 miles) north of La Serena, signposted just after turnoff for Incahuasi and before reaching Vallenar, La Higuera* ☎ *2/2463–3100* ⊕ *www.ls.eso.org.*

4

■**TIP→** Head up in the evening to see the surrounding hills in the Elqui Valley bathed in deep reds and oranges by the setting sun. ⊠ *Vicuña.*

Gran Observatorio Solar de Chile. This project of the Pangue Observatory claims to be the only solar tourist observatory in South America. Using a specialized Lunt Solar System Telescope—one of only seven in the world—visitors can observe phenomena such as sunspots, the equatorial bulge, and solar flares. Tours run all day and throughout the year, though observations are often hampered by overcast weather June to August. ⊠ *San Martín 233* ☎ *51/241–2584* ⊕ *www.observatoriodelpangue.blogspot.cl* ◻ *2500 pesos* ◷ *Closed July and Aug.*

Museo Gabriela Mistral. An expansive tribute to Vicuña's favorite daughter, the Gabriela Mistral Museum gathers a wide array of artifacts from the writer's life, including handwritten letters, poems, and a signed copy of *Canto General* given to her by her compatriot and fellow Nobel Prize winner, Pablo Neruda. A pleasant garden behind the main salon pays tribute to Mistral's love of nature. ⊠ *Gabriela Mistral 759* ☎ *51/241–1223* ⊕ *www.mgmistral.cl* ◻ *Free* ◷ *Closed Mon.*

Observatorio Cerro Mamalluca. The most welcoming of the Elqui Valley observatories and the one that attracts the most visitors, Mamalluca is 9 km (6 miles) north of Vicuña. On the Basic Astronomy tour, visitors are given an introductory talk before stargazing on the terrace and taking turns looking through a 12-inch digital telescope at sights including the moons of Jupiter and the rings of Saturn. Another tour focuses more on the Andean interpretation of the constellations. Tours should be booked at least a month in advance during spring and summer. You can either make your own way to the observatory or contract transport from the tour office in Vicuña at 3,000 pesos per person. ⊠ *Tour office, Gabriela Mistral 260* ☎ *51/267–0330* ◻ *7000 pesos.*

Fodor'sChoice ★ **Pangue Observatory.** One of the many tourist observatories to pop up across the region catering to the growing numbers of visitors keen to catch their own glimpse of the mysteries of the universe, Pangue—17 km (11 miles) south of Vicuña—boasts more firepower than most, with arguably the most powerful telescope in the region. Through the 16- and 25-inch telescopes, you can view solar systems, planets, galaxies, and nebulae. The standard tour allows enough time to see 8 to 10 such phenomena, while budding stargazers are welcome to bring their own list, and tour guides can help you find them. Tours can be organized from the tour office at San Martín 233 in Vicuña and are available in English, French, and Spanish. Note that tours do not run for the week around each full moon. ⊠ *17 km north of Vicuña, Ruta Antakari D445* ☎ *51/241–2584* ⊕ *observatoriodelpangue.blogspot.com* ◻ *From 24000 pesos* ◷ *Closed July and Aug.*

Fodor'sChoice ★ **Pisquera Aba.** This small, family-run distillery is known for producing several premium piscos that are consistently wining awards and international accolades. The free 40-minute tour includes a tasting; make sure you try the variety made with Maqui, a berry native to the southern forests of Chile and Argentina. The distillery is located just off the road between Vicuña and Pisco Elqui. ⊠ *Fundo San Juan, sector El Arenal, Km 66 Ruta 41* ☎ *51/241–1039* ⊕ *www.pisquera-aba.cl* ◻ *Free.*

Viña Cavas del Valle. A pleasant stop along the drive between Vicuña and Pisco Elqui, this boutique vineyard uses natural processes to produce several much-praised wines. Production is limited, and the wine is sold only here at the vineyard. Tours include a visit of the original ancestral home, which now houses the wine cellar. ⊠ *Ruta R-485, at Km 14.5; 1 km (1/2 mile) before Montegrande from Vicuña* ☎ *9/6842–5592* ⊕ *www.cavasdelvalle.cl* ⊠ *Free.*

WHERE TO EAT

$$ ✕ **Chivato Negro.** With cute decor and sprawling outdoor seating with rustic charm, this is the best place to find yourself for lunch or for a late-night jaunt. The menu serves Chilean classics, but there is also a daily set menu (including a smaller, cheaper menu) as well as great coffee. **Known for:** late-night events; smiling service; books to browse while you eat. ⑤ *Average main: 6000 pesos* ⊠ *Av. Gabriela Mistral 565* ☎ *9/7862–9439.*

CAFÉ
Fodor's Choice
★

$$ ✕ **Delicias del Sol.** Just outside of Vicuña is the small settlement of Villa Seca that has attracted attention in Chile due to their use of solar-powered ovens. Delicias del Sol is one such restaurant serving Chilean-style lunches and desserts all cooked outside beneath the sun's rays. **Known for:** ice-cold papaya juices; sun-baked fudge brownies; unique, eco-friendly dining experience. ⑤ *Average main: 7000 pesos* ⊠ *Chiloe 164, Villa Seca* ☎ *51/198–2184.*

CHILEAN

WHERE TO STAY

$ ☷ **Hostal Valle Hermoso.** Set in a beautiful turn-of-the-century house that seeps history and has some of the most reasonable rates in town, it's no wonder that Hostal Valle Hermoso has become a favorite with visitors. **Pros:** beautiful building; great value; near major museums. **Cons:** no garden; Wi-Fi signal can be patchy in rooms; no pool or cable television. ⑤ *Rooms from: 40000 pesos* ⊠ *Gabriela Mistral 706* ☎ *51/241–1206* ⊕ *www.hostalvallehermoso.com* ⟿ *9 rooms* ⫟⊘⫟ *Breakfast.*

B&B/INN
Fodor's Choice
★

$ ☷ **Hotel Halley.** In a pretty colonial house with wood trim and white walls, this inn has carefully decorated rooms filled with authentic circa-1950s radios and more doilies than you could possibly imagine. **Pros:** great for families; pool, cable, and Wi-Fi; central location. **Cons:** pool is small; disinterested staff; rooms a little musty. ⑤ *Rooms from: 45000 pesos* ⊠ *Gabriela Mistral 542* ☎ *51/241–2070* ⊕ *www.turismohalley.cl* ⟿ *12 rooms* ⫟⊘⫟ *Breakfast.*

B&B/INN

NIGHTLIFE

Antawara Restobar. While it admittedly has little competition, Antawara has cemented its position as Vicuña's principal spot for evening entertainment. Traditional Chilean fare is on the menu, while regular live music and a wide selection of locally produced piscos keep things lively in the only real nightlife spot in this otherwise permanently sleepy town. ⊠ *Gabriela Mistral 107* ☎ *51/241–2925.*

PISCO ELQUI

43 km (27 miles) east of Vicuña.

This idyllic village of fewer than 600 residents has two pisco plants. Once known as La Unión, the town, perched on a sun-drenched hillside, received its current moniker in 1939. Gabriel González Videla, at that time the president of Chile, renamed the village in a shrewd maneuver to ensure that Peru would not gain exclusive rights over the term "pisco." It's also a popular place for backpackers, so expect the usual run of hippie stores and plenty of hostels. Sunsets here are particularly beautiful.

GETTING HERE AND AROUND

From Vicuña, take Ruta 41 east to the turn for Paihuano (Ruta D-485). Follow this serpentine, narrow road south about 12 km (7½ miles) into Pisco Elqui. Buses and colectivos run with frequency between La Serena, Vicuña, and Pisco Elqui. A bus or colectivo between Vicuña and Pisco Elqui costs about 1,500 pesos. The small bus lines Via Elqui and Sol de Elqui make the 30-minute trip between La Serena and Pisco Elqui with 20-passenger buses.

Bus Contacts Sol de Elqui. ☎ *51/231–7499.* **Valle de Elqui Colectivos.** ☎ *51/222–0665.* **Via Elqui.** ☎ *51/231–2422.*

TOURS

Turismo Dagaz. With a wide range of specialized tours around Pisco Elqui, Turismo Dagaz is part of the town's booming tourism sector. Visits to Elqui Valley and the high Andean scenery of Agua Negra, close to the Argentine border, round out stargazing evenings and trekking activities. ⊠ *Arturo Prat s/n* ☎ *9/7399–4105* ⊕ *www.turismodagaz.com* 🖾 *From 15000 pesos.*

Fodor'sChoice ★ **Turismo Migrantes.** Trekking, bicycle hire, horse-riding, and astronomical tours are organized by this well-regarded operator, based close to Pisco Elqui's central plaza. ⊠ *Av. Libertador Bernardo O'Higgins s/n* ☎ *51/245–1917* ⊕ *www.turismomigrantes.cl* 🖾 *From 15000 pesos.*

EXPLORING

Casa Escuela. On the way to Pisco Elqui is the tiny village of Montegrande, where Gabriela Mistral grew up and considered her hometown. Her family lived in the schoolhouse where her elder sister taught. This was later turned into a museum and now displays some relics from the poet's life. Visitors can also visit the Nobel Prize–winning poet's tomb on a nearby hillside. ⊠ *Central Plaza, Gabriela Mistral 759, Monte Grande* 🖾 *500 pesos* ⊗ *Closed Mon.*

Fodor'sChoice ★ **Destilería Mistral.** In the older section of this pisco plant, maintained strictly for show, you can see the antiquated copper cauldrons and wooden barrels formerly used to distill the famous brand. The distillery arranges daily tours, followed by tastings of pisco sours. There is also a fantastic, top-rated restaurant. ⊠ *Av. Libertador Bernardo O'Higgins 746* ☎ *51/245–1358* ⊕ *www.destileriapiscomistral.cl/home* 🖾 *Tours 6000 pesos.*

Chile's National Drink

Distilled from muscat grapes grown in the sunbaked river valleys of El Norte Chico, pisco is indisputably Chile's national drink. This fruity, aromatic brandy is enjoyed here in large quantities—most commonly in a delightful elixir known as a pisco sour, which consists of pisco, lemon juice, and sugar. A few drops of bitters on top is optional. Some bars step it up a notch by adding whipped egg white to give the drink a frothy head. Another concoction made with the brandy is piscola—the choice of many late-night revelers—which is simply pisco mixed with soda. Tea with a shot of pisco is the Chilean answer to the common cold, and it may just do the trick to relieve a headache and stuffy nose. Whichever way you choose to take your pisco, expect a pleasant, smooth drink.

Chileans have enjoyed pisco, which takes its name from *pisku,* the Quechuan word for "flying bird," for more than 400 years. The drink likely originated in Peru—a source of enmity between the two nations. In 1939, Chilean President Gabriel González Videla went so far as to change the name of the town of La Unión to Pisco Elqui in an attempt to gain exclusive rights over the name pisco, but Peru already had its own town south of Lima named Pisco. The situation is currently at a standoff, with both countries claiming they have the better product.

The primary spots for pisco distillation in Chile are the Elqui and Limari valleys, which are particularly renowned for the quality of their grapes. The 300 days of sunshine per year here make it perfect for cultivating the muscat varietals. The distillation process has changed very little in the past four centuries. The fermented wine is boiled in copper stills, and the vapors are then condensed and aged in oak barrels for three to six months—pisco makers call the aging process "resting." The result is a fruity but potent brandy with between 30% and 50% alcohol.

Fodor's Choice ★ **Fundo Los Nichos.** About 4 km (3 miles) past Pisco Elqui lies this operational pisco distillery. Guided tours show you around its workings and culminate in the basement, where the original owner and his partners would raid the stock for prolonged, secretive drinking sessions. More clear-headed visitors should note that he and his friends also found time to amass a rather morbid collection of epithets, now displayed on the walls. ⊠ *Camino Público Pisco Elqui Horcón, at Km 3.5* ☎ *51/245–1085* ⊕ *www.fundolosnichos.cl* ☞ *3000 pesos (includes tour and tasting).*

WHERE TO EAT

$$$ CHILEAN ✕ **El Durmiente Elquino.** Just off the main square is this popular restaurant that serves delicious meat entrées, pizzas, and vegetarian options. Be sure to try the *costillar de cerdo al horno* (pork ribs) and if you can, nab a table in the pleasant courtyard with its excellent view of the surrounding hills. **Known for:** alfresco dining in a spectacular setting; vegetarian and meat dishes including great pork ribs; friendly staff. ⑤ *Average main: 10000 pesos* ⊠ *Las Carreras s/n* ☎ *9/8906–2754.*

WHERE TO STAY

$$$$
RENTAL
Fodor's Choice
★

⬚ **Elqui Domos.** Though the walls of these modern pods are made from heavy, translucent material, this is far from camping; each dome has a skylight so you can gaze at the stars from the comfort of your bed on the loftlike second floor. **Pros:** stargazing seclusion in a unique setting; unbeatable valley views; luxurious rooms. **Cons:** public transport required if you don't arrive by car; very secluded; no wheelchair access. $ *Rooms from: 120000 pesos* ✉ *Camino Público Pisco Elqui Horcón, at Km 3.5* ☎ *9/7709–2879* ⊕ *www.elquidomos.cl* ⇆ *7 domes, 4 cabins* ❖ *Breakfast.*

$
B&B/INN

⬚ **El Tesoro de Elqui.** Beautiful gardens with flowers of every imaginable shape and size surround this hotel's cabanas, which have gleaming pine floors and furniture and adobe walls. **Pros:** rooms with views of the stars; quiet; pretty garden. **Cons:** hard to navigate paths at night to reach rooms; unreliable Wi-Fi; not the most comfortable beds. $ *Rooms from: 45000 pesos* ✉ *Arturo Prat s/n* ☎ *51/245–1069* ⊕ *www.tesoro-elqui.cl* ⇆ *11 rooms, 2 apartments* ❖ *Breakfast.*

$$$
RESORT

⬚ **Refugio Misterios de Elqui.** The mountainside slopes up dramatically immediately behind these cabanas, making for dramatic views. **Pros:** a great spot to unwind; minigolfing green; on-site restaurant with extensive menu. **Cons:** only some rooms have fridges; footpaths a bit steep; no Wi-Fi in rooms. $ *Rooms from: 90000 pesos* ✉ *Arturo Prat s/n* ☎ *51/245–1126* ⊕ *www.misteriosdeelqui.cl* ⇆ *6 cabanas, 1 suite* ❖ *Breakfast.*

SHOPPING

Frutos de Elqui. Fresh fruit marmalade, jam, and preserves are sold at Frutos del Elqui, just off the town's main plaza. It's been a local institution for over 18 years. ✉ *Av. Libertador Bernardo O'Higgins, Local 1* ☎ *9/9011–9192.*

THE LIMARÍ VALLEY

The fertile Limarí Valley is a nice break after the bleak desert stretches of the Pan-American Highway, and you pass plenty of signs for *queso de cabra* (goat cheese), field after field of muscat grapes (used for pisco), and acre upon acre of avocado, creating a rich tapestry of greens as you travel inland. As one of the regions with the least annual rainfall, the valley has three dams to ensure it stays fertile and that the vineyards can cultivate the Pinot Noir, Viognier, Sangiovese, and Carménère grapes for which it is becoming famous.

The Limarí Valley also has the country's only lapis lazuli mine (lapis lazuli is a semiprecious stone found exclusively in Chile and Afghanistan), and is known for its production of combarbalita (a marblelike rock), which is fashioned into everything from jewelry boxes to chess pieces.

The Elqui Valley and The Limarí Valley

OVALLE

88 km (55 miles) south of La Serena via Ruta 43.

Ovalle always suffers in comparison to its fairer sister to the north, La Serena, as it has no beaches or breezes. However, it can be a good base for trips to Monumento Natural Pichasca and Valle del Encanto or a stopping-off point between Santiago and La Serena for lunch.

GETTING HERE AND AROUND

Ovalle is about an hour from La Serena via Ruta 43. A 15-minute drive on Ruta 45 out of Ovalle takes you to Valle del Encanto; just beyond that to the west, it intersects with the Pan-American Highway (Ruta 5). Many buses make daily trips between Ovalle and Santiago (five hours) or La Serena (one hour).

EXPLORING

Iglesia San Vicente Ferrer. On the Plaza de Armas, this church, constructed in 1849, is worth a visit if religious tourism is your thing. Its bells were made in the Chilean port town of Valparaíso in 1877 and, although damaged by an earthquake in 1997, the church was completely restored in 2002 and remains open. ✉ *Libertad 260.*

Monumento Natural Pichasca. Heading along the Hurtado River in the spectacular Limarí Valley, you come across this nature reserve covered

with a forest of petrified tree trunks imprinted with dozens of leaf and animal fossils. Nearby is a cave beneath a stone overhang that housed indigenous peoples thousands of years ago, and where cave paintings by the Molle people are still visible. ⊠ *50 km (31 miles) northeast of Ovalle on Camino Ovalle–Río Hurtado* ☏ *9/8923–0010, 51/224–4769 CONAF office* ⊕ *www.conaf.cl/parques/monumento-natural-pichasca* ☏ *6000 pesos* ⊘ *Closed Mon., Tues., and Wed. in high season.*

Termas de Socos. A tourist complex cut from the rough land, this hot spring is said to have waters with incredible healing powers, spouting from the earth at 28°C (82°F). Curative or not, a thermal bath here is extremely relaxing, even if the experience is the same as being in the tub in your bathroom at home (you sit in a bathtub in a private room indoors). Massages and use of the Jacuzzis are also available at an extra cost. ⊠ *Pan-American Highway at Km 370; 24 km (15 miles) west of Ovalle on Ruta 45* ☏ *53/198–2505* ⊕ *www.termasocos.cl* ☏ *4500 pesos for ½ hr.*

Fodor's Choice ★ **Valle del Encanto.** One of the more intriguing spots in all of Norte Chico, this isolated and sprawling reserve is crisscrossed by unexplained holes in the stone floor, made most likely by the Molle and Diaguita cultures. Also dotted all around the park are rock carvings known as petroglyphs and pictographs, which date back from about 4,000 years and feature everything from a (supposed) alien to people with elaborate headdresses. Wildlife roams everywhere here, so keep an eye out for the *liebre* (hare), *loica* (long-tailed meadowlark), and the *degu*, a native rodent.

Sometimes a guide waits near the petroglyphs and can show you the best of the carvings for a small fee. To reach the site, take Ruta 45 west from Ovalle. About 19 km (12 miles) out of town, head south for 5 km (3 miles) on a rough, dry road. ⊠ *24 km (15 miles) west of Ovalle* ☏ *53/266–1237* ☏ *2500 pesos* ⊘ *Closed Mon. and Tues.*

Fodor's Choice ★ **Viña Tabalí.** This small-scale winemaker is a Limari Valley pioneer, known for producing premium quality wines that highlight the character of each of their vineyards. The winery can be found on the same unpaved road that leads to the Valle del Encanto and makes a perfect place to relax after exploring the petroglyphs. Tours, which must be reserved at least one day in advance, include a tasting session in the impressive underground cellar. It's open only on weekends for appointments made in advance. ⊠ *Hacienda Santa Rosa de Tabalí s/n, Camino Monumento Histórico de Valle del Encanto; about 2 km (1 mile) after turnoff from Ruta 45, on right* ☏ *2/2477–5535, 9/9015–7960* ⊕ *www. tabali.com* ☏ *10000 pesos, includes tasting.*

WHERE TO EAT

$ ╳ **Mas Sabor.** A dizzying array of choices are available at this quirky empa-
CHILEAN nada haunt, which offers options that differ from the usual empanada fare. Try the Asian-inspired Oriental (with ginger and soy sauce), or the Queso de Cabra (goat cheese), a staple of the area. **Known for:** casual setting for quick food; empanadas with unusual flavor combinations; daily meal deals. ⑤ *Average main: 2000 pesos* ⊠ *Libertad 499* ☏ *53/262–9580.*

WHERE TO STAY

$$$
B&B/INN
Fodor's Choice
★

Hacienda Santa Cristina. One of the Limarí Valley's best-kept secrets, this homestead is a rural oasis just a few kilometers from the Pan-American Highway as it heads north from Ovalle toward La Serena. **Pros:** personalized attention with English spoken; beautiful, tranquil location; delicious food in a restaurant that serves only local wines. **Cons:** access by unpaved road (look out for the sign!); can get noisy; away from anything else. $ *Rooms from: 89000 pesos* ✉ *Ruta D-505, Quebrada Seca-Ovalle, at Km 4* ☎ *53/262–2335, 53/242–2270* ⊕ *www.haciendasantacristina.cl* ⤵ *12 rooms* ❂ *Breakfast.*

$
HOTEL
Fodor's Choice
★

Hostal Ovalle Suite Boutique. Set inside a revamped colonial building, this charming small hotel has big bedrooms with quality bedding, soft mattresses, and amenities such as Wi-Fi and on-site parking. **Pros:** Wi-Fi in every room; amazing showers; suites have small terraces. **Cons:** staff not always at reception; no wheelchair access; cramped bathrooms. $ *Rooms from: 50000 pesos* ✉ *Carmen 176* ☎ *53/262–7202* ⊕ *www.ovallesuite.cl* ⤵ *8 rooms* ❂ *Breakfast.*

$$
HOTEL

Hotel Limarí. This ranch-style hotel with only two floors opened at the forefront of a renewed effort to attract tourists to the area. **Pros:** a wide range of programs and activities to get to know the region better; great restaurant; attractive outdoor pool. **Cons:** outside town center; underwhelming free breakfast; rooms can get chilly. $ *Rooms from: 75300 pesos* ✉ *Camino Sotaqui at Km 5* ☎ *53/266–1400* ⊕ *www.hotellimari.cl* ⤵ *40 rooms* ❂ *Breakfast.*

NIGHTLIFE

Kata Bar & Resto. A sprawling family-friendly restaurant by day and lively bar by (late) night, this is the most happening place in Ovalle. While large, the place is divided into cozy sections marked by a wood motif; there are wooden benches and wooden crates on the walls and ceiling with lots of light streaming through. Food is an eclectic mix of schwarma sandwiches, pizzas, and empanadas. On weekends, it transforms into a karaoke bar. ✉ *Vicuña Mackenna 376* ☎ *9/9325–1732.*

PARQUE NACIONAL BOSQUES DE FRAY JORGE

110 km (68 miles) south of La Serena.

Seemingly defying the logic of El Norte Chico's otherwise barren landscapes, Parque Nacional Fray Jorge is a lush cloud forest formed by a unique microclimate. Calling this semidesert oasis home are the *chungungo* (South American sea otter), Humboldt penguins, and the Andean fox as well as almost 300 endemic plant species.

GETTING HERE AND AROUND

From the Pan-American Highway at Km 387, turn off onto an unpaved road and follow the signs to the park, which is 27 km (11 miles) west. Public transport to the park is not available.

EXPLORING

Parque Nacional Fray Jorge. A patch of land so rich in vegetation and animal life in the heart of El Norte Chico's dry, desolate landscape defies logic. But Parque Nacional Fray Jorge has been a UNESCO world biosphere reserve

since 1977, with a small cloud forest similar to those found in Chile's damp southern regions. The forest, perched 600 meters (1,968 feet) above sea level, receives its life-giving nourishment from the *camanchaca* (fog) that constantly envelops it. Within this forest, you will come across ferns and trees found nowhere else in the region as you maneuver a slightly slippery boardwalk on a 20-minute tour. Although Fray Jorge will not take a lot of time to see, it makes a pretty spot to stop at, and there is a picnic table from where you can watch the fog drift over the Pacific Ocean below. ⊠ *Pan-American Hwy. at Km 387* ✢ *Do not take route D560 as this is now closed* ☎ *51/224–4769* ⊕ *www.conaf.cl* ⊠ *6000 pesos* ☉ *Closed Dec. 25 and Jan. 1; Mon., Tues., Wed. in low season.*

RESERVA NACIONAL PINGÜINO DE HUMBOLDT

123 km (76 miles) north of La Serena

One of the top attractions in northern Chile, this national reserve comprises more than 2,000 acres spread across several islands, providing a home for a dazzling array of species, including sea otters, sea lions, birds, and the occasional whale and dolphin. But the star of the wildlife show is the Humboldt penguin, an endangered breed that mates only off the coasts of Chile and Peru, and which has suffered due to guano exploitation, overfishing, and habitat destruction.

GETTING HERE AND AROUND

Boat trips launch from Punta de Choros, a cold and dusty town with little else to recommend it, or you can visit as part of a tour from La Serena. If you come with your own wheels, keep an eye out as you drive down the dirt road from the highway as wild guanacos are often spotted. Be sure to take advantage of the olive oil for sale, as it's said to be some of the best in Chile.

■ TIP➔ The Chilean navy, which has a base in Punta de Choros, carefully monitors the boat trips, as weather can be volatile. High winds often prevent trips between September and October, so plan accordingly. Also be sure to bring cash as there are no ATM machines in the town and credit cards are not accepted at most establishments.

TOURS

Turismo Punta de Choros. There is a surprising number of fishermen turned tour guides in Punta de Choros, but this company can provide you with the best. Groups are led out to sea, passing by Isla Choros to spot the penguins and finishing with a visit to Isla Damas, the largest of the islands and home to gorgeous white-sand beaches. Tours last around three hours, and a separate fee of 6,000 pesos is needed to visit the penguin reserve. ⊠ *Caleta San Agustin, La Higuera* ☎ *9/899–6322* ⊕ *www.turismopuntadechoros.cl* ⊠ *From 17000 pesos.*

PARQUE NACIONAL LLANOS DE CHALLE

264 km (164 miles) north of La Serena.

The *desierto florido*, or flowering desert, is a jaw-droppingly vivid array of flowers that mysteriously bloom in the otherwise arid landscape of the Atacama Desert. More than 200 species have been recorded

blossoming in the area, predominately in the Parque Nacional Llano de Challe, including the pink *pata de guanaco* (guanaco hoof), and the native red *garra de león* (lion's claw). The stunning display is produced thanks to the El Niño phenomenom, which brings increased rainfall into the area most years, and occurs between late July and September. Locals are the best source to find out where the most spectacular spots are within the park, although most tour operators from Copiapo and La Serena will offer the trip when it is available. Even if you don't get to the park, patches of the desierto florido can be seen from the highway north of Vallenar most years, while the semi-arid land around Punta de Choros can also be spectacularly covered with plant life.

GETTING HERE AND AROUND

The best way to get to the park is with your own set of wheels. From Huasco, take the coastal highway C-360 40 km (25 miles) until you reach the CONAF (the national parks service) guardsite at Los Pozos. From Vallenar, you can drive on C-440. Either route takes around 1½ hours on decent roads. There is also a bus that leaves from the front of the Estadio Techado in Vallenar every Friday. Another alternative is a guided tour from La Serena or Copiapo.

EXPLORING

Parque Nacional Llanos de Challe. This coastal national park is home to 206 native plant species (14 of those are found only in the Atacama) and is famed primarily for its proliferation of flowers during the wetter months (a rarity in this part of the world). It's also home to various cacti species, foxes, peregrine falcons, and the guanaco, the largest of the wild South American camelids. There is one campsite in the park, with minimal facilities so you should come prepared with what you may need for an overnight stay. No buses run to the park, although it is possible to visit via tour groups from Copiapo or by private vehicle; it's accessible from either Huasco heading north or from the Pan-American Highway north of Vallenar. ⊠ *Parque Nacional Llanos de Challe, Copiapó* ☏ *52/221–3404* ⊕ *www.conaf.cl/parques/parque-nacional-llanos-de-challe* ⊒ *5000 pesos* ⊙ *Closed Mon.*

THE COPIAPÓ VALLEY

This region, once known as Copayapu, meaning "cup of gold" in the Andean Quechua language, was first inhabited by the Diaguitas around 1000 BC. The Incas arrived several hundred years later in search of gold. Conquistador Diego de Almagro, who passed this way in 1535, was the first European to see the lush valley.

During the 19th century, the Copiapó Valley proved to be a true cup of gold when prospectors started large-scale mining operations in the region. But today, the residents of the valley make their living primarily from copper.

The northernmost city in the region, Copiapó, lies at the end of the world. Here the semi-arid El Norte Chico gives way to the Atacama Desert. Continuing north from Copiapó, there is little but barren earth for hundreds of miles.

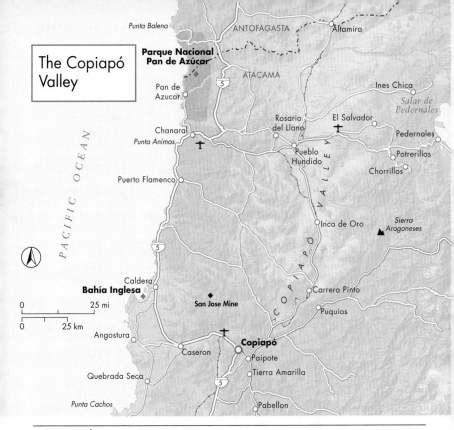

The Copiapó Valley

COPIAPÓ

145 km (90 miles) north of Vallenar.

Copiapó was officially founded in 1744 by Don Francisco Cortés, who called it Villa San Francisco de La Selva. Originally a *tambo,* or resting place, it was also the spot where Diego de Almagro recuperated after his grueling journey south from Peru in 1535. In the 19th-century silver strikes solidified Copiapó's status as an important city in the region, and today most residents make their living from copper mining. The city itself is modern and prosperous, with a lovely central park lined with 100-year-old pepper trees and plenty of flower-filled avenues. You can also see the site of South America's first train station, built in 1852, which once ran to the coastal port of Caldera.

GETTING HERE AND AROUND

Copiapó's Desierto de Atacama Airport (DAT) is a bit more than one hour's flying time from Santiago and connects to other points in El Norte Chico and El Norte Grande via Sky and LAN airlines. The DAT is about an hour from Copiapó but more like 30 minutes from Caldera—think of it as a big triangle. Several car rental companies have branches at DAT airport. Copiapó's bus terminal is serviced by all major bus lines. To the north (about 45 minutes via Ruta 5) lie the beaches of Caldera and Bahía Inglesa.

Air Contacts Desierto de Atacama Airport. ⊠ *Ruta 5 Norte, KM 863, Caldera* ☏ *52/252–3600* ⊕ *www.aeropuertodecaldera.cl/index.html.*

ESSENTIALS

Visitor Information Sernatur. ⊠ *Los Carrera 691* ☏ *51/221–2838* ⊕ *www. sernatur.cl/region-de-atacama.*

TOURS

Turismo Atacama. Regional flights and hotel bookings can be organized at this travel agency. They also recommend guides for excursions to Bahía Inglesa and Pan de Azucar National Park. ⊠ *Atacama 998* ☏ *9/9683–8586* ⊕ *www.turismoatacamaventura.cl.*

EXPLORING

Iglesia San Francisco. This red-and-white candy cane of a church was built in 1872, and although it looks as if it's made of cement, it's actually constructed of Oregon pine. The adjacent Plaza Godoy has a statue of wood-cutter Juan Godoy, who accidentally discovered huge silver deposits in nearby Chañarcillo in 1832, prompting thousands of people to move to the region to ignite the great silver boom of the day. ⊠ *Juan Godoy 65.*

Fodor's Choice **Museo Mineralógico.** This museum offers a geological history of the
★ region and the country's best collection of rocks and minerals. There are close to 2,500 samples, including some found only in the Atacama Desert. The museum even displays a few meteorites that fell in the area. ⊠ *Colipí 333, At Manuel Rodriguez* ☏ *52/220–6606* ⊕ *www.unap.cl/ museomin* 💲 *500 pesos* ⊗ *Closed weekends.*

Museo Regional de Atacama. A historic home that once belonged to the wealthy Matta family now houses this museum. The house, built by mining engineer Felipe Santiago Matta between 1840 and 1850, shows the history of the region through its reconstructions of 19th-century rooms. The exhibits themselves are dedicated to mining and archaeology. ⊠ *Atacama 98* ☏ *52/221–2313* ⊕ *www.museodeatacama.cl* ⊗ *Closed Mon.*

San Jose Mine. If you have your own car, you can make a road trip to this mind which made worldwide headlines in 2010, as the site where 33 miners were trapped underground and then rescued after a grueling 69 days. From the highway, the drive is a dusty one beside a stunning desert landscape until you reach the look-out, where there is an audiovisual guide and the rescue pod used to pull the miners out. One of the 33 is often on-site to speak to visitors (in Spanish only however); although site visits are free, it is recommended to leave a tip. ⊠ *Copiapó* ⊹ *Turn at Copec on Ruta 5 Norte toward San Jose* ☏ *52/221–2838* ⊗ *Closed Mon.–Wed.*

WHERE TO EAT

$$$ ✕**El Candil.** Located inside a former gas station, this restaurant has sea
CHILEAN food, Chilean classics, and pizza on the menu. While the overall experience here can be hit-or-miss, El Candil remains one of the more popular lunch and dinner spots for Copiapo locals. **Known for:** local hang-out; big pizzas; former gas station location. 💲 *Average main: 10000 pesos* ⊠ *Near exit ramp from highway, Pan America Norte 107–115* ☏ *52/221–1535.*

$ ✕ **Govindas.** A fun place to stop for a quick lunch, this café serves burg-
VEGETARIAN   ers, sandwiches, tacos, and empanadas, all served vegetarian-style. They
also have a daily set menu, a children's play area, and adult Hatha yoga
classes every day (kids sessions are on Tuesday). **Known for:** family-
friendly atmosphere; great vegan and vegetarian options; on-site yoga
classes. ⑤ *Average main: 5000 pesos* ✉ *Colipi 262* ☎ *52/233–6444*
☉ *Closed Mon.* ⊟ *No credit cards.*

WHERE TO STAY

$$$ ⊞ **Hotel Chagall.** Located half a block from the Copiapó's central plaza,
HOTEL   this well-equipped business hotel has clean, modern, and spacious rooms,
with colorful woven comforters in local designs. **Pros:** located right in the
center of the city; nice furnishings; large rooms with comfortable beds.
Cons: some rooms on street side may be noisy; no Wi-Fi in rooms; poorly
lit bedrooms. ⑤ *Rooms from: 99000 pesos* ✉ *Av. Bernardo O'Higgins
760* ☎ *52/235–2900* ⊕ *www.chagall.cl* ⤳ *88 rooms* ⦿*| Breakfast.*

$$$ ⊞ **Hotel Diego de Almeida.** Enjoying a privileged spot on the city's main
HOTEL   square, this hotel has comfortable and elegantly decorated rooms. **Pros:**
excellent location; large bedrooms; helpful staff. **Cons:** can be noisy;
parking is limited; decor is a bit run-down. ⑤ *Rooms from: 105000
pesos* ✉ *Av. Bernardo O'Higgins 640* ☎ *52/220–7700* ⊕ *www.daho-
teles.com* ⤳ *136 rooms* ⦿*| Breakfast.*

$$ ⊞ **Hotel La Casona.** Beautiful gardens surround this quaint country inn
B&B/INN   with a red facade. **Pros:** on-site restaurant; friendly service; secure park-
Fodor's Choice   ing. **Cons:** not in the center of town; rooms very hot in summer and
★   only some have fans; small bedrooms. ⑤ *Rooms from: 53000 pesos*
✉ *Av. Bernardo O'Higgins 150* ☎ *52/221–7277* ⊕ *www.lacasonahotel.
cl* ⤳ *12 rooms* ⦿*| Breakfast.*

BAHÍA INGLESA

68 km (42 miles) northwest of Copiapó.

Some of the most beautiful beaches in El Norte Chico are at Bahía
Inglesa, which was originally known as Puerto del Inglés because of the
number of English buccaneers using the port as a hideaway. It's not just
the beautiful white sand that sets these beaches apart, however: it's also
the turquoise waters, fresh air, and fabulous weather. Combine all this
with the fact that the town has yet to attract large-scale development
and you can see why so many people flock here in summer. If you are
fortunate enough to visit during the low season, you can experience a
tranquility rarely felt in Chile's other coastal towns.

GETTING HERE AND AROUND

Follow the Pan-American Highway about one hour north until the small
towns of Caldera and Bahía Inglesa come into view: you may smell the
salty Pacific before you see the buildings. Buses big and small, as well as
taxi colectivos, service Caldera, 5 km (3 miles) north of Bahía Inglesa.
From Caldera it's a 10-minute cab ride to Bahía Inglesa. To the north
lies Antofagasta, about six hours from both Caldera and Bahía Inglesa
by car or bus on the Pan-American Highway.

BEACHES

FAMILY **Playa La Piscina.** Stunningly pretty, impossibly calm, and perfect for swimming, Playa La Piscina is in many ways the ideal town beach. Bordering Bahía Inglesa's main drag, this beach—which translates as "the swimming pool"—enjoys perfect white sand and bright blue waters, all a short walk from most hotels and restaurants. Unsurprisingly, it gets very busy in the summer high season and suffers from quite a bit of littering. **Amenities:** food and drink; lifeguards (summer only); parking; toilets; water sports. **Best for:** swimming. ⊠ *Bahía Inglesa.*

Fodor's Choice
★ **Playa Las Machas.** Stretching from the southernmost tip of Bahía Inglesa right around the bay, Playa Las Machas has escaped the attention of the majority of tourists and is a relaxing alternative to the more crowded beaches in the town proper. Whether you decide to explore the long shoreline on foot, taking in the dramatic scenery as you go, or find yourself a secluded spot for sunbathing and to get away from it all, this white-sand beach is a great place to while away a lazy afternoon. **Amenities:** none. **Best for:** solitude; sunset; surfing; walking. ⊠ *Bahía Inglesa.*

4

WHERE TO EAT

$$$ ✕ **Domo Lounge.** The most happening spot on the waterfront, this sprawl-
EUROPEAN ing restaurant serves fresh sea food, pizzas, and shared plates of various European-inspired cuisine. It also transforms into a great spot to enjoy a few drinks, regular live music, and DJ events. **Known for:** live music and late-night events; freshly caught sea food; delicious drinks and desserts. ⑤ *Average main: 10000 pesos* ⊠ *Av. El Morro 610* ☎ *9/6244–6823.*

$$$ ✕ **El Plateao.** This bohemian bistro with ocean views is a must for
ECLECTIC anyone staying in the area. The innovative, contemporary menu lists such culinary non sequiturs as curry dishes and *tallarines con mariscos* (a pan-Asian noodle concoction served with shellfish and topped with cilantro). **Known for:** spicy, eclectic dishes; sunsets from the terrace. ⑤ *Average main: 10000 pesos* ⊠ *Av. El Morro 756* ☎ *09/826–0007.*

WHERE TO STAY

$$ 🏨 **Apart Hotel Playa Blanca.** If you are tired of indistinguishable chain hotels,
RENTAL a condo at Playa Blanca, complete with comfortable living room and full
FAMILY kitchen, may just do the trick. **Pros:** superclose to the water; fully equipped kitchens; excellent choice for families. **Cons:** location means a dark walk home from the action at night; no website; rooms with basic furnishings. ⑤ *Rooms from: 65000 pesos* ⊠ *Camino de Martín 1300* ☎ *9/5011–1235* ▭ *No credit cards* ⇲ *10 condos, 1 apartment* ⦿ *No meals.*

$$ 🏨 **Hotel Rocas de Bahía.** This sprawling modern hotel has Southwest
HOTEL style rooms with large beds and huge windows facing the sea. **Pros:** rooftop pool; good location right on the bay; free parking. **Cons:** can get noisy; poor breakfast; hit-and-miss service. ⑤ *Rooms from: 75000 pesos* ⊠ *Av. El Morro 888* ☎ *52/231–6005* ⊕ *www.rocasdebahia.cl* ⇲ *36 rooms* ⦿ *Breakfast.*

SPORTS AND THE OUTDOORS
WATER SPORTS
Oceano Aventura. Come here for scuba diving lessons and planned excursions to explore the stunning world beneath the waves. It's a great way to learn about the local flora and fauna as well as an excellent way to visit underwater statues. ⊠ *Av. El Morro* ☎ *9/9546–9848* ⊕ *www. oceanoaventura.cl* ✉ *From 40000 pesos.*

PARQUE NACIONAL PAN DE AZÚCAR

175 km (109 miles) north of Copiapó.

Some of the best coastal scenery in the country can be found at Parque Nacional Pan de Azúcar. Imposing cliffs give way to deserted white-sand beaches in this captivating reserve, which stretches for 40 km (25 miles) along the coast and is home to dolphins, sea otters, and many types of endangered birds.

GETTING HERE AND AROUND
You can take Route C-120 north from Chañaral for 29 km (18 miles) directly into the park, or take the Pan-American Highway north of Chañaral to Km marker 1,410, then cut toward the coast onto Route C-110 to the park.

EXPLORING
Fodor'sChoice **Parque Nacional Pan de Azúcar.** This national reserve stretching for 40
★ km (25 miles) along the coast north of the town of Chañaral has some of Chile's most spectacular coastal scenery. Steep cliffs fall into the crashing sea, their ominous presence broken occasionally by white-sand beaches made for picnics. Within the park is an incredible variety of flora and fauna, including sea lions, sea otters, foxes, and the very rare Peruvian Diving Petrel, as well as some 20 species of cacti including the rare copiapoa, which resembles a little blue pin cushion. At the tiny fishing village of Caleta Pan de Azúcar, you can find several local guides that can take you on boat trips to see colonies of Humboldt penguins. ⊠ *An unpaved but signposted road north of cemetery in Chañaral leads to park* ☎ *52/221–3404* ⊕ *www.conaf.cl* ✉ *5000 pesos.*

WHERE TO STAY
$ ⊡ **Lodge Pan de Azúcar.** Surrounded by the imposing "Sugar Loaf" moun-
RENTAL tain range to the rear and the crashing waves of the Pacific in front, you'd be hard pressed to find a more remote location to stay. **Pros:** gloriously remote; unbeatable views; environmentally friendly. **Cons:** no power other than lighting and kitchen; few dining alternatives available in the only nearby village; hard to get to without your own car. $ *Rooms from: 48600 pesos* ⊠ *Camino C-120, on left after passing park ranger's kiosk* ☎ *9/9280–3483* ⊕ *www.pandeazucarlodge.cl* ⤳ *5 cabanas* ⧉ *No meals.*

EL NORTE
GRANDE

WELCOME TO EL NORTE GRANDE

TOP REASONS TO GO

★ **San Pedro de Atacama:** This unassuming town in the middle of the desert is a world-class destination for the beautiful outdoor excursions nearby. Visit magical moonlike landscapes, large sand dunes, lush valleys filled with 900-year-old cactus plants, salt flats with blue lagoons, and surreal geysers with steam and bubbling water at dawn break.

★ **Flora and fauna:** Yes, the Atacama Desert is one of the driest places on earth. But head to the Chilean Altiplano, just a few hours east of Arica, and you'll find an abundance of fauna and, depending on the season, flora. Pink flamingos dot the edges of volcanic lakes like Lago Chungará on the Bolivian border, and slender brown vicuñas run in small herds through the sparse grasslands.

★ **Pristine beaches:** Pristine sands line the shore near Arica and Iquique. The beaches are packed during summer months, but in the off season you just might have the beach to yourself.

San Pedro de Atacama is one of the continent's gems, a hotspot for outdoor-sports enthusiasts, birdwatchers, and sandboarders. Resting between two giant branches of the Andean mountains is the *altiplano,* or high plains, where you'll see natural marvels such as crystalline salt flats, geysers, and volcanoes.

1 The Nitrate Pampa. This region was previously home to the nitrate plants that made Chile a mining powerhouse in the mid-20th century. These days, towns like Antofagasta and Chacabuco are fading testaments to an old way of life, but copper mines are turning places like Calama into modern-day boomtowns. These small towns make good stops on the way up to Atacama.

2 San Pedro and the Atacama Desert. Snowcapped volcanoes loom to the east, making mornings in this region especially memorable. Bird lovers will find the Reserva Nacional Los Flamencos well worth the high-altitude adjustment for a chance to see hundreds of pink flamingos wading in shimmering blue and green lakes. If you get beyond the hype and the hippies, San Pedro is a great place. The range of outdoor activities

and the breathtaking sights, including moonlike landscapes and Incan graveyards, make it a must-see stop in the North. Spend your mornings hiking, biking, and sandboarding, afternoons swimming, and nights beside a blazing outdoor fire in the patio of one of San Pedro's down-home but delicious eateries, gazing up at the star-filled heavens.

3 Iquique and Nearby. The port of Iquique is the world's largest exporter of fishmeal, but its heyday was as a nitrate center in the 19th century. Fading mansions remain, and this regional capital is still a popular destination. From here you can do a day trip to the hot springs of Mamiña, also glimpsing the ghost town of Humberstone, while getting to the petroglyph Gigante de Atacama—Chile's largest—in time for the sunset.

4 Arica and Nearby. Arica, at the intersection of Chile, Bolivia, and Peru, is part of the "land of eternal spring," and its pedestrian-mall eateries can ease even the most impatient traveler into a chair for a day. Sights include mummies dating to 6000 BC, Aymara markets, and national parks with alpine lakes and herds of vicuña.

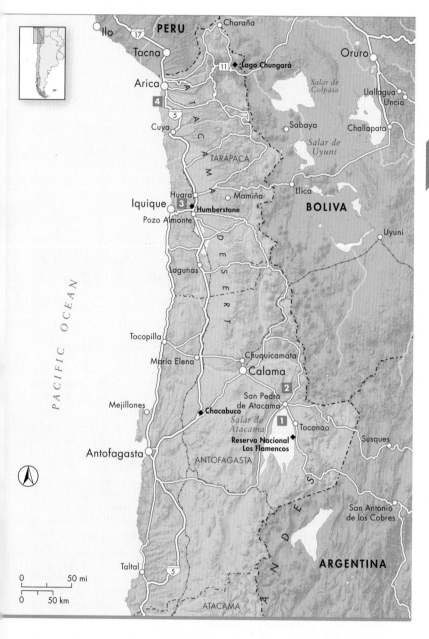

Ilo
PERU
Charaña
Tacna
17
Oruro
11 ◆ Lago Chungará
Salar de
Colpasa
Arica
Llallagua
Uncia
4
5
Cuya
Sabaya
Challapata
Salar de
TARAPACA
Uyuni
Huara
Mamiña
Llica
Iquique
3 ◆ Humberstone
BOLIVA
Pozo Almonte
Uyuni
Lagunas
D
E
S
Tocopilla
E
María Elena
Chuquicamata
R
Calama
T
2
San Pedro
de Atacama
Mejillones
◆ Chacabuco
Salar de
Atacama
1 Toconao
Reserva Nacional ◆
Susques
Los Flamencos
Antofagasta
ANTOFAGASTA
A
N
San Antonio
D
de los Cobres
E
S
Taltal
5
ARGENTINA
PACIFIC OCEAN

0   50 mi
0   50 km

ATACAMA

5

Updated by Amanda Barnes

The Norte Grande is as vast as it is remote, but don't be fooled by this seemingly empty landscape: the Atacama Desert is filled with natural wonders that make it one of most breathtaking destinations in the world. With a striking desert and volcano-lined horizon as your backdrop, you can discover otherworldly landscapes like salt-crusted white valleys, burnt-orange sand formations, stunning blue lagoons, lush oases, and picture-perfect beach destinations. Exhilarating hikes up volcanoes or through cactus-laden creeks and adrenaline-boosting bike rides attract outdoor sports enthusiasts, while relaxing thermal pools, a plethora of wildlife, calming beaches, and colorful native culture keep tamer travelers charmed.

Spanning some 1,930 km (1,200 miles), Chile's Great North stretches from the Río Copiapó to the borders of Peru and Bolivia. Here you will find the Atacama Desert, the driest place on Earth—so dry that in many parts no rain has ever been recorded.

Yet people have inhabited this desolate land since time immemorial. Indeed, the heart of El Norte Grande lies not in its geography but in its people. The indigenous Chinchorro people eked out a meager living from the sea more than 8,000 years ago, leaving behind the magnificent Chinchorro mummies, the oldest in the world. High in the Andes, the Atacameño tribes traded livestock with the Tijuanacota and the Inca. Many of these people still cling to their ways of life, though much of their culture was lost during the colonial period and by the abandonment of small villages as mining in the region boomed.

When huge deposits of nitrates were found in the Atacama region in the 1800s, the "white gold" brought boom times to towns like Pisagua, Iquique, and Antofagasta. Because most of the mineral-rich region lay beyond its northern border, Chile declared war on neighboring Peru and Bolivia in 1878. Chile won the five-year battle and annexed the land north of Antofagasta, a continuing source of national pride for many Chileans. With the invention of synthetic nitrates, the market for these fertilizers dried up and the nitrate barons abandoned their opulent mansions and returned to Santiago. El Norte Grande was once again left on its own.

What you'll see today is a land of both growth and decay. The glory days of the nitrate era are gone, but copper has stepped in to help fill that gap (the world's largest open-pit copper mine is here) and local lithium mining continues to show promise. El Norte Grande is still a land

of opportunity for fortune-seekers, as well as for tourists looking for a less traveled corner of the world. It is a place of beauty and dynamic isolation, a place where the past touches the present in a troubled yet majestic embrace.

PLANNER

WHEN TO GO

In the height of the Chilean summer, January and February, droves of Chileans and Argentines mob El Norte Grande's beaches. Although this is a fun time to visit, prices go up and finding a hotel can be difficult. Book your room a month or more in advance. The high season tapers off in March, an excellent time to visit if you're looking for a bit more tranquility. If you plan to visit the altiplano, bring the right clothing. Winter can be very cold, and summer sees a fair amount of rain. San Pedro is sunny year-round and pleasant to visit, but the best seasons are spring and fall when the crowds are gone and the days are not too hot, nor the nights too cold.

FESTIVALS

Every town in the region celebrates the day honoring its patron saint, Saint Peter, on June 29. Most are small gatherings attended largely by locals. One fiesta not to be missed takes place in La Tirana from July 12 to 18. During this time some 80,000 pilgrims converge on the town to honor the Virgen del Carmen with dancing in the streets.

PLANNING YOUR TIME

You'll have to hustle to see much of El Norte Grande in less than a week. You should spend at least two days in San Pedro de Atacama, visiting the incredible sights such as the bizarre moonscape of the Valle de la Luna and the desolate salt flats of the Salar de Atacama. For half a day soak in the hot springs in the tiny town of Pica, then head to the nitrate ghost town of Humberstone. On the way to Iquique, take a side trip to the Gigante de Atacama, the world's largest geoglyph. After a morning exploring Iquique, head up to Arica, the coastal town that bills itself as the "land of eternal spring." Be sure to visit the Museo Arqueológico de San Miguel de Azapa to see the Chinchorro mummies. Stop in Putre to catch your breath before taking in the flamingos at Parque Nacional Lauca or the vicuñas, llamas, and alpacas of Reserva Nacional Las Vicuñas.

GETTING HERE AND AROUND
AIR TRAVEL

There are no international airports in El Norte Grande, but from Santiago you can transfer to a flight headed to Antofagasta, Calama, Iquique, or Arica. Round-trip flights start from 80,000 pesos, and come run up to 300,000 pesos in peak season. The cities within El Norte Grande are far apart, so flying between them can save you time and provide more comfort. Sky and LATAM are the main airlines for the north and offer competitive pricing if you book in advance.

Air Contacts LAN. ☎ 600/526–2000 ⊕ www.latam.com. **Sky Airline.** ☎ 55/245–9090 ⊕ www.skyairline.cl.

BUS TRAVEL

Travel between the larger towns and cities in El Norte Grande is easy, but there may be no bus service to some smaller villages or the more remote national parks. No bus company has a monopoly, so shop around for the best price and note there are often several bus stations in each city.

Bus Contacts Pullman. ⊠ *Latorre 2827, Antofagasta* ☎ *600/600–0018* ⊕ *www.pullman.cl.* **Turbus.** ⊠ *Latorre 2751, Antofagasta* ☎ *600/660–6600* ⊕ *www.turbus.cl.*

CAR TRAVEL

A car is definitely the best way to see El Norte Grande. Driving in the cities can be a little hectic, but highway travel is usually smooth sailing and the roads are generally well maintained. Ruta 5, more familiarly known as the Pan-American Highway, bisects all of northern Chile. Ruta 1, Chile's answer to California's Highway 101, is a beautiful coastal highway running between Antofagasta and Iquique. Avis, Budget, and Hertz all have car rental offices in the region.

RESTAURANTS

The food of El Norte Grande is simple but quite good. Along the coast you can enjoy fresh seafood and shellfish, including *merluza* (hake), *corvina* (sea bass), *ostiones* (scallops), and *machas* (similar to razor clams but unique to Chile), to name just a few. Ceviche (a traditional dish made with raw, marinated fish) is a Chilean (and Peruvian) specialty found in much of El Norte Grande, but make sure you sample it in a place where you are confident that the fish is fresh. Fish may be ordered *a la plancha* (grilled in butter and lemon) or accompanied by a sauce such as *salsa margarita* (a butter-based sauce comprising almost every shellfish imaginable). As you enter the interior region you'll come across heartier meals such as *cazuela de vacuno* (beef stew served with corn on the cob and vegetables) and *chuleta con arroz* (porkchop with rice). In San Pedro, you'll find dishes that feature native meats like llama and vicuña.

People in the north generally eat a heavy lunch around 2 pm that can last two hours, followed by a light dinner around 10 pm. Reservations are seldom needed, except in the poshest of places. Leave a 10% tip if you enjoyed the service. *Restaurant reviews have been shortened. For full information, visit Fodors.com.*

HOTELS

The Atacama has seen a boom in luxury accommodations in recent years. San Pedro, in particular, hosts more than half a dozen luxury lodgings that range from lavish desert resorts to tasteful boutiques. Luxury hotels usually are full board with activities included and transfers to the airport in Calama. Otherwise, opt for one of the smaller hotels in town that offer reasonable prices. The gamut of hotels outside of San Pedro is less exciting, and be warned that some accommodations bill themselves as "luxury" despite not having seen a lick of clean paint for years. In rural towns, accommodation is relatively inexpensive and hotels are few and far between, so you might have to make do with guesthouses with basic rooms and shared bathrooms. *Hotel reviews have been shortened. For full information, visit Fodors.com.*

WHAT IT COSTS IN CHILEAN PESOS (IN THOUSANDS)			
	$	$$	$$$	$$$$
Restaurants	Under 6	6–9	10–13	over 13
Hotels	Under 51	51–85	86–115	over 115

Restaurant prices are the average cost of a main course price at dinner or, if dinner is not served, at lunch. Hotel prices are the lowest cost of a standard double room in high season, excluding tax.

HEALTH AND SAFETY

The main concern you should have in the North is the sun; a hat and sunblock are always a good idea, and be sure to drink plenty of fluids during any outdoor activity. The altitude can also be a problem for some, so take the first day slow and acclimatize.

Use common sense: don't be flashy with cash or expensive cameras. The North is relatively tranquil, but when venturing out from the center of any town into other neighborhoods, it's always safer to take a cab than to walk (ask an employee to call one for you). The main industry in El Norte Grande is mining, which means there is an inflated population of men and that foreign women often attract more than a few wandering gazes.

THE NITRATE PAMPA

The vast *pampa salitrera* is an atmospheric introduction to Chile's Great North. Between 1890 and 1925 this region was the site of more than 100 *oficinas de salitre,* or nitrate plants. For a glorious period, Chile was the king of production of the fertilizer saltpeter (sodium nitrate), led by the "Father of Nitrate," Englishman James Humberstone. The Dover-born chemist applied James Shanks' method of producing sodium nitrate, and soon it was used throughout Chile. The War of the Pacific fought by Chile, Peru, and Bolivia was caused at least in part by the desire for these rich deposits beneath the Atacama Desert. The invention of synthetic nitrates spelled the end for all but a few plants. Crumbling nitrate works now lay stagnant in the dry desert air, some disintegrating into dust, others remaining a fascinating testament to the white gold that, for a time, made this one of Chile's richest regions.

ANTOFAGASTA

565 km (350 miles) north of Copiapó.

Antofagasta is the most important—and the richest—city in El Norte Grande. It was part of Bolivia until 1879, when it was annexed by Chile in the War of the Pacific. The port town became an economic powerhouse during the nitrate boom. With the rapid decline of nitrate production, copper mining stepped in to keep the city's coffers filled.

Many travelers end up spending a night in Antofagasta on their way to the more interesting destinations like San Pedro de Atacama, Iquique, and Arica, but a few sights here are worth a look. Around two in the

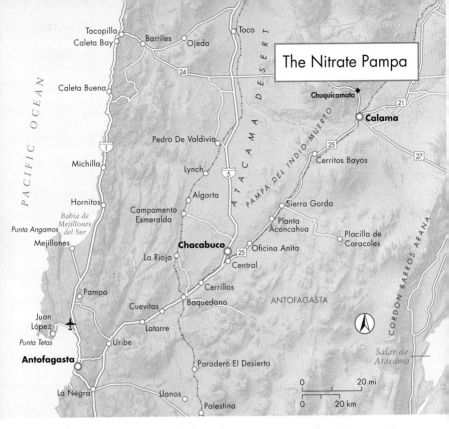

The Nitrate Pampa

afternoon the city shuts down most of the streets in the center of town, making for pleasant afternoon shopping and strolling.

GETTING HERE AND AROUND

Antofagasta's airport, 30 minutes from downtown, is a regular stop on Sky Airline's northern run, about a two-hour flight from Santiago. From Caldera in the south, it's a six- to seven-hour ride up the Pan-American Highway by bus or car, but at least on this stretch you'll see some of the ocean. The bus terminal on LaTorre is just a short walk from downtown. Regular buses leave to Calama (3 hours), San Pedro (4½ hours), and Iquique (6 hours). The beaches of Juan Lopez are 45 minutes up the coast road, and the famous "La Portada" a mere 16 km (10 miles) from downtown—minibuses run there from LaTorre 2723 frequently. The Turbus terminal, one of the bigger bus lines serving all of Chile, is just down the street on LaTorre. Desertica Expediciones arranges trips into the interior, including excursions to Parque Nacional Pan de Azúcar in El Norte Chico.

Air Travel Cerro Moreno Airport (Antofagasta) (CNF). ☎ *55/225-4998* ⊕ *www.aeropuertoantofagasta.cl.*

ESSENTIALS

Visitor Information Sernatur Antofagasta. ✉ *Prat 384, 1st fl.,* ☎ *55/245-1818* ⊕ *www.sernatur.cl.*

EXPLORING

Museo Regional de Antofagasta. Inside the historic customs house, this museum is the town's oldest building, dating back to 1866. It displays clothing and other bric-a-brac from the nitrate era. ⊠ *Balmaceda 2786* ☎ *55/222–7016* ⊕ *www.museodeantofagasta.cl* 🎟 *Free* ☉ *Closed Mon.*

Torre Reloj. High above Plaza Colón is this clock tower whose face is a replica of London's Big Ben. It was erected by British residents in 1910. ⊠ *Plaza Colón.*

WHERE TO EAT

$$$ ✕ **Amares Costafusion.** This trendy bistro is a top spot for fusion food that
CHILEAN mixes local seafood with different international cuisines. Try the crab lasagna, grilled octopus, Asian-style tuna, or tempura shrimp. **Known for:** fusion seafood menu; great ceviche; tasty pisco sours. ⑤ *Average main: 11000 pesos* ⊠ *Antonino Toro 995* ☎ *55/292–2376* ⊕ *www.amares.cl.*

$$ ✕ **Restaurant Arriero.** This classic Chilean barbecue joint serves up grilled
BARBECUE meats and fish, accompanied by live jazz on the piano each evening. A
FAMILY nice selection of homegrown wines supplements the menu. **Known for:** Chilean-style grilled meats and fish; hearty portions; live jazz. ⑤ *Average main: 8000 pesos* ⊠ *Condell 2644* ☎ *55/226–4371* ⊕ *www.arriero-afta.cl* ☉ *No dinner Sun.*

WHERE TO STAY

$$$ 🏨 **Enjoy Hotel del Desierto.** Although you may be sharing the spa and
HOTEL gym with many guests, you will get a spacious room to yourself and a comfortable big bed. **Pros:** big rooms; modern amenities; rooftop pool. **Cons:** slow service; limited bar; can be noisy outside. ⑤ *Rooms from: 88000 pesos* ⊠ *Av. Angamos 01455* ☎ *55/265–3000* ⊕ *www.enjoy.cl/ enjoy-antofagasta* ⤳ *100 rooms* ⦶ *Breakfast.*

$$$ 🏨 **Hotel Antofagasta.** Part of the Panamericana Hoteles chain, this high-
HOTEL rise on the ocean comes with first-class views and a lovely kidney-shaped pool. **Pros:** nice beachfront location; modern decor; big breakfast. **Cons:** mediocre restaurant; a bit sterile; bit overpriced. ⑤ *Rooms from: 88000 pesos* ⊠ *Av. Balmaceda 2575* ☎ *55/222–8811* ⊕ *www.hotelantofagasta. cl* ⤳ *153 rooms* ⦶ *Breakfast.*

CHACABUCO

70 km (43 miles) northeast of Antofagasta.

There are many ghost towns left from the nitrate boom in the early 20th century, and Chacabuco is one of them, although this deserted town has a darker history than most. Augusto Pinochet used the abandoned town, originally founded in 1924 for saltpeter plain exploitations, during his dictatorship as a concentration camp for almost 2,000 people between 1973 and 1974. The small town was surrounded by landmines to ensure no one attempted escape. Nowadays you can visit this unsettling place and see a display in the theater about life in Chacabuco when it was a nitrate plant, and get more information about its days as a concentration camp.

GETTING HERE AND AROUND

To reach Chacabuco from Antofagasta, head east through the coastal range until you hit the Panamerican Highway (Ruta 5 Norte) and follow it northeast in the direction of Calama.

EXPLORING

Chacabuco. A mysterious dot on the desert landscape, the ghost town of Chacabuco is a decidedly eerie place. More than 7,000 employees and their families lived here when the Oficina Chacabuco (a company mining town that was made a national monument in 1971) was in operation between 1922 and 1944.

During the first years of Augusto Pinochet's military regime, Chacabuco was used as a prison camp for political dissidents. The artwork of prisoners still adorns many of the walls. Do not walk around the town's exterior, as land mines from this era are still buried here.

Today you'll find tiny houses, their tin roofs flapping in the wind and their walls collapsing. You can wander through many of the abandoned and restored buildings and take a look inside the theater, which has been restored to its previous appearance as a boomtown. ✉ *70 km (43 miles) northeast of Antofagasta on Pan-American Hwy.* ✆ *1000 pesos.*

CALAMA

215 km (133 miles) northeast of Antofagasta.

The discovery of vast deposits of copper in the area turned Calama into the quintessential mining town, and therein lies its interest. People from the length of Chile flock to this dusty spot on the map in hopes of striking it rich in "the land of sun and copper"—most likely working for Codelco, Chile's biggest company, which has three mines in the surrounding area. A modern-day version of the boomtowns of the 19th-century American West, Calama is rough around the edges, but it does possess a certain energy.

Founded as a *tambo*, or resting place, at the crossing of two Inca trails, Calama still serves as a stopover for people headed elsewhere. Some people traveling to San Pedro de Atacama end up spending the night here, and the town does have a few attractions of its own.

GETTING HERE AND AROUND

Daily flights from Santiago via Sky, AirComet, and LAN arrive 20 minutes from downtown at Calama's El Loa Airport (CJC). Bus service to neighboring San Pedro is frequent and fast—it's about an hour between the two towns. To points north, you can fly to Iquique and Arica in an hour (if you can avoid the puddle-jumper service that adds a few stops), but a bus or car will take you seven and nine hours, respectively. Be very careful when passing the mining company trucks that may slow your journey. Mining companies own all the bright red pickups you'll no doubt notice around town.

ESSENTIALS

Visitor Information Municipal Tourism Office. ✉ *Latorre 1689* ☎ *55/253-1707* ⊕ *www.calamacultural.cl.*

EXPLORING

Catedral San Juan Bautista. The gleaming copper roof of this cathedral on Plaza 23 de Marzo, the city's main square, testifies to the importance of mining in this region. ⊠ *Ramírez at Av. Granaderos.*

OFF THE BEATEN PATH

Chuquicamata. The trucks never stop rolling and the machinery never stops grinding at Chuquicamata, the world's biggest open-pit mine, located just outside of Calama. Nine-hundred workers split three eight-hour shifts, digging, transporting, and processing the metal on which Chile runs.

When visiting, you are dwarfed by the sheer scale of "Chuqui," as locals call it: it's 5 km (3 miles) long, 2 km (1 mile) wide, and 1 km (1/2 mile) deep. It takes any of the 96 trucks, some of which have beds 12 meters (39 feet) wide, a half hour to navigate the winding road to the bottom of the pit. The monstrous German-made trucks cost a pretty penny, about $4 million, and are refueled by pressure-hoses in the same way Formula One cars are gassed up. After all, a 4,000-liter (1,000-gallon) tank could take a while to fill the conventional way. Even the tires cost about $20,000 apiece. Because they run night and day, the trucks require constant maintenance and generally only about 80 are in operation at any one time. The most modern cranes can shovel out up to 50 tons of rock at a time and require a single operator, while in years gone by 20-ton cranes required a crew of 12.

Stare into the vast pit of Chuquicamata and you'll be convinced that Chile uncovered untold riches below the barren Atacama Desert. But after decades of mining, production has fallen sharply due to structural problems and lower copper content. As the mine becomes too deep to exploit profitably, the industry is looking into other reserves and resources, most especially lithium mines, of which Chile currently has the world's largest reserves.

There is a small museum at the mine's entrance where you can get a close-up view of the machinery used to make such big holes. Tours are in Spanish and English. Reserve in advance by phone or by email. It's about a 20-minute taxi ride (5,000 pesos) from downtown Calama. ⊠ *16 km (10 miles) north of Calama* ☎ *55/232–2122* ⊕ *www.codelco. cl* ✉ *By donation* ⊗ *No tours weekends.*

Museo Historia Natural de Calamau. This small museum in El Loa Park has artifacts from Calama's history and pre-Columbian times. ⊠ *Parque El Loa (O'Higgins)* ✉ *500 pesos.*

WHERE TO EAT

$$$
CHILEAN

✕**Patagonia.** Decked with historic memorabilia, Patagonia is best known for its steak—large slices of steaming beef, cooked on the grill. Most people don't stray too far from the classics and it's probably best not to, as this is what Patagonia does best. **Known for:** huge, juicy steaks grilled to perfection; wooden decor; nice wine and beer lists. $ *Average main: 12000 pesos* ⊠ *Granaderos 2549* ☎ *55/234–1628* ⊗ *No dinner Sun.*

WHERE TO STAY

$$$
HOTEL

Park Hotel Calama. It's easy to see why international mining consultants frequent this modern hotel. **Pros:** nice swimming pool; relaxing lounge; comfortable rooms and beds. **Cons:** nothing within walking

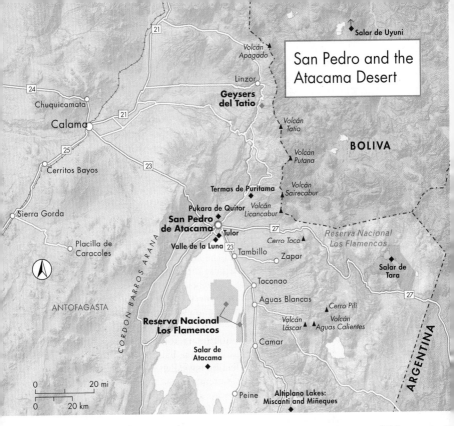

San Pedro and the
Atacama Desert

Salar de Uyuni

Volcán Apagado

Linzor

Geysers del Tatio

Chuquicamata

Calama

Cerritos Bayos

Volcán Tatio

Volcán Putana

BOLIVA

Termas de Puritama

Volcán Sairecabur

Pukara de Quitor

Volcán Licancabur

San Pedro de Atacama

Tulor

Valle de la Luna

Cerro Toco

Reserva Nacional Los Flamencos

Tambillo

Zapar

Salar de Tara

Sierra Gorda

Placilla de Caracoles

ANTOFAGASTA

CORDON BARROS ARANA

Reserva Nacional Los Flamencos

Toconao

Aguas Blancas

Cerro Pili

Volcán Láscar

Volcán Aguas Calientes

Camar

Salar de Atacama

ARGENTINA

0   20 mi
0   20 km

Peine

Altiplano Lakes: Miscanti and Miñeques

distance; some street noise; no air-conditioning in rooms. $ *Rooms from: 86000 pesos* ✉ *Alcalde Jose Lira 1392* ☎ *55/271–5800* ⊕ *www. parkcalama.cl* ➥ *108 rooms* ⦿ *Breakfast.*

SAN PEDRO AND THE ATACAMA DESERT

It might seem to be a strange phenomenon that the world's driest desert has become one of Chile's greatest tourist attractions; when you fly into the region and see the barren, scorched earth below, it's tempting to tell the pilot to turn back around and head to the lush central valleys and crystal-blue seas of Chile instead. But those who do traverse into the wilderness of the Atacama Desert are rewarded with otherworldly landscapes, a tapestry of colorful fauna and flora, and extraordinary night skies. San Pedro de Atacama sits in the heart of the Atacama Desert, where a string of towering volcanoes, some of which are still active, stands watch to the east. To the west is La Cordillera de Sal, a mountain range composed almost entirely of salt. Here you'll find such marvels as the Valle de la Luna (Valley of the Moon) and the Valle de la Muerte (Valley of Death), part of the Reserva Nacional Los Flamencos. The desolate Salar de Atacama, Chile's largest salt flat, lies to the south. The number of attractions in the Atacama area does not end there:

alpine lakes, steaming geysers, colonial villages, and ancient fortresses all lie within easy reach.

The area's history goes back to pre-Columbian times, when the Atacameño people scraped a meager living from the fertile delta of the San Pedro River. By 1450 the region had been conquered by the Incas, but their reign was cut short by the arrival of the Europeans. Spanish conquistador Pedro de Valdivia, who eventually seized control of the entire country, camped here in 1540 while waiting for reinforcements. By the 19th century San Pedro had become an important trading center and was a stop for llama trains on their way from the altiplano to the Pacific coast. During the nitrate era, San Pedro was the main resting place for cattle drives from Argentina.

SAN PEDRO DE ATACAMA

100 km (62 miles) southeast of Calama.

Fodor's Choice It is not an exaggeration to call San Pedro de Atacama a once-in-a-★ lifetime destination, as after all, there's nowhere else quite like the Atacama Desert in the entire world. The quiet town of San Pedro is an oasis in the desert in the both literal and metaphorical sense: greenery and rushing irrigation channels give life to this dusty town, and the intriguing community of travelers, artisans, and natives have created a stress-free paradise far removed from the burdens of normal life. Over the last decade San Pedro has exploded in tourism, now offering more than 100 accommodation options, three dozen restaurants, and more tourism operators than you'll care to count.

What is so attractive about San Pedro? For adventurists, it is the opportunity to do high-altitude climbing, sandboarding, and mountain biking. For sightseers, it is the volcano-lined horizon, the salt-encrusted valleys, the clear blue salt lakes dotted with flamingos, and the billowing geysers. And for pleasure seekers, it is simply soaking in the beautiful Atacama sun and landscapes while moving to the San Pedro pace: nice and slow.

GETTING HERE AND AROUND

San Pedro is an hour's bus or car ride from Calama. You can either take the private (50,000 pesos) or shared (12,000 pesos) shuttle services from the airport, or the cheaper option of a bus ride (1,500). There's no need to book in advance. You'll find four shuttle companies as you arrive at the baggage claim in the airport. If you want to take the public bus you'll need to travel into Calama bus station first. Turbus and a few other companies serve San Pedro, and the bus terminal is just a few blocks from downtown at the intersection of Lincacabur and Domingo Atienz. If planning other trips around Chile, there's a Turbus ticket window here.

ESSENTIALS

Visitor Information Sernatur San Pedro de Atacama. ✉ *Toconao at Gustavo LePaige* ☎ *55/285–1420* ⊕ *www.chile.travel.*

TOURS

Every corner you turn in San Pedro, someone is offering a tour. Most of them offer the same classic routes—geysers, flamingos, Valle de la Luna—and all seem to have surprisingly low prices. But if it seems too good to be true, it probably is.

Make sure to ask how many people will be on the tour and how long you will spend at each place. Avoid unlicensed companies or agencies that sell into other company's tours. Try to stick with reputable companies that employ guides who have been in San Pedro long enough to know the best lookout points.

If you don't want to go with a group, hire a private driver and guide. A car and chauffeur should cost around 60,000 pesos per half-day, excluding gas. Ask the tourism office or your hotel for their recommendations.

Atacama Mistica. Focusing on volcano treks, Atacama Mistica takes small groups up volcanoes to peer into craters and enjoy the sweeping views of the desert beneath. Half-day, full-day, and even two-day treks are on their agenda. They also offer trips to Uyuni in Bolivia, stopping at lagoons, hot springs, and salt flats along the way over the three-day excursion. ⊠ *Caracoles 238* ☎ *55/285–1966* ⊕ *www.atacamamistica. cl* 🖃 *From 60000 pesos.*

Cosmo Andino Expediciones. Operating for more than 30 years, Cosmo is one of the most established and reliable tour operators. All guides and drivers are contracted (not freelance) and the vehicles are their own. The classic tours are all covered, although Cosmo prides itself on beating the crowd with earlier start times and spending longer in each location than the other companies. They offer multiple hiking options, as well as a full-day Tara tour where you can enjoy volcanos, llamas, and spectacular views. ⊠ *Caracoles s/n, At Tocapilla* ☎ *55/285–1069* ⊕ *www.cosmoandino.cl* 🖃 *From 16000 pesos.*

TurisTour. This reliable chain has the biggest fleet of vehicles in San Pedro. It offers classic group tours (up to 35 people) that show you to the highlights of San Pedro—the geysers, the salar, Valle de la Luna, and Laguna Cejar. The company also offers a less common half-day archaeological tour, which visits small settlements and a typical farm. Another option is to hire a driver to head into the desert. ⊠ *Caracoles at Calama* ☎ *55/242–4748* ⊕ *www.turistour.cl* 🖃 *From 44,000 pesos.*

EXPLORING

Iglesia San Pedro. To the west of the square is one of the altiplano's largest churches. It was miraculously constructed in 1744 without the use of a single nail—the builders used cactus sinews to tie the roof beams and door hinges. ⊠ *Gustavo Le Paige s/n.*

Pukara de Quitor. Just 3 km (2 miles) north of San Pedro lies this ancient fortress at the entrance to the Valle de Catarpe, which was built in the 12th century to protect the Atacameños from invading Incas. It wasn't the Incas but the Spanish who were the real threat, however. Spanish conquistador Pedro de Valdivia took the fortress by force in 1540. The crumbling buildings were carefully reconstructed in 1981 and declared a national monument in 1982. ⊠ *On road to Valle Catarpe* 🖃 *3000 pesos.*

Tulor. This archaeological site, 9 km (6 miles) southwest of San Pedro, marks the remains of the oldest known civilization in the region. Built around 800 BC, the village of Tulor was home to the Linka Arti people, who lived in small mud huts resembling igloos. The site was uncovered only in the middle of the 20th century, when Jesuit missionary Gustavo Le Paige excavated it from a sand dune. Archaeologists hypothesize that the inhabitants left because of climatic changes and a possible sand storm. Little more about the village's history is known, and only one of the huts has been completely excavated. As one of the well-informed guides will tell you, even this hut is sinking back into the obscurity of the Atacama sand. ⊠ *9 km (6 miles) southwest of San Pedro, then 3 km (2 miles) down road leading to Valle de la Luna* ⌑ *3000 pesos.*

WHERE TO EAT

$$

CHILEAN

Fodor's Choice

★

✕**Baltinache.** Offering "indigenous fusion" food, Baltinache is a unique option in San Pedro. Its daily menu incorporates native ingredients as well as typically Chilean preparations like *curanto* (seafood, meat, and veggies prepared in a hole in the ground), *merkin* (smoked chile peppers), and *la patasca* (pork stew with corn). **Known for:** native cuisine with unusual ingredients; intimate and relaxed charm; hard to find location. Ⓢ *Average main: 9000 pesos* ⊠ *Domingo Atienza, Allyu de Larache* ☎ *9/9871–0103* ⊗ *Closed Mon.*

$$$

LATIN AMERICAN

✕**Café Adobe Restaurante.** One of the most popular restaurants in San Pedro, Adobe gets extra points for its atmospheric fire pit and local Andean band. The food reflects international and local tastes with quesadillas, salads, and pizzas, alongside the calorific Chilean favorite of steak *a la pobre* (topped with fried egg, onions, and fries). **Known for:** cozy outdoor fireplace; Atacama-fusion dishes like roast lamb kofte; pisco sours with local ingredients. Ⓢ *Average main: 13000 pesos* ⊠ *Carcoles 211* ☎ *55/285–1164* ⊗ *No lunch Wed.*

$$

PIZZA

✕**Charrua.** While you may not have come to San Pedro to eat pizza, this busy joint serves respectable thin-crust pies. The restaurant itself is not classy, but if you are looking for a bit of home comfort or takeout for your hotel patio, Charrua is the place. **Known for:** decent pizza; quick meals; small setting. Ⓢ *Average main: 8000 pesos* ⊠ *Tocopilla 442* ☎ *55/285–1443.*

$$

CHILEAN

✕**Delicias de Carmen.** Owner Carmen has managed to attract locals and tourists alike with her immensely popular restaurant that serves affordable, typically Chilean home-style dishes, ranging from soups and stews to roast meats and fish. Warm bread is served with a killer *pebre* (spicy salsa), and the lunch specials are the best value in San Pedro. **Known for:** Chilean comfort food; local favorite; affordable lunches. Ⓢ *Average main: 7000 pesos* ⊠ *Calama 360* ☎ *9/089–5673.*

$$

CHILEAN

✕**Kunza.** This might be a bit out of town, but the volcanic views and delicious Chilean cuisine are worth the trip. Part of the Cumbres Hotel, Kunza is open every day so you can enjoy interesting dishes like guanaco carpaccio, llama jerky, and fish cooked in Atacama salt served with a traditional corn tamale. **Known for:** local cuisine that takes risks; tasty pisco sours; outdoor fire pits great for star-gazing. Ⓢ *Average main: 9000 pesos* ⊠ *Cumbres, Las Chilcas s/n* ☎ *55/285–2136* ⊕ *www.cumbressanpedro.com.*

5

WHERE TO STAY

$$$$
RESORT
Fodor's Choice
★
🏨 **Alto Atacama Desert Lodge & Spa.** No other hotel makes you feel quite as much part of the Atacama Desert landscape as Alto; set in the middle of the Salt Mountains Range (Cordillera de la Sal), this 42-room luxury retreat is a surprising oasis in a desert that seems to extend endlessly in every direction. **Pros:** one-of-a-kind desert escape; excellent facilities; fantastic restaurant and service. **Cons:** expensive; far from town; weak Wi-Fi in rooms. $ *Rooms from: 900000 pesos* ✉ *Camino Pukará, Sector Suchor* ☎ *02/2912–3945* ⊕ *www.altoatacama.com* ⇆ *42 rooms* ❙❖❙ *All-inclusive; Breakfast.*

$$$$
RESORT
🏨 **Cumbres San Pedro de Atacama.** Atacama's largest resort features 60 large and comfortable rooms spread over the vast property, offering peace and privacy, with each room having its own patio looking onto native flora and an indoor/outdoor shower. **Pros:** gorgeous facilities including spa and pools; plenty of excursions offered; private and peaceful rooms. **Cons:** spa can get full; slow service; busy meal times. $ *Rooms from: 251000 pesos* ✉ *Av. Las Chilcas s/n Lote 10, Parcela 2* ☎ *55/285–2160* ⊕ *www.cumbressanpedro.com* ⇆ *63 rooms* ❙❖❙ *All-inclusive; Breakfast.*

$$$$
HOTEL
🏨 **explora Atacama.** This all-inclusive hotel looks more like an estancia or even a stable from the outside, but inside spacious rooms and airy interiors look out onto the volcanoes in the distance and the friendly staff is there to help you plan your excursions in the altiplano and desert. **Pros:** excellent excursions; great pool area; great social scene in bar area. **Cons:** expensive; no Wi-Fi in rooms; restaurant disappointing for price. $ *Rooms from: 900000 pesos* ✉ *Domingo Atienza s/n, Ayllu de Larache* ☎ *2/2395–2800 in Chile, 866/750–6699 in U.S.* ⊕ *www. explora.com/explora-atacama* ⇆ *54 rooms* ❙❖❙ *All-inclusive.*

$$$
HOTEL
FAMILY
🏨 **Hotel Altiplánico.** This hotel village outside the center of San Pedro has the look and feel of a pueblo: a labyrinth of walkways leads you from room to room, which are each constructed with typical mud-color adobe and adorned with private terraces and often outdoor showers. **Pros:** refreshing pool; plenty of privacy; great stargazing at night. **Cons:** long walk from town (no provided transfers); rooms quite dark; noise travels between rooms. $ *Rooms from: 155000 pesos* ✉ *Domingo Atienza 282* ☎ *55/285–1212* ⊕ *www.altiplanico. cl* ⇆ *32 rooms* ❙❖❙ *Breakfast.*

$$$$
HOTEL
🏨 **Lodge Andino Terrantai.** Right behind the main plaza, Terrantai is a real gem combining the historical and modern; the historical part is a 200-year-old colonial house with high cane ceilings supported by entire tree trunks, and the modern part (constructed in 1996) opens out into a maze of river-stone walls with secret fountains and gardens. **Pros:** unique design; great location for walking to the plaza; plenty of homey touches. **Cons:** noise travels; rooms are basic for price; slow Wi-Fi. $ *Rooms from: 187000 pesos* ✉ *Tocopilla 411* ☎ *55/285–1045* ⊕ *www.terrantai.com* ⇆ *21 rooms* ❙❖❙ *Breakfast.*

$$$$
RESORT
🏨 **Tierra Atacama.** This stylish hotel has an imaginative take on design, services, and excursions to give it a touch of luxury and originality without losing that atacameño feel or respect for local places, people, and traditions. **Pros:** down-to-earth luxury; excellent spa; great tours.

Cons: small bathrooms; expensive; communal areas not very inviting. $ *Rooms from: 970000 pesos* ⊠ *Calle Séquitor s/n, Ayllú de Yaye* ☎ *55/555–975* ⊕ *www.tierraatacama.com* ⟿ *32 suites* ⍾ *All-inclusive.*

NIGHTLIFE

The bohemian side of San Pedro gets going after dinner and generally ends around midnight. Afterward, locals move to the outskirts for clandestine raves. There is an increasing problem with trafficked cocaine from Bolivia through San Pedro, so be careful if anyone tries to offer you some. Back in the legal sphere, most of the bars and small cafés are on Caracoles and it is all pretty mellow. Your choices are pretty much limited to whether you want to sit outside by a fire or inside, where it's a bit warmer.

Cervecería St. Peter. If drinking artisanal beers around a warm fire sounds like your ideal night, then head to Cervecería St. Peter where you can try microbrews created used native plants including rica rica and algarrobo. ⊠ *Toconao 479* ☎ *9/4287–9893.*

Chelacabur. Yes, you can find a true pub even in the desert. At Chelacabur, football shirts hang from the mud walls, sports constantly play on the television, and lots of cheap beers are on tap. This place fills up fast on the weekends so be sure to get there early if you want a seat. There's no food on-site, but they let you bring in pizza from the place next door. ⊠ *Caracoles 212* ☎ *9/9489–8191.*

La Estaka. A hippie bar with funky decor, La Estaka has a true local feel. Reggae music rules, and the international food isn't half bad either. ⊠ *Caracoles 259B* ☎ *55/285–1286.*

SPORTS AND THE OUTDOORS

San Pedro is an outdoors lover's dream. There are great places for biking, hiking, and horseback riding in every direction. Extreme-sports enthusiasts can try their hand at sandboarding on the dunes of the Valle de la Muerte. Climbers can take on the nearby volcanoes, which provide an exhilarating high-altitude ascent; the only trouble is the crowds. At the Valle de la Luna, for example, sunset at the large dune is somewhat spoiled by the large tourist vans that dump a couple hundred sightseers there for the renowned sundown. The number of tour agencies and outfitters in San Pedro can be a bit overwhelming: shop around, pick a company you feel comfortable with, ask questions, and make sure the company is willing to cater to your needs.

Whatever your sport, keep in mind that San Pedro lies at 2,400 meters (7,900 feet) above sea level. If you're not acclimated to the high altitude, you'll feel tired much sooner than you might expect, so save excursions to the altiplánico or geysers until your last days. Also, remember to slather on the sunscreen and drink plenty of water.

BIKING

An afternoon ride to the Valle de la Luna is unforgettable, as is a quick trip to the ruins of Tulor, or the Laguna Cejar. Bike rentals can be arranged at most hotels and tour agencies. A bike can be rented for a half day for 5,000 pesos and for an entire day for upward of 10,000 pesos. There are also several bike rentals on offer in the city center (look

around Caracoles and Toconao streets). You can go ride on your own to the local sites (Valle de la Luna, Valley de la Muerte, Tulor, Pukara de Quitor, and Laguna Chaxa), or you can book a bike tour with most of the local tourism agencies. La Bicicleta Verde (⊕ *www.labicicletaverde. com*) offers tours to different local villages. Don't forget sunscreen, sunglasses, a scarf for the dust and wind, and plenty of water.

HIKING

There is fantastic hiking throughout San Pedro, whether you want to spend a half-day trekking the Valle de Luna, an afternoon in the Cactus Valley, or a full day hiking up a volcano.

Lascar Volcano. There are several volcano ascents you can attempt in San Pedro de Atacama, but Lascar is one of the more accessible and rewarding hikes. You'll need a few days of acclimation to the higher altitude to reach the 18,346 foot summit, but the hike isn't particularly rigorous if the weather is on your side. It's always advisable to summit with a group, and most tours will drive you out to just before the start of the summit. This leaves you with a couple hours to reach the summit, where you can peer into the belly of one of northern Chile's most active volcanoes. ⊠ *San Pedro de Atacama.*

Quebrada de Guatin. Informally known as Cactus Valley, the Quebrada de Guatin is a steep gorge where you can follow the Puritama River through the stunning rocky landscape where century-old cacti loom overhead. Don't let the small waterfalls and eagle nests distract you too much; this is a tricky walk with curves, turns, and a couple of jumps between rocks. The most rewarding route is heading uphill and finishing in the Puritama Hot Springs. It takes about three hours (over 3 miles) from the road. ⊠ *San Pedro de Atacama.*

FAMILY **Valle de la Luna and Valle de la Muerte.** This is a popular afternoon and sunset walking spot for when the heat dies down and the colors of the landscape change. Although you have to stick to the paths, there are numerous different tracks through the valleys that will take you away from the busloads of tourists and into complete isolation staring up, or down, at the Cordillera de la Sal (Salt Mountains). You can make this a quick trek or spend a few hours exploring the valleys. ⊠ *San Pedro de Atacama* ⊡ *3000 pesos.*

HORSEBACK RIDING

Atacama Horse. San Pedro has the feeling of a Wild West town, so why not hitch up your horse and head out on an adventure? Although the sun is quite intense during the middle of the day, sunset is a perfect time to visit Pukara de Quitor or Tulor. You can do day rides or multiple day rides and crossings. ⊠ *Tocopilla 406* ☎ *55/285–1956* ⊕ *www.atacama-horseadventure.com* ⊡ *From 23000 pesos per person.*

SANDBOARDING

Sandboarding in the Atacama is surprisingly popular among back-packers, despite the occasional heat rash and painful abrasions. Many agencies offer a three-hour sandboarding excursion into the Valle de la Muerte from 4 pm to 9 pm—the intelligent way to beat the desert heat. These tours run about 15,000 pesos and include an instructor. If you're brave and have your own transportation, you can rent just the board

for 7,000 pesos. There are several combination tours with Valle de la Luna. Since a fall on the sand can be hard, you should wear a helmet and board with caution.

Sandboard San Pedro. One of the more reliable outfitters in town, Sandboard San Pedro offers tours and board for hire, along with experienced guides and proper board boots. ⊠ *Caracoles 362* ☎ *55/2983–669* ⊕ *www.sandboardsanpedro.com.*

STARGAZING

The Atacama Desert is one of the best places for stargazing in the world due to its clear skies, high altitude, and isolation from light pollution. So good is the stargazing here that San Pedro de Atacama is home to one of the world's biggest space ventures, the international ALMA observatory.

While the naked eye is perfectly good for spotting constellations, planets, and shooting stars (there's an average visibility of four every hour here), you shouldn't miss out on an opportunity to look through one of the many powerful telescopes here. Luxury hotels sometimes have their own telescopes and outdoor observatories.

ALMA. The biggest astronomic observatory in the world, ALMA (Atacama Large Millimeter Aray) has 66 antennas that produce imagery of the coldest, most hidden parts of the sky. The public can visit on weekends and see the back-of-house operations in this international observatory, but you must reserve in advance. ⊠ *ALMA* ⊕ *www.alma. cl* ▧ *Free.*

SPACE. SPACE (San Pedro de Atacama Celestial Explorations) offers one of the best astronomical tours in San Pedro. The complete darkness allows you to observe the night sky with the naked eye and through a dozen powerful telescopes. The tour finishes with an astronomy chat over hot chocolate. Popular with backpackers, tours are nightly (weather depending) and depart from the city center with native English-speaking specialist guides. ⊠ *166 Caracoles* ☎ *55/256–6278* ⊕ *www.spaceobs. com* ▧ *From 25000 pesos (includes transport).*

SHOPPING

Just about the entire village of San Pedro is an open-air market. Shopping here is fun, but prices are probably about 20% to 30% higher than in neighboring areas, and you'll find many of the same products: the traditional altiplano ponchos (aka *serapes*), jewelry, and even musical instruments. If you are taking a tour out to some of the smaller villages you might find the same products being sold at a much lower price. Most upscale hotels also have a small shop with high-quality goods, often at an even higher price.

Feria Artesenal. Just off the Plaza de Armas, the Feria Artesenal is bursting at the seams with artisan goods. Here, you can buy high-quality knits from the altiplano, such as sweaters and other woolen items. ⊠ *Off plaza.*

Galería Cultural de Pueblos Andinos. This open-air market sells woolen goods and crafts. ⊠ *Caracoles s/n, east of town.*

Fodor's Choice ★ **Libreria del Desierto.** For a unique literary experience, head out to this eclectic bookshop and library in the small *ayllu* (village) of Solor. It's an hour walk or 20-minute bike ride out of town, but you'll be rewarded with an impressive collection of books in multiple languages, eco-friendly architecture, stunning volcano views, and philosophical conversation with the passionate and intellectual owner, Diego. ⊠ *Calle Volcan Lascar 67, Solor Ayllu* ☎ *9/7749–8473* ⊕ *www.libreriadeldesierto.cl.*

Mallku. This pleasant store carries traditional altiplano textiles, some up to 20 years old. ⊠ *Caracoles 190c* ☎ *55/285–1417.*

GEYSERS DEL TATIO

95 km (59 miles) north of San Pedro.

Fodor's Choice ★ Witnessing the fumaroles at daybreak here is one of the best experiences Chile has to offer. The geysers pump out boiling water throughout the day, and seeing the steam rise against the stark landscapes is breathtaking.

GETTING HERE AND AROUND

El Tatio is open all day for visits, but nearly everyone arrives just before sunrise, when the cold night air gives the steaming geysers an imposing presence. Tour groups depart San Pedro around 4 or 5 am, depending on the time of year. Most tours start with a walk through the geyser field and end with a simple breakfast. Tours usually return to San Pedro at midday.

EXPLORING

Fodor's Choice ★ **Geysers del Tatio.** The world's highest geothermal field, the Geysers del Tatio is a breathtaking natural phenomenon. The sight of dozens of geysers throwing columns of steam into the air is unforgettable. A trip to El Tatio usually begins at 4 or 5 am, on a guided tour, when San Pedro is still cold and dark (any of the tour agencies in San Pedro can arrange this trip). After a two-hour bus ride on a relentlessly bumpy road, you reach the high plateau around daybreak. (The entrance fee is covered if you are on a tour, otherwise it is 10,000 pesos.) The jets of steam are already shooting into the air as the sun slowly peeks over the adjacent cordillera. The rays of light illuminate the steam in a kaleidoscope of chartreuses, violets, reds, oranges, and blues. The vapor then silently falls onto the sulfur-stained crust of the geyser field. As the sun heats the cold, barren land, the visibility and force of the geysers gradually diminish, allowing you to explore the mud pots and craters formed by the escaping steam. Be careful, though—the crust is thin in places and people have died falling into the boiling-hot water. ⊠ *Geysers El Tatio, San Pedro de Atacama* ☎ *10000 pesos.*

Termas de Puritama. On your way back to San Pedro, you may want to stop at the Termas de Puritama hot springs. A hot soak may be just the thing to shake off that early morning chill. A relaxing day trip in itself, the termas are a series of eight pools, each one connected by wooden platforms and surrounded by foliage in the middle of a natural valley that is also a popular hiking area. If you don't have your own transport, you can book a transfer or group tour from many agencies in San Pedro. If you're staying at Hotel Explora, you'll have exclusive access to the first (and warmest) spring. ⊠ *Termas de Puritama, San Pedro de Atacama* ☎ *15000 pesos (discounted after 2 pm).*

RESERVA NACIONAL LOS FLAMENCOS

10 km (6 miles) south and east of San Pedro.

Fodor's Choice ★ In the middle of one of the largest salt flats in the world, crowds of pink flamingos flock to a couple pretty lagoons. While the flamingos often get the most attention, the whole setting is stunning, with volcanoes in the backdrop and vast, white stretches of land that paint a beautiful picture at sunset.

GETTING HERE AND AROUND
Nearly all San Pedro tour companies take you to the Reserva, but if you're in your own vehicle, take the road toward Toconao for 33 km (21 miles) to the park entrance.

ESSENTIALS
CONAF. You can get information about the Reserva Nacional Los Flamencos at the station run by CONAF, the Chilean forestry service. ⊠ *CONAF station near Laguna Chaxa* ⊕ *www.conaf.cl* ✉ *2500 pesos.*

EXPLORING
Altiplánico Lakes: Miscanti and Miñeques. At more than 13,000 feet above sea level, these lakes are in a completely different climate than San Pedro below. The altiplánico has much more moisture in the air and while that means you are likely to experience rain and snow in certain seasons, it also means the area is alive with color and wildlife. The pastel-color backdrop is picture-perfect with the large blue lagoons and volcanoes in the distance. The largest of the lagoons is Miscanti, at 4,350-meter-high (14,270-foot-high), which merits a few moments of contemplation and is one of the prettiest spots in Atacama (on a sunny day). The smaller lake, Miñeques, is equally spectacular and is home to wildlife like vicuña and huge flocks of flamingos. The altiplánico lakes are usually a full-day excursion from San Pedro. ⊠ *Laguna Miscanti, San Pedro de Atacama* ✉ *3000 pesos.*

Fodor's Choice ★ **Reserva Nacional Los Flamencos.** Many of the most astounding sights in El Norte Grande lie within the boundaries of the protected Reserva Nacional Los Flamencos. This sprawling national reserve to the south and east of San Pedro encompasses a wide variety of geographical features, including alpine lakes, salt flats, and volcanoes. And of course, here is where you will find the most stunning collection of pink flamingos on the planet.

Fodor's Choice ★ **Salar de Atacama.** About 10 km (6 miles) south of San Pedro you arrive at the edge of Chile's largest salt flat. The rugged crust measuring 3,000 square km (1,158 square miles) formed when salty water flowing down from the Andes evaporated in the stifling heat of the desert. Unlike other salt flats, which are smooth surfaces of crystalline salt, the Salar de Atacama is a jumble of jagged rocks that look rather like coral. **Laguna Chaxa,** in the middle of Salar de Atacama, is a very salty lagoon that is home to three of the New World's four species of flamingos. The elegant pink-and-white birds are mirrored by the lake's glassy surface. Near Laguna Chaxa, beautiful plates of salt float on the calm surface of **Laguna Salada.** Visiting the salar is a half-day excursion from San Pedro and often better at sunset when the sky can paint pretty pink colors, reflected in the

5

mirrorlike lagoons. Arrive early before the crowds scare off the birds, and bring your binoculars. ⊠ *Laguna Chaxa, San Pedro de Atacama.*

Salar de Tara. More than 14,000 feet high, Salar de Tara has some similarities to the Altiplánico Lakes, but what makes it unique is the unusual rock formations that appear like castles in the sky, surreal sculptures among the sand flats, and flamingo-spotted lagoons. It is a full day from San Pedro on the way to Bolivia, and involves a long and bumpy road both ways. ⊠ *Salar de Tara, San Pedro de Atacama.*

Fodor's Choice   **Valle de la Luna.** This surreal landscape of barren ridges, soaring cliffs, ★   sand dunes, and pale valleys could be from a canvas by Salvador Dalí. Originally a small corner of a vast inland sea, the valley rose up with the Andes. The water slowly drained away, leaving deposits of salt and gypsum that were folded by the shifting of the Earth's crust and then worn away by wind and rain. The vastness and grandeur of some of the formations is quite breathtaking, and listening carefully to the cracking of the salt crystals as the sun warms up and cools down the surfaces is quite awe-inspiring. Visiting the Valle de la Luna is fabulous at sunset, although this is also when truckloads of tourists arrive, so if you want the valley to yourself visit in the morning when there is barely a soul there. You can visit by car, by bike (bring a big hat for shade!), or horseback. ⊠ *14 km (9 miles) west of San Pedro, San Pedro de Atacama* ☜ *3000 pesos.*

Valle de la Muerte. Not far from the Valle de la Luna, just on the other side of Ruta 98 leading to Calama, are the reddish rocks of the Valle de la Muerte (Death Valley). Jesuit missionary Gustavo Le Paige, who in the 1950s was the first archaeologist to explore this desolate area, discovered many human skeletons. These bones are from the indigenous Atacameño people, who lived here before the arrival of the Spanish. He hypothesized that the sick and the elderly may have come to this place to die. The name of the valley comes from its Mars-like, red appearance and was originally called Valle de Martes (Mars Valley), but Gustavo's foreign pronunciation of Martes (Mars) was heard as Muerte (dead). ⊠ *San Pedro de Atacama* ☜ *3000 pesos.*

OFF THE BEATEN PATH   **Salar de Uyuni.** It's possible to take a three- to five-day, four-wheel-drive organized tour from San Pedro into Bolivia's massive and mysterious salt flat, the largest in the world. Beware: the accommodations—usually clapboard lodgings in small oasis towns—are rustic to say the least, but speeding along the Salar de Uyuni, which is chalkboard flat, is a treat. Nearby are geysers, small Andean lagoons, and islands of cactus that stand in sharp contrast to the sealike salt flat.

IQUIQUE AND NEARBY

The waterside town of Iquique itself is rather dreary, but the area holds many sights that merit a visit. Wander down to the port and *muelles* (fishing piers) and watch the fishing boats come in; while you're there, imagine the key battle of the War of the Pacific being waged offshore in 1879, or Sir Francis Drake and his gang of brigands arriving to sack the town in 1577. You can find out more about this history at the Museo Naval.

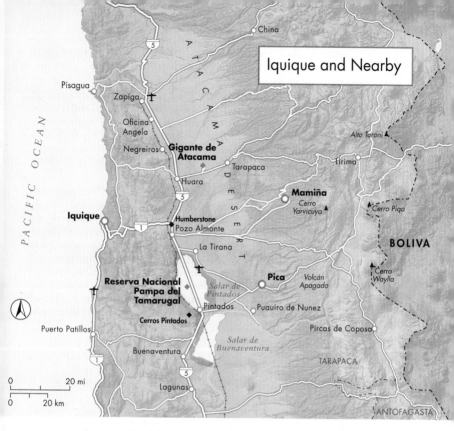

A stone's throw from Iquique, nitrate ghost towns like Humberstone sit in eternal silence. Farther inland you encounter the charming hot-spring oases of Pica and Mamiña and the enigmatic Gigante de Atacama, the world's largest geoglyph.

IQUIQUE

390 km (242 miles) northwest of Calama.

Iquique is the capital of Chile's northernmost region, but it wasn't always so important. For hundreds of years it was a tiny fishing community. After the arrival of the Spanish, the village grew slowly into a port. The population, however, never totaled more than 100. It was not until the great nitrate boom of the 19th century that Iquique became a major port. Many of those who grew rich on nitrate moved to the city and built opulent mansions, almost all of which still stand today. Many of the old mansions are badly in need of repair, however, giving the city a rather worn-down look. The boom went bust, and those who remained turned again to the sea to make a living. Today Iquique is the world's largest exporter of fishmeal.

At the base of a coastal mountain range, Iquique is blessed with year-round good weather. This may explain why it's popular with vacationing

Chilean families, who come for the long stretches of white beaches as well as the *zona franca,* or duty-free zone.

GETTING HERE AND AROUND

Iquique's Diego Aracena airport (IQQ) is about 45 minutes from downtown proper (35 km [22 miles]; 17,000 pesos in taxi fare) and is served by the country's two major airlines: Sky and LATAM. Iquique is about seven hours via bus or car from Calama (400 km [249 miles]); once you've turned off the Pan-American Highway it's a narrow, serpentine road down to the town, so don't try passing any of the big trucks or other vehicles that may be slowing you down.

The tourist sights of Mamiña, Pica, and the Gigante de Atacama can all be done in one day's driving, and if you don't want to drive yourself, tour companies in town offer all-inclusive tours. There are two official taxi stands, one on Plaza Prat and one on the pedestrian street of Baquedano. Both will quote you rates to and from the airport, as well as day tours to nearby sites like the Gigante de Atacama, Humberstone, and Mamiña. To get to Pica, La Tirana, and the surrounding sights from Iquique, head south on Ruta 5 (Pan-American Highway) to Km 1,800 (Cruce Sara). Then head east on Ruta 685. As for rental cars, the best deals are in Iquique, but cars rented here can't be taken out of the area.

Air Travel Diego Aracena Airport (IQQ). ☎ *57/247–3473.*

ESSENTIALS

Visitor Information Sernatur Iquique. ✉ *Aníbal Pinto 436* ☎ *57/231–2238* ⊕ *www.sernatur.cl.*

TOURS

Avitours. Offering full- or multiday tours to local attractions like Isluga Volcano, the Pampa Calichera, and Humberstone, Avitours can also organize paragliding over Iquique. ✉ *Patricio Lynch 563* ☎ *9/7861–6806* ⊕ *www.avitours.cl* 🎫 *From 25,000 pesos.*

EXPLORING

Calle Baquedano. Leading out from Plaza Prat is this pedestrian mall with wooden sidewalks. This is a great place for an afternoon stroll past some of Iquique's *salitrera*-era mansions or for a leisurely cappuccino in one of the many sidewalk cafés. An antique trolley runs the length of the mall. ✉ *Iquique.*

Museo Corbeta Esmeralda. Located on a beautifully maintained historical naval ship, this museum is a highlight in Iquique as the long lines will tell you. Professional and passionate guides detail the inner workings of the ship and its important role in Chile's history and the 1879 battle of the War of the Pacific. ✉ *49 Av. Arturo Prat Chacón* ☎ *57/253–0812* ⊕ *www.museoesmeralda.cl* 🎫 *3500 pesos* ⊗ *Closed Mon. in Mar.–Dec.*

Museo Regional. Along the historic Calle Baquedano is this natural-history museum of the region. It showcases pre-Columbian artifacts such as deformed skulls and arrowheads, as well as an eclectic collection from the region's nitrate heyday. ✉ *Baquedano 951* ☎ *57/253–654* 🎫 *Free* ⊗ *Closed Sun.*

Palacio Astoreca. For a tantalizing view into the opulence of the nitrate era, visit this Georgian-style palace. Built in 1903, it includes highlights

CLOSE UP

Geoglyphs of the Atacama Desert

In addition to the Gigante de Atacama, the world's largest geoglyph at 86 meters (282 feet) high, there are geoglyphs throughout El Norte Grande. The rock art at Cerros Pintados comprises the largest collection of geoglyphs in South America. More than 400 images adorn this hill in Reserva Nacional Pampa del Tamarugal. Figures representing birds, animals, people, and geometric patterns appear to dance along the hill. Farther north, the Tiliviche

geoglyphs decorate a hill sitting not far from the modern-day marvel of the Pan-American Highway. These geoglyphs, most likely constructed between AD 1000 and 1400 during the Inca reign, depict a large caravan of llamas. All of these llamas are headed in the same direction—toward the sea—a testament, perhaps, to the geoglyphs' navigational use during the age when llama trains brought silver down to the coast in exchange for fish.

such as the likeness of Dionysus, the Greek god of revelry; a giant billiard table; and a beautiful skylight over the central hall. An art- and natural-history museum on the upper level houses rotating exhibitions by Chilean artists and artifacts such as pottery and textiles. ⊠ *Av. Bernardo O'Higgins 350* ☎ *57/242–5600* ⊠ *Free* ⊗ *Closed Mon.*

Plaza Prat. Life in the city revolves around this plaza, where children ride bicycles along the sidewalks and adults chat on nearly every park bench. The 1877 **Torre Reloj,** with its gleaming white clock tower and Moorish arches, stands in the center of the plaza. ⊠ *Iquique.*

Teatro Municipal. Unlike most cities, Iquique does not have a cathedral on the main plaza. Instead, you'll find the sumptuous Teatro Municipal, built in 1890 as an opera house. The lovely statues on the Corinthian-columned facade represent the four seasons. ⊠ *Plaza Prat* ☎ *57/241–1292* ⊠ *Free.*

BEACHES

Playa Blanca. Thirteen km (8 miles) south of the city center on Avenida Balmaceda, Playa Blanca is a sandy spot that you can often have all to yourself and enjoy the active sealife. **Amenities:** food and drink; parking. **Best for:** snorkeling; swimming. ⊠ *Iquique.*

Playa Brava. If you crave privacy, head south on Avenida Balmaceda to Playa Brava, a pretty beach that's often deserted except for young people lighting bonfires in the evening. The currents here are quite strong, so swimming is not recommended. **Amenities:** parking; food and drink; toilets. **Best for:** sunset; surfing. ⊠ *Iquique.*

FAMILY

Fodor's Choice

★

Playa Cavancha. Just south of the city center on Avenida Balmaceda is Playa Cavancha, a long stretch of white, sandy beach that's great for families and often crowded. You can stroll along the boardwalk and touch the llamas and alpacas at the petting zoo. There's also a walk-through aquarium housing a group of *yacares,* small crocodiles that inhabit the rivers of Bolivia, Argentina, and Uruguay. **Amenities:** food and drink; showers; toilets. **Best for:** partiers; surfing; swimming. ⊠ *Iquique.*

WHERE TO EAT

$ ✕ **Cafe Cioccolatá.** Chock-full of espresso drinks and cakes, you'll also find
CAFÉ specialty concoctions like Café Verdi, Café Rossini, the "Rolling Stone,"
FAMILY and the "Monkie." This is a good people-watching spot with decent snacks
as well. **Known for:** tasty and affordable cakes; hearty sandwiches; great
coffee. ⑤ *Average main: 3000 pesos* ⊠ *Anibal Pinto 487* ☎ *57/253–2290.*

$$$ ✕ **Casino Español.** This venerable gentleman's club on Plaza Prat has been
SPANISH transformed into a palatial Spanish restaurant, with beautiful Moorish
architecture that calls to mind the Alhambra in Granada. The service is
good, though rather fussy, and the food is extravagant in the traditional
Andalucian style. **Known for:** Spanish-style dishes like paella; ornate
decor; excellent pisco sours. ⑤ *Average main: 12000 pesos* ⊠ *Plaza Prat
584* ⊕ *www.casinoespanoliquique.cl* ⊗ *Closed Mon. No dinner Sun.*

$$$ ✕ **Club Nautico Cavancha.** Located away from the center of the city, this
SEAFOOD seafood restaurant treats you to views of Playa Cavancha. Try the sole
in Cleopatra sauce, with shrimp, capers, and olive oil; the Thai-style
sautéed shrimp; or the paella for two, served by friendly bow-tied waiters. **Known for:** great views; local seafood; hearty stews. ⑤ *Average
main: 12000 pesos* ⊠ *Los Rieles 110* ☎ *57/231–1456.*

$$ ✕ **La Mulata.** This hip eatery creatively combines Peruvian, Japanese,
PERUVIAN and Chilean flavors in dishes served straight on the waterfront. You can
Fodor'sChoice expect Chilean classics like ceviche and empanadas as well as Peruvian
★ and Nikkea staples of *lomo saltado*and rich seafood broth. **Known for:**
Asian and Southern American fusion dishes; sunset views; top-notch
cocktails. ⑤ *Average main: 9000 pesos* ⊠ *Av. Arturo Prat Chacon 902*
☎ *57/247–3727* ⊕ *www.lamulata.cl* ⊗ *No lunch Sun.*

$$ ✕ **Neptuno.** When the doors open at lunchtime, locals fill this seafood
SEAFOOD lovers' paradise for tasty dishes including swordfish ceviche, mussels in
green sauce, and a *marinera,* a seafood stew. A large selection of Chilean
wines complements the food. **Known for:** fresh seafood and must-try
seafood stew; local Chilean wine list; nautical decor. ⑤ *Average main:
9000 pesos* ⊠ *Riquelme 234* ☎ *57/232–3264.*

WHERE TO STAY

$$ ⊡ **Hotel Terrado Arturo Prat.** In the heart of Iquique's historic district, the
HOTEL highlight of this modern hotel is a very pleasant rooftop pool area deco-
rated with white umbrellas and navy-blue sails. **Pros:** central location;
friendly staff; lovely pool area. **Cons:** noise from plaza travels; some rooms
nicer than others; small gym. ⑤ *Rooms from: 58000 pesos* ⊠ *Anibal Pinto
695* ☎ *600/582–0500* ⊕ *www.terrado.cl* ⇆ *175 rooms* ⊙⃝ *Breakfast.*

$ ⊡ **Sunfish.** On Playa Cavancha, Sunfish has large, modern rooms,
HOTEL many with views of the beach. **Pros:** close to the beach; rooftop pool;
good breakfast. **Cons:** outdated decor; rooms lack character; disap-
pointing restaurant. ⑤ *Rooms from: 48500 pesos* ⊠ *Amunategui 1990*
☎ *57/254–1000* ⊕ *www.sunfish.cl* ⇆ *75 rooms* ⊙⃝ *Breakfast.*

$$$ ⊡ **Terrado Suites.** A skyscraper at the southern end of Playa Cavan-
HOTEL cha, the Terrado is in a great location for Iquique. **Pros:** everything
you'd need in one place; on the beach with pool; good breakfast.
Cons: poor Wi-Fi; pricey restaurant; a bit run-down. ⑤ *Rooms from:
88500 pesos* ⊠ *Los Rieles 126* ☎ *600/582–0500* ⊕ *www.terrado.cl*
⇆ *98 rooms* ⊙⃝ *Breakfast.*

NIGHTLIFE

Iquique really gets going after dark. Young vacationers stay out all night and then spend the next day lazing around on the beach.

BARS

Bar Sovia. This bar is popular with a wide range of ages thanks to live music, dancing, and lots of different beers on tap. ⊠ *Vivar 1406* ☎ *57/242–1373.*

Runas-Valhalla. Runas (also known as Valhalla) caters to the 30-plus crowd with DJs and live bands playing rock music. They also serve monster burgers. Thursday is karaoke night. ⊠ *Arturo Prat 2996* ☎ *9/7388–8831.*

SHOPPING

Zona Franca. Many Chileans come to Iquique with one thing on their minds—shopping. About 3 km (2 miles) north of the city center is the Zona Franca—known to locals as the Zofri—the only duty-free zone in the country's northern tip. This big, unattractive mall is stocked with cheap cigarettes, alcohol, and electronic goods. Remember that large purchases, such as personal computers, are taxable upon leaving the country. ⊠ *Av. Salitrera Victoria* ☎ *57/515–100* ⊕ *www.zofri.cl.*

EN ROUTE

Humberstone. One of the last nitrate plants in the region, Humberstone closed in 1960 after operating for nearly 200 years. Now it's a ghost town where ancient machines creak and groan in the wind. You can wander through the central square and along the streets of the company town, where almost all of the original buildings survive. The theater, with its rows of empty seats, is particularly eerie. ⊠ *45 km (28 miles) east of Iquique on the Pan-American Hwy.* 🎟 *4000 pesos.*

MAMIÑA

125 km (78 miles) east of Iquique.

An oasis cut from the brown desert, the tiny village of Mamiña has hundreds of hot springs. Renowned throughout Chile for their curative powers, these springs draw people from around the region. Every hotel in town has the thermal water pumped into its rooms, so you can enjoy a soak in the privacy of your own *tina,* or bathtub. The valley also has several public pools fed by thermal springs. The town itself is perched on a rocky cliff above a terraced green valley where locals grow alfalfa.

GETTING HERE AND AROUND

Mamiña is 125 km (78 miles) from Iquique proper: go back to Ruta 5, and head south briefly before taking Ruta A-65 directly east into Mamiña. If you'd also like to see Tambillo (a resting spot on the Inca trail), take the turnoff for Ruta A-651. There are also (admittedly uncomfortable) minivans that head to Mamiña from Iquique.

EXPLORING

Most directions in town are given in relation to the Mamiña bottling plant, which produces the popular mineral drinking water sold in many Chilean shops.

Iglesia Nuestra Señora del Rosario. This simple and charming church in the central plaza dates to 1632. The church's twin bell towers are unique in Andean Chile. A garish electric sign mars the front of the building. ⊠ *Mamiña.*

Termas Mamiña. Ipla is the hottest of the *termas* (thermal baths) with a direct channel of thermal water practically going straight to the large public baths. The Barros El Chino is where you can relax covered in therapeutic mud, bake it off on the drying rack, and then wash clean in the plunge pools. There are basic changing facilities, showers, and a snack bar. ⊠ *Near Mamiña bottler* ☜ *2000 pesos.*

Vertiente del Radium. This fountain near the Baños Ipla has slightly radioactive spring water (because it occurs naturally, it's fine to bathe in but not drink), that is said to cure every type of eye malady. ⊠ *Mamiña.*

PICA

114 km (71 miles) southeast of Iquique.

From a distance, Pica appears to be a mirage. This oasis cut from the gray and brown sand of the Atacama Desert is known for its fruit—the limes used to make pisco sours are grown here. A hint of citrus hangs in the air because the town's chief pleasure is sitting in the Plaza de Armas and sipping a *jugo natural,* fresh-squeezed juice of almost any fruit imaginable, including mangoes, oranges, pears, and grapes. You can buy a bag of any of those from a vendor for the bus trip back to Iquique.

EXPLORING

Cocha Resbaladero. Most people come to Pica not for the town itself but for the incredible hot springs at Chocha Resbaladero. Tropical green foliage surrounds this lagoonlike pool cut out of the rock, and nearby caves beckon to be explored. It is quite a walk, about 2 km (1 mile) north of town, but well worth the effort. You can also drive here or catch a bus from town. ⊠ *Gen. Ibañez* ☜ *3000 pesos* ☉ *Closed Wed.*

WHERE TO EAT

$ ✕ **El Pomelo.** You'll find simple, homemade food at good prices here at
CHILEAN El Pomelo. The fresh juices are particularly worth trying. **Known for:** tasty fresh juices; good value Chilean food; large portions. ⑤ *Average main: 5000 pesos* ⊠ *Maipu, at Bolivar* ☎ *9/9894–3134.*

$$ ✕ **Yatiri.** Abundant dishes of northern Chilean cuisine at Yatiri make for
CHILEAN a great and affordable meal in Pica. Expect roast meats, colorful salads, and fresh seafood. **Known for:** standard northern Chilean cuisine; rich stews; friendly service. ⑤ *Average main: 6000 pesos* ⊠ *Balmaceda 319* ☎ *57/226–0368.*

RESERVA NACIONAL PAMPA DEL TAMARUGAL

96 km (60 miles) southeast of Iquique.

This large forest in the middle of the desert is a unique sight. One of the highlights of the Reserva is the enormous geoglyphs that were created 500–1,500 years ago in the Cerros Pintados.

GETTING HERE AND AROUND

From Iquique, drive to the Pan-American Highway and head south. The entrance, which is 2 km east of the highway, lies 24 km (15 miles) south of Pozo Almonte.

EXPLORING

Fodor'sChoice **Cerros Pintados** (*Painted Hills*). The amazing Cerros Pintados, the larg-
★ est group of geoglyphs in the world, within the Reserva Nacional Pampa del Tamarugal are well worth a detour. These figures, which scientists believe helped ancient peoples navigate the desert, date from AD 500 to 1400. They are also quite enormous—some of the figures are decipherable only from the air. Drawings of men wearing ponchos were probably intended to point out the route to the coast to the llama caravans coming from the Andes. More than 400 figures of birds, animals, and geometric patterns adorn this 4-km (3-mile) stretch of desert. There is a CONAF kiosk on a dirt road 2 km (1 mile) west of the Pan-American Highway. ⊠ *45 km (28 miles) south of Pozo Almonte* ☎ *57/275–1055* ☞ *4000 pesos.*

Reserva Nacional Pampa del Tamarugal. The tamarugo tree is an anomaly in the almost lifeless desert. These bushlike plants survive where most would wither because they are especially adapted to the saline soil of the Atacama. Over time they developed extensive root systems that search for water deep beneath the almost impregnable surface. Reserva Nacional Pampa del Tamarugal has dense groves of tamarugos, which were almost wiped out during the nitrate era when they were felled for firewood. At the entrance to this reserve is a CONAF station. ⊠ *24 km (15 miles) south of Pozo Almonte on Pan-American Hwy* ☎ *57/275–1055* ☞ *Free.*

GIGANTE DE ATACAMA

84 km (52 miles) northeast of Iquique.

Although there are more than 5,000 geoglyphs in the Atacama, this one is the most iconic. The Gigante de Atacama is an 86-meter depiction of a giant man (or perhaps Pachamama, otherwise known as Mother Earth) that looks like a computer-game character from the 1980s. Of course, this geoglyph is far older—most likely dating back to 900 AD—and was created by the area's indigenous peoples.

GETTING HERE AND AROUND

To get here from Iquique, head north on Ruta 5, take Ruta A-483 toward Chusmiza (east), then turn west at Huara and travel for 14 km (8 miles).

EXPLORING

Fodor'sChoice **Gigante de Atacama.** The world's largest geoglyph, the Gigante de Atac-
★ ama, measures an incredible 86 meters (282 feet). The Atacama Giant, thought to represent a chief of an indigenous people or perhaps created in honor of Pachamama (Mother Earth), looks a bit like a video game space alien. It is adorned with a walking staff, a cat mask, and a feathered headdress that resembles rays of light bursting from his head. The exact age of the figure is unknown, but it certainly hails from before the arrival of the Spanish, perhaps around AD 900. The

geoglyph, which is on a hill, is best viewed just before dusk, when the long shadows make the outline clearer. ⊠ *Cerro Unita, 14 km (8 miles) west of turnoff to Chusmiza* 🖂 *Free.*

ARICA AND NEARBY

At the very tip of Chile, Arica is the country's northernmost city, and a pleasant community on a rocky coast that once belonged to Peru. In 1880, during the War of the Pacific, Chilean soldiers stormed El Morro, a fortress set high atop a cliff in Arica. Three years later, much of the land north of Antofagasta that was once part of Peru and Bolivia, belonged to Chile. Though the Arica of today is fervently Chilean, you can still see the Peruvian influence in the streets and market stalls of the city. Indigenous women still sell their goods and produce in the town's colorful markets.

Inland from Arica, the Valle Azapa cuts its way up into the mountains, a strip of green in a land of brown. Here, the excellent Museo Arqueológico de San Miguel de Azapa contains the world's oldest mummies. They were left behind by the Chinchorro people who inhabited Chile's northern coast during pre-Hispanic times. Ascending farther up the mountains toward the Bolivian border you pass through the pleasant indigenous communities of Socoroma and Putre. These towns, though far from picturesque, are good resting points if you're planning to make the journey to the 4,000-meter-high (13,120-foot-high) Parque Nacional Lauca and the neighboring Reserva Nacional Las Vicuñas. The beautiful Lago Chungará, part of Parque Nacional Lauca, lies near Bolivia, creating what is probably the country's most impressive border crossing.

ARICA

301 km (187 miles) north of Iquique.

Arica boasts that it is "the land of the eternal spring," but its temperate climate and beaches are not the only reason to visit this small city. Relax for an hour or two on the Plaza 21 de Mayo. Walk to the pier and watch the pelicans and sea lions trail the fishing boats as the afternoon's catch comes in. Walk to the top of the Morro and imagine battles of days gone by, or wonder at the magnitude of modern shipping as Chilean goods leave the port below by container ship.

GETTING HERE AND AROUND

Arica is a true international crossroads: planes arrive daily from Santiago (via Sky and LATAM airlines), buses pull in from La Paz, and colectivos laden with four passengers head in both directions for Tacna and the Peruvian border. The airport is about 15 minutes north of town (a taxi fare is about 7,000 pesos). The bus terminal is a quick five-minute taxi ride to downtown. Vans leave in the morning from Patricio Lynch if you want a local's experience of getting to Putre; you can also take colectivos there for a bargain rate (about US$1) to the museum out in Azapa Valley (a 15- to 20-minute ride). Arica is about four or five hours north of Iquique by auto or bus (300 km [187 miles]).

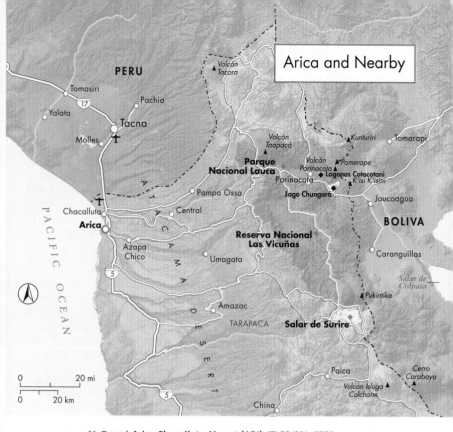

Air Travel Arica Chacalluta Airport (ARI). ☏ 58/221-2773.

ESSENTIALS

Visitor Information Sernatur, Chilean Tourism. ✉ San Marcos 101 ☏ 58/225-2054.

TOURS

Geotour. This well-respected agency arranges trips from Arica to Parque Nacional Lauca, the Salar de Surire, and the Reserva Nacional Las Vicuñas. ✉ *Bolognesi 421* ☏ *58/225-3927* ⊕ *www.geotour.cl* ✉ *From 50000 pesos.*

EXPLORING

Aduana de Arica. Across from the Parque General Baquedano, the Aduana de Arica, the city's former customs house, is one of Alexandre Gustave Eiffel's creations. It currently contains the town's cultural center, where you can find exhibits about northern Chile, old photographs of Arica, and works by local painters and sculptors. ✉ *Arica* ✉ *Free.*

El Morro de Arica. Hanging over the town, this fortress is impossible to ignore. This former Peruvian stronghold was the site of one of the key battles in the War of the Pacific. The fortress now houses the **Museo de las Armas**, which commemorates that battle. As you listen to the proud drum roll of military marches, you can wander among

the uniforms and weapons of past wars. ✉ *Reached by footpath from Calle Colón* 🎫 *600 pesos.*

Estacíon Ferrocarril. North of Parque General Baquedano is the defunct train station for the Arica–La Paz railroad. Though trains no longer run across the mountains to the Bolivian capital, there are round-trip journeys four times a week to the altiplano. The 1913 building houses a small museum with a locomotive and other remnants of the railroad. ✉ *Arica* 🎫 *Free.*

Iglesia de San Marcos. Located on the Plaza Colón, the Iglesia de San Marcos was erected in 1876 and constructed entirely from iron. Alexandre Gustave Eiffel, designer of that famed eponymous Parisian tower, had the individual pieces cast in France before bringing them to Arica. ✉ *Arica.*

Fodor'sChoice
★ **Museo Arqueológico de San Miguel de Azapa.** A visit here is a must for anyone who travels to El Norte Grande. In an 18th-century olive oil refinery, this museum houses an impressive collection of artifacts from the cultures of the Chinchorros (a coastal people) and Tijuanacotas (a group that lived in the antiplano). Of particular interest are the Chinchorro mummies, the oldest in the world, dating to 6000 BC. The incredibly well-preserved mummies are arranged in the fetal position, which was traditional in this area. To look into their wrinkled, expressive faces is to get a glimpse at a history that spans more than 8,000 years. The tour ends at an olive press that functioned until 1956, a reminder of the still thriving industry in the surrounding valley. The museum is a short drive from Arica. You can also make the 20-minute journey by colectivo from Patricio Lynch for about 1,200 pesos. ✉ *12 km (7 miles) south of town en route to Putre* 📞 *58/220–5555* 🌐 *masma. uta.cl* 🎫 *2000 pesos.*

Fodor'sChoice
★ **Museo del Mar.** This museum houses a well-maintained and colorful collection of more than 1,000 seashells and oceanic oddities from around the world. The owner has traveled the globe for more than 30 years to bolster his collection, which includes specimens from Africa, Asia, and you guessed it—Arica. ✉ *Sangra 315* 📞 *9/6909–5863* 🌐 *www. museodelmardearica.cl* 🎫 *2000 pesos* 🕑 *Closed Sun.*

BEACHES

Part of the reason people flock to Arica is the beaches. The surf can be quite rough in some spots, so look for—and heed—signs that say "no apta para bañarse" ("no swimming").

Playa Brava. The long stretch of Playa Brava is renowned for its consistent waves (which are too strong for swimming) and beautiful sunsets. **Amenities:** parking. **Best for:** solitude; sunset; surfing. ✉ *Arica.*

FAMILY **Playa Chinchorro.** The white sands of Playa Chinchorro, 2 km (1 mile) north of the city are popular with families and swimmers. You can also rent Jet Skis in high season. **Amenities:** food and drink; parking; toilets. **Best for:** swimming. ✉ *Arica.*

FAMILY **Playa El Laucho.** South of El Morro, Playa El Laucho is the closest to the city, and thus the most crowded. It's also a bit rocky at the bottom

but waters are calm and inviting. **Amenities:** food and drink; lifeguards; parking; showers; toilets. **Best for:** swimming. ✉ *Arica.*

WHERE TO EAT

$$
SEAFOOD

✗ **El Rey de Mariscos.** Locals love this seafood restaurant, and for good reason. The *corvina con salsa margarita* (sea bass in a seafood-based sauce) is a winner, as is the *paila marina,* a hearty soup stocked with all manner of fish. **Known for:** affordable seafood dishes; down-to-earth ambience; great ceviche. ⑤ *Average main: 8500 pesos* ✉ *Colon 565, 2nd fl.* ☎ *58/222–9232.*

$$$
SEAFOOD
Fodor's Choice
★

✗ **Maracuyá.** Wicker furniture enhances the cool South Pacific atmosphere of this pleasant, open-air restaurant that literally sits above the water on stilts. The seafood, lauded by locals, is always fresh; ask the waiter what the fishing boats brought in that day. **Known for:** seaside views; international cuisine with a focus on seafood; sea bass with pineapple. ⑤ *Average main: 12000 pesos* ✉ *Av. Comandante San Martin 0321* ☎ *58/222–7600.*

WHERE TO STAY

$$
HOTEL
FAMILY

🏨 **Hotel Arica.** Sitting on the ocean between Playa El Laucho and Playa Las Liseras, this hotel has a sense of somewhat faded grandeur with elegant but dated rooms, although the views of the ocean are top-notch and the staff are courteous and attentive. **Pros:** beautiful setting; nice restaurant; good breakfast. **Cons:** somewhat dated; far from downtown; a bit worn and scruffy. ⑤ *Rooms from: 75000 pesos* ✉ *Av. Comandante San Martin 599* ☎ *58/225–4540* ⊕ *www.panamericanahoteles.cl* ⤳ *128 rooms, 20 cabanas* ❧❘ *Breakfast.*

$$
HOTEL

🏨 **Hotel Aruma.** This modern boutique hotel is located in the city center and has minimalist furnishings with a splash of color in the comfortable communal spaces and outdoor sun terrace and pool. **Pros:** central location; modern amenities and decor; comfy beds. **Cons:** rooms are a little small; no elevator; small closet space. ⑤ *Rooms from: 65000 pesos* ✉ *Calle Patricio Lynch 530* ☎ *58/225–0000* ⊕ *www.aruma.cl* ⤳ *16 rooms* ❧❘ *Breakfast.*

NIGHTLIFE

You can join the locals for a beer at one of the cafés lining the pedestrian mall of 21 de Mayo. These low-key establishments, many with outdoor seating, are great places to spend afternoons watching the passing crowds. An oddity in Arica is the attire of the servers in various tranquil cafés and tea salons (usually called "café con piernas" or "cafés with legs"); women serve coffee and tea dressed in lingerie.

Barrabas. For a more refined setting, try the lively, funky Barrabas, a bar and adjoining disco that attracts Arica's younger set. ✉ *Av. Comandante San Martin 222* ☎ *58/225–1531.*

Discoteca SoHo. Located near Playa Chinchorro, Discoteca SoHo livens things up on weekends with the sounds of pop and cumbia. ✉ *Buenos Aires 209* ☎ *9/8905–1806.*

SHOPPING

Calle Bolognesi. This street is crowded with artisan stalls that sell handmade goods. ✉ *Bolognesi.*

Calle Chacabuco. The length of Calle Chacabuco is closed to traffic on Sunday for a market featuring everything from soccer jerseys to bootleg CDs. ⊠ *Chacabuco.*

Calle 21 de Mayo. This is a good place for window-shopping. ⊠ *21 de Mayo.*

Feria Internacional. This shop on Calle Máximo Lira sells everything from bowler hats (worn by Aymara women) to blankets to batteries. The Terminal Pesquero next door offers an interesting view of fishing, El Norte Grande's predominant industry. ⊠ *Maximo Lira.*

Poblado Artesenal. Located outside the city in the Azapa Valley, the Poblado Artesenal is an artisan cooperative designed to resemble an altiplano community. This is a good place to pick up traditionally styled ceramics and leather. ⊠ *Hualles.*

PARQUE NACIONAL LAUCA

47 km (29 miles) southeast of Putre.

The Parque Nacional Lauca offers dramatic landscapes and eye-catching wildlife. Stunning volcanic landscapes and colorful desert scrubland are dotted with llamas, flamingos, and all sorts of flora.

GETTING HERE AND AROUND
Follow the CH-11 International Highway out of Arica toward Bolivia. Just after the town of Putre, take the right-hand turning toward Palca. The park entrance lies 47 km (29 miles) southeast of Putre.

TOURS
Raíces Andinas. Along with full-day trips, Raíces Andinas offers longer trips running up to two weeks between Chile and Argentina. Most tours include lunch and guides. ⊠ *Héroes del Morro 632, Arica* ☎ *58/223–3305* ⊕ *www.raicesandinas.com* ⊠ *From 25000 pesos.*

EXPLORING
Lago Chungará. This lake sits on the Bolivian border at an amazing altitude of 4,600 m (15,100 feet) above sea level. Volcán Parinacota, at 6,330 m (20,889 feet), casts its shadow onto the lake's glassy surface. Hundreds of flamingos make their home here. There is a CONAF-run office at Lago Chungará on the highway just before the lake. ⊠ *From Ruta 11, turn north on Ruta A-123* ⊕ *www.conaf.cl* ⊠ *Free.*

Lagunas Cotacotani. About 8 km (5 miles) east of Parinacota are the beautiful Laguna Cotacotani, which means "land of many lakes" in the Quechua language. This string of ponds—surrounded by a desolate moonscape formed by volcanic eruptions—attracts many species of bird, including Andean geese.

Parinacota. Within the park, off Ruta 11, is the altiplano village of Parincota, one of the most beautiful in all of Chile. In the center of the village sits the whitewashed **Iglesia Parinacota**, dating from 1789. Inside are murals depicting sinners and saints and a mysterious "walking table," which parishioners have chained to the wall for fear that it will steal away in the night. An interesting Aymara cultural commentary can be found in the Stations of the Cross, which depict

Christ's tormenters not as Roman soldiers, but as Spanish conquistadors. Opposite the church you'll find crafts stalls run by Aymara women in the colorful shawls and bowler hats worn by many altiplano women. Only 18 people live in the village, but many more make a pilgrimage here for annual festivals such as the Fiesta de las Cruces, held on May 3, and the Fiesta de la Virgen de la Canderlaria, a three-day romp that begins on February 2.

Fodor's Choice ★ **Parque Nacional Lauca.** On a plateau more than 4,000 meters (13,120 feet) above sea level, the magnificent Parque Nacional Lauca shelters flora and fauna found in few other places in the world. Cacti, grasses, and a brilliant emerald-green moss called *llareta* dot the landscape. Playful *vizcacha*—rabbitlike rodents with long tails—laze in the sun, and llamas, graceful vicuñas, and alpacas make their home here as well. About 10 km (6 miles) into the park is a CONAF station with informative brochures. ⊠ *Off Ruta 11* ☎ *58/220–1201 in Arica* ⊕ *www.conaf.cl* ✉ *Free.*

RESERVA NACIONAL LAS VICUÑAS

121 km (75 miles) southeast of Putre.

This 100-km (62-mile) reserve is filled with vicuñas that graze in the high plains near the blue alpine lakes. There are also volcanoes in the distance and salt flats in the forefront.

GETTING HERE AND AROUND

From the town of Putre, follow the international highway to Bolivia for a few kilometers, then take the turn southeast on a unpaved road that leads to the Lauca National Park. The entrance to the Las Vicuñas National Reserve lies 121 km (75 miles) past Putre.

EXPLORING

Fodor's Choice ★ **Reserva Nacional Las Vicuñas.** Although it attracts far fewer visitors than neighboring Parque Nacional Lauca, Reserva Nacional Las Vicuñas contains some incredible sights—salt flats, high plains, and alpine lakes. And you can enjoy the vistas without running into buses full of tourists. The reserve, which stretches some 100 km (62 miles), has a huge herd of graceful vicuñas. Although quite similar to their larger cousins, llamas and alpacas, vicuñas have not been domesticated. Their incredibly soft wool, among the most prized in the world, led to so much hunting that these creatures were threatened with extinction, and today it is illegal to kill a vicuña. Getting to this reserve, unfortunately, is quite a challenge. There is no public transportation, and the roads are passable only in four-wheel-drive vehicles. Many people choose to take a tour out of Arica. ⊠ *From Ruta 11, take Ruta A-21 south to park headquarters* ☎ *58/2201–201 in Arica* ⊕ *www.conaf.cl.*

SALAR DE SURIRE

126 km (78 miles) southeast of Putre.

From a distance, Surire looks like a giant white lake, but as you approach you'll see the small white crystals of salt that define this intriguing nature spot.

EXPLORING

Salar de Surire. After passing through the high plains, where you'll spot vicuña, alpaca, and the occasional desert fox, you'll catch your first glimpse of the sparkling Salar de Surire. Seen from a distance, the salt flat appears to be a giant white lake. Unlike its southern neighbor, the Salar de Atacama, it's completely flat. Three of the four New World flamingos (Andean, Chilean, and James's) live in the nearby lakes. ⊠ *South from Reserva Nacional Las Vicuñas on Ruta A-235* ☎ *58/220–1201 in Arica* ⊕ *www.conaf.cl* ⌨ *Free.*

THE CENTRAL VALLEY

WELCOME TO THE CENTRAL VALLEY

TOP REASONS TO GO

★ **Wine tasting:** The Central Valley is the heart of Chile's wine country. Vineyards for both table and wine grapes cover the landscape—in fact, the Pan-American Highway runs through some of the longest continuous vineyards in the world. There is ample opportunity to taste the delicious product, too, from full-bodied reds at BBQs to crisp whites by the pool.

★ **Rowdy rodeos:** The Central Valley is also home to the *huaso*, a cousin of the Argentine gaucho. Huasos, in their typical flat-topped, wide-brimmed hats, are a common sight around Rancagua, where they flock to the national Medialuna (rodeo arena) for their favorite sport.

★ **Scenic countryside:** The Central Valley is not limited to vineyards. Rivers and lakes lie between hillsides dotted with cactus and fruit trees. East in the Andes countryside, dirt roads weave the high mountaintops, passing pretty waterfalls and swimming holes; it's perfect for exploring on foot, bike, or horseback.

Geographically speaking, the Central Valley isn't really a valley at all, but rather an "Intermediate Depression" between two mountain ranges—the Andes to the east, and Coastal Range to the west. The two separate just north of Santiago, leaving a fertile flatland between them that runs south to the Bío Bío, where the Coastal Mountains gradually descend into the Pacific Ocean. The large Central Valley is divided into the four subregions: the Maipo Valley (Santiago sits in its center), the Rapel Valley (divided into Cachapoal and Colchagua), the Curicó Valley (around the city of Curicó), and the Maule Valley (south from Talca).

1 Rapel Valley. Chile's agricultural heartland is the rodeo country home of the *huaso*, known for their wide-brimmed hats and jaunty smiles. There's some mighty fine wine, too. The valley is divided into two wine appellations, Cachapoal and Rancagua to the north and Santa Cruz and Colchagua to the south.

2 Curicó Valley. Dormant volcanoes make a gorgeous backdrop for the valley's extensive vineyards, and Curicó city's charming plaza fills with excitement and grape stomping each April for one of the country's most traditional wine fests. If wine's not your thing, try the upscale resorts on Vichuquén Lake near the coast or camping at Radal Siete Tazas National Park.

3 Maule Valley. Scratch any surface in this subregion and find plenty of rural tradition and natural beauty. The O'Higginiano Museum and the Villa Huilquilemu in Talca beautifully portray the area's cultural heritage, and Chile's only local train still makes daily runs to the coast. Vineyards old and new pepper the stunning countryside.

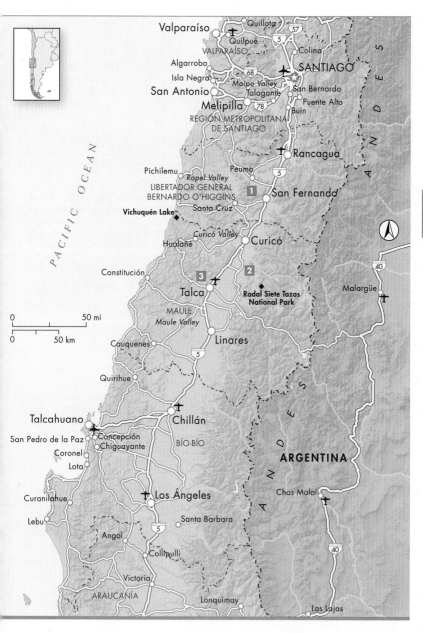

6

Updated
by Amanda
Barnes

The Central Valley is the most abundant valley in Chile, not just for fruit and grape production, but also for its wealth of opportunities for adventure: hiking the Andes, steaming in thermal pools, scaling rocks, or heli-skiing down snowy slopes. At the coast, you can tan on the lovely beaches, surf world-class waves, and nosh on outstanding seafood. In between, indulge in some of the finest wines South America has to offer while enjoying the laid-back charm of rural life.

The Central Valley is Chile's agricultural heartland. The rich soil benefits from ample spring melt-water for irrigation and long, warm, and dry summers. Grapes especially thrive, and wine has been an important product in much of the Central Valley for the past four centuries.

The Central Valley is a straight shot down the Pan-American Highway between the volcanic cones of the Andes on the west and the lower Coastal Mountains to the east. As you head south, the relatively dry foliage of the short, scrubby indigenous bushes gives way to verdant pastures and thick pine and eucalyptus forests.

It's about a five-hour drive straight south from Santiago to Chillán and nearly another hour east to Concepción, but plan to stop and explore along the way. Most valleys have Wine Route (Ruta del Vino) associations, which are happy to help visitors plan tours of the wineries, as are most hotels.

PLANNING

WHEN TO GO

Timing your visit to the Central Valley really depends on what you want to do there. January and February are peak summer vacation months in Chile, so parks are open and beaches are full. The weather is clear and sunny—cool on the mountains and coast, and quite hot in between, making this the best time for many outdoor activities. If winter sports are on the bucket list, it's best to come from June to September, although climate change is making the season more variable.

If wineries draw you to the Central Valley, however, consider that grapes are picked from late February through early May, depending on the varietal and area. This is certainly the best time to visit area vineyards, since you can see everything from crushing to bottling. Visit on a weekend, and there's a good chance of joining one of the many harvest festivals that take place throughout the region at this time of year. But don't overlook a visit another time of year, as wineries offer tastings and fun activities year-round.

FESTIVALS

The harvest season is the most important time of the year in wine country. Most of Chile's wine-producing regions mark the moment with a *Fiesta de la Vendimia,* or harvest festival, which take place in March and April. The biggest and most spectacular events are held in Colchagua and Curicó, including grape-stomping competitions and harvest-queen contests. Maule, another notable festival, kicks off the year with its Carmenère Festival in January, in honor of the very Chilean red wine grape.

Not every fiesta is wine related, of course. Catholic roots run deep here, and many traditional religious festivals remain, such as those in honor of San Pedro and San Pablo, the patron saints of fishermen (on June 29 in fishing villages all along the coast). San Sebastian, the much persecuted, arrow-pierced saint, draws thousands of devotees to Yumbel (108 km [68 miles] from Concepción) on January 20. And during the fiesta de San Francisco, held October 4 in the small colonial-era village of Huerta de Maule, 38 km (24 miles) southwest of Talca, more than 200 huasos gather from all over Chile for a day of horseback events, including races around the central square. Fiestas Patrias, Chile's independence day (September 18), spills into a week of festivities all over the country.

GETTING HERE AND AROUND

6

BUS TRAVEL

The two big bus companies in the region, Pullman Bus and Turbus, offer regular departures that leave precisely on time from Santiago's Alameda Terminal bound for Rancagua, Talca, Curicó, Chillán, and Concepción. One-way fare from Santiago to Chillán runs about 10,000 pesos.

Bus Contacts Pullman del Sur. ✉ *Camilo Henríquez 253, Curicó* ☎ *75/231–0387* ⊕ *www.pdelsur.cl.* **Tur Bus.** ✉ *Av. Bernardo O'Higgins 0484, Rancagua* ☎ *72/235–1221* ⊕ *www.turbus.cl.*

CAR TRAVEL

Traveling by car is often the most convenient way to see the region. The Central Valley is sliced in half by Chile's major highway, the Pan-American Highway, also called Ruta 5, which passes through all of the major towns in the region. Be sure to have local cash on hand for the frequent tolls, which are rather high and increase on weekends and holidays.

TRAIN TRAVEL

The train remains an excellent way to travel through the Central Valley. Express trains from Estación Central in Santiago to the cities of Rancagua, Curicó, Talca, Chillán, and Concepción are comfortable and faster than taking the bus or driving.

RESTAURANTS

No matter where or when you eat in the Central Valley, a good bottle of local wine is likely to be on the table, so a handful of wine-related words will doubtless come in handy. *Vino* is the Spanish word for wine; red is *tinto* (never *rojo*) and white is *blanco*. Drink them by the *copa,* or wine glass, or take part in more formal wine tasting called *desgustación* and *cata.*

Central Valley cuisine consists of hearty fare based on locally raised beef and pork, served with local vegetables and followed by fruit-based

desserts. These are always accompanied by regional—usually red—wine. Most Chileans eat a big lunch around 1 pm and have a light dinner late in the evening. If you want to try real, home-style Chilean cooking, your best bet is to follow suit and look for lunch at the same time. Afterward you may need to adopt the local siesta habit as well.

In the summer look for popular favorites such as *porotos granados* (fresh cranberry beans with corn, squash, and basil), *humitas* (Chilean tamales) with fresh-sliced tomatoes, or *pastel de choclo* (a savory ground-beef base served in a clay bowl, sometimes with a piece of chicken, and always generously slathered with a rich grated corn topping). Desserts are often simply fresh fruits served in their own juice. Do watch for the refreshing *mote con huesillo* served cold as a drink or dessert. Begin by eating the *mote,* a type of wheat hominy; then slurp up the juice from the *huesillo,* a large dried peach, which serves as the final act of this three-course treat. *Restaurant reviews have been shortened. For full information, visit Fodors.com.*

HOTELS

Accommodation ranges from simple B&Bs, beautiful old estancias, rustic-chic mountain lodges, and basic hotels in between. While in wine country, you might want to opt for lodgings at the wineries themselves, whether in resorts, guesthouses, or boutique hotels. *Hotel reviews have been shortened. For full information, visit Fodors.com.*

WHAT IT COSTS IN CHILEAN PESOS (IN THOUSANDS)				
	$	**$$**	**$$$**	**$$$$**
Restaurants	Under 6	6–9	10–13	over 13
Hotels	Under 51	51–85	86–115	over 115

Restaurant prices are the average cost of a main course at dinner or, if dinner is not served, at lunch. Hotel prices are the lowest cost of a standard double room in high season, excluding tax.

TOURS

Most wineries in the Central Valley allow you to make your own direct booking, and the relatively easy-to-navigate road network makes renting a car a good option for you to get around. However, Chile has a zero tolerance law for drunk driving, so booking a taxi for the day is often preferable, and safer. Alternatively, each of the agencies below organizes private and group tours to the different wine regions.

Ruta Valle de Luz. This alternative wine tourism company organizes visits to garage wineries and organic producers; an artisan route to see the local craftsmen can also be incorporated into the tour. Hearty lunches exploring local cuisine are an added highlight. If you want to get away from the big producers, this is the tour agency for you. ⊠ *Av. Errazuriz 1172, Santa Cruz* ☎ *09/7698–0801* ⊕ *Facebook/Turismo-Ruta-Valle-de-Luz* ⊠ *From 45000 pesos.*

Upscape. This tourism outfitter organizes wine tours from Santiago to the different wine routes either in full-day or multiday trips. Visits

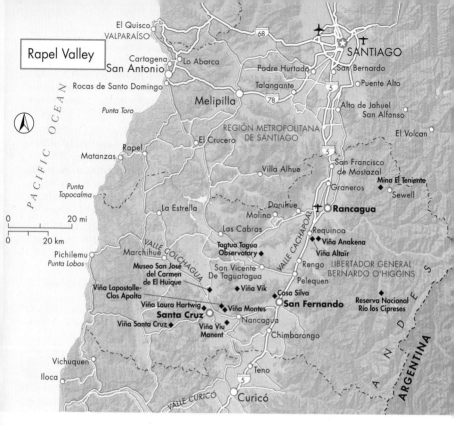

usually come with premium wine pours, your own bilingual guide, private transfer, and pick-up from your hotel doorstep. ✉ *Tegualda 1352, Providencia* ☎ *2/2244–2750* ⊕ *www.upscapetravel.com* ⛵ *From 193000 pesos.*

RAPEL VALLEY

The Rapel Valley—which includes Colchagua and Cachapoal—is the largest denomination in Chile, covering over a quarter of the country's vineyards.

RANCAGUA

87 km (54 miles) south of Santiago along Pan-American Hwy.

In 1814, the hills around Rancagua were the site of a battle in the War of Independence known as the *Desastre de Rancagua* (Disaster of Rancagua). Chilean independence fighters, including Chile's independence leader Bernardo O'Higgins, held off the powerful Spanish army for two days before surrendering, but escaping to fight another day. In the resulting blaze, much of the town was destroyed.

Despite its historical significance and current importance as a regional commercial center, the city has relatively little to offer in terms of tourism. By all means, visit the historic area around the central plaza or take in a rodeo in the national *Medialuna*, or rodeo arena, but otherwise skip the city and head straight for one of the more interesting attractions outside of town such as a copper mine, hot spring, nature reserve, or winery.

GETTING HERE AND AROUND

Rancagua is a one-hour hop due south from Santiago by car or bus. It's a bit faster by train and much too close to justify flying. Wheeled transport takes the Pan-American Highway, while rail options go beside it. Traffic heading out of Santiago is often sluggish, and delays due to roadwork are frequent, but the highway is generally in good condition and allows for speeds of 120 kph (75 mph) for most of the route.

Bus Contacts Rancagua Terminal al Sur. ✉ *Ocarrol 1175* ☎ *72/222–5425.* **Rancagua Terminal de Buses.** ✉ *Av. O'Higgins 0484* ☎ *72/222–5425* ⊕ *www. terminalohiggins.cl.*

ESSENTIALS

Visitor and Tour Information Sernatur Rancagua. ✉ *German Riesco 350* ☎ *72/222–7261* ⊕ *www.sernatur.cl.*

EXPLORING
TOP ATTRACTIONS

Viña Altaïr. Inspired by the brightest star in the Aquila constellation, this French-Chilean joint venture was formed to produce one excellent wine: Altaïr. Today the winery offers a second celestial bottling called Sideral. Both are red blends from grapes grown in the foothills of the Andes. The winery runs three different types of tours, ranging from a straightforward winery tour and tasting to horseback riding through the vineyards and high into the hills. There's even a spectacular nocturnal version that includes a moonlight ride on horseback through the vineyards and a tasting under the stars. All tours include tastings of one or both house wines. ✉ *Fundo Totihue, Camino Pimpinela s/n, Requinoa* ☎ *97/518–6554* ✎ *From 18000 pesos* ⚞ *Reservations essential.*

Viña Anakena. Based in the Andean sector of the Cachapoal Valley known as "Alto Cachapoal," this winery has properties in a number of Chilean wine regions to ensure the finest results for each variety. Their labels include symbols inspired by the motifs found in Chile's various indigenous cultures. Visits include a tour of the vineyards, cellars, varietal garden, and scenic overlook, along with tastings of *reserva* or premium lines. You can also reserve ahead for lunch, horseback riding, or wine-and-food-pairing classes. ✉ *Camino Pimpenela s/n, Requinoa* ☎ *2/2433–8600* ⊕ *www.anakenawines.cl* ✎ *From 10000 pesos* ⚞ *Reservations essential.*

WORTH NOTING

Casa del Pilar de la Esquina. Located across the street from the Museo Regional de Rancagua, Casa del Pilar de la Esquina once belonged to Fernando Errázuriz Aldunate, who helped draft the country's constitution. In addition to displays on the area's history and indigenous cultures, there are often modern-art exhibits on the first floor. ✉ *Estado 682, at Ibieta* ☎ *72/222–1524* ✎ *Free.*

Iglesia de la Merced. A block north of the plaza along Calle Estado is this 18th-century church that was declared a national monument for its beauty and significance in the city's fateful history. It was in this bell tower that O'Higgins waited in vain for reinforcements during the Battle of Independence. The somber, neoclassical twin spires are a fitting memorial. Parts of the church were unfortunately damaged in the 2010 earthquake. ⊠ *At Cuevas and Estado.*

Mina El Teniente and Sewell. High in the mountains north of Termas de Cauquenes, 60 km (37 miles) northeast of Rancagua, the El Teniente Mine is the world's largest subterranean copper mine, in operation since colonial times. In 1905 the city of Sewell, known as the "city of stairs," was constructed at 2,130 meters (6,988 feet) above sea level to house miners. Abandoned in the early 1970s, Sewell was declared a UNESCO World Heritage Site in 2006. Rancagua tour operator VTS offers guided tours of both the mine and the city every day (except Monday), with transport from Santiago or Rancagua. ⊠ *Millán 1020* ☎ *72/295–2692 VTS* ⊕ *www.vts.cl* ✉ *From 30000 pesos.*

Museo Regional de Rancagua. This three-room museum re-creates a typical 18th-century home, complete with period furniture and religious artifacts. A small collection of 19th-century weaponry is the type that would have been used in the momentous Battle of Rancagua. Dioramas illustrate this dramatic moment in the country's quest for independence. The whitewashed colonial building is a few blocks south of Plaza de los Héroes. ⊠ *Estado 685, at Ibieta* ☎ *72/222–1524* ⊕ *www.museorancagua.cl* ✉ *Free.*

Plaza de los Héroes. Today's Rancagüinos enjoy relaxing in the city's central square, the Plaza de los Héroes. A statue of the valiant war hero and future first president Bernardo O'Higgins on horseback stands proudly in the center of the plaza. Although each side of the statue base contains one of his famous sayings, curiously enough, there is nothing to indicate to visitors and newcomers that it is a statue of O'Higgins. ⊠ *Plaza de los Heroes.*

Reserva Nacional Río los Cipreses. Numerous trails lead through thick forests of cypress trees at this 92,000-acre national reserve 50 km (31 miles) east of Rancagua. Some of the trails come to clearings where you are treated to spectacular views of the mountains above. CONAF, the national parks service, has an office here with informative displays and maps. Hiking, swimming, and horseback riding are all available, and you can camp overnight. Just south of the park is the spot where a plane carrying Uruguayan university students crashed in 1972. The story of the group, some of whom survived three months in a harsh winter by resorting to cannibalism, was told in the book and film *Alive.* ⊠ *Carretera del Cobre s/n* ☎ *72/220–4610* ⊕ *www.conaf.cl* ✉ *5000 pesos.*

WHERE TO EAT

$$
CHILEAN
FAMILY

✗ **Juan y Medio.** On the north-bound side of the Pan-American Highway, between the towns of Requinoa and Rosario, this well-loved Chilean diner caters to hearty appetites. It began as a humble truck stop in 1946 and established a tremendous reputation for its trucker-size portions of Chilean favorites—whopping steaks and ribs grilled over a wood fire,

slow-cooked *cazuelas,* and stews that leave you wanting nothing more than a hammock and a long nap. **Known for:** large portions; Chilean dishes; family-friendly atmosphere. $ *Average main: 8000 pesos* ✉ *Ruta 5, Km 109, Rengo* ☎ 72/252–1726 ⊕ *www.juanymedio.cl.*

WHERE TO STAY

$$$$
HOTEL

🏨 **Puma Lodge.** This large mountain lodge set right in the middle of the Andes offers heli-skiing in winter and mountain treks in the summer. **Pros:** peaceful location; valley views; outdoor pool. **Cons:** remote location requires 4x4 in winter; expensive; poor road access. $ *Rooms from: 120000 pesos* ✉ *Reserva Nacional Rio Los Cipreses, Fundo Sierra Nevada, Km 22* ☎ 2/2799–8932 ⊕ *www.noihotels.com* 🛏 *24 rooms* ❘○❘ *Breakfast.*

SPORTS AND THE OUTDOORS

RODEO

National Rodeo Arena. One of the great highlights of life in Rancagua includes excursions to the National Rodeo Arena: the *Medialuna Monumental,* especially in late March, when it hosts the national championship. This is a great opportunity to glimpse huaso tradition in its full glory: horsemanship, riding, and cow-herding skills, traditional foods, crafts, music, and dance. ✉ *Av. Germán Ibarra s/n, at Av. España* ⊕ *www.caballoyrodeo.cl.*

SAN FERNANDO AND NEARBY

152 km (94 miles) south of Santiago.

San Fernando is surrounded by popular wineries, handsome hotels, colonial estancias, and beautiful nature spots. The city is a convenient stopping point alongside Ruta 5. The gateway to Colchagua Valley, San Fernando city has an attractive plaza and all the necessary conveniences, although the main attractions lie in the surrounding rural areas, vineyards, and fruit plantations. Streets are colorfully lined with fruit stands selling eye-catching citrus fruits, melons, and ripe avocados. West of San Fernando is where the wine route to Santa Cruz begins, but there is much to discover toward the Andes, too.

GETTING HERE AND AROUND

San Fernando is almost two hours by car, more than two hours by bus, and a bit faster by train. If you are moving farther south by public transport, chances are you might have to stop off in San Fernando first to change buses at the terminal.

Bus Contacts **San Fernando Terminal de Buses.** ✉ *Manso de Velasco, (corner of Rancagua)* ☎ 72/271–3912.

EXPLORING

Casa Silva. The Silva family is a true wine dynasty of Chile and the family winery, just five minutes off the main Ruta 5, is one of the most convenient area wineries to visit. The atmospheric wine cellar is one of the oldest in Colchagua, and the colonial architecture has been tastefully refurbished throughout the winery and production rooms, where a tour shows the main facilities as well as the family's collection of classic cars.

Finish up with a tasting in the modern tasting room and wine shop, or cycle, drive, or walk through the vineyards to the excellent restaurant overlooking the polo fields. ⊠ *Hijuela Norte, (El Tambo exit from Ruta 5)* ☎ *72/291–3117* ⊕ *www.casasilva.cl.*

FAMILY **Tagua Tagua Observatory.** On a clear night, the Colchagua Valley can be excellent for stargazing. Eccentric expat Ian Hutcheon runs an observatory just outside of Tagua Tagua, where family-friendly events begin with a welcome glass of wine (made with meteorites in the barrel), after which there is entertaining discussion, presentation, and observation through advanced telescopes. During the day, Hutcheon leads nature hikes in the area with a buried treasure surprise. ⊠ *Observatorio Tagua Tagua, Tunca Arriba s/n, San Vicente de Tagua Tagua* ☎ *9/9452–0291* ⊕ *www.taguatagua.com* ⊴ *5000 pesos.*

Viña Vik. Jaw-dropping architecture and stunning views over the valley make this one of Chile's most handsome wineries. Nestled in a private 11,000-acre estate, the VIK winery is pure luxury and the Norwegian owners don't do anything by half measures. A visit includes a barrel tasting of the individual components before a taste of the final blend. Make a day of your visit with horseback riding in the stunning estate and lunch in the hotel restaurant, one of Chile's best. ⊠ *Millahue s/n, San Vincente de Tagua Tagua* ☎ *9/5668–4852* ⊕ *www.vinavik.com* ⊴ *From 25000 pesos.*

6

WHERE TO EAT

$$$ ✗ **Casa Silva Restaurant.** This sunny restaurant overlooking the vineyards
CHILEAN and polo field serves tasty dishes of local delicacies including fresh ceviche, Chilean beef on the BBQ, seafood salads, beef jerky empanadas, an
Fodor's Choice eclectic mix of tapas dishes, and indulgent Chilean desserts. The wine
★ list is all from the Casa Silva winery, of course, but it's an enormous portfolio of varieties and the prices carry attractive discounts. **Known for:** modern Chilean cuisine; tasty desserts; polo views. Ⓢ *Average main: 10000 pesos* ⊠ *Hijuelas Norte* ☎ *9/6847–5786* ⊕ *www.casasilva.cl.*

$$ ✗ **Hydro.** If you're looking for new flavor combinations, this fusion
INTERNATIONAL sushi bar is a great spot for creative cuisine and craft beers. A range of fresh ceviches, delicious octopus tacos, imaginative sushi rolls and skyscraper burgers are just some of the regular menu items. **Known for:** creative sushi; flavorful ceviche; craft beer. Ⓢ *Average main: 6000 pesos* ⊠ *Av. Bernardo O'Higgins Sur 0280* ☎ *72/271–6663* ⊕ *www.hydrorestobar.cl* ☉ *Closed Sun.*

$$$$ ✗ **Milla Milla.** It takes quite a drive to get here, but Milla Milla—the
CHILEAN restaurant at VIK winery—is worth the trip. Fabulous valley views are the only thing pulling your eyes away from the colorful plates of contemporary Chilean cuisine, which uses ingredients sourced from the local sea, mountains, and on-site garden. **Known for:** beautiful presentation; locally sourced organic ingredients; fine dining. Ⓢ *Average main: 25000 pesos* ⊠ *Milla Milla restaurant, Vina VIK* ☎ *9/5668–4853* ⊕ *www.millamilla.cl.*

WHERE TO STAY

$$$$
HOTEL
🖼 **Hacienda Los Lingues.** This tastefully restored 17th-century hacienda is one of the oldest in Chile, and its sweeping 20,000-acre estate exudes an old-world charm. **Pros:** history handsomely restored; beautiful estate; Wi-Fi in bedrooms. **Cons:** service can be stuffy; some facilities a bit tired; lacks some mod cons. ⑤ *Rooms from: 170000 pesos* ⊠ *Ruta 5 S, Km 124.5 s/n* ☎ *72/2977–080* ⊕ *www.loslingues.com* ⟿ *16 rooms* ⟉⊙⟊ *Breakfast.*

$$$$
HOTEL
Fodor's Choice
★
🖼 **Viña Vik Hotel.** With a grand, swooping titanium roof and rooms that are individually decorated by different artists, this statement hotel is one of Chile's most luxurious. **Pros:** stunning valley views; quirky art design; excellent restaurant and food. **Cons:** expensive; impersonal reception; far from other wineries. ⑤ *Rooms from: 800000 pesos* ⊠ *Millahue s/n, San Vincente de Tagua Tagua* ☎ *9/6193–1754 cell phone* ⊕ *www.vinavik.com* ⟿ *22 suites, 1 family cabin* ⟉⊙⟊ *All-inclusive; All meals.*

SANTA CRUZ

180 km (112 miles) southwest of Santiago; 104 km (65 miles) south-west of Rancagua via the Pan-American Hwy. to San Fernando, then southwest on I–50.

Fodor's Choice
★
This once sleepy village has become the height of rural chic in recent years, due, in large part, to the booming Colchagua Valley wine indus-try, which produces many of Chile's award-winning red wines. It has an attractive central plaza surrounded by a mix of modern and tradi-tional architecture, including the town hall, the Colchagua Museum, the Wine Route office, and the grand Hotel Santa Cruz Plaza. The church still stands on the Plaza although little of the 19th-century building survived the 2010 earthquake; it has been completely refur-bished and rebuilt since.

Santa Cruz is the perfect home base for visiting the Colchagua wineries that extend out to the east and west, mostly along Route I–50.

GETTING HERE AND AROUND

Getting to Santa Cruz is easiest by car. After reaching San Fernando on Ruta 5 you need to pass the first exit north of the city and continue another 2 km (1 mile) to the exit marked "Santa Cruz, Carretera del Vino, Pichilemu." This is I–50, the "Wine Highway," which takes you west through wine country along the coast to Pichilemu, surf capital of Chile. It is very easy to visit most of the valley's wineries by car; in fact, you see a number of them along the way on this aptly named route.

If using public transportation, take a bus or train to San Fernando and then the local bus or *colectivo* (a shared taxi with a fixed route) to Santa Cruz.

Bus Contacts Santa Cruz Terminal. ⊠ *Rafael Casanova 480* ☎ *72/282–2191.*

EXPLORING

Museo de Colchagua. One of the best museums in Chile if not Latin America, this attractive, colonial-style, 20th-century museum focuses on the history of the region. It's the largest private natural-history collec-tion in the country and second only in size to Santiago's Museo Nacio-nal de Historia Natural. Exhibits include pre-Columbian mummies,

HISTORY OF CHILEAN WINE

Fans of Chilean wines owe a debt to missionaries who arrived here in the 16th century. Spanish priests, who needed wine to celebrate the Catholic Mass, planted the country's first vineyards from Copiapó in the north to Concepción in the south. Of course, not all the wine was intended for religious purposes, and vines were quickly sent north and planted in the Maipo Valley around Santiago to fill the "spiritual void" experienced by the early Spanish settlers—many of whom were soldiers and sailors.

With the rise of cross-Atlantic travel and trade that began in the 19th century, some Chileans made fortunes in the mining industry. They returned from Europe with newfound appreciation for French food, dress, architecture, and lifestyles. Many began building their own Chilean-style chateaux, particularly on the outskirts of Santiago. French varietals such as Cabernet Sauvignon, Malbec, and Carménère thrived in the Central Valley's rich soils and the near-perfect climate, and thus Chile's second "wine boom" was launched.

Chilean wineries did not keep pace with the rest of the world and stagnated throughout much of the 20th century. However, the introduction of modern equipment such as stainless steel tanks in the late 1980s caught the country some global attention. Fresh national and international investment in the industry made Chilean wine a tasty and affordable option. Continued advances in growing techniques and wine-making methods throughout the 1990s and into the early 21st century have resulted in the production of exceedingly excellent wines of premium and ultrapremium quality, with increasingly hefty price tags. Wine exports increase annually, and Chile has been named one of the top five wine exporters worldwide since 2010, shipping its wine to more than 90 countries around the globe.

extinct insects set in amber viewed through special lenses, the world's largest collection of silver work by the indigenous Mapuche, and the only known original copy of Chile's proclamation of independence. A few early vehicles and wine-making implements surround the building. The museum is the creation of Santa Cruz native and international businessman Carlos Cardoen. Expect to spend around four hours here. ⊠ *Av. Errázuriz 145* ☎ *72/282–1050* ⊕ *www.museocolchagua. cl* 🎫 *7000 pesos.*

Museo San José del Carmen de El Huique. Here you can look into the lifestyle of Chile's 19th-century rich and famous. Construction began on the current house in 1829 and was completed with the inauguration of the chapel in 1852. The Errázuriz family, who can trace the 2,600-acre estate back through family lines to 1756, donated it to the Chilean Army in 1975. It was reopened as a museum in the 1990s and is now the only remaining preserved, intact estate of its kind in Chile open to the public. Inside, sumptuous suites are filled with opal glass, lead crystal, bone china, antique furniture, and family portraits evoking Chile's aristocratic past. Servants' quarters are also part of the tour, as are the

kitchens and 16 working patios, each dedicated to a specific household chore, such as laundry, butchering, or cheese making. Guides are knowledgeable and have tales to tell, as many grew up hearing family stories about working at the estate. The tour ends with a visit to the chapel, which has Venetian blown-glass balustrades around the altar and the choir loft. Visits are by prior reservation only, and English-speaking guides are available with sufficient notice. ⊠ *26 km (16 miles) north of Santa Cruz to Palmilla, turn left to Estación Colchagua, then turn right and follow signs to museum* ☎ *09/733–1105 cell phone* ⊕ *www. museoelhuique.cl* 🖫 *2000 pesos.*

Ruta del Vino de Colchagua. Right on the main square, the Ruta del Vino office organizes tours and tastings at 13 of Colchagua's best-known wineries. The office arranges tour and lunch packages from Santiago and locally that start from 12,000 pesos per person up to almost 200,000, depending on the complexity of the tour. The harvest season—March and April—kicks off with the *Fiesta de la Vendimia* (Grape Harvest Festival) and is always a great time to visit. ■ **TIP→ Though most wineries have their own guides, few of the guides speak English, and some wineries only accept visits arranged by Ruta del Vino.** ⊠ *Plaza de Armas 298* ☎ *72/282–3199* ⊕ *www.colchaguavalley.cl.*

Viña Lapostolle-Clos Apalta. Lapostolle's showcase winery rises impressively from the vineyards in a wooden nest formation, offering a memorable view from the outside and inside of this gravity-flow winery. The prized grapes are picked from the biodynamic vineyards and taken to the top floor, where they are separated by hand, dropped into tanks on the floor below, then racked to barrels on the floor below, and so on until the grapes are six floors down into the hillside, where they are finally trucked out and shipped around the world. Join one of the four daily tours with tastings, or stay for a fabulous lunch at the Lapostolle Residence with a fresh and organic menu picked straight from its own garden. ⊠ *Apalta, Km 4* ☎ *72/295–3300* ⊕ *www.lapostollewines.com* 🖫 *From 20000 pesos* ⚑ *Reservations essential.*

Viña Laura Hartwig. This small winery rests on lands where grapes have been grown for more than a century. The likeness of Laura Hartwig, the elegant owner of the estate, is beautifully drawn on the winery's labels by the famous Chilean artist Claudio Bravo. After a tour of the facilities, sample the red wines, including Chile's unique Carménère variety, a tasty Petit Verdot, juicy Malbec, and rich Cabernet Sauvignon. ⊠ *Camino Barreales s/n* ☎ *72/282–3179* ⊕ *www.laurahartwig. cl* 🖫 *From 12000 pesos per person.*

Fodor's Choice **Viña Montes.** Montes is one of most recognized wine brands in Chile
★   today, but it started with humble roots in 1987 in the Curicó Valley with a group of young entrepreneurs. Today it is in the heart of Apalta, Colchagua, where the second generation of the Montes family helps run this feng shui–designed winery and restaurant. Deep, rich, and concentrated red wines and bright whites offer a diverse portfolio from around Chile. Enjoy the wines with food at one of the restaurants: Angel's Kitchen, serving a smart bistro menu, or Fuegos de Apalta with its showstopping fire-themed menu. The regular tour takes you through

the winery processes and finishes with a wine tasting inside, or there is also a more active wine tour that involves a mountain hike followed by a picnic and wine tasting at the summit. ⊠ *Parcela 15, Millahue de Apalta* ☎ *72/281–7815* ⊕ *www.monteswines.com* ☐ *12000 pesos* ⚭ *Reservations essential.*

FAMILY **Viña Santa Cruz.** In the lesser-visited Lolol region, this winery is owned by the same business man who has the Santa Cruz Plaza Hotel and Museum. The highlight to this winery is the flamboyant replica "indigenous village" at the top of the hill (reachable by cable car). A tour finishes with wine tasting, although the view is more overwhelming than the wine. ■**TIP→ Visit at night and you can stargaze from the observatory (open all year, depending on weather).** ⊠ *Carretera I–72, Km 25, Lolol* ☎ *72/235–4920* ⊕ *www.vinasantacruz.cl* ☐ *From 22000 pesos* ⚭ *Reservations essential* ☞ *Astronomy tour Wed.–Sat. at 6:30.*

FAMILY **Viña Viu Manent.** What better way to visit the vineyards at Viu Manent than via a horse-drawn carriage ride? The stylish equestrian entrance is part of the tour package, which also includes a wine tasting in the beautiful colonial-style house. Focusing mainly on red wines from the Colchagua Valley, Viu also includes a couple of coastal wines from Casablanca and even a Malbec from Argentina. Pick wines to taste after the tour or over lunch at the excellent Rayuela restaurant, which keeps live oysters in freezing-cold Jacuzzis out back. ⊠ *Carretera del Vino, Km 37* ☎ *72/285–8350 general, 2/2840–3181 tours and wine shop* ⊕ *www.viumanent.cl* ☐ *16000 pesos (or 13000 without horses)* ☞ *Tours: 10:30, 12, 3, and 4:30 year-round.*

WHERE TO EAT

$$ ✕ **Casa Colchagua.** Surrounded by vineyards, this small restaurant is
CHILEAN a countryside culinary experience serving contemporary Chilean cuisine that celebrates native ingredients: seaweed ceviche, scallop and quinoa risotto, and *carne mechada* (pulled beef) among them. There's inside seating in this cozy country home, but most diners want to take advantage of the clement Colchagua weather and the vineyard view from the garden. **Known for:** modern Chilean dining; local ingredients; intimate setting. ⑤ *Average main: 7500 pesos* ⊠ *Camino a los Boldos* ☎ *9/424–5007* ⊕ *www.casacolchagua.cl* ⊗ *No dinner Tues.–Sat.*

$ ✕ **Club Social de Santa Cruz.** One of the most traditional restaurants
CHILEAN in town, the social club specializes in simple, hearty Chilean fare like *conejo guisada* (rabbit stew) and *arrollado* (rolled roast pork). In summer, the courtyard fills with locals lunching under the shady pergola. **Known for:** local flavor; hearty dishes; old-school service. ⑤ *Average main: 5000 pesos* ⊠ *Plaza de Armas 178* ☎ *72/822–5295.*

$$ ✕ **Vino Bello.** This stylish restaurant—one of the best in Santa Cruz—
MODERN ITALIAN features an eclectic range of clay oven–cooked pizzas, as well as pastas,
Fodor'sChoice salads, and fish and meat dishes, alongside local wines and don't-miss
★ cocktail offerings (try the chili-laced version of a pisco sour). Smooth music, attractive surroundings, and some nice twists on the classics make Vino Bello a taste of *la dolce vita* in Colchagua. **Known for:** creative pizza toppings; wicked pisco sours; romantic atmosphere. ⑤ *Average main: 8500 pesos* ⊠ *Barreales s/n* ☎ *72/282–2755* ⊕ *www. vino-bello.com.*

WHERE TO STAY

$$
B&B/INN

☷ **Hotel Boutique Bellavista de Colchagua.** In the wine region of Lolol, this peaceful countryside getaway has value, comfort, and warm hospitality that begins with a welcome glass of wine. **Pros:** countryside location; you can reserve a massage; charming hospitality. **Cons:** car required for remote location; breakfast is simple (but you can get eggs to order); far from restaurants. ⑤ *Rooms from: 72500* ⊠ *San Pedro de Callihue Lote 5 J* ☎ *9/7808–3785* ⊕ *www.bellavistadecolchagua.cl* ⇋ *9 rooms* ⦿ *Breakfast.*

$$$
HOTEL
FAMILY

☷ **Hotel Santa Cruz Plaza.** Right on the Plaza de Armas, this beautiful, colonial-style hotel is certainly Santa Cruz's most central, but it isn't the most historical. **Pros:** great location; handsome decor; quirky museum displays. **Cons:** rooms can be small; some street noise in back rooms; labyrinthine layout makes some rooms hard to find. ⑤ *Rooms from: 99000 pesos* ⊠ *Plaza de Armas 286* ☎ *72/220–9600* ⊕ *www.hotelsanta-cruzplaza.cl* ⇋ *116 rooms* ⦿ *Breakfast.*

$$$
HOTEL
FAMILY

☷ **Hotel TerraViña.** This pretty Spanish-style boutique hotel is only minutes outside of Santa Cruz, yet it's peacefully surrounded by its own vineyards and gardens. **Pros:** buffet breakfast; late check-out; convenient location. **Cons:** small bathrooms; noise travels between rooms; some beds could do with replacing. ⑤ *Rooms from: 95000 pesos* ⊠ *Camino Los Boldos s/n, Barreales* ☎ *72/282–1284* ⊕ *www.terravina.cl* ⇋ *19 rooms* ⦿ *Breakfast.*

$$$$
RESORT
Fodor's Choice
★

☷ **Lapostolle Residence.** Overlooking the stunning Apalta Valley and Lapostolle winery, the Lapostolle Residence is one of South America's most upscale wine residences, where fresh, made-to-order cuisine is prepared daily in a four-course, wine-paired menu for breakfast, lunch, and dinner. **Pros:** excellent homegrown food; beautiful valley; fantastic service. **Cons:** expensive; limited activities; late check-in. ⑤ *Rooms from: 600000 pesos* ⊠ *Camino Apalta, Km 4* ☎ *72/295–3360* ⊕ *www.lapostolle.com* ⊗ *Closed Aug.* ⇋ *4 rooms* ⦿ *Breakfast; All meals.*

$$
B&B/INN
FAMILY

☷ **Posada Colchagua.** With a large, sunny garden, a pool, and a fountain, this cheerful family posada in the rural Isla de Yaquil area provides both good value and a peaceful stay in the Colchagua Valley. **Pros:** good value; kind hospitality; experience of rural Chile. **Cons:** car required; limited mod cons; far from restaurants. ⑤ *Rooms from: 70000 pesos* ⊠ *Isla de Yaquil* ☎ *9/9223–2196* ⊕ *www.posadacolchagua.cl* ⇋ *10 rooms* ⦿ *Breakfast.*

SPORTS AND THE OUTDOORS

HORSEBACK RIDING

FAMILY **Cabalgatas Santa Cruz.** Expat Ian Garrett organizes three-hour horseback rides at his 1,500-acre family farm near Santa Cruz. The 40 horses bear riders up the foothills to a vantage point over the valley, where a picnic spread of cheese and wine from the family vineyard awaits. ⊠ *Isla de Yaquil* ☎ *9/7667–2595 cell* ⊕ *www.cabalgatassantacruz.com* ✉ *From 30000 pesos (hotel or Santa Cruz transfer included).*

SHOPPING

Alpaca Artesania Chilena. If you want authentic Chilean leather goods, alpaca wool, huaso hats, and colorful artisan products, this small shop on the main square carries them all—and more. ⊠ *Plaza de Armas 276* ☎ *9/8348–8983.*

La Lajuela. For a souvenir you can't find elsewhere, head to La Lajuela, a hamlet 8 km (5 miles) southeast of Santa Cruz. Residents here weave *chupallas*, straw hats made from a fiber called *teatina* that is cut, dyed, dried, and braided by hand. ⊠ *La Laguela*.

CURICÓ VALLEY

Curicó Valley may play second fiddle to Colchagua in terms of glamor, but it is a sizable region with both nature and vinous delights ready to be discovered between the mountains and coast. With its own national park and Lago Vichuquén nearby, there are plenty of outdoor sports to keep the adrenaline flowing between a few glasses of the region's famed Cabernet Sauvignon.

CURICÓ

113 km (71 miles) south of Rancagua along Pan-American Hwy.

Founded in 1743, Curicó means "black water" in Mapudungún, the native Mapuche language. Today this agroindustrial center is the provincial capital and the gateway to the Curicó wine valley. The Plaza de Armas is one of the most attractive in the Central Valley; it is a center of activity year-round but fills to capacity for the Fiesta de la Vendimia (Wine Harvest Festival) each March. Most of the wineries are south of the city and easily reached from the Pan-American Highway. Other points of interest are found toward the Andes or on the coast.

GETTING HERE AND AROUND

From Santa Cruz, head south on the Pan-American Highway for just a short 50 km (31 miles) to Curicó. You can also take an interurban bus to Curicó, or head to San Fernando and hop the train for the very quick trip south. Once you're in Curicó, you can get around by local bus, taxi, or colectivo. If you're visiting wineries, be sure to contact the Ruta del Vino de Curicó, which can help make arrangements for visits and transport to other sights, such as Radal Siete Tazas or Vichuquén.

Bus Contacts Curicó Terminal. ⊠ *Arturo Prat 780* ☎ *75/255–8118.*

ESSENTIALS

Visitor Information Curicó Tourism Office. ⊠ *Manso de Velasco 449* ☎ *75/254–7690* ⊕ *www.curico.cl.*

EXPLORING
TOP ATTRACTIONS

Viña Miguel Torres. Curicó's star winery is owned by the Spanish wine mogul, Miguel Torres, and he hasn't spared a peso in building this large winery just south of Curicó and immediately off the Pan-American Highway. There are a handful of wine tours on offer—from a classic winery tour to wine and chocolate pairings to one with a sparkling wine focus—and in each you'll get a glimpse into the pioneering nature of Torres, who was the first in Chile to use a stainless-steel tank (now de rigueur). He also brought another tradition from his native Iberia: the annual Wine Harvest Festival that takes place in Curicó's main plaza.

■TIP→ Be sure to visit the restaurant, definitely one of the finest in

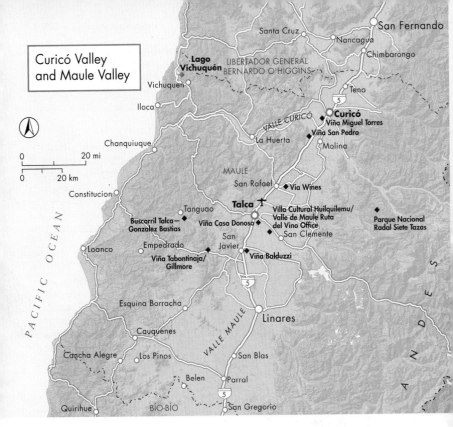

Curicó Valley
and Maule Valley

the area. The overnight guesthouse welcomes the public. ⊠ *Ruta 5 S, Km 195* ☎ *75/256–4100* ⊕ *www.migueltorres.cl* 🍷 *From 5000 pesos.*

Viña San Pedro. Surrounded by a vineyard that was first planted in 1701, San Pedro is one of Chile's largest producers, second only to Concha y Toro. San Pedro's top of the line is the premium Cabo de Hornos (which is Spanish for Cape Horn), followed by 1865 (the year the winery was founded), and Castillo de Molina. The bottling plant has a sleek glass dome and a second-floor viewing platform, and you can feel small alongside the 28 half-million-liter stainless-steel tanks in the winery. There's also a great little wine shop just off the highway where you can pick up some bargains. Tours can be arranged through the Ruta del Vino office in Curicó. ⊠ *Ruta 5 S, Km 205, exit to Lontue* ☎ *9/7518–6554* ⊕ *www.sanpedro.cl* 🍷 *From 9000 pesos* ☉ *Closed Sun.*

WORTH NOTING

Parque Nacional Radal Siete Tazas. This 10,000-acre national reserve, 70 km (43 miles) southeast of Curicó, is famous for the unusual "Seven Teacups," a series of pools created by waterfalls along the Río Claro (although it is more accurately five teacups since the 2010 earthquake displaced two). The falls are a short hike from the park entrance, where you'll find a CONAF station. Farther along the trail are two other impressive cascades: the Salto Velo de la Novia (Bridal Veil Falls) and

Salto de la Leona (Lioness Falls). Black woodpeckers, hawks, and eagles are common throughout the park, and condors nest in the highest areas. If you're lucky, you might glimpse the scarce *loro tricahue*, an endangered species that is Chile's largest and most colorful parrot. Camping is permitted in the park, which is snowed over in winter. October–March is the best time to visit. ⊠ *Camino Molina–Parque Inglés* ☎ *75/249–1179 CONAF* ⊕ *www.conaf.cl* ☙ *5000 pesos.*

Plaza de Armas. The lovely Plaza de Armas has a pretty fountain ringed by statues of dancing nymphs. Nearby is an elaborate bandstand constructed in New Orleans in 1904. ⊠ *Plaza de Armas.*

Ruta del Vino. The local Ruta del Vino office provides basic information and a variety of tours that range from simple half-day visits to a single winery to combination packages that include hiking, biking, and rafting. English-speaking guides are available. ⊠ *Carmen 727* ☎ *75/232–8972* ⊕ *www.rutadelvinocurico.cl* ☙ *From 60000 pesos (2 wineries, lunch, transport).*

LAGO VICHUQUÉN

112 km (69 miles) west of Curicó.

An hour's drive from Curicó, this lake is a popular place for water sports such as sailing and water-skiing. The town itself, about 8 km (5 miles) away, is worth a visit for its museum but has little to offer in terms of dining or lodging. Black-necked swans are a common sight on meandering Lago Vichuquén and nearby Laguna Torca, which is a protected area.

EXPLORING

Museo Colonial de Vichuquén. Ceramics, stone tools, and other artifacts collected from pre-Hispanic peoples are on display. ⊠ *Av. Manuel Rodríguez s/n, Vichuquén* ☎ ☙ *1500 pesos.*

WHERE TO STAY

$$
HOTEL
Fodor'sChoice
★

Marina Vichuquén. The comfortable Marina Vichuquén has an enviable location right on the shore and makes use of it with its own marina, where there are plenty of opportunities for water sports, including a sailing school for children. **Pros:** plenty to do here; well kept; good restaurant. **Cons:** somewhat remote location; no beach; some tired facilities. $ *Rooms from: 120000 pesos* ⊠ *Sector Aquelarre, Lago Vichuquén, Vichuquén* ☎ *75/240–0265* ⊕ *www.marinavichuquen.cl* ☞ *18 rooms* ⟋ *Breakfast.*

MAULE VALLEY

Talca is the capital of Maule, Chile's largest wine valley. Dozens of wineries are scattered throughout the region, which begins north of Talca in San Rafael and extends south to the regional border at the Perquilauquén River, just south of Parral. Most are roughly grouped into two areas: east of the highway around San Clemente, or slightly west of the highway around San Javier and Villa Alegre. Long ignored as backward, Maule is now an up-and-coming region, as insightful winemakers have discovered its value in producing excellent red wines with some of the oldest vines in the Americas.

6

TALCA

56 km (35 miles) south of Curicó on Ruta 5.

Straddling the banks of the Río Claro, Talca is not only Maule's most important industrial center; it is also one of the most appealing towns in the Central Valley. It was founded in 1692 and intelligently designed on a regimented grid pattern divided into quadrants—*poniente* means west, *oriente* east, *sur* south, and *norte* north—centered around the pretty Plaza de Armas. Be sure to take some time to check out its native and exotic trees.

GETTING HERE AND AROUND

No surprises here; once again it's back to the Ruta 5 (Pan-American Highway) for an easy ride to Talca, about 65 km (40 miles) south of Curicó.

ESSENTIALS

Visitor Information Sernatur. ⊠ *1 Oriente 1150, 1st fl.* ☎ *71/223-3669, 71/222-6940* ⊕ *www.sernatur.cl.*

EXPLORING

TOP ATTRACTIONS

Valle del Maule Ruta del Vino Office. The information center, east of Talca, arranges visits to about a dozen wineries. It can provide transportation and an English-speaking guide, which simplifies and enriches a visit. The office is in the **Villa Cultural Huilquilemu**, a hacienda built in 1850 that also holds a small museum of religious art and local culture. ⊠ *Villa Cultural Huilquilemu, Camino a San Clemente, Km 7* ☎ *9/8157-9951* ⊕ *www.valledelmaule.cl* ☜ *1000 pesos.*

Via Wines. The modern tasting room overlooks the vineyards and an artificial lake, and you can stop by for a traditional Chilean lunch as well as a tasting of its wines—which include Via Wines' most recognizable brand, Oveja Negra, which means black sheep. A visit takes you through the modern winery and gorgeous vineyards with the Andes as a backdrop. ⊠ *Fundo Las Chilcas, San Rafael* ⊕ *www.viawines.com/via_experience* ⌂ *Reservations essential.*

FAMILY **Viña Balduzzi.** Albano Balduzzi, descended from 200 years of Italian winemakers, built this 40-acre estate in San Javier in 1900; today it is run by his great-grandson and produces more than a million liters a year. Tours include a peek at the cellars that stretch underneath the property, and a collection of antique machinery, as well as a tasting of the varied portfolio. Within the estate is a beautiful expanse of oak and cedar trees perfect for a picnic, and if you want to get a bird's-eye view of the estate you can take a flying tour of the vineyards in a private airplane. Lunches can be organized on request. ⊠ *Av. Balmaceda 1189, San Javier* ☎ *73/232-2138* ⊕ *www.balduzzi.cl* ☜ *From 4500 pesos.*

FAMILY **Viña Casa Donoso.** Ten minutes east of Talca along a dirt road are the massive iron gates that mark the entrance to this red hacienda with barrel-tile roof. The estate was once called Domain Oriental because it is east of the city, but today it bears the name of the family who owned it for generations before it was purchased by four Frenchmen in 1989. The vineyards themselves climb up into the Andean foothills.

The oenological work is performed by a skilled Chilean staff. ⊠ *Fundo La Oriental, Camino a Palmira, Km 3.5* ☎ 71/234–1400 ⊕ *www.casa-donoso.cl* ⊠ *From 6000 pesos* ⌂ *Reservations essential.*

FAMILY
Fodor's Choice
★

Viña Tabontinaja/Gillmore. The Gillmores, who own this winery, are a creative bunch. In addition to making fine red wines (sold as Viña Gillmore), they have created a fun place to stop and spend a couple of hours or stay on for a night or two. There's an impressive zoo on-site that includes a pair of puma, a rare Chilean deer called a *pudu,* and a raucous group of peacocks. An adobe chapel has been turned into a museum. This is a great place to stay while on the way south. Its odd-looking guest houses made from ancient recycled fermentation tanks provide all the comforts of home, as well as a wood-burning hot tub and great food. Take the Pan-American Highway to the "Camino a Constitución" turnoff, south of San Javier. Head east over the Loncomilla River and through the rolling hills of the Coastal Mountains for 20 km (13 miles); Tabontinaja is on the right. ⊠ *Camino a Constitución, Km 20, San Javier* ☎ 73/197–5539 ⊕ *www.gillmore.cl* ⊠ *From 5000 pesos* ⌂ *Reservations essential.*

WORTH NOTING

Avenida Bernardo O'Higgins. A cedar-lined boulevard popular with joggers, skaters, and strolling couples, the Avenida Bernardo O'Higgins is a pleasant stretch of green. At its western tip is the Balneario Río Claro, where you can hire a boat to paddle down the river. ⊠ *Talca.*

Buscarril Talca-Gonzalez Bastias. There may be no better way to get to know the Central Valley than by taking a ride on one of Chile's few remaining *buscarril* lines, which runs from Talca to the wine region of Gonzalez Bastias in Maule. It departs from Talca's Estación de Tren daily at 12:15 pm, reaching Gonzalez Bastias at 2:42 pm; it returns at 5 pm. A good option is to visit Gonzalez Bastias winery on arrival and get in a tasting before a traditional *campestre* (countryside) lunch. ⊠ *11 Oriente 1000* ⊕ *www.trencentral.cl* ⊠ *10000 pesos return.*

Cerro de la Virgen. You can make out the city's orderly colonial design from this hill that affords a panoramic view of Talca and the vineyards in the distance. ⊠ *Talca.*

San Clemente. This town 16 km (10 miles) southeast of Talca, hosts the best rodeo in the region, with riding, roping, dances, and beauty-queen competitions. The events take place 11–6 on weekends from September to April. The national championship selections are held here near the end of the season. ⊠ *Talca.*

Tren Central. Take the train on a scenic route from Santiago into the Araucania and Temuco, in the heart of Maule, where you pass vineyards and hillsides. It departs twice a day from Santiago at 8:30 am and 7:30 pm. ⊠ *Estación de Ferrocarriles de Talca* ☎ 2/2585–5000 ⊕ *www.tren-central.cl* ⊠ *24000 pesos return from Alameda, Santiago.*

WHERE TO EAT

$$$
SUSHI

✗ **Ryoshi Sushi Bar Marisqueria.** In southern Chile, where fresh fish and seafood come in daily from the port, Ryoshi puts a contemporary twist on Chilean seafood classics, including scallop sashimi, flame-grilled octopus maki, tuna ceviche, and a truly Chilean delicacy—fresh sea

urchin. **Known for:** fresh seafood; Chilean-style sushi; good soups. ⑤ *Average main: 12000 pesos* ✉ *Av. Isidoro del Solar 260* ☎ *71/268–2018* ⊕ *www.ryoshi.cl* ⊘ *Closed Sun.*

WHERE TO STAY

$ 🏨 **Hostal del Puente.** This quiet, family-run hotel, at the end of a dusty
HOTEL   street two blocks west of the Plaza de Armas, is quite a bargain. **Pros:** good budget option; central; clean. **Cons:** no frills; simple breakfast; weak Wi-Fi. ⑤ *Rooms from: 30000 pesos* ✉ *1 Sur 407* ☎ *41/2131–091* ⊕ *www.hostaldelpuente.cl* ▭ *No credit cards* ⇨ *18 rooms* ⭐ *Breakfast.*

$$$ 🏨 **Hotel Casino Talca.** 🏨 **Tabonko.** Designed to look like two large wine
HOTEL   barrels, this boutique hotel right in the Gillmore vineyard is owned and run by the Gillmore family, who have created a warm space with plenty of personal touches. **Pros:** personally attended by the owners; vineyard setting; garden, pool, and small zoo. **Cons:** closed in winter; a bit remote; weak Wi-Fi. ⑤ *Rooms from: 110000 pesos* ✉ *Camino a Constitución, Km 20, San Javier* ☎ *73/2197–5539* ⊕ *www.tabonko.cl* ⊘ *Closed Apr.–Oct.* ⇨ *15 rooms* ⭐ *Breakfast.*

NIGHTLIFE

Casa Alameda. This busy resto-bar is a popular spot for late-night mojitos and beer on the outdoor patio; frequently in the evenings there's live music. Supplement your liquid indulgences with the stream of sushi and burgers from the kitchen. ✉ *4 Norte 1065* ☎ *71/268–0592.*

THE LAKE DISTRICT

WELCOME TO THE LAKE DISTRICT

TOP REASONS TO GO

★ **Volcanoes:** Volcán Villarrica and Volcán Osorno are the conical, iconic symbols of the northern and southern Lake District, respectively, but some 50 other volcanoes loom and fume in this region. Not to worry; eruptions are rare.

★ **Stunning summer nights:** Southern Chile's austral summer doesn't get more glorious than January and February, when sunsets don't fade until well after 10 pm, and everyone is out dining, shopping, and enjoying the outdoors.

★ **Lakes and rivers:** The region may sport a long Pacific coastline, but everyone flocks to the inland lakes to swim, sunbathe, kayak, sail, and more. The region also hosts numerous wild rivers that are, among other things, excellent for fly-fishing.

★ **Soothing hot springs:** Chile counts some 280 thermal springs, and a good many of the well-operated ones are in the Lake District, the perfect place to pamper yourself after a day of outdoor adventure and sightseeing.

Throughout the Lake District, volcanoes burst into view alongside large lakes and winding rivers. Architecture and gastronomy here are unlike anywhere else in Chile, much of it influenced by the large-scale German colonization of the 1850s and '60s. the Pan-American Highway (Ruta 5) runs down the middle, making travel to most places in the region relatively easy. It connects the cities of Temuco, Osorno, and Puerto Montt, but bypasses Valdivia by 50 km (30 miles). A drive from Temuco to Puerto Montt should take less than four hours. Flying between the hubs is a reasonable option. The region also has a passenger train connecting Temuco and Puerto Montt, plus many towns in between.

1 La Araucanía. This region contains some of Chile's most spectacular lake scenery. Several volcanoes, among them Villarrica and Llaima, two of South America's most active, loom over the region. Burgeoning Pucón, on the shore of Lake Villarrica, has become the tourism hub of southern Chile. Other quieter alternatives exist, however. Lago Calafquén, farther south, begins the *Siete Lagos* (Seven Lakes) chain that stretches across the border to Argentina.

2 Los Lagos and Los Ríos. The southern half of the Lake District is a land of snowcapped volcanoes, rolling farmland, and the shimmering lakes that give the region its name. This landscape is literally a work in progress, as it's part of the so-called Ring of Fire encircling the Pacific Rim. Most of the region's active volcanoes are here.

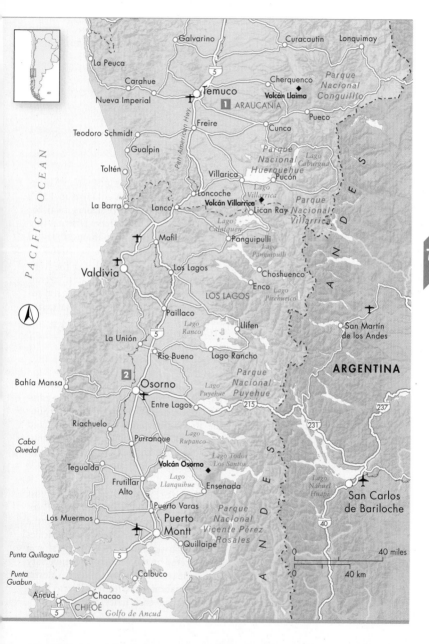

Updated
by Jimmy
Langman

As you travel the winding roads of the Lake District, the snowcapped shoulders of volcanoes emerge, mysteriously disappear, then materialize again, peeping through trees or towering above broad valleys. With densely forested national parks, a dozen large lakes, vastly improved hotels and restaurants, and easy access to roads and public transportation, Chile's Lake District has come pretty close to perfecting tourism. It's great for adventure travel and outdoor sports, but also has outstanding local cuisine, especially seafood, and a rich cultural past.

The Lake District is the historic homeland of Chile's indigenous Mapuche people, who revolted against the early Spanish colonists in 1598, driving them from the region. The Mapuche kept foreigners away for nearly three centuries. Though small pockets of the Lake District were controlled by Chile after it won its independence in 1818, most viewed the forbidding region south of the Río Bío Bío as a separate country.

Eventually, an 1881 treaty ended the Mapuche control over the territory, and in the middle of the 18th century Santiago began to recruit waves of German, Austrian, and Swiss immigrants to settle the so-called empty territory. The Lake District quickly took on the Bavarian-Tyrolean sheen that is still evident today.

PLANNER

WHEN TO GO

Most Chileans head here during southern Chile's glorious summer, between December and March. For fishermen, the official season commences the second Friday of November and runs through the first Sunday of May. Visiting during the off-season is no hardship, though, and lodging prices drop dramatically. An increasing number of Santiaguinos flee the capital in winter to enjoy the Lake District's brisk, clear air or to ski and snowboard down volcanoes and Andean hills.

FESTIVALS AND EVENTS

Summer means festival season in the Lake District. Communities across the region hold their own festivals in January and February, but the Festival Costumbrista in Castro, Chiloé, held the third week of February, is the can't-miss event. In late January and early February, Semanas Musicales de Frutillar brings together the best in classical music. Verano en Valdivia is a two-month-long celebration centered on the February 9 anniversary of the founding of Valdivia. During the second week of October, Valdivia also hosts a nationally acclaimed international film festival. Puerto Varas hosts an entertaining and fun Rain Festival each June.

GETTING HERE AND AROUND
AIR TRAVEL
None of the Lake District's airports—Osorno, Puerto Montt, Temuco, and Valdivia—receives international flights; flying here from another country means connecting in Santiago. Of the five cities, Puerto Montt has the greatest frequency of domestic flights.

BUS TRAVEL
There's no shortage of bus companies traveling the Pan-American Highway (Ruta 5) from Santiago south to the Lake District. The buses, which are very comfortable, have assigned seating and aren't too crowded. Tickets may be purchased in advance. If you are traveling overnight, consider spending extra dough on a "cama" bus; the seats are wider, fold back like a bed, and therefore are much more comfortable.

Bus Contacts Buses JAC. ⊠ *Balmaceda 1005, Temuco* ☎ *45/299–3117* ⊕ *www.jac.cl.* **Cruz del Sur.** ⊠ *Bus Terminal, Av. Vicente Pérez Rosales 1609, Temuco* ☎ *45/273–0310* ⊕ *www.busescruzdelsur.cl.* **Turbus.** ⊠ *Bus Terminal, Vicente Pérez Rosales 1609, Puerto Montt* ☎ *45/220–1521* ⊕ *www.turbus.cl.*

CAR TRAVEL
It's easier to see more of the Lake District if you have your own vehicle. The Pan-American Highway through the region is a well-maintained four-lane toll highway. Bring plenty of small bills for the frequent toll booths.

Rental Car Contacts Castillo Rent a Car. ⊠ *Valentin Letelier 585, Villarrica* ☎ *45/241–1618* ⊕ *www.castillorentacar.cl.* **Econorent.** ⊠ *Blanco Encalada 838, Temuco* ☎ *45/221–5997* ⊕ *www.econorent.cl.* **Europcar.** ⊠ *Panamericana Sur 4750, Padre Las Casas, Temuco* ☎ *45/291–8940* ⊕ *www.europcar.cl.*

RESTAURANTS
Meat and potatoes are popular in the cuisine of southern Chile. The omnipresent *cazuela* (a plate of rice and potatoes with beef or chicken) and *pastel de choclo* (a corn, meat, and vegetable casserole) are solid, hearty meals. But it is the seafood that most sets this region apart from other places. In Puerto Montt, tourists regularly fall in love with the local shellfish offerings, especially when served in traditional plates like *curanto* (cooked by hot stones) and *paila marina* (seafood stew).

Among the greatest gifts from the waves of German immigrants were their tasty *küchen,* rich fruit-filled pastries (raspberry and local *murta* berries are a special favorite here). Sample them during the late-afternoon *onces,* the coffee breaks locals take to tide them over until dinner. The Germans also brought their beer-making prowess to the New World; Valdivia, in particular, is where the popular Kunstmann brand got its start. *Restaurant reviews have been shortened. For full information, visit Fodors.com.*

HOTELS
Many hotels, even the newly built ones, are constructed in Bavarian-chalet style echoing the region's Germanic heritage. Central heating is a much-appreciated feature whenever it's available in lodgings here in winter and on brisk summer evenings. If not, you grow to appreciate the wood-heated stoves that abound all over the region. Air-conditioning is uncommon, but it's rarely necessary this far south. Rates usually include

a continental breakfast of coffee, cheese, bread, and jam. Although most of the places listed here stay open all year, call ahead to make sure the owners haven't decided to take a well-deserved vacation during the April–October off-season. *Hotels reviews have been shortened. For full information, visit Fodors.com.*

WHAT IT COSTS IN CHILEAN PESOS (IN THOUSANDS)			
$	$$	$$$	$$$$
Restaurants	Under 6	6–8	9–11	over 11
Hotels	Under 46	46–75	76–105	over 105

Restaurant prices are the average cost of a main course price at dinner or, if dinner is not served, at lunch. Hotel prices are the lowest cost of a standard double room in high season, excluding tax.

TOURS

Awash in rivers, mountains, forests, gorges, and its namesake lakes, this part of the country is one of Chile's outdoors capitals. Outfitters traditionally are concentrated in the northern resort town of Pucón and the southern Puerto Varas, but companies up and down this 400-km-long (240-mile-long) swath of Chile can rent you equipment or guide your excursions.

The increasing popularity of such excursions means that everybody wants a slice of the adventure pie. Quality varies widely, especially in everybody's-an-outfitter destinations such as Pucón or Puerto Varas. Ask questions about safety and guide-to-client ratios. (A few unscrupulous businesses might take 20 climbers up the Villarrica Volcano with a single guide.) Also, be brutally frank with yourself about your own capabilities: Are you really in shape for rappelling? Or is bird-watching more your style? This is nature at its best and sometimes most powerful.

LA ARAUCANÍA

La Araucanía is the historic home of the Mapuche indigenous people. The Spanish both feared and respected the Mapuche, and this nomadic society, always in search of new terrain, was a moving target that the Spaniards found impossible to defeat. Beginning with the 1598 battle against European settlers, the Mapuche kept firm control of the region for almost 300 years. After numerous peace agreements failed, a treaty signed near Temuco ended hostilities in 1881 and paved the way for the German, Swiss, and Austrian immigration that would transform the face of the Lake District.

TEMUCO

675 km (405 miles) south of Santiago.

This northern gateway to the Lake District acquired a bit of pop-culture cachet as the setting for a scene in *The Motorcycle Diaries*, a film

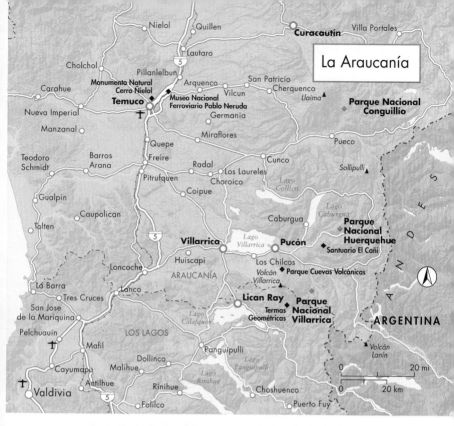

depicting Che Guevara's prerevolutionary travels through South America in the early 1950s. But with its office towers and shopping malls, today's Temuco would hardly be recognizable to Guevara. The city has a more Latin flavor than the communities farther south (it could be the warmer weather and the palm trees swaying in the pleasant central park). It's also an odd juxtaposition of modern architecture and indigenous markets, with traditionally clad Mapuche women darting across the street and business executives talking on cell phones, but oddly enough it all works. It warrants a day in town if you have the time.

GETTING HERE AND AROUND

At least a dozen bus lines serve Temuco; it's an obligatory stop on the long haul between Santiago and Puerto Montt. The city also hosts Manquehue Airport, 6 km (4 miles) southwest of town, which has daily connections to Santiago and other Chilean cities. At the airport, in addition to taxis, there are several transfer services that can take you into town. If going to Villarrica or Pucón, you probably come through here as well. The Pan-American Highway, Ruta 5, runs through the city and is paved, but several of the outlying roads connecting Temuco to smaller, rural towns are two-lanes and unpaved. Be careful on such roads, as the Chilean auto accident rate due to passing cars is high.

ESSENTIALS

Visitor Information Sernatur. ⊠ *Manuel Bulnes 590* ☎ *45/240–6215* ⊕ *www. sernatur.cl.* **Temuco Tourist Office.** ⊠ *Plaza Aníbal Pinto* ☎ *45/220–3345, 9/6238–0660.*

EXPLORING

Cholchol. The experience of visiting this small village 29 km (18 miles) northwest of Temuco begins the moment you board the bus. Expect to share space with Mapuche vendors and their enormous sacks and baskets of fruits and vegetables, all returning from market. A trip in your own vehicle is much less wearing but infinitely less colorful. Regardless of your chosen mode of transport, you arrive in Cholchol to the sight of *rucas,* traditional indigenous thatch huts, plus claptrap wooden houses, horse-drawn carts, and artisan vendors lining the dusty streets—all of whom sell their wares from 9 until about 6. Photo opportunities are plentiful, but be unobtrusive and courteous with your camera. Locals dislike being treated as merely part of the scenery. ⊠ *Temuco.*

Monumento Natural Cerro Ñielol. This imposing hillside site is where the 1881 treaty between the Mapuche and the Chilean army was signed, allowing the city of Temuco to be established. Trails bloom with bright red *copihues* (a bell-like flower with lush green foliage), Chile's national flower, in autumn (March–May). The monument, not far from downtown, is part of Chile's national park system. ⊠ *Av. Arturo Prat, 5 blocks north of Plaza Teodoro Schmidt* ☎ *45/229–8222* 🎫 *2000 pesos.*

Fodor'sChoice ★ **Museo Nacional Ferroviario Pablo Neruda.** Author Pablo Neruda was Chile's most famous train buff; he spent his childhood in Temuco, and his father was a rail worker. Accordingly, the city has transformed its old rail yard into this well-laid-out museum documenting Chile's rail history and dedicated it to the author's memory. Thirteen locomotives (one diesel and 12 steam) and nine train carriages are housed in the round engine building. Scattered among the exhibits are snippets from Neruda's writings: "Trains were dreaming in the station, defenseless, sleeping, without locomotives," reads one. Exhibits are labeled in Spanish, but an English-speaking guide is on hand if you need translation. The museum lies a bit off the beaten path, but if trains fascinate you, as they did Neruda, it's worth the short taxi ride from downtown. Twice-monthly tourist rail excursions to Valdivia, using the museum's restored 1940 steam locomotive, are worth an afternoon of your time. ⊠ *Av. Barros Arana 0565* ☎ *45/297–3940* 🎫 *1000 pesos* ☉ *Closed Mon.*

Museo Regional de la Araucanía. Housed in a 1924 mansion, this museum covers the history of the area. It has an eclectic collection of artifacts and relics, including musical instruments, utensils, and the country's best collection of indigenous jewelry. Upstairs, exhibits document the Mapuche people's three-century struggle to keep control of their land. The presentation could be more evenhanded: the rhetoric glorifies the Central European colonization of this area as the *pacificación de la Araucanía* (taming of the Araucanía territories). But the museum gives you a reasonably good Spanish-language introduction to Mapuche history, art, and culture. ⊠ *Av. Alemania 84* ☎ *45/274–7948* ⊕ *www. museoregionalaraucania.cl* 🎫 *Free* ☉ *Closed Mon.*

Plaza Aníbal Pinto. Temuco's bustling central square is ringed with imported palm trees—a rarity in this part of the country. A monument to the 300-year struggle between the Mapuche and the Spaniards sits in the center. ⊠ *Temuco.*

WHERE TO EAT

$
CAFÉ
✕ **Confitería Central.** Coffee and homemade pastries are the specialties of this café, but old-school (and big) sandwiches, excellent hot dogs, ice cream, and other simple dishes are also available. A classic stop in Temuco since the 1940s, it seems the whole town stops by for a quick lunch during the week, among the clattering of dishes and the army of waitresses maneuvering their way around the tables. **Known for:** great coffee; classic Chilean pastries; plenty of Temuco history. ⑤ *Average main: 4000 pesos* ⊠ *Manuel Bulnes 442* ☎ *45/221–0083* ⊕ *www.confiteriacentral.cl.*

$$$$
STEAKHOUSE
✕ **La Pampa.** Wealthy local professionals frequent this upscale modern steak house for its huge, delicious cuts of beef, abundant salads, and the best *papas fritas* (french fries) in Temuco. Although most Chilean restaurants douse any kind of meat with a creamy sauce, this is one of the few exceptions; the entrées are served without anything but the simplest of seasonings. **Known for:** huge bife de chorizo steaks; excellent salads; friendly service. ⑤ *Average main: 12400 pesos* ⊠ *San Martin 0137* ☎ *45/232–9999* ⊕ *www.lapampa.cl* ⊘ *No dinner Sun.*

$
CHILEAN
✕ **Las Muñecas del Ñielol.** This place has been an institution in Temuco since 1975, attaining legendary status for its homemade food. The kitchen puts its own tasty spin on traditional Chilean dishes like *guatitas a la española,* a stew of cow's stomach, bacon, sausage, and tomato cooked in wine. **Known for:** authentic Chilean dishes; great prices; friendly service. ⑤ *Average main: 3200 pesos* ⊠ *Caupolicán 1347* ☎ *45/223–7368* ⊘ *Closed Sun.*

$$$
ITALIAN
Fodor's Choice
★
✕ **Mercato.** With its extensive Italian menu and lively atmosphere, this is a place not to be missed when in Temuco. The pizza and pasta are spectacular, but do try their desserts as well (churro with manjar and nutella is heavenly). **Known for:** great traditional pizza and pastas; fresh juices; big crowds on the weekends so reserve ahead. ⑤ *Average main: 10000* ⊠ *Hochstetter 425* ☎ *45/248–2617* ⊕ *www.mercato.cl.*

$$$
SPANISH
✕ **Toro Bravo.** At this eclectic-looking restaurant steaks are huge and delicious, and there's also a variety of seafood and pasta dishes on the menu. Upon arrival, be sure to start it all off with a pisco sour. **Known for:** diverse menu; eclectic decor; crowded on weekends so it's best to make reservations. ⑤ *Average main: 9000 pesos* ⊠ *San Martín 468* ☎ *45/232–0161* ⊘ *No dinner Sun.*

WHERE TO STAY

$$
B&B/INN
⌂ **Goblin's House Hotel.** Situated above an Irish bar and restaurant of the same name, this boutique hotel is a fun spot for your overnight stay in Temuco. **Pros:** attentive service from the owner; relaxed environment; pool table in the bar. **Cons:** no gym or other services; simple breakfasts; rooms are poorly lit. ⑤ *Rooms from: 52000 pesos* ⊠ *Pirineos 0841* ☎ *45/232–0044* ⊕ *www.hotelgoblin.cl* ⇥ *7 rooms* ⑩ *Breakfast.*

$$
HOTEL
⌂ **Hotel Don Eduardo.** This orange, classic nine-story hotel is close to the city center and has rooms that are clean, pleasant, and mostly spacious.

The Mapuche People

The Mapuche profoundly affected the history of southern Chile. For almost 300 years this indigenous group fought to keep colonial, then Chilean powers out of their land. The Spanish referred to these people as the Araucanos, from a word in the Quechua language meaning "brave and valiant warriors." In their own Mapudungun language, today spoken by some 260,000 people, the word *mapuche* means "people of the land." In colonial times only the Spanish missionaries, who were in close contact with the Mapuche, seemed to grasp what this meant. "There are no people in the world," one of them wrote, "who so love and value the land where they were born."

Chilean schoolchildren learning about the Mapuche are likely to read about Lautaro, a feared and respected young chief whose military tactics were instrumental in driving out the Spanish. He cunningly adopted a know-thy-enemy strategy that proved tremendously successful in fending off the colonists. Students are less likely to hear about the tightly knit family structure or nomadic lifestyle of the Mapuche. Even the region's two museums dedicated to Mapuche culture, in Temuco and Valdivia, traditionally focused on the three-century war with the Spaniards. They toss around terms like *pacificación* (meaning "to pacify" or "to tame") to describe the waves of European immigrants who settled in the Lake District at the end of the 1800s, the beginning of the end of Mapuche dominance in the region.

Life has been difficult for the Mapuche since the signing of a peace treaty in 1881. Their land was slowly usurped by the Chilean government. Some 200,000 Mapuche today are living on small settlements known as *reducciones* (literally meaning "reductions"). Other Mapuche have migrated to the cities, in particular fast-growing Temuco, in search of employment. Many have lost their identity in the urban landscape, assimilating to the popular Chilean way of life.

A resurgence in Mapuche pride these days takes several forms, some peaceful, some militant. Mapuche demonstrations in Temuco are now commonplace, many calling attention to deplorable living conditions. Some are seeking the return of their land, while others are fighting against the encroachment of power companies damming the rivers and logging interests cutting down the forests. News reports occasionally recount attacks and counterattacks between indigenous groups and police in remote rural areas far off the beaten tourist path. The courts have become the newest battleground as the Mapuche seek legal redress for land they feel was wrongfully taken.

Awareness of Mapuche history is increasing. (Latest census figures show that about 1 million of Chile's population of 17 million can claim some Mapuche ancestry.) There is also a newfound interest in the Mapuche language and its seven dialects. Mapudungun poetry movingly describes the sadness and dilemma of integration into modern life and of becoming lost in the anonymity of urban life. Never before really understood by others who shared their land, the Mapuche have finally begun to make their cause known.

Pros: central location; very clean; parking available. **Cons:** no gym; restaurant closed on weekends; furnishings and decor need an update. $ *Rooms from: 68000 pesos* ✉ *Andres Bello 755* ☎ *45/221–4133* ⊕ *www.hoteldoneduardo.cl* ➩ *46 rooms* ⟨○⟩ *Breakfast.*

$$$
HOTEL

🏨 **Hotel Frontera.** This lovely old hotel is really two in one, with *nuevo* (new) and *clásico* (classic) wings facing each other across Avenida Bulnes in the city center. **Pros:** centrally located; great restaurant; modern, clean rooms. **Cons:** service slow at times; not all rooms are the same quality; parking is limited. $ *Rooms from: 95000 pesos* ✉ *Av. Bulnes 733–726* ☎ *45/220–0400* ⊕ *www.hotelfrontera.cl* ➩ *91 rooms* ⟨○⟩ *Breakfast.*

$$
HOTEL
FAMILY

🏨 **Hotel RP.** In a central location, this hotel has fine rooms, attentive service, and secure parking on-site. **Pros:** comfortable, ample rooms; central location; more amenities than other hotels in the area. **Cons:** street noise; breakfasts could be better; Wi-Fi connection comes and goes. $ *Rooms from: 63000 pesos* ✉ *Diego Portales 779* ☎ *45/297–7777* ⊕ *www.hotelrp.cl* ➩ *24 rooms* ⟨○⟩ *Breakfast.*

$
B&B/INN

🏨 **Posada Selva Negra.** This bed-and-breakfast run by a German-Chilean couple is a good option. **Pros:** super affordable; great breakfast; comfy beds. **Cons:** pretty far from the city center; not much privacy; small rooms. $ *Rooms from: 34000 pesos* ✉ *Tirzano 110* ☎ *9/9453–0200* ▭ *No credit cards* ➩ *7 rooms* ⟨○⟩ *Breakfast.*

NIGHTLIFE

Caravan. This bar has more than 50 beers available and excellent food. It's also open for lunch. ✉ *Alemania 0740* ☎ *45/224–0666* ⊕ *caravantemuco.cl.*

Lagerhaus. A great spot to sample Chilean microbrews, Lagerhaus also features excellent live music from local rock, blues, and funk bands. ✉ *Alemania 0425* ☎ *9/8803–1071.*

Sanseacabó. There's live music here every night, from blues to Latin rock, and generous cocktails. ✉ *Hoschtetter 435* ☎ *45/224–1010.*

SHOPPING

Temuco is ground central for the Mapuche Nation. Here you will find the gamut of Mapuche Indian handicrafts, from carpets to sweaters to sculpture.

Casa de la Mujer Mapuche. This indigenous women's center lets you shop for textiles, ponchos, and jewelry in a display room, with a minimum of fuss (the organization even handles catalog sales). Proceeds support social development programs. ✉ *Arturo Prat 283* ☎ *45/223–3886.*

Farmacia Mapuche Lawen Kiyen. This shop sells ancestral Mapuche remedies for everything from simple head colds to cancers and improving sexual performance. ✉ *Aldunate 245* ☎ *45/221–6030.*

Feria Libre. At the Feria Libre, you can bargain hard with the Mapuche vendors, who sell their crafts and produce in the blocks surrounding the railroad station and bus terminal. Leave the camera behind, as the vendors aren't happy about being photographed. ✉ *Barros Arana at Miraflores.*

Padre Las Casas. Across the Río Cautín from Temuco is the suburb of Padre Las Casas, a Mapuche community whose center is populated by artisan vendors selling locally crafted woodwork, textiles, and pottery under the auspices of the town's rural development program. You can purchase crafts here weekdays 9 to 5. ✉ *2 km (1 mile) southeast of Temuco.*

PARQUE NACIONAL CONGUILLÍO

126 km (78 miles) northeast of Temuco.

One of southern Chile's most beautiful and oldest tree species, the arau-caria tree thrives in the native forest that blankets one of Chile's best national parks. This natural paradise is a wonderful place for hiking, with lakes surrounded by forest and steep mountains. It's also home base for Llaima Volcano, one of Chile's most active volcanoes.

GETTING HERE AND AROUND

About 126 km (78 miles) northeast of Temuco, the roads are paved until the town of Curacautín; from there it's 40 km (25 miles) on gravel and dirt roads, marked with signs, to the park.

ESSENTIALS

CONAF. Chile's national parks are administered by CONAF, which pro-vides maps and other information about them. In summer the organization arranges hikes in Parque Nacional Conguillío. The agency is strict about permits to ascend the nearby volcanoes, so expect to show evidence of your climbing ability and experience. ✉ *Bilbao 931, Temuco* ☎ *45/229–8114.*

EXPLORING

Fodor'sChoice **Parque Nacional Conguillío.** Volcán Llaima, which has shown constant but
★ not dangerous levels of activity since 2002, is the brooding centerpiece of Parque Nacional Conguillío. One of Chile's most active volcanoes, the 3,125-meter (10,200-foot) monster has created the moonscape of hardened lava flow that characterizes the park's southern portion. In the 610-square-km (235-square-mile) northern sector, there are thou-sands of umbrella-like araucaria pines, also known as monkey puzzle trees. The Sierra Nevada Trail is the most popular for short hikes. The three-hour trek begins at park headquarters on Laguna Conguillío and continues northeast to Laguna Captrén. Heavy snow can cut off the area in winter, so November to May is the best time to visit the park's eastern sector. Conguillío's western sector, Los Paraguas, comes into its own in winter because of a small ski center.

The main entrance to the park is in the Melipeuco sector, which is reached from Temuco via a paved road that passes through the towns of Cunco and Melipeuco before becoming a gravel road over its final sec-tion. In Melipeuco, a private company, Sendas Conguillío, administers excellent cabins and camping facilities. ✉ *Parque Nacional Conguillío, Melipeuco* ☎ *45/229–8114* 🗓 *6000 pesos.*

WHERE TO STAY

$$$ 🛏 **Sendas Conguillío.** The official lodging concession at the park, Sen-
B&B/INN das Conguillío rents 11 rustic but comfortable cabins in the spectacu-lar Araucaria forest. **Pros:** quality cabins in the middle of stunning nature; outdoor hot tubs for each cabin; cabins are well-equipped.

Cons: can't get supplies in the park; you need a vehicle and patience to arrive; hot tubs available only if climatic conditions are not a fire risk. $ *Rooms from: 96,000 pesos* ✉ *Parque Nacional Conguillío, Melipeuco* ☎ *2/2840–6852* ⊕ *www.sendasconguillio.cl* ⇥ *11 cabins* ❄ *All-inclusive; Breakfast.*

CURACAUTÍN AND NEARBY

90 km (56 miles) northeast of Temuco.

The ancient homeland of the proud indigenous Pehuenche people, Curacautín province is one of the most spectacular places in southern Chile for adventuring into wild nature, with the ever-present Llaima and Lonquimay volcanoes towering over the landscape. Here you will find several reserves and parks, hot springs, and increasing tourism activities, which are beginning to rival the more well-known area to the south around Villarrica and Pucón.

GETTING HERE AND AROUND

You can get to Curacautín via Temuco, going north from Temuco on Ruta 5 for about 30 km (18 miles) until you reach the Lautaro exit. From there it's about 60 km (37 miles) on a paved road through hilly, scenic countryside landscape before arriving in the small town of Curacautín, the starting point for adventures at the many nature parks and reserves in the zone.

WHERE TO STAY

$$$$
B&B/INN

Endemiko. The cabins at Endemiko are quite plush, with all the creature comforts you'd expect yet fresh, minimalist, and attractive in their design. **Pros:** attractive design; cabins have top-quality comfort; personalized service. **Cons:** no Wi-Fi in cabins; expensive; no pool. $ *Rooms from: 160000 pesos* ✉ *Ruta Internacional 181, Km 89, Malalcahuello* ☎ *9/9825–2577* ⊕ *www.endemiko.cl* ⇥ *5 cabins* ❄ *Breakfast.*

$$$
B&B/INN
Fodor's Choice
★

La Baita Conguillío. Located in the heart of Conguillío National Park, this tranquil and rustic eco-lodge is powered almost entirely by renewable energy. **Pros:** proximity to nature trails; eco-friendly facilities; excellent food and service. **Cons:** difficult and dirt roads; strict energy diet means some luxuries are sacrificed; no Internet or television. $ *Rooms from: 90000 pesos* ✉ *Camino Laguna Verde, Km 18, Melipeuco* ☎ *45/258–1073* ⊕ *www.labaitaconguillio.com* ⊘ *Closed June* ⇥ *14 rooms* ❄ *Breakfast.*

$$$$
RESORT

Valle Corralco Hotel & Spa. This modern, spiffy hotel and spa is in a privileged mountain setting with some of the best skiing in the Southern Hemisphere during winter months. **Pros:** great skiing; gorgeous views; modern facilities. **Cons:** Internet connection is weak; restaurant menu is limited; prices skyrocket in ski season. $ *Rooms from: 115000 pesos* ✉ *Reserva Nacional Forestal Malalcahuello, Malalcahuello* ☎ *45/294–0310* ⊕ *www.corralco.com* ⇥ *58 rooms* ❄ *Breakfast; All-inclusive.*

7

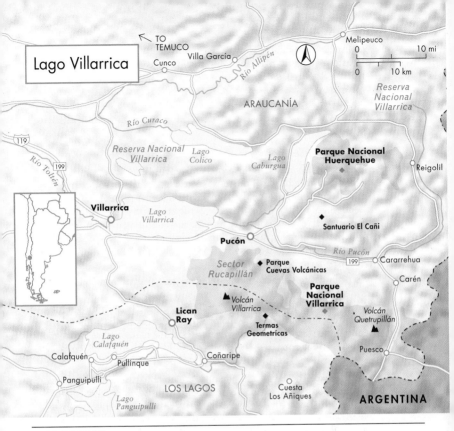

VILLARRICA

87 km (52 miles) southeast of Temuco.

Villarrica was founded in 1552, but the Mapuche wars prevented extensive settlement of the area until the early 20th century. Founded by the Spanish conqueror Pedro de Valdivia, it was a Spanish fortress built primarily to serve as a base for gold mining in the area. The fortress's mission succeeded until 1599, when the Mapuche staged an uprising and destroyed the original town. On December 31, 1882, a historic meeting between more than 300 Mapuche chiefs and the Chilean government was held in Putue, a few kilometers outside of the town. The next day, the town was refounded.

Today this pleasant town of about 35,000 people, situated on the lake of the same name, is in one of the loveliest, least-spoiled areas of the southern Andes and has stunning views of the Villarrica and Llaima volcanoes. To Villarrica's eternal chagrin, it lives in the shadow of Pucón, a flashier neighbor several miles down the road. Many travelers drive through without giving Villarrica a glance, but it has some wonderful hotels that don't give you a case of high-season sticker shock. Well-maintained roads and convenient public transportation make the town a good base for exploring the area.

GETTING HERE AND AROUND

Located southeast of Temuco, Villarrica can be reached by a paved, two-lane road, from the town of Freire, or farther to the south, from Loncoche. Several bus lines serve the town. For about 2,000 pesos, buses leave every hour from the Temuco bus terminal and arrive in Villarrica about one hour later.

ESSENTIALS

Visitor Information Villarrica Tourist Office. ☒ *Pedro de Valdivia 1070* ☏ *45/220–6619.*

TOURS

Amity Tours. This tour company runs several worthy day trips around Villarrica, including a Villarrica Volcano hike lumped together with a visit to a hot springs. There's also a full-day family rafting trip and barbecue on the mild but pretty Tolten River, which runs alongside the town. ☒ *Camino Internacional #1470 Interior, Pucón* ☏ *45/244–4574* ⊕ *www.amity-tours.com* ✉ *From 96000 pesos per person, with minimum 4 people.*

EXPLORING

Museo Histórico y Arqueológico de Villarrica. The municipal museum displays an impressive collection of Mapuche ceramics, masks, leather, and jewelry. A replica of a *ruca* hut graces the front yard. It's made of thatch so tightly entwined that it's impermeable to rain. ☒ *Pedro de Valdivia 1050* ☏ *45/241–5706* ✉ *Free* ⊘ *Closed weekends.*

WHERE TO EAT

$$ ╳ **Café 2001.** For a filling sandwich, a homemade *küchen* cake, and an
CAFÉCAFÉ espresso or cappuccino brewed from freshly ground beans, this is the place to stop in Villarrica. Pull up around a table in front or slip into one of the quieter booths by the fireplace in the back. **Known for:** one of the best lomito completo sandwiches in southern Chile; great coffee; quaint setting. ⑤ *Average main: 6000 pesos* ☒ *Camillo Henríquez 379* ☏ *45/241–1470.*

$$$ ╳ **Fuego Patagon.** On the outskirts of town near the lake, this stellar
BARBECUE restaurant serves exceptional steaks. The menu has good and generous
Fodor's Choice barbecue plates (including wild boar, goat, and lamb); there is a nice
★ variety of seafood and pasta dishes, too. **Known for:** friendly owner; great barbecue and steaks; tasty tiramisu. ⑤ *Average main: 11000 pesos* ☒ *Pedro Montt 40* ☏ *45/241–2207* ⊕ *www.fuegopatagon.cl.*

$$$ ╳ **Mesa del Mar.** This upscale restaurant in the center of town specializes
SEAFOOD in gourmet seafood. The menu also includes other diverse offerings, but
FAMILY it is the colorful, exquisitely prepared fish and shellfish that deserve your close attention. **Known for:** some of the region's best seafood; great choices for kids; sophisticated ambience. ⑤ *Average main: 10000 pesos* ☒ *Geronimo de Alderete 835* ☏ *45/241–9515* ⊕ *www.mesadelmar.cl.*

$$ ╳ **The Travellers.** Martín Golian and Juan Pereira met by happenstance
ECLECTIC and decided to open a place serving food from their homelands—and a few other countries. The result is a place that serves one or two dishes from Germany, Thailand, China, Italy, Mexico, and many countries in between. **Known for:** multiethnic cuisine; outdoor dining in summer; retro dance nights. ⑤ *Average main: 7000 pesos* ☒ *Valentín Letelier 753* ☏ *45/241–3617.*

WHERE TO STAY

$
B&B/INN
Hostal & Turismo Don Juan. This is an inexpensive option in the center of Villarrica that gives you all you need; rooms are simply furnished but clean, with Wi-Fi, cable, and parking on-site. **Pros:** central location; helpful staff; affordable. **Cons:** rooms are simple; light breakfast; thin walls. *⑤ Rooms from: 44000 pesos ⊠ General Korner 770 ☎ 45/241–1833 ⊕ www.hostaldonjuan.cl ➘ 23 rooms ⑩ No meals.*

$$$
B&B/INN
FAMILY
Hostería de la Colina. Attentive service as well as special little touches like homemade ice cream and bountiful breakfasts give this place an edge over others. **Pros:** friendly service; lovely ambience; scenic views. **Cons:** rooms could use new furnishings; some rooms are small; weak Wi-Fi in cabins. *⑤ Rooms from: 83000 pesos ⊠ Las Colinas 115 ☎ 45/241–1503 ⊕ www.hosteriadelacolina.com ➘ 9 rooms ⑩ Breakfast; Some meals.*

$$$
B&B/INN
Fodor'sChoice
★
La Codorniz. This lovely, wooden home is set upon a spectacular 25-acre private property with tremendous organic gardens and volcano views. **Pros:** outstanding meals prepared by owners; tranquil, lovely setting; warm hospitality. **Cons:** Wi-Fi is poor; cash only; can be hard to find. *⑤ Rooms from: 97000 pesos ⊠ Km 13.9 Segunda FAJA, Molco Alto ☎ 9/68341102 ⊕ www.lacodorniz.cl ➘ 6 rooms ⑩ Some meals ▤ No credit cards.*

$$$$
HOTEL
FAMILY
Villarrica Park Lake Hotel. This classic, European-styled hotel and spa, now part of the Enjoy chain, has the perfect mix of old-world luxury and clean, uncluttered design. **Pros:** lake views; lots of activities on-site; spacious rooms. **Cons:** understaffed; restaurant open Friday and Saturday only; no shuttle to town. *⑤ Rooms from: 120000 pesos ⊠ 13 km (8 miles) east of Villarrica on road to Pucón ☎ 600/700–6000 ⊕ www.enjoy.cl/villarrica/en/enjoy-park-lake ➘ 70 rooms ⑩ Breakfast.*

SPORTS AND THE OUTDOORS

Fodor'sChoice
★
Aurora Austral. Spectacular dog-sledding trips pulled by huskies are run by this tour agency, from one-day dog sledding below Villarrica Volcano to seven days crossing the Andes from Chile to Argentina. In summer, the dogs pull carriages. *⊠ Novena Region Husky Farm Patagonia, 19 km (12 miles) from Villarrica on road to Lican Ray ☎ 9/8901–4518 ⊕ www.auroraaustral.com.*

SHOPPING

Feria Mapuche. This market features some of the best local artisans that make all manner of Mapuche handicrafts, from sweaters and ponchos to wooden figurines. *⊠ At Pedro de Valdivia with Julio Zegers.*

PUCÓN

25 km (15 miles) east of Villarrica.

Fodor'sChoice
★
The resort town of Pucón, on the southern shore of Lago Villarrica, attracts Chileans young and old. By day, there are loads of outdoor activities in the area. The beach on Lago Villarrica feels like one of Chile's popular coastal beach havens near Viña del Mar. By night, young people flock to the major night spots and party until dawn while the older crowd has a large array of fine restaurants and trendy shops to visit. Pucón has many fans, though some lament the town's meteoric

rise to fame. Be warned that accommodations are hard to come by in February, which is easily the busiest month. Outside of summer, most stores, restaurants, and pubs here close down.

With Volcán Villarrica looming south of town, a color-coded alert system on the Municipalidad (city hall) on Avenida Bernardo O'Higgins signals volcanic activity, and signs around town explain the colors' meanings: green—that's where the light almost always remains—signifies "normal activity," indicating steam being let off from the summit with sulfuric odors and constant, low-level rumblings; yellow and red indicate more dangerous levels of activity. But remember that the volcano sits a good 15 km (9 miles) away, and you are scarcely aware of any activity. Indeed, ascending the volcano is the area's most popular excursion.

GETTING HERE AND AROUND

Pucón has only a small air strip 2 km (1 mile) outside of town for private planes, but national airlines such as LAN and Sky fly regularly to Temuco. From Temuco, Buses JAC has frequent service to Pucón. Roads that connect Pucón to Ruta 5, the Pan-American Highway, are paved from Loncoche and Freire. In Pucón, there are several taxis that can move you about, but the town itself is small and in most cases you just need your two feet.

ESSENTIALS

Visitor Information Pucón Tourist Office. ⊠ *Av. Bernardo O'Higgins 483* ☎ *45/229–3002.*

7

EXPLORING

Parque Cuevas Volcánicas. Halfway up Volcán Villarrica, you find this cave right next to a very basic visitor center. It first opened up in 1968 for spelunkers to explore, but eventually tourism proved more lucrative. A short tour takes you deep into the electrically illuminated cave via wooden walkways that bring you close to the crystallized basalt formations. Your tour guide may make occasional hokey references to witches and pumas hiding in the rocks, but it's definitely worth a visit—especially if uncooperative weather prevents you from partaking of the region's other attractions and activities. ⊠ *Volcán Villarrica National Park, Camino al Volcán Km 14.5* ☎ *45/244–2002* ⊕ *www.cuevasvolcanicas.cl* 🔛 *18000 pesos.*

Fodor's Choice **Termas Geométricas.** Chile's volcanoes have endowed the area around
★ Pucón with numerous natural hot springs. About a two-hour drive from Pucón, this is one of the best and most beautiful. Seventeen natural hot-spring pools, many of them secluded, dot the dense native forest. Each thermal bath has its own private bathrooms, lockers, and deck. ⊠ *3 km (2 miles) south of Villarica National Park* ☎ *9/7477–1708* ⊕ *www.termasgeometricas.cl* 🔛 *24000 pesos.*

WHERE TO EAT

$$ ✕**Cassis.** This wonderful café and restaurant is dessert heaven, with
CAFÉ assorted pastries baked fresh every day, chocolates galore, and an excellent selection of ice cream. The restaurant also has a varied menu of sandwiches, pizza, and more, and an extensive wine list. **Known for:**

some of the best desserts in the area; sidewalk seating; late nights in summer. $ *Average main: 6500 pesos* ✉ *Fresia 223* ☎ *45/244–9088* ⊕ *www.chocolatescassis.com.*

$$$
MEDITERRANEAN
✕ **Hestia and Bacco.** The chef here impresses diners from all over the world with the inventive and abundant Mediterranean dishes served at Hestia and Bacco. Always made with fresh, often organic, ingredients, the meals are truly delicious and well-presented. **Known for:** excellent beef short ribs; inventive Mediterranean dishes; growing popularity so reserve a table in advance. $ *Average main: 11000 pesos* ✉ *Fresia 246* ☎ *9/9200–3235.*

$$$$
STEAKHOUSE
✕ **La Maga.** Argentina claims to prepare the best *parrillada,*or grilled beef, but here's evidence that Uruguayans are no second best. Watch the beef cuts turn slowly over the wood fire at the entrance. **Known for:** traditional parrillada with a Uruguayan flair; great chimichurri sauce; huge portions. $ *Average main: 12500 pesos* ✉ *Gerónimo de Alderete 276* ☎ *45/244–4277* ⊕ *www.lamagapucon.cl.*

$$
ECLECTIC
✕ **Latitude 39.** Inventive hamburgers, sandwiches, burritos, tacos, and all-day breakfast are served at this California-inspired restaurant. Check out the Buddha burger, which is topped with popcorn shrimp and spicy sriracha sauce, the beer-battered fish tacos, or the delicious *huevos rancheros,* fried eggs on Mexican tortillas. **Known for:** all-day breakfast dishes like huevos rancheros; unique burgers; big crowds. $ *Average main: 6500 pesos* ✉ *Gerónimo de Alderete 324* ☎ *9/7430–0016* ⊙ *Closed Sun.*

$$
PIZZA
✕ **Pizza Cala.** The excellent pizza here is cooked in a wood-fired oven, making for exquisite crust. A host of great toppings is exactly the way Italy meant a pizza to be. **Known for:** classic pizza; craft beers; outdoor seating. $ *Average main: 7900 pesos* ✉ *Lincoyan 361* ☎ *45/246–3024.*

$$$
CONTEMPORARY
Fodor's Choice
★
✕ **Trawen Restaurant.** This solar-powered, creative restaurant features fresh and organic ingredients. Breakfasts include homemade yogurt, free-range eggs, and Italian coffee, while lunch and dinner present everything from over-size empanadas and sandwiches to meat, fish, and pasta. **Known for:** eco-friendly ethos; diverse menu; vegetarian and vegan options. $ *Average main: 8200 pesos* ✉ *Bernardo O'Higgins 311* ☎ *45/244–2024* ⊕ *www.trawen.cl.*

$$$
PERUVIAN
✕ **Viva Perú.** As befits the name, Peruvian cuisine reigns supreme at this restaurant with rustic wooden tables. Try the *ají de gallina* (hen stew with cheese, milk, and peppers), ceviche , or the splendid *saltado nikkei* , a Japanese-style dish of fish, shrimp, squid, and stir-fried vegetables. **Known for:** classic Peruvian dishes; lovely porch dining; two-for-one pisco sours. $ *Average main: 10000 pesos* ✉ *Lincoyan 372* ☎ *45/244–4025.*

WHERE TO STAY

$$$
HOTEL
🛏 **Apart Hotel Del Volcán.** In keeping with the region's immigrant heritage, the furnishings of this chalet-style hotel look like they come straight from Germany. **Pros:** kitchen available for use; central location; large apartments. **Cons:** no restaurant; street noise in summer; no air-conditioning. $ *Rooms from: 99000 pesos* ✉ *Fresia 420* ☎ *45/244–2055* ⊕ *www.aparthoteldelvolcan.cl* ⇗ *18 apartments* ⦿ *Breakfast.*

$ 🛏 **¡école!** This lively, nonprofit hostel has several shared rooms, but
B&B/INN opt for one of the excellent private rooms and stay in good style. **Pros:**
Fodor'sChoice great food in restaurant; easy to meet other travelers; eco-conscious
★ ethos. **Cons:** some rooms are noisy; hostel environment not for every-
one; breakfast not included in room rate. 💲 *Rooms from: 36000 pesos*
✉ *General Urrutia 592* ☎ *45/244–1675* ⊕ *www.ecole.cl* ⤴ *22 rooms*
🍽 *No meals.*

$$ 🛏 **Hostal Gerónimo.** This hotel is a solid choice and well-located in the
HOTEL town, an easy walk to everything yet on a quiet street. **Pros:** central
location; good value; excellent service. **Cons:** small rooms; Wi-Fi issues;
could use more light in some rooms. 💲 *Rooms from: 61000 pesos*
✉ *Gerónimo Alderete 665* ☎ *45/244–3762* ⊕ *www.geronimo.cl* ⤴ *34*
rooms 🍽 *Breakfast.*

$$$$ 🛏 **Hotel Antumalal.** A young Queen Elizabeth stayed here in the 1950s,
B&B/INN as did actor Jimmy Stewart—and the Antumalal hasn't changed much
since then. **Pros:** secluded location and views; fireplace in room; unique
architecture. **Cons:** old-fashioned decor not for everyone; could offer
more variety in restaurant; Wi-Fi unstable. 💲 *Rooms from: 219000*
pesos ✉ *Km 2, Camino Pucon-Villarica* ☎ *45/244–1011* ⊕ *www.antum-*
alal.com ⤴ *20 rooms* 🍽 *Breakfast; Some meals.*

$$$$ 🛏 **Hotel Boutique CasaEstablo.** A true boutique hotel, with just 10 rooms,
B&B/INN the CasaEstablo is personally managed by the owners and their two
lovely dogs, who provide service above and beyond. **Pros:** friendly hosts;
spacious rooms; lake views. **Cons:** road to hotel is very steep (don't go
here without your own vehicle); extra fee to use the wood-fired hot tub;
dogs on-site not great for those with allergies. 💲 *Rooms from: 150000*
pesos ✉ *Camino Villarica, Km 6* ☎ *45/244–3084* ⊕ *www.casaestablo.*
cl ⤴ *10 rooms* 🍽 *Breakfast.*

$$ 🛏 **Hotel O Gudenschwager.** Built in 1923, this old dame was remodeled to
B&B/INN become one of the town's finest bed-and-breakfasts. **Pros:** excellent loca-
tion; attentive service; some rooms have great views. **Cons:** no television
in rooms; can get cold at night; rooms are pretty small. 💲 *Rooms from:*
70000 pesos ✉ *Pedro de Valdivia 12* ☎ *45/244–9073* ⊕ *www.hogu.cl*
⤴ *17 rooms* 🍽 *Breakfast.*

$$$ 🛏 **Hotel Posada del Río.** This hotel has good quality rooms and cabins
B&B/INN on its beautiful, 4-hectare (10-acre) private park, Metreñehue, which
FAMILY is covered with native forest and skirts along the Trancura River. **Pros:**
good facilities; secluded riverside location near Pucón; spacious cabins.
Cons: no air-conditioning; Wi-Fi and cell phone service is weak here;
road to hotel needs better signage. 💲 *Rooms from: 77500 pesos* ✉ *Km*
11, Camino Pucon-Calburga ☎ *9/5821–5306* ⊕ *www.parquemetrene-*
hue.com ⤴ *13 rooms* 🍽 *Breakfast; Some meals.*

$$$$ 🛏 **Mirador los Volcanes.** In a gorgeous, rural setting, complete with sheep
B&B/INN outside your spacious cabin, this is an idyllic spot to relax and stay close
to several of the best sights in the Pucón area, like Lake Caburga, Huer-
quehue National Park, and numerous natural hot springs. **Pros:** tran-
quil, beautiful countryside setting; nearby lake and park; great pools.
Cons: 18 km (11 miles) from Pucón; some furnishings need upgrade;
Wi-Fi doesn't always work. 💲 *Rooms from: 110000 pesos* ✉ *Km 17.5,*

7

Camino Pucon-Caburgua ☎ *9/8189–8801* ⊕ *www.miradorlosvolcanes. com* ⇆ *10 rooms* ꫶⊙꫶ *Breakfast.*

$$$
B&B/INN
Fodor's Choice
★

⊞ **Peumayen Lodge & Termas Boutique.** This hotel is truly a sight to behold, set on a stunning, 48-hectare (119-acre) property dominated by native forests and biking and hiking trails. **Pros:** a great place to relax; award-winning restaurant; beautiful surroundings. **Cons:** can be too couple-focused for single or family travelers; pretty far from the amenities of Pucón; some furnishings in rooms need an update. ⑤ *Rooms from: 85000 pesos* ⊠ *Camino Pucón Huife, Km 28* ☎ *45/197–0060* ⊕ *www. termaspeumayen.cl* ⊗ *Closed June* ⇆ *12 rooms* ꫶⊙꫶ *Breakfast; All meals; Some meals.*

NIGHTLIFE

Beanies & Bikinis. A fun local hang-out, this is where the drinks flow, the music blares, and soccer games are always on the televisions. ⊠ *Fresia 477* ☎ *45/244–1109.*

Kamikaze. This is one of Pucón's great discos to party the night away. Summer brings big crowds and often special promotions on drinks. ⊠ *Camino Internacional 5* ⊹ *Sector El Claro* ⊕ *www.kamikaze.cl/ pucon.*

Mamas & Tapas. A local favorite is the friendly Mamas & Tapas, which is de rigueur among the expat crowd. Light Mexican dining morphs into DJ sets or live music at night, which lasts into the wee hours. ⊠ *Av. Bernardo O'Higgins 597* ☎ *45/244–9002.*

Sala Murano. This discotheque chain in Chile has one of the liveliest party centers in Pucón, with fiestas and drink specials throughout the year. ⊠ *Pasaje Las Rosas 175* ☎ *9/9561–6073* ⊕ *www.salamurano.cl.*

SPORTS AND THE OUTDOORS

Just 20 minutes from the 2,847-meter-high (9,341-foot) Villarrica Volcano, Pucón is one of Chile's top spots for adventure travel. The active volcano has itself become an obligatory climb for the many nature- and adventure-seeking tourists who come to Chile. In winter, the volcano is a favorite spot for skiing and snowboarding. Nearby Trancura River is a rafting, kayaking, and fishing paradise. Villarrica and Caburgua lakes are outstanding for fishing, swimming, kayaking, and water-skiing. There are several worthy nature hikes close to Pucón, featuring some of the most beautiful forests in Chile, including the El Cani Sanctuary and Huerquehue National Park.

At first glance Pucón's myriad outfitters look the same and sell the same slate of activities and rentals; quality varies, however. The firms we recommend get high marks for safety, professionalism, and friendly service. Although a given outfitter might have a specialty, it usually offers other activities as well. Pucón is the center for rafting expeditions in the northern Lake District, with Río Trancura 15 minutes away, making for easy half-day excursions on Class III–V rapids.

FLY-FISHING

Mario's Fishing Zone. This operator guides fly-fishing day trips on the Trancura and Liucura rivers near Pucón. Transport, boat, and a snack is included. ✉ *Av. Bernardo O'Higgins 590* ☎ *9/760–7280* ⊕ *www.flyfishingpucon.com* ⌨ *From 90000 pesos.*

HORSEBACK RIDING

Huepilmalal. This operator arranges horseback riding in the nearby Cañi mountain range, with everything from half-day to six-day excursions. ✉ *Km 27, Carretera a Huife* ☎ *9/643–2673* ⊕ *www.huepilmalal.cl.*

MULTISPORT OPERATORS

Aguaventura. Friendly, French-owned Aguaventura outfits for rafting, as well as canyoning, kayaking, snowshoeing, and snowboarding. They specialize in trekking up Volcan Villarrica, including some trips combined with a ski descent, although you should be an expert skier if you want to join them. ✉ *Palguín 336* ☎ *45/244–4246* ⊕ *www.aguaventura.com* ⌨ *From 25000.*

Captura Chile. This tour operator specializes in heli-skiing and heli-fishing, but also provides individuals and private groups with flight tours of the Pucón area via small plane or helicopter. ✉ *Pucón* ☎ *9/699–3686* ⊕ *www.capturachile.com.*

Politur. This tour operator can take you rafting or zip-lining at the Río Trancura, trekking in nearby Parque Nacional Huerquehue, and hiking up Volcán Villarrica, not to mention skiing and skydiving. They also offer a laid-back tour of the natural attractions in the Pucón area that includes a dip in a local hot spring. ✉ *Av. Bernardo O'Higgins 635* ☎ *45/244–1373* ⊕ *www.politur.com* ⌨ *From 15000 pesos.*

Sol y Nieve. For rafting trips, canyoning, hiking, and skiing expeditions, sign up with this tour operator. It takes groups up Villarrica Volcano. ✉ *Lincoyan 361* ☎ *45/244–4761* ⊕ *www.solynievepucon.cl* ⌨ *From 20000 pesos.*

Summit Chile. The experienced guides at Summit Chile rent gear and lead treks to the Villarrica Volcano summit; they also offer other outdoor adventures. It's the only agency with rock-climbing excursions in Pucón. ✉ *Urrutia 585* ☎ *45/244–3259* ⊕ *www.summitchile.org* ⌨ *From 36000 pesos.*

PARQUE NACIONAL HUERQUEHUE

35 km (21 miles) northeast of Pucón.

Unless you have a four-wheel-drive vehicle, this 124-square-km (48-square-mile) park is accessible only in summer (even then, a jeep isn't a bad idea). It's worth a visit for the two-hour hike on the Lago Verde trail beginning at the ranger station near the park entrance. You head up into the Andes through groves of araucaria trees, eventually reaching three startlingly blue lagoons with panoramic views of the whole area, including distant Villarrica Volcano.

GETTING HERE AND AROUND

Take the Caburgua road from Pucón, following the signs to Huerquehue, which is about 22 km (14 miles) northeast of Pucón.

WHERE TO STAY

Those not staying the night near the park can still use the hot springs at Termas de Huife for a 20,000 pesos entry fee. The office in Pucón offers twice-daily shuttle service for 26,000 pesos round-trip.

$$$$
B&B/INN

⊞ **Termas de Huife.** Just outside Parque Nacional Huerquehue, this resort lets you relax in three steaming pools set beside an icy mountain stream. **Pros:** access to hot springs and park; large pools; comfy beds. **Cons:** price is steep; no Wi-Fi in rooms; service in general is slow. $ *Rooms from: 189000 pesos* ⊠ *33 km (20 miles) from Pucón on road to Calburga, Pucón* ☎ *45/244–1222* ⊕ *www.termashuife.com* ⊅ *14 rooms* ⊌ *Breakfast.*

PARQUE NACIONAL VILLARRICA

15 km (9 miles) south of Pucón.

Dominated by Villarrica Volcano, this park is on the outskirts of Pucón and has become Chile's most popular place to climb a volcano, as well as a great destination for skiing, treks, and other outdoor adventures.

EXPLORING

Parque Nacional Villarrica. The main draw of this popular 610-square-km (235-square-mile) national park, which has skiing, hiking, and many other outdoor activities, is the volcano. Happily, you don't need to have any climbing experience to reach the 3,116-meter (9,350-foot) summit, but a guide is a good idea. The volcano sits in the park's Sector Rucapillán, a Mapuche word meaning "house of the devil." That name is apt, as the perpetually smoldering volcano is one of South America's most active. CONAF closes off access to the trails at the slightest hint of volcanic activity deemed out of the ordinary. It's a steep uphill walk to the snow line, but doable any time of year. All equipment is supplied by any of the Pucón outfitters that organize daylong excursions for about 50,000 pesos per person. Your reward for the six-hour climb is the rare sight of an active crater, which continues to release clouds of sulfur gases and explosions of lava. You're also treated to superb views of the nearby volcanoes, the less visited Quetrupillán and Lanín. ☎ *45/244–3781* ▧ *5000 pesos.*

Fodor's Choice
★

Santuario El Cañi. Chile's first private nature preserve, this park hosts one of the last remaining, extensive Araucaria forests, a magnificent tree species that can live up to 2,000 years and that is oft nicknamed "monkey puzzle" because of its tangled branches which swirl around its treetop. With about 500 hectares (1,235 acres) altogether, this is one of the best treks you can do in southern Chile. The hike to El Cañi's highest ground (1,600 meters), called El Mirador, is a three- to four-hour steep climb, but rewards you with some of the most beautiful views to be found of the region's lakes and volcanoes. The sanctuary can provide a guide (required in winter) and prices start at 45,000 pesos. There are camping sites and a *refugio* for overnight stays. Located about 20 km (12 miles) east of Pucón, the park is accessible via the road to Lago Caburgua (take the turnoff at Km 14). Then turn on the paved road with the sign "Termas Huife" and drive until you reach El Cañi. It is also possible to arrive by bus. ⊠ *Santuario El Cañi, Pucón* ☎ *9/9837–3928, 9/897–38147* ⊕ *www.santuariocani.cl* ▧ *5000 pesos.*

SPORTS AND THE OUTDOORS
SKIING

Ski Pucón. This popular ski resort, in the lap of Volcán Villarrica, has 20 runs of varying levels of expertise, but they're mostly for beginners and intermediate skiers. There are nine ski lifts, but note that these lifts are quite slow-going. There's also equipment rental and good snowboarding too. The ski season usually begins early July and often runs through mid-October. High-season rates are 38,000 pesos per day and 33,000 pesos per half day. There is also a restaurant, coffee shop, and boutique for skiing accessories, as well as skiing and snowboarding classes. ⊠ *Parque Nacional Villarrica, Pucón* ☎ *45/244–1901.*

LICAN RAY

30 km (18 miles) south of Villarrica.

In the Mapuche language, Lican Ray means "flower among the stones." This pleasant, unhurried little resort town of 2,169 inhabitants is on Lago Calafquén, the first of a chain of seven lakes that spills over into Argentina. You can rent rowboats and sailboats along the shore, which is also a fine spot to soak up sun.

GETTING HERE AND AROUND

You can reach Lican Ray via the paved Ruta 199 from Temuco and Villarrica. From Valdivia and points south, take Ruta 203 to Panguipulli, then travel on dirt and gravel roads north to Lican Ray. There is daily and frequent bus service to the town from nearby locales such as Villarrica.

7

ESSENTIALS

Visitor Information Lican Ray Tourist Office. ⊠ *General Urrutia 310, At Cacique Marichanquin* ☎ *45/243–1516.*

WHERE TO EAT

$$ ✕ **Cábala Restaurant.** Impeccable service is the hallmark of this Italian
ITALIAN   restaurant on Lican Ray's main street. The brick-and-log building has indoor and outdoor seating, perfect to watch the summer crowds stroll by as you enjoy pizza and pasta. **Known for:** classic Italian dishes; nice outdoor seating; friendly service. $ *Average main: 7500 pesos* ⊠ *General Urrutia 201* ☎ *9/9158–8636* ⊘ *Closed Apr.–Nov.*

$$ ✕ **Restaurant Mi Fundo.** Southern Chilean hospitality at its finest, this
CHILEAN   restaurant was actually constructed using wood from trees taken from the bottom of Lake Calafquén. The gregarious owners are on-site serving up stories and exquisite food, from diverse dishes using local trout fish and salmon to roast beef covered with a delicious mushroom sauce. **Known for:** friendly and proudly local service; tasty trout dishes; ice-cream cake for dessert. $ *Average main: 8000 pesos* ⊠ *Lican Conaripe, Km 1* ☎ *9/9450–3948.*

WHERE TO STAY

$$ 🛏 **Harris Hotel.** After more than two decades in operation, this rustic
B&B/INN   hotel on the lakefront is a good choice for Lican Ray. **Pros:** terrace views of lake; clean and comfortable; nice restaurant on-site. **Cons:** rooms are simply furnished; on the small side; some noise pollution in summer.

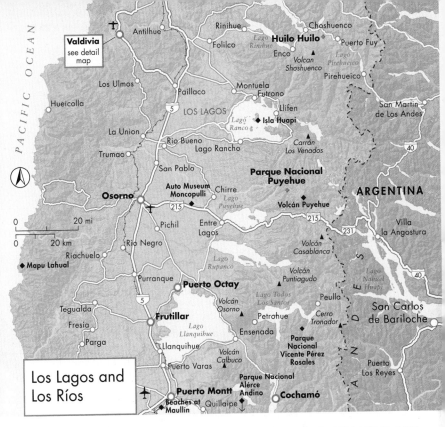

Los Lagos and Los Ríos

⑤ *Rooms from: 55000 pesos* ✉ *Cacique Manquel 105* ☎ *45/243–1553*
⊕ *www.hotelharris.cl* ⤻ *8 rooms* ❑ *Breakfast.*

$$
B&B/INN
🏠 **Hostal Hofmann.** The bright, airy rooms at this house just outside
town are built for extra comfort with lots of pillows and thick, color-
ful quilts on the beds. **Pros:** comfortable rooms; friendly owner; nice
sitting area. **Cons:** no restaurant; breakfasts could be improved; Wi-Fi
comes and goes. ⑤ *Rooms from: 48000 pesos* ✉ *Camino a Coñaripe
100* ☎ *45/243–1109* ⤻ *11 rooms* ❑ *Breakfast.*

SPORTS AND THE OUTDOORS
Playa Chica. This smaller of the beaches near Lican Ray is south of town
and popular for swimming. ✉ *Lican Ray.*

Playa Grande. This beach stretches a few blocks on the west side of Lican
Ray and has choppy water. Swimming is best avoided here. ✉ *Lican Ray.*

LOS LAGOS AND LOS RÍOS

Some of Chile's oldest cities are in the Los Lagos and Los Ríos regions
yet you may be disappointed if you come looking for colonial grandeur.
Wars with indigenous peoples kept the Spaniards, then Chileans, from
building here for 300 years. An earthquake of magnitude 9.5, the largest

recorded in history, was centered near Valdivia and rocked the region on May 22, 1960. It destroyed many older buildings in the region and produced a tsunami felt as far away as Japan.

Eager to fill its *tierras baldías* (uncultivated lands) in the 19th century, Chile worked tirelessly to promote the country's virtues to German, Austrian, and Swiss immigrants looking to start a new life. The newcomers quickly set up shop, constructing breweries, foundries, shipyards, and lumberyards. By the early part of the 20th century, Valdivia, which is now capital of the Los Ríos region, became one of the country's foremost industrial centers, aided in large part by the construction of a railroad from Santiago. Puerto Montt, capital of the Los Lagos region, is today the fastest growing city in Chile and the principal port for the country's large-scale farmed salmon exports. To this day, there remains a distinctly Germanic flair in this part of Chile, and you might swear you've taken a wrong turn to Bavaria when you pull into towns like Frutillar or Puerto Octay.

VALDIVIA

120 km (72 miles) southwest of Villarrica.

One of Chile's most scenic cities, it gracefully combines Chilean woodshingle construction with the architectural style of the well-to-do German settlers who colonized the area in the late 1800s. The historic appearance is a bit of an illusion, as the 1960 earthquake destroyed all but a few old riverfront structures. The city painstakingly rebuilt its downtown area, seamlessly mixing old and new buildings. Today you can enjoy evening strolls through its quaint streets and along two rivers, the Valdivia and the Calle-Calle.

Various tour boats leave from the docks at Muelle Schuster along the Río Valdivia for a one-hour tour around nearby Isla Teja. Expect to pay about 7,000 pesos. If you have more time, a five-hour excursion takes you to Niebla near the coast for a visit to the colonial-era forts. A four-hour tour north transports you to Punucapa, the site of a 16th-century Jesuit church and a nature sanctuary at San Luis de Alba de Cruces. Most companies charge around 29,000 pesos for either of the longer tours (depending on whether the tour includes a meal). Each tour company offers all three excursions daily during the December–March high season, and you can always sign on to one at the last minute. Most will not operate tours for fewer than 15 passengers, however, which makes things a bit iffy during the rest of the year.

GETTING HERE AND AROUND

Like most other major cities in the Lake District, Valdivia is served by Ruta 5, the Pan-American Highway. The city also has an airport with frequent flights by national airlines such as LAN, and the nation's bus lines regularly stop here as well. Valdivia's bus terminal is by the river at the cross section of Muñoz and Prat. Some outlying towns and sites around Valdivia you may want to visit, however, are connected only by dirt roads.

ESSENTIALS

Visitor Information Sernatur. ✉ *Arturo Prat s/n, in front of Feria Fluvial* ☎ *63/223–9060* ⊕ *www.sernatur.cl*. **Valdivia Tourist Office.** ✉ *Arturo Prat s/n , in front of Mercado Municipal* ☎ *63/227–8748*.

EXPLORING

TOP ATTRACTIONS

Catedral de Nuestra Señora del Rosario. Valdivia's imposing modern cathedral faces the west side of the central plaza. A small museum inside documents the evangelization of the region's indigenous peoples from the 16th through 19th centuries. ✉ *Independencia 514* ☎ *63/223–3663* ⊕ *www.obispadodevaldivia.cl* ☞ *Free.*

Cervecería Kunstmann. Valdivia has a long history of producing beer, and this brewery brews the country's beloved lager. The Anwandter family emigrated from Germany a century-and-a-half ago, bringing along their beer-making know-how. The *cervecería* (brewery), on the road to Niebla, hosts interesting guided tours by prior arrangement. There's also a small museum and a souvenir shop where you can buy the requisite caps, mugs, and T-shirts, plus a pricey restaurant serving German fare. ✉ *Ruta 350 No. 950* ☎ *63/229–2969* ⊕ *www.cerveza-kunstmann.cl* ☞ *10000 pesos.*

Mercado Fluvial. This awning-covered market in the southern shadow of the bridge leading to Isla Teja is a perfect place to soak up the atmosphere of a real fish market. Vendors set up early in the morning; you hear the thwack of fresh trout and the clatter of oyster shells as they're piled on the side of the market's boardwalk fronting the river. If the sights, sounds, and smells are too much for you, fruit and vegetable vendors line the other side of the walkway opposite the river. ✉ *Av. Arturo Prat at Libertad* ☎ *63/221–2151* ☉ *Closed Sun.*

Museo de Arte Contemporáneo. Fondly known around town as the "MAC," this is one of Chile's foremost modern-art museums. The complex on Isla Teja was built on the site of the old Anwandter brewery destroyed in the 1960 earthquake. The minimalist interior, formerly the brewery's warehouses, contrasts sharply with a modern glass wall fronting the Río Valdivia, completed for Chile's bicentennial. The museum has no permanent collection; it's a rotating series of temporary exhibits by contemporary Chilean artists. ✉ *Los Laureles* ✛ *Isla Teja* ☎ *63/222–1968* ☞ *1500 pesos* ☉ *Closed on Mon. in Mar.–Dec.*

Museo Histórico y Antropológico Maurice van de Maele. For a historic overview of the region, visit this museum on neighboring Isla Teja. The collection focuses on the city's colonial period, during which time it was settled by the Spanish, burned by the Mapuche, and invaded by Dutch corsairs. Downstairs, rooms re-create the interior of the late-19th-century Anwandter mansion that belonged to one of Valdivia's first immigrant families; the upper floor delves into Mapuche art and culture. ✉ *Los Laureles, Isla Teja* ☎ *63/221–2872* ⊕ *www.museosaustral.cl/index.php/museos/museo-historico-y-antropologico-mauricio-van-de-maele-valdivia* ☞ *1500 pesos* ☉ *Closed Mon. in Mar.–Dec.*

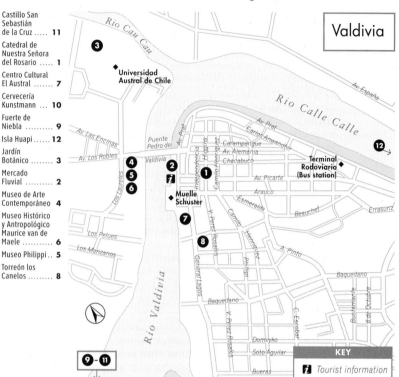

WORTH NOTING

Castillo San Sebastián de la Cruz. Across the estuary from the Fuerte de Niebla is this large and well-preserved fort from 1645. In the January through February summer season, historic reenactments of Spanish military maneuvers take place daily at 4 and 6. To get there, you need to rent a small boat, which costs only about 1,000 pesos at the marina near Fuerte de Niebla. ✉ *1 km (½ mile) north of Corral* ☎ *63/247–1828* 🎫 *1000 pesos* ⊘ *Closed Mon.*

Centro Cultural El Austral. A walk south of downtown on Yungay and General Lagos takes you through a neighborhood of late-19th- and early-20th-century houses that were spared the ravages of the 1960 earthquake. One of these houses dates to 1870 and accommodates the Centro Cultural El Austral. It's worth the stop if you have an interest in period furnishings. ✉ *Yungay 733* ☎ *63/213–6588* ⊕ *www.ccultural-valdivia.cl* 🎫 *Free* ⊘ *Closed Mon.*

Fuerte de Niebla. To protect the all-important city of Valdivia, the Spanish constructed a series of strategic fortresses at Niebla, where the Valdivia and Tornagaleones rivers meet. Portions of the 1671 Fuerte de Niebla and its 18 cannons have been restored. The ground on which the cannons sit is unstable; you can view them from the ramparts above. The old commander's house serves as a small museum documenting

the era's military history. ⊠ *1 km (½ mile) west of entrance to Niebla* ☎ *63/228–2084* ⊕ *www.museodeniebla.cl* ✆ *Free* ☉ *Closed Mon.*

OFF THE
BEATEN
PATH

Isla Huapi. Some 20% of Chile's 1 million Mapuche live on *reducciones,* or reservations. One of the most welcoming communities is on Isla Huapi, a leafy island in the middle of deep-blue Lago Ranco. It's out of the way—about 80 km (48 miles) southeast of Valdivia—but worth the trip for those interested in Mapuche culture. A boat departs from Futrono, on the northern shore of the lake, at 7 am Monday, Wednesday, and Friday, returning at 5 pm. The pastoral quiet of Isla Huapi is broken once a year in January or February with the convening of the island council, in conjunction with the Lepún harvest festival. You are welcome during the festival, but be courteous and unobtrusive with your camera. ⊠ *Valdivia.*

Jardín Botánico. North and west of the Universidad Austral campus, this garden is awash with 1,000 species of flowers and plants native to Chile. It's a lovely place to wander among the alerce, cypress, and laurel trees whatever the season. If you can't make it to Conguillío National Park to see the monkey puzzle trees, this is the place to see them. It's particularly enjoyable in spring and summer. ⊠ *Isla Teja* ☎ *63/222–1344* ⊕ *www. jardinbotanicouach.cl* ✆ *Free.*

FAMILY **Museo Philippi.** Behind the history and anthropology museum, this museum bears the name of 19th-century Chilean explorer and scientist Rudolph Amandus Philippi and is designed to foster an interest in science among young people. ⊠ *Los Laureles s/n* ☎ *63/221–2872* ⊕ *www.museosaustral.cl/index.php/museos/museo-r-a-philippi-de-la-exploracion* ✆ *1500 pesos* ☉ *Closed Mon. in Mar.–Dec.*

Torreón Los Canelos. Just south of the Centro Cultural El Austral lies one of two fortress towers constructed in 1774 to defend Valdivia from constant indigenous attacks. Both towers—the other sits on Avenida Picarte between the bus terminal and the bridge entering the city over the Río Calle Calle—were built in the style of those that guarded the coasts of Andalusia, in southern Spain. A wall and moat connected the two Valdivia towers in the colonial era, effectively turning the city into an island. ⊠ *General Lagos at Yerbas Buenas.*

WHERE TO EAT

$ ✕**Café Haussmann.** The excellent *crudos* (steak tartare), German-style
GERMAN sandwiches, and delicious *küchen* cakes here are testament to the fact that Valdivia was once a mecca for German immigrants. The place is small—a mere four tables and a bar—but the authentic ambience is special. **Known for:** German-style dining; excellent steak tartare; intimate seating. ⑤ *Average main: 4500 pesos* ⊠ *Av. Bernardo O'Higgins 394* ☎ *63/221–3878* ⊕ *www.cafehaussmann.cl* ☉ *Closed Sun.*

$$$ ✕**La Parrilla de Thor.** This riverfront institution is constantly packed with
STEAKHOUSE locals, which is always a good sign that you've come to the right res-
Fodor'sChoice taurant. The Argentine owner Teodoro Poulsen serves beef and chicken
★ in delicious Argentine *parrilla* style. **Known for:** one of the best steakhouses in Chile; river views; great wine list. ⑤ *Average main: 10000 pesos* ⊠ *Arturo Prat 653, Costanera* ☎ *63/227–0767.*

$ ✕**La Ultima Frontera.** The creative and wide variety of sandwiches in
CAFÉ this bohemian café have made it a national legend. On first glance,

La Ultima Frontera appears to be nothing more than a college hangout or a trendy place for the artsy crowd, but the abundant, reasonably priced, and delicious food attracts young and old. **Known for:** creative sandwiches; artsy, youthful ambience; locally brewed beers on tap. $ *Average main: 3500 pesos* ⊠ *Vicente Perez Rosales 787* ☎ *63/223–5363* ⊘ *Closed Sun.*

$$$ ✕ **New Orleans.** Louisiana Cajun cooking in southern Chile is far from
CAJUN common, but this place pulls it off and has become a must-stop on
FAMILY the tourist trail. Excellent meats and seafood with a spicy, Cajun twist populate the extensive menu, like *filete Mardi Gras* or red curry shrimp. **Known for:** Cajun cuisine; seafood straight from a NOLA menu; Mardi Gras–inspired ambience. $ *Average main: 9000 pesos* ⊠ *Esmeralda 682* ☎ *63/221–8771.*

$$ ✕ **Salón de Té Entrelagos.** This swanky café caters to Valdivian business
CAFÉ executives who come here to make deals over sandwiches, decadent crepes, and desserts. In the evenings, the atmosphere feels less formal—the menu is exactly the same—as the Entrelagos becomes a place to meet friends who converse well into the night. **Known for:** Isla Teja sandwich with grilled chicken and vegetables; chocolate shop next door; business lunches. $ *Average main: 8000 pesos* ⊠ *Vicente Pérez Rosales 640* ☎ *63/221–8333* ⊕ *www.entrelagos.cl.*

WHERE TO STAY

$$ 🏨 **Hotel Diego de Almagro Valdivia.** A good value in a superb location on
HOTEL the riverfront and near the city center, this hotel is part of a national chain. **Pros:** near the city center; great value option; nice views. **Cons:** interior decor is old-fashioned; not many amenities; no local character. $ *Rooms from: 71000 pesos* ⊠ *Arturo Prat 433, Costanera* ☎ *2/235–59250* ⊕ *www.dahoteles.com* ⇨ *105 rooms* ❑ *Breakfast.*

$$$$ 🏨 **Hotel Dreams Valdivia.** This swanky hotel is the tallest in Valdivia and
HOTEL thus has tremendous views no matter the vantage point. **Pros:** rooms
Fodor's Choice with a view; modern comforts; near the action. **Cons:** casino gets noisy;
★ no privacy between balconies; service could be more attentive. $ *Rooms from: 119000 pesos* ⊠ *Carampangue 190* ☎ *2/2346–4300, 600/626–0000* ⇨ *88 rooms* ❑ *Breakfast.*

$$$ 🏨 **Hotel Naguilán.** Located on the banks of the Río Valdivia, this is an
HOTEL entertaining and pretty spot, and the hotel itself is overall one of good quality. **Pros:** attentive service; river location; outdoor pool in summer. **Cons:** 15-minute walk to downtown; outdated furnishings in older wing; traffic noise in rooms facing main road. $ *Rooms from: 89000 pesos* ⊠ *General Lagos 1927* ☎ *63/221–2851* ⊕ *www.hotelnaguilan. com* ⇨ *33 rooms* ❑ *Breakfast.*

$$$ 🏨 **Hotel Puerta del Sur.** In a near perfect location, on a secluded spot on
HOTEL Isla Teja, yet only eight blocks from downtown Valdivia, this highly regarded lodging has spacious, pleasant rooms, decorated in soft lavender tones, and views of the river. **Pros:** central location; great service; lots of activity options. **Cons:** maintenance issues due to advancing age of property; in need of a decor update; no gym. $ *Rooms from: 102000 pesos* ⊠ *Los Lingues 950, Isla Teja* ☎ *63/222–4500* ⊕ *www. hotelpuertadelsur.com* ⇨ *40 rooms* ❑ *Breakfast.*

7

$$$
B&B/INN

🛏 **Pilolcura Lodge.** Just 25 km (15 miles) from Valdivia, Pilolcura Lodge comes with a tremendous beachside location and five immaculate rooms facing the ocean. **Pros:** location on a quiet, lovely beach; world-class mountain biking; clean and relaxing rooms. **Cons:** road to lodge is in poor condition in spots; located far from actual city; no television in rooms. ⓢ *Rooms from: 82000 pesos* ⊠ *Playa Pilolcura* ☎ *9/7378–0103* ⊕ *www.pilolcuralodge.cl* ⟿ *5 rooms* ⦿*| Breakfast.*

NIGHTLIFE

Here in the hometown of Austral University of Valdivia, a major Chilean university, the nightlife is lively and fun, particularly in and around the downtown area known as Calle Esmeralda. Bars, discos, and pubs are not just student-oriented, though; there are also many establishments in Esmeralda and elsewhere in the city that cater to older folks.

Carre Social Club. This fun club with an outdoor terrace, indoor pub, and disco has generous happy hour specials before 11 pm. ⊠ *Esmeralda 677* ☎ *63/223–9288* ⊕ *www.valdivia.carre.cl.*

Fodor's Choice
★

El Growler. Opened by an ex-pat from Oregon, this microbrew pub has taken Chile by storm and brushed to the side the old traditional German beers the area had previously been known for. The Growler's own IPA beer is offered in-house only, and is a bar highlight. They also have a plethora of other beers, and good pub food like fish-and-chips. ⊠ *Saelzer 41* ☎ *63/222–9545* ⊕ *www.elgrowler.cl.*

Rio Music Bar. This vibrant bar is popular with the twentysomething crowd, thanks to the live music and good food. ⊠ *Alemania 290* ☎ *63/221–1229.*

SPORTS AND THE OUTDOORS

A complex network of 14 rivers cuts through the landscape in and around this southern Chilean city, forming dozens of small islands. About 160 km (99 miles) of the river system are navigable in waters ranging from 5 to 20 meters (16½ to 66 feet) deep. That makes ideal territory for kayaking, canoeing, and sailing, among other water sports. Valdivia is also near the Pacific coast. Curiñanco beach, 25 km (16 miles) from Valdivia, is considered a prime spot for fishing. Then there are the intact coastal temperate rainforests on the outskirts of town, secluded areas with beautiful scenery for long hikes and camping trips. At the private Oncol Park, 22 km (14 miles) from Valdivia, are hiking trails and an 870-meter (2,854-foot) tree-top canopy course.

Bird-watching is a joy here, particularly when you witness the rare black-necked swans, one of the world's smallest, which have made the Valdivia area their main habitat despite past pollution problems from a nearby pulp mill.

Panchito El Lobo Marino. A young, local veterinarian founded this unique eco-tourism company that aims to show and explain the region's wildlife species and natural ecosystems through bike and kayaking tours. ⊠ *Valdivia* ☎ *9/7296–0188* ⊕ *www.panchitoellobomarino.cl.*

Pueblito Expediciones. This Valdivia-based tour operator organizes marvelous rafting, kayaking, and nature-appreciation trips on nearby rivers. ⊠ *San Carlos 188* ☎ *63/224–5055* ⊕ *www.pueblitoexpediciones. cl* ⟿ *From 25000 pesos.*

Turismo Hua Hum. This veteran tour operator runs city tours, bike rentals, and hiking excursions to nearby Parque Oncol and the Coastal Alerce Reserve. ⊠ *Carelmapu 2133* ☎ *9/9771–5083* ⊕ *www.huahum.cl* ⊠ *From 30000 pesos.*

SHOPPING

Entrelagos. Affiliated with the restaurant of the same name next door, Entrelagos has been whipping up sinfully rich chocolates for decades and arranging them with great care in the storefront display windows. Most of what is sold here is actually made at Entrelagos's factory outside town, but a small army of chocolate makers is on-site to let you see, on a smaller scale, how it's done, and to carefully package your purchases for your plane ride home. ⊠ *Vicente Pérez Rosales 622* ☎ *63/221–2047* ⊕ *www.entrelagos.cl.*

Mercado Municipal. The city's 1918 Mercado Municipal barely survived the 1960 earthquake intact, but it thrives again after extensive remodeling and reinforcement as a shopping-dining complex. A few restaurants, mostly hole-in-the-wall seafood joints (but some quite nice) share the three-story building with artisan and souvenir vendors. ⊠ *Block bordered by Av. Arturo Prat, Chacabuco, Yungay, and Libertad* ☎ *63/222–0353.*

HUILO HUILO

165 km east of Valdivia.

Fodor's Choice ★ At this private nature reserve, which spans nearly 120,000 hectares (300,000 acres), you find some of the last and best stands of Chile's native evergreen forest, a temperate rain-forest ecosystem rich in plants and unique wildlife like the world's smallest deer, the pudu, and the *monito del monte*, the only surviving member of an otherwise extinct marsupial order. In addition, Huilo Huilo has undergone an ambitious project to restore the endangered huemul deer to the landscape. The reserve is home to rivers ideal for rafting and fishing, plus the spectacular Lake Pirihueico, which can be crossed by ferry to get to Argentina's tourist resort San Martin de Los Andes. Snow at the top of the park's Mocho Volcano is year-round, making it one of the country's best destinations for snowboarding. In the nearby town of Neltume and at the park store, you can purchase unique local handicrafts based on forest mythological characters known as *duendes* and *hadas.*

GETTING HERE AND AROUND

Travel east from Valdivia by car, pass by picturesque country farms along Ruta 5, going through Lanco until you reach the town of Panguipulli. From there, pick up the Panguipulli–Puerto Fuy International Highway, which becomes gravelly and narrow, with wicked curves, over the last stretch of 10 km (6 miles) leading into Huilo Huilo.

WHERE TO STAY

$$$$
RESORT
FAMILY
Fodor's Choice ★

Huilo Huilo. This massive eco-tourism complex boasts four hotels, numerous cabins, and several camping sites amid the beautiful temperate forest, rivers, and lakes at the Huilo Huilo Biological Reserve. **Pros:** close access to nature; unique architecture; amazing views. **Cons:** no Wi-Fi in rooms; customer service is inconsistent; a long drive to get

there. $ *Rooms from: 108290 pesos* ✉ *Camino Internacional, Huilo Huilo, between Netulme and Puerto Fuy* ☎ *2/2887–3536* ⊕ *www.huilo-huilo.com* ⇄ *109 rooms* ⦿| *Breakfast.*

OSORNO

107 km (65 miles) southeast of Valdivia, via Ruta 5, Pan-American Hwy.

Although the least visited of the Lake District's four major cities, Osorno is one of the oldest in Chile, but the Mapuche prevented foreigners from settling here until the late 19th century. Like other communities in the region, it bears the imprint of the German settlers who came here in the 1880s. The 1960 earthquake left Osorno with little historic architecture, but a row of 19th-century houses miraculously survived on Juan Mackenna between Lord Cochrane and Freire. Their distinctively sloped roofs, which allow adequate drainage of rain and snow, are replicated in many of Osorno's newer houses. Situated in a bend of the Río Rahue, the city makes a convenient base for exploring the nearby national parks.

GETTING HERE AND AROUND
Osorno is about a 1½-hour flight from Santiago. By car, Osorno is reached by the paved Ruta 5, or Pan-American Highway. There is also passenger train service via Temuco. All the main bus lines serve Osorno on a frequent basis.

ESSENTIALS
Visitor Information Sernatur. ✉ *Av. Bernardo O'Higgins 667* ☎ *64/223–4104* ⊕ *www.sernatur.cl.*

TOURS
Osorno Tourist Office. The friendly people at the tourist office arrange free daily tours in summer. Each day has a different focus, including walks around the city, fruit orchards, or nearby farms. ✉ *North side of Plaza de Armas, Mackenna and Freire* ☎ *64/221–8740* ⌑ *Free.*

EXPLORING
Catedral de San Mateo Apostol. This modern cathedral fronts the Plaza de Armas and is topped with a tower resembling a bishop's mitre. "Turn off your cell phone," the sign at the door admonishes those who enter. "You don't need it to communicate with God." ✉ *Plaza de Armas.*

Fodor's Choice **Mapu Lahual.** On the Pacific coast, about a three-hour drive from
★   Osorno, is a network of indigenous parks spread over nine Huilliche Indian communities amid 50,000 hectares (124,000 acres) of pristine temperate rainforest. Day trips include a sail up the coast to visit a Huilliche settlement. The eight-person boat leaves from Bahía Mansa, but keep an eye on the weather as the boat won't run if it's really windy. Exploring the indigenous parks by land is a more intrepid trip, although trekking, horseback rides, and homestays (simple, basic accommodations) with descendants of the Huilliche are possible. Nature lovers will appreciate the native alerce forest as you cross the Chilean Coastal Range, home to 30 different bird species and an equal number of mammals, including the Molina's hog-nosed skunk, mountain monkeys, and

pumas. A highlight for those going by water is the beautiful, white-sand Condor Beach. ⊠ *Oficina de Turismo, Puaucho, Ruta U400, San Juan de la Costa* ☎ *9/8731–3418* ⊕ *www.turismosanjuan.cl.*

Museo Municipal Osorno. This museum contains a decent collection of Mapuche artifacts, Chilean and Spanish firearms, and exhibits devoted to the German settlement of Osorno. Housed in a pink neoclassical building dating from 1929, this is one of the few older structures in the city center. ⊠ *Manuel Antonio Matta 809* ☎ *64/223–8615* ⊕ *www. osornomuseos.cl* ⊠ *Free.*

WHERE TO EAT

$$ × **Café Central.** You can dig into a hearty American-style breakfast in the
CAFÉ morning and burgers and sandwiches the rest of the day at this diner on the Plaza de Armas. It's most famous around town for its *completos*— Chilean hot dogs topped with gobs of mayo, guacamole, and whatever else you desire. **Known for:** huge, tasty breakfasts; famous Chilean hot dogs; local favorite (not much English). ⑤ *Average main: 6000 pesos* ⊠ *Av. Bernardo O'Higgins 610* ☎ *64/225–7711.*

$$$$ × **El Galpón.** This is a good place to eat barbecue, steaks, and chicken
BARBECUE (and just that, as it's meat only here). The design intrigues as well,
Fodor's Choice resembling a *galpón,* which means "barn" in English. **Known**
★ **for:** best dining option in Osorno; meat-centric menu; fun, rustic ambience. ⑤ *Average main: 11500 pesos* ⊠ *Lord Cochrane 816* ☎ *64/223–4098* ◷ *Closed Mon.*

WHERE TO STAY

$$ ⌂ **Hotel García Hurtado de Mendoza.** Long one of Osorno's better lodg-
HOTEL ings, this stately hotel built in 1988 is a good option in the center of town, just two blocks from the Plaza de Armas. **Pros:** excellent location; friendly service; comfortable rooms. **Cons:** hotel restaurant closed on weekends; no gym; parking is limited. ⑤ *Rooms from: 63000 pesos* ⊠ *Juan Mackenna 1040* ☎ *64/223–7111* ⊕ *www.hotelgarciahurtado. cl* ⊅ *31 rooms* ⦿ *Breakfast.*

$$ ⌂ **Hotel Waeger.** In operation for nearly seven decades, this German
HOTEL hotel has seemingly become synonymous with travel to Osorno. **Pros:** best restaurant in town; close to center; decent prices. **Cons:** classic decor and atmosphere is not for everyone; like many old hotels, needs some renovation; lacking sufficient electric outlets in some rooms. ⑤ *Rooms from: 64000 pesos* ⊠ *Lord Cochrane 816* ☎ *64/223–3721* ⊕ *www.hotelwaeger.cl* ⊅ *45 rooms* ⦿ *Breakfast.*

$$$ ⌂ **Sonesta Hotel Osorno.** Part of the upscale, international hotel chain
HOTEL of the same name, this modern, high-quality hotel overlooks the
Fodor's Choice Rahue River and is adjacent to Plaza de Los Lagos, a shopping cen-
★ ter with a large casino. **Pros:** spacious rooms; high-quality facilities; next to casino and shops. **Cons:** service is sometimes slow; loca-tion is not near city center; thin walls. ⑤ *Rooms from: 89500 pesos* ⊠ *Ejercito 395* ☎ *64/255–5000* ⊕ *www.sonesta.com/osorno* ⊅ *106 rooms* ⦿ *Breakfast.*

7

SPORTS AND THE OUTDOORS

No outdoor wonder, this city is within an hour's drive of Puyehue National Park, one of Chile's best hiking areas, and several lakes for fishing and boating, such as Rupanco. To the west, there is horseback riding, fishing, and hiking along the Pacific coast and at the indigenous network of parks, Mapu Lahual, which is managed by Huilliche native communities.

SHOPPING

Centro de Artesanía Local. Osorno's city government operates this complex of 46 artisan vendors' stands built with steeply sloped roofs. Woodwork, leather, and woolens abound. Prices are fixed but fair. ⊠ *Juan MacKenna at Ramón Freire.*

EN ROUTE

Auto Museum Moncopulli. An Osorno business executive's love for tailfins and V-8 engines led him to establish this auto museum. His particular passion is the little-respected Studebaker, which accounts for more than half of the 100 vehicles on display. Elvis and Buddy Holly bop in the background to put you in the mood. ⊠ *Ruta 215, 25 km (16 miles) east of Osorno, Puyehue* ☎ *64/221–0744* ⊕ *www.moncopulli. cl* ⊠ *4500 pesos.*

PARQUE NACIONAL PUYEHUE

81 km (49 miles) east of Osorno, via Ruta 215

One of Chile's most popular national parks, Parque Nacional Puyehue draws crowds who come to bask in its famed hot springs. Most never venture beyond them, and that's a shame. A dozen miles east of the Aguas Calientes sector lies a network of short trails leading to spectacular moonlike volcanic landscapes and evergreen forests with dramatic waterfalls.

GETTING HERE AND AROUND

From Osorno, the park is about 80 km (50 miles) to the east off Highway 215. There are also several buses and travel agencies in Osorno that can help with transport to the park.

EXPLORING

Volcán Puyehue. Truly adventurous types attempt the five-hour hike to the summit of 2,240-meter (7,350-foot) Volcán Puyehue. As with most climbs in this region, CONAF rangers insist on ample documentation of experience before allowing you to set out. Access to the 1,070-square-km (413-square-mile) park is easy; head east from Osorno on the highway leading to Argentina. ⊠ *Ruta 215* ☎ *65/248–6101* ⊠ *1500 pesos.*

WHERE TO STAY

$$$$
B&B/INN
Cantarias Lodge & Spa. An exclusive boutique lodge on the south shore of Lake Puyehue, Cantarias combines personalized service and an excellent restaurant with outdoor excursions like fly-fishing, kayaking, trekking, and skiing. **Pros:** great selection of outdoor activities; superior restaurant; located close to entrance of Puyehue park. **Cons:** lodge is oriented toward longer stays; often booked solid; expensive. ⑤ *Rooms from: 291000 pesos* ⊠ *Km 63.5, Ruta Internacional 215* ☎ *9/9159–1367* ⊕ *www.cantarias.com* ⟿ *8 suites* ⦿ *All-inclusive; Breakfast; Some meals.*

$$$
B&B/INN
Fodor's Choice
★
⊞Lodge El Taique. This B&B run by a friendly French couple is situated in a charming country setting with tremendous lake and volcano views. **Pros:** excellent French cuisine; gorgeous views; good value rooms. **Cons:** located 8 km (5 miles) from the main road; no guides for outdoor activities; no television. ⑤ *Rooms from: 78000 pesos* ⊠ *Sector El Taique, Km 4, Puyehue* ☎ *9/9213–8105* ⊕ *www.lodgeeltaique.cl* ⇌ *10 rooms* ⋈ *Breakfast.*

$$$$
RESORT
FAMILY
⊞Termas Puyehue Wellness and Spa Resort. This grandiose stone-and-wood hot springs resort sits on the edge of Parque Nacional Puyehue. **Pros:** near Puyehue Park; thermal pools; all-inclusive. **Cons:** some of the older rooms could benefit from upgrading; pools can get crowded; summer rates are high. ⑤ *Rooms from: 270000 pesos* ⊠ *Ruta 215, Km 76, Puyehue* ☎ *64/233–1400, 2/2293–6000 in Santiago* ⊕ *www.puyehue.cl* ⇌ *137 rooms* ⋈ *All-inclusive.*

PUERTO OCTAY

50 km (30 miles) southeast of Osorno, via Ruta 5, Pan-American Hwy.

The story goes that a German merchant named Ochs set up shop in this tidy community on the northern tip of Lago Llanquihue. A phrase uttered by customers looking for a particular item, "¿Ochs, hay...?" ("Ochs, do you have...?"), gradually became "Octay." With spectacular views of the Osorno and Calbuco volcanoes, the town was the birthplace of Lake District tourism. A wealthy Santiago businessman constructed a mansion (now the famed Hotel Centinela) outside town in 1912, using it as a vacation home to host his friends.

GETTING HERE AND AROUND
Puerto Octay is easily accessible on paved roads from Ruta 5, the Pan-American Highway. It's about an hour north of Puerto Montt.

WHERE TO EAT

$$$$
BARBECUE
FAMILY
Fodor's Choice
★
✕Rancho Espantapajaros. Midway between Puerto Octay and Frutillar, this countryside restaurant has an all-you-can eat buffet, which includes the tasty, rarely offered *carne de jabali,* or wild boar meat. But the entire menu is worthy, including homemade integral bread, organic fruits and vegetables, and other meat and chicken dishes done up with regional flavors like quinoa and merquen, plus a plethora of cakes and desserts. **Known for:** extensive all-you-can-eat buffet; wild boar meat; reservations recommended on weekends. ⑤ *Average main: 12000 pesos* ⊠ *Quilanto, Km 6* ☎ *65/233–0049* ⊕ *www.espantapajaros.cl.*

WHERE TO STAY

$$$$
B&B/INN
FAMILY
⊞Los Lingues Lodge. Offering much more than just four spacious, well-equipped cabins, Los Lingues Lodge also comes with a southern Chilean breakfast delivered right to your door and a full-on outdoor adventure in a beautiful setting. **Pros:** well-equipped cabins; outdoor adventure options on-site; beautiful natural setting. **Cons:** long road to the lodge; Internet connection is not always the best; other meals not included. ⑤ *Rooms from: 116000 pesos* ⊠ *Rte. U-55-V, Km 27.5, Cruce El Escudo* ☎ *9/9642–8604* ⊕ *www.loslingueslodge.com* ⇌ *4 cabins* ⋈ *Breakfast.*

7

$ ☒ **Zapato Amarillo.** This modern alerce-shingled house and accompany-
B&B/INN   ing cabins with grassy roofs give a drop-dead gorgeous view of Volcán
Fodor's Choice   Osorno outside town. **Pros:** amazing food; fantastic views; kitchen
★   available for use. **Cons:** neighbor noise through thin walls; cash only;
located about 30 minutes from town. ⑤ *Rooms from: 42000 pesos*
☒ *Ruta U-55, Km 2.5* ☎ *64/221–0787* ⊕ *www.zapatoamarillo.cl* ▭ *No
credit cards* ⊗ *Closed June–Aug.* ⮩ *6 rooms* ⑩ *Breakfast; Some meals.*

FRUTILLAR

30 km (18 miles) southwest of Puerto Octay.

Halfway down the western edge of Lago Llanquihue lies the small
town of Frutillar, a destination for European immigrants in the late
19th century and, today, arguably the most picturesque Lake District
community. The town—actually two adjacent hamlets, Frutillar Alto
and Frutillar Bajo—is known for its perfectly preserved German architecture. Don't be disappointed if your first sight of the town is the
nondescript neighborhood (the Alto) on the top of the hill; head down
to the charming streets of Frutillar Bajo that face the lake, with their
picture-perfect view of Volcán Osorno. The town has rapidly developed
its touristic infrastructure, and it is worth a stop.

GETTING HERE AND AROUND
The town is about 45 minutes north of Puerto Montt, on Ruta 5, the
Pan-American Highway. Several bus lines make stops here on Santiago–
Puerto Montt routes.

ESSENTIALS
Visitor and Tour Information Información Turística. ☒ *Costanera Philippi
in front of boat dock.* **Secretaria Municipal de Turismo.** ☒ *Av. Philippi 753*
☎ *65/242–1685.*

EXPLORING
Fodor's Choice   **Museo Colonial Alemán.** Step into the past at one of southern Chile's
★   best museums. Besides displays of 19th-century agricultural and household implements, this open-air museum has full-scale reconstructions
of buildings—a smithy and barn, among others—used by the original
German settlers. Exhibits at this complex administered by Chile's Universidad Austral are labeled in Spanish and German, but there are also
a few signs in English. A short walk from the lake up Avenida Arturo
Prat, the museum also has beautifully landscaped grounds and great
views of Volcán Osorno. ☒ *Av. Vicente Pérez Rosales at Av. Arturo Prat*
☎ *65/242–1142* ▭ *2500 pesos.*

WHERE TO EAT
$$ ✗ **Club Alemán.** One of the German clubs that dot the Lake District,
GERMAN   Alemán serves up ample portions alongside prompt service. This is the
perfect spot to try Germanic pork and sauerkraut dishes. **Known for:**
traditional German cuisine; rotating prix-fixe menus; tasty küchen cake
for dessert. ⑤ *Average main: 7500 pesos* ☒ *Philippi 747* ☎ *65/242–1249.*

$$$$ ✗ **Restaurante Cocina Frau Holle.** Get a table with an incredible view of
BARBECUE   the lake during the day if you can, and prepare to enjoy the out-of-this-
FAMILY   world homemade bread and a delicious pisco sour. Then, go for one of

their huge steaks, pork chops, or short ribs, along with the homemade french fries. **Known for:** succulent steaks; tasty homemade bread and awesome desserts; lake views. $ *Average main: 15000 pesos* ⊠ *Antonio Varas 54* ☎ *65/242–1345.*

$$$
CONTEMPORARY
Fodor's Choice
★

✕ **Se Cocina.** The gourmet meals at Se Cocina, made with fresh local ingredients from the organic garden on-site, are excellent, but it's worth coming here for the experience alone. The food is prepared right in front of you at the open kitchen, which is next to the dining room tables. **Known for:** local organic ingredients and open kitchen; lake views; microbrews made on-site. $ *Average main: 10500 pesos* ⊠ *Camino a Tortal Km 2, sector Quebrada Honda* ☎ *9/8972–8195* ⊕ *www.secocina.cl.*

WHERE TO STAY

$$$
B&B/INN
Fodor's Choice
★

🏠 **Hotel Ayacara.** This attractive yellow-and-green house built at the turn of the 19th century has tasteful design and beautiful views of the lake and Osorno Volcano. **Pros:** historic, remodeled home; great views; good food. **Cons:** limited parking; can hear noise from other rooms; lots of stairs. $ *Rooms from: 85000 pesos* ⊠ *Philippi 1215* ☎ *65/242–1550* ⊕ *www.hotelayacara.cl* ➡ *8 rooms* ⦿ *Breakfast.*

$$$$
B&B/INN

🏠 **Hotel Frau Holle.** This 1940s German colonial house, remodeled into a boutique hotel, is surrounded by lush gardens and has a privileged location on a hill with stunning views close to the lakeshore and Teatro del Lago. **Pros:** excellent service; attention to detail; fantastic restaurant. **Cons:** more expensive than other boutique hotels in the area; staff inattentive at times; outside doors kept locked. $ *Rooms from: 160000 pesos* ⊠ *Antonio Varas 54* ☎ *65/242–1345* ⊕ *frauholle-frutillar.cl* ➡ *9 rooms* ⦿ *Breakfast; Some meals.*

$$$
HOTEL
FAMILY

🏠 **Hotel Frutillar.** This centrally located hotel is the perfect place to base an extended trip in the area, offering both comfortable rooms and private apartments with a kitchen. **Pros:** centrally located; friendly service; lovely decor. **Cons:** limited parking; thin walls; not much in the way of amenities. $ *Rooms from: 80000* ⊠ *Vicente Pérez Rosales 673* ☎ *65/242–1649* ➡ *16 rooms* ⦿ *Breakfast.*

$$$
B&B/INN

🏠 **Hotel Serenade de Franz Schubert.** The names of the guest rooms here reflect musical compositions—like Fantasia and Wedding March—and each door is painted with the first few sheet-music bars of the work it's named for. **Pros:** quiet, historic home; good breakfasts; central, lakeside location. **Cons:** rooms have an old, formal decor; lacking in services; no television in rooms. $ *Rooms from: 95000 pesos* ⊠ *Pedro Aguirre Cerda 50* ☎ *65/242–0332* ⊕ *www.hotelserenade.cl* ➡ *6 rooms* ⦿ *Breakfast.*

$$
B&B/INN

🏠 **Playa Maqui Lodge.** In the countryside, this excellent lodging combines quiet nights, great views, and private access to a lakeside beach. **Pros:** secluded location with private lakefront; rural ambience; great service. **Cons:** off-the-beaten track vibe not for everyone; you may feel isolated without your own vehicle; old house with thin walls. $ *Rooms from: 74112 pesos* ⊠ *Km 6, Ruta V155* ☎ *65/233–9166, 9/9567–8446* ⊕ *www.playamaqui.cl* ➡ *7 rooms* ⦿ *Breakfast; Some meals.*

$$
B&B/INN

🏠 **Salzburg Hotel & Spa.** A good value option, the rooms at this Tyrolean-style lodge command excellent views of the lake. **Pros:** great views; tranquil spa; brewery on-site. **Cons:** no TV in rooms; thin walls;

7

maintenance issues with some of the older facilities. $ *Rooms from: 65000 pesos* ✉ *Costanera Norte* ☎ *65/242–1589* ⊕ *www.salzburg.cl* ⌁ *31 rooms* ❏ *Breakfast.*

PERFORMING ARTS

Fodor's Choice
★

Teatro del Lago. Culture in Frutillar, and the southern Lake District in general, nowadays follows the lead of Teatro del Lago, which hosts a year-round schedule of concerts, art shows, and film. Events take place every week, and the state-of-the-art building is considered one of the finest of its kind in the world. Even if you can't attend an event, it's worth a look when walking along the lakefront in Frutillar. ✉ *Av. Philippi 1000* ☎ *65/242–2900* ⊕ *www.teatrodellago.cl.*

SPORTS AND THE OUTDOORS

Playa Frutillar. Packed with summer crowds, the gray-sand Playa Frutillar stretches for 15 blocks along Avenida Philippi. From this point along Lago Llanquihue you have a spectacular view due east of the conical Volcán Osorno, as well as the lopsided Volcán Puntiagudo. ✉ *Frutillar.*

PUERTO VARAS

27 km (16 miles) south of Frutillar via Ruta 5, Pan-American Hwy.

Fodor's Choice
★

A fast-growing resort town on the edge of Lake Llanquihue, Puerto Varas is renowned for its view of both the Osorno and Calbuco volcanoes. Stunning rose arbors and Germanic-style architecture grace the many centuries-old houses and churches that dot this tranquil town. Well-situated, it's not far to Chiloé, Puerto Montt, Vicente Pérez Rosales National Park, Cochamó, and other regional hot spots. With literally dozens of big hotels and smaller B&Bs added in recent years, as well as several cafés and trendy restaurants, a modern casino, and an interesting bar scene, the town is now an honest rival to Pucón as the region's top vacation spot.

GETTING HERE AND AROUND

Puerto Varas is only about a 20-minute drive from the center of nearby Puerto Montt. You can get to the Puerto Montt airport via a 25-minute drive on Camino Las Lomas just north of the town. Most of the bus lines that serve Puerto Montt make obligatory stops in Puerto Varas on their way north or south. Around town, there are numerous taxis and several minivan buses, which make several stops, the most prominent being on Avenida Salvador near the corner of Santa Rosa. Both taxis and buses can take you to countryside locations such as Ensenada and Puerto Montt for a minimal cost. You can cross to Argentina via bus or boat.

ESSENTIALS

Visitor and Tour Information Casa del Turista. ✉ *Piedra Plen, in front of Plaza de Armas* ☎ *65/223–7956.* **Oficina de Turismo.** ✉ *Del Salvador 320* ☎ *65/236–1194.*

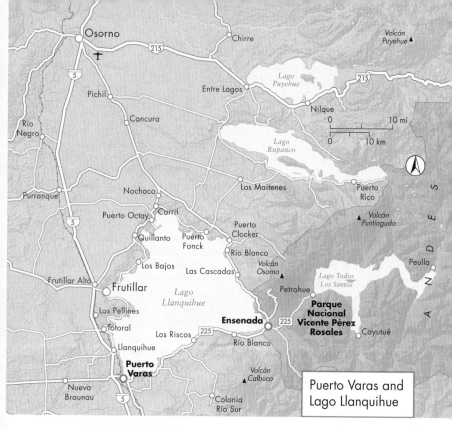

Puerto Varas and
Lago Llanquihue

WHERE TO EAT

$$ ✕ **Café Danes.** This friendly café-restaurant next to Santa Isabel Super-
CHILEAN market on Puerto Varas's main drag, Calle del Salvador, serves a set
lunch menu and a range of plates, from sandwiches to beef and chicken
dishes. The large beef and vegetarian empanadas and the illustrious
küchen cakes are not to be missed. **Known for:** Chilean classics; excel-
lent empanadas; affordable lunch deals. ⑤ *Average main: 8000 pesos*
✉ *Del Salvador 441* ☎ *65/223–2371.*

$$$ ✕ **Casa Valdes.** Start your dinner off right with a cool pisco sour at this
SEAFOOD fine dining, lakeside restaurant with great views. The cooking style is
influenced in part by Basque cuisine, with its fish and other plates often
accompanied by peppers, beans, and potatoes. **Known for:** Basque-
inspired seafood; lake views; crowds at dinnertime. ⑤ *Average main:
10000 pesos* ✉ *Santa Rosa 040* ☎ *65/223–7551.*

$$$$ ✕ **La Marca.** For quality steaks, this is the top spot in town. Start it
STEAKHOUSE all off with a pisco sour and sopaipillas, a sort of sweet fried bread,
Fodor's Choice before moving on to the *bife chorizo* or *lomo vetado*—both are tasty
★ cuts of meat. **Known for:** parrilla-style grilled meats; great pisco sour
menu; attentive service. ⑤ *Average main: 12000 pesos* ✉ *Santa Rosa
539* ☎ *65/223–2026.*

$$$ ╳ **La Olla.** This Puerto Varas institution serves the best fish in Chile,
SEAFOOD according to its legion of fans. The specialties of the house also include
a variety of seafood plates, empanadas, and Chilean-style beef dishes.
Known for: excellent fish dishes; tasty empanadas; big crowds on weekends, so book ahead. ⑤ *Average main: 9000 pesos* ⊠ *R-225, Km 1
(Camino a Ensenada)* ☏ *65/223-4605.*

$$$ ╳ **Mercado 605.** The gourmet cuisine served here is best described as
INTERNATIONAL international fusion that uses local ingredients. The presentation of the
food is beautiful; there is a pleasant ambience; and the service is friendly.
Known for: diverse, locally sourced menu; whiskey-glazed salmon; on-site wine shop where you can buy a bottle for dinner. ⑤ *Average main:
9000 pesos* ⊠ *Imperial 605* ☏ *65/223-1980* ⊕ *www.mercado605.cl.*

$$ ╳ **Mesa Tropera.** Situated on a lone pier jutting out into the lake, Mesa
PIZZA Tropera offers up quality Italian-Patagonian cuisine that features a wide
Fodor'sChoice array of creative toppings on their thin crust pizzas, inventive pasta
★ dishes, and abundant salads. Mesa Tropera is also a connoisseur of
fine beer, brewing their own flavors as well as keeping a selection of
microbrews in stock from others in the region. **Known for:** creative
pizzas with a Patagonian flair; great microbrew menu; large crowds
and no reservations. ⑤ *Average main: 7500 pesos* ⊠ *Santa Rosa 161*
☏ *65/223-7973* ⊕ *www.mesatropera.cl* ⊙ *Closed Sun.*

WHERE TO STAY

$$ ⛺ **Casa Kalfu.** This bright-blue cozy B&B is in one of the many distinctive, old-style German homes found throughout the older sections
B&B/INN of Puerto Varas. **Pros:** location close to the town center; welcoming,
friendly environment; comfortable rooms. **Cons:** breakfast area can get
crowded; limited parking; noise from creaky wooden floors. ⑤ *Rooms
from: 67000 pesos* ⊠ *Tronador 1134* ☏ *65/275-1261* ⊕ *www.casa-
kalfu.cl* ⇱ *11 rooms* ⑩ *Breakfast.*

$$ ⛺ **Estancia 440.** In a beautiful, restored German colonial mansion less
B&B/INN than a 10-minute walk from downtown Puerto Varas, this B&B pays
Fodor'sChoice close attention to detail throughout. **Pros:** tasty breakfast; restored home
★ with lots of character; clean and comfortable rooms. **Cons:** not in downtown; surrounding area not very charming; rooms are mostly small.
⑤ *Rooms from: 61000 pesos* ⊠ *Decher 440* ☏ *65/223-3921* ⊕ *www.
estancia440.cl* ⊙ *Closed May and June* ⇱ *7 rooms* ⑩ *Breakfast.*

$$$$ ⛺ **Hotel Cumbres Puerto Varas.** A towering hotel on a hill overlooking the
HOTEL lake, Cumbres Puerto Varas is part of a leading hotel chain in Chile that
has gained a sterling reputation for their impeccable customer service.
Pros: service is exemplary; impressive views of lake; modern infrastructure. **Cons:** pool is small; restaurant food is average; lacks unique character. ⑤ *Rooms from: 115000 pesos* ⊠ *Imperial 0565* ☏ *2/2414-5000*
⊕ *www.cumbrespuertovaras.cl* ⇱ *90 rooms* ⑩ *Breakfast.*

$$$$ ⛺ **Hotel Dreams de Los Volcanes.** In the center of town next to the casino,
HOTEL this hotel has exceptional rooms with excellent views and many have
their own private terrace overlooking the lake. **Pros:** lake views; spa and
pool; downtown location. **Cons:** casino environment not for everyone;
limited parking; restaurant needs more variety. ⑤ *Rooms from: 116000
pesos* ⊠ *Del Salvador 21* ☏ *65/249-2000* ⊕ *www.mundodreams.com*
⇱ *50 rooms* ⑩ *Breakfast.*

$$$$
HOTEL
FAMILY
Fodor's Choice
★

⊞ Enjoy Puerto Varas Hotel. This upscale hotel on a lovely residential street just minutes to downtown comes with many rooms that have commanding views of the lake and volcanoes. **Pros:** spacious rooms; tranquil location; great on-site services. **Cons:** gym and spa are small; some rooms lack lake views; frequent events at the hotel draw crowds. $ *Rooms from: 122000 pesos* ⊠ *Klenner 349* ☎ *65/220–1000* ⊕ *www. enjoy.cl/puerto-varas* ⤳ *91 rooms* ⦿| *Breakfast.*

$$$$
B&B/INN
FAMILY

⊞ Gracias a la Vida Lodge. These four plush, beautiful cabins are located on stilts on the banks of Lago Pichilaguna, complete with a dramatic view of Osorno Volcano and all the peace and tranquility one could desire. **Pros:** beautiful lake setting; spacious cabins for up to six people; bird-watching and other excursions offered. **Cons:** really best if you have your own car; use of sauna is extra; road to lodge is unpaved. $ *Rooms from: 115000 pesos* ⊠ *Fundo Pichilaguna Parcela 44* ☎ *9/9826–1268, 9/9292–1521* ⊕ *www.graciasalavidalodge.com* ⤳ *4 cabins* ⦿| *Breakfast.*

$$$$
B&B/INN

⊞ Los Caiquenes Hotel Boutique. This high-end boutique hotel on the shore of Lake Llanquihue is just outside of Puerto Varas. **Pros:** maximum comfort; big, luxurious rooms; lakeside location. **Cons:** hotel is on the outskirts of town; lacks extra amenities of the bigger hotels; small staff. $ *Rooms from: 197000 pesos* ⊠ *Camino Ensenada, Km 9.5* ☎ *9/8159–0489* ⊕ *www.hotelloscaiquenes.cl* ⤳ *8 rooms* ⦿| *Breakfast.*

NIGHTLIFE

Bravo Cabrera. This lively bar-restaurant packs a nice local crowd most nights, with music getting louder as the night goes on. But do not underestimate the excellent restaurant here as well. The pizzas are the most popular choice by the locals, but the menu also includes soups, salads, sandwiches, ribs, pasta, and more—all for a reasonable price. ⊠ *Vicente Perez Rosales 1071* ☎ *65/223–3441* ⊕ *www.bravocabrera.cl.*

Fodor's Choice
★

Casino Dreams Puerto Varas. The flashy Casino Dreams Puerto Varas has the most prestigious address in town, facing the center of the waterfront. For a small-town casino, it's actually a modern, well-done place, with all the Vegas-style trappings, from slot machines to roulette, along with a restaurant, bar, weekly music, comedy, and other entertainment. ⊠ *Del Salvador 21* ☎ *65/249–2000.*

Club Orquidea. Near the center of town, this is the trendiest nightlife spot in Puerto Varas, with drinks constantly flowing at the long bar, two outdoor seating areas for smokers, karaoke or live music on most evenings, and good pizza and bar food. ⊠ *San Pedro 537.*

La Buena Vida Bistró. Most nights, this club has the best live music in town, with jazz, blues, rock, and Latin music. There's also decent international cuisine on tap. ⊠ *Walker Martinez 551* ☎ *9/9700–8843.*

SPORTS AND THE OUTDOORS

Puerto Varas has a plethora of outdoor options. Fly-fishing is prominent in the region, with many rivers and the huge Lago Llanquihue making attractive targets. The region has still more to offer, including mountain biking, canyoning, wind surfing, sailing, hiking in Vicente Pérez Rosales Park, or just enjoying the lake by kayak. You can also hike up the nearby volcanoes. With so much attractive nature in its backyard, it's

7

no wonder Puerto Varas has become a global destination for outdoor-adventure enthusiasts.

The lake itself frequently boasts strong winds suitable for first-class windsurfing and sailing. At Canopy Lodge of Cascadas, the largest canopy area in Chile, not far from Puerto Varas, you can zip-line 70 meters (230 feet) above canyons and forest. The Petrohué River offers the opportunity for rafting, and along with numerous other rivers in the area, great fishing. Biking alongside the lake is a popular trip, too. Vicente Pérez Rosales Park and Alerce Andino Park have good trails for hiking and camping, while Osorno Volcano excels for treks, skiing, and snowboarding. Some two hours from Puerto Varas is Cochamó Valley, a fantastic spot that has drawn comparisons to Yosemite Park in California for its high granite mountain cliffs, waterfalls, and overall landscape. This is a rock climber's paradise and a hiker's dream, with exceptional horseback-riding trails as well. Just south from Cochamó is Puelo, a river valley in the shadow of the Andes Mountains. It's the launching point for some of Chile's best fly-fishing, in addition to great hiking and other outdoor action.

BIRD-WATCHING

BirdsChile. Go on bird-watching excursions throughout the Lake District with BirdsChile. ⊠ *San Pedro 311* ☎ *9/9269–2606* ⊕ *www.birdschile. com* ✉ *From 25000 pesos.*

FLY-FISHING

Saltos del Maullín. Go exclusive fly-fishing on the Maullin River, located about 24 km (15 miles) outside of Puerto Varas. Take lessons, go boating on the river, take a guided hike in the nearby forest, and enjoy a Patagonian barbecue. ⊠ *Fundo la Isla, Río Maullin, Nueva Braunau* ☎ *9/9325–9490* ✉ *From 160000 pesos.*

Tres Piedras. This longtime fly-fishing agency in Puerto Varas organizes day- and multiday trips at nearby lakes and rivers. ⊠ *Puerto Varas* ☎ *65/233–0157, 9/7618–7826* ⊕ *www.trespiedras.cl* ✉ *From 150000 pesos.*

HORSEBACK RIDING

Alanca. This company offers two-hour horseback trips through native forest, wetlands, and on the lake shore in a rural park just 10 minutes from Puerto Varas. ⊠ *Puerto Varas* ☎ *9/6496–5291* ⊕ *www.alancachile. com* ✉ *From 48000 pesos.*

MULTISPORT OPERATORS

Jass Puerto Varas. Trekking and kayaking tours in the region are offered by Jass, from half-day to multiday trips. Their guides provide special expertise in nearby areas such as Cochamo, Puelo, Volcán Osorno, and Alerce Andino Park. ⊠ *San Jose 192, Office 203* ☎ *9/6590–6458* ⊕ *www.jasspuertovaras.com* ✉ *From 65000 pesos.*

Ko'Kayak. This company offers sea and river kayaking, as well as white-water rafting trips, from half-day excursions to multiday trips. Ko'Kayak is the leading provider for excursions on the Petrohue River, but they also do longer trips to other places in the region, like Pumalin National Park. ⊠ *Ruta 225, Km 40* ☎ *65/223–3004* ⊕ *www.kokayak. cl* ✉ *From 35000 pesos.*

TREKKING

Huella Andina Expeditions. These experts guide excursions to the major volcanoes of southern Chile, including trekking to the summit of Osorno Volcano. ✉ *Camino Volcán Calbuco, Km 3.8* ☎ *44/890–6571* ⊕ *www.huellandina.com* 💰 *From 180000 pesos.*

ENSENADA

47 km (28 miles) east of Puerto Varas.

A drive along the southern shore of Lago Llanquihue to Ensenada takes you through the heart of Chile's *murta*-growing country. Queen Victoria is said to have developed a fondness for these tart red berries, and today you find them used as ingredients in syrups, jams, and küchen. Frutillar, Puerto Varas, and Puerto Octay might all boast about their views of Volcán Osorno, but you can really feel up close and personal with the volcano when you arrive in the town of Ensenada, which also neighbors the jagged Volcán Calbuca. The lake drive to Ensenada is also without doubt one of the prettiest in southern Chile.

GETTING HERE AND AROUND

By car, it's a beautiful scenic ride about 48 km (30 miles) east of Puerto Varas on the Camino Ensenada. In Puerto Varas, a regular, hourly mini-bus (until 9 pm) also provides transport to Ensenada.

WHERE TO STAY

$$$
B&B/INN

🏠 **Biosfera Volcanica Lodge.** Rest and relax under the volcano, moon, and stars in a wood-fired hot tub next to your personal dome-shape, luxury accommodations at Biosfera Volcánica. **Pros:** excellent service; Wi-Fi, television, and other amenities in unique dome lodging; near parks and other nature attractions. **Cons:** breakfast included only, though some units have their own kitchens; hot tubs require three to four hours of preparation; no bike rental on-site. ⑤ *Rooms from: 95000 pesos* ✉ *Ruta 225, Km 39.5, Parcela 5-D, La Ensenada* ⚓ *Valle Los Ulmos* ☎ *9/7668–5266* ⊕ *www.biosferavolcanicalodge.cl* ⊗ *Closed July* 💤 *3 rooms* ⑩ *Breakfast* ▤ *No credit cards.*

$$$$
HOTEL
Fodor's Choice
★

🏠 **Hotel AWA.** Thanks to an attentive staff, great food, a variety of services that cater to each guest's interest, and design that maximizes comfort and quality with clean sensibility, Hotel AWA has all the makings of one of the world's finer hotels. **Pros:** fine dining at its best; floor-to-ceiling views of the lake and volcano; creative and attractive design. **Cons:** 45-minute drive to Puerto Varas; meals extra; limited parking. ⑤ *Rooms from: 255000 pesos* ✉ *Km 27, Camino Ensenada, La Ensenada* ⚓ *Sector Los Riscos* ☎ *65/229–2020* ⊕ *www.hotelawa.cl* 💤 *15 rooms* ⑩ *Breakfast.*

$
B&B/INN

🏠 **Quila Hostal.** This hostal, run by a local photographer and longtime ex-pat originally form France, offers a quiet and relaxed place to base your excursions. **Pros:** knowledgeable host; tranquil vibe; volcano views. **Cons:** vehicle required to get here; some rooms do not have private baths; no television in rooms. ⑤ *Rooms from: 45000 pesos* ✉ *Km 37, Camino Ensenada, La Ensenada* ☎ *9/6760–7039* ⊕ *www.quilahostal.com* ▤ *No credit cards* ⊗ *Closed June and July* 💤 *6 rooms* ⑩ *Breakfast; Some meals.*

7

PARQUE NACIONAL VICENTE PÉREZ ROSALES

3 km (2 miles) east of Ensenada.

Chile's oldest national park, with its spectacular Lago Todos Los Santos, forests, and Andean mountain backdrop, Vicente Perez Rosales is a real treasure for hiking, fly-fishing, and more.

GETTING HERE AND AROUND

Take a one-hour drive along Ruta 224, Camino a Ensenada, from Puerto Varas. Several agencies in Puerto Varas run guided trips and transport to the park.

EXPLORING

Parque Nacional Vicente Pérez Rosales. Chile's oldest national park was established in 1926. South of Parque Nacional Puyehue, the 2,538-square-km (980-square-mile) preserve includes the Osorno and lesser-known Puntiagudo volcanoes, as well as the deep-blue Lago Todos los Santos. The Volcán Osorno appears in your car window soon after you drive south from Osorno and doesn't disappear until shortly before your arrival in Puerto Montt. The visitor center opposite the Hotel Petrohué provides access to some fairly easy hikes. The Rincón del Osorno trail hugs the lake while the Saltos de Petrohué trail runs parallel to the river of the same name. Rudimentary campsites are available for 10,000 pesos per person. ☎ *65/248–6102* 🌐 *4000 pesos.*

WHERE TO STAY

$$$$
B&B/INN
Petrohué Lodge. The common areas in this rustic orange chalet have vaulted ceilings and huge fireplaces. **Pros:** inside Vicente Pérez Rosales Park; organized outdoor excursions; nice views. **Cons:** no elevator to upper floors; Wi-Fi unstable; no television in rooms. ⑤ *Rooms from: 116000 pesos* ✉ *Parque Nacional Vicente Perez Rosales, Ruta 225, Km 60, Petrohué* ☎ *9/9887–6896* 🌐 *www.petrohue.com* ✪ *Closed May and June* 🛏 *31 rooms* ⑩ *Breakfast; All meals.*

SPORTS AND THE OUTDOORS

Canopy Chile. Make like Tarzan and swing through the treetops in the shadow of Volcán Osorno with Canopy Chile. A helmet, a very secure harness, 2 km (1 mile) of zip line strung out over 11 platforms (the second-longest in South America), and experienced guides give you a bird's-eye view of the forest below. ✉ *Ruta U99-V, Camino Cascadas Km 60, Puerto Varas* ☎ *9/9909–5269* 🌐 *www.canopychile.cl* 🌐 *From 25000 pesos.*

Cruce Andino. This all-day crossing of the spectacular Andean mountain lakes between Puerto Varas and Bariloche is the classic trip of the area and worth doing. It leaves out of Lake Todos los Santos in Vicente Perez Rosales National Park at 10:30 am every day. There is a stop for lunch at an island called Peulla before eventually arriving in Bariloche at around 9 pm. The operator can also pick you up at your hotel if in Puerto Varas or Bariloche. ✉ *Del Salvador 72, Puerto Varas* ☎ *2/2387–7035* 🌐 *www.cruceandino.com* 🌐 *From 150000 pesos.*

Fodor's Choice
★
Ski & Outdoor Volcán Osorno. About 60 kilometers (37 miles) from Puerto Varas, Volcán Osorno is the setting for entertaining skiing with breathtaking vistas of the Lake District. The Ski & Outdoor Center on the volcano has two ski lifts, 11 ski trails with varied levels of difficulty,

and a store that rents equipment and provides ski and snowboard lessons. The Mirador restaurant has hot lunch and coffee. Daily ski passes are 26,000 pesos. In summer, the volcano is a great spot for hiking, zip-lining, and mountain biking. ⊠ *Volcán Osorno, Puerto Varas* ☎ *9/9158–7337, 9/6679–2284* ⊕ *www.volcanosorno.com.*

PUERTO MONTT

20 km (12 miles) south of Puerto Varas via Ruta 5, Pan-American Hwy.

For most of its history, windy Puerto Montt was the end of the line for just about everyone traveling in the Lake District. Now the Carretera Austral carries on southward, but for all intents and purposes Puerto Montt remains the region's last significant outpost, a provincial city that is a hub for the nation's salmon farming industry as well as local fishing, farming, and forestry.

Today the city center is full of malls, condos, and office towers (it's the fastest-growing city in Chile) but away from downtown, Puerto Montt consists mainly of low clapboard houses perched above its bay, the Seno de Reloncaví. If it's a sunny day, head east to Playa Pelluco or one of the city's other beaches. If you're more interested in exploring the countryside, drive along the shore for a good view of the surrounding hills.

GETTING HERE AND AROUND

Puerto Montt is a main transit hub in the region. Buses from Santiago and all points in southern Chile ramble through here at some point, while many cruise ships dock at the port. Puerto Montt's El Tepual Airport has daily air traffic from all the major airlines that serve Chile. The Pan-American Highway also stops here, while the mostly unpaved Carretera Austral, which winds it ways through Chilean Patagonia, begins south of the city. To cross over into Argentina, buses leave from here and from Puerto Varas. There is also regular ferry service to Chaiten from the port. Chiloé Island is less than two hours' drive from Puerto Montt. Take the last part of Ruta 5, or the Pan-American Highway, to Pargua, where two ferries cross the Chacao Channel every hour.

CRUISE TRAVEL TO PUERTO MONTT

The many large cruise ships that arrive to the public port of Puerto Montt, the most important in southern Chile, must anchor offshore and use smaller tender boats to carry passengers to the dock. The port is located at the western end of the city near Caleta Angelmo, which conveniently for travelers is also the best place to shop for local handicrafts and try local seafood in numerous small restaurants at the tail end of the waterfront.

Downtown Puerto Montt, where all the malls, office buildings, and hubbub is located, is about nine blocks, or 1 mile away. You can walk there in about 20 minutes or so, but buses or cheap taxis (usually about 1,500 pesos per person) are prevalent near the port and can whisk you to the city center within minutes. Moreover, many of the taxis and local tour operators are often waiting at the port to offer you deals on day trips in the city or nearby tourism destinations like Puerto Varas, Volcán Osorno, and Frutillar.

ESSENTIALS

Visitor and Tour Information **Puerto Montt Tourist Office.** ⊠ *Plaza de Armas, Antonio Varas 415* ☎ *65/222–3016.* **Sernatur.** ⊠ *San Martin 80* ☎ *65/222–3016* ⊕ *www.sernatur.cl.*

EXPLORING

Beaches at Maullín. About 70 km (43 miles) southwest of Puerto Montt, at this small town near Pargua—the ferry crossing to Chiloé—the Maullín River merges with the Pacific Ocean in spectacular fashion. Be sure to visit the expansive Pangal Beach, with large sand dunes teeming with birds. If staying overnight, there are cabins and a campground. ⊠ *Ruta 5 south from Puerto Montt, about a 1-hr drive.*

Fodor's Choice
★

Caleta Angelmó. About 3 km (2 miles) west of downtown along the coastal road lies Puerto Montt's fishing cove. This busy port serves small fishing boats, large ferries, and cruisers carrying travelers and cargo southward through the straits and fjords that form much of Chile's shoreline. On weekdays, small launches from Isla Tenglo and other outlying islands arrive early in the morning and leave late in the afternoon. There are dozens of stalls selling local handicrafts and the fish market here has one of the most varied seafood selections in all Chile. ⊠ *Puerto Montt.*

Catedral de Puerto Montt. Latin America's ornate church architecture is nowhere to be found in the Lake District. More typical of the region is Puerto Montt's stark 1856 Catedral. The alerce-wood structure, modeled on the Pantheon in Paris, is the city's oldest surviving building. ⊠ *Plaza de Armas.*

Museo Juan Pablo II. This museum, east of the city's bus terminal, has a collection of crafts and relics from the nearby archipelago of Chiloé. Historical photos of Puerto Montt give a sense of the area's slow and often difficult growth, plus the impact of the 1960 earthquake, which virtually destroyed the port. Pope John Paul II celebrated Mass on the grounds during his 1987 visit; one exhibit documents the event. ⊠ *Av. Diego Portales 997* ☎ *65/222–3029* 🖼 *Free.*

**OFF THE
BEATEN
PATH**

Parque Nacional Alerce Andino. Close to Puerto Montt, the mountainous 398-square-km (154-square-mile) Parque Nacional Alerce Andino, with more than 40 small lakes, was primarily established to protect the endangered alerce trees that are spread out upon some 20,000-hectares (49,421 acres) of the park. Comparable to California's redwood trees, alerce grow to average heights of 50 meters (165 feet) and can reach 5 meters (16 feet) in diameter. Immensely popular as building material for houses and furniture in southern Chile, they have been nearly wiped out from the landscape. They are also the world's second-oldest living tree species, many living up to 4,000 years. ⊠ *Carretera Austral, 35 km (21 miles) east of Puerto Montt* ☎ *65/248–6102* 🖼 *4000 pesos.*

WHERE TO EAT

$$$
ITALIAN

✕ **Azzurro.** This great Italian restaurant serves mouth-watering pizzas and pasta, but also on the menu are some beef and fish plates. The restaurant is housed in a modest blue building, with a rustic wooden interior and informal atmosphere. **Known for:** simple, classic Italian dishes; good meat options; casual ambience. 🛈 *Average main: 9000 pesos* ⊠ *Liborio Guerrero 1769* ☎ *65/231–8989* ⊕ *www.azzurro.cl.*

$ ✕ **Caleta Angelmó.** More than a dozen small kitchens and eateries at
CHILEAN this enclosed market 3 km (2 miles) west of Puerto Montt along the
coast road prepare southern Chilean seafood favorites like *curanto*, a
potpourri of shellfish, meat, and potatoes, and *paila marina,*a hearty
seafood stew with mainly shellfish. Each kitchen has separate tables
and counters. **Known for:** food stalls serving Chilean specialities; no
set hours but usually open for lunch and dinner in high season; fish
market and handicraft stores also on-site. $ *Average main: 4000 pesos*
⊠ *Caleta Angelmó* ⊟ *No credit cards.*

$$$ ✕ **Chile Picante.** Nestled on a steep hill in a nondescript neighborhood, the
CHILEAN decor here is no frills, but the view of the city is spectacular and the food
is some of the best in Puerto Montt. They offer daily set menus for 9,000
pesos, including an appetizer, drink, and dessert. **Known for:** awesome
views; regularly changing menu of spicy Chilean classics; affordable prices.
$ *Average main: 9000 pesos* ⊠ *Vicente Perez Rosales 567* ☎ *9/8454–8923*
⊕ *www.chilepicanterestoran.cl* ⊗ *Closed Sun.* ⊟ *No credit cards.*

$$$ ✕ **Cotelé.** On a hill overlooking the Puerto Montt bay, Cotelé has the
STEAKHOUSE look and feel of a typical *quincho* (barbecue), with wooden walls and
Fodor's Choice tables with the grill in the middle. Here, it is strictly about meticulously
★ preparing the best possible steaks. **Known for:** one of the top-rated steak
houses in Chile; selection of prime meats you can then watch be grilled
in front of you; nice selection of wines and pisco sours. $ *Average main:*
11000 pesos ⊠ *Juan Soler Manfredini 1661* ☎ *65/227–8000* ⊕ *www.*
cotele.cl ⊗ *Closed Sun.*

$$$$ ✕ **El Fogón de Pepe.** If you need a change of pace from the ubiquitous sea-
STEAKHOUSE food in Puerto Montt, this is a great option. Roast-beef plates, roasted
ribs, chicken, and steaks are all great. **Known for:** excellent meats;
friendly service; big weekend crowds. $ *Average main: 12000 pesos*
⊠ *Rengifo 845* ☎ *65/227–1527* ⊗ *Closed Sun.*

$$ ✕ **Entre Mar y Pasta.** This reasonably priced restaurant specializes in all
FUSION manner of fish, seafood, and homemade pastas (filled with seafood).
Especially noteworthy is the delicious crab lasagna. **Known for:** tasty
seafood pasta; friendly service; parking lot on-site. $ *Average main:*
8000 pesos ⊠ *Egaña 311* ☎ *65/271–4302* ⊗ *Closed Mon.*

$$$ ✕ **Restaurant Kiel.** Founded in 1973, this Chilean-German seafood res-
SEAFOOD taurant is located on the coast about 15 minutes west of Puerto Montt,
Fodor's Choice and is considered an institution in the area. The interesting decor and
★ sea views are nice, but it's the beautifully prepared seafood and, in
particular, the curanto that draws crowds. **Known for:** great seafood
curanto; fresh produce from on-site garden; reservations necessary in
summer. $ *Average main: 9200 pesos* ⊠ *Camino Chinquihue, Km 8,*
Chinquihue ☎ *65/225–5010* ⊕ *www.kiel.cl.*

WHERE TO STAY

$$$ 🏨 **Holiday Inn Express.** Stunning views of Puerto Montt Bay and the city
HOTEL make this place an excellent choice. **Pros:** amazing views; walking distance
to city center; movie theater and shopping in mall below. **Cons:** few extras
like a pool; not much character; fitness center is small. $ *Rooms from:*
86000 pesos ⊠ *Av. Costanera* ✛ *Above Mall Paseo Costanera* ☎ *65/256–*
6000 ⊕ *www.holidayinnexpress.cl* ⊅ *105 rooms* ⊙l *Breakfast.*

7

$$ ⊞**Hotel Central.** Close to the bus station, this is a good, low-price
HOTEL option for a night or two in Puerto Montt. **Pros:** excellent service;
good value; central location. **Cons:** decor is old-fashioned; neighbor-
hood is not the most attractive; simple breakfast. ⑤ *Rooms from:*
52000 pesos ⊠ *Juan José Mira 1092* ☎ *65/225–7516* ⊕ *www.hotel-*
central.cl ⤶ *29 rooms* ⦿ *Breakfast.*

$$$ ⊞**Hotel Gran Pacífico.** Thanks to an ideal location just steps away from
HOTEL downtown, Hotel Gran Pacífico is a great choice in Puerto Montt,
especially with its awesome views of the bay. **Pros:** nice views; good restaurant on top floor; centrally located. **Cons:** the lobby is unattractive;
spa and gym are small; decor is nothing special. ⑤ *Rooms from: 86000*
pesos ⊠ *Urmeneta 719* ☎ *65/248–2100* ⊕ *www.hotelgranpacifico.cl*
⤶ *48 rooms* ⦿ *Breakfast.*

$$$ ⊞**Manquehue Hotel Puerto Montt.** Mainly set up to be the premier business
HOTEL hotel in Puerto Montt, this hotel goes above and beyond by offering
travelers good value and comfort. **Pros:** good business hotel; heated
pool; safer part of town. **Cons:** outside of the city center; slow elevators;
hard to find if arriving by car. ⑤ *Rooms from: 76611 pesos* ⊠ *Semi-*
nario 252 ☎ *65/233–1000* ⊕ *puertomontt.manquehuehoteles.cl* ⤶ *142*
rooms ⦿ *Breakfast.*

NIGHTLIFE

Boulebar. This is a fun bar in the city center for music, tapas, and drinks.
There's a second, more modern branch at Rengifo 920. ⊠ *Benavente*
435, 2nd fl. ☎ *9/5626–1611.*

Baradero. This is the best place to catch live music in the city. You'll
find diverse music styles and a large selection of microbrews at the
bar, along with the occasional DJ or karaoke night. ⊠ *Rengifo 964*
☎ *9/4294–0230.*

Taytao. This longtime bar and disco at Pelluco beach is a lively night
spot, with two dance floors, six rooms, karaoke, a restaurant, and live
music. ⊠ *Juan Soler Manfredini 1881* ☎ *9/4408–2536.*

SHOPPING

Feria Artesanal Angelmó. An excellent selection of handicrafts is sold at
the best prices in the country at the Feria Artesanal Angelmó, on the
coastal road near Caleta Angelmó. Chileans know there's a better selec-
tion of crafts from Chiloé for sale here than in Chiloé itself. Baskets,
ponchos, figures woven from different kinds of grasses and straw, and
warm sweaters of raw, hand-spun, and hand-dyed wool are all for sale.
Much of the merchandise is geared toward tourists, so look carefully for
more authentic offerings. Haggling is expected. It's open daily 9–dusk.
⊠ *Puerto Montt.*

COCHAMÓ

94 km (59 miles) southwest of Puerto Varas.

The small fishing villages of Cochamó are blessed with friendly people
but little infrastructure. Only a few farms dot the countryside. In short,
nature with a capital "N" is the real reason to come here. Civilization
has barely touched these great, vast nature areas, some of Chile's (and

the world's) last. Think of Yosemite National Park in California without the crowds. Granite walls and domes are prevalent throughout the valley. At Río Puelo, the emerald-blue water seems like a dream amid the rare, ancient alerce forests and Andean mountain scenery. An old frontier cattle trail in Cochamó Valley, once used as a hideout by Butch Cassidy and the Sundance Kid, reminds the visitor that the only way through this natural wonderland is by foot or horse. You don't find any cars or roads here.

GETTING HERE AND AROUND

There are few cars in Cochamó, and even fewer gas stations (though you can get gas by the container). Walking is probably the most efficient way to get around. Nearby Puelo is even smaller than Cochamó. If you must, rent a car in Puerto Montt or Puerto Varas. Roads in the region are mostly gravel and dirt, so four-wheel drive would be good. Buses do service these towns, however. If you take the bus, arrange with a travel agency or outfitter beforehand to help with transport to the nature areas on your wish list.

ESSENTIALS

Visitor Information Cochamó Oficina de Turismo. ⊠ *Casa del Turista, Plaza de Puelo* ☎ *65/256–2586.*

WHERE TO STAY

$$$$
B&B/INN
🏠**Campo Aventura Cochamó.** The longest-running lodge and tour operator in Cochamó, Campo Aventura is a great resource for guided hikes, horseback treks, kayaking, rafting, bicycling, and bird-watching activities. **Pros:** oldest accommodations in Cochamó; assistance with organizing outdoor activities; staff provides nice intro to Patagonian culture and food. **Cons:** no frills rooms; some guests may find the lodge too quiet; no Wi-Fi or televisions. ⑤ *Rooms from: 110000 pesos* ⊠ *5 km (3 miles) south of Cochamó on Ruta 225 (Camino a Ensenada)* ☎ *9/9289–4318* ⊕ *www.campo-aventura.com* ☉ *Closed mid-Mar.–mid-Oct.* ⇂ *8 rooms* ⍀⍁ *All meals.*

$$$$
HOTEL
FAMILY
🏠**Mítico Puelo Lodge.** Built in 1991 as a private getaway for fly-fishing enthusiasts on the shores of Tagua Tagua Lake, this lodge is reached by private boat or plane (the hotel has its own motorboat, and transfers are included in rates), and now offers activities like biking, horseback riding, trekking, and kayaking. **Pros:** facilitates trips to nearby Tagua Tagua Park; quiet and remote; good for families. **Cons:** two hours from closest airport; only satellite phone service (extra charge); excursions are extra (except for all-inclusive plans). ⑤ *Rooms from: 338119 pesos* ⊠ *Lago Tagua Tagua* ☎ *65/256–6646* ⊕ *www.miticopuelo.com* ⇂ *21 rooms* ⍀⍁ *All-inclusive; Some meals.*

$$$$
B&B/INN
🏠**Posada Puelo Lodge.** This cozy lodge is on the banks of the beautiful Puelo River. **Pros:** excellent service; beautiful surroundings; great fly-fishing. **Cons:** three-hour drive from airport on difficult roads; geared primarily to fly-fishermen; can get windy and rainy in the area. ⑤ *Rooms from: 233000 pesos* ⊠ *Río Puelo* ☎ *9/9265–0665* ⊕ *www.posadapuelo.cl* ☉ *Closed June–Aug.* ⇂ *5 rooms* ⍀⍁ *All-inclusive.*

$$
B&B/INN
🏠**Refugio Cochamó.** The small, rustic Refugio Cochamó was built by a climber from Colorado and has been providing one of the few lodging alternatives to camping under the stars at Cochamó for more than

a decade. **Pros:** one of the only indoor places to sleep in the area; hot showers; great pizza. **Cons:** lacking the thrill of sleeping under a starry night; place is often booked solid; shared bathrooms. $ *Rooms from: 48,000 pesos* ✉ *Cochamó Valley* ⊕ *www.cochamo.com/refugio* ⊗ *Closed mid-Mar.–Nov.* ⇆ *3 rooms.*

SPORTS AND THE OUTDOORS

Cochamó and Río Puelo's vast forests, fast-flowing rivers, and mountains are an outdoors-lover's mecca. Before you pursue any of the myriad activities available, though, be sure to get your bearings. Unlike national parks, these areas are not formally protected and maintained, and therefore often lack well-marked trails. Check with a local outfitter or travel agency to get more information on where to go and how. Because of growing tourism in the Cochamó nature area, any potential campers must first reserve campsites ahead of time online (⊕ *www. reservasvallecochamo.org*).

Southern Trips. Run by Cochamó locals, this outfitter is often cited as the best and most experienced guiding company for horseback rides and treks throughout the Cochamó Valley nature area. ✉ *Cochamó* ☎ *9/8407–2559* ⊕ *www.southern-trips.cl.*

Trekka. Led by an accomplished local mountaineer, Trekka can take you on multiday backpacking trips through the incredible landscapes of Cochamó and Puelo as well as rock climbing to the summit of Cochamó's fabled granite peaks. ✉ *Puerto Montt* ☎ *9/989–40820* ⊕ *www.trekka.cl.*

CHILOÉ

WELCOME TO CHILOÉ

TOP REASONS TO GO

★ **Charming churches:** Within Chile, Chiloé is known for the simply elegant churches that dot Isla Grande. Almost all are open to the public, and a visit is essential.

★ **Traditional crafts:** Chiloé's sweaters, ponchos, blankets, and rugs are a defining feature of the island. There's nothing warmer, woollier, or more wonderful anywhere else in Chile.

★ **Nature:** Chiloé's close proximity to breeding grounds for blue whales, a globally endangered species, makes it one of the planet's top destinations for whale-watching. Many other animals call Chiloé home, too; there's spectacular bird-watching, including massive penguin colonies and rare birds like the Chucao Tapaculo.

★ **Fantastic folklore:** Spirits of all stripes haunt Chiloé—or at least populate its colorful folklore, which is full of trolls, witches, mermaids, and ghost ships.

Most people explore Chiloé by car. Major towns and landmarks are no more than an hour or two apart. The Pan-American Highway (Ruta 5) that meanders through northern Chile ends at the Golfo de Ancud and continues again on Isla Grande. It connects the cities of Ancud, Castro, and Chonchi before ending in Quellón. Paved roads connect the Pan-American to Quemchi and Dalcahue, and Achao on Isla Quinchao. The coastal route connecting the village of San Antonio de Chacao with Dalcahue is now mostly paved. A more scenic route leads from Chacao to Caulín and Ancud, via Huicha. The road west from Ancud every year is paved farther and pavement should eventually extend to the lighthouse at Corona Point.

1 **Ancud and Nearby.** Your ferry may arrive on Chiloé at Chacao, but Ancud is the area's main transportation hub and the island's second-largest city. Explore here the penguins of Puñihuil, the fog- and folklore-steeped towns of Quemchi and Quicaví, and northeastern Chiloé's famous churches. If you venture to Isla Quinchao, stop in Achao, a busy fishing town.

2 **Castro and Nearby.** Castro is the capital and the larger more cosmopolitan answer to Ancud. You can see a lot near here, including Chonchi's brightly painted houses and the Parque Nacional Chiloé. Other small towns dot the east coast down to Quellón, home to nearby Parque Tantauco and where you can take ferries to Chaitén and the mainland.

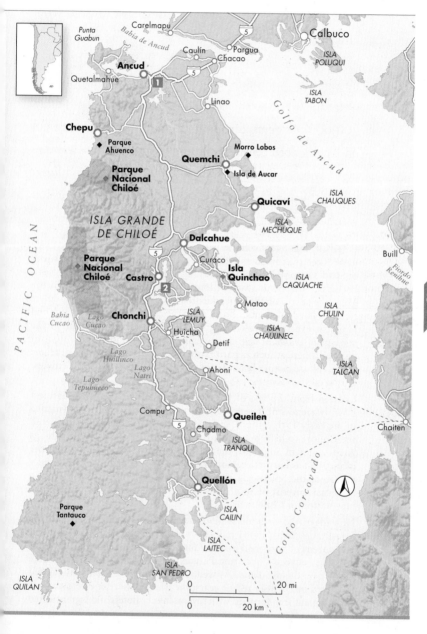

Updated
by Jimmy
Langman

Steeped in magic, shrouded in mist, the 41-island archipel-ago of Chiloé is that proverbial world apart, isolated not so much by distance from the mainland as by the quirks of history. It's also fast becoming one of Chile's favorite travel destinations. Chiloé is packed with fascinating nature, from wild beaches to thick, temperate forests. Opportunities abound for trekking, horseback riding, kayaking, bird-watching, whale-watching, and more. Much of the island's 200,000 residents are descendants of blended colonial and indigenous cultures with fascinating traditions in farm-ing, fishing, and devout Catholicism, not to mention finely crafted woolen sweaters, rich seafood stews, unique wooden churches, and palafito, or houses poised on stilts.

Originally inhabited by the indigenous Chono people, Chiloé was grad-ually taken over by the Huilliche. Though Chiloé was claimed as part of Spain's empire in the 1550s, colonists dismissed the archipelago as a backwater despite its strategic importance. The 1598 rebellion by the Mapuche people on the mainland drove a contingent of Spanish settlers to the isolated safety of Chiloé. Left to their own devices, Spaniards and Huilliche lived and worked side by side. Their society was built on the concept of *minga*, a help-thy-neighbor spirit resembling traditions of pioneer America, such as barn raisings and quilting bees. The outcome was a culture neither Spanish nor indigenous, but Chilote—a quintes-sential mestizo society.

Isolated from the rest of the continent, islanders had little interest in or awareness of the revolutionary fervor sweeping Latin America in the early 19th century. In fact, the mainland Spaniards recruited the Chilote to help put down rebellions in the region. When things got too hot in Santiago, the Spanish governor took refuge on the island, just as his predecessors had done two centuries earlier. Finally defeated, the Spaniards abandoned Chiloé in 1826, surrendering their last outpost in South America, and the island soon joined the new nation of Chile.

Nowadays, the isolation is more psychological than physical. Chiloé is just more than 2 km (1 mile) from the mainland at its nearest point, and dozens of buses and frequent ferries every day make the half-hour crossing between Chiloé and Pargua, near Puerto Montt in the Lake District on the mainland. As well, a modern airport was inaugurated in Castro in 2013. In recent years, the island's tourism offerings have taken a giant leap forward with several luxury hotels and sophisticated

gourmet restaurants opening in the Castro area and the massive private park Tantauco drawing droves of trekkers near Quellón. Today, Chiloé is embracing the world while firmly preserving its cultural past.

PLANNER

WHEN TO GO

Chiloé is increasingly a year-round destination, but like the rest of southern Chile, the ideal time to go is during the summer months, from December to March. Summer is sunnier and the prime time for cultural festivals all over the island. Although Chiloé is known to be rainy—some parts receive more than 150 inches annually—periods of sunshine regularly break the spells. Year-round, however, mist and fog prevail and deepen the mystery of the islands, while the crisp, breezy air is refreshing.

FESTIVALS AND EVENTS

Like elsewhere in southern Chile, most of Chiloé's festivals take place in summer. Fiestas Costumbristas, which celebrate Chilote customs and folklore, take place over several weekends between December and February in Ancud, Castro, and other towns. There are still other special events, such as a biodiversity fair in Castro the third week of February and a small open-air film festival in Ancud during the first few days of February.

PLANNING YOUR TIME

After crossing the Golfo de Ancud on the morning ferry on your first day, drive south to Ancud. Soak up the port town's atmosphere, but do try to visit the colony of penguins at nearby Puñihuil. Head to Dalcahue the next day, and have lunch at the colorful artisans' market. Then, take the short ferry ride to Isla Quinchao and visit the colorful church of Santa María de Loreto. Back on Isla Grande, proceed to Castro. Spend the next day relaxing, shopping, or visiting the capital's museums and the lovely church, then head south to tour Chonchi, known to locals as the "City of Three Stories." From there it's just a one-hour drive to the Pacific coast to visit the Parque Nacional Chiloé, where you can enjoy a hike through the forest and go horseback riding on the beach. If you have another day or two, consider going to Parque Tantauco near Chiloé's southernmost town, Quellón.

GETTING HERE AND AROUND
AIR TRAVEL

In November 2012, Chiloé added the modern Mocopulli Airport near Castro that connects the island with national and international flights four times a week via Aeropuerto El Tepual in Puerto Montt. Chiloé also has several small airports for regional flights and private planes.

BOAT AND FERRY TRAVEL

Since Chiloé is an archipelago, the only way to arrive by car is to take one of the frequent ferries across the eastern end of the Chacao Channel. Both Cruz del Sur and Transmarchilay operate the frequent ferry service that connects mainland Pargua with Chacao.

Ferry Service Cruz del Sur. ✉ *Los Carrera 850, Ancud* ☎ *65/262–2249* ⊕ *www.busescruzdelsur.cl.*

BUS TRAVEL

Cruz del Sur and its subsidiary Transchiloé operate some 30 buses per day between Ancud and the mainland, usually terminating in Puerto Montt. Many routes continue north to Temuco, and a few travel all the way to Santiago. Buses arriving from the mainland provide local service once they reach the island, making frequent stops.

Bus Contacts Buses Gallardo. ⊠ *San Martín 667, Of. 8, Castro* ☎ *9/9967–1706.* **Buses JAC.** ⊠ *San Martín 667, Castro* ☎ *45/246–5463* ⊕ *www.jac.cl.* **Cruz del Sur.** ⊠ *Los Carrera 850* ☎ *65/262–2249* ⊕ *www.busescruzdelsur.cl.* **ETM.** ⊠ *Bus terminal, Aníbal Pinto 1200, Ancud* ☎ *65/262–0997* ⊕ *www.etm.cl.* **Queilén Bus.** ⊠ *San Martín 667, Castro* ☎ *65/263–2173* ⊕ *www.queilenbus.cl.*

CAR TRAVEL

Rather than terminating in Puerto Montt, the Pan-American Highway skips over the Golfo de Ancud and continues through Ancud, Castro, and Chonchi before stopping in Quellón. Paved roads also lead to Quemchi, Dalcahue, and Achao on Isla Quinchao. There are rental car agencies in Castro and Ancud.

Rental Car Contacts Rent a Car Chiloé. ⊠ *Calle Dieciocho 182, Ancud* ☎ *9/9069-9675.* **SalfaSur.** ⊠ *Arturo Prat 270, Ancud* ☎ *65/262-4028* ⊕ *www.salfasur.cl.*

RESTAURANTS

As befits an island culture, seafood reigns in Chiloé. The signature Chilote dish is the *curanto*, a hearty stew of shellfish, chicken, sausages, and smoked pork ribs. It's served with plenty of potato-and-flour patties, known as *milcao* and *chapaleles*. *Salmón ahumado* (smoked salmon) is another favorite, though salmon is not native to this area. Avoid any uncooked shellfish unless you're certain you can trust the chef.

Breakfast here is often a humble menu of instant Nescafe coffee with warm bread, rolls, jam, and butter. Like the rest of Chile, most residents take their lunch between 1 pm and 3 during the week and often do so with gusto. In addition to seafood, Chilotes enjoy empanadas—baked or fried bread stuffed with meat, chicken, seafood, and other fillings. Roasted lamb is another favorite, with sheep raising still a common livelihood throughout the island.

The archipelago is also known for its tasty fruit liqueurs, usually from the central Chiloé town of Chonchi. Islanders take berries and apples and turn them into the *licor de oro* that often awaits you at your hotel. *Restaurant reviews have been shortened. For full information, visit Fodors.com.*

HOTELS

Over the past five years, Chiloé's hotel offerings have taken a quantum leap, with world-class luxury lodgings beginning to appear on the mainland. But the islands are still mostly dominated by smaller, more reasonably priced hotels. Castro and Ancud have the most choices; Chonchi, Achao, and Quellón less so. Central heating and a light breakfast are standard in better hostelries. Not all places, especially in rural towns, take credit cards, but ATMs are more readily available than you might expect.

Outside the major cities, *hospedaje* (lodgings) are few and far between. But in summer, they seem to sprout in front of every other house in Castro and Ancud, as homeowners rent rooms to visitors. Quality varies, so inspect the premises before agreeing to take a room from someone who greets you at the bus station. *Hotel reviews have been shortened. For full information, visit Fodors.com.*

WHAT IT COSTS IN CHILEAN PESOS (IN THOUSANDS)				
	$	**$$**	**$$$**	**$$$$**
Restaurants	Under 6	6–8	9–11	over 11
Hotels	Under 46	46–75	76–105	over 105

Restaurant prices are the average cost of a main course at dinner or, if dinner is not served, at lunch. Hotel prices are for the lowest cost of a standard double room in high season.

ANCUD AND NEARBY

Although it's the second-largest city in Chiloé, Ancud feels like a small town. With its hills, irregular streets, and commanding ocean views, it gets raves for its quiet charm.

Raw nature is on tap at Chepu, while Chiloé's tranquil and mystical heart is at Quemchi and Quicaví. It's also worth taking a drive along the picturesque coast, ducking into some of the beaches tucked away from development.

8

ANCUD

90 km (54 miles) southwest of Puerto Montt.

The village of Chacao (where your ferry arrives) was actually the site of one of the first Spanish shipyards in the Americas, but it was moved in 1769 to Ancud, which was deemed a more defensible location. Ancud was repeatedly attacked during Chile's war for independence and remained the last stronghold of the Spaniards in the Americas—as well as the seat of their government-in-exile after they fled from Santiago, until 1826—when the island was finally annexed by Chile.

GETTING HERE AND AROUND

Boats leave Pargua, on the mainland, every 15 minutes from 7 am until late in the evening. Trips take about 30 minutes. An additional 30 minutes down the road from Chacao, Ancud is the first real stop on Chiloé Island for most visitors. Roads from Chacao to Ancud are paved, but if you venture north or west of town to visit attractions such as the lighthouse at Faro Corona or the penguin colony at Puñihuil, the road eventually turns into gravel. There are several bus lines that serve Chiloé cities, particularly Ancud and Castro. Most visitors board buses in Puerto Montt, which is about 2½ hours from Ancud. Add another hour to get to Castro. The main bus line serving Chiloé, Cruz del Sur, has frequent service throughout the island, including Chonchi and Quellón.

Chiloé's Chapels

More than 150 wooden churches are scattered across the eastern half of Chiloé's main island and the smaller islands nearby. Jesuit missionaries came to the archipelago after the 1598 Mapuche rebellion on the mainland, and the chapels they built were an integral part of the effort to convert the indigenous peoples. Pairs of missionaries traveled the region by boat, making sure to celebrate Mass in each community at least once a year. Franciscan missionaries continued the tradition after Spain expelled the Jesuits from its New World colonies in 1767.

The architectural style of the churches calls to mind those in rural Germany, the home of many of the missionaries. The complete lack of ornamentation

is offset only by a steep roof covered with wooden shingles called *tejuelas* and a three-tier hexagonal bell tower. An arched portico fronts most of the churches. Getting to see more than the outside of many of the churches can be a challenge. Many stand seemingly forlorn in their solitude on the coast and remain locked most of the year; others are open only for Sunday services. There are two main exceptions: Castro's orange-and-lavender Iglesia de San Francisco, dating from 1906—it's technically not one of the Jesuit churches but built in the same style—opens its doors to visitors; and Achao's Iglesia de Santa María de Loreto gives daily guided Spanish-language tours.

ESSENTIALS

Visitor Information Sernatur. ⊠ *Libertad 665* ☎ *65/262–2800* ⊕ *www. sernatur.cl.*

EXPLORING

Fuerte de San Antonio. Northwest of downtown Ancud, the 16 cannon emplacements of this fort are nearly all that remain of Spain's last outpost in the New World. Constructed in 1786, the fort was a key component in the defense of the Canal de Chacao, especially after the Spanish colonial government fled to Chiloé during Chile's war for independence. ⊠ *Lord Cohrane at San Antonio* 🎫 *Free.*

Museo Regional de Ancud. Statues of mythical Chilote figures, such as the Pincoya and Trauco, greet you on the terrace of this fortress-like museum, just uphill from the Plaza de Armas. The replica of the schooner *La Goleta Ancud* is the museum's centerpiece; the ship carried Chilean settlers to the Strait of Magellan in 1843. Inside is a collection of island handicrafts. ⊠ *Libertad 370* ☎ *65/262–2413* ⊕ *www.museoancud.cl* ☾ *Closed Mon.*

Fodor's Choice ★ **Puñihuil.** One of the best nature excursions on Chiloé is at Puñihuil. Located 29 km (18 miles) southwest of Ancud, the three small islets here are home to an abundant colony of Humboldt and Magellanic penguins, along with a variety of other birds and wildlife. From December to May, a local tour operator, Ecomarine Puñihuil (www.ballenaschiloe. cl), takes out up to eight people in the mornings to search for blue whales, which have been extensively tracked in the area by scientists. ⊠ *Ancud* ☎ *9/8174–7592 mobile* ⊕ *www.pinguineraschiloe.cl.*

WHERE TO EAT

$ ✕**Kuranton.** This intimate establishment specializes in *curanto* (a Chil-
CHILEAN ean feast cooked in the ground), available at both dinner and lunch
(most restaurants only have it for lunch). A variety of other dishes fill
out the menu, from standard Chilote seafood to pizza, beef, chicken,
and sandwiches. **Known for:** curanto; Chiloé memorabilia; cozy spot.
⑤ *Average main: 5000 pesos* ✉ *94 Arturo Prat* ☎ *65/262–3090.*

$$ ✕**Mascaron de Proa Restaurant.** For excellent seafood and sea views, this
SEAFOOD is the place. Founded in 1992 in front of Arena Gruesa beach on the
northern end of the coastal road (behind Cabañas las Golondrinas), the
restaurant serves its food against the backdrop of volcanoes emerging in
the horizon on a clear day. **Known for:** seafood platter; fresh fish; great
views. ⑤ *Average main: 7500 pesos* ✉ *Baquedano 560* ☎ *65/262–1979*
▭ *No credit cards* ⊘ *Closed Sun.*

$$$ ✕**Ostras Caulin.** Just 12 miles outside of Ancud, this now classic spot
SEAFOOD cracks open some of the world's best oysters, taken each day from the
Fodor's Choice coast in front of the small, wooden restaurant. Oysters come in multiple
★ forms: fried, poached, creamed, and raw. **Known for:** fresh oysters;
good spot for bird-watching. ⑤ *Average main: 10000 pesos* ✉ *Caulin (9*
km from Chacao) ☎ *9/9643–7005* ⊕ *www.ostrascaulin.cl* ⊘ *No dinner.*

WHERE TO STAY

$ ⌂**Cabañas y Hostel Isla Magica.** Located near the town center with excel-
B&B/INN lent views, Isla Magica's cozy cabins and apartments are each warmed by
FAMILY their own wood stoves and decorated with local crafts and flair. **Pros:** wood
stoves; centrally located with parking; full kitchens. **Cons:** showers are
small; Wi-Fi is slow; no breakfast. ⑤ *Rooms from: 45000 pesos* ✉ *Bellav-*
ista 438 ☎ *65/262–1326* ⊕ *www.islamagica.cl* ⇴ *9 rooms* ⦿ *Some meals.*

$$ ⌂**Faros del Sur.** This rustic, wooden hotel that bills itself as a "bou-
HOTEL tique hostal" is a worthy choice for the views alone. **Pros:** ocean
views; family atmosphere; tranquil location. **Cons:** no elevator; bath-
rooms could use a face-lift; hard to get to without a car. ⑤ *Rooms*
from: 49000 pesos ✉ *Costanera Norte 320* ☎ *65/262–5799* ⊕ *www.*
farosdelsur.cl ⇴ *18* ⦿ *Breakfast.*

$ ⌂**Hotel Balai.** Facing the town plaza, this hotel has an ideal location in the
B&B/INN center of town. **Pros:** good location; well-maintained rooms; friendly ser-
vice. **Cons:** paper-thin walls; parking is two blocks away; small bathrooms.
⑤ *Rooms from: 36000 pesos* ✉ *Pudeto 169* ☎ *65/262–2541* ⊕ *www.hotel-*
balai.cl ⊘ *Closed on some holidays* ⇴ *12 rooms* ⦿ *Breakfast.*

$$ ⌂**Hotel Galeón Azul.** On a bluff overlooking Ancud's waterfront, this
HOTEL older hotel is conveniently located and fine for a brief stay. **Pros:**
waterfront views; proximity to downtown; pisco sours. **Cons:** thin
walls; street noise; hotel is showing its age. ⑤ *Rooms from: 55000*
pesos ✉ *Libertad 751* ☎ *65/262–2567* ⊕ *www.hotelgaleonazul.cl*
⇴ *15 rooms* ⦿ *Breakfast.*

$$ ⌂**Panamericana Hotel Ancud.** A solid choice for your stay, the vener-
HOTEL able Panamericana Hotel Ancud has long been one of Chiloé's top
hotels. **Pros:** privileged views of Ancud Bay; good restaurant; excellent
service. **Cons:** rooms are on the small side; hotel is older; not much
storage space for luggage. ⑤ *Rooms from: 65000 pesos* ✉ *San Antonio*
30 ☎ *65/262–2340* ⊕ *www.hotelancud.cl* ⇴ *24 rooms* ⦿ *Breakfast.*

8

NIGHTLIFE

L'Chinchel Bar and Cafe. A friendly, laid-back bar with great local beers on tap, tasty bar food, and trendy tunes in the background as it fills up. ⊠ *Eleuterio Ramirez 317* ☎ *65/262–4749* ⌁ *Closed Sun.*

Retro's Pub. Bar tunes blare loudly at the smoky, crowded Retro's Pub. Its Mexican food offerings—burritos, fajitas, and nachos—are a nice change of pace from Chiloé's ubiquitous seafood. ⊠ *Maipu 615* ☎ *65/262–6410.*

SPORTS AND THE OUTDOORS

Water sports such as sailing or sea kayaking are popular in the Ancud area. There are several fishing and trekking possibilities as well. Along the coastline you can see dolphins, penguins, and often whales from the area's picturesque beaches.

MULTISPORT OPERATORS

Austral Adventures. Austral Adventures arranges bilingual, tailor-made kayaking, trekking, and bird-watching trips. ⊠ *Ave. Salvador Allende 904* ☎ *65/262–5977* ⊕ *www.austral-adventures.com.*

Fodor'sChoice
★ **Chiloé Natural.** This sustainable tour operator offers a diverse array of excursions, from birding and trekking to tours of the island's historic churches, and does so with creativity, insight, and authenticity. ⊠ *Blanco 100, Castro* ☎ *65/253–4973* ⊕ *www.chiloenatural.com.*

Turismo Pehuén. A pioneer on the island, the leading tourism operator on Chiloé has long been Turismo Pehuén. It runs a variety of top-notch nature and culture excursions of Castro, Ancud, and the surrounding region. ⊠ *Chacabuco 498, Castro* ☎ *65/263–5254* ⊕ *www.turismopehuen.cl.*

SHOPPING

Feria Municipal Rural y Artesanal. Shopping in Ancud is nothing extraordinary, though there's a fine artisans' market just below the town plaza and a few blocks up from the waterfront. There you find woolen blankets, sweaters, dolls, wooden figurines, and other items by Chiloé artisans. ⊠ *At Libertad and Dieciocho.*

QUEMCHI

62 km (37 miles) southeast of Ancud.

On the protected interior of the Golfo de Ancud, Quemchi is a small, tranquil fishing village that makes for a good stopover when visiting churches and other tourist sites in northeastern Chiloé. There are several historic churches and scenic islands nearby.

GETTING HERE AND AROUND

You can reach Quemchi via paved roads from Ancud in less than an hour by car. To get to nearby tourist sites, be prepared for gravelly, dusty country roads that require careful driving, preferably in a four-wheel-drive vehicle. Additionally, there are a few small islands nearby worth seeing. You can hire a boat at the town port, where there is usually a handful of captains on hand ready to negotiate a fee for the service.

EXPLORING

Isla de Aucar. This tiny forested islet 6 km (4 miles) south of Quemchi is reached by walking across a stunning wooden bridge some 510 meters (1,673 feet) long. Black-necked swans and other birds frequent the area. The island hosts a botanical garden and Jesuit chapel and cemetery that date to 1761. ⊠ *Isla de Aucar.*

Morro Lobos. Reached by a 45-minute boat ride from the port of Quemchi, this immense rock outcrop juts out of the sea off the coast of Caucahue Island. Hundreds of sea lions and marine birds call it home. Boats at the port can be hired for about 12,000 pesos. ⊠ *Quemchi.*

OFF THE BEATEN PATH

Parque Ahuenco. This 1,120-hectare (2,768-acre) private reserve is a magic landscape with windswept, old-growth temperate rainforest bumping up to a coastline that attracts a Humboldt and Magellanic penguin colony from September to February. A unique conservation initiative involving 46 different private owners, the park hosts the majority of the flora and fauna found on the big island of Chiloé, including the endangered Darwin's fox and the tiny pudú deer. Get here by taking a 30-minute boat ride from the Club de Pesca y Caza in Chepu, then once you reach the mouth of the river it's a three-hour hike into the park. ⊠ *Chepu* ☎ *9/8464–7374* ⊕ *www.ahuenco.cl.*

WHERE TO EAT

$$
CHILEAN
Fodor's Choice
★

✕ El Chejo. The guest book at this small, waterfront restaurant is jammed with raves and compliments about its Chiloé seafood dishes, but it's the dozen types of empanadas—filled with beef, cheese, clams, salmon, or crab meat, to name a few—that impress most. **Known for:** empanadas; local seafood dishes; waterfront dining. Ⓢ *Average main: 7000 pesos* ⊠ *Diego Bahmonde 251* ☎ *65/269–1490* ⊕ *www.elchejo. cl* ▭ *No credit cards.*

QUICAVÍ

25 km (15 miles) southeast of Quemchi.

The center of all that is magical and mystical about Chiloé, Quicaví sits forlornly on the eastern coast of Isla Grande. Superstitious locals strongly advise against going anywhere near the coast to the south of town, where miles of caves extend to the village of Tenaún. They believe that witches, and evil ones at that, inhabit them. On the beaches, local lore says, are mermaids that lure fishermen to their deaths. (These are not the beautiful and benevolent Pincoya, also a legendary kelp-covered mermaid. A glimpse of her is thought to portend good fishing for the day.) Many Quicaví denizens claim to have glimpsed Chiloé's notorious ghost ship, the *Caleuche,* roaming the waters on foggy nights, searching for its doomed passengers. Of course, a brief glimpse of the ship is all anyone dares admit, as legend holds that a longer gaze could spell death.

GETTING HERE AND AROUND

From Ancud, Quicaví is reached by going first to Quemchi, then driving south along a two-lane dirt road through the Chiloé countryside for about 40 minutes.

8

EXPLORING

Iglesia de San Pedro. In an effort to win converts, the Jesuits constructed this enormous church on the Plaza de Armas. The original structure survives from colonial times, though it underwent extensive remodeling in the early 20th century. It's open for services on the first Sunday of every month at 11 am, which is your best bet for getting a look inside. ⊠ *Quicaví.*

DALCAHUE

44 km (27 miles) southwest of Quicaví; 74 km (44 miles) southeast of Ancud; 20 km (12 miles) northeast of Castro.

Most days travelers in the laid-back port town of Dalcahue stop only long enough to board the ferry that deposits them 15 minutes later on Isla Quinchao. But the artisan market here is a worthy stop, if only to sample the local food. Dalcahue is a pleasant coastal town—one that deserves a longer visit.

GETTING HERE AND AROUND

Dalcahue is about an hour from Ancud along paved roads. There is also frequent bus service, particularly from Castro, which is about a 15-minute drive from Dalcahue. Dalcahue Expreso buses can be caught at Castro's bus terminal (at the corner of Freire and O'Higgins) or at several bus stops along the road between Dalcahue and Ancud.

EXPLORING

Iglesia de Nuestra Señora de los Dolores. This 1850 church, modeled on the churches constructed during the Jesuit era, sits in the main square (Plaza de Armas). A portico with nine arches, an unusually high number for a Chilote church, fronts the structure. The church holds a small museum with historic town and church documents and old church ornaments. ⊠ *Dalcahue* ☎ *65/264–1456* 🆓 *Free.*

Museo Histórico Etnográfico de Dalcahue. A *fogón*—a traditional indigenous cooking pit—sits in the center of the small *palafito* (a shingled house built on stilts and hanging over the water) housing this museum that displays historical exhibits about the indigenous peoples of Chiloé—the Chonos and Huilliche. ⊠ *Pedro Montt 40* ☎ *65/264–2375* 🆓 *Free.*

WHERE TO STAY

$
B&B/INN

Hotel la Isla. A friendly attitude greets you at this wood-shingled hotel with a cozy sitting room and big fireplace off the lobby. **Pros:** comfortable; friendly service; centrally located. **Cons:** staff does not speak English; not on the waterfront; street noise. $ *Rooms from: 45000 pesos* ⊠ *Mocopulli 113* ☎ *65/264–1241* ⊕ *www.hotellaisladalcahue.com* ⤳ *19 rooms* ⦿ *Breakfast.*

$$$
B&B/INN
Fodor'sChoice
★

Refugio de Navegantes. Close to both the historic church and the waterfront, this boutique hotel has just five rooms, and is run with a very personal touch by its owners. **Pros:** contemporary decor; near the town plaza; excellent café. **Cons:** Wi-Fi sometimes falters; limited café menu; lacks local Chilote character. $ *Rooms from: 97969 pesos* ⊠ *San Martín 165* ☎ *65/264–1128* ⊕ *www.refugiodenavegantes.cl* ⤳ *5 rooms* ⦿ *Breakfast.*

SHOPPING

Feria Artesanal in Dalcahue. Dalcahue's crafts market, near the waterfront municipal building, draws crowds who come to shop for Chilote handicrafts, woolens, baskets, and woven mythical figures. It's open every day, but the best time to go is on Sunday mornings as more vendors travel from surrounding areas to sell their wares. Don't miss the lively food stalls at the Cocinería behind the market. Bargaining is expected, though the prices are already quite reasonable. ⊠ *Av. Pedro Montt.*

ISLA QUINCHAO

1 km (1 mile) southeast of Dalcahue.

For many visitors, the elongated Isla Quinchao, the easiest to reach of the islands in the eastern archipelago, defines Chiloé. Populated by hardworking farmers and fisherfolk, Isla Quinchao provides a glimpse into the region's past. Head to Achao, Quinchao's largest community, to see the *alerce*-shingle (a wood native to Chile) houses, busy fishing pier, and colonial church. And if you have more time, visit one of the nine outlying islands near Quinchao.

GETTING HERE AND AROUND

The roads from Dalcahue, and the main road through Isla Quinchao, are paved. About two hours from Ancud, Achao is a 30-minute journey from Dalcahue, the town from which you catch the ferry to cross Ayacara Bay. The ride is a mere five minutes, and there are frequent departures from 7 am to midnight. It's free for pedestrians and 2,500 pesos each way for cars. Once on the island, the road to Achao winds its way through verdant countryside, often with tremendous views of the surrounding sea.

EXPLORING

Iglesia de Nuestra Señora de Gracia. About 10 km (6 miles) south of Achao is the archipelago's largest church. As with many other Chilote churches, the 200-foot structure sits in solitude near the coast. The church has no tours but may be visited at anytime during the summer months, and the rest of the year when they celebrate Sunday Mass at 11 am. ⊠ *7 km (4 miles) north of Castro, Nercon.*

Fodor'sChoice ★ **Iglesia de Santa María de Loreto.** Achao's centerpiece is this 1730 church, the oldest house of worship in Chile. In addition to the alerce wood so commonly used to construct buildings in the region, the church also uses cypress and *mañío* trees. Its typically unadorned exterior contrasts with the deep-blue ceiling embellished with gold stars and rich baroque carvings on the altar inside. Mass is celebrated Sunday at 11 am and Tuesday at 7 pm, but docents give guided tours while the church is open. An informative Spanish-language museum behind the altar is dedicated to the period of Chiloé's Jesuit missions. ⊠ *Plaza de Armas, Delicias at Amunategui, Achao* ☎ *65/266–1143* ⊠ *Free* ⊗ *Closed Mon. Mar.–Nov.*

WHERE TO EAT

$$
SEAFOOD
× **Hostería la Nave.** Inside this rambling beachfront building that arches over the street, this restaurant serves seafood, beef, and other dishes. Try the oysters or *merluza margarita*, hake fish in a shellfish sauce.

Known for: merluza margarita; beachfront location; basic hotel upstairs. $ *Average main: 8000 pesos* ✉ *Arturo Prat at Sargento Aldea, Achao* ☎ *65/266–1219.*

$$
SEAFOOD

✕ **Mar y Velas.** Scrumptious oysters and a panoply of other gifts from the sea are served on the top floor of this big wooden house at the foot of Achao's dock (accessible via a side stairway). Open late and serving generous portions, many in town maintain the food here is the best around. **Known for:** fresh seafood; late dining; local favorite. $ *Average main: 7000 pesos* ✉ *Serrano 2, Achao* ☎ *65/266–1375.*

WHERE TO STAY

$
B&B/INN

🏨 **Hospedaje Sol y Lluvia.** If you plan to stay in Isla Quinchao overnight, this is the best option. **Pros:** clean; friendly service; secure parking. **Cons:** not close to the beach; small place; less privacy. $ *Rooms from: 25000 pesos* ✉ *Ricardo Jara 9* ☎ *65/266–1383* ▭ *No credit cards* ⤴ *8 rooms, 3 with bath* ⧆ *Breakfast.*

CASTRO AND NEARBY

With a population of 43,500, Castro is now Chiloé's largest city. Though hardly an urban jungle, this is big-city life Chiloé-style. Residents of more rural parts of the island, who visit the capital no more often than necessary, return home with tales of traffic so heavy that it has to be regulated with stoplights.

South of Castro, Chonchi's colorful wooden houses climb the hillside. Parque Nacional Chiloé, one of the island's main attractions, is a great place to visit before the ferry ride back to the mainland from Quellón.

CASTRO

45 km (28 miles) west of Achao; 88 km (55 miles) south of Ancud.

Founded in 1567, Castro is Chile's third-oldest city. Its history has been one of destruction, with three fires and three earthquakes laying waste to the city over four centuries. The most recent disaster was in 1960, when a tidal wave caused by an earthquake on the mainland engulfed the city.

Castro's future as Isla Grande's governmental and commercial center looked promising after the 1598 Mapuche rebellion on the mainland drove the Spaniards to Chiloé, but then Dutch pirates sacked the city in 1600. Many of Castro's residents fled to the safety of more isolated parts of the island. It wasn't until 1982 that the city finally became Chiloé's administrative capital.

Next to its wooden churches, *palafitos,* shingled houses on stilts in the water along the coast, are the best-known architectural symbol of Chiloé. Avenida Pedro Montt, which becomes a coastal highway as it leads out of town, is the best place to see palafitos in Castro. Many of these ramshackle structures have been transformed into restaurants, boutique hotels, and artisan markets.

GETTING HERE AND AROUND

In the center of the Isla Grande de Chiloé, Castro is only about a one-hour drive from Ancud along Ruta 5, the Pan-American Highway. For a more interesting journey, consider the mostly unpaved coastal road to Castro via Quemchi, which takes twice as long but passes numerous historic churches and other tourist sites.

In late 2012, Castro opened Mocupulli Airport, which four days a week receives commercial flights from the mainland. There is also regular and frequent bus service from the terminal in Puerto Montt to Castro, which takes almost four hours. Buses Queilén and Gallardo operate on Chiloé Island only. Various buses go to Dalcahue from the Castro bus terminal. Buses JAC and ETM can take you to the main cities of Chiloé and several cities in Chile. Cruz del Sur have routes nationwide and even into Argentina. Reserve ahead for buses.

ESSENTIALS

Visitor Information **Tourism Office of the Castro Municipality.** ✉ *Plaza de Armas* ☎ *65/254–7706.*

EXPLORING

Fodor's Choice **Iglesia de San Francisco.** Any tour of Castro begins with this much-pho-
★ tographed 1906 church, constructed in the style of the archipelago's wooden churches, only bigger and grander. Depending on your perspective, terms like "pretty" or "garish" describe the orange-and-lavender exterior colors chosen when the structure was spruced up before Pope John Paul II's 1987 visit. It's infinitely more reserved on the inside. The dark-wood interior's centerpiece is the monumental carved crucifix hanging from the ceiling. In the evening, a soft, energy-efficient external illumination system makes the church one of Chiloé's most impressive sights. ✉ *Plaza de Armas, corner of Freire and Caupolicán.*

Museo de Arte Moderno de Chiloé. Housed in five refurbished barns in a city park northwest of downtown, this modern-art complex—referred to locally as the MAM—exhibits works by Chilean artists. The museum opens to the public only when there are exhibitions or special events. ✉ *Pasaje Díaz 181* ☎ *65/263–5454* ⊕ *www.mamchiloe.cl* 🎫 *Free.*

Museo Regional de Castro. This museum, one block from the Plaza de Armas, gives a good (Spanish-only) introduction to the region's history and culture. Packed into a fairly small space are artifacts from the Huilliche era (primarily farming and fishing implements) through the 19th century (looms, spinning wheels, and plows). One exhibit displays the history of the archipelago's wooden churches; another shows black-and-white photographs of the damage caused by the 1960 earthquake that rocked southern Chile. The museum has a collection of quotations about Chiloé culture by outsiders. "The Chilote talks little, but thinks a lot. He is rarely spontaneous with outsiders, and even with his own countrymen he isn't too communicative," wrote one ethnographer. ✉ *Esmeralda 255* ☎ *65/263–5967* 🎫 *Free* ☉ *Closed Sun., Mar.- Dec.*

WHERE TO EAT

$$$$ ✕ **Cazador.** With a charming ambience, Cazador is an intimate dining
CONTEMPORARY experience that features inventive food made with fresh, often organic, local ingredients. Be sure to try the duck with garden vegetables and

8

roasted pumpkin. **Known for:** duck with garden vegetables; merluza austral fish; cozy atmosphere. $ *Average main: 15000 pesos* ⊠ *Ernesto Riquelme 1212* ☎ *65/253–1770* ⊗ *Closed Sun.*

$$$
CONTEMPORARY
Fodor's Choice
★

✕ **El Mercadito.** With a fresh, creative approach to traditional Chilote cuisine, this restaurant is a nice change of pace in the island's restaurant scene—and, most importantly, it serves up really good food. El Mercadito is in a restored house overlooking the waterfront in the historic Pedro Montt barrio. **Known for:** spicy conger eel stew; waterfront setting; tradition with a twist. $ *Average main: 9000 pesos* ⊠ *Pedro Montt 210* ☎ *65/253–3866* ⊕ *www.elmercaditodechiloe.cl* ⊗ *Closed Sun.*

$$
SEAFOOD

✕ **Sacho Restaurant.** Going strong since the late 1970s, Sacho features the favorite seafood plates Chiloé is known for, cooked in the traditional style, from fish and curanto to *chupe de jaiba* (crab stew). Service is friendly and mostly prompt, even when it fills up at lunch time with locals. **Known for:** local institution; traditional seafood; popular lunch spot. $ *Average main: 8000 pesos* ⊠ *Thomson 213* ☎ *65/263–2079* ⊕ *www.sachorestaurant.cl* ⊗ *Closed Sun.*

$$$
CHILEAN
Fodor's Choice
★

✕ **Travesia.** Co-owned by the authors of an award-winning cook book about Chiloé cuisine, Travesia is a wonderful way to experience Chiloé dishes that are prepared with inventive, modern twists by a young team of chefs. A favorite is the out-of-this-world *chancho ahumado* (smoked pork), which is served with a delightful sauce made of local murta berries together with potatoes (a star ingredient here—Chiloé hosts 90% of the world's known potato varieties). **Known for:** creative Chilote food; hancho ahumado (smoked pork); cookbook owners. $ *Average main: 10000 pesos* ⊠ *Eusebio Lillo 188* ☎ *65/263–0137* ⊕ *www.restaurantravesia.wordpress.com* ⊗ *No dinner Sun.*

WHERE TO STAY

$$
HOTEL

🏨 **Hotel de Castro.** Looming over downtown near the estuary, this hotel has a sloped chalet-style roof with a long skylight, which makes the interior seem bright and airy even on a cloudy day. **Pros:** central location; bay views; spa. **Cons:** older building is dated; weak Wi-Fi signal on some floors; limited parking space. $ *Rooms from: 65000 pesos* ⊠ *Chacabuco 202* ☎ *65/263–2301* ⊕ *www.hoteldecastro.cl* ⤶ *69 rooms* ⦿| *Breakfast.*

$$$$
HOTEL

🏨 **Hotel de la Isla Enjoy Chiloé.** This five-star hotel, part of Chile's Enjoy casino chain, rents a mix of rooms and self-catering apartments that tastefully blend into the landscape. **Pros:** bay views; amenities and entertainment on-site; updated, comfortable rooms. **Cons:** lacking authentic local feel; casino attracts large crowds; not near the city center. $ *Rooms from: 115000 pesos* ⊠ *Ruta 5 Sur 2053* ☎ *65/258–4500* ⤶ *76 rooms* ⦿| *Breakfast.*

$$$$
HOTEL

🏨 **Hotel Parque Quilquico.** Across the Dalcahue Channel at Rilan Peninsula, Hotel Parque Quilquico incorporates the colorful style of Chiloé architecture into a hotel with a green conscience. **Pros:** indoor pool and outdoor hot tubs; private trail; all rooms have terraces. **Cons:** spotty Wi-Fi connection; some rooms are small; no TVs. $ *Rooms from: 210000 pesos* ⊠ *Quilquico Rural s/n* ☎ *65/297–1000* ⊕ *www.hpq.cl* ⤶ *37 rooms* ⦿| *Breakfast.*

$$$$ 🏠 **Ocio Territorial Hotel.** A tremendous place to disconnect and relax while
B&B/INN   exploring Chiloé, this beautiful, countryside hotel rents various types of
Fodor's Choice   lodging. **Pros:** privacy; stunning view of the city and estuary; luxurious
★   setting. **Cons:** Wi-Fi only in common area; hard to get here; restaurant
is in a separate building. $ *Rooms from: 250000 pesos* ✉ *Península de
Rilán* 🕾 *65/297–1911, 9/7300–7056* ⊕ *www.ocioterritorial.com* 🛏 *18
rooms* ❍ *Some meals; Breakfast.*

$$$ 🏠 **Palafito 1326 Hotel Boutique.** A renovated *palafito* (traditional stilt
B&B/INN   house) in the Gambo neighborhood, this hotel inside Castro is a small,
quiet alternative to the bigger, luxury options in the area. **Pros:** views
from the terrace; central heating; excellent breakfasts. **Cons:** often
sold out; no TV; street noise. $ *Rooms from: 83000 pesos* ✉ *Ernesto
Riquelme 1326* 🕾 *65/253–0053* ⊕ *www.palafito1326.cl* 🛏 *12 rooms*
❍ *Breakfast.*

$$ 🏠 **Patio Palafito.** This small, but cozy boutique palafito (traditional house
B&B/INN   on stilts) hotel is a laid-back, low-frills place to stay for a night or two.
Pros: unique architecture; on the water; great café. **Cons:** limited parking space; rooms are small; thin wooden walls. $ *Rooms from: 60000
pesos* ✉ *Pedro Montt 465* 🕾 *65/268–2777* ⊕ *www.patiopalafito.com*
🛏 *8 rooms* ❍ *Breakfast.*

$$$$ 🏠 **Tierra Chiloé.** Tranquility and absorbing views of verdant farmland
HOTEL   and Chiloé coastline make this truly upscale home-away-from-home
Fodor's Choice   quite intimate, as does the reading room, fireplace lounge, and dining
★   area in the main lodge. **Pros:** impressive architecture; beautiful setting
and views; new indoor–outdoor spa. **Cons:** occasional salmon farming
pens amid the sea views; most of the excursions are group trips; can
be difficult to find. $ *Rooms from: 290000 pesos* ✉ *San José Playa,
Castro, Casilla* 🕾 *2/2207–8861* ⊕ *www.tierrachiloe.com* 🛏 *24 rooms*
❍ *All-inclusive; Breakfast.*

SPORTS AND THE OUTDOORS

Sea kayaking around the outlying islands near Castro has become one
of Chiloé's main draws. There are also interesting options for fishing,
horseback riding, and hiking in the surrounding countryside, particularly in and around Chiloé National Park.

KAYAKING

Altue Sea Kayaking. Altue Sea Kayaking is one of Chile's oldest adventure
travel operators. From December to March, the outfitter leads five-day/
four-night trips around the Chiloé archipelago, departing from its sea-
kayaking center near Dalcahue. ✉ *Dalcahue* 🕾 *9/419–6809* ⊕ *www.
seakayakchile.com.*

MULTISPORT OPERATORS

Chiloetnico. This agency runs a variety of nature and culture tours
throughout Chiloé, with both day-trip and multiday options, including
trekking, cycling, kayaking, city tours, and visits to historical churches.
✉ *Ernesto Riquelme 1228* 🕾 *65/263–0951* ⊕ *chiloetnico.cl* 🗺 *From
70000 pesos.*

8

SHOPPING

Feria Artesanal Castro. The city's Feria Artesanal, a lively, often chaotic crafts market, is regarded by most as the best place on the island to pick up the woolen sweaters, woven baskets, and straw figures for which Chiloé is known. Prices are already quite reasonable, but vendors expect some bargaining. The stalls share the place with several food vendors. It's open daily 9–dusk though the best time to come is Saturday morning, when artisans from all over the island come to sell their wares. ⊠ *Eusebio Lillo s/n.*

CHONCHI

23 km (14 miles) south of Castro.

The colorful wooden houses of Chonchi are on a hillside so steep that it's known in Spanish as the Ciudad de los Tres Pisos (City of Three Stories). The town's name means "slippery earth" in the Huilliche language, and if you tromp up the town's steep streets on a rainy day you can understand why. Arranged around a scenic harbor, Chonchi wins raves as one of Chiloé's most picturesque towns.

GETTING HERE AND AROUND

Chonchi is 15 minutes south of Castro via the Pan-Amercan Highway, Ruta 5.

EXPLORING

Iglesia de San Carlos. The town's centerpiece, this church on the Plaza de Armas was started by the Jesuits in 1754 but left unfinished until 1859. Rebuilt in the neoclassical style, the church is now a national monument. An unusually ornate arcade with five arches fronts the church, and inside are an intricately carved altar and wooden columns. The church contains Chonchi's most prized relic, a statue of the Virgen de la Candelaria. According to tradition, this image of the Virgin Mary protected the town from the Dutch pirates who destroyed neighboring Castro in 1600. Townspeople celebrate the event every February 2 with fireworks and gunpowder symbolizing the pirate attack. The building is open for mass Sunday at 11 am. ⊠ *Plaza de Armas, at Centenario and Francisco Corral.*

Museo de las Tradiciones Chonchinas. This small but interesting museum documents early life in Chonchi through furnishings and photos in a 19th-century house. ⊠ *Centenario 116* ☎ *65/267–2802* 🕅 *700 pesos* 🕙 *Closed Sun.*

WHERE TO EAT

$

SEAFOOD

✕ **Mercado Chonchi.** In a tidy building, this market with four restaurants is a great spot for an informal lunch, though it's also open for dinner. The restaurants, in a food court overlooking the water, mainly serve standard Chiloé fare such as curanto and assorted seafood. **Known for:** classic Chiloé fare; casual vibe; convenient to stores selling local crafts. ⑤ *Average main: 5000 pesos* ⊠ *Irarrázabal 47* ▭ *No credit cards.*

WHERE TO STAY

$$$$
B&B/INN

Espejo de Luna. About a 40-minute drive south of Castro, this hotel has astounding vistas of the Gulf of Corcovado with volcanoes and mountains crowning the horizon. **Pros:** excellent restaurant; privacy; natural beauty. **Cons:** poor Internet connection; limited menu; not a lot of amenities. ⑤ *Rooms from: 190000 pesos* ⊠ *Pan-American Hwy., Km 35; just south of Castro and town of Altyuy, Queilén* ☎ *9/9040–5888* ⊕ *www.espejodeluna.cl* ↪ *5 rooms, 3 cabins* ⑩ *Some meals.*

$
B&B/INN

Hotel & Cabanas Huildin. Given Chonchi's relatively short distance to both Castro and Chiloé National Park, this is a good value option for travelers moving through the island by car. **Pros:** historic building; views of the bay; cozy ambience. **Cons:** some rooms are small; no restaurant; no frills. ⑤ *Rooms from: 20000 pesos* ⊠ *Centenario 102* ☎ *65/267–1388* ↪ *12 rooms, 8 cabins* ⑩ *Breakfast.*

PARQUE NACIONAL CHILOÉ

35 km (21 miles) west of Chonchi.

The Parque Nacional Chiloé comprises a huge swath of Chiloé's Pacific coast. It's a wonderful mix of broad beaches, rolling sand dunes, lush temperate rain forest, and, to the north, extensive wetlands, that come together to form one of the country's most visually compelling parks. It's a draw for eco-tourists. But even though the climate is often windy and rainy, this is also just a spectacular place to roam the beautiful beach.

GETTING HERE AND AROUND

To get to Chiloé National Park, take the Pan-American Highway, or Ruta 5, south from Ancud or Castro. A paved side road from the highway leading to the park is found at Notuco, near the town of Chonchi, which is only 22½ km (14 miles) south of Castro.

EXPLORING

Fodor's Choice
★

Parque Nacional Chiloé. This 430-square-km (166-square-mile) park hugs Isla Grande's sparsely populated Pacific coast. The park's two sectors differ dramatically. Heavily forested with evergreens, Sector Anay, to the south, is most easily entered from the coastal village of Cucao. A road heads west to the park from the Pan-American Highway at Notuco, just south of Chonchi. Popular among backpackers is its short woody Tepual Trail, which begins at the Chanquín Visitor Center, 1 km (1 mile) north of the park entrance and winds through a rare, intact forest of tepu trees (*Tepualia stipularis*), whose large, twisted trunks are visible above and below your walking path. Along the path as well are signs explaining the significance of the forest and what it holds. The longer Dunas Trail leads through the forest to the beach dunes near Cacao. Keep an eye out for the Chiloé fox, native to Isla Grande; more reclusive is the pudú , a miniature deer. Some 3 km (2 miles) north of the Cucao entrance is a Huilliche community on the shore of Lago Huelde. Unobtrusive visitors are welcome. At the southern end of the park is one of Chile's best beaches, Cucao Beach , where dunes extend along the unusually wide sand. Camping is permitted. The northern Sector Chepu contains primarily wetlands and a large bird population (most notably penguins) and sea-lion colony. Get there via Ruta 5, but take

8

the crossroad toward Río Chepu, then continue west on a gravel road until Puerto Anguay. ⊠ *North of Cucao and south of Chepu, Parque Nacional Chiloe* ☎ 65/253–2501 ⊠ *4000 pesos.*

WHERE TO STAY

$ **El Fogon de Cucao.** Founded in 1997 by a former newspaper reporter in Chile, El Fogon de Cucao has a friendly atmosphere with rustic decor and big beds. **Pros:** excellent service; lakeside; good food. **Cons:** few rooms so bookings must be made in advance; no Wi-Fi; reservations only by telephone. ⑤ *Rooms from: 35000 pesos* ⊠ *Within Chiloé National Park, near Cucao entrance at southern end of park, Chiloé National Park* ☎ 9/9946–5685 ⊟ *No credit cards* ⇄ *9 rooms, 1 cabin* ⎮⊙⎮ *Breakfast.*

B&B/INN

$$ **Palafito Cucao Hostel.** With nine rooms, each with private bathroom and a view of Cucao Lake, this is an excellent option for overnight visits to Chiloé National Park. **Pros:** lake views; good place to meet people; well-designed. **Cons:** neighbor noise; heating system erratic; Wi-Fi is slow. ⑤ *Rooms from: 54000 pesos* ⊠ *Chiloe National Park, Cucao* ☎ 65/297–1164 ⊕ *www.hostelpalafitocucao.cl* ⊟ *No credit cards* ⇄ *9 rooms* ⎮⊙⎮ *Breakfast.*

B&B/INN

QUEILÉN

47 km (29 miles) southeast of Chonchi.

This town named for the red cypress trees that dot the area sits on an elongated peninsula and, as such, is the only town on Isla Grande with two seafronts. Though Chiloé's windy, rainy, and cold climate is mostly unfavorable for typical beach activities, the beauty of the unspoiled seaside is unquestionable. Two of Isla Grande's best beaches are the **Playa de Queilén**, in the center of town, and the **Playa Lelbun**, 15 km (9 miles) northwest of the city.

GETTING HERE AND AROUND

From Castro, go south on Ruta 5 until you get to the Chonchi exit; from Chonchi a gravel road heads southeast to Queilén.

EXPLORING

Mirador. Uphill on Calle Presidente Kennedy, this scenic overlook has stupendous views of the Golfo de Ancud, the smaller islands in the archipelago, and, on a clear day, the Volcán Corcovado on the mainland. ⊠ *Calle Presidente Kennedy.*

Refugio de Navegantes. The town's cultural center contains a small museum with artifacts and old black-and-white photographs. Nothing is very colorful here—the muted tones of the pottery, fabrics, and farm implements reflect the stark life of colonial Chiloé. ⊠ *Av. Alessandri s/n* ☎ 65/253–5300 ⊠ *Free.*

WHERE TO STAY

$$$ **El Coo Lodge.** If your lodging criteria includes peace, empty beaches, abundant nature, and magical views, this small but stylish hotel is the perfect escape. **Pros:** magnificent views; private beach; peace and quiet. **Cons:** only breakfast is offered; few services; just three rooms. ⑤ *Rooms from: 76000* ⊠ *Sector Rural ñida* ✛ *2 km from center of Queilen* ☎ 9/6867–8334 ⊕ *www.elcoolodge.com* ⇄ *3 rooms* ⎮⊙⎮ *Breakfast.*

B&B/INN

QUELLÓN

99 km (60 miles) south of Castro.

The Pan-American Highway, which begins in Alaska and stretches for most of the length of North and South America, ends without fanfare here in Quellón, Chiloé's southernmost city. Quellón was the famed "end of Christendom" described by Charles Darwin during his 19th-century visit. Just a few years earlier it had been the southernmost outpost of Spain's empire in the New World. For most visitors today, Quellón is also the end of the line. But for hikers and nature lovers, there's plenty to explore along the coast and Parque Tantauco nearby. It's also the starting point for ferries that head to the Southern Coast.

GETTING HERE AND AROUND

Quellón is about a one-hour drive south of Castro, on the paved Ruta 5. From Quellón, you can also catch a ferry with Naviera Austral to Chaitén (Thursday), Puerto Cisnes (Tuesday), or Chacabuco (Wednesday and Saturday) along the Carretera Austral.

ESSENTIALS

Ferry Information Ferry dock. ☒ *Pedro Montt 48* ☎ *65/268–2207.*

EXPLORING

Sendero Antipani. About 20 miles outside of Quellón, in Compu, join Huilliche guide Sandra Antipani on a two-hour native forest trek as she explains her family's indigenous traditions and the diverse native flora and fauna of the Fundo Cohuin private nature reserve. The trek can be followed by a grand curanto lunch, a visit to the first indigenous church in Chiloé, and kayaking. ☒ *Ruta 5, Sector Compu* ☎ *9/8900–8841* ✐ *antipani.s@gmail.com.*

OFF THE BEATEN PATH

Parque Tantauco. This vast, 118,000-hectare (300,000-acre) park founded by former Chile President Sebastián Piñera has added an attractive guesthouse, campground with modern bathrooms, and a series of hiking trails and overnight shelters for those who wind their way through the park's thick Valdivian temperate rain forests and rocky coastline. Serious hiking and camping enthusiasts should consider the five-day, 32-mile Transversal Trail from Chaiguata (also reachable by bus from Quellón) to Caleta Inío, the park headquarters, where you can get a boat back to Quellón. En route, you can sleep at four simple shelters, complete with bunks, cooking facilities, and latrines. Park entrance for adults costs 3,500 pesos and children 500 pesos. Trekking shelters run 15,000 pesos per night, while Caleta Ines Guesthouse has rooms for 60,000 pesos per night. There are also six geothermal domes for overnight stays at Lake Chaiguata that have central heating, from four to eight beds, and include access to a restaurant and hot tubs on-site (from 84,000 pesos). You can also rent tents and kayaks and take guided, multiday tours from the park. ☒ *Ruta 5 camino a Quellón* ☎ *65/263–3805* ⊕ *www.parquetantauco.cl* ☞ *Information office in Castro (Ruta 5 Sur 1826, Gamboa).*

8

WHERE TO EAT

$ ✕ **Sandwicheria Mitos.** The giant sandwiches here have attained mythical
FAST FOOD status in these parts. The restaurant also has an extensive daily menu
featuring a variety of traditional Chilean dishes like cazuela, roasted
chicken, *lentejas* (lentils), and more. **Known for:** giant sandwiches; traditional Chilean cuisine; fun atmosphere. $ *Average main: 6500 pesos*
✉ *Jorge Vivar 235* ☎ *65/268–0798* ⊕ *www.mitoschiloe.cl.*

WHERE TO STAY

$$ ⌂ **Hotel Patagonia Insular.** Owner Anita Azocar has transformed this
HOTEL somewhat plain-Jane hotel into a warm and inviting space, and the
most modern lodging in Quellón. **Pros:** Quellón Bay views; good food;
friendly owner. **Cons:** no gym or spa; unstable Wi-Fi signal; plain rooms.
$ *Rooms from: 55000 pesos* ✉ *Av. Juan Ladrilleros 1737* ☎ *65/268–
1610* ⊕ *www.hotelpatagoniainsular.cl* ⇱ *34 rooms* ⏐◯⏐ *Breakfast.*

$ ⌂ **Hotel Tierra del Fuego.** This rambling alerce-shingle house, dating
B&B/INN from the 1920s, is on Quellón's waterfront. **Pros:** great location;
good restaurant; cheap. **Cons:** rooms vary in quality; decor is in
need of an update; hot water is sometimes an issue. $ *Rooms from:
32000 pesos* ✉ *Av. Pedro Montt 445* ☎ *65/268–2079* ▭ *No credit
cards* ⇱ *25 rooms* ⏐◯⏐ *Breakfast.*

SPORTS AND THE OUTDOORS

Ana Villosa Sea Tours. Quellón is considered one of the best starting
points for whale-watching. Also present in the canals and islands off
the spectacular coast here are a plethora of marine birds and Peale's and
Chilean dolphins. On-board the *Ana Villlosa*, Ana Jaramillio, a Chilean
who's lived much of her life in the United States, runs day tours to view
these charismatic animals. The tour culminates with a visit (and lunch)
on the scenic Cailin Island. ✉ *Quellón* ☎ *9/824–67340* ✎ *amjaramil-
lobecker@yahoo.com.*

SHOPPING

Feria Artesanal Llauquil. Quellón's market doesn't have the hustle and
bustle of similar ones in Castro and Dalcahue, but there are some good
buys on woolens and straw folkloric figures. Don't bother to bargain;
the prices are already extremely reasonable. ✉ *Av. Gómez García*
◷ *Closed Sun. Mar.–Nov.*

THE SOUTHERN COAST

WELCOME TO THE SOUTHERN COAST

TOP REASONS TO GO

★ **Scenery:** The Carretera Austral, a dusty dirt road that was blazed through southern Chile in the 1970s and '80s, has opened up one of the most beautiful places in the world to tourists.

★ **Glaciers:** There's a world-class network of national parks with amazing attractions, such as the breathtaking mountainscapes of Cerro Castillo National Park, the wildlife and spectacular ecology of Patagonia National Park, and the glaciers merging with the sea at Laguna San Rafael National Park.

★ **Fishing:** Fly-fishing fanatics were among the first to explore this area thoroughly. At any number of lodges, you can step right outside your door for great fishing or take a short boat trip to more isolated spots.

★ **Rafting and kayaking:** The Futaleufú River is beautiful, turquoise blue, and Class V-plus (that's raft speak for very fast-moving water). The surrounding countryside is a magnificent setting for it.

The Southern Coast is a tranquil, expansive region covered with pristine nature, much of it protected in national parks and reserves. By and large, this is territory for people who love the outdoors and rural tourism. Here you find unparalleled fishing, kayaking, white-water rafting, and mountain biking through natural beauty. Intrepid explorers are rewarded with relatively untrammeled trails and spectacular vistas.

1 Chaitén, Futaleufú, and Puerto Puyuhuapi. Chaitén is the beginning point for most journeys down the Carretera Austral. From there, head to Futaleufú, located next to a world-class river for rafting, kayaking, and fishing, and Puerto Puyuhuapi, a scenic Patagonian town near Queulat National Park.

2 Coyhaique and Nearby. Where Río Simpson and Río Coyhaique come together is Coyhaique, by far the largest settlement on the Carretera Austral. The capital city of the Aysén Region, Coyhaique has some 60,000 residents—more than half of the region's population.

9

Updated
by Jimmy
Langman

The sliver of land known as the Southern Coast stretches for more than 1,000 km (620 miles), from the southern-most part of the Lakes District through southernmost Aysén. For travelers driving along the Carretera Austral, or Southern Highway, it's like a seemingly boundless tour through a natural playground. Many of its wondrous places are preserved in numerous national parks and reserves, making the region a growing, global hot spot for outdoors sports and eco-tourism.

In the Southern Coast, also known as the Aysén region, thick green forested mountains dominate, some of which rise dramatically from the shores of shimmering lakes. Slender waterfalls and nearly vertical streams, often seeming to emerge from the rock itself, tumble and slide from neck-craning heights. Some dissipate into misty nothingness before touching the ground, while others flow into innumerable rivers—large and small, wild and gentle—heading westward to the sea.

With the expansion of the Carretera Austral, migration has jumped to the region. Still, this is one of the least-populated areas in South America, with a population density said to be lower than the Sahara Desert. The infrequent hamlets scattered along the low-lying areas of this rugged region subsist mainly from fishing or farming, but increasingly cater to tourism. Coyhaique, the only town here of any size, has lots of dining and lodging options. Several intrepid entrepreneurs have also established excellent accommodations in remote locations throughout the region, frequently near spectacular rivers, mountain peaks, lakes, volcanoes, and glaciers.

Planning a visit to the region's widely separated points of interest can be challenging, as getting from place to place is often difficult. Creating a logical itinerary in southern Chilean Patagonia is as much about choosing how to get here as it is about choosing where you want to go. The most rewarding mode of transport through this area is a combination of boat and plane, with an occasional car rental if you want to journey a little deeper into the hinterlands.

PLANNER

WHEN TO GO

Late spring through summer—mid-November to mid-March—is considered high season in this part of southern Chile. It's highly recommended that you make advance reservations if your intention is to stay at high-end hotels or resorts during this time. Although the weather is likely to be cooler and rainier in the spring (September into November) and fall (March to May), it's also a fine time for travel here.

PLANNING YOUR TIME

On your first day head straight to Futaleufú, home to one of the world's fastest and most spectacular rivers and situated among breathtaking Patagonian mountain valleys. After a few nights there, spend a day going down the Carretera Austral, or Southern Highway, to Puerto Puyuhuapi, preferably in a rented, four-wheel-drive truck or jeep to give you more flexibility. A stay at Puyuhuapi Lodge & Spa, a resort accessible only by boat, is a great way to relax and recharge for the next phase of your journey. While in Puyuhuapi, consider spending an extra day there to visit the "hanging glacier" at Parque Nacional Queulat. Afterward, go to Coyhaique, located about five hours south. The largest city in the region, Coyhaique will be a good place for shopping and eating a nice meal before heading south to Lake General Carrera and Patagonia National Park, or to nearby Puerto Chacabuco, where you can board a boat bound for the unforgettable glaciers at Laguna San Rafael National Park. Consider returning to Puerto Montt via a ferry boat that departs from Puerto Chacabuco.

GETTING HERE AND AROUND

AIR TRAVEL

LATAM has flights to the region from Santiago, Puerto Montt, and Punta Arenas. They arrive at the Southern Coast's only major airport, 55 km (34 miles) south of Coyhaique, in the town of Balmaceda. Other carriers serving southern Chile include Sky Airlines, Latin American Wings, Jetsmart, DAP, and Pewen.

BOAT AND FERRY TRAVEL

Be warned that ferries in southern Chile can be slow and sometimes suffer delays, but they are reliable. If you're touring the region by car, the ferry is a good choice. The main companies serving this area are Navimag, Naviera Austral, and Transmarchilay.

BUS TRAVEL

Service between Puerto Montt and Coyhaique is by private operators such as Kemel and Becker. A nearly 48-hour journey including fjord crossings via ferry, it is a long haul but very scenic; you *must* overnight in the town of Chaitén before heading south to Coyhaique. Another option to get to Coyhaique are buses departing from Bariloche, Argentina.

Bus Contacts Buses Becker. ⊠ *General Parra 335, Coyhaique* ☏ *67/223–2167.* **Don Carlos.** ⊠ *Subteniente Cruz 63, Coyhaique* ☏ *67/223–1981.* **Suray.** ⊠ *Prat 265, Coyhaique* ☏ *67/223–4085.* **Transfer Valencia.** ⊠ *Lautaro 828, Coyhaique* ☏ *67/223–3030.*

CAR TRAVEL

In Chile, the northern part of the Southern Coast must be done with the aid of a ferry, which departs from Puerto Montt, Hornopiren, or Quellón, Chiloé. Another route is to loop through Argentine Patagonia, crossing back into Chile near Futaleufú. This Argentine route takes you to Bariloche, crossing over the Argentina border near Osorno and Puyehue, just north of Puerto Montt.

The Carretera Austral, the road that runs through the southern coast, is mostly a dirt road and during rainy periods requires especially careful

9

driving. The road cuts through awesome virgin nature though, connecting tiny fishing towns and quaint villages all the way from Puerto Montt to Villa O'Higgins.

Navigating the Carretera Austral requires some planning, as communities along the way are sometimes few and far between. Some parts of the highway, especially in the southernmost reaches, are deserted. Check out your car thoroughly, especially the air in the spare tire. Make sure you have a jack and jumper cables. Plan your refueling stops ahead of time and bring along food in case you find yourself stuck far from the nearest restaurant.

Rental Car Contacts Europcar. ⊠ *Aeropuerto Balmaceda and Errázuriz 454, Coyhaique* ☎ *67/267–8640* ⊕ *www.europcar.cl.* **Varona.** ⊠ *Riquelme 438, Coyhaique* ☎ *67/221–6674* ⊕ *www.varona.cl.*

RESTAURANTS

All manner of fish, lamb, beef, and chicken dishes are available in the Southern Coast. By and large, entrées are simple and hearty. Given the area's great distance from Chile's Central Valley, where the majority of Chile's fruits and vegetables are grown, most things that appear on your plate probably grew somewhere nearby. Many dishes are prepared from scratch when you order. *Restaurant reviews have been shortened. For full information, visit Fodors.com.*

HOTELS

This region offers a surprisingly wide choice of accommodations. What you don't find is the blandness of chain hotels. Most of the region's establishments reflect the distinct personalities and idiosyncrasies of their owners.

Some of the most humble homes in villages along the Carretera Austral are supplementing their family income by becoming bed-and-breakfasts. A stay in one of these *hospedajes* is an ideal way to meet the people and experience the culture. These accommodations are not regulated, so inquire about the availability of hot water and confirm that breakfast is included. Don't hesitate to ask to see the room—you may even get a choice.

WHAT IT COSTS IN CHILEAN PESOS (IN THOUSANDS)				
	$	**$$**	**$$$**	**$$$$**
Restaurants	Under 6	6–8	9–11	over 11
Hotels	Under 46	46–75	76–105	over 105

Restaurant prices are the average cost of a main course at dinner or, if dinner is not served, at lunch. Hotel prices are the lowest cost of a standard double room in high season, excluding tax.

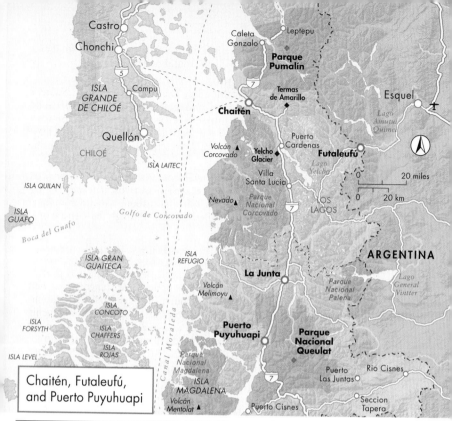

Chaitén, Futaleufú,
and Puerto Puyuhuapi

CHAITÉN, FUTALEUFÚ, AND
PUERTO PUYUHUAPI

Many people overlook Chaitén in a hurry to go elsewhere, but this town makes for a good base to explore the coast or Pumalin Park. A few hours south along the Carretera Austral is Futaleufú, one of the world's top destinations for white-water sports but also a spectacular mountain valley that the locals say is so beautiful it must have been painted by God. La Junta is nearby; it's home to several lakes and rivers that are among the best anywhere for fishing. Meanwhile, Puyuhuapi is a great place to rest in the hot springs or trek to the hanging glaciers at nearby Quelat National Park.

CHAITÉN

201 km (125 miles) south of Puerto Montt.

If you are traveling by ferry to and from Chiloé or Puerto Montt, you will likely pass through Chaitén. In May 2008, a volcano erupted near the town, forcing its residents to evacuate. Today, however, many have returned and Chaitén is springing back to life, with the remnants of the disaster a tourist attraction in its own right. It's an interesting and

pleasant place to stay for a night or two. You can also buy food and other supplies in town before your southbound journey.

GETTING HERE AND AROUND

Four days a week (Sunday, Monday, Thursday, and Friday), Naviera Austral (⊕ *www.navieraustral.cl*) operates a ferry service between Chaitén and Puerto Montt in the Lake District and Quellón on Chiloé. Flying is also an option; a few small airlines like Aerocord, Cielo-MarAustral, and Pewen Servicios Aéreos run flights between Chaitén and Puerto Montt.

It's also possible to drive to Chaitén from Puerto Montt via the Carretera Austral, but you have to make use of two-car ferries run by Transportes Austral (⊕ *www.taustral.cl*). It's about a six-hour journey. You must reserve your ticket ahead of time through the website or a travel agency.

TOURS

Chaitur Excursions. Vermont native Nicolas La Penna is a pioneer in the tourist trade on the Carretera Austral, leading tours and providing transport on the mostly dirt roads of northern Patagonia for well more than two decades. His office doubles as the Chaitén bus station, making him an especially rich source for tips on the region. Among his destinations in the Chaitén area are Pumalin Park, Futaleufú River, the Yelcho and Michimahuida glaciers, and still-smoking Chaitén Volcano. Tour prices start from 30,000 pesos. ⊠ *Av. Bernardo O'Higgins 67* ☏ *65/273–1429, 9/7468–5608* ⊕ *www.chaitur.com*.

EXPLORING

Lago Yelcho. One of the best places in the region to fish, this lake is constantly packed with brown trout. It runs along the Carretera Austral south of Chaitén, and there are several lodges nearby catering to anglers. ⊠ *Chaitén*.

Termas del Amarillo. These natural hot springs about 31 km (19 miles) southeast of Chaitén provide a nice respite for weary muscles. Situated along a river running through a heavily forested valley, the springs are warmed by Michimahuida Volcano. In addition to the natural baths, there are dressing rooms, cabins, a sauna, and a pool on-site. ⊠ *Off Carretera Austral, 6 km (4 miles) inland from Puerto Cardenas* ☏ *3700 pesos*.

Yelcho Glacier. Just 2 km (1 mile) past the village of Puerto Cárdenas is Puente Ventisquero Yelcho (Glacier Bridge), the beginning of a moderate three-hour round-trip hike to Ventisquero Cavi (Hanging Glacier). The trail is clearly marked, but Chaitur Excursions (*www.chaitur.com*) also organizes group treks to the glacier. ⊠ *Carretera Austral*.

WHERE TO EAT

$$$
CHILEAN
✕ **Cabañas Tranqueras del Monte.** Here you can enjoy high-quality, home-cooked meals prepared by the owners—such as incredible steaks, crab stew, and freshly caught fish—as well as yummy pastries, including apple cinammon rolls straight from the oven. **Known for:** steaks; pastries; friendly service. ⑤ *Average main: 10000 pesos* ⊠ *Carretera Austral 178* ☏ .

CLOSE UP

The Carretera Austral: Chile's Road to Riches

The Pan-American Highway, which snakes its way through the northern half of Chile, never quite makes it to the Southern Coast. To connect this remote region with the rest of the country, former President Augusto Pinochet proposed a massive public works project to construct a highway called the Carretera Austral. But the $300 million venture had another purpose as well. Pinochet was afraid that without a strong military presence in the region, neighboring Argentina could begin chipping away at Chile's territory. The highway would allow the army easier access to an area that until then was accessible only by boat.

Ground was broken on the Carretera Austral in 1976, and in 1982 the first section, running from Chaitén to Coyhaique, opened to great fanfare. The only trouble was that you still couldn't get there from the mainland. It took another five years for the extension from Chaitén north to Puerto Montt to be completed. An extension from Coyhaique south to Cochrane was finished the following year.

The word *finished* is misleading, as construction continues to this day. Although the Carretera Austral is nicely paved near Puerto Montt, it soon reveals its true nature as a two-lane gravel surface that crawls inexorably southward for 1,156 km

(718 miles) toward the outpost of Villa O'Higgins. Nor is the highway contiguous. In places the road ends abruptly at water's edge—ferries link these broken stretches of highway. The segment from Chaitén to Coyhaique is mostly gravel road, but every year the paved sections grow longer.

The Carretera Austral is lauded in tourism brochures as "a beautiful road studded with rivers, waterfalls, forests, lakes, glaciers, and the occasional hamlet." This description is accurate—you may live the rest of your life and never see anything half as beautiful as the scenery. However, the highway itself is far from perfect. The mostly unpaved road has dozens of single-lane, wide-board bridges over streams and rivers. Shoulders are nonexistent or made of soft, wheel-grabbing gravel. Periodically, traffic must wend its way through construction, amid heavy equipment and workers.

What the Carretera Austral gives adventurous travelers is a chance to see a part of the world where relatively few have ventured. The views from the highway are truly amazing, from the conical top of Volcán Corcovado near Chaitén to the sprawling valleys around Coyhaique. Here you also find a spectacular network of national parks, such as Pumalín National Park and Patagonia National Park.

9

WHERE TO STAY

$$$$
B&B/INN
Fodor's Choice
★

🏔 **Chucao Lodge.** The all-inclusive Chucao Lodge is a high-end way to experience fly-fishing and more at Lago Yelcho and other top spots in the Palena area. **Pros:** fishing at diverse spots; all-inclusive; great views. **Cons:** a long journey to get here; mostly a destination for fly-fishermen; Wi-Fi connection is unstable. $ *Rooms from: 250000 pesos* ⊠ *Lago Yelcho, Puerto Cárdenas* ☏ *801/415–9617* ⊕ *www.chucaolodge.com* ▭ *No credit cards* ⊘ *Closed May–mid-Oct.* ⇱ *5 rooms* ⦿ *All-inclusive.*

$$ **Hospedaje and Cabañas Pudu.** Open year-round, this warm and inviting (but not fancy) place takes you in while you wait for the ferry boat out of Chaitén. **Pros:** big and comfortable beds; friendly owners; independence. **Cons:** often booked solid; no breakfast included; located at the end of the waterfront. [$] *Rooms from: 65000 pesos* ⊠ *Corcovado 668* ☎ *9/8227–9602, 65/273–1336* ✉ *puduchaiten@hotmail.com* ⇦ *3 rooms, 8 cabins* ❤ *No meals.*

B&B/INN

$$ **Hotel Mi Casa.** The friendly owner, a former Olympic gymnast, makes you feel right at home at this simple rustic hotel, giving you access to bicycles for exploring and serving you pancakes for breakfast. **Pros:** friendly owner; attention to detail; town views. **Cons:** thin walls; some rooms are small; not a lot of storage space. [$] *Rooms from: 57450 pesos* ⊠ *Av. Norte 206* ☎ *65/273–1285* ⊕ *www.hotelmicasa.cl* ⇦ *17 rooms* ❤ *Breakfast.*

HOTEL

$$ **Posada de Expediciones Kahuel.** Located inside a forest and just steps from the seashore, this rustic B&B is a nice setting for a stay and yet it's just a five-minute drive from town. **Pros:** friendly service; steps away from the coast; good food. **Cons:** walls are thin; no Wi-Fi; expensive for what you get. [$] *Rooms from: 65000 pesos* ⊠ *Km 4 Camino Chaitén-Sta. Bárbara, sector Fandango* ☎ *9/8156–6148* ⊕ *www.posadakahuel.cl* ⇦ *6 rooms* ❤ *Breakfast.*

B&B/INN

PARQUE PUMALÍN

56 km (35 miles) north of Chaitén.

The world's largest privately owned nature preserve, the future Pumalín National Park (it will officially become a national park in April 2019) in northern Chaitén hosts a pristine set of mountains, temperate rain forests, volcanoes, lakes, and rivers. Kayaking around the park's coastal fjords is a popular activity, as is hiking through some of the last intact alerce forest anywhere. The park also has excellent camping facilities, first-class cabins, and a superb café and restaurant at its headquarters in Caleta Gonzalo.

GETTING HERE AND AROUND

Caleta Gonzalo, headquarters of Pumalín Park, is about 60 km (37 miles) north of Chaitén. The road from Chaitén to Caleta Gonzalo is well maintained but not paved. You can also reach Caleta Gonzalo by ferry. To venture to the northernmost areas of the park, such as Cahuelmo hot springs, you need to rent a boat in Hornopirén, a small town about 110 km (68 miles) southeast of Puerto Montt.

TOURS

Alsur Expeditions. This longtime tour operator in Puerto Varas runs tours to the park, with all-inclusive tours including treks and sea kayaking of four days or more. ⊠ *Puerto Varas* ☎ *65/223–2300, 9/871–8827* ⊕ *www.alsurexpeditions.com* ✉ *From 1000 pesos.*

Chaitur. This agency in Chaitén knows the park better than almost anyone, outside of the park administrators. Tours include an inexpensive, one-day hike at three trails (Sendero los Alerces, Sendero Cascadas Escondidas, and Sendero el Volcán). ⊠ *Av. Bernardo O´Higgins 67, Chaitén* ☎ *9/7468–5608* ⊕ *www.chaitur.com* ✉ *From 10000 pesos.*

Yak Expediciones. This reputable tour operator in Puerto Varas runs sea kayaking trips off the fjordal coast of the northern section of Pumalín Park, with camping along the way and visits to the natural hot springs at Cahuelmo. ⊠ *Puerto Varas* ☎ *9/8332–0574* ⊕ *www. yakexpediciones.cl* ✉ *Prices vary.*

EXPLORING

Fodor's Choice
★

Parque Pumalín. Funded and organized by the late American conservationist Douglas Tompkins, this park covers 296,081 hectares (731,632 acres) and shelters the largest—and one of the few remaining—intact alerce forests in the world. Alerces, the world's second-longest-living tree species at up to 4,000 years, are often compared to the equally giant California redwood. Tompkins, who founded the clothing companies ESPRIT and The North Face, died in a kayaking accident in December 2015, and was posthumously lauded as an environmental hero in Chile and the world over. Pumalin Park represents the biggest parcel of altogether 1 million acres of land officially donated to Chile in March 2017 by Conservation Land Trust, the foundation set up to manage Tompkins's park projects in South America. Thanks in part to lands bought up and preserved by Tompkins, Pumalín will become a full-fledged national park in April 2019. The Pan-American Highway, which trundles all the way north to Alaska, is interrupted at Pumalín, though the government plans to expand the highway through it. Meanwhile, there's a well-maintained road stretching 60 km (37 miles) from Chaitén to the northern entrance of the park at Caleta Gonzalo.

Parque Pumalín encompasses some of the most pristine landscape in the region, if not the world. There are a dozen trails that wind past lakes and waterfalls. Stay in excellent wooden cabins, or at one of the 17 campsites, or put up your tent on one of the local farms scattered across the area that welcome travelers. After the Chaitén Volcano eruption here in 2008, the main entrance to the park was moved to El Amarillo, some 30 km (18 miles) south of Chaitén. But one can still arrive via the more developed Caleta Gonzalo entrance to the north, where a ferry from Hornopirén can drop you off, and where the cabins and a park restaurant are located. ⊠ *Information center, Klenner 299, Puerto Varas* ☎ *65/225–0079* ⊕ *www.parquepumalin.cl* ✉ *Free.*

WHERE TO STAY

$$$
B&B/INN

Cabañas Caleta Gonzalo. Seven gray-shingled cabanas, each designed to be distinct from its neighbor, sit high on stilts against the backdrop of the misty mountains. **Pros:** attractive design; close to nature; ocean views. **Cons:** often booked up; no Wi-Fi; no kitchen. $ *Rooms from: 95000 pesos* ⊠ *Caleta Gonzalo, Parque Pumalin* ☎ *65/225–0079* ✉ *reservas@parquepumalin.cl* ↪ *7 cabins* ○ *Breakfast.*

FUTALEUFÚ

159 km (99 miles) east of Chaitén.

Near the town of Villa Lucia, Ruta 231 branches east from the Carretera Austral and winds around Lago Yelcho. About 159 km (99 miles) later, not far from the Argentine border, it reaches the tiny town of Futaleufú.

9

Despite being barely five square blocks, Futaleufú is high on many global travelers' itineraries. World-class adventure sports await here, where the Río Espolón and the Río Futaleufú collide. It's the staging center for serious river kayaking and white-water rafting, as well as a glorious spot for mountain biking, fly-fishing, hiking, and horseback riding. The small community also has surprisingly nice lodging and dining options.

GETTING HERE AND AROUND

The road from Chaitén to Futaleufú, now partially paved, takes about three hours to drive. However, it's also possible to enter Futaleufú from Argentina, which is about 190 km (118 miles) southwest of Esquel. From Bariloche, Argentina, drive south for about five hours through pleasant Argentine tourist towns like El Bolson and Esquel. After Esquel you come upon the road that leads to Futaleufú. The roads are paved throughout the Argentine portion of the trip, and a car rented in Puerto Montt costs less than 40,000 pesos per day, although better deals can be had in Santiago. Kemel Bus (☎ 65–2253530 ⊕ www.kemelbus.cl) offers service to Futaleufú from Puerto Montt. In Chaitén, Chaitur Excursions (☎ 746–85608 ⊕ www.chaitur.com) runs minivan service to Futaleufú.

ESSENTIALS

Visitor Information Tourist Office. ⊠ Av. Bernardo O'Higgins 596 ☎ 65/272–1610.

TOURS

Patagonia Elements. Recognized for its experience and professionalism on the Futaleufú, this Chilean-owned outfitter offers rafting, floating, fly-fishing, trekking, and kayaking. Rafting day trips are an especially inexpensive way to experience the river. ⊠ Pedro Aguirre Cerda 549 ☎ 9/9261–9441 ⊕ www.patagoniaelements.com ⊠ From US$99.

WHERE TO EAT

$ ╳ **Cafe Mandala.** On a cold, rainy day nothing is finer than partaking
CAFÉ of a rico coffee and küchen cake at Cafe Mandala in Futaleufú. The café also has cakes and fast-food fare like pizza and sandwiches featuring delicious homemade bread. **Known for:** coffee; pastries; homemade bread. ⑤ Average main: 4000 pesos ⊠ Pedro Aguirre Cerda 545 ☎ 9/6168–4925 ▭ No credit cards.

$$$ ╳ **Martin Pescador.** The restaurant's fireplace and library supply ambience
CHILEAN while you dine on some of the finest food on the Carretera Austral, such as Chilean and regional dishes like grilled trout and roasted lamb, which are prepared with style and mostly organic ingredients. An added benefit is that the restaurant is run by a longtime American rafting guide who can give inside info on outdoor activities in the area. **Known for:** gourmet fare; ambience. ⑤ Average main: 10000 pesos ⊠ Balmaceda 603 ☎ 65/272–1279 ✍ restaurantemartinpescador@yahoo.com.

WHERE TO STAY

$ ▥ **Hostal Las Natalias.** Part hostal, part B&B, this warm and welcoming
HOTEL place just outside of town is a good value option. **Pros:** friendly owners; ample parking; spacious house. **Cons:** lacks the creature comforts; a 10-minute hike to town; communal living. ⑤ Rooms from: 32000 pesos ⊠ Sector Noroeste s/n ☎ 9/6283–5371 ⊕ www.hostallasnatalias.cl ☾ Closed May–Oct. ↰ 7 rooms ⦿ Breakfast.

$$$ **Hotel El Barranco.** This hotel stands out for its first-class rooms and
B&B/INN facilities, including a pool, gym, sauna, and bikes for guests. **Pros:**
good food; pool and sauna; central location. **Cons:** Wi-Fi unstable;
some rooms not well lit; simple breakfast. ⑤ *Rooms from: 95000
pesos* ⊠ *Av. Bernardo O'Higgins 172* ☎ *65/272–1314* ⊕ *www.elbar-
rancochile.cl* ⊘ *Closed June–August* ⤺ *10 rooms* ⦿| *All-inclusive;
Breakfast; Some meals.*

$$ **La Gringa Carioca.** This small, rustic B&B within walking distance of
B&B/INN the town plaza provides a countryside homey ambience with pictur-
esque views of the surrounding mountains and Espolon River. **Pros:**
patio with great views; homelike atmosphere; service in three languages. **Cons:** rooms get cold at night; poor ventilation in some rooms;
some bathrooms small. ⑤ *Rooms from: 65000 pesos* ⊠ *Sargento Aldea
498* ☎ *65/272–1260* ⊕ *hostallagringacarioca.cl* ⊘ *Closed June–Aug.*
⤺ *5 rooms* ⦿| *Breakfast.*

$$$$ **Uman Lodge.** This five-star lodge in the middle of some of Pata-
HOTEL gonia's most beautiful scenery has 16 large suites, each impeccably
Fodor'sChoice designed and with all the amenities of a high-end hotel, including
★ cable TV (unusual for this area), plus a private deck with tremendous views of the mountain and river valley. **Pros:** views of the
Futaleufú River; luxurious rooms; five-star amenities in a remote
setting. **Cons:** a long trip to get here; not close to town; limited
menu. ⑤ *Rooms from: 350000 pesos* ⊠ *Fundo La Confluencia*
☎ *65/272–1700* ⊕ *www.umanlodge.cl* ⊘ *Closed June–Sept.* ⤺ *16
suites* ⦿| *All-inclusive; Breakfast; Some meals.*

SPORTS AND THE OUTDOORS

The main reason to visit Futaleufú is to partake in the plethora of sports
and outdoor options in the area.

Bio Bio Expeditions. With offices in California and Chile, Bio Bio Expeditions runs nine-day multisport outings based out of its excellent river-
side lodge facilities in the Futaleufú countryside. The trip can include
rafting, kayaking, fly-fishing, trekking, horseback riding, yoga, and
mountain biking. Rates start at US$3,600. ⊠ *Futaleufú* ☎ *800/246–
7238* ⊕ *www.bbxrafting.com.*

Earth River Expeditions. This popular eco-conscious river outfitter offers
nine-day rafting trips down the Futaleufú. Earth River owns four "wilderness camps" along the river, each decked out with hot tubs and
access to a variety of other sports in addition to the rafting. ⊠ *Futaleufú*
☎ *800/643–2784* ⊕ *www.earthriver.com* ⤇ *From US$4500.*

Fodor'sChoice **Expediciones Chile.** Founded by former Olympic kayaker Chris Spelius,
★ who was one of the first ever to kayak the entire river, this outfitter
offers rafting itineraries ranging from three days to two weeks. Moun-
tain-biking and horseback-riding trips are available, too. ⊠ *Gabriela
Mistral 296* ☎ *208/629–5032* ⊕ *www.exchile.com* ⤇ *Prices vary.*

9

LA JUNTA

150 km (93 miles) south of Chaitén.

If you're traveling by car or jeep down Carretera Austral, this small town of approximately 1,200 residents is a good place to stop for gas, meals, or an overnight rest. The town itself doesn't offer much more in terms of touristic value, but it is within close proximity to top fishing and eco-tourism spots, such as the Palena River and the 12,725-hectare (31,444-acre) Reserva Nacional Lago Rosselot.

GETTING HERE AND AROUND

There is only one road in and out of La Junta, the Carretera Austral. There are several minibus transport options to La Junta, leaving from Chaitén and Coyhaique.

WHERE TO STAY

$$$
B&B/INN
Fodor's Choice
★

Espacio y Tiempo Hotel de Montaña. This is a great find after a long day driving down the Carretera Austral. **Pros:** telephone service in rooms; modern comforts; excellent in-house restaurant. **Cons:** Internet connection can be slow; rooms on first floor are sometimes noisy; surrounding town has few touristic attractions. $ *Rooms from: 114000 pesos* ✉ *Carretera Austral 399* ☎ *67/231–4141* ⊕ *www.espacioytiempo.cl* ⤶ *9 rooms* ⦿ *Breakfast.*

$$$$
B&B/INN
FAMILY

Fundo Los Leones. This lodge provides a stunning, quiet place to relax and engage in outdoor excursions, such as fishing, bird-watching, and hiking in pristine natural surroundings. **Pros:** natural beauty; quiet spot; friendly service. **Cons:** remote location; Internet connection is slow; 75 km (47 miles) on a one-lane, gravel road from main highway. $ *Rooms from: 129000 pesos* ✉ *58 km (36 miles) west of La Junta, near small fishing village called Raúl Marín Balmaceda* ☎ *9/7898–2956* ⊕ *www.fundolosleones.cl* ⤶ *4 rooms* ⦿ *Breakfast.*

$$$$
ALL-INCLUSIVE

Melimoyu Lodge. Near the spectacular, rarely explored Melimoyo Volcano, this lodge built in 2016 offers unique access to some of the most spectacular natural areas of southern Chile. **Pros:** access to virgin nature; fly-fishing program; free airport shuttle. **Cons:** requires extensive travel to get there; no Internet; guided activities are extra charge. $ *Rooms from: 294000 pesos* ✉ *Km 37, Camino La Junta a Puerto Raúl Marín Balmaceda* ☎ *9/9609–5977* ⊕ *www.melimoyulodge.com* ⤶ *4 rooms* ⦿ *All-inclusive.*

PUERTO PUYUHUAPI

196 km (123 miles) south of Chaitén.

This mossy fishing village of about 500 residents is one of the oldest along the Carretera Austral. It was founded in 1935 by German immigrants fleeing the economic ravages of post–World War I Europe. As in much of Patagonia, Chile offered free land to settlers with the idea of making annexation by Argentina more difficult. Those early immigrants ventured into the wilderness to clear the forests and make way for farms.

Today this sleepy town near Queulat National Park and Termas de Puyuhuapi is a convenient stopover for those headed farther south in

the region. It has a few modest guesthouses, as well as some markets and a gas station.

GETTING HERE AND AROUND

The mostly unpaved 210-km (130-mile) drive from Coyhaique to Puerto Puyuhuapi along the Carretera Austral can be undertaken by car or bus. A small landing strip nearby serves private planes only.

WHERE TO STAY

$ **Casa Ludwig.** Built in the 1950s by one of the town founders, this
B&B/INN historical home with a big fireplace and living room is stunning with its big, low-hanging roof and wonderful views of the bay and surrounding landscape. **Pros:** good breakfasts; authentic atmosphere; owner is knowledgeable about local history. **Cons:** can be difficult to get a room during summer months; gets cold at night; a full house can be noisy. $ *Rooms from: 44000 pesos* ⊠ *Otto Uebel 202, Puyuhuapi* ☎ *67/232–5220* ⊕ *www.casaludwig.cl* ▬ *No credit cards* ☾ *Closed Apr.–Oct.* ☝ *10 rooms* �‖ *Breakfast.*

$ **Hostería Alemana.** The home of Ursula Flack, the last of the town's
B&B/INN original German settlers, is a great choice for travelers who are looking for simple but charming rooms with a touch of European flavor. **Pros:** friendly host; good breakfast; cozy atmosphere. **Cons:** located just outside of town; thin walls; small home. $ *Rooms from: 45000 pesos* ⊠ *Otto Uebel 450, Puyuhuapi* ☎ *67/232–5118* ⊕ *www.hosteriaalemana.cl* ☝ *8 rooms* �‖ *Breakfast.*

$$$$ **Puyuhuapi Lodge & Spa.** Located 13 km (8 miles) south of Puerto
RESORT Puyuhuapi, this first-class lodge takes care of your every need, whether you're in the mood for hiking and kayaking, excursions to glaciers at nearby Queulat National Park, or just relaxing with a massage and splashing in one of three indoor and outdoor hot-spring pools. **Pros:** quality spa treatments; three pools; views of the bay and mountains. **Cons:** no Internet; wellness facilities cost extra; food menu is limited. $ *Rooms from: 203278 pesos* ⊠ *Bahia Dorita s/n, Puyuhuapi* ☎ *67/232–5103, 2/2225–6489 in Santiago* ⊕ *www.puyuhuapilodge.com* ☝ *30 rooms* �‖ *Breakfast.*

SPORTS AND THE OUTDOORS

More than 50 rivers are within easy driving distance of Puerto Puyuhuapi, making this a cherished destination among fishing enthusiasts. Poles reel in rainbow and brown trout, silver and steelhead salmon, and local species such as the *robalo*. The average size is about six pounds, but it's not rare to catch some twice that size. Daily trips are organized by the staff at Puyuhuapi Lodge & Spa (☎ *67/325–103, 2/225–6489 in Santiago* ⊕ *www.puyuhuapilodge.com*).

SHOPPING

Alfombras de Puyuhuapi. Carpets at Alfombras de Puyuhuapi are handwoven by four generations of women from Chiloé, who use only natural wool thread and cotton fibers. The rustic vertical looms, designed and built specifically for this shop, allow the weavers to make carpets with a density of 20,000 knots per square meter. Trained by his father and grandfather, who opened the shop in 1945, proprietor Helmut E. Hopperdietzel proudly displays the extensive stock of finished carpets

of various sizes and designs. Carpets can be shipped. The shop is closed in June. ⊠ *Calle Aysén s/n, Puyuhuapi* ☎ *9/935–9915, 67/232–5131* ⊕ *www.puyuhuapi.com* ⊙ *Closed June.*

PARQUE NACIONAL QUEULAT

175 km (109 miles) south of Chaitén.

Many tourists mistakenly neglect to stop at this vastly underrated park, yet it is a good place to camp and hike. If you do make time for a visit, you can experience rich temperate rain forest, hidden lakes, huge waterfalls, white-water rivers, and high mountains. The highlight is Ventisquero Colgante, or Hanging Glacier, which is among Chile's most memorable sights. Although camping is a fun way to visit the park, there are also some good lodging options within a short drive.

EXPLORING

Fodor's Choice ★ **Parque Nacional Queulat.** The rugged 154,000-hectare (380,000-acre) Parque Nacional Queulat begins to rise and roll to either side of the Carretera Austral some 20 km (12 miles) south of Puyuhuapi. The rivers and streams crisscross dense virgin forests. At the higher altitudes, brilliant blue glaciers can be found in the valleys between snowcapped peaks. If you're lucky, you'll spot a *pudú*, one of the diminutive deer that make their home in the forest. Less than 1 km (about a mile) off the east side of the Carretera Austral, you are treated to a close-up view of the hanging glacier, Ventisquero Colgante, which slides a sheet of ice between a pair of gentle rock faces. Several waterfalls cascade down the cliffs to either side of the glacier's foot. There is an easy 15-minute walk leading to one side of the lake below the glacier, which is not visible from the overlook. A short drive farther south, where the Carretera Austral makes sharp switchback turns as it climbs higher, a small sign indicates the trailhead for the Salto Padre García. There is no parking area, but you can leave your car on the shoulder. This short hike through dense forest is worth attempting for a close-up view of this waterfall of striking proportions. There are three CONAF stations (the national forestry service), and an informative Environmental Information Center at the parking lot for the Ventisquero Colgante overlook and the southern and northern entrances to the park. ⊠ *Parque Nacional Quelat, Puyuhuapi* ☎ *67/221–2109, 9/2221–7948* ⊕ *www.conaf.cl* 🖻 *5000 pesos.*

COYHAIQUE AND NEARBY

The capital of the Aysén region, Coyhaique is the center of transport and commerce in this sparsely populated part of Chilean Patagonia. Get organized here before your travel southward, where the natural beauty and the friendliness of the people only gets better the further south you go.

Along the Carretera Austral you will pass by Chile's next great trekkers paradise, Cerro Castillo National Park, and most likely bump up against sheep herders that occasionally take over roads. There is the brilliant blue Lago General Carrera with its spectacular caves at

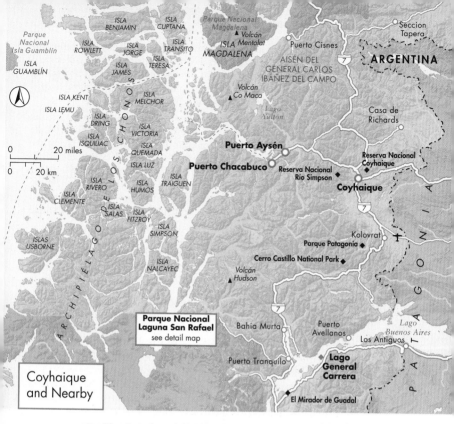

Coyhaique and Nearby

Capillas de Mármol. But keep going farther if you can, you don't want to miss Patagonia National Park, the Baker River, and Caleta Tortel, a charming town where instead of cars residents get around on wooden walkways built from the local cypress trees.

COYHAIQUE

224 km (140 miles) south of Puerto Puyuhuapi.

The hub of the Aysén region in Patagonia, this is a city in contrast, with modernity mixing with a traditionally slower rhythm in the shadow of the Andes. Within minutes of departing Coyhaique you can be fly-fishing on the Simpson River or trekking and horseback-riding amid magnificent countryside scenery. The town itself is constantly improving its shopping and cultural offerings for tourists. Throughout the year there are regular cultural festivals of all kinds, outdoor sports competitions, and surprisingly lively night spots on weekends.

GETTING HERE AND AROUND

There are regular domestic flights every day to the Southern Coast's only major airport, 55 km (34 miles) south of Coyhaique in the town of Balmaceda. Ferry lines operating in southern Chile sail the interwoven fjords, rivers, and lakes of the region. Navimag (short for "Navegación

Magallanes") operates a cargo and passenger fleet throughout the region. Transmarchilay operates a cargo and passenger ferry fleet similar to that of Navimag, with ships starting in Puerto Montt and sailing to nearby Puerto Chacabuco. Tour companies often have more luxurious transport that includes stops in Chacabuco.

Renting a car, although expensive, is a worthwhile option for getting around. At Balmaceda airport there are several rental agencies. Make sure you understand the extent of your liability for any damage to the vehicle, including routine events such as a chipped or cracked windshield. As well, plan ahead for fueling stops, which are few and far between on the Carretera Austral. If you want to visit one of the more popular parks, check out tour prices. They may prove far cheaper than driving yourself. A number of bus companies with offices in Coyhaique serve most destinations in the area.

ESSENTIALS

Visitor Information Sernatur. ⊠ *Bulnes 35* ☎ *67/224–0290* ⊕ *www.sernatur. cl.*

TOURS

Geoturismo Patagonia. This veteran tour operator based in Coyhaique runs tours from 5 to 12 nights; tours include transport, guides, accommodations, breakfast, and dinner. Destinations include Capillas de Marmol, Caleta Tortel, Quelat Park, Chile Chico, and Villa O'Higgins. ⊠ *21 de Mayo 398* ☎ *9/6636–7733* ⊕ *www.geoturismopatagonia.cl* ⊠ *From 412900 pesos.*

FAMILY
Fodor'sChoice
★
Patagona Rafting Excursiones. This local tour operator is run by Marcela Rios, who knows virtually every nook and corner of Aysén and explores them through rafting, trekking, kayaking, horseback riding, skiing, boating, and more. Of particular expertise is the Lago General Carrera–Cochrane area; trips go to the Capillas de Marmol, Valle de Exploradorse, Baker River, and Mount San Lorenzo, among others. ⊠ *Paseo Horn 48, Interior* ☎ *9/7848–2132* ⊕ *www.patagonaexcursiones.com.*

Purapatagonia. Tour operator Purapatagonia runs diverse guided tours along the Carretera Austral, including a city tour of Coyhaique and a half-day excursion devoted to bird-watching for the Andean condor, a majestic species with one of the largest wing spans of any bird. ⊠ *General Parra 202* ☎ *67/224–6000* ⊕ *www.purapatagonia.cl.*

EXPLORING

Fodor'sChoice
★
Cerro Castillo National Park. Just 64 km (40 miles) south of Coyhaique, this new national park is home to one of the most beautiful mountain chains in the region, crowned majestically by the rugged Cerro Castillo. Glacier runoff fills the lakes below the mountain, and the reserve is also home to several species of deer, puma, and guanaco. Cerro Castillo could be called one of the best hikes in Patagonia, but it gets only a tiny percent of visitors compared to its more popular counterpart to the south, Torres del Paine. One excellent hiking route begins at Las Horquetas Grandes, 8 km (5 miles) south of the park entrance. From there, go along La Lima River until Laguna Cerro Castillo, where you can begin your walk around the peak and then head toward the nearby village of Villa Cerro Castillo. There is bus service from Coyhaique, but

it's better to come here in your own rented vehicle. It's also preferable to hike with a guide, as trails are not always clearly marked. ☒ *Parque Nacional Cerro Castillo, Villa Cerro Castillo* ☏ *67/221–2139* ☏ *3000 pesos; camping 5000 pesos.*

Museo Regional de Aysén. This small museum has an interesting collection of black-and-white photos of early 20th-century pioneering in this region, as well as sections devoted to archaeology and geology of Aysén. One of the most fascinating collections features Father Antonio Ronchi, an Italian Catholic missionary who assisted communities throughout the region during the 1960s. ☒ *Cochrane 233* ☏ *9/4526–7721* ⊕ *www. museoregionalaysen.cl* ☏ *Free* ⊗ *Closed weekends.*

Plaza de Armas. This is the center of town and the nexus for its attractions, including the town's cathedral and government building. ☒ *Coyhaique.*

Reserva Nacional Coyhaique. The 2,150-hectare (5,313-acre) Reserva Nacional Coyhaique, about 4 km (2½ miles) north of Coyhaique, provides hikers with some stunning views when the weather cooperates. If it's raining you can drive a 9-km (5½-mile) circuit through the park. ☒ *Reserva Nacional Coyhaique* ☏ *67/221–2160* ⊕ *www.conaf. cl/parques/reserva-nacional-coyhaique* ☏ *3000 pesos.*

Reserva Nacional Río Simpson. This classic fishing spot in Aysén is dotted with waterfalls tumbling down steep canyon walls. A lovely waterfall called the Cascada de la Virgen is a 1-km (about a mile) hike from the information center, and another called the Velo de la Novia is 8 km (5 miles) farther. About 1 km from Coyhaique, along the banks of the Simpson River, you can also see the Piedra del Indio, a rock shaped in the profile of an indigenous individual. Get to the park via the highway that connects Coyhaique with Puerto Aysén; the park entrance is 32 km (20 miles) northeast of Coyhaique. ☒ *Reserva Nacional Rio Simpson* ☏ *67/233–2743* ⊕ *www.conaf.cl/parques/reserva-nacional-rio-simpson* ☏ *3000 pesos* ⊗ *Closed Mon.*

WHERE TO EAT

$$$$
FUSION
Fodor's Choice
★

✗ **Dalí.** Founded in 2007 by local chef Cristian Balboa, this is one of the top restaurants in Chile. The dressed-up regional dishes served here are not merely good, they are culinary works of art. **Known for:** regional dishes; world-class gourmet cooking; local ingredients. ⑤ *Average main: 12000 pesos* ☒ *Lautaro 82* ☏ *67/224–5422* ⊗ *Closed Sun.* ⊟ *No credit cards.*

$$$
CHILEAN

✗ **La Casona.** This restaurant is run by the González family—the mother cooks, her husband and son serve—and they all exude a genuine warmth to everyone who walks in the door. There's plenty of traditional Chilean fare on the menu, including Patagonian cordero (roasted lamb), their standout *centolla* (king crab) and *langostino* (lobster), and the hearty *filete casona*—roast beef with bacon, mushrooms, and potatoes. **Known for:** regional dishes; Patagonian lamb; prompt service. ⑤ *Average main: 11000 pesos* ☒ *Obispo Vielmo 77* ☏ *67/223–8894.*

$$
PIZZA

✗ **Mamma Gaucha.** This "Italo-Patagon" pizzeria in the heart of Patagonia mixes the best of Italian cuisine with local ingredients and cooking methods. There is the excellent, clay-oven baked pizza (the one

9

with *cordero* meat is a running favorite), heaping salads, and inventive plates like grilled camembert smothered in *calafate* (a local berry) sauce and homemade panzotti pasta stuffed with crab. **Known for:** pizza; big salads; craft beer. ⑤ *Average main: 8000 pesos* ⊠ *Horn 47-D* ☎ *67/221–0721* ⊕ *www.mammagaucha.cl* ☾ *Closed Sun.*

WHERE TO STAY

$$$$
B&B/INN
🏠 **Cinco Rios Lodge.** Just 8 km (5 miles) outside of Coyhaique, yet in a countryside setting, this lodge gives you the best of both worlds, with a selection of outdoor activities offered for all, especially fly-fishermen. **Pros:** rural setting; fly-fishing experts; big rooms with beautiful views. **Cons:** primarily a place for fishermen; transportation is difficult without your own vehicle; rooms difficult to get in summer months. ⑤ *Rooms from: 141000 pesos* ⊠ *Km 5, Camino Balmaceda* ☎ *9/7408–9483* ⊕ *www.cincorios.cl* ⇌ *6 rooms* ⍢ *All-inclusive; Breakfast; Some meals.*

$$$
B&B/INN
🏠 **El Reloj.** Rooms at this hotel along the river (yet just four blocks from the town center) are simple, clean, and paneled in wood, while the salon is warmly decorated with Patagonian flair, with local antiques and a cozy, large fireplace. **Pros:** on the river; good food; comfortable. **Cons:** no frills; parking is limited; restaurant closed on Sun. ⑤ *Rooms from: 85000 pesos* ⊠ *Av. General Baquedano 828* ☎ *67/223–1108* ⊕ *www. elrelojhotel.cl* ⇌ *16 rooms* ⍢ *Breakfast.*

$$$
B&B/INN
🏠 **Hostal Belisario Jara.** You realize how much attention has been paid to detail in this quaint lodging when the proprietor points out that the weather vane on the peak of the single turret is a copy of one at Chilean poet Pablo Neruda's home in Isla Negra. **Pros:** good parking; central location; excellent service. **Cons:** some rooms are small; mornings sometimes are noisy; small breakfast area. ⑤ *Rooms from: 96000 pesos* ⊠ *Francisco Bilbao 662* ☎ *67/223–4150* ⊕ *www.belisariojara.cl* ⇌ *8 rooms* ⍢ *Breakfast.*

$$$
B&B/INN
FAMILY
Fodor's Choice
★
🏠 **Raices Bed and Breakfast.** This B&B with a thick Patagonian accent is not just warm because of its big, open fireplace but because of its service: the friendly owner and her staff help you with whatever you need. **Pros:** friendly service; big breakfast; local flair. **Cons:** no parking on-site; street noise at front of hotel; some rooms are small. ⑤ *Rooms from: 80000 pesos* ⊠ *Baquedano 444* ☎ *67/221–0490* ⇌ *12 rooms* ⍢ *Breakfast.*

NIGHTLIFE

Café Peña Quilantal. For music and dancing to the tunes and traditions of down-home Aysén Patagonia, try Café Peña Quilantal. Admission includes a sit-down dinner and dancing all night to the varied tunes of the Quilantal band. ⊠ *Baquedano 791* ☎ *67/223–4394* 🎟 *5000 pesos.*

Piel Roja. The outrageous stylishness of this bar and disco, whose name translates as "red skin," is given a boost by its remote location. Opening relatively early, at 7 pm, it fills four levels with several bars, a large dance floor, and private nook with sculptural decor, eclectic oversize furnishings, and a mix of art nouveau and Chinese motifs. The weekend cover price of 3,000 pesos for men is credited toward drinks. ⊠ *Moraleda 495* ☎ *67/223–6635* ⊕ *www.pielroja.cl.*

SPORTS AND THE OUTDOORS

SKIING

El Fraile Ski Center. The only ski center in the Aysén region is located on Camino Lago Pollux, about 29 km (18 miles) outside of Coyhaique. There are two lifts for five slopes surrounded by native forest on the 1,600-meter (5,250-foot) Cerro Fraile. This small, government-run ski center has equipment available for rent and there is a ski school. There are no accommodations, but there is a cafeteria on-site for meals. The season runs June through September. Ski tickets begin at 16,000 pesos. ✉ *Cerro Fraile* ☎ *67/221–3187* ⊕ *www.skielfraile.com.*

SHOPPING

Coyhaique is no shopping mecca, but as it's the largest settlement around, you should stock up on general supplies here if you're heading off on a long exploring expedition.

Feria Artesanal. This market hosts several stalls selling unique woolen clothing, small leather items, and pottery, making it a good place to search for gifts. ✉ *Plaza de Armas between Dussen and Horn.*

PUERTO CHACABUCO AND PUERTO AYSÉN

68 km (43 miles) northwest of Coyhaique.

The drive from Coyhaique to the town of Puerto Aysén and its port, Chacabuco, is beautiful. The mist hangs low over farmland, adding a dripping somnolence to the scenery. Dozens of waterfalls and rivers wend their way through mountain formations. Yellow poplars surround charming rustic lodges, and sheep and cattle graze on mossy, vibrant fields. The picture of serenity terminates at the sea, where the nondescript town of Puerto Aysén and its port Chacabuco—Coyhaique's link to the ocean—sits. This harbor ringed by snowcapped mountains is where you board the ferries that head north to Puerto Montt in the Lake District and Quellón on Chiloé, as well as boats going south to the spectacular Laguna San Rafael.

GETTING HERE AND AROUND

Puerto Chacabuco is less than an hour's drive from Coyhaique, and about 10 minutes from nearby Puerto Aysén. Several bus lines in Coyhaique serve Chacabuco. The town is also the jumping-off point for Laguna San Rafael, although the boats going to the park are almost all luxury tour vessels, which you need to contract in Coyhaique or in Santiago. Consult a travel agent beforehand if you plan to use one of these.

EXPLORING

Puerto Aysén. A hanging bridge leads from Chacabuco to Puerto Aysén, founded in 1928 to serve the region's burgeoning cattle ranches. Devastating forest fires that swept through the interior in 1955 filled the once-deep harbor with silt, making it all but useless for transoceanic vessels. Nowadays, fishing and salmon farming are the leading economic activities. The town gained some fame in February 2012, when protests here sparked a region-wide revolt over an array of social issues. The busy main street is a good place to stock up on supplies for boat trips to the nearby national parks. ✉ *Puerto Aisén.*

WHERE TO STAY

$$$$
HOTEL

Hotel Loberías del Sur. On a hill overlooking the modest port, this upscale four-star hotel was born because the owner, who runs a catamaran service to Parque Nacional Laguna San Rafael, needed a place to pamper foreign vacationers for the night. **Pros:** well-equipped spa; boat tours to Laguna San Rafael Park; modern facilities. **Cons:** nothing to do in port itself; pool is small; meals extra. $ *Rooms from: 135000 pesos* ⊠ *Carrera 50, Puerto Chacabuco* ☎ *67/235–1112* ⊕ *www.loberiasdelsur.cl* ⊲ *60 rooms* ⏐○⏐ *Breakfast.*

$$
B&B/INN
Fodor's Choice
★

Patagonia Green. There are few hotels in Aysén that combine good service, quality facilities, delicious food, and environmental responsibility like this one does. **Pros:** cabins well equipped; good base for exploring the area; excellent restaurant on-site. **Cons:** not many entertainment options in town; Internet not always reliable; noisy neighbors sometimes. $ *Rooms from: 65000 pesos* ⊠ *Av Lago Riesco s/n, Puerto Chacabuco* ☎ *67/233–6796* ⊕ *www.patagoniagreen.cl* ⊘ *Closed July* ⊲ *10 rooms* ⏐○⏐ *Breakfast.*

SPORTS AND THE OUTDOORS

The principal reason to come here for many travelers is to board a boat bound for the spectacular glaciers and ice at Laguna San Rafael Park. To do so, you must arrange with one of three tour operators or organize your own private boat. But given that it's a 10-hour round-trip, organizing your own transportation can be quite expensive. That said, the area around Puerto Aysén is nature-rich and worth checking out. Nearby, for example, is Parque Aiken del Sur, a small private park on the banks of Riesco Lake with excellent walks through native flora and strong fly-fishing possibilities. For fishermen, the area is bountiful in prime fishing spots at the numerous rivers and lakes.

Catamaranes del Sur. This agency arranges day trips by boat to Laguna San Rafael, part of an all-inclusive package deal including a three- or four-night stay at its Loberías del Sur Hotel in Puerto Chacabuco. There is also a half-day hike at nearby Aiken del Sur park. Rates begin at US$885. ⊠ *Carrera 50, Puerto Chacabuco* ☎ *67/235–1112, 2/2231–1902 in Santiago* ⊕ *www.catamaranesdelsur.cl.*

Patagonia Green. This hotel can arrange all kinds of excursions to nature attractions around Puerto Aysén, including an overflight of glaciers at nearby Laguna San Rafael Park. ⊠ *Puerto Chacabuco* ☎ *67/233–6796* ⊕ *www.patagoniagreen.cl.*

Rio Exporadores. If you're planning on exploring Lake General Carrera and other gorgeous places further south, this agency based in Puerto Tranquilo is a good option. For starters, they can provide a scenic way to take a day trip to Laguna San Rafael if you don't have time to go to Puerto Aysén. It's run by Ian Farmer, a Brit who has worked in outdoor adventure travel in Aysén since 2000. Full-day tours start from 145,000 pesos. ☎ *9/6205–0534* ⊕ *www.exploradores-sanrafael.cl.*

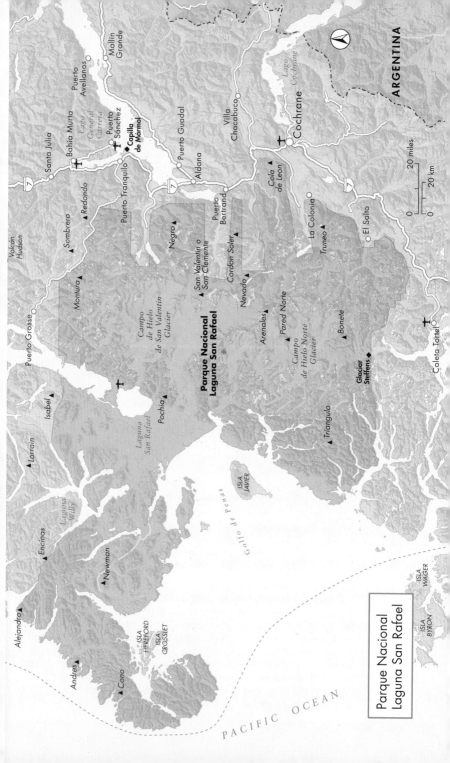

Parque Nacional
Laguna San Rafael

PACIFIC OCEAN

Golfo de Penas

Laguna San Rafael

Campo de Hielo de San Valentin Glacier

Parque Nacional Laguna San Rafael

Campo de Hielo Norte Glacier

ARGENTINA

Cochrane

Lago Cochrane

20 miles
20 km

Mallin Grande
Puerto Avellanos
Puerto Murta
Santa Julia
Bahía Murta
Lago General Carrera
Puerto Sánchez
Capilla de Mármol
Redondo
Sombrero
Puerto Tranquilo
Puerto Guadal
Aldana
Puerto Bertrand
Villa Chacabuco
Cola de Leon
La Colonia
El Salto
Truneo
Negro
San Valentín o San Clemente
Cordón Soler
Nevado
Montura
Arenales
Pared Norte
Bonete
Glaciar Steffens
Caleta Tortel
Volcán Hudson
Puerto Grosse
Isabel
Pochia
Larrain
Laguna Willi
Encinas
Newman
Triángulo
Alejandro
Andrés
Cono
ISLA HEREFORD
ISLA CROSSLET
ISLA JAVIER
ISLA WAGER
ISLA BYRON
7
7
7

PARQUE NACIONAL LAGUNA SAN RAFAEL

5 hrs by boat from Puerto Chacabuco.

One of Chile's largest parks, extending 168 square km (65 square miles), Laguna San Rafael encompasses the length of Chile's vast northern Patagonia ice fields. The main attraction at this park is the San Rafael glacier, which begins 4,056 meters (13,310 feet) above sea level at Mount San Valentín. Also located within the park, San Valentín is the highest peak in the southern Andean mountain range. While there are opportunities for serious hikers to go trekking here, it's the glacier that most visitors stop at to breathlessly watch gigantic chunks of ice continually split off its brilliant blue sides and thunderously crash into the lagoon.

GETTING HERE AND AROUND

Several different companies make the trip to Laguna San Rafael. The cheapest are Navimag and Transmarchilay, which offer two-night trips from Puerto Chacabuco and four-night trips from Puerto Montt. More luxurious are the three-night cruises from Puerto Chacabuco and the six-night cruises from Puerto Montt run by Skorpios (⊕ *www.skorpios. cl*). For those with less time, Patagonia Connection has day trips from Chacabuco on a deluxe catamaran.

EXPLORING

Parque Nacional Laguna San Rafael. Nearly all of the 1,742,000-hectare (3,832,400-acre) Parque Nacional Laguna San Rafael is inaccessible fields of ice, and only a handful of the people have ever set foot on land. Most travel by boat from Puerto Chacabuco or Puerto Montt through the maze of fjords along the coast to the expansive San Rafael Lagoon. Floating on the surface of the brilliant blue water are scores of icebergs that rock from side to side as boats pass. Most surprising is the variety of forms and colors in each iceberg, including a shimmering, translucent cobalt blue. The massive Ventisquero San Rafael glacier measures 4 km (3 miles) from end to end but is receding about 182 meters (600 feet) a year. Paint on a bordering mountain marks the location of the glacier in past years. It's a noisy beast, roaring like thunder as the sheets of ice shift. If you're lucky, you can see huge pieces of ice calve off, causing violent waves that should make you glad your boat is at a safe distance.

Wildlife lovers can glimpse black-browed albatross and elegant black-necked swans here, as well as sea lions, dolphins, elephant seals, and *chungungos*—the Chilean version of the sea otter. ⊠ *Parque Nacional Laguna San Rafael* ☎ *67/221–2109* ⌨ *7000 pesos.*

WHERE TO STAY

$$$$

B&B/INN

Fodor's Choice

★

Entre Hielos Lodge. Halfway up a hill in the center of Caleta Tortel in southern Aysén, Entre Hielos is the best option for your stay in this roadless (but charming) village, where residents move about on cypress, wooden walkways. **Pros:** great views; managed directly by the owner; best quality lodging in town. **Cons:** town has infrastructure problems; uphill climb to the lodge; if you have trouble walking, don't go here. ⑤ *Rooms from: 116000 pesos* ⊠ *Sector Centro s/n, Caleta Tortel* ☎ *9/9579–3779, 9/9599–5730* ⊕ *www.entrehielostortel.cl* ☉ *Closed May 15–Sept. 15* ⇄ *5 rooms* ⑩| *Breakfast; Some meals.*

LAGO GENERAL CARRERA AND NEARBY

280 km (174 miles) southeast of Coyhaique.

It takes a 280-km (174-mile) drive from Coyhaique along the rutted, mostly unpaved Carretera Austral to reach Lago General Carrera—a beautiful, almost surreally blue lake, the biggest in Chile (and the second-largest in South America, after Lake Titicaca). This spectacular place is more than worth the trip. Every year, more and more travelers have been making the pilgrimage in four-wheel-drive vehicles to fish, hike, and gasp at the mountains, glaciers, and waterfalls that dot the landscape.

TOURS

Fodor'sChoice **Patagonia Adventure Expeditions.** Founded and led by American Jonathan ★ Leidich, Patagonia Adventure Expeditions has been guiding in Patagonia for more than two decades, specializing in glacier excursions to the dramatic and highly beautiful Aysén Glacier Trail and raft trips down the Baker River. ⊠ *Cochrane* ☎ *9/8182–0608* ⊕ *www.adventurepatagonia.com.*

EXPLORING

$$$
B&B/INN
🏨 **El Mirador de Guadal.** With spacious rooms and a spectacular location on the southern end of Lake General Carrera, this hotel is a great place to relax, reflect, or honeymoon—and to use as the perfect base for excursions in the southern part of the Carretera Austral. **Pros:** personalized service; the view; spacious cabins. **Cons:** unstable Wi-Fi connection; low water pressure in shower; Internet is slow. ⑤ *Rooms from: 80000 pesos* ⊠ *Km 2, Camino a Chile Chico, Puerto Guadal* ☎ *9/9234–9130* ⊕ *www.elmiradordeguadal.com* ☉ *Closed May–Sept.* ⇩ *10 rooms, 2 suites* ⎟◯⎟ *Breakfast.*

OFF THE
BEATEN
PATH
Parque Patagonia. Located on 81,000 hectares (200,000 acres) of the former Valle Chacabuco sheep ranch in southern Aysén, this private conservation iniative led by Kris Tompkins McDivitt, former CEO of outdoor clothing company Patagonia and wife of the late nature philanthropist Doug Tompkins, will combine with an additional 186,000 hectares (460,000 acres) in the adjacent Jeinimeni and Tamango National Reserves to become a national park in 2019. Already, it is fast joining Torres del Paine as one of Chile's most important eco-tourism destinations. With a landscape reminiscent of the American Southwest, the Parque Patagonia includes semiarid steppe, temperate beech forests, grasslands, wetlands, and high mountains. The park includes unique fauna such as *huemul,* an endangered Chilean deer species; pumas; the hairy armadillo; and numerous birds species such as the Andean condor and Pygmy owl. Guanacos especially abound here. Like other parks created by Tompkins and their Conservación Patagónica in the region, the trails and infrastructure are setting not just a national standard but a global one. For longer stays, the park has a stately, six-room, stone-and-wood lodge (from 325,000 pesos) patterned after the Ahwahnee Lodge in Yosemite National Park. Admission to the park is free; camping is 8,000 pesos. ⊠ *Valle Chacabuco* ☎ *65/225–0079* ⊕ *www.parquepatagonia.org* ☉ *Closed May–Sept.*

9

WHERE TO STAY

$$$ ⊞ **Green Baker Lodge.** Overlooking the magnificent Baker River—one
B&B/INN of Chile's best destinations for fly-fishing and rafting—this lodge rents comfortable rooms. **Pros:** great access to river; cozy cabins; friendly, attentive service. **Cons:** excursions are expensive; meals are extra; rooms are basic. $ Rooms from: 84000 pesos ⊠ Lote C, Km 3, Puerto Bertrand ☎ 9/4444–6874 ⊕ www.greenlodgebaker.com ⇨ 5 rooms, 7 cabins ⦿ No meals.

$$$ ⊞ **Mallin Colorado Ecolodge.** Rustic, native wood cabins with tremen-
B&B/INN dous views of Lake General Carrera highlight this tranquil spot to relax when you're not on your Patagonia adventures. **Pros:** views from cabins; tranquil location; opportunities for excursions. **Cons:** need independent transportation to get here; sometimes issues with maintenance of facilities; hot water hit and miss. $ Rooms from: 101000 pesos ⊠ Lago General Carrera ☎ 2/2263–2370 ⊕ www.mallincolorado.com ⊟ No credit cards ⊘ Closed June and July ⇨ 4 cabins, 6 rooms ⦿ Breakfast; Some meals.

$$ ⊞ **Terra Luna Lodge.** Occupying 15 peaceful acres at the southeastern
B&B/INN edge of the Lake General Carrera, this property boasts charming but basic redwood cabins, grazing horses, and a beautiful main lodge, where all meals are served. **Pros:** good value; location is ideal; offer several excursions in the area. **Cons:** room quality varies; Wi-Fi only in main lodge; temperatures chilly in the mornings. $ Rooms from: 60000 pesos ⊠ Hijuelas 10, Puerto Guadal ⊹ Camino a Mallín Grande ☎ 9/8449–1092 bookings, 9/9883–6285 lodge ⊕ www.terraluna.cl ⇨ 25 rooms ⦿ All-inclusive; Breakfast; Some meals.

$$$$ ⊞ **Robinson Crusoe Deep Patagonia.** At the southernmost end of the
B&B/INN Carretera Austral, or Southern Highway, this upscale oasis combines wooden floors and ceilings with tasteful decor, comfortable beds, and exceptional vistas. **Pros:** quality facilities; attractive interior design; organized area excursions. **Cons:** due to extreme remote location, fresh vegetables and fruit are not always available; often booked solid in summer months; weak Internet connection. $ Rooms from: 145000 pesos ⊠ Carretera Austral, Km 1.240, Villa O'Higgins ☎ 2/2334–1504 ⊕ www.robinsoncrusoe.com ⇨ 12 rooms ⦿ Breakfast.

SOUTHERN CHILEAN PATAGONIA AND TIERRA DEL FUEGO

WELCOME TO SOUTHERN CHILEAN PATAGONIA AND TIERRA DEL FUEGO

TOP REASONS TO GO

★ **Natural wonders:** With jaw-dropping mountains, gravity-defying glaciers, milky blue lakes, and dark, deep forests, there's no end to Patagonia's wonders. Be prepared to feel astounded.

★ **Bird-watching:** Southern Chile enjoys one of the richest populations of sea birds in the world. Perhaps most dazzling is the largest of all sea birds, the albatross, eight species of which migrate through Chilean waters.

★ **Glaciers:** One of the prime justifications for traveling thousands of miles via sea, air, and land is to set yourself opposite an impossibly massive wall of ice, contemplating the blue-green-turquoise spectrum trapped within.

★ **Penguins:** Humboldt, Rockhopper, and Magellanic penguins congregate around the southern Patagonian coast—at the noisy, malodorous colony of Isla Magdalena you'll find a half-burned lighthouse and more than 120,000 of our waddling friends.

Punta Arenas, more than 2,000 km (1,360 miles) south of Santiago, is the capital of this Chilean province. The only other settlement of any size in Magallanes is Puerto Natales, 240 km (149 miles) to the northwest, a well-positioned gateway to Parque Nacional Torres del Paine. Frequent bus service links the two cities. At the bottom end of the continent, separated by the Magellan Strait and split between Chile and Argentina, lies Tierra del Fuego. It's comprised of a number of islands; Isla Grande attracts the vast bulk of visitors. The resort town of Ushuaia, Argentina, is by a long stretch the leading tourist attraction of the region.

1 Puerto Natales and Torres del Paine. Puerto Natales serves as the last stop before what many consider the finest national park in South America, Parque Nacional Torres del Paine. A worthy break in your journey is the city itself, which has an isolated charm to it and boasts an array of fine eateries.

2 Punta Arenas. Lord Byron's legendary mariner grandfather gave Chile's southernmost city its name. Situated at the foot of the Andes, monument-laden Punta Arenas faces the island of Tierra del Fuego, where the Atlantic and Pacific oceans convene—and there it thrived as a key 19th-century refueling port for maritime traffic.

3 El Calafate, El Chaltén, and Parque Nacional los Glaciares. The wild, icy expanse of the Hielo Continental ice-cap and the exquisite turquoise surface of Lago Argentino exist in dramatic contrast to the tourist boomtown atmosphere of El Calafate, where international visitors flock for the modern hotels and for legendary Argentine steak.

4 Ushuaia and Tierra del Fuego. The common name of Isla Grande, the largest island of southern Patagonia's archipelago, this is where the world's longest mountain chain peters out to become *el fin del mundo* (the end of the world). Part-Chilean, part-Argentinean, Tierra del Fuego is synonymous with seclusion and natural beauty, though you will find plenty of company in Ushuaia, the world's most southern city.

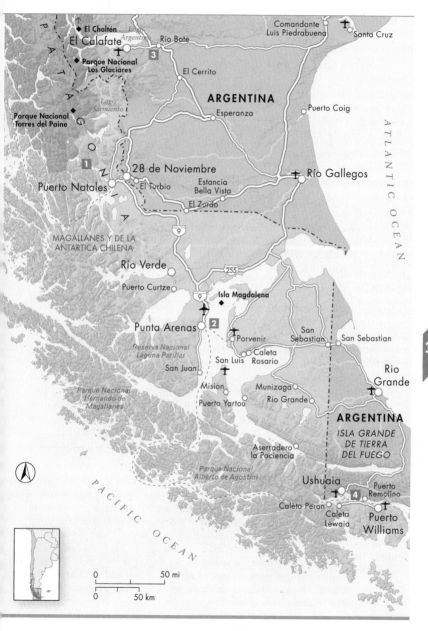

10

Updated
by Amanda
Barnes

There's no doubt about it that Patagonia is striking in its beauty—the constantly changing sky throws a different light on the landscape from one minute to the next, completely changing the hues of gray, blue, green, and purple found in the ground, water, and ice here. No two pictures of Patagonia are ever the same, whether you're looking onto the iconic Torres del Paine and their multicolored rocky spires; being wowed by the stunning Perito Moreno glacier and many surrounding ice formations in one of the biggest glacier parks on the planet; or visiting the tiny farming and fishing communities that offer a glimpse into a fast-disappearing lifestyle of solitude.

While the population is one of the least dense in the world, those that inhabit Patagonia have introduced exquisite cuisine and world-class activities. Cuisine is based around the natural bounty in these parts: succulent king crab; richly flavored and freely roaming Patagonian lamb; and a host of native vegetation and sea dwellers. Outdoor activities involve the sea and land, too: from trekking through deep forests, rivers, and mountain ranges, to sea-kayaking past icebergs and along fjords, to spotting wildlife like penguins and flamingos.

Although Patagonia is the most isolated part of South America (Tierra del Fuego is physically cut off from the rest of the continent by two vast ice caps and the Strait of Magellan), that doesn't stop visitors from flocking here. If you make it as far as the southernmost tip of Tierra del Fuego, you'll encounter sheep-wrangling gauchos, islands inhabited solely by elephant seals and penguin colonies, and austere landscapes that captivated everyone from Charles Darwin to Butch Cassidy and the Sundance Kid.

PLANNER

WHEN TO GO

In each season Patagonia has its own magic. November to March—summer in the Southern Hemisphere—is considered high season in Patagonia, when there is generally more sunshine and clearer skies. Demand for accommodations is highest in January and February, so advance reservations are vital. The weather in Patagonia can change in an instant no matter the season, so always bring layers. Summer weather in these latitudes swings between warm and pleasantly cool, although strong winds are common, and on or near Antarctic waters, these breezes can be quite biting.

In spring (September to November) and fall (March to May) the weather is usually delightfully mild, but can also be downright cold, depending on clouds and the wind. These seasons do, however, bring wonderful colors to the landscape, and the population shrinks by more than half. The winter months of June, July, and August are blissfully free of tourists, although many attractions and hotels go into hibernation.

GETTING HERE AND AROUND

If you want to begin your trip in Chile, fly into Punta Arenas, the region's principal city, or drive in from Argentina—if you've been visiting El Calafate—and head directly to Puerto Natales and Torres del Paine. Plans to expand the airport in Puerto Natales will also open up more direct routes from Santiago, Punta Arenas, and El Calafate. If you'd rather begin touring the area in Argentina, head on down to Ushuaia: many fly or cruise from Punta Arenas to Ushuaia or vice versa. Remote spots, such as Isla Magdalena or Puerto Williams, can be reached only by boat or airplane.

AIR TRAVEL

LATAM (⊕ *www.lan.com*) operates flights daily between Punta Arenas and Santiago, Coyhaique, and Puerto Montt. Sky (⊕ *www.skyairline.cl*) also offers competitive fares and flights to Puerto Natales in summer. Aerovías DAP (⊕ *www.aeroviasdap.cl*) has regularly scheduled flights exclusively in Patagonia, between Punta Arenas, Porvenir, and Puerto Williams. Aerolíneas Argentinas (⊕ *www.aerolineas.com.ar*) has service between Buenos Aires, El Calafate, and Ushuaia, Argentina.

BOAT TRAVEL

Boat tours are a popular way to see otherwise inaccessible parts of Patagonia and Tierra del Fuego. **Cruceros Australis** (⊕ *www.australis. com*) runs ships between Punta Arenas and Ushuaia, Argentina, and other destinations along the coast lines. **Navimag** (⊕ *www.navimag. com*) runs a service between Puerto Natales and Puerto Montt to the north. In Punta Arenas, **Transbordadora Austral Broom** (⊕ *www.tabsa.cl*) offers daily crossings to Porvenir (two to three hours) and crossings to Puerto Williams.

BUS TRAVEL

The four-hour trip between Punta Arenas and Puerto Natales is serviced several times a day by small private companies. The best is Buses Fernández. To travel the longer haul between Punta Arenas, Río Gallegos, and Ushuaia, Argentina, your best bet is Tecni-Austral, based in Argentina and the only regular bus service that crosses the Magellan Strait. Book your ticket in advance.

Bus Contacts Buses Fernández. ⊠ *Eleuterio Ramirez 399, Puerto Natales* ☎ *612/411–111* ⊕ *www.busesfernandez.com.* **Cootra.** ⊠ *Bus station, Puerto Natales* ☎ *612/412–785* ⊕ *www.cootra.com.ar.* **Transportes María José.** ⊠ *Av. España 1455, Puerto Natales* ☎ *612/410–951* ⊕ *www.busesmariajose.com.*

CAR TRAVEL

If you truly enjoy the call of the open road, there are few places that can rival the vast emptiness and jaw-dropping beauty of Patagonia. Be prepared for miles and miles of semidesert steppes with no gas stations, towns, or even restrooms. Always carry plenty of water, snacks,

10

a jack, and tire-changing tools, with at least one spare. Take extra care when driving on *ripio* (gravel roads); it's easy to flip small cars at speeds over 80 kmh (55 mph). Fill your tank at every opportunity. If you're not driving, consider simply paying for a *remis* (car with driver) for day excursions.

Rental Cars Avis (Emsa). ✉ *Barros Arana 118, Puerto Natales* ☎ *612/614–388* ⊕ *www.emsarentacar.com.*

CRUISE TRAVEL

Cruising is a leisurely and comfortable way to take in the rugged marvels of Patagonia and the southernmost region of the world. Sailing through remote channels and reaching islands virtually untouched by man, you'll witness fjords, snowcapped mountains, granite peaks, and their reflections dominating the glacial lakes. You'll get a close look at elephant seals and colonies of Magellanic penguins and cormorants from the comfort of your vessel and during shore excursions taken in Zodiacs (small motorized boats) led by naturalist guides.

Most short cruises depart from Ushuaia, Argentina, or Punta Arenas, Chile, while longer and more luxurious itineraries typically depart from either Buenos Aires or Santiago. The majority of cruisers plan their trips four to six months ahead of time. Book a year ahead if you're planning to sail on a small adventure vessel, as popular itineraries may be full six to eight months ahead. Cruise Lines International Association (⊕ *www. cruising.org*) lists recognized agents throughout the United States.

Ever since Lars-Eric Lindblad operated the first cruise to the "White Continent" in 1966, Antarctica has exerted an almost magnetic pull for serious travelers. From Ushuaia, the world's southernmost city, you'll sail for two (often rough) days through the Drake Passage. Most visits are to the Antarctic Peninsula, the continent's most accessible region. Accompanied by naturalists, you'll travel ashore in motorized rubber craft called Zodiacs to view penguins and nesting seabirds. More adventurous cruisers can kayak between icebergs and walk, or even camp, on the ice. Founded to promote environmentally responsible travel to Antarctica, the **International Association of Antarctica Tour Operators** (☎ *401/841–9700*) ⊕ *iaato.org* is a good source of information, including suggested readings. Most companies operating Antarctica trips are members of this organization and display its logo in their brochures.

Cruising the southern tip of South America and along Chile's western coast north to the Lake District reveals fjords, glaciers, lagoons, lakes, narrow channels, waterfalls, forested shorelines, fishing villages, and wildlife. Boarding your vessel in Punta Arenas, Chile, or Ushuaia, Argentina, you'll cruise the Strait of Magellan and the Beagle Channel, visiting glaciers, penguin rookeries, and seal colonies before heading north along the fjords of Chile's western coast.

Some ships set sail in the Caribbean and stop at one or two islands before heading south; a few transit the Panama Canal en route. West Coast (U.S.) departures might include one or more Mexican ports before reaching South America. Fourteen- to 21-day cruises are the norm. Vessels vary in the degree of comfort or luxury as well as in what is or isn't included in the price.

RESTAURANTS

Menus tend to be extensive, although two items in particular might be considered specialties: *centolla* (king crab) and moist, tender *cordero magallánico* (Magellanic lamb). Many Chilean restaurants offer salmon *a la plancha* (grilled), a satisfying local delicacy. If you hop the border into Argentina, the dining options are cheaper and similar. You'll find the same fire-roasted cordero (in Argentina it's *cordero a la cruz* or *al asador*), but you'll also get a chance to try the famous Argentine *parrillas* (grilled-meat restaurants). Many restaurants close for several hours in the afternoon and early evening (3–8).

Huge numbers of foreign visitors mean that vegetarian options are getting better; *woks de verdura* (vegetable stir-fries) are a newly ubiquitous option. Most cafés and bars serve quick bites known as *minutas*. The region is also famous for its stone fruits, which are used in various jams, preserves, sweets, and *alfajores* (a chocolate-covered sandwich of two cookies with jam in the middle). When in El Calafate, be sure to nibble on some calafate berries (or drink them in cocktails like the Calafate Sour)—legend has it if you eat them in El Calafate you are destined to return one day soon. *Restaurant reviews have been shortened. For full information, visit Fodors.com.*

HOTELS

Punta Arenas has many historic hotels offering luxurious amenities and fine service. A night or two in one of them should be part of your trip, although Puerto Natales or accommodations within Torres del Paine National Park is where you should spend most of your time.

There aren't many budget options in Patagonia; the luxury market, on the other hand, is booming. Patagonia is a "once-in-a-lifetime" destination that most people are happy to splurge on, and the increasing cruise culture doesn't ease accommodation prices. The inaccessible nature of Patagonia also means that all-inclusive packages (which usually include expeditions, excursions, and transfers) are often preferable, if you can afford them. In most cities and towns you'll find a mix of big, expensive hotels with comfortable resorts, local flavor estancias, and small B&B-style *hosterías*.

The terms *hospedaje* and *hostal* are used interchangeably in the region, so don't make assumptions based on the name. Many *hostals* are fine hotels—not youth hostels with multiple beds—just very small. By contrast, some *hospedajes* are little more than a spare room in someone's home. *Hotel reviews have been shortened. For full information, visit Fodors.com.*

WHAT IT COSTS IN CHILEAN PESOS (IN THOUSANDS)				
	$	$$	$$$	$$$$
Restaurants	Under 6	6–9	10–13	over 13
Hotels	Under 51	51–85	86–115	over 115

Restaurant prices are the average cost of a main course price at dinner or, if dinner is not served, at lunch. Hotel prices are the lowest cost of a standard double room in high season, excluding taxes.

10

HEALTH AND SAFETY

Emergency services and hospitals are widely available in the cities. At Torres del Paine, there is an emergency clinic during the summer at the National Park administration office. The closest hospital is in Puerto Natales. Additionally, every park guide is trained in first aid.

Most mountains are not high enough to induce altitude sickness, but the weather can turn nasty quickly. Sunglasses and sunscreen are essential. Although tap water is safe to drink throughout the region, most travelers still choose to drink bottled water. Do not approach or let your children approach sea lions, penguins, or any other animals, no matter how docile or curious they might seem.

VISITOR INFORMATION

Sernatur, Chile's national tourism agency has offices in Punta Arenas and in Puerto Natales (⊕ *www.sernatur.cl*). You can also try the helpful folks at the Punta Arenas City Tourism Office, in an attractive kiosk (with free Internet) in the main square. Sometimes they offer last-minute specials to fill remaining seats on popular tours. Ask for complete printouts of transportation timetables; information sometimes changes on short notice.

PUERTO NATALES AND TORRES DEL PAINE, CHILE

Serious hikers often come to this area and use Puerto Natales as their base for hiking the classic "W" or circuit treks in Torres del Paine, which take between four days and a week to complete. You can camp within Torres del Paine, or break the trip up into daily hikes while staying in more luxurious accommodations inside or outside the park.

If you have less time, however, it's possible to spend just one day touring the park, as many people do, with Puerto Natales as your starting point. In that case, rather than drive, you'll want to book a one-day Torres del Paine tour with one of the many tour operators here. Most tours pick you up at your hotel between 8 and 9 am and follow the same route, visiting several lakes and mountain vistas, seeing Lago Grey and its glacier, and stopping for lunch in Hostería Lago Grey or one of the other hotels inside the park. These tours return around sunset. A budget option is the daily bus tour (year-round) from the bus station with Transportes María José, which also offers hop-on, hop-off options for hikers and campers.

While visiting Torres del Paine remains the most popular excursion, nearby Parque Bernardo O'Higgins is also ripe for exploration with popular boat tours to glaciers with companies like Turismo 21 de Mayo (year-round) and Agunsa (September through April).

Argentina's magnificent Glaciar Perito Moreno, near El Calafate, can be visited on a popular (but extremely long) one-day tour, leaving at the crack of dawn and returning late at night—don't forget your passport. It's a four-hour-plus trip in each direction; some tours sensibly include overnights in El Calafate.

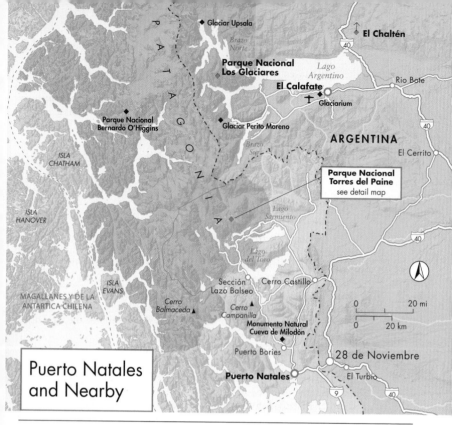

Puerto Natales and Nearby

PUERTO NATALES

242 km (150 miles) northwest of Punta Arenas.

While known for being a rather unimpressive town on its own, the proximity of Puerto Natales to Parque Nacional Torres del Paine and Parque Nacional Bernardo O'Higgins has made it the main base for exploring this part of the world, with a surge of boutique hotels and hip eateries giving it a much needed lift. The medium-size fishing town offers picturesque views of the Seno Última Esperanza (Last Hope Sound) channel, which was named by Spanish navigator Juan Ladrillero in the 16th century as it was his last hope to reach the Strait of Magellan.

Since the opening of the small airport in Puerto Natales, the town is starting to challenge the more staid larger city of Punto Arenas as a hub for exploring Patagonia.

GETTING HERE AND AROUND

The trip to Puerto Natales from El Calafate, whether via bus or rental car, is a beautiful journey through color-washed Patagonian landscapes with white-peaked mountains in the distance and picturesque estancias and cattle ranches dotted along the way.

Puerto Natales centers on the Plaza de Armas, a lovely, well-landscaped sanctuary. A few blocks west of the plaza on Avenida Bulnes you'll find the small Museo Histórico Municipal. On a clear day, an early morning walk along Avenida Pedro Montt, which follows the shoreline of the Seno Última Esperanza (or Canal Señoret, as it's called on some maps), can be a soul-cleansing experience. The rising sun gradually casts a glow on the mountain peaks to the west.

ESSENTIALS

Rental Cars Avis (Emsa). ⊠ *Barros Arana 118, Puerto Natales* ☎ *612/614–388* ⊕ *www.emsarentacar.com.*

Visitor and Tour Information Sernatur Puerto Natales. ⊠ *Av. Pedro Montt and Phillip, Puerto Natales* ☎ *61/241–2125* ⊕ *www.patagonia-chile.com.*

EXPLORING

Iglesia Parroquial. Across from the Plaza de Armas is the squat little Iglesia Parroquial. The ornate altarpiece in this church depicts the town's founders, indigenous peoples, and the Virgin Mary all in front of the Torres del Paine. ⊠ *Arturo Prat and Eberhard, Puerto Natales.*

Plaza de Armas. A few blocks east of the waterfront overlooking Seno Última Esperanza is the not-quite-central Plaza de Armas. An incongruous railway engine sits prominently in the middle of the square. ⊠ *Arturo Prat at Eberhard, Puerto Natales.*

Monumento Natural Cueva de Milodón. In 1896, Hermann Eberhard stumbled upon a gaping cave that extended 200 meters (650 feet) into the earth. Venturing inside, he discovered the bones and dried pieces of hide (with deep red fur) of an animal he could not identify. It was later determined that what Eberhard had discovered were the extraordinarily well-preserved remains of a prehistoric herbivorous mammal, *mylodon darwini,* about twice the height of a man, which they called a *milodón.* The discovery of a stone wall in the cave, and of neatly cut grass stalks in the animal's feces led researchers to conclude that 10,000 years ago a group of Tehuelche Indians captured this beast. The cave is at the Monumento Natural Cueva de Milodón. The cathedral-size space was carved out of a solid rock wall by rising waters. Its dusty floor and barren walls are unspectacular, and the tacky life-size fiberglass model at the cave mouth is useful only as a reference to the size of the gigantic animal that lived here. ⊠ *5 km (3 miles) off Ruta 9 signpost, 28 km (17 miles) northwest of Puerto Natales, Puerto Natales* ⊕ *www. cuevadelmilodon.cl* ✉ *5000 pesos.*

Museo Historico Municipal. A highlight in the small but interesting Museo Historico Municipal is a room filled with antique prints of Aonikenk and Kaweshkar indigenous peoples. Another room is devoted to the exploits of Hermann Eberhard, a German explorer considered the region's first settler. Check out his celebrated collapsible boat. In an adjacent room you will find some vestiges of the old Bories sheep plant, which processed the meat and wool of more than 300,000 sheep a year. ⊠ *Av. Bulnes 285, Puerto Natales* ☎ *61/220–9548* ✉ *1000 pesos* ⊗ *Closed Sun.*

WHERE TO EAT

$$$
INTERNATIONAL

✕ Afrigonia. The idea of a "taste of Africa in Patagonia" might sound cheesy, but the unusual fusion menu here is well rehearsed and flavor combinations are well-tuned and tasty. With bamboo shoots adorning the walls, you might forget you are in Puerto Natales, but then you'll see the local seafood, Patagonian lamb, and king crab on the menu, presented with enticing ingredients like masala curry, mango, and coconut cream. **Known for:** interesting flavor combos; friendly service; long wait times. ⑤ *Average main: 12000 pesos* ✉ *Magallanes 247, Puerto Natales* ☎ *61/241–2877* ⊘ *Closed Apr.–Sept.*

$$$$
CHILEAN
Fodor's Choice
★

✕ Aldea. This hip eatery is the real deal, from the local and slow food that is served with passion and flavor to an authentic and lively ambience. Tasteful local dishes show flair and imagination while respecting Chile's gastronomic traditions like slow-cooked lamb rich in spices and Patagonian herbs or fresh scallop ceviche sealed with hot *leche de tigre* (citrus-based marinade). **Known for:** creative flavor combinations; best wine list in town; well-seasoned meats. ⑤ *Average main: 14000 pesos* ✉ *Barros Arana 132, Puerto Natales* ☎ *61/241–4027* ⊘ *Closed May–Sept. and Tues.*

$$$
CHILEAN

✕ Asador Patagónico. This bright spot in the Puerto Natales dining scene is zealous about meat; so zealous, in fact, that there's no seafood on the menu. Incredible care is taken with the excellent *lomo* and other grilled steaks, and the room is filled with the smell of roasting meat. **Known for:** mouthwatering meats; cozy open fire; friendly service. ⑤ *Average main: 10000 pesos* ✉ *Prat 158, Puerto Natales* ☎ *61/241–3553* ⊘ *Closed June.*

$$
SEAFOOD

✕ Cangrejo Rojo. Although it requires a taxi drive to the other side of town, this nautical-chic café is worth it for its maritime feel, good music and atmosphere, and the tasty, feel-good food prepared lovingly by the marine biologist owners, Francisco and Nuriys. As well as a plethora of sea dwellers, you'll find lamb and other meats on the contemporary menu. **Known for:** excellent king crab; homemade waffles; organic wine menu. ⑤ *Average main: 9000 pesos* ✉ *Santiago Bueras Av. 782, Puerto Natales* ☎ *612/412–436* ⊘ *Closed Sun.*

$$
BURGER

✕ Cerveza Baguales. This microbrewery offers a cozy spot for beer and comfort food in the form of burgers, hearty sandwiches, Mexican food, wings, and fries by the kilo. Popular with locals and tourists alike, it's the best spot in town for a pint, whether you try the rotating selection of four or five homebrews on tap or the much wider portfolio of imported beers by the bottle. **Known for:** craft beer menu including homebrews; calorific comfort food; amazing burgers. ⑤ *Average main: 7500 pesos* ✉ *Bories 430, Puerto Natales* ☎ *61/241–1920* ⊕ *www. cervezabaguales.cl* ⊘ *Closed Sun.*

$
CAFÉ
Fodor's Choice
★

✕ The Coffee Maker. It is no exaggeration to say that this coffee bar is the best spot for a steaming cup of joe in Patagonia, thanks to its well-sourced beans, expert baristas, and some of the best views in town. The Coffee Maker also serves breakfasts, cakes, afternoon snacks, and cocktails, making it a good spot to enjoy the view and take advantage of the Wi-Fi anytime of the day. **Known for:** the area's best coffee; unique pisco sours; great views. ⑤ *Average main: 4000 pesos* ✉ *Kau, Pedro*

10

Montt 161, Puerto Natales ☎ *61/241–4611* ⊕ *www.the-coffeemaker. com* ☽ *No lunch in winter.*

$$
VEGETARIAN

✕ **El Living.** This bohemian, loft-style café offers comfy couches and tables covered in gossip magazines and tour info. The gluten-free and vegetarian options on the menu will tick the box in comfort and health. **Known for:** healthy juices; tasty curries; huge salads. ⑤ *Average main: 6000 pesos* ✉ *Arturo Prat 156, Puerto Natales* ⊕ *www.el-living.com* ☽ *Closed Apr.–Oct. and Sun.*

$$
CHILEAN
FAMILY

✕ **Espacio Ñandu.** Right on the corner of the plaza, this modern artisan shop doubles as a restaurant, bar, café, post office, and the best Wi-Fi spot in town, where you can surf on your own computer or rent one of theirs. With empanadas, tacos, seafood, and salads, you've got all bases covered for lunch, dinner, or just coffee and a snack. **Known for:** quick bites; souvenir shopping over lunch; local beers. ⑤ *Average main: 7000 pesos* ✉ *Eberhard and Arturo Prat, Puerto Natales* ☎ *61/241–031.*

$$$$
CHILEAN

✕ **Kosten.** You'll watch the wind whip the Seno Última Esperanza from a comfortable lounge in front of the fireplace at this modern café and bar attached to Indigo Hotel. With a well-stocked bar upstairs, this is a nice spot for a calafate sour, and if you are feeling lazy, just amble downstairs to the small restaurant where they serve simple, modern Chilean cuisine. **Known for:** good views; fun cocktail list; simple but tasty Chilean food. ⑤ *Average main: 14000 pesos* ✉ *Indigo Hotel, Ladrilleros 105, Puerto Natales* ☎ *612/740–670* ⊕ *www.indigopatagonia.cl* ☽ *Closed in winter; months vary.*

$
ECLECTIC

✕ **Last Hope Distillery.** After falling in love with Patagonia while doing the famed "W" trail, Australian tourists Keira and Matt decided to stay, and opened the world's southernmost distillery and whisky and gin bar. Local cheese platters and home-smoked jerky mean you can spend most of the evening here imbibing. **Known for:** creative cocktails with Patagonian spirits; great selection of world gins and whisky; good bar food. ⑤ *Average main: 5000 pesos* ✉ *Esmeralda 882, Puerto Natales* ☎ *9/7201–8585* ⊕ *www.lasthopedistillery.com* ☽ *Closed Mon. and Tues.*

$$
CHILEAN

✕ **Restaurant Última Esperanza.** Named for the strait on which Puerto Natales is located, Restaurant Última Esperanza is perhaps your last chance to try Patagonian seafood classics in a town being overrun by hip eateries. This traditional restaurant is well known for attentive, if formal, service, and top-quality, typical dishes. **Known for:** classic king crab stew; poached conger eel in shellfish sauce; old-school service. ⑤ *Average main: 9000 pesos* ✉ *Av. Eberhard 354, Puerto Natales* ☎ *61/241–1391* ☽ *Closed July.*

$$$$
CHILEAN
Fodor's Choice
★

✕ **The Singular.** An evening dining at The Singular is a quintessential Puerto Natales experience where old-world charm meets modern Chilean cuisine in a stylish and historical setting. Smartly dressed and attentive waiters welcome you with a long list of aperitifs and hand you fur-bound menus that list exquisitely original Patagonian dishes like ceviche of fresh king crab and seafood; guanaco steak with native cracked wheat; and locally caught rabbit with homemade pickles. **Known for:** unforgettable food; stylish setting; exceptional overall dining experience. ⑤ *Average main: 17000 pesos* ✉ *Puerto Bories s/n, Puerto Natales* ☎ *61/272–2030* ⊕ *www.thesingular.com* ☽ *Closed May–Sept.*

$ ╳**Wine & Market.** If wine tasting at the end of the world is what you
WINE BAR are after, this smart wine bar and shop offers personal wine tastings to
get to know all the main valleys and varieties of Chile. Select a bottle
from the excellent range of Chilean wines and brews, and enjoy it at the
informal bar with some of the local delicacies and nibbles on sale in the
shop. **Known for:** best wine selection in Puerto Natales; local cheeses
and cold cuts; artisan beers. ⓢ*Average main: 6000 pesos* ⊠ *Magallanes
, at Senoret, Puerto Natales* ☎ *61/269–1138* ⊕ *www.wmpatagonia.cl*
☾ *Closed Sun. in May–Aug.*

WHERE TO STAY

$$ ⌞⌝**Hostal Lady Florence Dixie.** Named after an aristocratic English immi-
B&B/INN grant and tireless traveler, this long-established hotel with an alpine-
inspired facade is on the town's main street; its bright, spacious upstairs
lounge is a good people-watching perch. **Pros:** convenient location; relaxed
atmosphere; good value. **Cons:** simple amenities; dowdy rooms; basic
breakfast. ⓢ*Rooms from: 85000 pesos* ⊠ *Av. Bulnes 655, Puerto Natales*
☎ *612/411–158* ⊕ *www.hotelflorencedixie.cl* ↪ *19 rooms* ⎮⊘⎮*Breakfast.*

$$$$ ⌞⌝**Hotel CostAustralis.** This old grande dame of Puerto Natales has been
HOTEL somewhat superseded by more modern, eye-catching hotels, but its
peaked, turreted roof and distinctive architecture still dominate the
waterfront. **Pros:** great views from bay-facing rooms; courteous and
professional staff; startlingly low off-season rates. **Cons:** rooms are
somewhat bland; endless corridors a little impersonal; wind and street
noise. ⓢ*Rooms from: 150000 pesos* ⊠ *Av. Pedro Montt 262, at Av.
Bulnes, Puerto Natales* ☎ *612/412–000* ⊕ *www.hotelcostaustralis.com*
↪ *112 rooms* ⎮⊘⎮*Breakfast.*

$$$ ⌞⌝**Hotel Martín Gusinde.** Don't let the dowdy exterior put you off—inside
HOTEL this is a modern hotel with a good downtown location and simple but
well-equipped rooms. **Pros:** urbane atmosphere; comfortable beds; central location. **Cons:** weak Wi-Fi; simple breakfast; noise travels. ⓢ*Rooms
from: 115000 pesos* ⊠ *Carlos Bories 278, Puerto Natales* ☎ *61/271–2100*
⊕ *www.hotelmartingusinde.com* ↪ *28 rooms* ⎮⊘⎮*Breakfast.*

$$$$ ⌞⌝**Índigo.** Chilean architect Sebastian Irarrazabel was given free rein to
HOTEL redesign this building along a nautical theme; inside, a maze of gang-
planks, ramps, and staircases shoot out across cavernous open spaces,
minimalist wood panels line walls and ceilings, and water burbles down
a waterfall that borders the central walkway. **Pros:** rooftop spa; great
views; excellent guiding on excursions. **Cons:** weak Wi-Fi; standard
rooms do not have bathtubs; can get noisy. ⓢ*Rooms from: 164000
pesos* ⊠ *Ladrilleros 105, Puerto Natales* ☎ *61/274–0670* ⊕ *www.indi-
gopatagonia.cl* ↪ *29 rooms* ⎮⊘⎮*Breakfast.*

$$ ⌞⌝**Kau Lodge.** One of the best B&B offerings in town comes with excel-
B&B/INN lent views over the lake, comfy and large beds draped in wool throws,
and insider touring tips from the mountain-guide owner. **Pros:** cozy
rooms; good value; fantastic coffee. **Cons:** wind can be noisy on win-
dows; basic breakfast; small showers. ⓢ*Rooms from: 61,000 pesos*
⊠ *Pedro Montt 161, Puerto Natales* ☎ *612/414–611* ⊕ *www.kaulodge.
com* ↪ *9 rooms* ⎮⊘⎮*Breakfast.*

10

OUTSIDE PUERTO NATALES

Several lodges have been constructed on a bluff overlooking the Seno Última Esperanza, about a mile outside of town. The views at these hotels are spectacular, with broad panoramas and unforgettable sunsets. While some might complain about the 10- to 30-minute trek into town, it is an easy walk along the seafront. A taxi will set you back around 2,000–4,000 Chilean pesos.

$$$
HOTEL

Altiplánico Sur. This is the Patagonian representative of the Altiplánico line of thoughtfully designed eco-hotels, and nature takes center stage: the hotel blends so seamlessly with its surroundings, it's almost subterranean. **Pros:** eco-friendly; stellar views; outdoor Jacuzzi on request. **Cons:** slow service; few technological amenities, including television; patchy Wi-Fi. ⑤ *Rooms from: 115000 pesos* ⊠ *Ruta 9 Norte, Km 1.5, Huerto 282, Puerto Natales* ☎ 61/241–2525 ⊕ *www.altiplanico.cl* ⊙ *Closed May–Sept.* ⟿ *22 rooms* ⦿| *Breakfast.*

$$$$
HOTEL
Fodor's Choice
★

Remota. The eye-catching architecture of Remota competes with stunning views over the Última Esperanza for your attention, especially at night when the soft orange lighting beckons. **Pros:** great spa area; restaurant menu of delicious, native ingredients; inspiring design. **Cons:** wind noises can be wild in the common areas; no Wi-Fi in rooms; expensive. ⑤ *Rooms from: 225000 pesos* ⊠ *Ruta 9 Norte, Km 1.5, Huerto 279, Puerto Natales* ☎ 612/414–040 ⊕ *www.remota.cl* ⟿ *72 rooms* ⦿| *All-inclusive; Breakfast.*

$$$$
HOTEL
Fodor's Choice
★

The Singular Patagonia. Inhabiting the former Bories Cold-Storage Plant, which used to process and export more than 250,000 sheep a year and practically built Puerto Natales as a town, the Singular may well be Puerto Natales's most luxurious and tasteful hotel. **Pros:** one-of-a-kind historic setting; expeditions and tours for all levels of fitness; fantastic restaurant. **Cons:** taxi ride from town; super pricey; breakfast can get busy. ⑤ *Rooms from: 530000 pesos* ⊠ *Y-300 Rd., toward Torres del Paine National Park, Puerto Bories* ☎ 61/722–030 ⊕ *www.thesingular. com* ⟿ *57 rooms* ⦿| *All-inclusive; Breakfast.*

$$$$
HOTEL

Weskar Patagonian Lodge. Weskar stands for "hill" in the language of the indigenous Kaweskar, to whom owner Juan José Pantoja, a marine biologist, pays homage in creating and maintaining this cozy lodge, which is high on a ridge overlooking the Ultima Esperanza fjord. **Pros:** great views from your room; cozy log-cabin decor; rustic and cozy design. **Cons:** less luxurious than neighbors; no lunch offerings; poor temperature regulation. ⑤ *Rooms from: 145000 pesos* ⊠ *Ruta 9 Norte, Km 1/Puerto Natales, Puerto Natales* ☎ 612/414–168 ⊕ *www.weskar. cl* ⊙ *Closed May–Sept.* ⟿ *30 rooms* ⦿| *Breakfast.*

PARQUE NACIONAL TORRES DEL PAINE

80 km (50 miles) northwest of Puerto Natales.

A top global destination for hikers and nature spotters, Torres del Paine National Park is, quite simply, outstanding. With breathtaking mountains, glaciers, and lakes, along with wildlife like guanacos, rheas, and pumas, the Park offers plenty of picture-perfect moments. Frequently

changeable Patagonian weather is the only blemish in this UNESCO World Heritage Site, which attracts more than 200,000 visitors a year.

ESSENTIALS

Visitor Information CONAF. ⊠ *CONAF station in southern section of the park past Hotel Explora* 📞 *61/269–1931* ⊕ *www.conaf.cl* ✉ *Baquedano 847, Puerto Natales* 📞 *61/241–1438* ✉ *Av. Bulnes 0309, 4th fl., Punta Arenas* 📞 *61/223–8581.*

EXPLORING

Fodor's Choice
★

Parque Nacional Torres del Paine. About 12 million years ago, lava flows pushed up through the thick sedimentary crust that covered the southwestern coast of South America, cooling to form a granite mass. Glaciers then swept through the region, grinding away all but the twisted ash-gray spire, the "towers" of Paine (pronounced "pie-nay"; it's the old Tehuelche word for "blue"), which rise over the landscape to create one of the world's most beautiful natural phenomena, now the Parque Nacional Torres del Paine. The park was established in 1959. Snow and rock formations dazzle at every turn of road, and the sunset views are spectacular. The 2,420-square-km (934-square-mile) park's most astonishing attractions are its lakes of turquoise, aquamarine, and emerald waters; and the Cuernos del Paine ("Paine Horns"), the geological showpiece of the immense granite massif.

Another draw is the park's unusual wildlife; creatures like the guanaco and the ñandú abound. They are acclimated to visitors, and don't seem to be bothered by approaching cars and people with cameras. Predators like the gray fox make less frequent appearances. You may also spot the dramatic aerobatics of falcons and the graceful soaring of endangered condors. The beautiful puma, celebrated in a National Geographic video filmed here, is especially elusive, but sightings have grown more common.

The vast majority of visitors come during the summer months of January and February, which means the trails can get congested. Early spring, when wildflowers add flashes of color to the meadows, is an ideal time to visit because the crowds have not yet arrived. In summer, the winds can be incredibly fierce. During the wintertime of June to September, the days are sunnier yet colder (averaging around freezing) and shorter, but the winds all but disappear. The park is open all year, but some trails are not accessible in winter. Storms can hit without warning, so be prepared for sudden rain or snow. The sight of the Paine peaks in clear weather is stunning; if you have any flexibility in your itinerary, visit the park on the first clear day.

OFF THE
BEATEN
PATH

Parque Nacional Bernardo O'Higgins. Bordering the Parque Nacional Torres del Paine on the southwest, Parque Nacional Bernardo O'Higgins marks the southern tip of the vast Campo de Hielo Sur (Southern Ice Field). As it is inaccessible by land, the only way to visit the park is to take a boat up the Seno Última Esperanza. The Navimag boat passes through on the way to Puerto Montt, but only the Puerto Natales–based, family-run outfit Turismo 21 de Mayo operates boats that actually stop here—the *21 de Mayo* and the *Alberto de Agostini.* (Several operators run trips to just the Balmaceda Glacier.) These well-equipped

10

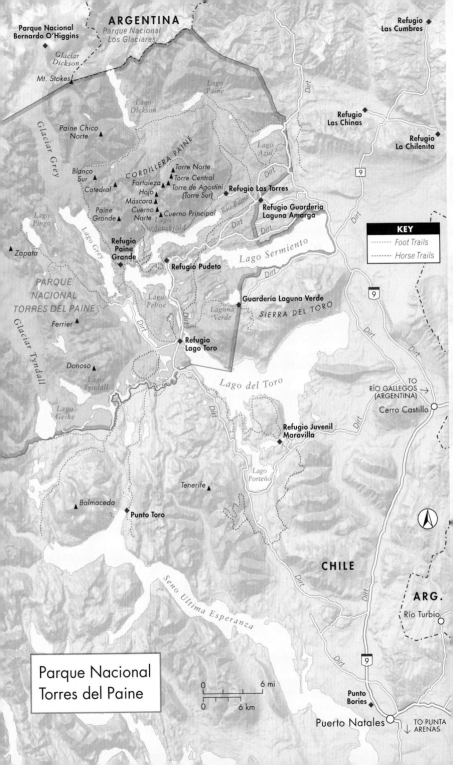

CLOSE UP

Exploring Parque Nacional Torres del Paine

There are three entrances to the park: Laguna Amarga (all bus arrivals), Lago Sarmiento, and Laguna Azul. You are required to sign in when you arrive, and pay your entrance fee (around US$42 in high season for three consecutive days). *Guardaparques* (park rangers) staff six stations around the reserve, and can provide a map and up-to-the-day information about the state of various trails. A regular minivan service connects Laguna Amarga with the Hostería Las Torres, 7 km (4 miles) to the west.

Although considerable walking is necessary to take full advantage of Parque Nacional Torres del Paine, you need not be a hard-core trekker. Many people choose to hike the **"W" route,** which takes four days, but others prefer to stay in one of the comfortable lodges and hit the trails in the morning or afternoon. **Glaciar Grey,** with its fragmented icebergs, makes a rewarding and easy hike; equally rewarding is the spectacular boat or kayak ride across the lake, past icebergs, and up to the glacier, which leaves from Hostería Lago Grey. Another great excursion is the 900-meter (3,000-foot) ascent to the sensational views from **Mirador Las Torres,** four hours one way from Las Torres Patagonia.

If you do the "W," you'll begin (or end, if you reverse the route) at Laguna Amarga and continue to Mirador Las Torres and Los Cuernos, then continue along a breathtaking path up Valle Frances to its awe-inspiring and fiend-ishly windy lookout (hold on to your hat!) and finally Lago Grey. The W runs for 100 kilometers (62 miles), but always follows clearly marked paths, with gradual climbs and descents at relatively low altitude. The challenge

comes from the weather. Winds whip up to 90 mph, and a clear sky can suddenly darken with storm clouds, producing rain, hail, or snow in a matter of minutes. An even more ambitious route is the "Circuito," which essentially leads around the entire park and takes from a week to 10 days. Along the way some people sleep at the dozen or so humble *refugios* (shelters) evenly spaced along the trail, and many others bring their own tents.

Driving is an easy way to enjoy the park; one road cuts the distance to Puerto Natales from a meandering 140 km (87 miles) to a more direct 80 km (50 miles). Inside the national park more than 100 km (62 miles) of roads leading to the most popular sites are safe and well maintained, though unpaved.

You can also hire horses from the Hostería Las Torres and trek to the Torres, the Cuernos, or along the shore of Lago Nordenskjold (which offers the finest views in the park, as the lake's waters reflect the chiseled massif). Alternatively, many Puerto Natales–based operators offer multiday horseback tours. Water transport is also available, with numerous tour operators offering sailboat, kayak, and inflatable Zodiac speedboat options along the Río Serrano toward the Paine massif and the southern ice field. Additionally, the Hostería Lago Grey operates the *Grey II,* a large catamaran making a three-hour return trip to Glaciar Grey four times daily as well as dinghy runs down the Pingo and Grey rivers; reaching Lago Grey without your own transport requires hiking. Another boat runs between Refugio Pudeto and Refugio Lago Pehoé.

10

boating day trips are a good option if for some reason you don't have the time to make it to Torres del Paine. On your way to the park you approach a cormorant colony with nests clinging to sheer cliff walls, venture to a glacier at the foot of Mt. Balmaceda, and finally dock at Puerto Toro for a 1-km (½-mile) hike to the foot of the Serrano Glacier. Congratulations, you made it to the least-visited national park in all of Chile. In recognition of the feat, on the trip back to Puerto Natales the crew treats you to a *pisco sour* (brandy mixed with lemon, egg whites, and sugar) served over a chunk of glacier ice. As with many full-day tours, you must bring your own lunch. Warm clothing, including gloves, is recommended year-round, particularly if there's even the slightest breeze.

WHERE TO STAY

$$$$
HOTEL
🏨 **Hostería Lago Grey.** The panoramic view from the restaurant and bar, past the lake dappled with floating icebergs to the glacier beyond, is worth the somewhat difficult journey here. **Pros:** great views in communal areas; excellent location; heated bathroom floors. **Cons:** thin walls; older rooms are not very attractive; hard to access without own transport. $ *Rooms from: 178000 pesos* ⊠ *Lago Grey* 🕿 *612/712–100* ⊕ *www.lagogrey.com* 🛏 *60 rooms* ¶◯| *Breakfast.*

$$$$
HOTEL
Fodor's Choice
★
🏨 **Hotel Explora—Salto Chico.** There's no better location in the park than Hotel Explora: on top of a gently babbling waterfall on the southeast corner of Lago Pehoé with a shimmering lake offset by tiny rocky islets and a perfect view of Torres del Paine. **Pros:** the grande dame of Patagonian hospitality; heart-stopping views from the center of the national park; adventurous park excursions. **Cons:** a bank breaker; poor Wi-Fi and none in rooms; simple breakfast. $ *Rooms from: 1300000 pesos* ⊠ *Lago Pehoé, Parque Nacional Torres Del Paine* 🕿 *2/2395–2800 in Santiago, 2/395–2580 in Lake Pehoé* ⊕ *www.explora.com* 🛏 *49 rooms* ¶◯| *All-inclusive.*

$$$$
HOTEL
🏨 **Hotel Río Serrano.** The main draw of this grand hotel are the views, which take in the entire Torres del Paine mountain range, with the Serrano River and a wind-stunted forest in the foreground. **Pros:** stunning location and all-encompassing views; comfortable rooms; Wi-Fi in rooms. **Cons:** standard rooms are tight on space; pricey for facilities; not always good water temperature. $ *Rooms from: 220000 pesos* ⊠ *Lago Toro, Torres del Paine* 🕿 *61/222–4181 for reservations (Puerto Natales)* ⊕ *www.hotelrioserrano.cl* 🛏 *95 rooms* ¶◯| *All-inclusive; Breakfast.*

$$$$
HOTEL
🏨 **Las Torres Patagonia.** Owned by one of the earliest families to settle in what eventually became the park, Las Torres has a long history, and is the closest hotel to the main trails into the heart of the Torres del Paine itself. **Pros:** friendly and efficient; homey atmosphere; couldn't be closer to the mountains. **Cons:** not cheap and prices keep rising; poor Wi-Fi; noisy bar. $ *Rooms from: 310000 pesos* ⊠ *Lago Amarga* 🕿 *61/261–7450* ⊕ *www.lastorres.com* ☾ *Closed mid-Apr.–mid-Sept.* 🛏 *84 rooms* ¶◯| *All-inclusive; Breakfast.*

$$$$
RESORT
Fodor's Choice
★
🏨 **Patagonia Camp.** These luxury yurts fully immerse you in the romance and wilderness of the Patagonian landscape; enjoy the sounds of the whistling winds and patter of rain, gaze onto the expanse of stars on a peaceful night, and awake to a spectacular sunrise over the blue glacial waters of Del Toro lake, all from the comfort of your king-size

bed in a heated yurt with a full tub and rain shower. **Pros:** beautiful location and stunning views; immersive nature experience; good restaurant. **Cons:** more than an hour to park activities; yurts can be noisy; expensive (and some tours cost extra). $ *Rooms from: 460000 pesos* ✉ *Camino al Milodón, Km 74, Parque Nacional Torres Del Paine* ☎ *2/2594–0591* ⊕ *www.patagoniacamp.com* ⊘ *Closed mid-May–mid-Sept.* ➪ *20 rooms* ⦿ *All-inclusive; Breakfast.*

$$$$
RESORT

🔲 **Tierra.** With stunning views of Lago Sarmiento and the Torres del Paine range from the huge interior windows, this luxurious hotel and spa keeps nature directly in the foreground at all times. **Pros:** gorgeous architecture and design; excellent spa; fabulous views. **Cons:** expensive; transfers in/out are limited; food a bit bland. $ *Rooms from: 490000 pesos* ✉ *Lago Sarmiento, Ruta Y, Parque Nacional Torres Del Paine* ☎ *2/3705–301* ⊕ *www.tierrapatagonia.com* ⊘ *Closed May–Sept.* ➪ *43 rooms* ⦿ *All-inclusive; Breakfast.*

PUNTA ARENAS, CHILE

Founded more than 150 years ago, Punta Arenas was Chile's first permanent settlement in Patagonia. Great developments in cattle-keeping, mining, and wood production led to an economic and social boom at the end of the 19th century; today, though the port is no longer an important stop on trade routes, it exudes an aura of faded grandeur. Plaza Muñoz Gamero, the central square (also known as the Plaza de Armas), is surrounded by evidence of its early prosperity: buildings whose then-opulent brick exteriors recall a time when this was one of Chile's wealthiest cities.

The newer houses here have colorful tin roofs, best appreciated when seen from a high vantage point such as the Mirador Cerro la Cruz. Although the city as a whole is not particularly attractive, look for details: the pink-and-white house on a corner, the bay window full of potted plants, and schoolchildren in identical naval pea coats reminding you how the city's identity is tied to the sea.

Although Punta Arenas is 3,141 km (1,960 miles) from Santiago, daily flights from the capital make it an easy journey. As the transportation hub of southern Patagonia, Punta Arenas is within reach of Chile's Parque Nacional Torres del Paine (a four-hour drive) and Argentina's Parque Nacional los Glaciares. It's also a major base for penguin-watchers and a key embarkation point for boat travel to Ushuaia and Antarctica.

10

The sights of Punta Arenas can be done in a day or two. The city is mainly a jumping-off point for cruises, and while tours to Torres del Paine do operate from here, a visit to Chilean Patagonia's main attraction is much more pleasantly done from Puerto Natales, a town that's gaining ground over Punta Arenas as a vacation destination and will likely affect the traffic into Punta Areas as the new airport there gains traction.

GETTING HERE AND AROUND

Most travelers will arrive at Aeropuerto Presidente Carlos Ibañez del Campo, a modern terminal approximately 12 miles from town. On a clear day you'll get a memorable fly-by view of Torres del Paine. Public bus service from the airport into the central square of Punta Arenas is 3,000 pesos although private transfers by small companies running minivans out of the airport (with no other pick-up points or call-in service) are most reliable and cost around 5,000 pesos per person, while a taxi for two or more is your best deal at 8,000 pesos.

Set on a windy bank of the Magellan Strait, eastward-facing Punta Arenas has four main thoroughfares that were originally planned wide enough to accommodate flocks of sheep. Bustling with pedestrians, Avenida Bories is the main drag for shopping, and O'Higgins for dining. Overall, the city is quite compact, and navigating its central grid of streets is fairly straightforward.

CRUISE TRAVEL TO PUNTA ARENAS

Arturo Prat Port is not far from the main drag of town. You can either walk five minutes from the pier or take a taxi for around US$6. Stroll along the portside a few minutes until you reach Calle O'Higgins, where you'll find many bars and restaurants, and then head up Calle Roca or Pedro Montt to the main plaza.

The small town center is easy to walk around, although you'll want to bring layers with you, as you never know when the wind might pick up. Also remember to bring a warm jacket for the evening, as nighttime temperatures are cold year-round.

ESSENTIALS

Visitor and Tour Information Punta Arenas City Tourism. ⊠ *Plaza Muñoz Gamero, Punta Arenas* ☏ *61/220–0619* ⊕ *www.puntaarenas.cl.* **Sernatur Punta Arenas.** ⊠ *Monseñor José Fagnano 643, Punta Arenas* ☏ *61/222–5385* ⊕ *www. sernatur.cl.*

EXPLORING

Cementerio Municipal (*Municipal Cemetery*). The fascinating history of this region is chiseled into stone at the Municipal Cemetery. Set among long paths lined with eerily sculpted cypress trees, ornate mausoleums honor the original families who built Punta Arenas. In a strange effort to recognize the region's indigenous past, there's a shrine in the northern part of the cemetery where the last member of the Selk'nam tribe was buried (look for the copper dome). Local legend says that rubbing the statue's left knee brings good luck. ⊠ *Av. Bulnes 949, Punta Arenas* 🖾 *Free.*

Fodor's Choice **Monumento Natural Los Pingüinos** (*Penguin Natural Monument*). Punta
★ Arenas is the launching point for a boat trip to see the more than 120,000 Magellanic penguins at the Monumento Natural Los Pingüinos on Isla Magdalena. Visitors walk a single trail, marked off by rope, and penguins are everywhere—wandering across your path, sitting in burrows, skipping along just off the shore, strutting around in packs. The trip to the island, in the middle of the Estrecho de Magallanes, takes about two hours. To get here, you must take a tour boat. If you

Punta Arenas

Angamos

Burnes

Maipú

Sarmiento

Armando Sanhueza

Chiloé

Borries

Magallanes

Navarro

O'Higgins

Jorge Montt

Quillota

Yugoslavia

Mejicana

Carrera Pinto

Av. España

Av. Colón

José Menéndez

TO
ISLA MAGDALENA

Pedro Montt

Fagnano

Armando Sanhueza

Chiloé

José Nogueira

21 de Mayo

Navarro

Roca

Errázuriz

Balmaceda

Av. Independencia

Estrecho de Magallanes

haven't booked in advance, you can stop at any of the local travel agencies and try to get on a trip at the last minute, which is often possible. You can go only from November to the end of March; the penguin population peaks in January and February. Almost all cruise ships that stop at Punta Arenas visit the colony. However you get here, bring warm clothing, even in summer; the island can be chilly, and it's definitely windy, which helps with the occasional penguin odor. ⊠ *Punta Arenas* 🖅 *7000 pesos.*

Museo Naval y Marítimo (*The Naval and Maritime Museum*). This museum extols Chile's high-seas prowess, particularly where Antarctica is concerned. In fact, a large chunk of ice from the great white continent is kept just below freezing in a glass case. The exhibits are worth a visit by anyone with an interest in merchant or military ships and sailing, but the real highlight is in the screening room, where you can watch Irving Johnson's incredible film *Around Cape Horn*—his account of the hardship faced by crews in frigid southern waters in the early 20th century. His astounding black-and-white footage of daredevil crew members and mountainous seas is accompanied by a gruff and often hilarious voiceover. ⊠ *Av. Pedro Montt 981, Punta Arenas* 🕾 *61/224–5987* 🖅 *1200 pesos* ⊘ *Closed Sun. and Mon.*

Fodor'sChoice   **Museo Regional de Magallanes** (*Regional Museum of Magallanes*). ★   Housed in what was once the mansion of the powerful Braun-Menéndez family, the Regional Museum of Magallanes is an intriguing glimpse into the daily life of a wealthy provincial family in the early 1900s. Lavish Carrara marble hearths, English bath fixtures, a billiard room that was a social hub in the city's glory days, and cordovan leather walls are all kept in immaculate condition, helped by the sockettes you wear over your shoes. The museum has an excellent group of displays depicting Punta Arenas's past, from prehistoric animals to European contact to its decline with the opening of the Panama Canal. The museum is half a block north of the main square. ⊠ *Av. Magallanes 949, Punta Arenas* 🕾 *61/224–4216* ⊕ *www.museodemagallanes.cl* 🖅 *1000 pesos* ⊘ *Closed Thurs.–Sun.*

QUICK BITES   **Chocolatta.** Tea and coffee house, chocolate shop, and bakery, Chocolatta is a perfect refueling stop during a day of wandering Punta Arenas. The interior is warm and cozy, the staff is fast and friendly, but there's no pressure. ⊠ *Bories 852, Punta Arenas* 🕾 *61/224–8150* ⊕ *www.chocolatta. cl.*

Mirador Cerro la Cruz. The white cross that gives this hill its name marks a pretty good vantage point over the city, but it's not the best; to get to the best spot, climb down the stairs to the road just in front on the cross and turn right, until you reach a novelty road sign showing the distance to far-flung points of the globe. You'll have a panoramic view of the city's colorful corrugated rooftops and across the Strait of Magellan. Stand with the amorous local couples gazing out toward the flat expanse of Tierra del Fuego in the distance. ⊠ *Fagnano at Señoret, Punta Arenas* 🖅 *Free.*

Museo Salesiano de Maggiorino Borgatello. Commonly referred to simply as El Salesiano, this museum is operated by Italian missionaries whose order arrived in Punta Arenas in the 19th century. The Salesians, most of whom spoke no Spanish, proved to be daring explorers. Traveling throughout the region, they collected the artifacts made by indigenous tribes that are currently on display. They also relocated many of the indigenous people to nearby Dawson Island, where they died by the hundreds (from diseases like influenza and pneumonia). The museum contains an extraordinary collection of everything from skulls and native crafts to stuffed animals. ⊠ *Av. Bulnes 336, Punta Arenas* ☎ *61/222–1001* ⊕ *www.museomaggiorinoborgatello.cl* 🖃 *2500 pesos* ⊙ *Closed Mon.*

Palacio Sara Braun. This resplendent 1895 mansion, a national landmark and architectural showpiece of southern Patagonia, was designed by French architect Numa Meyer at the behest of Sara Braun (the wealthy widow of wool baron José Nogueira). Materials and craftsmen were imported from Europe during the home's four years of construction. The city's central plaza and surrounding buildings soon followed, ushering in the region's golden era. The Club de la Unión, a social organization that now owns the building, opens its doors to nonmembers for tours of some of the rooms and salons, which have magnificent parquet floors, marble fireplaces, and hand-painted ceilings. Unfortunately, the staff aren't all that friendly or enthusiastic. After touring the rooms, head to the cellar tavern for a drink or snack. ⊠ *Plaza Muñoz Gamero 716, Punta Arenas* ☎ *61/224–2049* 🖃 *1000 pesos* ⊙ *Closed Sun.*

Plaza Muñoz Gamero. A canopy of pine trees shades this grandiose main square, which is surrounded by splendid baroque-style mansions from the 19th century. The heart of the city gives perhaps the strongest impression of Punta Arenas at its peak of wealth and power. A grandiose bronze sculpture commemorating the voyage of Hernando de Magallanes dominates the center of the plaza. Local lore has it that a kiss on the shiny toe of Calafate, one of the Fuegian statues at the base of the monument, will one day bring you back to Punta Arenas. ⊠ *José Nogueira at 21 de Mayo, Punta Arenas.*

10

WHERE TO EAT

$$ ✕ **Café Tapiz.** This colorful and cozy café has a warm, inviting atmosphere, aided by the steaming hot chocolates and coffee on offer alongside sweet treats and Chilean sandwiches. You can buy local handicrafts here as well and take advantage of the Wi-Fi. **Known for:** tasty warm beverages; hip ambience; nice spot for Chilean teatime. ⑤ *Average main: 7000 pesos* ⊠ *Roca 912, Punta Arenas* ☎ *9/6565–5294* ⊙ *Closed Sun.*

CAFÉ

$ ✕ **Kiosko Roca.** This little bar is always packed with locals who come here for their specialty: a small sandwich with chorizo paste and béchamel sauce, and a banana milk shake. It might not seem like much, but Kiosko Roca is an institution in Punta Arenas. **Known for:** local flavor; amazing banana milk shakes; cash-only policy. ⑤ *Average main: 1000 pesos* ⊠ *Roca 875, Punta Arenas* ⊟ *No credit cards* ⊙ *Closed Sun. No dinner Sat.*

CAFÉ

$$$ ✕ **La Cuisine.** This place became one of the most popular restaurants in
FRENCH Punta Arenas by adding a French and European twist to typical Chilean
Fodor'sChoice seafood and meat dishes. Layered king crab lasagna and guanaco with
★ calafate berry reduction are house favorites, as well as their signature
pâté and three-flavor crème brûlée. **Known for:** creative dishes like
three-flavor crème brûlée; intimate atmosphere; reservations necessary
in summer. ⑤ *Average main: 11000 pesos* ✉ *Av. Bernardo O'Higgins
1037, Punta Arenas* ☎ *61/222–8641* ☾ *Closed Sun.*

$$$ ✕ **La Marmita.** Fronting a small plaza lined with topiary, La Marmita
CHILEAN is a family business just a short distance from downtown—but a long
Fodor'sChoice way from the usual Punta Arenas dining experience. The short menu
★ leans heavily on seafood, but with a twist; *ceviche de salmón* and crab
dishes served with quinoa show a Peruvian influence, and the *pulmai*
is a southern take on the famous seafood hot pot *curanto* from Chiloé.
Known for: cozy and rustic atmosphere; creative seafood menu; reser-
vations needed for small space. ⑤ *Average main: 10000 pesos* ✉ *Plaza
Sampaio 678, Punta Arenas* ☎ *61/222–2056* ⊕ *www.marmitamaga.cl*
⊟ *No credit cards* ☾ *Closed Sun.*

$$$$ ✕ **Parrilla Los Ganaderos.** This bright restaurant resembles a rural *estan-*
CHILEAN *cia* (ranch), with retro decor and waiters dressed in gaucho costumes
FAMILY serving up spectacular *cordero al ruedo* (spit-roasted lamb) cooked over
a big fire in the dining room. A lamb serving comes with three different
cuts of meat, or you can pick your way through other barbecue dishes.
Known for: traditional ranch-inspired decor and menu; spectacular
roast lamb; extensive Chilean wine list. ⑤ *Average main: 14000 pesos*
✉ *Av. Bernardo O'Higgins 1166, Punta Arenas* ☎ *61/222–5103.*

$$ ✕ **Sotito's Restaurant.** An institution in Punta Arenas, Sotito's is a typical
SEAFOOD old-school Chilean diner. Attentive, bow-tied waiters serve large grilled
meat dishes and mouthwatering plates of *centolla* (king crab). **Known
for:** waterfront location; king crab entrées; hearty portions. ⑤ *Aver-
age main: 8000 pesos* ✉ *Av. Bernardo O'Higgins 1138, Punta Arenas*
☎ *61/224–3565* ☾ *No dinner Sun.*

$$ ✕ **Taberna Club de la Unión.** A jovial, publike atmosphere prevails in this
CAFÉ wonderful, labyrinthine cellar down the side stairway of Sara Braun's
old mansion on the main plaza. Patagonian beers like Austral are served
cold in frosted mugs while you eat tapas-style meat, cheese, and seafood
appetizers. **Known for:** excellent drinks; historical setting; old-school
decor. ⑤ *Average main: 9000 pesos* ✉ *Plaza Muñoz Gamero 716, Punta
Arenas* ☎ *61/224–1317* ☾ *Closed Sun. No lunch.*

WHERE TO STAY

$$ ⊡ **Hotel Cabo de Hornos.** This hotel towers impressively over the main
HOTEL plaza, but unlike the bland sameness many large hotels fall into, there's
Fodor'sChoice a quirk around every corner here—from the dramatic slate-walled lobby
★ with tube lighting to the open-plan bar/lounge with cowhide high-
backed chairs and the blackened wreck of an old skiff. **Pros:** friendly,
professional service; bargain if booked early; central location. **Cons:**
standard rooms don't match the brave design choices downstairs; can
be noisy; rooms have basic amenities. ⑤ *Rooms from: 70000 pesos*

⊠ *Plaza Muñoz Gamero 1025, Punta Arenas* ☎ *61/271–5000* ⊕ *www. hotelcabodehornos.com* ⇱ *110 rooms* ⦿ *Breakfast.*

$$$$ ⊡ **Hotel Dreams.** Equipped with a big casino, convention center, and
HOTEL disco, Hotel Dreams is one of the flashiest hotels in Punta Arenas.
Pros: great location and amenities; modern; sea views. **Cons:** can fill
up with cruise passengers; noise from the casino crowds; restaurant is
a bit mediocre. ⑤ *Rooms from: 155000 pesos* ⊠ *Av.O'Higgins 1235,
Punta Arenas* ☎ *600/626–0000* ⊕ *www.mundodreams.com/ciudad/
punta-arenas* ⇱ *104 rooms* ⦿ *Breakfast.*

$$$ ⊡ **Hotel José Nogueira.** Originally the home of Sara Braun, this opulent
HOTEL 19th-century mansion has a superior location—just steps off the main
plaza. **Pros:** central location; historic; ample breakfast buffet. **Cons:**
small rooms; can have street noise; uncomfortable mattresses. ⑤ *Rooms
from: 115000 pesos* ⊠ *Bories 967, Punta Arenas* ☎ *61/271–1000*
⊕ *www.hotelnogueira.com* ⇱ *22 rooms* ⦿ *Breakfast.*

$$$$ ⊡ **Hotel Rey Don Felipe.** This hotel is a popular choice in Punta Arenas for
HOTEL its comfortable rooms, gym and spa, and friendly staff. **Pros:** nice spa
area; quiet surroundings; comfortable beds. **Cons:** overpriced; uninspir-
ing views; simple breakfast. ⑤ *Rooms from: 140000 pesos* ⊠ *Armando
Sanhueza 965, Punta Arenas* ☎ *61/229–5000* ⊕ *www.hotelreydonfe-
lipe.com* ⇱ *47 rooms* ⦿ *Breakfast.*

NIGHTLIFE

Jekus. This gastro pub is a popular nightspot, where locals come for
beer on the tap, live music, and karaoke at the weekends. They have
a menu of local cuisine for when you get a bit peckish, too. ⊠ *Av.
Bernardo O'Higgins 1021, Punta Arenas* ☎ *61/224–5851* ⊕ *www.res-
taurantypubjekus.cl.*

La Taberna Club de la Unión. The city's classic speakeasy, La Taberna Club
de la Unión, hops into the wee hours with a healthy mix of younger and
older patrons. It is also open for an early evening drink if you just want
an aperitif before dinner. ⊠ *Plaza de Armas, Punta Arenas.*

Pub 1900. If you can't stay up late, try Pub 1900, which attracts an early
crowd. It's a decent place for audible conversation. ⊠ *Bories at Colon,
Punta Arenas* ☎ *61/2226–200.*

10

SHOPPING

You don't have to go far to find local handicrafts, pricey souvenirs,
wool clothing, hiking gear, postcards, custom chocolates, or semipre-
cious stones like lapis lazuli. You will see penguins of every variety,
from keychain size to larger than life. Warm wool clothing is for sale
in almost every shop, but it isn't cheap. Unfortunately, few things are
actually made in Chile—often a design is sent to England to be knitted
and then returned with a handsome markup.

Plaza de Armas. The pretty Plaza de Armas in the center of town has a
dozen small artisan kiosks that offer a wide range of tourist trinkets
and souvenirs. ⊠ *Plaza de Armas, Punta Arenas.*

Quilpué. This shoe-repair shop also sells *huaso* (cowboy) supplies such as bridles, bits, and spurs. Pick up some boots for folk dancing. ✉ *José Nogueira 1256, Punta Arenas* ☎ *61/222–0960.*

Zona Franca. You can find real bargains on electronic goods, from digital cameras and laptops to thumb drives and USB devices, at the Zona Franca, a free-trade zone about 3 miles out of town along Bulnes. ✉ *Punta Arenas* ⊕ *www.zonaustral.cl/en/zona-franca.*

PUERTO HAMBRE

50 km (31 miles) south of Punta Arenas.

In an attempt to gain a foothold in the region, Spain founded Ciudad Rey Don Felipe in 1584. Pedro Sarmiento de Gamboa constructed a church and homes for more than 100 settlers. But just three years later, British navigator Thomas Cavendish came ashore to find that all but one person had died of hunger, which some might say is a natural result of founding a town where there isn't any fresh water. He renamed the town Port Famine. Today a tranquil fishing village, Puerto Hambre still has traces of the original settlement, a sobering reminder of bad government planning.

EXPLORING

Fuerte Bulnes. In the middle of a Chilean winter in 1843, a frigate under the command of Captain Juan Williams Rebolledo sailed southward from the island of Chiloé carrying a ragtag contingent of 11 sailors and eight soldiers. In October, on a rocky promontory called Santa Ana overlooking the Estrecho de Magallanes, they built a wooden fort, which they named Fuerte Bulnes, thereby founding the first Chilean settlement in the southern reaches of Patagonia. Much of the fort has since been restored. ✉ *5 km (3 miles) south of Puerto Hambre, Puerto Hambre* ☎ *61/272–3195* ⊕ *www.parquedelestrecho.cl* 🎟 *14000 pesos park entrance.*

Monolith. About 2 km (1 mile) west of Puerto Hambre is a small white monolith that marks the geographical center of Chile, the midway point between northernmost Arica and the South Pole. ✉ *Puerto Hambre.*

Reserva Nacional Laguna Parrillar. The 47,000-acre Reserva Nacional Laguna Parrillar, west of Puerto Hambre, stretches around a shimmering lake in a valley flanked by hills. It's a great place for a picnic, if the weather cooperates. A number of well-marked paths lead to sweeping vistas over the Estrecho de Magallanes. ✉ *Off Ruta 9, 52 km (32 miles) south of Punta Arenas, Puerto Hambre* 🎟 *1500 pesos.*

EL CALAFATE, EL CHALTÉN, AND PARQUE NACIONAL LOS GLACIARES, ARGENTINA

The Hielo Continental (Continental Ice Cap) spreads its icy mantle from the Pacific Ocean across Chile and the Andes into Argentina, covering an area of 21,700 square km (8,400 square miles). Approximately 1.5 million acres of it are contained within the Parque Nacional los Glaciares (Glaciers National Park), a UNESCO World Heritage Site. The

park extends along the Chilean border for 350 km (217 miles), and 40% of it is covered by ice fields that branch off into 47 glaciers feeding two enormous lakes—the 15,000-year-old **Lago Argentino** (Argentine Lake, the largest body of water in Argentina and the third largest in South America) at the park's southern end, and **Lago Viedma** (Lake Viedma) at the northern end near **Cerro Fitzroy**, which rises 11,138 feet.

Plan on a minimum of two to three days to see the glaciers and enjoy El Calafate—more if you plan to visit El Chaltén or any of the other lakes. Entrance to the southern section of the park, which includes Perito Moreno Glacier, costs around US$30 for non-Argentineans.

Prices for restaurants and hotels in the Argentina sections are given in U.S. dollars. As of this writing, the exchange rate was US$1 to 634 Chilean pesos and US$1 to 17 Argentine pesos.

WHAT IT COSTS IN U.S. DOLLARS				
	$	$$	$$$	$$$$
Restaurants	Under $9	$9–$12	$13–$18	over $18
Hotels	Under $116	$116–$200	$201–$300	over $300

Restaurant prices are the average cost of a main course at dinner or, if dinner is not served, at lunch. Hotel prices are the lowest cost of a standard double room in high season.

EL CALAFATE AND PARQUE NACIONAL LOS GLACIARES

320 km (225 miles) north of Río Gallegos; 253 km (157 miles) east of Río Turbio on Chilean border; 213 km (123 miles) south of El Chaltén.

Founded in 1927 as a frontier town, El Calafate is the base for excursions to the Parque Nacional Los Glaciares, which was created in 1937 as a showcase for one of South America's most spectacular sights, the Glaciar Perito Moreno. Because it's on the southern shore of Lago Argentino, the town enjoys a microclimate much milder than the rest of southern Patagonia.

To call El Calafate a boomtown would be a gross understatement. In the first decade of this millennium the town's population exploded from 4,000 to more than 25,000, and it shows no signs of slowing down; at every turn you'll see new construction, with many luxury and boutique hotels cropping up. As a result, the downtown has a new sheen to it, although most buildings are constructed of wood, with a rustic aesthetic that respects the majestic natural environment. One exception is the casino in the heart of downtown, the facade of which seems to mock the face of the Glaciar Perito Moreno. Farther out of the city is another glacier lookalike, the Glaciarium Museum, architecturally modeled on Perito Moreno and with Argentina's only ice bar.

Now with a paved road between El Calafate and the glacier, the visitors continue to flock in to see the creaking ice sculptures. These visitors include luxury-package tourists bound for handsome estancias in the park

10

surroundings, backpackers over from Chile's Parque Nacional Torres del Paine, and *porteños* (from Buenos Aires) in town for a long weekend.

For a town that lives and dies on tourism, one of the most infuriating elements of the boom is the cash shortage that strikes El Calafate every weekend during high season. The four ATMs in town frequently run out of money starting as early as Friday evening, and there's often no respite until midday Monday. The shortage is compounded by tour companies who offer steep discounts for cash on combined glacier, ice-trekking, and estancia tours. Apart from stocking up during the week, the best plan to ensure that you won't run out is to bring all the cash you'll need for your stay here. If worse comes to worst, most hotels and many restaurants will accept credit cards, or exchange dollars.

GETTING HERE AND AROUND

Daily flights from Buenos Aires, Ushuaia, and Río Gallegos, and direct flights from Bariloche transport tourists to El Calafate's 21st-century glass-and-steel airport with the promise of adventure and discovery in distant mountains and glaciers. El Calafate is so popular that the flights sell out weeks in advance, so don't plan on booking at the last minute.

If you can't get on a flight or are looking for a cheaper option, there are daily buses between El Calafate, El Chaltén, Río Gallegos, Ushuaia, and Puerto Natales in Chile—all of which can be booked at the bus terminal. El Calafate is also the starting (or finishing) point for the legendary Ruta 40 journey to Bariloche. If you can bear the bus travel for a few days, you'll pass some exceptional scenery, and most operators allow you to hop on and hop off at canyons, lakes, and the famous handprint-covered caves en route.

Driving from Río Gallegos takes about four hours across desolate plains enlivened by occasional sightings of *ñandú* (rheas), shy llamalike guanacos, silver-gray foxes, and fleet-footed hares the size of small deer. Esperanza is the only gas, food, and bathroom stop halfway between the two towns. Driving from Puerto Natales is similar, although snow-topped mountains line the distance; arriving by road from Ushuaia requires four border crossings and more than 18 hours.

A staircase ascends from the middle of Libertador to Avenida Julio Roca, where you'll find the bus terminal and a very busy Oficina de Turismo with a board listing available accommodations and campgrounds; you can also get brochures and maps, and there's a multilingual staff to help plan excursions. The tourism office has another location on the corner of Rosales and Libertador; both locations are open daily from 8 to 8 (during high season). The Oficina Parques Nacionales, open weekdays 8 to 4, has information on the Parque Nacional Los Glaciares, including the glaciers, area history, hiking trails, and flora and fauna.

Bus Contacts Cal Tur. ⊠ *Terminal Ómnibus, El Calafate* ☎ *2962/491–842* ⊕ *www.caltur.com.ar* ⊠ *Av. Libertador 1080, El Calafate* ☎ *2902/491–368* ⊕ *www.caltur.com.ar.* **Freddy.** ☎ *2902/492–127.* **TAQSA.** ⊠ *Bus terminal, El Calafate* ☎ *2902/491–843, 2902/491–843* ⊕ *www.taqsa.com.ar.* **Turismo Zaahj.** ⊠ *Bus terminal, El Calafate* ☎ *2902/491–631* ⊕ *www.turismozaahj.co.cl.*

Rental Cars **Fiorasi.** ⊠ *Av. Libertador 1319, El Calafate* ☏ *0280/15–430–2958* ⊕ *www.fiorasirentacar.com.* **ServiCar.** ⊠ *Av. Libertador 695, El Calafate* ☏ *2902/492–541.*

Taxis **El Calafate.** ⊠ *Av. Roca 1004, El Calafate* ☏ *2902/490–905.*

TOURS

In El Calafate, each tour has to be approved by the local government and is assigned to one tour operator only. On the upside you'll never fall foul of a shady operator, but on the downside there is no competition to keep prices low. Whether you book a tour directly with the operator who leads it, with another operator, or through your hotel or other tour agency, the price should remain the same. Take note that most tour prices do not include the park entrance fee, an extra US$30 for foreigners.

ESSENTIALS

Visitor and Tour Information **Oficina de Turismo.** ⊠ *Rosales at Libertador, El Calafate* ☏ *2902/491–090* ⊕ *www.elcalafate.gov.ar* ✉ *Bus terminal, El Calafate* ☏ *2902/491–476.* **Oficina Parques Nacionales.** ⊠ *Av. Libertador 1302, El Calafate* ☏ *2902/491–005, 2902/491–005, 2902/491–545* ⊕ *www.parquesnacionales.gov.ar.*

EXPLORING

Glaciarium. This out-of-town glacier museum gives you an educational walk through the formation and life of glaciers (particularly in Patagonia) and the effects of climate change, as well as temporary art exhibitions. A 3-D film about the national park and plenty of brightly lit displays, along with the stark glacier-shaped architecture, give it a modern appeal. Don't miss the Glaciobar—the first ice bar in Argentina—where you can don thermal suits, boots, and gloves, and where a whisky on the rocks means 200-year-old glacier rocks from Perito Moreno. ⊠ *Ruta 11, Km 6, El Calafate* ✛ *Arrive by taxi (US$10 each way), 1 hr walking, or by shuttle service from tourism office leaving every hr ($5 return)* ☏ *2902/497–912* ⊕ *www.glaciarium.com* ▱ *Museum $20; bar $14 for 25 minutes with 1 drink.*

Fodor'sChoice ★ **Glaciar Perito Moreno.** Eighty km (50 miles) away on R11, the road to the Glaciar Perito Moreno has now been entirely paved. From the park entrance the road winds through hills and forests of lenga and ñire trees, until all at once the glacier comes into full view. Descending like a long white tongue through distant mountains, it ends abruptly in a translucent azure wall 5 km (3 miles) wide and 240 feet high at the edge of frosty green Lago Argentino.

Although it's possible to rent a car and go on your own (which can give you the advantage of avoiding large tourist groups), virtually everyone visits the park on a day trip booked through one of the many travel agents in El Calafate. The most basic tours start at $50 for the round-trip and take you to see the glacier from a viewing area composed of a series of platforms wrapped around the point of the Península de Magallanes. The platforms, which offer perhaps the most impressive view of the glacier, allow you to wander back and forth, looking across the Canal de los Tempanos (Iceberg Channel).

10

Here you listen and wait for nature's number-one ice show—first, a cracking sound, followed by tons of ice breaking away and falling with a thunderous crash into the lake. As the glacier creeps across this narrow channel and meets the land on the other side, an ice dam sometimes builds up between the inlet of Brazo Rico on the left and the rest of the lake on the right. As the pressure on the dam increases, everyone waits for the day it will rupture again.

In recent years the surge in the number of visitors to Glaciar Perito Moreno has created a crowded scene that is not always conducive to reflective encounters with nature's majesty. Although the glacier remains spectacular, savvy travelers would do well to minimize time at the madhouse that the viewing area becomes at midday in high season, and instead encounter the glacier by boat or on a mini-trekking excursion. Better yet, rent a car and get an early start to beat the tour buses, or visit Perito Moreno in the off-season when a spectacular rupture is just as likely as in midsummer and you won't have to crane over other people's heads to see it. ⊠ *El Calafate* 🖾 *$30 park entrance.*

Glaciar Upsala. The largest glacier in South America, Glaciar Upsala is 55 km (35 miles) long and 10 km (6 miles) wide, and accessible only by boat. Daily cruises depart from Puerto Banderas (40 km [25 miles] west of El Calafate via R11) for the 2½-hour trip. Dodging floating icebergs (*tempanos*), some as large as a small island, the boats maneuver as close as they dare to the wall of ice that rises from the aqua-green water of Lago Argentino. The seven glaciers that feed the lake deposit their debris into the runoff, causing the water to cloud with minerals ground to fine powder by the glacier's moraine (the accumulation of earth and stones left by the glacier). Condors and black-chested buzzard eagles build their nests in the rocky cliffs above the lake. When the boat stops for lunch at Onelli Bay, don't miss the walk behind the restaurant into a wild landscape of small glaciers and milky rivers carrying chunks of ice from four glaciers into Lago Onelli. Glaciar Upsala has diminished in size in recent years. ⊠ *El Calafate* 🖾 *Cruises start from $50.*

Lago Roca. This little-visited lake is inside the national park just south of Brazo Rico, 46 km (29 miles) from El Calafate. The area receives about five times as much annual precipitation as El Calafate, creating a relatively lush climate of green meadows by the lakeshore, where locals come to picnic and cast for trophy rainbow and lake trout. Don't miss a hike into the hills behind the lake—the view of dark-blue Lago Roca backed by a pale-green inlet of Lago Argentino with the Perito Moreno glacier and jagged snowcapped peaks beyond is truly outstanding. ⊠ *El Calafate.*

Nimez Lagoon Ecological Reserve. A marshy area on the shore of Lago Argentino just a short walk from downtown El Calafate, the Nimez Lagoon Ecological Reserve is home to many species of waterfowl, including black-necked swans, buff-necked ibises, southern lapwings, and flamingos. Road construction along its edge and the rapidly advancing town threaten to stifle this avian oasis, but it's still a haven for birdwatchers and a relaxing walk in the early morning or late afternoon. Strolling along footpaths among grazing horses and flocks of birds may

not be as intense an experience as, say, trekking on a glacier, but a trip to the lagoon provides a good sense of the local landscape. During high season the nature reserve is open from 8 am until 9 pm. Don't forget your binoculars and a telephoto lens. ✉ *1 km (½ miles) north of downtown, just off Av. Alem, El Calafate* ☎ *2902/495–536* 🎟 *$9.*

Fodor's Choice **Parque Nacional Los Glaciares** (*Los Glaciares National Park*). As the name
★ suggests, this national park is renowned for being the home of 47 glaciers, with almost a third of the entire park covered in ice. A giant ice cap located in the Andes Mountains, the world's largest outside of Antarctica and Greenland, feeds all 47 of the glaciers, which snake through the Patagonian steppe and sub-polar forests, eventually crumbling into milky blue glacial lakes. A UNESCO World Heritage Site, it is also the largest national park in Argentina and spans over 2,500 square miles, encompassing the territories running from El Chaltén down to El Calafate, on the border of Chile's Torres del Paine. Spotting the glaciers is the highlight of any visit to the park, with the most accessible one being **Perito Moreno**, which can be reached by road. Visiting the **Upsala** and **Spegazzini** glaciers requires a boat journey, and the **Viedma Glacier** can be seen from hiking paths on the shore of Lake Viedma, a route that is particularly popular with trekkers and climbers who journey onward to Mount Fitz Roy and Cerro Torre (which are also within the park limits). **Lago del Desert** and **Lago Roca** are the other two most visited sites in the park, but outside of these locations the majority of the park is left wonderfully unexplored and untouched. There are few places to stay in the park with the exception of a few estancias and campsites at Lago Roca and on the hiking routes of El Chaltén. Beyond the stunning landscapes, the park is the natural habitat of guanacos, ñandúes, cougars, and the South American grey fox, as well as more than 100 different species of birds. The park is open all year-round, although winter frequently sees snowfall as the temperature drops below freezing. ✉ *Los Glaciares National Park* ☎ *02902/491–005* ⊕ *www.losglaciares. com/en/parque* 🎟 *$30.*

WHERE TO EAT

$$$$ ✕ **Casimiro Biguá.** This restaurant and wine bar boasts a hipper-than-
ARGENTINE thou interior and modern menu serving such delights as Patagonian lamb with *calafate* sauce (calafate is a local wild berry). The Casimiro Biguá Parrilla, down the street from the main restaurant, has a similar trendy feel but you can recognize the *parrilla* by the *cordero al asador* (spit-roasted lamb) displayed in the window. **Known for:** fantastic roast lamb; big portions; typical asado atmosphere. ⑤ *Average main: US$22* ✉ *Av. Libertador 963, El Calafate* ☎ *2902/492–590* ⊕ *www. casimirobigua.com.*

$$$ ✕ **Isabel.** It takes a lot of moxie to open a restaurant not serving *cor-*
ARGENTINE *dero*, barbecue, or pizza in Patagonia, and former "fancy" chefs José
Fodor's Choice and Leandro show they have just that with their homely restaurant,
★ Isabel. They use vintage plow wheels to cook a traditional and ultimately delicious stew-style dish known as *al disco*. The *al disco* menu offers all sorts of meats and veggies cooked in beer, red wine, or white wine; more creative and quasi-modern options like Bife al Napolitana; or you can create your own. **Known for:** signature stew dish cooked

10

several creative ways; charming and lively atmosphere; massive portions. $ *Average main: US$15* ✉ *Gob. Moyano 1020, at 25 Mayo, El Calafate* ☎ *2902/489–000.*

$$$ ✕ **La Lechuza.** This bustling spot is where locals go for their pizza joint
ARGENTINE fix, thanks to the typical Argentine-style pizza of thick crust, and layered
FAMILY with stringy cheese. Their empanadas are just as good—pick up a few and you have the perfect pastry pick-me-up during a long day of exploring. **Known for:** fantastic empanadas; classic Argentine pizza; crowds of locals. $ *Average main: US$15* ✉ *Av. Libertador at 1 de Mayo, El Calafate* ☎ *2902/491–610.*

$$$$ ✕ **La Tablita.** It's a couple of extra blocks from downtown and across a
ARGENTINE little white bridge, but this *parrilla* is where the locals go for a special night out. The highlight is being able to watch your food as it's cooking; Patagonian lamb and beef ribs roast gaucho-style on frames hanging over a circular asador, and an enormous grill along the back wall is full of steaks, chorizos, and *morcilla* (blood sausage). **Known for:** great traditional parilla; tasty empanadas; big crowds on weekends. $ *Average main: US$25* ✉ *Coronel Rosales 28, El Calafate* ☎ *2902/491–065* ⊕ *www.la-tablita.com.ar.*

$$$$ ✕ **La Zaina.** With a focus on modern and well-presented Patagonian
ARGENTINE cuisine, good cocktails, and a range of wines from Argentina, there's a lot to love at La Zaina. Hearty meats like Patagonian lamb and Argentine steak are served with a delicate touch. **Known for:** modern and healthy Patagonian cuisine; nice wine list; artfully presented dishes. $ *Average main: US$20* ✉ *Gdor Gregores 1057, El Calafate* ☎ *2902 /496–789* ⊗ *No lunch.*

$$$ ✕ **Pura Vida.** Bohemian music, homey cooking, and colorful patchwork
ARGENTINE cushions set the tone for this unpretentious, vegetarian-friendly restaurant several blocks from downtown. You'll be surrounded by funky artwork, couples whispering under low-hung lights, and laid-back but efficient staff as you try to decide which big-enough-to-share dish you'll order while working your way through a great dome of steaming bread. **Known for:** signature pumpkin stew; great vegetarian options; fun and eclectic decor. $ *Average main: US$15* ✉ *Av. Libertador 1876, El Calafate* ☎ *2902/493–356* ⊗ *Closed Wed. No lunch.*

WHERE TO STAY

$$$$ ⊞ **Eolo.** A luxury lodge on the road to Perito Moreno, Eolo offers full-
HOTEL board stays in handsome accommodations where you can take in the beauty of Patagonia's vast, empty lands and see Lago Argentino in the distance. **Pros:** beautiful location; luxury service; endless acres of estate to explore. **Cons:** expensive; no drinks included in meal plans; far from town or any services. $ *Rooms from: US$980* ✉ *Ruta Provincial N 11, Km 23,000, El Calafate* ☎ *2902/492–042* ⊕ *www.eolo.com.ar* ⊗ *Closed mid-Apr.–mid-Oct.* ⤳ *17 rooms* ⦿ *All-inclusive; Some meals.*

$$$$ ⊞ **Estancia Cristina.** Boarding a catamaran for the four-hour journey
HOTEL across Lago Argentina, you pass a field of giant icebergs in front of the Upsala Glacier—as spectacular as Perito Moreno, minus the crowds— then disembark at Punta Bandera for a short drive up to these three guest lodges, their stark green roofs mirroring the mountain ridges beyond. **Pros:** combines a glacier visit with a stay in a genuine estancia;

knowledgeable guides; incredible mountain views from comfortable, well-appointed rooms. **Cons:** long boat journey to get here; expensive; no alcohol drinks included in (high) price. $ *Rooms from: US$1360* ✉ *Punta Bandera, El Calafate* ☎ *2902/491–133* ⊕ *www.estanciacristina.com* ⊗ *Closed mid-Apr.–mid-Nov.* ⇆ *20 rooms* ¶⊙¶ *All-inclusive.*

$$$$
HOTEL
Fodor's Choice
★

Helsingfors. This luxurious converted ranch house has an absolutely spectacular location in the middle of the national park on the shore of Lago Viedma. **Pros:** unique location; wonderful staff; comfy atmosphere. **Cons:** three hours by dirt road from El Calafate; rooms are dated and basic; expensive. $ *Rooms from: US$780* ✉ *Lago Viedma, 3 hrs by dirt road from El Calafate, El Calafate* ☎ *11/2021–506927* ⊕ *www. helsingfors.com.ar* ⊗ *Closed May–Oct.* ⇆ *9 rooms* ¶⊙¶ *All-inclusive.*

$$
HOTEL

Hotel Kau-Yatun. From the homemade chocolates and wildflower bouquets that appear in the rooms each evening to the sweeping backyard complete with swing sets for the kids, there are many thoughtful details in this converted ranch. **Pros:** good value; nice details; central location. **Cons:** water pressure is only adequate; lost a bit of personality from chain takeover; Wi-Fi and modern amenities sparse. $ *Rooms from: US$120* ✉ *25 de Mayo, El Calafate* ☎ *2902/491–059* ⊕ *www.kauyatun.com* ⊗ *Closed Apr.–Sept.* ⇆ *44 rooms* ¶⊙¶ *Breakfast.*

$$
HOTEL

Kosten Aike. Lined with wooden balconies, high beamed ceilings, and a slate floor, this hotel is a paragon of Andean Patagonian architecture. **Pros:** large rooms and spa; central location; good value at this price point. **Cons:** dining room decor is uninspired; rooms are simply furnished; some rooms get outside noise. $ *Rooms from: US$120* ✉ *G. Moyano 1243, at 25 de Mayo, El Calafate* ☎ *2902/492–424* ⊕ *www. kostenaike.com.ar* ⊗ *Closed May–Sept.* ⇆ *80 rooms* ¶⊙¶ *Breakfast.*

$$
B&B/INN

Los Ponchos Apart Boutique. Cozy and handsomely designed two-floor apartments in this boutique complex have beautiful views over Lago Argentina and offer some independence and privacy with a self-catering kitchen and homey, gaucho-chic decoration. **Pros:** warm service; cozy atmosphere; private. **Cons:** a bit of a walk from town; street dogs noisy at night; low ceilings. $ *Rooms from: US$200* ✉ *Los Alamos 3321, El Calafate* ☎ *2902/496–330* ⊕ *www.losponchosapart.com.ar* ⊗ *Closed June–mid-Sept.* ⇆ *8 rooms, 2 double apartments, 1 cabin* ¶⊙¶ *Breakfast.*

$$$$
RESORT

Nibepo Aike. This lovely estancia is an hour and a half from El Calafate in a bucolic valley overlooking Lago Roca and backed by snow-capped mountain peaks; sheep, horses, and cows graze among purple lupine flowers, and friendly gauchos give horse-racing and sheep-shearing demonstrations. **Pros:** spectacular scenery; classic estancia experience; friendly guides. **Cons:** expensive for simple amenities; basic food; no Wi-Fi. $ *Rooms from: US$380* ✉ *For reservations:, Av. Libertador 1215, El Calafate* ☎ *11/5031–0755 reservations (Buenos Aires), 290/492–797 day visits* ⊕ *www.nibepoaike.com.ar* ⊗ *Closed May–Sept.* ⇆ *10 rooms* ¶⊙¶ *All-inclusive; Breakfast.*

SPORTS AND THE OUTDOORS
BOAT TOURS

Glaciares Gourmet. If fine dining and sipping wine while admiring the glaciers is more your style, this is the no-effort-required cruise for you. With a maximum of 28 passengers, the deluxe cruise liner is never

overcrowded. You get a full day of cruising around the Spegazzini and Upsala glaciers, a short leg-stretching walk at beauty spot Puesto de las Vacas, and a six-course gourmet lunch with wine. If a full day isn't enough, you can opt for the two-night cruise option where you'll visit four glaciers (Spegazzini, Upsala, Perito Moreno, and Mayo) and access views that no one else can. ⊠ *Cruceros Marpatag, 9 de Julio (Local 4, Galleria de los Pajaros), El Calafate* ☎ *2902/492–118* ⊕ *www.cruceros-marpatag.com* ✉ *From $230.*

Safari Náutico. Boats depart from a small port 7 km (4 miles) from Perito Moreno glacier and take tourists on an hour-long cruise around the glacier's south face for a closer inspection of the advancing glacier and floating icebergs. On a good day, you can stand on the deck for the best up-close photo opportunities. Tours happen all year and can be reserved at the port or in advance in the downtown office or other tour agencies. ⊠ *Hielo y Aventura, Av. Libertador 935, El Calafate* ☎ *2902/492–205* ⊕ *www.hieloyaventura.com* ✉ *From $60.*

Solo Patagonia. With two different full-day boat excursions, Solo Patagonia has been navigating the milky waters for years. Their fleet of large cruisers offers access to some of the best views of the Perito Moreno, Upsala, and Spegazzini glaciers from October to March. ⊠ *Av. Libertador 867, El Calafate* ☎ *2902/491–155* ⊕ *www.solopatagonia.com* ✉ *From $70.*

CAMPING

Camping Lago Roca. There are gorgeous campsites, simple cabins, fishing-tackle rentals, hot showers, and a basic restaurant at Camping Lago Roca. Make reservations in advance if visiting over the Christmas holidays; at other times the campground is seldom crowded. In high season Cal Tur offer shuttles from Lago Roca to Perito Moreno. For more comfortable accommodations, you can arrange to stay at the Nibepo Aike Estancia at the western end of Lago Roca, about 5 km (3 miles) past the campground. The national park entrance fee is collected only on the road to Perito Moreno Glacier or at Puerto Banderas, where cruises depart, so admission to the Lago Roca corner of the park is free. ⊠ *El Calafate* ☎ *2902/499–500* ⊗ *Closed May–Sept.*

HIKING

Although it's possible to find trails along the shore of Lago Argentino and in the hills south and west of town, these hikes traverse a rather barren landscape and are not terribly interesting. The mountain peaks and forests are in the park, an hour by car from El Calafate. If you want to lace up your boots in your hotel, walk outside, and hit the trail, go to El Chaltén—it's a much better base than El Calafate for hikes in the national park. Good hiking trails are accessible from the camping areas and cabins by Lago Roca, 50 km (31 miles) from El Calafate.

HORSEBACK RIDING AND ESTANCIAS

Cabalgata en Patagonia. Anything from a short day ride along Lago Argentino to a weeklong camping excursion in and around the glaciers can be arranged in El Calafate via phone, their Facebook page, or through the tourist office. ⊠ *Av. Libertador 4315, El Calafate* ☎ *2902/493–278.*

Estancia El Galpón del Glaciar. This estancia welcomes guests overnight or for the day—for a horseback ride, bird-watching, or an afternoon program that includes a demonstration of sheep dogs working, a walk to the lake with a naturalist, sheep-shearing, and dinner in the former sheep-shearing barn served right off the asador by knife-wielding gauchos. ⊠ *Ruta 11, Km 22, El Calafate* ☎ *11/5217–6720* ⊕ *www. elgalpondelglaciar.com.ar.*

Nibepo Aike. This pretty estancia an hour and a half from El Calafate offers a range of horseback experiences from hour-long excursions to full-day, nine-hour rides to view glaciers in the distance. It's possible to visit Nibepo Aike by booking a day trip at the office in downtown El Calafate, or you can stay overnight at the estancia. ⊠ *53 km (31 miles) from El Calafate near Lago Roca on Ruta 15, El Calafate* ☎ *2902/492– 797, 2902/492–859* ⊕ *www.nibepoaike.com.ar.*

Provincial Tourist Office. *Estancias turísticas* (tourist ranches) are ideal for a combination of horseback riding, ranch activities, and local excursions. Information on all the estancias can be obtained from Estancias de Santa Cruz in Buenos Aires, or on the website. ⊠ *Reconquista 642* ☎ *11/5237–4043* ⊕ *www.estanciasdesantacruz.com.*

ICE TREKKING

Hielo y Aventura. For the most unusual and up-close-and-personal experience with Perito Moreno glacier, book yourself onto an ice trekking day where you'll don crampons and walk over the glacier studying crevasses and ice lakes before finishing with a whisky on the rocks using ice from the glacier. The Mini Trekking excursion is a 10-hour trip and includes a 90-minute ice trek, a short trek in the forest, a 20-minute boat ride, and a transfer to the park from your hotel. You'll have to pay your own park entrance, bring a packed lunch, and wear the right clothing (crampons are provided), but you also get over an hour to enjoy the view of Perito Moreno Glacier from the park. For a more in-depth and challenging ice day, Hielo y Aventura also offers the Big Ice trek, which includes more time on the ice and ducking through bright-blue ice tunnels. This excursion has around seven hours' walking in total and is a longer day (ages 18–50 only). During high season, tours can get a bit crowded, but with a glacier the size of Buenos Aires, there is plenty of white space to feel true isolation. Ice trekking is available May to mid-September. ⊠ *Av. Libertador 935, El Calafate* ☎ *2902/492–205* ⊕ *www.hieloyaventura.com* ☜ *From $150.*

KAYAKING

Mil Outdoor. Those brave enough to get in the milky ice waters can get dropped off by a boat on the glacier's edge and take a two-hour guided kayaking excursion with this outfitter. Available November through March, weather permitting. ⊠ *Calafate Mountain Park/Mil Outdoor, Av. Libertador 1037, El Calafate* ☎ *2902/491–446* ⊕ *www.miloutdoor. com.ar* ☜ *From $50.*

LAND ROVER EXCURSIONS

Mil Outdoor. If pedaling uphill sounds like too much work, check out the Land Rover expeditions offered by Mil Outdoor October to April. These trips use large tour trucks to follow dirt tracks into the hills

10

above town for stunning views of Lago Argentino. On a clear day, you can even see the peaks of Cerro Torre and Cerro Fitzroy on the horizon. Mil's Land Rovers are converted to run on vegetable oil, so environmentalists can enjoy bouncing up the trail with a clean conscience. During the winter, the same company (also known as Calafate Mountain Park) runs a children's snow park with sledding, beginners' slopes, and more advanced off-piste skiing, snowshoeing, and snowmobiling. Open in winter only, the snow park is 15 kms (9 miles) from El Calafate proper. ⊠ *Mil Aventura (Calafate Mountain Park/ Viva Patagonia), Av. Libertador 1037, El Calafate* ☎ *2902/491–446* ⊕ *www.miloutdoor.com.ar* ⊠ *From $110.*

MOUNTAIN BIKING

Bike Rental. Mountain biking is popular along the dirt roads and mountain paths that lead to the lakes, glaciers, and ranches. There are several places to rent bikes in town; two options are HLS (Perito Moreno 95) and E Bike (Avenida Libertador 1319). ⊠ *El Calafate.*

EL CHALTÉN

222 km (138 miles) north of El Calafate.

Founded in 1985, El Chaltén is Argentina's newest town, and it's growing at an astounding rate. Originally just a few shacks and lodges built near the entrance to Parque Nacional Los Glaciares, the town is starting to fill a steep-walled valley in front of Cerro Torre and Cerro Fitzroy, two of the most impressive peaks in Argentina.

Famous for the exploits of rock climbers who started their pilgrimage to climb some of the most difficult rock walls in the world in the 1950s, the range is now drawing hikers whose more earthbound ambitions run to dazzling mountain scenery and unscripted encounters with wildlife including condors, Patagonian parrots, red-crested woodpeckers, and the *huemul,* an endangered deer species.

GETTING HERE AND AROUND

The three-hour car or bus trip to El Chaltén from El Calafate makes staying at least one night here a good idea. The only gas, food, and restroom facilities en route are at La Leona, a historically significant ranch 110 km (68 miles) from El Calafate where Butch Cassidy and the Sundance Kid once hid from the long arm of the law.

Before you cross the bridge into town over Río Fitzroy, stop at the Parque Nacional office. It's extremely well organized and staffed by bilingual rangers who can help you plan your mountain treks and point you to accommodations and restaurants in town. It's an essential stop; orientation talks are given in coordination with arriving buses, which automatically stop here before continuing on to the bus depot.

There's only one ATM in town (it's in the bus station), and it's in high demand; because of servicing schedules, on the weekend El Chaltén runs into the same cash availability problems that El Calafate does, though on a smaller scale. ■TIP➔ **During the week, stockpile the cash you'll need for the weekend, or bring it with you if you're arriving between midday Friday and midday Monday.**

ESSENTIALS

Visitor Information Parque Nacional Office. ⊠ *Av. M.M. de Güemes 21, El Chaltén* ☎ *2962/493–004* ⊕ *www.losglaciares.com/en.*

EXPLORING

Cerro Torre and Cerro Fitzroy. You don't need a guide to do the classic treks to Cerro Torre and Cerro Fitzroy, each about six to eight hours round-trip out of El Chaltén. If your legs feel up to it the day you do the Fitzroy walk, tack on an hour of steep switchbacks to Mirador Tres Lagos, the lookout with the best views of Mt. Fitzroy and its glacial lakes. Both routes, plus the Mirador and various side trails, can be combined in a two- or three-day trip. ⊠ *El Chaltén.*

Chorillo del Salta (*Trickling Falls*). Just 4 km (3 miles) north of town on the road to Lago del Desierto, the Chorillo del Salta waterfall is no Iguazú, but the area is extremely pleasant and sheltered from the wind. A short hike uphill leads to secluded river pools and sun-splashed rocks where locals enjoy picnics on their days off. If you don't feel up to a more ambitious hike, the short stroll to the falls is an excellent way to spend the better part of an afternoon. Pack a bottle of wine and a sandwich and enjoy the solitude. ⊠ *El Chaltén.*

Laguna del Desierto (*Lake of the Desert*). A lovely lake surrounded by lush forest, complete with orchids and mossy trees, the Laguna del Desierto is 37 km (23 miles) north of El Chaltén on R23, a dirt road. Hotels in El Chaltén can arrange a trip for about $50 for the day. Locals recommend visiting Lago del Desierto on a rainy day, when more ambitious hikes are not an option and the dripping green misty forest is extra mysterious. ⊠ *El Chaltén.*

WHERE TO EAT

$$$
ARGENTINE
FAMILY
✕ **Aonikenk.** In a dark wooden dining hall you'll share hearty steaks, warming soups, and wine poured from penguin-shaped ceramic jugs in a family restaurant that includes a hostel upstairs. It's rustic, and the food is not spectacular, but you can't beat the friendly atmosphere in what is easily El Chaltén's largest and most popular restaurant. **Known for:** family-friendly atmosphere; standard Chilean cuisine; open hours even in the off-season. ⑤ *Average main: US$16* ⊠ *Av. M.M. de Güemes 23, El Chaltén* ☎ *2962/493–070* ⊟ *No credit cards.*

$$
ARGENTINE
Fodor's Choice
★
✕ **La Cervecería.** While El Chaltén is still building all it needs to become a full-fledged town, it already has a successful microbrewery that is famous in the region for its brews and comfort food. Of course, it's not just the hops bringing in the crowds; they also cook up delicious soups, snacks, empanadas, and a great *locro* (hearty traditional northern Argentine stew). **Known for:** impressive craft beer; hearty comfort food; welcoming atmosphere. ⑤ *Average main: US$10* ⊠ *San Martín 320, El Chaltén* ☎ *2962/493–109* ⊘ *Closed June–Oct.*

WHERE TO STAY

$$$$
HOTEL
▥ **Aguas Arriba Lodge.** Accessible only by boat or a three-hour trek, Aguas Arriba has a privileged location right on the Lago del Desierto, with a glimmer of Mt. Fitzroy in the distance. **Pros:** fantastic location; attended by owners; excellent excursions. **Cons:** noise travels between rooms; private shuttle to lake required in addition to walk/boat; no

10

phone signal. ⑤ *Rooms from: US$800* ✉ *Lago del Desierto, El Chaltén* ☎ *11/4152–5697 Buenos Aires* ⊕ *www.aguasarribalodge.com* ⊙ *Closed mid-Apr.–Sept.* ➷ *6 rooms* ⦿ *Breakfast.*

$

B&B/INN

⊡ **Nothofagus.** A simple B&B off the main road, Nothofagus is named after the southern beech tree, and the lodge has a rough-hewn, woodsy feel with exposed beams and leaves stamped into the lampshades. **Pros:** great views; bright and sunny breakfast room; good value. **Cons:** staff energy too low for some; spartan rooms and bathrooms, some of which are shared; simple breakfast. ⑤ *Rooms from: US$90* ✉ *Hensen, at Riquelme, El Chaltén* ☎ *2962/493–087* ⊕ *www.nothofagusbb.com. ar* ▭ *No credit cards* ⊙ *Closed May–Sept.* ➷ *9 rooms* ⦿ *Breakfast.*

$$

HOTEL

⊡ **Posada Lunajuim.** A traditional A-frame roof keeps the lid on a funky, modern lodge filled with contemporary artwork, exposed brick masonry, and a spacious lounge and dining room complete with a roaring fireplace and a library stacked with an intriguing mix of travel books. **Pros:** great lounge area; friendly staff; awesome food and wine list. **Cons:** not all rooms have views; baths are quite small; slow Wi-Fi. ⑤ *Rooms from: US$140* ✉ *Trevisan 45, El Chaltén* ☎ *2962/493–047, 2962/493–047* ⊕ *www.lunajuim.com* ➷ *26 rooms* ⦿ *Breakfast.*

SPORTS AND THE OUTDOORS

El Chaltén owes its existence to those who wanted a base for trekking into this corner of Los Glaciares National Park, specifically Cerro Torre and Cerro Fitzroy. It's no surprise that nearly everyone who comes here considers hiking up to those two mountains to be the main event—though the *locro* (hearty stew) and microbrews at the end of the day are a plus.

HIKING

Both long and short hikes on well-trodden trails lead to lakes, glaciers, and stunning viewpoints. There are two main hikes, one to the base of Cerro Fitzroy, the other to a windswept glacial lake at the base of Cerro Torre. Both hikes climb into the hills above town, and excellent views start after only about an hour on either trail. The six-hour round-trip hike to the base camp for Cerro Torre at Laguna Torre has (weather permitting) dramatic views of Torres Standhart, Adelas, Grande, and Solo.

Trails start in town and are very well marked, so if you stick to the main path there is little danger of getting lost. Just be careful of high winds and exposed rocks that can get slippery in bad weather. The eight-hour hike to the base camp for Cerro Fitzroy passes Laguna Capri and ends at Laguna de los Tres, where you can enjoy an utterly spectacular view of the granite tower. If you have time for only one ambitious hike, this is probably the best choice, though the last kilometer of trail is very steep. At campsites in the hills above town, hardy souls can pitch a tent for the night and enjoy sunset and dawn views of the mountain peaks. Ask about current camping regulations and advisories at the national park office before setting off with a tent in your rucksack. Finally, use latrines where provided, and under no circumstance should you ever think about starting a fire—a large section of forest near Cerro Torre was devastated several years ago when a foolish hiker tried to dispose of toilet paper with a match.

MOUNTAIN CLIMBING

Casa de Guias. A guide is required if you want to enter the ice field or trek on any of the glaciers in Los Glaciares National Park. Casa de Guias is a group of professional, multilingual guides who offer fully equipped multiday treks covering all the classic routes in the national park, and longer trips exploring the ice field. They even offer a taste of big-wall climbing on one of the spires in the Fitzroy range. ⊠ *Av. San Martín 310, El Chaltén* ☎ *2962/493–118* ⊕ *www.casadeguias.com.ar.*

El Chaltén Mountain Guides. Five mountain guides offer expeditions in and around El Chaltén, as well as many other destinations in Argentina. One-day and multiday treks and ascents to rock and ice-climbing expeditions are available. In the winter they also offer backcountry skiing tours. ⊠ *Rio de las Vueltas 212, El Chaltén* ☎ *2962/493–329* ⊕ *www.ecmg.com.ar.*

USHUAIA AND TIERRA DEL FUEGO, ARGENTINA

Tierra del Fuego, a more or less triangular island separated from the southernmost tip of the South American mainland by the twists and bends of the Estrecho de Magallanes, is indeed a world unto itself. The vast plains on its northern reaches are dotted with trees bent low by the savage winds that frequently lash the coast. The mountains that rise in the south are equally forbidding, traversed by huge glaciers slowly making their way to the sea.

The first European to set foot on this island was Spanish explorer Hernando de Magallanes, who sailed here in 1520. The smoke that he saw coming from the fires lighted by the native peoples prompted him to call it Tierra del Humo (Land of Smoke). King Charles V of Spain, disliking that name, rechristened it Tierra del Fuego, or Land of Fire.

Tierra del Fuego is split in half. The island's northernmost tip, well within Chilean territory, is its closest point to the continent. The only town of any size here is Porvenir. Its southern extremity, part of Argentina, points out into the Atlantic toward the Falkland Islands. Here you'll find Ushuaia, the main destination, on the shores of the Canal Beagle. Farther south is Cape Horn, the southernmost point of land before Antarctica (still a good 500 miles across the brutal Drake Passage).

10

USHUAIA

914 km (567 miles) south of El Calafate.

At 55 degrees latitude south, Ushuaia (pronounced oo-swy-ah) is closer to the South Pole than to Argentina's northern border with Bolivia. It is the capital and tourism base for Tierra del Fuego, the island at the southernmost tip of Argentina.

The city rightly (if perhaps too loudly) promotes itself as the southernmost city in the world (Puerto Williams, a few miles south on the Chilean side of the Beagle Channel, is a small town). You can make

your way to the tourism office to get your clichéd, but oh-so-necessary, "Southernmost City in the World" passport stamp. Ushuaia feels like a frontier boomtown, at heart still a rugged, weather-beaten fishing village, but exhibiting the frayed edges of a city that quadrupled in size in the '70s and '80s and just keeps growing. Unpaved portions of Ruta 3, the last stretch of the Pan-American Highway, which connects Alaska to Tierra del Fuego, are finally being paved. The summer months (December through March) draw more than 120,000 visitors, and dozens of cruise ships. The city is trying to extend those visits with events like March's Marathon at the End of the World and by increasing the gamut of winter activities buoyed by the excellent snow conditions.

A terrific trail winds through the town up to the Martial Glacier, where a ski lift can help cut down a steep kilometer of your journey. The chaotic and contradictory urban landscape includes a handful of luxury hotels amid the concrete of public housing projects. Scores of "sled houses" (wooden shacks) sit precariously on upright piers, ready for speedy displacement to a different site. But there are also many small, picturesque homes with tiny, carefully tended gardens. Many of the newer homes are built in a Swiss-chalet style, reinforcing the idea that this is a town into which tourism has breathed new life. At the same time, the weather-worn pastel colors that dominate the town's landscape remind you that Ushuaia was once just a tiny fishing village, snuggled at the end of the Earth.

As you stand on the banks of the Canal Beagle (Beagle Channel) near Ushuaia, the spirit of the farthest corner of the world takes hold. What stands out is the light: at sundown the landscape is cast in a subdued, sensual tone; everything feels closer, softer, and more human in dimension despite the vastness of the setting. The snowcapped mountains reflect the setting sun back onto a stream rolling into the channel, as nearby peaks echo their image—on a windless day—in the still waters.

Above the city rise the last mountains of the Andean Cordillera, and just south and west of Ushuaia they finally vanish into the often-stormy sea. Snow whitens the peaks well into summer. Nature is the principal attraction here, with trekking, fishing, horseback riding, wildlife spotting, and sailing among the most rewarding activities, especially in the Parque Nacional Tierra del Fuego (Tierra del Fuego National Park).

GETTING HERE AND AROUND

Arriving by air is the preferred option. Ushuaia's Aeropuerto Internacional Malvinas Argentinas (*Península de Ushuaia 2901/431–232*) is 5 km (3 miles) from town and is served daily by flights to and from Buenos Aires, Río Gallegos, El Calafate, Trelew, and Comodoro Rivadavía. There are also flights to Santiago via Punta Arenas in Chile. A taxi into town costs about US$8.

Arriving by road on the Ruta Nacional 3 involves Argentine and Chilean immigrations/customs, a ferry crossing, and a lot of time. Buses to and from Punta Arenas make the trip five days a week in summer, four in winter. Daily buses to Río Gallegos leave in the predawn hours, and multiple border crossings mean an all-day journey. Check prices on the

55-minute flight, which can be a much better value. There is no central bus terminal, just individual company locations.

There is no regular passenger transport (besides cruises) by sea.

Bus Services Tecni-Austral. ⊠ *Roca 157, Ushuaia* ☎ *2901/431–408.*

CRUISE TRAVEL TO USHUAIA

As you sail into Ushuaia, the captain almost always takes you around the picturesque lighthouse at the "end of the world": a beacon for the southernmost city perched on the edge of the Canal Beagle. The port is just two blocks from the main street, leaving you in a central location once you disembark.

Before undertaking the five-minute walk into town, stop at the tourism office (right in front of the port), where you can gather information and take advantage of the free Wi-Fi. Most city attractions can be reached on foot, although if you're spending the night here, you may need to take a taxi to your hotel. If you're in Ushuaia only for the day, lace on some good shoes, as the city is built on a hill and requires calves of steel.

ESSENTIALS

Visitor Information Ushuaia Tourist Office. ⊠ *Prefectura Naval 470, Ushuaia* ☎ *2901/437–666* ⊕ *www.turismoushuaia.com.*

EXPLORING
TOP ATTRACTIONS

Canal Beagle. Several tour operators run trips along the Canal Beagle, on which you can get a startling close-up view of sea mammals and birds on **Isla de los Lobos, Isla de los Pájaros,** and near **Les Eclaireurs Lighthouse.** Catamarans, motorboats, and sailboats usually leave from the tourist pier at 9:30, 10, 3, and 3:30 (trips depend on weather; few trips go in winter). Trips start at US$70 and some include hikes on the islands. Check with the tourist office for the latest details; you can also book through any of the local travel agencies or scope out the offers yourself by walking around the kiosks on the tourist pier. ⊠ *Ushuaia.*

Estancia Harberton (*Harberton Ranch*). This property—50,000 acres of coastal marshland and wooded hillsides—was a late-19th-century gift from the Argentine government to Reverend Thomas Bridges, who authored a Yamana–English dictionary and is considered the patriarch of Tierra del Fuego. His son Lucas wrote *The Uttermost Part of the Earth*, a memoir about his frontier childhood. Today the ranch is managed by Bridges's great-grandson, Thomas Goodall, and his American wife, Natalie, a scientist and author who has cooperated with the National Geographic Society on conservation projects and operates the impressive marine mammal museum, **Museo Acatushun.** Most people visit as part of organized tours, but you'll be welcome if you arrive alone. They serve up a tasty tea in their house, the oldest building on the island. For safety reasons, exploration of the ranch can be done only on guided tours (45–90 minutes). Lodging is available, either in the Old Shepherd's House or the Old Cook's House. Additionally, you can arrange a three-course lunch at the ranch by calling two days ahead for a reservation. Most tours reach the estancia by boat, offering a rare opportunity to explore the Isla Martillo penguin colony and a sea-lion refuge on Isla de los Lobos

10

(Seal Island) along the way. ⊠ *85 km (53 miles) east of Ushuaia, Ushuaia* ☎ *2901/422–742* ⊕ *www.estanciaharberton.com* 🖃 *$14.*

Glaciar Martial. It might pale in comparison to the glaciers in El Calafate, but if you've never seen a glacier up close before, you should check out Glaciar Martial, in the mountain range just above Ushuaia. Named after Frenchman Luís F. Martial, a 19th-century scientist who wandered this way aboard the warship *Romanche* to observe the passing of the planet Venus, the glacier is reached via a panoramic *aerosilla* (ski lift) or by foot. Take the Camino al Glaciar (Glacier Road) 7 km (4 miles) out of town until it ends (this route is also served by the local tour companies). Stop off at one of the teahouses en route (at the foot of the ski lift, when it is functioning) because this is a steep, strenuous 90-minute hike to the top. You can cool your heels in one of the many gurgling, icy rivulets that cascade down water-worn shale shoots or enjoy a picnic while you wait for sunset (you can walk all the way down if you want to linger until after the *aerosilla* closes). When the sun drops behind the glacier's jagged crown of peaks, brilliant rays beam over the mountain's crest, spilling a halo of gold-flecked light on the glacier, valley, and channel below. Moments like these are why this land is so magical. Note that temperatures drop dramatically after sunset, so come prepared with warm clothing. ⊠ *Glaciar Martial, Ushuaia.*

Museo Marítimo (*Maritime Museum*). Part of the original penal colony, the Presidio building was built to hold political prisoners, murderous estancia owners, street orphans, and a variety of Buenos Aires's most violent criminals. Some even claim that singer Carlos Gardel landed in one of the cells for the petty crimes of his misspent youth. In its day it held 600 inmates in 380 cells. Today it's on the grounds of Ushuaia's naval base and holds the Museo Marítimo, which starts with exhibits on the canoe-making skills of the region's indigenous peoples, tracks the navigational history of Tierra del Fuego and Cape Horn and the Antarctic, and even has a display on other great jails of the world. You can enter cell blocks and read about the grisly crimes of the prisoners who lived in them and measure yourself against their eerie life-size plaster effigies. Of the five wings spreading out from the main guard house, one has been transformed into an art gallery and another has been kept untouched—and unheated. Bone-chattering cold and bleak, bare walls powerfully evoke the desolation of a long sentence at the tip of the continent. Well-presented tours (in Spanish only) are conducted at 11:30 am, 4:30 pm, and 6:30 pm daily. ⊠ *Gobernador Paz at Yaganes, Ushuaia* ☎ *2901/437–481* ⊕ *www.museomaritimo. com* 🖃 *$23 (valid for 2 days).*

WORTH NOTING

Antigua Casa Beban (*Old Beban House*). One of Ushuaia's original houses, the Antigua Casa Beban long served as the city's social center. Built between 1911 and 1913 by Fortunato Beban, it's said he ordered the house through a Swiss catalog. In the 1980s the Beban family donated the house to the city to avoid demolition. It was moved to its current location along the coast and restored, and is now a cultural center with art exhibits. ⊠ *Maipú at Pluschow, Ushuaia* ☎ *2901/431–386* 🖃 *Free* ☉ *Closed weekends.*

Canal Fun. This unconventional tour goes to Monte Olivia, the tallest mountain along the Canal Beagle, rising 1,358 meters (4,455 feet) above sea level. You also pass the Five Brothers Mountains and go through the Garibaldi Pass, which begins at the Rancho Hambre, climbs into the mountain range, and ends with a spectacular view of Lago Escondido. From here you continue on to Lago Fagnano through the countryside past sawmills and lumber yards. To do this tour in a four-wheel-drive truck with an excellent bilingual guide, contact Canal Fun; you'll drive *through* Lago Fagnano (about 3 feet of water at this point) to a secluded cabin on the shore and have a delicious asado, complete with wine and dessert. In winter they can also organize tailor-made dogsledding and cross-country-skiing trips. ⊠ *Roca 136, Ushuaia* ☎ *2901/435–777* ⊕ *www.canalfun.com.*

Lago Escondido (*Hidden Lake*). One good excursion in the area is to Lago Escondido and Lago Fagnano (Fagnano Lake). The Pan-American Highway out of Ushuaia goes through deciduous beech forests and past beavers' dams, peat bogs, and glaciers. The lakes have campsites and fishing and are good spots for a picnic or a hike. This can be done on your own or as a seven-hour trip, including lunch, booked through the local travel agencies (around $75 for standard tour or $110 with lunch and 4x4 transportation). ⊠ *Ushuaia.*

Museo del Fin del Mundo (*End of the World Museum*). Here you can see a large taxidermied condor and other native birds, indigenous artifacts, maritime instruments, a reconstruction of an old Patagonian general store, and such seafaring-related objects as an impressive mermaid figurehead taken from the bowsprit of a galleon. There are also photographs and histories of El Presidio's original inmates, such as Simon Radowitzky, a Russian immigrant anarchist who received a life sentence for killing an Argentine police colonel. The museum is split across two buildings—the first, and original, is in the 1905 residence of a Fuegonian governor at Maipú 173. The newer museum building is farther down the road at Maipú 465, where you can see extended exhibitions of the same style. ⊠ *Maipú 173, at Rivadavía, Ushuaia* ☎ *2901/421–863* 🖰 *$10.*

Tren del Fin del Mundo (*End of the World Train*). Heavily promoted but a bit of a letdown, the Tren del Fin del Mundo purports to take you inside the Parque Nacional Tierra del Fuego, 12 km (8 miles) away from town, but you have to drive to get there, and it leaves visitors a long way short of the most spectacular scenery in the national park. The touristy 40-minute train ride's gimmick is a simulation of the trip El Presidio prisoners were forced to take into the forest to chop wood; but unlike them, you'll also get a good presentation of Ushuaia's history (in Spanish and English). The train departs daily at 9:30, noon, and 3 (only 10 and 3 in low season). One common way to do the trip is to hire a remis that will drop you at the station for a one-way train ride and pick you up at the other end, then drive you around the Parque Nacional for two or three hours of sightseeing (which is far more scenic than the train ride itself). ⊠ *Ruta 3, Km 3042, Ushuaia* ☎ *2901/431–600* ⊕ *www. trendelfindelmundo.com.ar* 🖰 *$45, one-way.*

10

OFF THE
BEATEN
PATH

Tres Marias Excursions. Although there are a number of boat tours through the Canal Beagle or around the bays to Tierra del Fuego National Park, one offers an experience that will put you in the shoes of the earliest explorers to visit the far south. The operators of Tres Marias Excursions offer a half-day sailing trip to Island H, an outcrop in the middle of the channel, with cormorant colonies, families of snow geese, seaweed stands, and a weather station that records the howling winds blowing in from the misnamed Pacific Ocean. The guides are skillful sailors and storytellers. On a gusty day you'll marvel at the hardiness of the Yamana people, who survived frigid winters wearing little or no clothing by setting fires behind natural and man-made windbreaks. You'll find the same plant and moss species that grow in the high Andes; they thrive here at sea level because the conditions kill off less hardy, temperate species. On the way back you visit a sea lion colony, but won't soon forget arriving in Ushuaia under full sail as the late sun hits the mountains. At $75, it's only a little more expensive, and a lot more adventurous, than the motorized alternatives trawling for business at the dock. Tours only October to March. ⊠ *Port, Ushuaia* ☎ *2901/582–060* ⊕ *www. tresmariasweb.com* ✉ *$75.*

WHERE TO EAT

$$$$

ARGENTINE

✕ **Bodegón Fueguino.** A mustard-yellow pioneer house that lights up the main street, this traditional eatery is driven by its ebullient owner Sergio Otero, a constant presence bustling around the bench seating, making suggestions, and revving up his staff. Sample the *picada* plate (king crab rolls, Roma-style calamari, marinated rabbit) over an artisanal Beagle Beer—the dark version is the perfect balm on a cold windy day. **Known for:** large and hearty portions; famous Patagonian lamb; no-reservations but a quick wait. ⑤ *Average main: US$22* ⊠ *San Martín 859, Ushuaia* ☎ *2901/431–972* ⊕ *www.tierradehumos.com* ⊙ *Closed Mon.*

$$$$

SEAFOOD

Fodor'sChoice

★

✕ **Chez Manu.** *Herbes de provence* in the greeting room, a tank of lively king crabs in the dining room: French chef Manu Herbin gives local seafood a French touch and creates some of Ushuaia's most memorable meals with views to match. The first-rate wine list includes Patagonian selections, while all dishes are created entirely with ingredients from Tierra del Fuego. **Known for:** amazing views of Beagle Channel; excellent king crab gratin and other fresh seafood; fantastic wine list. ⑤ *Average main: US$38* ⊠ *Camino Luís Martial 2135, Ushuaia* ☎ *2901/432–253* ⊕ *www.chezmanu.com* ⊙ *Closed Mon. No lunch Tues. Closed 2 wks in May and June.*

$$$$

MODERN
ARGENTINE

✕ **Kalma Resto.** Beautiful dishes and a contemporary twist on traditional Patagonian flavors meet at this funky little restaurant at the end of the world. Owner and chef Jorge says that recipes are inspired by his grandma's classics, but there is also a hint of Peruvian and Mediterranean with signature dishes like octopus ceviche, centolla and Beagle Channel mussels, and paella. **Known for:** creative cuisine with wines to match; fantastic tasting menu; sophisticated service. ⑤ *Average main: US$28* ⊠ *Antártida Argentina 57, Ushuaia* ☎ *2901/425–786* ⊕ *www. kalmaresto.com.ar* ⊙ *Closed May and June and Sun.*

$$$$

ARGENTINE

✕ **Kaupé.** The white picket fence, manicured lawns, and planter boxes play up the fact that this out-of-the-way restaurant used to be a family

home. Inside, the star ingredient is *centolla* (king crab), best presented as chowder with a hint of mustard. **Known for:** seafood served with elegance and sophistication; sunset views over the city; hard-to-find location. ⑤ *Average main: US$28* ✉ *Roca 470, Ushuaia* ☎ *2901/422–704* ⊕ *www.kaupe.com.ar* ⊘ *Closed Sun.*

$$ ✕**La Cabaña Casa de Té.** This impeccably maintained riverside cottage
ARGENTINE is nestled in a verdant stand of lenga trees and overlooks the Beagle Channel. It provides a warm, cozy spot for delicious loose leaf tea or comforting snacks before or after a hike to the Martial Glacier (it's conveniently located at the end of the Martial road that leads up from Ushuaia, tucked in behind the ski lift). **Known for:** countryside setting and views; traditional afternoon tea menu; lunchtime fondue. ⑤ *Average main: US$12* ✉ *Camino Luís Martial 3560, Ushuaia* ☎ *2901/424–779* ⊕ *www.lacabania.com.ar* ⊘ *Closed Apr. and May.*

$$$ ✕**Ramos Generales.** Entering this café on the waterfront puts you in
ARGENTINE mind of a general store from the earliest frontier years of Ushuaia, which is why locals call it the *viejo almacen* (old grocery store). As you walk from room to room admiring the relics (like the hand-cranked Victrola phonograph), the hubbub around the bar reminds you that a warehouse like this was not just a store to pick up supplies; it was also a place for isolated pioneers to socialize and gather all the latest news from the port. **Known for:** old-school frontier vibe; sweet treats like lemon croissants; submarino drink, dark chocolate bar dipped in hot milk. ⑤ *Average main: US$18* ✉ *Maipú 749, Ushuaia* ☎ *2901/424–317, 2901/424–317* ⊘ *Closed 3 wks in May.*

$$$$ ✕**Tia Elvira.** On the street that runs right along the Beagle Channel,
ARGENTINE Tia Elvira is a good place to sample the local catch. Garlicky shellfish appetizers and centolla are delicious; even more memorable is the tender *merluza negra* (black sea bass). **Known for:** good local seafood; attentive service; kitschy decor. ⑤ *Average main: US$28* ✉ *Maipú 349, Ushuaia* ☎ *2901/424–725* ⊘ *Closed Sun.*

$$$$ ✕**Volver.** A giant king crab sign beckons you into this red-tin-walled
ARGENTINE restaurant, where the maritime bric-a-brac hanging from the ceiling can be a little distracting. The name means "return" and it succeeds in getting repeat visits on the strength of its seafood; the culinary highlight is the centolla, which comes served with a choice of five different sauces. **Known for:** great place to try signature dish of Tierra del Fuego, centolla (king crab); waterfront views; cozy maritime atmosphere. ⑤ *Average main: US$28* ✉ *Maipú 37, Ushuaia* ☎ *2901/423–977* ⊘ *No lunch Sun. Closed Mon.*

WHERE TO STAY

$$$$ 🏨**Arakur.** You can see this luxury hotel towering in the distance in front
RESORT of Monte Olivia; it's one of the most extensive spa-and-resort complexes in Ushuaia and overlooks the entire bay and town from its own nature reserve out of town on the road to Cerro Castor. **Pros:** modern design with luxury fittings; sweeping views; nature reserve at doorstep. **Cons:** expensive; sterile atmosphere; far from town. ⑤ *Rooms from: US$330* ✉ *Cerro Alarken, Access via Av. Héroes de Malvinas 2617, Ushuaia* ☎ *2901/442–900* ⊕ *www.arakur.com* ⇌ *131 rooms* ⦿*Breakfast.*

10

$$$
B&B/INN

⌂ **Cumbres de Martial.** This charming complex of cabins and bungalows, painted a deep berry purple, is high above Ushuaia in the woods at the base of the ski lift to the Martial Glacier; each spacious room has an extremely comfortable bed and a small wooden deck with terrific views down to the Beagle Channel. **Pros:** easy access to the glacier and nature trails; romantic cabins; lovely spa. **Cons:** you need to cab it to and from town; few restaurant options or services within walking distance; slow service. ⑤ *Rooms from: US$210 ⌧ Camino Luís Martial 3560, Ushuaia ☎ 2901/424–779 ⊕ www.cumbresdelmartial.com.ar ⊗ Closed Apr. and May ⇆ 6 rooms, 4 cabins* ⎮○⎮ *Breakfast.*

$$
B&B/INN

⌂ **Hostería Patagonia Jarké.** Jarké means "spark" in a local native language, and this B&B is a bright, electric addition to Ushuaia; the three-story lodge cantilevers down a hillside on a dead-end street in the heart of town. **Pros:** warm, welcoming rooms with decent views; good price for Patagonia; friendly staff. **Cons:** steep walk home; can't compete with the views from the larger hotels farther uphill; noise travels through walls. ⑤ *Rooms from: US$125 ⌧ Sarmiento 310, at G. Paz, Ushuaia ☎ 2901/437–245 ⊕ www.patagoniajarke.com.ar ⇆ 15 rooms* ⎮○⎮ *Breakfast.*

$$
HOTEL

⌂ **Hotel Fueguino.** In downtown Ushuaia, the Fueguino boasts all the modern amenities: a conference center; a gym; a spa; shuttle service; outgoing, professional, multilingual staff; and one of the better Wi-Fi signals in town. **Pros:** all the modern conveniences; central location; friendly staff. **Cons:** some street noise; small rooms; weak Wi-Fi in rooms. ⑤ *Rooms from: US$180 ⌧ Gobernador Deloqui 1282, Ushuaia ☎ 2901/424–894 ⊕ www.fueguinohotel.com.ar ⇆ 53 rooms* ⎮○⎮ *Breakfast.*

$$$
HOTEL

⌂ **Hotel Los Yámanas.** This cozy hotel 4 km (3 miles) from the center of town is named after the local tribe and offers a rustic mountain aesthetic. **Pros:** some stunning views from rooms; peaceful location; sauna is very nice. **Cons:** far from town; questionable taste in decoration; Wi-Fi not strong in rooms. ⑤ *Rooms from: US$230 ⌧ Costa de los Yámanas 2850, Km 4, Ushuaia ☎ 2901/446–809 ⊕ www.hotelyamanas.com.ar ⊗ Closed May ⇆ 41 rooms* ⎮○⎮ *Breakfast.*

$$
HOTEL

⌂ **Hotel y Resort Las Hayas.** In the wooded foothills of the Andes, Las Hayas is slightly dated in its facilities, but the views overlooking the town and channel below still make it worth the trip. **Pros:** great views; delicious restaurant; relaxing spa. **Cons:** decor doesn't suit everyone; facilities dated; rooms could use some revamping. ⑤ *Rooms from: US$170 ⌧ Camino Luís Martial 1650, Km 3, Ushuaia ☎ 2901/442–000 ⊕ www.lashayashotel.com ⇆ 88 rooms* ⎮○⎮ *Breakfast.*

$$$
B&B/INN

⌂ **La Tierra de Leyendas.** This adorable B&B is a honeymooners' delight, thanks to the multiple personal touches, from homecooked cuisine to family photos on the walls. **Pros:** tasty food in restaurant; enthusiastic, personal, and attentive service; all seven rooms have views. **Cons:** the street name is no joke—it's insanely windy; immediate surroundings are a bit barren; closed during winter. ⑤ *Rooms from: US$208 ⌧ Tierra de Vientos 2448, Ushuaia ☎ 2901/446–565 ⊕ www.tierradeleyendas.com.ar ⊗ Closed mid-Apr.–mid-July ⇆ 7 rooms* ⎮○⎮ *Breakfast.*

$$ ⊞ **Los Acebos.** From the owners of Las Hayas (just around the corner
HOTEL on the winding mountain road), Los Acebos is a modern hotel on a
FAMILY forested ridge with a commanding view over the Beagle Channel; spa-
cious and superclean rooms feature the same iconoclastic decor as Las
Hayas, including the trademark fabric-padded walls, only this time with
a '60s-style color scheme. **Pros:** spacious rooms; expansive views of the
channel; friendly staff. **Cons:** out of town; no spa; simple breakfast.
$ *Rooms from: US$185* ⊠ *Luis F. Martial 1911, Ushuaia* ☎ *2901/442–
200, 2901/430–710* ⊕ *www.losacebos.com.ar* ⇌ *60 rooms.*

$$$$ ⊞ **Los Cauquenes Resort and Spa.** Right on the shore of the Beagle Chan-
HOTEL nel about 8 km (5 miles) west of town, this resort is in a private com-
Fodor'sChoice munity with privileged beach access and a nature hike that starts right
★ outside your room. **Pros:** luxurious spa offers comprehensive range of
treatments and massages; free transfer into city; private boat excur-
sions offered. **Cons:** rooms can get uncomfortably hot; thin walls can
make for noisy nights; outside of town. $ *Rooms from: US$320* ⊠ *De
la Ermita 3462, Barrio Bahía Cauquén, Ushuaia* ☎ *2901/441–300*
⊕ *www.loscauquenesushuaia.com.ar* ⇌ *54 rooms* ⦿ *Breakfast.*

NIGHTLIFE

Bar Ideal. This cozy and historic bar and café opens from 9 am onward.
⊠ *San Martín 393, at Roca, Ushuaia* ☎ *2901/437–860* ⊕ *www.elba-
rideal.com.*

El Náutico. The biggest and most popular pub in town, El Náutico
attracts a young crowd with disco and techno music. ⊠ *Belgrano 21,
Ushuaia* ⊘ *Closed Sun.–Thurs.*

Tante Sara. This popular café-bar in the heart of town has a casual, old-
world feel. Locals kick back with a book or a beer; they pour the local
artisanal brews, too. During the day it's one of the few eateries to defy
the 3–6 pm siesta and stays open late. Their other branch, at San Martín
175, closes at 8:30 pm. ⊠ *San Martín 701, Ushuaia* ☎ *2901/423–912,
2901/433–710* ⊕ *www.tantesara.com.*

SHOPPING

Boutique del Libro–Antartida y Patagonia. Part of a bookstore chain, this
branch specializes in Patagonian and polar exploration. Along with
dozens of maps and picture books, postcards, and posters, it offers
adventure classics detailing every Southern expedition from Darwin's
Voyage of the Beagle to Ernest Shackleton's incredible journeys of Ant-
arctic survival. While books in English are hard to come by in the rest
of Argentina, here you're spoiled for choice, and the Antarctica trip
logbooks on sale at the counter might inspire you to extend your travel
farther south. ⊠ *San Martín 1120, Ushuaia* ☎ *2901/4245–750.*

Laguna Negra. If you can't get to South America's chocolate capital Bari-
loche, you'll find some of the best sweets in Argentina at this boutique/
café in the center of town. Planks of homemade chocolate include coco-
nut crunches, fudges, and brittles, along with Tierra del Fuego's best
selection of artisanal beers, chutneys, and spices. In the small coffee shop
at the back, drop a glorious slab of dark chocolate into a mug of pip-
ing hot milk—one of the best *submarinos* in town. Locals pop in for a
quick cup of hot chocolate at all hours, even as other cafés close for the

10

lull between 3 and 8 in the evening. If you get hooked, there's another branch on the main street of El Calafate. ✉ *San Martín 513, Ushuaia* ☎ *02901/431–144, 2901/431–144* ⊕ *www.lagunanegra.com.ar.*

PARQUE NACIONAL TIERRA DEL FUEGO, ARGENTINA

21 km (13 miles) west of Ushuaia.

This park is one of the main reasons that travelers make a trip to the tip of Argentina. Its deep forests, glistening lakes, and wind-whipped trees will not disappoint. An easy day trip from Ushuaia, this 60,000-hectare park offers varied outdoor experiences and many wildlife-spotting opportunities.

EXPLORING

Fodor's Choice ★ **Parque Nacional Tierra del Fuego.** The pristine park offers a chance to wander through peat bogs, stumble upon hidden lakes, trek through native *canelo, lenga,* and wild cherry forests, and experience the wonders of wind-whipped Tierra del Fuego's rich flora and fauna. Everywhere, lichens line the trunks of the ubiquitous lenga trees, and "chinese lantern" parasites hang from the branches.

Another thing you'll see everywhere are the results of government folly, in the form of *castoreros* (beaver dams) and lodges. Fifty beaver couples were first brought here from Canada in 1948 so that they would breed and create a fur industry. In the years since, without any predators, the beaver population has exploded to plague proportions (more than 100,000) and now represents a major threat to the forests, as the dams flood the roots of the trees; you can see their effects on parched dead trees on the lake's edge. Believe it or not, the government used to pay hunters a bounty for each beaver they killed (they had to show a tail and head as proof). To make matters worse, the government, after creating the beaver problem, introduced weasels to kill the beavers, but the weasels killed birds instead; they then introduced foxes to kill the beavers and weasels, but they also killed the birds. With eradication efforts failing, some tour operators have accepted them as a permanent presence and now offer beaver-viewing trips.

Visits to the park, which is tucked up against the Chilean border, are commonly arranged through tour companies. Trips range from bus tours to horseback riding to more adventurous excursions, such as canoe trips across Lapataia Bay. Entrance to the park is about $20.

Several private bus companies travel through the park making numerous stops; you can get off the bus, explore the park, and then wait for the next bus to come by or trek to the next stop (the service operates only in summer; check providers with the tourism office). Another option is to drive to the park on R3 (take it until it ends and you see the famous sign indicating the end of the Pan-American Highway, which starts 17,848 km [11,065 miles] away in Alaska, and ends here). If you don't have a car, you can also hire a private *remis* (taxi) to spend a few hours driving through the park, including the Pan-American terminus, and perhaps combining the excursion with the Tren del Fin del Mundo. Trail and camping information is available at the park-entrance ranger

station or at the Ushuaia tourist office. At the park entrance is a gleaming restaurant and teahouse set amid the hills, Patagonia Mia (⊕ *www.patagoniamia.com*); it's a great place to stop for tea or coffee, or a full meal of roast lamb or Fuegian seafood. A nice excursion in the park is by boat from lovely Bahía Ensenada to **Isla Redonda**, a wildlife refuge where you can follow a footpath to the western side and see a wonderful view of the Canal Beagle. This is included on some of the day tours; it's harder to arrange on your own, but you can contact the tourist office to try. While on Isla Redonda you can send a postcard and get your passport stamped at the world's southernmost post office. You can also see the Ensenada bay and island (from afar) from a point on the shore that is reachable by car.

Other highlights of the park include the spectacular mountain-ringed lake, **Lago Roca**, as well as **Laguna Verde**, a lagoon whose green color comes from algae at its bottom. Much of the park is closed from roughly June through September, when the descent to Bahía Ensenada is blocked by up to 6 feet of snow. Even in May and October, chains for your car are a good idea. No hotels are within the park—the only one burned down in the 1980s, and you can see its carcass as you drive by—but there are three simple camping areas around Lago Roca. Tours to the park are run by **All Patagonia** (⊕ *www.allpatagonia.com*). ⊕ *www.parquesnacionales.gob.ar* ✉ *$20.*

EN ROUTE

If you're in Ushuaia in the days leading up to New Year's Eve, drop in on **La Pista del Andino** campsite, on the edge of town. You'll be dwarfed by a mad mix of four-wheel-drive vehicles, enormous customized German trucks, and worn-out bicycles with beaten panniers. It's a tradition among overland explorers to spend Christmas and New Year's in the southernmost city in the world, and this turns out to be one of the most unusual "motorhog" celebrations around. Their routes zigzag across South America and are often painted on the sides of their vehicles—which have been known to be equipped with everything from rooftop tents to satellite dishes. Travelers share stories of crossing places like Siberia or northern Africa, and if you're lucky you'll encounter some who've ridden, driven, or pedaled the Pan-American Highway all the way from Alaska down to Ushuaia, a 17,000-mile journey that takes years to complete.

10

SPORTS AND THE OUTDOORS
FISHING

The rivers of Tierra del Fuego are home to trophy-size freshwater trout—including browns, rainbows, and brooks. Both fly- and spin-casting are available. The fishing season runs November through April; license fees range from $50 per week to $65 per season for nonresidents. Fishing expeditions are organized by the various local companies.

Asociación de Caza y Pesca. Founded in 1959, the Asociación de Caza y Pesca is the principal hunting and fishing organization in the city. ✉ *Av. Maipú 822* ☎ *2901/423–168* ⊕ *www.cazaypescaushuaia.org.*

Rumbo Sur. The city's oldest travel agency can assist in setting up fishing trips. ✉ *Av. San Martín 350* ☎ *2901/421–139* ⊕ *www.rumbosur.com.ar.*

Wind Fly. In summer this outfitter is dedicated exclusively to fishing, and offers classes and arranges trips. ⊠ *Av. 25 de Mayo 155, Ushuaia* ☏ *2901/431–713* ⊕ *www.windflyushuaia.com.ar.*

MOUNTAIN BIKING

A mountain bike is an excellent mode of transport in Ushuaia, giving you the freedom to roam without the rental car price tag. Good mountain bikes normally cost about $12 for a half day or $20 for a full day. Guided tours are about the same price.

All Patagonia. Guided bicycle tours (including rides through the national park) are organized by All Patagonia. ⊠ *Juana Fadul 58, Ushuaia* ☏ *2901/433–622* ⊕ *www.allpatagonia.com.*

Rumbo Sur. One of the city's biggest travel agencies, Rumbo Sur can arrange cycling trips. ⊠ *San Martín 350, Ushuaia* ☏ *2901/421–139* ⊕ *www.rumbosur.com.ar.*

Ushuaia Extreme. You can rent bikes or do a tour with Ushuaia Extreme. ⊠ *San Martín 830, Ushuaia* ☏ *2901/434–373* ⊕ *www. ushuaiaextremo.com.*

SCENIC FLIGHTS

The gorgeous scenery and island topography of the area is readily appreciated on a Cessna tour.

Aeroclub Ushuaia. Half-hour- and hour-long trips are available through Aeroclub Ushuaia. The half-hour flight ($95 per passenger with a group; $125 for single passengers) with a local pilot takes you over Ushuaia, Tierra del Fuego National Park, and the Beagle Channel with views of area glaciers, waterfalls, and snowcapped islands south to Cape Horn. A 60-minute flight ($155 per passenger with a group; $205 for single passengers) crosses the Andes to Escondida and Fagnano lakes. ⊠ *Antiguo Aeropuerto, Luis Pedro Fique 151, Ushuaia* ☏ *2901/421–717* ⊕ *www.aeroclubushuaia.org.ar.*

Heli-Ushuaia. All sorts of helicopter trips are available from Heli-Ushuaia, beginning with a seven-minute spin at $99 per person. There are plenty of longer trips and excursions if you have money to burn. ⊠ *Laserre 108, Ushuaia* ☏ *2901/444–444, 2901/444–444* ⊕ *www. heliushuaia.com.ar.*

SKIING

Canopy Ushuaia. Located at the Martial Glaciar, Canopy Ushuaia offers skiing in winter and canopy lines in summer. ⊠ *Cerro Martial, Luis Fernando Martial 3551, Ushuaia* ☏ *2901/1550–3767* ⊕ *www.canopyushuaia.com.ar.*

Cerro Castor. With off-piste and alpine skiing and almost guaranteed snow, this has become a popular ski haunt for European Olympic teams looking for summer snow. Pistes range from beginners to black-diamond runs with more than 31 trails and four high-speed lifts. You can rent skis and snowboards and take ski lessons at this resort 26 km (17 miles) northeast of Ushuaia on R3. Day passes are around 850 pesos in high season, and there are restaurants, bars, and a ski lodge on-site. The resort is open June to October, depending on snow. ⊠ *Ruta 3 Km 26, Ushuaia* ☏ *2901/499–301* ⊕ *www.cerrocastor.com.*

Club Andino. Ushuaia is the cross-country skiing (*esqui de fondo* in Spanish) center of South America, thanks to enthusiastic Club Andino members who took to the sport in the 1980s and made the forested hills of a high valley about 20 minutes from town a favorite destination for skiers. It's a magnet for international ski teams who come from Europe to train in the northern summer. ✉ *Fadul 50, Ushuaia* ☎ *2901/440–732* ⊕ *www.clubandinoushuaia.com.ar.*

Haruwen. Here, you can snowmobile in the winter, and ride a buggie in the summer. Countryside lamb cookouts are offered all year-round. ⊕ *www.haruwen.com.ar.*

PUERTO WILLIAMS, CHILE

82 km (50 miles) southeast of Ushuaia, Argentina.

On an island southeast of Ushuaia, the town of Puerto Williams is the southernmost permanent settlement in the world (it's closer to the South Pole than to the northern border of Chile). Even though Ushuaia in Argentina often makes this claim, Ushuaia is in fact the southernmost *city,* although many here consider Puertio Williams to be a city, too. Originally called Puerto Luisa, it was renamed in 1956 in honor of the military officer who took possession of the Estrecho de Magallanes for Chile in 1843, just after the country was founded. Most of the 2,500 residents are troops at the naval base, but there are several hundred civilians in the adjacent village. A tiny community of indigenous Yaghan peoples makes its home in the nearby Ukika village.

GETTING HERE AND AROUND

Even though it's a short distance across the Canal Beagle from Ushuaia, there are no regular ferry services from Argentina to Puerto Williams. This is due in part to, according to whom you talk to, the desire among tour operators in Ushuaia to restrict the smaller Chilean town's claims to the lucrative tourist market. Aeroclub Ushuaia can organize private flights to Puerto Williams, as can Ushuaia Boating, although both are quite pricey.

Stop in at the Oficina de Turismo at Ibáñez 130 (☎ *61/2621–011*), but don't expect much beyond maps. Accommodation offerings are simple and huddled around the center of town.

EXPLORING

Aerovís DAP. Weather permitting, Aerovís DAP offers charter flights over Cabo de Hornos, the southernmost tip of South America. Although the water looks placid from the air, strong westerly winds make navigating around Cape Horn treacherous. Over the last few centuries, hundreds of ships have met their doom here trying to sail to the Pacific. ✉ *Av. Bernardo O'Higgins 891, Punta Arenas* ☎ *61/2616–100* ⊕ *www.dapairline.com.*

Museo Martín Gusinde. For a quick history lesson on how Puerto Williams evolved, and some insight into the indigenous peoples, visit the Museo Martín Gusinde, named for the renowned anthropologist who traveled and studied in the region between 1918 and 1924. ✉ *Aragay 1, Puerto Williams* ☎ *61/2621–043* ⊕ *www.museomartingusinde.cl* 🎫 *500 pesos.*

WHERE TO STAY

🖼 **Lakutaia Hotel.** The most southern luxury hotel in the world, Hotel Lakutaia takes advantage of the area's beautiful surroundings to offer a range of unique outdoors activities including kayaking and trekking in Lauta, mountain biking, golf, horseback riding, sailing, walks to Castors Lagoon, and matches of Rayuela, a typical Chilean sport. **Pros:** offers an impressive range of activities; reaching untouched parts of Tierra del Fuego; lovely decor. **Cons:** comes with a high price tag; transfers are bumpy; excursions are all weather-dependent. $ *Rooms from: 160000 pesos* ✉ *Seno Lauta s/n, Puerto Williams* ☎ *61/2621–721* ⊕ *www.lakutaia.cl* ⤴ *24 rooms* ❘O❘ *Breakfast.*

SPORTS AND THE OUTDOORS

HIKING

Cerro Bandera. A hike to the top of Cerro Bandera is well worth the effort if you have the stamina. The trail is well marked but very steep. The view from the top toward the south to the Cordón Dientes del Perro (Dog's Teeth Range) is impressive, but looking northward over the Beagle Channel to Argentina—with Puerto Williams nestled below and Ushuaia just visible to the west—is truly breathtaking. Near the start of the trail, 3 km (2 miles) west of Puerto Williams, is the Parque Etnobotánico Omora visitor center, which got its name from the Yahgan word for hummingbird. In the Yahgan cosmology, Omora was more than a bird; he was also a revered mythological hero. The Omora Foundation is a Chilean NGO dedicated to biocultural conservation in the extreme southern tip of South America. Their work led UNESCO to designate the Cape Horn Biosphere Reserve in 2005. Within the park's interpretive trails, explore the various habitats of the Isla Navarino region: coastal coigue forests, lenga parks, nirre forests, sphagnum bogs, beaver wetlands, and alpine heath. Additionally, the Robalo River runs through the park and provides potable water to the town. ✉ *3 km (2 miles) west of Puerto Williams, Puerto Williams.*

EASTER ISLAND

WELCOME TO EASTER ISLAND

TOP REASONS TO GO

★ **Astounding archaeology:** Whether it's the ubiquitous moai statues, petroglyphs, or cave paintings, Easter Island is an open-air museum with a turbulent and mysterious past.

★ **Wonderful walking:** Easter Island's rolling hills, with the white-flecked ocean rarely out of sight, hold some glorious walking trails, especially along the north coast.

★ **Extraordinary diving:** Diving into the cobalt-blue waters is one of the most popular pastimes on Easter Island. Visibility is up to 120 feet, so you don't miss the bright tropical fish or the turtles. Coral formations like the Cavern of the Three Windows make for an unforgettable underwater experience.

★ **Souvenir shopping:** Locals have carved a living out of the stone and driftwood, making handicrafts like miniature moai, elaborate bowls, eerie masks, and shell jewelry.

It's nearly impossible to get lost on Easter Island. It's just 22 km (14 miles) from end to end and has only three roads that fan out from Hanga Roa: one crosses the island northeast to Anakena Beach; another curves along the southeastern coast before turning north and then west to Anakena; and the third snakes around Rano Kau volcano to the southwest.

1 **Hanga Roa.** Almost all hotels on Easter Island are in or near Hanga Roa, the only town, as are the offices of tour operators and car rental companies. Hanga Roa also has its own sights, including the Iglesia Hanga Roa, which has a magnificent view of the Pacific Ocean. Next door is the better of the town's two craft markets. A short walk along the coast to the north leads to the unique town cemetery, the Tahai moai statue, and the island's small but attractively didactic anthropology museum.

2 **The Southeastern Circuit.** Most of the archaeological sites on the island are along its southeastern coast. Lined with moai, including Ahu Tongariki with its 15 statues, re-erected after being toppled by a tidal wave, this road also leads to Ankena Beach and the so-called moai factory in the side of Rano Raraku volcano.

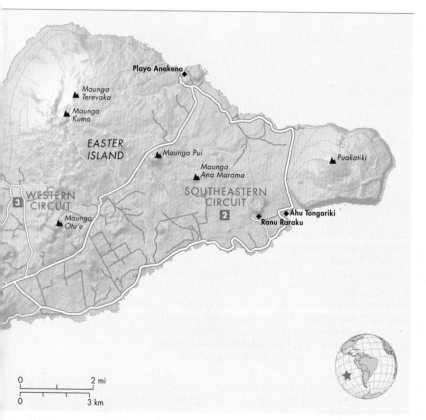

Playa Anakena

Maunga
Terevaka

Maunga
Kuma

EASTER
ISLAND

Maunga Pui

Maunga
Ana Marama

Puakatiki

3 WESTERN
CIRCUIT

SOUTHEASTERN
CIRCUIT

2

Maunga
Otu'u

Ahu Tongariki

Ranu Raraku

0   2 mi

0   3 km

3 **The Western Circuit.**
A visit to the west of the
island has really only one
objective—to see the stone
houses and petroglyphs in
Orongo ceremonial village,
the center of the island's
birdman cult. On the way
is the water-filled crater of
the now-extinct Rano Kau
volcano.

Updated by
Sorrel
Moseley-
Williams

Easter Island, the most isolated inhabited island in the world—2,985 km (1,850 miles) from its nearest populated neighbor and 3,700 km (2,295 miles) off the Chilean coast—is a tiny speck in the Pacific ocean. Dotted over the island are hundreds of giant stone statues called moai, which overlook the ruins of the settlements that constructed them. The mystery of the moai, why the Rapa Nui (as the locals call themselves) constructed and later toppled them, plus the area's natural beauty, continue to attract explorers, archaeologists, and tourists to this far-flung destination.

The practice of carving, transporting, and erecting the large-headed, small-bodied stone moai, sometimes reaching 37 feet high, was central to the historical culture of Easter Island. Said to represent deceased leaders, the statues stand on an ahu, or burial platform, to watch over the communities they had once ruled. Several reconstructions and archaeological digs have confirmed the Rapa Nui had strong engineering skills, because the moai weigh many tons, and putting them in place using traditional materials and techniques must have been a tremendous strain on human and natural resources.

Various ahus and their moai have been reconstructed, inviting visitors to marvel at the enormous effort required to build them. Many travelers visit, or leave, with various questions; first, how did the Rapa Nui get here? Then, why did they build and how did they move the moai? Why were the moai later toppled?

Theories abound, and a combination of local oral history as well as European observations and guesswork tell the following story. King Hotu Matu'a and his family sailed here, and landed on a beach at the north shore, which began the population of the land. Norwegian explorer Thor Heyerdahl believed that these original settlers came from South America, and he sailed from Peru in a balsa-wood boat called the Kon-Tiki in 1947, to prove that it was possible. However, it is now commonly believed that the Rapa Nui are of Polynesian descent, and indeed this influence is seen in the traditional dance, food names and preparation, and the greeting used all over the island: *iorana*.

Easter Island's peak population is estimated to have once been between 10,000 and 15,000 people but from 1722, when the first European, Dutch Jacob Roggeveen set foot on the island, to the 1774 arrival of British Captain James Cook, there was extreme population loss and many moai were toppled. Less than a hundred years later, 1,000 islanders were captured by Peruvian slave traders to work in guano mines. When they were eventually returned to the island, these freed slaves brought smallpox with them, further decimating the population down to just 110 people.

11

Chile claimed the island in 1888, and, with little regard for the inhabitants, leased it to a British sheep company, which corralled the Rapa Nui people into the village of Hanga Roa. The company departed in 1953, but it wasn't until 1967, when the airport was constructed, that the quality of life began to improve again for the people of Easter Island.

Today, geographical isolation and archaeological history are the two main draws for travelers. A visit to the quarry at Rano Raraku, where most moai were sourced and sculpted, is especially impressive, considering the engineering effort and know-how required. The Rapa Nui also had the only written language in Polynesia, called rongo rongo, which still hasn't been deciphered; petroglyphs can be seen at sites such as the ceremonial village of Orongo where the "birdman" culture thrived.

The culture of the Rapa Nui is another attraction to Easter Island, which despite its tumultuous history, continues to thrive, in language, cuisine, carving, dance, song, and the summer festival of Tapati, which takes place every February. There is also a special energy or mana (as it is locally called) at Te Pito o Te Henua (the navel of the world) that adds an intangible element to visits here, making a journey to Easter Island a once-in-a-lifetime trip that few get to share.

PLANNER

WHEN TO GO

Most people visit in summer, between December and March, often coinciding with Tapati Rapa Nui, a two-week celebration of music and dancing in the first two weeks of February. Temperatures can soar above 27°C (81°F) in summer. In winter, temperatures reach an average of 22°C (72°F), although brisk winds can often make it feel much cooler. Be sure to bring a light jacket. The wettest months are May and June.

FESTIVALS

The annual Tapati Rapa Nui festival, a two-week celebration of the island's heritage, takes place every year in February. The normally laid-back Hanga Roa bursts to life in a colorful music and dance festival. The Día de la Lengua (Language Day), which usually takes place in early November, celebrates the Rapa Nui language.

PLANNING YOUR TIME

In a few days, you can visit the island's major sights. Spend one day in Hanga Roa, stopping by the Iglesia Hanga Roa, the cemetery, and the Museo Antropológico Padre Sebastián Englert. Finish the day with sunset at Tahai. On your second day, tour the coastal road, visiting the hundreds of moai in the quarry at Rano Raraku and the lineup of 15 at nearby Ahu Tongariki. On your last day, visit Rano Kau volcanic crater, where the ceremonial village of Orongo is. In the afternoon head inland to the small quarry of Puna Pau to see the seven statues of Ahu Akivi and where the red *pukao* (topknots) that crown some moai were crafted.

Almost all businesses close for a few hours in the afternoon. Most are open 9 to 1 and 4 to 8, but a few stay open late into the evening. Many are closed Sunday. Smaller restaurants and shops don't usually accept

credit cards. Be aware that outside of Hanga Roa, the only place to buy anything to eat or drink is at Anakena, or at one of the more remote luxury hotels, which are quite off the beaten path.

GETTING HERE AND AROUND

AIR TRAVEL

Easter Island's shoe-box-size Aeropuerto Internacional Mataveri is on the southern edge of Hanga Roa. LATAM Airlines operates all flights from Santiago to the east and Tahiti to the west. Eight flights a week arrive from Santiago throughout the year (twice on Monday and Thursday, none on Tuesday), and one from Tahiti. Planes are often full in January and February, so it's best to book well in advance.

Tickets to Easter Island are expensive—up to $1,000 for a round-trip flight from Santiago. There are better deals, however, if you buy your Santiago to Easter Island ticket as part of a multileg ticket that includes your flight from your city of departure to Santiago.

At the airport, the CONAF (national parks service) office outpost sells tickets for Rapa Nui National Park, which you need to get into all archaeological sites. As these tickets are sold in only two other places (Central Comunidad Indígena Ma'u Henua on Atamu Tekena Street and the CONAF office in the Mataveri neighborhood), it's usually best to pay the US$80 fee right at the airport.

Contacts Aeropuerto Internacional Mataveri. ⊠ *Av. Hotu Matu'a s/n, Hanga Roa* ☎ *32/2210–0277, 32/2210–0278.* **LATAM.** ⊠ *Av. Atamu Tekena s/n, Hanga Roa, Hanga Roa* ☎ *32/2210–0279* ⊕ *www.latam.com.*

CAR TRAVEL

To see Easter Island's less traveled areas, a four-wheel-drive vehicle is sometimes a necessity. There are three well-maintained, paved roads. The first traverses the island from Hanga Roa to Playa Anakena, the second goes to Ahu Akivi and forks off of the Anakena road, and the third runs along the southern coast. Other roads are loose gravel or packed dirt (or mud if it has rained recently), particularly those that take visitors to some of the most isolated spots. Though in some cases, there are no roads at all.

There are no international car rental chains with offices on Easter Island, but there are two reputable local agencies, Insular and Oceanic, which have vehicles for rent, as do the main tour operators. The minimum charge is about 50,000 pesos per day for a basic Jeep. Helmet use is mandatory on an ATV or scooter, which rent for 50,000 pesos and 30,000 pesos, respectively. If you plan on visiting during January and February, call a few days ahead to reserve a car.

You can also rent cars at many restaurants, souvenir shops, and guesthouses. If you ask around, you may find a significantly cheaper rate than what the rental companies charge. It is important to note that there is no vehicle insurance on Easter Island and any damage is charged to the client.

Contacts Aku Aku. ⊠ *Av. Tu'u Koihu s/n, Hanga Roa, Hanga Roa* ☎ *3/2210–0770* ⊕ *www.akuakuturismo.cl.* **Insular.** ⊠ *Av. Atamu Tekena s/n, Hanga Roa* ☎ *3/2100–0480* ⊕ *www.rentainsular.cl.* **Kia Koe.** ⊠ *Av. Atamu Tekena s/n,*

Hanga Roa ☏ 3/2210–0852 ⊕ *www.kiakoetour.cl.* **Oceanic Rapa Nui.** ✉ *Av. Atamu Tekena s/n, Hanga Roa, Hanga Roa* ☏ 3/2210–0985 *Atamu Tekena, 3/2255–1392 Te Pito O Te Henua* ⊕ *www.rentacaroceanic.com.*

TAXI TRAVEL

With no buses on Easter Island, taxis are a common form of transport, so it's never difficult to flag one down. Vehicles of the three main companies are identified by a yellow sign on the roof, but many local car owners also work as taxi drivers. They have a cardboard sign on the windscreen (and tend to be cheaper than radio taxis). Most trips to destinations in Hanga Roa should cost no more than 3,000 pesos (rates are lower for residents), but after 8 or 9 pm the price generally goes up to 5,000.

RESTAURANTS

Compared to mainland Chile, Easter Island is expensive. Almost everything from petrol to vegetables has to be shipped or flown in, and you may sometimes feel you're not getting value for money. The upside to dining here is wonderful fresh fish and, in summer, mangoes and small, sweet pineapples. The guavas on the bushes are ripe (and plentiful) when yellow, and there are some other interesting island-only fruits around, which you can often try in the ice cream. Don't leave Easter Island without trying the local banana bread known as *poe* (best bought at the Riro bakery opposite the church), at 1,000 pesos per hearty square.

At restaurants, local fish such as kana kana and tuna are nearly always on the menu. The only restaurants are in Hanga Roa or at the luxury hotels. There are some simple snack bars at Playa Anakena, and a few other fast food places around town, serving sandwiches and empanadas. Most other restaurants serve fish, salads, ceviche, and international dishes like pasta; there are plenty of imported ingredients, such as shrimp, which tend to come from Ecuador.

Most restaurants are open for lunch and dinner, and a few scattered cafés open for breakfast. At restaurants, check your bill before leaving a tip; most places add a 10% service charge (which you are not legally obliged to pay). *Restaurant reviews have been shortened. For full information, visit Fodors.com.*

HOTELS

A key factor in where to stay is whether you're prepared to rent a car or bike or do quite a lot of walking. There are a few good hotels in the center of Hanga Roa, the only town, but most others are on the town's outskirts, a 15-minute walk or a 3,000-peso taxi ride away. Budget accommodation can be found at *residenciales*—often a few rooms attached to a private home—but standards vary enormously; rather than booking ahead, try to arrive on an early plane and talk to the representatives of the residenciales, or take a taxi into town and scout out the best bargains. Except in January and February, rooms are always available. The three main luxury hotels require a vehicle, though they, like most other hotels, provide transportation to and from the airport.

Most hotels now take credit cards, but quite a few add a surcharge (as much as 10%). Ask ahead and, if there's a surcharge, consider getting money out of one of the two ATMs. *Hotel reviews have been shortened. For full information, visit Fodors.com.*

WHAT IT COSTS IN CHILEAN PESOS (IN THOUSANDS)			
$	**$$**	**$$$**	**$$$$**
Restaurants			
Under 6	6–9	10–13	over 13
Hotels			
Under 51	51–85	86–115	over 115

Restaurant prices are the average cost of a main course price at dinner or, if dinner is not served, at lunch. Hotel prices are the lowest cost of a standard double room in high season, excluding tax.

ESSENTIALS

Visitor Information Sernatur. ⊠ *Av. Policarpo Toro s/n, Hanga Roa, Hanga Roa* ☎ *3/2210–0255* ⊕ *www.sernatur.cl.*

TOURS

There are several ways visitors arrange tours on Easter Island. Book ahead of time before setting foot on the island, which is recommended even for the plan-averse, especially for more strenuous, time-consuming hikes or horseback rides to the north coast and Poike. Fans of the all-inclusive experience can make the most of hotel-based tours, while more spontaneous travelers can arrange tours on-site with hotels and agencies, which can get you out the following, or even same day, depending on the activity. Before visiting Rapa Nui National Park, make sure you purchase your national park ticket from CONAF as agencies do not include them in packages.

Another option is to simply wander the streets of Hanga Roa, looking for storefronts that offer tours, which can also yield good results, but may not be the most time-efficient and keeps you away from some of the smaller, more innovative agencies. Sernatur, the local tourist office, has extensive knowledge of options and opportunities, and can point you in the right direction.

Easter Island Travel. An unlikely transplant to Easter Island, Marcus Edensky, a Swedish man married to a Rapa Nui woman, runs some of the best-reviewed tours on the island. An outdoorsman, he leads multiday hiking tours, horseback riding, and spiritual tours, among others, often on the north coast. He speaks Swedish, Spanish, English, and Rapa Nui. Easter Island Travel specializes in small group tours, and the north coast tour ends (optionally) with *tunu ahi*, or food cooked directly on hot rocks. Private day-long hiking tours cost 91,000 pesos, and three-day adventure tours start at 875,000 pesos; both have a two-person minimum. ⊠ *Policarpo Toro, Hanga Roa* ☎ *9/7510–3841* ⊕ *www.easterisland.travel* ✉ *From 90000 pesos.*

Kava Kava Tours. This local company runs small full- and half-day tours taking in major sights, including moai and caves. One half-day tour goes to Puna Pau, the quarry from which the red stone topknots that

sat atop the moai were carved. Another day-long tour goes around the Poike Peninsula, the oldest part of the island, and one of two areas open to hikers or people on horseback with guides only and not accessible by vehicle. Prices are steep so team up with others to form a group of four and bring down costs. ⊠ *Av. Ana Tehe Tama, Hanga Roa* ☎ *9/7216–5015* ⊕ *www.kavakavatours.com* ✉ *From 193000 pesos.*

Kia Koe. One of the largest and oldest tour companies on the island, this company runs full- and half-day excursions with pick-up and drop-off from some of the major hotels. ⊠ *Av. Atamu Tekena s/n, Hanga Roa* ☎ *3/2210–0852* ⊕ *www.kiakoetour.cl* ✉ *From 20000 pesos.*

Makemake Tours & Rental. A metal sculpture of a bike signals the entrance to this shop, slightly hidden from the street. It rents mountain bikes and surfboards, both to use alone or with a guide and instructor. Guided walks, private tours, snorkeling, and boat and fishing tours are also available. A mountain bike rental runs 11,000 pesos for eight hours, 13,000 pesos for a day, and 21,000 pesos for two days. A guided day-tour on mountain bike is 26,000, and a horseback-riding tour over the north coast is 80,000 pesos per person, with a two-person minimum. ⊠ *Atamu Tekena s/n, Hanga Roa* ☎ *9/6212–7132* ✉ *From 25000 pesos.*

HANGA ROA

Hugging the coast on the northwest side is the island's capital of Hanga Roa. Of the 9,000 residents, about 3,000 are indigenous Rapa Nui and the rest are from continental Chile or abroad. Few people live outside Hanga Roa because the bulk of the island forms the Rapa Nui National Park or is state owned. The town's two main roads intersect a block from the ocean at a small plaza. Avenida Atamu Tekena, the road that runs the length of the village, is where to find most of the tourist-oriented businesses. Avenida Te Pito o Te Henua begins near the fishing pier and extends two blocks uphill to the church.

Buildings are not numbered and signs are nonexistent (street names are sometimes painted on curbstones), so finding a particular building can be frustrating at first. Locals give directions in terms of landmarks, so it's not a bad idea to take a walk around town as soon as you arrive to get your bearings. Important landmarks in town are the fishing cove and pier, the Catholic church, Cruz Verde pharmacy, and the LATAM (airline) office. A little farther away to the south and southeast, respectively are Hanga Pika pier and the airport.

EXPLORING

Caleta Hanga Roa. Colorful fishing boats bob up and down in the water at Hanga Roa's tiny jetty. Here you may see fisherfolk hauling in the day's tuna catch, or a boatload of divers returning from a trip to neighboring islets. Nearby is Ahu Tautira, a ceremonial platform with a restored moai. ⊠ *Av. Policarpo Toro at Av. Te Pito o Te Henua, Hanga Roa.* .

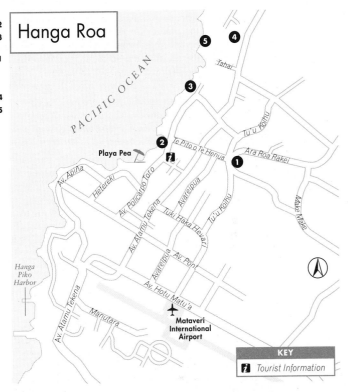

Cementerio. Hanga Roa's colorful walled cemetery occupies a prime position overlooking the Pacific and is visually unlike most. With artificial flower arrangements, white tombstones, and even some replica moai, the cemetery has a cheerful feeling. The central cross is erected on a *pukao*, the reddish topknot or hat that likely topped a moai at some point. The cemetery keeps expanding toward the ocean, but by 2020, the newly deceased will have to be buried elsewhere, as it will likely be full. Some Rapanui bury family members around the island, such as near Playa Ovahe, so you should be respectful should you come across burial sites. ⊠ *Av. Policarpo Toro at Petero Atamu, Hanga Roa.*

Iglesia Hanga Roa. Missionaries might have brought Christianity to Easter Island, but the Rapa Nui people brought their own beliefs to Christianity. Find the two intertwined in this white church on the hill overlooking Hanga Roa. The paintings of the Via Crucis on the walls are what you would find in any Catholic church, but the wood figures have a clear Rapa Nui flavor and one of the altars rests on a block of local volcanic stone. At the first mass on Sunday morning at 9 am, hymns are sung in Rapa Nui. ⊠ *Av. Te Pito o Te Henua s/n, Hanga Roa.*

FAMILY

Fodor's Choice

★

Museo Antropológico Padre Sebastián Englert. This small museum, named for a German priest who dedicated his life to improving conditions on Rapa Nui and is buried beside the church, provides an excellent

summary of the history of Easter Island and its way of life, as well as its native flora and fauna. Here, too, is one of the few female moai on the island and the replica of a coral eye found during the reconstruction of an ahu at Playa Anakena (the original is in storage after an attempted robbery). Texts are in Spanish and English, and the museum can easily overcrowd given its small size. ⊠ *Tahai s/n, Hanga Roa* ☎ *3/2255–1020* ⊕ *www.mapse.cl* ⊗ *Closed Mon.*

Tahai. The ancient ceremonial center of Tahai, where much of the annual Tapati Rapa Nui festival takes place, was restored in 1968 by archaeologist William Mulloy, who is buried nearby. Tahai consists of three separate ahus facing a wide plaza that once served as a community meeting place. You can still find the foundations of the boat-shape dwellings where religious and social leaders once lived. In the center is Ahu Tahai, which holds a single weathered moai. To the left is Ahu Vai Uri, where five moai, one little more than a stump, cast their stony gaze over the island. Also here is Ahu Kote Riku, with a splendid moai and red topknot intact; this is the only moai on the island to have its gleaming white eyes restored. ■TIP→ **This is an especially good place to come to see the island's blazing yellow sunsets.** ⊠ *On coast near Museo Antropológico Sebastián Englert, Hanga Roa.*

BEACHES

FAMILY **Playa Pea.** Hanga Roa has only two tiny beaches: Playa Pea, a stretch of sand near the bay where surfers go to catch waves, and another small beach on the northern edge of the town, with a sea pool for swimming. Both are popular among local families with small children. **Amenities:** food and drink. **Best for:** snorkeling; sunset; swimming. ⊠ *Policarpo Toro, Hanga Roa.*

WHERE TO EAT

$$$$ ✕ **Au Bout du Monde.** This Belgian–Polynesian restaurant serves some of
BELGIAN Easter Island's best food from the fish- and meat-based menu. Try the seared tuna with Tahitian vanilla sauce, and one of the many chocolate-based desserts. **Known for:** classy and eclectic dishes; buzzy atmosphere; ocean views. $ *Average main: 15000 pesos* ⊠ *Av. Policarpo Toro s/n, Hanga Roa* ☎ *3/2255–2060.*

$ ✕ **Café Caramelo.** This airy, colorful café serves the island's best home-
CAFÉ made cakes, including a fantastic cheesecake and fruit pie. The coffee is also better than most on the island, with beans sourced from major international roasters. **Known for:** excellent pastry selection; quick breakfasts; great coffee and smoothies. $ *Average main: 3500 pesos* ⊠ *Av. Atanu Tekena, Hanga Roa.*

$$$ ✕ **Haka Honu.** This festive restaurant on the street that runs along the
SEAFOOD beach serves hearty portions of local foods like *kana kana* (fish) and seafood. It is rumored to get some of the best picks of fish on the island. **Known for:** some of the island's best seafood; great cocktail menu; huge desserts. $ *Average main: 12000 pesos* ⊠ *Policarpo Toro s/n, Hanga Roa* ☎ *3/2255–2260* ⊗ *Closed Mon.*

$ ✕ **Kona Tunu Kai Hua María Pika.** This spot looks like a small, no-frills,
CHILEAN rustic shack, but at lunchtime it is always full, which speaks to the
food's quality. The menu is written on a flowery whiteboard on the wall
of the raw-wood interior and includes owner María Luisa Ikanakoi's
big, filling Chilean sandwiches as well as ceviche and a daily menu
for 5,000 pesos. **Known for:** well-priced lunches; huge sandwiches;
local crowd. $ *Average main: 5000 pesos* ⌂ *Av. Apiña s/n, Hanga Roa*
☎ 9/9140–6767 ⊟ No credit cards ⊘ No dinner.

$$$$ ✕ **La Kaleta.** This restaurant draws in patrons with its unbeatable,
SEAFOOD secluded views from the point of Caleta Hanga Roa, seen from the
deck by the breaking waves. Fish dishes can include prawn curry, warm
fish salad, and the grilled catch of the day. **Known for:** excellent seafood; panoramic view of the beach; spacious patio. $ *Average main:*
14000 pesos ⌂ *Caleta Hanga Roa, Hanga Roa* ☎ 3/2255–2244 ⊕ *www.*
lakaletarestaurant.com.

$ ✕ **Mikafe.** This coffee shop with outdoor seating down on the jetty
CAFÉ does swift business with hungry divers coming off the boats, locals
FAMILY needing coffee, and school kids in search of after-school ice cream.
Those ice-cream flavors include strawberry and cream, the unusual
pepino (a melonlike fruit), and occasionally, island-specific flavors
like *tipanie* (a flower). **Known for:** unique ice cream flavors; nice tea
selection; classic sandwiches for lunch. $ *Average main: 5000 pesos*
⌂ *Caleta Hanga Roa, Hanga Roa.*

$$ ✕ **Tataku Vave.** At Hanga Piko, the next bay south from Hanga Roa,
SEAFOOD this delicious, all-fish restaurant is worth the 15-minute walk. At
6,000 pesos, the set main course at lunchtime is a good value, but the
large portions of ceviche are even more popular. **Known for:** fresh
seafood; turtle-spotting on the restaurant grounds; amazing ocean
views. $ *Average main: 6000 pesos* ⌂ *Hanga Piko Jetty, Hanga Roa*
☎ 3/2255–1544 ⊟ No credit cards.

$$$$ ✕ **Te Moana.** If you stay any length of time on Easter Island, you may
SEAFOOD find yourself returning to this inviting blue and wood restaurant on
Fodor's Choice the waterfront with an expansive ocean view. The portions of fish,
★ meat, and pasta are generous, and the service is efficient. **Known for:**
wonderful views; great ceviche and Thai fish soup; nice cocktails and
beer list. $ *Average main: 14000 pesos* ⌂ *Policarpo Toro s/n, Hanga*
Roa ☎ 3/2255–1578 ⊘ Closed Sun.

WHERE TO STAY

$$$$ 🏨 **Altiplánico Rapa Nui.** This hotel, part of a chain of boutique hotels
HOTEL in popular Chilean vacation spots, has minimalist design—beds are
mattresses on a cement platform and some rooms have indoor–out-
door showers—and rooms that are really more like standalone cab-
ins, each one painted with a pattern representing the eye of a moai.
Pros: expansive coastal views; total peace and quiet; Aka Pu moai
visible from the hotel. **Cons:** 40-minute walk from Hanga Ro; car
or taxi needed to get elsewhere on the island; pricey for what you
get. $ *Rooms from: 175000 pesos* ⌂ *Sector Hinere s/n, Easter Island*
☎ 3/2255–2190 ⊕ *www.altiplanico.cl/altiplanico-rapa-nui-isla-de-*
pascua ⇥ 17 cabins ⦿ Breakfast.

Mysteries of the Moais

Most people are drawn to Easter Island by the moai, the stone statues that have puzzled and intrigued outsiders since the first Europeans arrived there over three centuries ago. These squat, minimalist figures with oversize heads are believed to have been the crowning glory of a family shrine, standing on an ahu—or stone platform—beneath which ancestors were buried and transmitted their mana, or power, to the living family chief. They most likely overlooked the settlements that erected them.

Most of the moai were carved at the Rano Raraku quarry in the east of the island, where many can still be seen at different stages of completion. That, in itself, was a mammoth task, with only stone tools to chisel the statues laboriously out of the volcanic hillside. It was, however, nothing compared to transporting the finished statues to their ahu. Oral tradition used to claim the moai "walked" to their destination, but most archaeologists believe they were either dragged on wooden platforms or rolled along on top of tree trunks. It's not clear how they could have been moved miles without damaging the statues en route, though the eye sockets were not carved until they arrived at the ahus.

Once the moai arrived at their ahu, how were they lifted into place? In 1955, Norwegian explorer Thor Heyerdahl and a team of a dozen men were able to raise the single moai on Ahu Ature Huki in 18 days. In 1960 archaeologists William Mulloy and Gonzalo Figueroa and their men raised the seven moai at Ahu Akivi. They struggled for a month to lift the first, but the last took only a week.

Both teams used the same method—lifting them with a stone ramp and wooden poles. This technique would be unwieldy for lifting the larger moai, however. It also fails to explain how the pukao, or topknots, were placed on many of the heads.

Why were the moai subsequently toppled? The reason posited by some is that creating them required a tremendous amount of natural resources, particularly wood, and as these were depleted, family groups that had once worked in harmony began to squabble, attacking the source of their opponent's mana—their moai.

That, at least, is the theory put forward by Jared Diamond in his book *Collapse: How Societies Choose to Fail or Succeed.* If that is the case, the moai are not only Easter Island's glory but, as the island was deforested, the cause of the decline of the civilization that created them. But, in a way, the moai are still serving their original purpose. Mana meant prosperity, and the moai continue to bring this today in the form of tourism.

It is unlikely that any additional moai will ever be stood back up. Archaeologists, such as Sergio Rapu, are looking at the possibility of leaving them where they are and using digital platforms to show both past (moais upright) and present (moais toppled) without damaging the statues.

$$
B&B/INN
Fodor'sChoice
★

Aukara Lodge. Located just behind the LATAM airline office, this *residencial* is owned by a history professor and a local sculptor, whose work is displayed in the adjacent art gallery. **Pros:** tours available; contact with local artists in the workshop; airport transport included. **Cons:** few rooms and high popularity make it difficult to get a space here; early booking is essential; credit cards not accepted. ⑤ *Rooms from: 70000 pesos* ✉ *Av. Pont s/n, Hanga Roa* ☎ *3/2210–0539* ⊕ *www.aukara.com* ▭ *No credit cards* ⤳ *5 rooms* ⦿ *Breakfast.*

$$
B&B/INN

Cabañas Manatea. These four cabins couldn't be more basic, with just a bed, a shower, and a shared kitchen, but they're spotlessly clean. **Pros:** right beside the Tahai moai, it's the perfect place to watch an Easter Island sunset; airport transfer included; great budget option. **Cons:** 15-minute walk or a 3,000-peso taxi ride from Hanga Roa; very basic; shared common spaces. ⑤ *Rooms from: 53000 pesos* ✉ *Sector Tahai s/n, Hanga Roa* ☎ *32/255–2234* ⊕ *www.cabanasmanatea.com* ▭ *No credit cards* ⤳ *4 cabins* ⦿ *No meals.*

$$
B&B/INN

Chez María Goretti. The beautiful garden and lovely, airy, plant-filled dining room are the main attractions of this guesthouse on the northern edge of town between Hanga Roa and Museo Antropológico Padre Sebastián Englert. **Pros:** newer rooms are good value; friendly atmosphere. **Cons:** older rooms could use a paint job; about a 10-minute uphill walk from town. ⑤ *Rooms from: 68000 pesos* ✉ *Av. Atamu Tekena s/n, Hanga Roa* ☎ *3/2210–0459* ⤳ *20 rooms* ⦿ *Breakfast.*

$$$$
RESORT

Explora Rapa Nui. This luxury property is built with local volcanic stone and imported wood, and curves along a hillside overlooking the island's south coast in an emulation of the ceremonial village at Orongo. **Pros:** well-guided hikes; excellent food; superb service. **Cons:** a 15-minute drive from Hanga Roa; somewhat isolated; incredibly expensive. ⑤ *Rooms from: 1575000 pesos* ✉ *Sector Vaihu s/n, Hanga Roa* ☎ *2/2395–2800* ⊕ *www.explora.com* ⤳ *30 rooms* ⦿ *All-inclusive.*

$$$$
RESORT
Fodor'sChoice
★

Hangaroa Eco Village & Spa. Green initiatives meet traditional architecture and hospitality at this peaceful retreat on the coast. **Pros:** fantastic luxury; environmentally sustainable; incredible spa. **Cons:** dinner menu doesn't vary much; minimum three-night stay; very expensive. ⑤ *Rooms from: 252000 pesos* ✉ *Av. Pont s/n, Hanga Roa* ☎ *2/2957–0300* ⊕ *www.hangaroa.cl* ⤳ *75 rooms* ⦿ *All-inclusive.*

$
B&B/INN

Hostal Taniera. The guest book of this little house, located by the side of the church, testifies to more than a decade of satisfied customers. **Pros:** awesome garden of coffee, cotton, and different varieties of banana trees; attractively decorated; environmentally friendly. **Cons:** very basic rooms; no free breakfast; might be too intimate for some. ⑤ *Rooms from: 50000 pesos* ✉ *Simón Paoa s/n, Hanga Roa* ☎ *3/2210–0491* ⊕ *www.taniera.cl* ▭ *No credit cards* ⤳ *3 rooms* ⦿ *No meals.*

$$$$
HOTEL

Hotel Gomero. A drive lined by palm and papaya trees leads to this charming small hotel. **Pros:** an inviting swimming pool sits in a beautifully attended garden; owners run a tour service; impeccably tidy. **Cons:** on the outskirts of town and up a hill; pool is a bit small; design is basic. ⑤ *Rooms from: 129500 pesos* ✉ *Av. Tu'u Koihu s/n, Hanga Roa* ☎ *3/2210–0313* ⊕ *www.hotelgomero.com* ⤳ *17 rooms* ⦿ *Breakfast.*

11

$$$$ **Hotel Iorana.** Perched high on a cliff jutting out into the ocean, this
HOTEL hotel entices its visitors with unmatched views. **Pros:** lovely setting;
rooms are attractively, if simply, decorated; airport transfer available. **Cons:** more expensive than other similar midrange hotels; 15- to
20-minute walk from town; can be crowded with tour groups. $ *Rooms
from: 127000 pesos ⊠ Ana Magaro s/n, Hanga Roa* ☎ *3/2210–0608*
⊕ *www.ioranahotel.cl ⇲ 52 rooms* ◉ *Some meals.*

$$$$ **Hotel Manavai.** This hotel has 30 simple wood-paneled rooms around
HOTEL a long garden that's perfect for kids to play in. **Pros:** perfect for fami-
FAMILY lies; peaceful garden; knowledgeable hosts. **Cons:** no ocean view from
rooms; simple decor; no free breakfast. $ *Rooms from: 123000 pesos*
⊠ *Av. Te Pito o Te Henua, Hanga Roa* ☎ *3/2210–0670* ⊕ *www.hotel-
manavai.cl ⇲ 30 rooms* ◉ *No meals.*

$$$$ **Hotel O'Tai.** Although the hotel is right in the center of town, its
HOTEL beautiful gardens make you feel like you're miles from anywhere.
Pros: great location; good value for money; views of the ocean. **Cons:**
some of the standard rooms could do with an update; bar not open
at night; no free Wi-Fi. $ *Rooms from: 121000 pesos* ⊠ *Av. Te Pito
o Te Henua s/n, Hanga Roa* ☎ *3/2210–0250* ⊕ *www.hotelotai.com
⇲ 40 rooms* ◉ *Breakfast.*

$$$$ **Hotel Taha Tai.** Open and airy, this hotel seems to have sunlight
HOTEL streaming in from everywhere. **Pros:** rooms are spacious, clean, and
comfortable; staff are friendly and helpful; private bungalows are a
nice option. **Cons:** a 10-minute walk from the center of town; small
bathrooms; basic decor. $ *Rooms from: 147200 pesos* ⊠ *Av. Apina
Nui s/n, Hanga Roa* ☎ *3/2255–1192* ⊕ *www.hoteltahatai.cl ⇲ 30
rooms, 10 bungalows* ◉ *Breakfast.*

$$$$ **Hotel Taura'a.** This lovely hotel on Hanga Roa's main street is owned
HOTEL by Bill Howe, an Australian, and his Rapanui wife, Edith Pakarati. **Pros:**
good breakfasts—they're different every day of the week—and coffee
(a rarity on Easter Island); airport transport available; owners run a
tour service. **Cons:** no pool; no air-conditioning in rooms; decor a bit
basic. $ *Rooms from: 113000 pesos* ⊠ *Av. Atamu Tekena s/n, Hanga
Roa* ☎ *9/6622–8129 ⇲ 17 rooms* ◉ *Breakfast.*

$$$ **Hotel Tupa.** Owned and managed by local archaeologist and former
HOTEL governor of the island, Sergio Rapu, this hotel has three kinds of
rooms: budget, garden, and beach. **Pros:** lovely location overlook-
ing the Hanga Roa bay; owner-run tour service; very connected and
knowledgeable owners. **Cons:** long, twisty hallways; some areas not
in perfect repair; no Wi-Fi in rooms. $ *Rooms from: 91350 pesos*
⊠ *Taniera Teave s/n, Hanga Roa* ☎ *3/2210–0225* ⊕ *www.tupahotel.
com ⇲ 40 rooms* ◉ *Breakfast.*

$$$$ **Mana Nui Inn.** This collection of seven rooms and three simply fur-
B&B/INN nished cabins are laid out in a grassy yard with paved paths, banana
trees, and blooming bougainvillea and hibiscus. **Pros:** friendly owner;
ocean-view breakfast room; lots of homey touches. **Cons:** the 10-minute
walk from town on a dirt road gets muddy in the rain; breakfast is only
included in rooms and not cabins; basic accommodations. $ *Rooms
from: 123000 pesos* ⊠ *Sector Tahai s/n, Hanga Roa* ☎ *3/2210–0811*
⊕ *www.mananui.cl ⇲ 10 rooms* ◉ *Breakfast.*

$$$$
HOTEL
⊡ **Puku Vai.** Within walking distance of the airport, Puka Vai is clean, airy, bright, and spacious. **Pros:** clean, efficient construction; owners have a good relationship with taxi companies, car rental, and tour agencies. **Cons:** 15-minute walk from town; few elements of Easter Island culture present. $ *Rooms from: 148000 pesos* ⊠ *Hotu Matu'a s/n, near the airport, Hanga Roa* ☎ *3/2255–1838* ⊕ *www.pukuvaihotel. com* ⤳ *13 rooms* |◯| *Breakfast.*

$$$$
RESORT
⊡ **Vai Moana.** The name of this lodging means "blue sea," and it's easy to see why, as a long stretch of azure ocean can be seen from just about everywhere. **Pros:** owner is interested in the living culture (not just historical culture) of Easter Island; very art-centric; great views. **Cons:** a 15-minute walk from the center of Hanga Roa; basic rooms; no Wi-Fi in rooms. $ *Rooms from: 115000 pesos* ⊠ *Av. Policarpo Toro s/n, Hanga Roa* ☎ *3/2210–0626* ⊕ *www.vai-moana.cl* ⤳ *26 rooms* |◯| *Breakfast.*

NIGHTLIFE AND PERFORMING ARTS

NIGHTLIFE

You're in for a late night if you want to sample the scene in Hanga Roa. There are two sets of nightlife: one that goes on at restaurants until around midnight, and a second one that starts at around 2 am at the few clubs on the island. These are mainly frequented by locals, as tourists tend to go to sleep early to make the most of daylight hours on the island.

DANCE CLUBS

Piriti. This dance club close to the airport appeals to both locals and visitors. The soundtrack is a mix of Latin and pop early in the night; later on at around 2 or 3 am, live bands play. There are two parts of the club: the outer, rustic part, and the inside, which could be a disco anywhere in the world. ⊠ *Av. Hotu Matu'a s/n, Easter Island.*

Toroko. On weekends, the younger set heads to Toroko, a dance club a stone's throw from the beach. You won't need directions—just follow the thumping disco beat. This is where young Rapanui come to dance and enjoy a few beers. ⊠ *Av. Policarpo Toro s/n, Hanga Roa.*

PERFORMING ARTS
DANCE SHOWS

Ballet Cultural Kari Kari. The island's longest-running dance group spends most of the show getting members of the audience on the stage to dance with the performers. It's done with little technology (no flashing lights or microphones), and is in a fairly small space on the main street. Members also perform a very good *sau sau,* the island's famous courtship dance. They perform on Monday, Tuesday, Thursday, and Saturday. ⊠ *Av. Atamu Tekena, Hanga Roa* ☎ *32/2210–0767* ⤳ *15000 pesos.*

Grupo Maori Tupuna. One of three traditional dance groups on the island, this one performs at the Vai te Mihi cultural center next to Au Bout du Monde restaurant. Part of every show involves willing participants pulled up onto the stage to dance with the traditional Rapanui dancers. The dances are supposed to be among the least influenced by other Polynesian styles, and feature traditionally (read: barely) clad, body-painted

men and women telling stories through dance. They perform Monday, Thursday, and Saturday. ■TIP➔ **If you'd like to be pulled up on stage, increase your chances by sitting in the front row for 199,000 pesos extra (you need a reservation).** ✉ *Vai te Mihi, Policarpo Toro s/n, Hanga Roa* ☎ *3/2255–0556* ⊕ *www.maoritupuna.cl* ✉ *From 16000 pesos.*

Peu Tepuna Tongariki (Tongariki Cultural Center). This cultural center is aimed at the island's school-aged children, to keep Rapa Nui traditions, including songs, poetry, and dance, alive. Performances are frequent (often by the children themselves) and free to the public. You can usually find the kids rehearsing in the garden outside. ✉ *Policarpo Toro s/n, Hanga Roa* ☎ *3/2210–0226* ⊕ *www.culturarapanui.cl.*

Te Ra'ai. This dance group brings participants off the tourist track right to the host's home, where there is traditional face painting, an explanation of the ceremonial type of cooking called *umu par*, and finally a dance performance put on by the Haha Varua Collective (you can also just attend the dance performance). The dance is traditional Polynesian and Rapa Nui and interactive with the audience. Performances take place Monday, Wednesday, and Friday. ✉ *Av. Kaituoe s/n, Hanga Roa* ☎ *3/2255–1460* ⊕ *www.teraai.com* ✉ *Dance performance 20000 pesos; performance and dinner 50000 pesos.*

SPORTS AND THE OUTDOORS

Haka pei, or sliding down hillsides on banana trunks, is one of the more popular activities during the Tapati Rapa Nui festival. Another is racing across the reed-choked lake that's hidden inside the crater of Rano Raraku.

Visitors who take to the water usually prefer swimming at one of the sandy beaches or snorkeling near one of the offshore islets. The astroturf soccer pitch is usually filled with teams practicing, but if it's an informal game, you might be able to join in.

DIVING

The crystal-clear waters of the South Pacific afford great visibility for snorkelers and divers. Dozens of types of colorful fish as well as turtles flourish in the warm waters surrounding the island's craggy volcanic rocks. Some of the most spectacular underwater scenery is at Motu Nui and Motu Iti, two adjoining islets just off the coast.

Mike Rapu Diving Center. This center arranges first dives (no certification necessary) for 40,000 pesos, and for those with NAUI or PADI certification (they are a PADI partner), it's 35,000 pesos. A photographer can be provided for an additional 10,000 pesos. Snorkeling trips are available as well for 25,000 pesos. ✉ *Caleta de Hanga Roa, Hanga Roa* ☎ *3/2255–1055* ⊕ *www.mikerapu.cl.*

Orca Diving Center. This place will provide a boat, guide, and gear for 55,000 pesos per person or 45,000 for a night dive. The outfitter also rents snorkeling masks and fins if you'd like to go out independently, but the guided boat trips let you see much more. ✉ *Caleta de Hanga Roa, Hanga Roa* ☎ *3/2255–0877, 3/2255–0375* ⊕ *www.orcadivingcenter.cl.*

HIKING

The breezes that cool the island even in the middle of summer make this a perfect place for hikers, and because such a large part of the island is a national park, you can walk more or less wherever you want without worrying if you might be on private property. Be careful, though, as the sun is much stronger than it feels. Slather yourself with sunblock and take plenty of water.

Numerous hikes leave from Hanga Roa. You can take a short walk roughly north along the coast and onto the grassy field before it takes you to Ahu Tahai. More strenuous is the hike on the unpaved road from Ahu Te Peu to the seven moai at Ahu Akivi, about 10 km (6 miles) north of town. One of the most rewarding treks is along a rough dirt path on the northern coast that leads from Ahu Te Peu to Playa Anakena. The six-hour journey around Terevaka takes you past many undisturbed archaeological sites that few tourists ever see. CONAF (the parks service) recommends a guide for this route. If you insist on going without one, pick up an *Easter Island Trekking Map* at any local shop.

HORSEBACK RIDING

One popular way to see the island is on horseback, which typically costs around 35,000 pesos for a half-day or 70,000 pesos for a group tour with a guide, but you may get a discount if you pay cash. Trips past Ahu Akivi and up to Terevaka (the highest point on the island) are popular, and full-day tours of the north coast are also possible. Some outfitters may offer multiday tours, with a minimum of two passengers.

MOUNTAIN BIKING

Mountain biking is a great way to get around Easter Island's sights. Most car rental agencies also rent mountain bikes for 11,000 pesos for 8 hours or 13,000 pesos for 24 hours. Remember to pack water, as you won't find much (if any) outside of town.

SURFING

When the weather is right, you can find surfboard rentals near Playa Pea for about 20,000 pesos for the board or 25,000 pesos with a lesson. Alicia Ika, at Easter Island Travel, teaches surfing as well. Vendors at beachfront stands near SERNATUR (the local tourism office) can also take you out.

SHOPPING

Souvenir shops line Hanga Roa's two main streets, Avenida Atamu Tekena and Avenida Te Pito o Te Henua. The most popular souvenirs and gifts are reproduction stone moai in a variety of formats (keychain size to the length of your forearm), and shell necklaces. Go farther afield to the sculptor Bene Tuki's workshop at Aukara Lodge or visit Amaya Vai's art studio two streets back from Atamu Tekena on Tu'u Koihu.

Amaya Art Gallery. Originally from mainland Chile, Amaya Vai has lived on Easter Island for almost 30 years and creates colorful paintings, some on paper made from local products. Her work tends toward natural designs, flowers, and some from the petrolyphs found on the island, in acrylic, watercolor, and mixed media. ⊠ *Tu'u Koihu, Hanga Roa* ☎ *9/9136–6102.*

Feria Municipal. The Feria Municipal, the town's fruit, vegetable, and fish market, also houses a crafts section. ⊠ *Av. Atamu Tekena s/n, Hanga Roa* ☎ *3/2255–2049.*

Mercado Artesanal. Next to the church is the Mercado Artesanal, a large building filled with crafts stands. Here, local artisans whittle wooden moai and string together seashell necklaces. It's open Monday–Saturday 9–8 (until 7 May–October) and Sunday 10–1:30. When specific vendors step out briefly, they cover their wares with a blanket. ⊠ *Ara Roa Rakei s/n, Hanga Roa* ☎ *3/2255–1346.*

Rapa Nui Natural Products. This quirky natural products store is filled with everything from local soaps and scented oils to jams (such as guava), candy, and the world's healthiest honey. English, Spanish, and German are spoken. ■TIP➔ **Pick up some white and dark chocolate moai here.** ⊠ *Ana o Ruhi s/n, Hanga Roa* ☎ *3/2255–2084* ⊕ *www. rapanui-shop.com.*

Vai a Heva. This small store stocks professional and souvenir-quality carvings of moai and other important symbols of the Rapa Nui culture, as well as jewelry made of shells and bone, pearls from the South Pacific, and imitation *rongo rongo* (glyph writing system) tablets on wood. ⊠ *Te Pito O Te Henua s/n, Hanga Roa* ☎ *3/2255–1385.*

THE SOUTHEASTERN CIRCUIT

Most archaeological sites on the island line the southeastern coast. Driving along it, you pass many ahus, where moai once stood, most of which have not been reconstructed and most likely never will be. Busloads of tourists hurry past these on their way to Rano Raraku, the volcanic quarry where around 400 moai wait in stony silence, and Ahu Tongariki, where 15 moai famously stand in line.

Heading out of Hanga Roa along the island's southern coast, the road leads to Ahu Vaihu, with its eight fallen moai; Ahu Akahanga, the burial site of the island's first ruler; and Ahu Hanga Tetenga's large, unfinished moai. Farther along, at Ahu Tongariki, encounter your first standing moai, but that's just a warm-up for the jackpot at Rano Raraku quarry where the moai were carved out of the hillside. Grab a guide to take you to the caverns of Ana O Keke and Ana O Neru; then, visit the magnetic "navel of the world" stone at Ahu Te Pito Kura and the beautiful, pink-sand Playa Ovahe before ending the day at Playa Anakena.

EXPLORING

Ahu Akahanga. Tradition holds that this is the burial site of Hotu Matu'a, the first of the island's rulers. The 13 moai lying facedown on the ground once stood on the four long stone platforms. There are also several "boat houses," oblong, boat-shaped outlines that were once the foundations of homes. ⊠ *5 km (5 miles) east of Ahu Vaihu on coastal road, Easter Island.*

Ahu Hanga Tee (Vaihu). Eight fallen moai lie face down in front of this ahu, the first you encounter on the southern coastal road. Three reddish

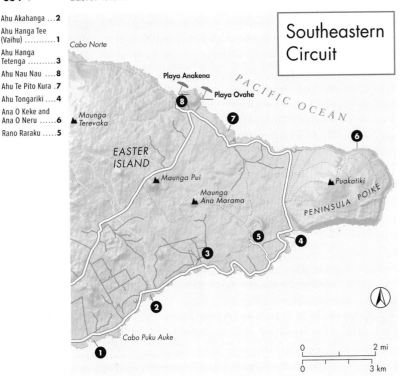

Southeastern Circuit

topknots are strewn around them. Even after the ahu was destroyed, this continued to be a burial chamber, shown by the rocks piled on the toppled moai. ⊠ *10 km (6 miles) southeast of Hanga Roa on coastal road, Easter Island.*

Ahu Hanga Tetenga. Lying here in pieces is the largest moai ever transported to a platform, measuring nearly 10 meters (33 feet). The finishing touches were never made to its eye sockets, so researchers believe it fell while being erected. ⊠ *3 km (2 miles) east of Ahu Akahanga on coastal road, Easter Island.*

Ahu Nau Nau. Beside the swaying palm trees on Playa Anakena stand the island's best-preserved moai on Ahu Nau Nau. Buried for centuries in the sand, these five statues were protected from the elements. Minute details of the carving—delicate lips, flared nostrils, gracefully curved ears—are still visible. On their backs, fine lines represent belts. It was here during a 1978 restoration that a white coral eye was found, leading researchers to speculate that all moai once had them; a replica of that eye is now on display at the Museo Antropológico Padre Sebastián Englert; the original is in storage for safe-keeping following an attempted robbery. Staring at Ahu Nau Nau is a solitary moai on nearby Ahu Ature Huki, the first statue to be re-erected on its ahu. Thor Heyerdahl conducted this experiment in 1955 to test whether the

techniques islanders claimed were used to erect the moai could work. It took 12 islanders nearly three weeks to lift the moai into position using rocks and wooden poles. ✉ *1 km (about 1 mile) west of Playa Ovahe, at Playa Anakena, Easter Island.*

Ahu Te Pito Kura. The largest moai ever successfully erected stands at Ahu Te Pito Kura. Also here is the perfectly round magnetic stone (believed to represent the navel of the world) that Hotu Matu'a is said to have brought with him when he arrived on the island. ✉ *9 km (6 miles) north of Ahu Tongariki on coastal road, Easter Island.*

Fodor'sChoice ★ **Ahu Tongariki.** One of the island's most breathtaking sights is Ahu Tongariki, where 15 moai stand side by side on a 200-foot-long ahu, the longest ever built. Tongariki was painstakingly restored after being destroyed for the second time by a massive tidal wave in 1960. These moai, some whitened with a layer of sea salt, have holes in their extended earlobes that might have once been filled with chunks of obsidian. They face an expansive ceremonial area where you can find petroglyphs of turtles and fish, and the entrance is guarded by a single moai, which has traveled to Japan and back for exhibition. ■TIP➔ **The perfect morning sunrise behind the moai at Tongariki lasts only from December 21 to March 21.** ✉ *2 km (1 mile) east of Rano Raraku on coastal road, Easter Island.*

Ana O Keke and Ana O Neru. Legend has it that young women awaiting marriage were kept here in the Caves of the Virgins so that their skin would remain as pale as possible. You need an experienced guide to find the caverns, which are accessible only on foot and hidden in the cliffs along the coast. Take a flashlight to see the haunting petroglyphs of flowers and fish thought to have been carved by these girls. ✉ *Reached via dirt road through ranch on Poike, Poike.*

Fodor'sChoice ★ **Rano Raraku.** When it comes to moai, this is the motherlode. Some 400 have been counted at the quarry of this long-extinct volcano, both on the outer rim and clustered inside the crater. More than 150 are unfinished, some little more than faces in the rock. Among these is El Gigante, a monster measuring 22 meters (72 feet). Also here is Moai Tukuturi, the only statue in a kneeling position; it's thought to predate most others. Look out also for the moai with a three-masted boat carved on its belly; the anchor is a turtle. CONAF checks but does not sell tickets here. They are sold at the airport upon arrival or at the CONAF office near the Anthropological Museum, paid in dollars. The same ticket gives access to all archeological sights on the island. ■TIP➔ **It's best to buy your national parks ticket upon arrival at the airport.** ✉ *5 km (3 miles) east of Ahu Hanga Tetenga on coastal road, Easter Island* 💲 *US$80 for non-Chileans.*

BEACHES

FAMILY Fodor'sChoice ★ **Playa Anakena.** Easter Island's earliest settlers are believed to have landed on idyllic Playa Anakena. Legend has it that the caves in the cliffs overlooking the beach are where Hotu Matu'a dwelled while constructing his home. It's easy to see why the island's first ruler might have selected this spot: on an island ringed by rough volcanic rock, Playa

Anakena is the widest swath of sand. Ignoring the sun-worshipping tourists are five beautifully carved moai standing on nearby Ahu Nau Nau. On the northern coast, Playa Anakena is reachable by a paved road that runs across the island or by the more circuitous coastal road. For 20,000 pesos (or ask your hotel to negotiate a better price), a taxi takes you from Hanga Roa and picks up at the agreed-upon time later. ■**TIP→** **Bring snacks and water from Hanga Roa. Amenities:** parking; toilets. **Best for:** snorkeling; swimming. ⊠ *Easter Island.*

Playa Ovahe. A lovely strip of pink sand, Playa Ovahe isn't as crowded as neighboring Playa Anakena. The fact that most tourists pass it by is what makes this secluded beach so appealing. Families head here on weekends for afternoon cookouts, but swimming is dangerous because of strong undercurrents. The cliffs that tower above the beach were once home to many of the island's residents. Locals proudly point out caves that belonged to their relatives. ■**TIP→** **Come in the morning if you want to sunbathe; the position of the sun means that by afternoon, you'll be sitting in the shade. Amenities:** none. **Best for:** solitude; sunrise. ⊠ *Easter Island.*

THE WESTERN CIRCUIT

On the western tip of the island are the cave paintings of Ana Kai Tangata and the petroglyphs near the ceremonial village of Orongo. You'll also be treated to a spectacular view of the crater lake inside the long-dormant volcano of Rano Kau as well as the three islets or motu in the ocean below.

Divide this circuit into two, with a break for lunch in Hanga Roa. In the morning, start by visiting Ahu Vinapu, with its unusual masonry, before heading up the Rano Kau volcano, with its water-filled crater and wonderful views, to Orongo. On the way down, consider stopping by the cave paintings at Ana Kai Tangata. After lunch, visit the Puna Pau quarry, origin of the moai's red topknots, and the inland moai at Ahu Huri a Urenga, before carrying on north to Ahu Akivi's seven moai, the underground caverns at Ana Te Pahu, and the remains of the so-called boat houses at Ahu Te Peu.

EXPLORING

Ahu Akivi. These seven stoic moai—believed by some to represent explorers sent on a reconnaissance mission by King Hotu Matu'a— are among the few that gaze out to sea, though researchers say they face a ceremonial site. Others say the oral history of the explorers has morphed into stories about the moai, and that there isn't an actual connection between statues and explorers. Archaeologists William Mulloy and Gonzalo Figueroa restored the moai in 1960. ⊠ *Past Puna Pau on road branching north from paved road to Playa Anakena, Easter Island.*

Ahu Huri a Urenga. One of the few ahus to be erected inland, Ahu Huri a Urenga appears to be oriented toward the winter solstice. Its lonely moai is exceptional because it has two sets of hands, the second carved above the first. Archaeologists believe this is because the lower set was

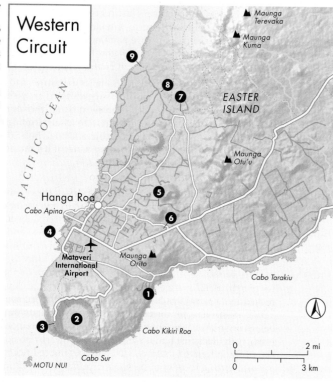

Western
Circuit

Maunga
Terevaka

Maunga
Kuma

9

8
7

EASTER
ISLAND

Maunga
Otu'u

Maunga
Orito

Hanga Roa

Cabo Apina

5

6

4

Mataveri
International
Airport

Cabo Tarakiu

1

3 **2**

Cabo Kikiri Roa

MOTU NUI

Cabo Sur

PACIFIC OCEAN

| 0 | | 2 mi |
| 0 | | 3 km |

damaged during transport to the ahu. ✉ *3 km (2 miles) from Av. Hotu Matu'a on paved road to Playa Anakena, Easter Island.*

Ahu Te Peu. As at Ahu Vinapu, the tightly fitting stones at the unrestored Ahu Te Peu recall the best work of the Incas. The foundations for several boat-shape houses, including one that measures 40 meters (131 feet) from end to end, are clearly visible. From here you can begin the six-hour trail-less hike around the island's northern coast to Playa Anakena. CONAF (national parks service) recommends a guide, and you may walk past many of the archaeological sites without one. ✉ *Past Ana Te Pahu on gravel road branching north from paved road to Playa Anakena, Easter Island.*

Ahu Vinapu. The appeal of this crumbled ahu isn't apparent until you notice the fine masonry on the rear wall. Anyone who has seen the ancient Inca city of Machu Picchu in Peru can note the similar stonework. This led Norwegian archaeologist Thor Heyerdahl to theorize that Rapa Nui's original inhabitants may have sailed here from South America. By now it has been established that the first settlers were Polynesian, though evidence points to contact with South America early on. The moai here still lie where they were toppled, including one face up, which is unusual, as most were knocked face-down. ✉ *Southeast of Hanga Roa along Av. Hotu Matu'a, Easter Island.*

Ana Kai Tangata. A small sign just past the entrance of Hotel Iorana points toward Ana Kai Tangata, a seldom-visited cavern on the coast that holds the island's only cave paintings. Directly over your head are images of red and white birds in flight. Dramatic cliffs shelter the cave from the crashing surf. ⊠ *South of Hanga Roa, Easter Island.*

Ana Te Pahu. A grove of banana trees marks the entrance to these underground caverns that once served as dwellings. Partly shielded from the blazing sun, a secret garden of tropical plants thrives in the fissure where the caves begin. Below ground is a passage leading to a second cave where the sunlight streams through a huge hole. ■TIP➔ **Bring a flashlight, and be careful of dripping water if it's rained in the past week.** ⊠ *Past Ahu Akivi on gravel road branching north from paved road to Playa Anakena, Easter Island.*

Fodor's Choice ★ **Orongo.** A small museum kickstarts the story of the ceremonial village of Orongo, likely constructed in the late 1600s and used by locals until 1866; the 48 oval stone houses here were occupied only during the ceremony honoring the god Make-Make. Many of these abodes have since been reconstructed. The high point of the annual event was a competition in which prominent villagers sent servants to Motu Nui, the largest of three islets just off the coast. The first servant to find an egg of the sooty tern, a bird nesting on the islets, would swim back with the prize tucked in a special headdress. His master would become the *tangata manu*, or birdman, for the next year. The tangata manu was honored by being confined to a cave until the following year's ceremony. Dozens of petroglyphs depicting birdlike creatures cover nearby boulders along the rim of Rano Kau. CONAF checks, but does not sell tickets here. They are sold at the airport or at the CONAF office near the Padre Sebastián Englert Anthropological Museum, and are good for all archaeological sites on the island. ⊠ *South of Hanga Roa on Rano Kau, Easter Island* ⊠ *US$60 for non-Chileans.*

Puna Pau. Scoria, the reddish stone used to make topknots for the moai, was once excavated at this quarry. About two dozen finished topknots are still here. ■TIP➔ **The views of the island from the top of the hill are worth the short climb.** ⊠ *Off road branching north from road to Playa Anakena, signposted "Puna Pau" and "Ahu Akivi,", Easter Island.*

Fodor's Choice ★ **Rano Kau.** This huge volcano on the southern tip of the island affords wonderful views of Hanga Roa. The crater, which measures a mile across, holds a lake nearly covered over by reeds. The opposite side of the crater has crumbled a bit, revealing a crescent of the deep blue ocean beyond. Entering the crater is forbidden, except in signposted areas. It is protected, and the ground is unstable. ⊠ *South of Hanga Roa, Easter Island.*

TRAVEL SMART CHILE

Visit Fodors.com for advice, updates, and bookings

GETTING HERE AND AROUND

▌ AIR TRAVEL

Traveling between the Americas is usually less tiring than traveling to Europe or Asia because you cross fewer time zones. Miami (8½ hour flight), New York (11 hours), Dallas (9½ hours), and Atlanta (9½ hours) are the primary departure points for flights to Chile from the United States, though there are also frequent flights from Los Angeles, Boston, Washington, D.C., and other cities. Other international flights often connect through other major South American cities like Buenos Aires and Lima.

Arriving from abroad, Australian citizens must pay US$117 on entry as a "reciprocity fee." Credit cards and cash are accepted for payment. Since 2014, U.S. and Canadian citizens are exempt from paying the fee.

Always confirm international flights at least 72 hours ahead of the scheduled departure time. This is particularly true for travel within South America, where flights tend to operate at full capacity and passengers often have a great deal of baggage to process.

LAN offers the LANPASS program, where customers can earn miles (actually, kilometers) by flying with LAN or other members of the One World Alliance (American Airlines, British Airways, Qantas, and others) or through car rentals or hotel stays with affiliated companies.

AIRPORTS

Most international flights head to Santiago's Arturo Merino Benítez International Airport (SCL) about 30 minutes west of the city. Domestic flights leave from the same terminal. Expect long customs queues on arrival and remember that it's prohibited to bring fresh produce (dairy, fruit, meat, jams) into Chile.

Airport Information Comodoro Arturo Merino Benítez International Airport. ✉ *Pudahuel, Pudahuel* ☎ *2/2690–1796* ⊕ *www.nuevopudahuel.cl.*

FLIGHTS

The largest North American carrier is American Airlines, which has direct service from Dallas, New York, and Miami; Delta flies from Atlanta. United flies from Houston. LATAM flies nonstop to Santiago from Miami, Dallas, and New York and with a layover in Lima from Los Angeles. Air Canada flies nonstop from Toronto. Most of the major Central and South American airlines also fly to Santiago, including Aerolíneas Argentinas, Avianca (Taca), and Copa.

LATAM and Sky have daily flights from Santiago to most cities throughout Chile.

▌ BOAT TRAVEL

Boats and ferries are the best way to reach many places in Chile, such as Chiloé and the Southern Coast. They are also a great alternative to flying when your destination is a southern port like Puerto Natales or Punta Arenas. Navimag and Transmarchilay are the two main companies operating routes in the south. They both maintain excellent websites with complete schedule and pricing information. You can buy tickets online, or book through a travel agent.

Boat Information Navimag. ☎ *2/2869–9900 in Santiago* ⊕ *www.navimag.com.* **Transmarchilay.** ☎ *65/270–700 in Puerto Montt* ⊕ *www.transmarchilay.cl.*

CRUISES

Several international cruise lines, including Celebrity Cruises, Holland America, Norwegian Cruise Lines, Princess Cruises, and Silversea Cruises, call at ports in Chile or offer cruises that start in Chile. Itineraries typically start in Valparaíso, following the coastline to the southern archipelago and its fjords. Some companies, such as Holland America, have itineraries that include Antarctica. Victory Adventure Expeditions and Adventure Associates are tour companies that offer cruises to Antarctica.

You can spend a week aboard the luxury *Skorpios,* which leaves from Puerto Montt and sails through the archipelago to the San Rafael glacier. In Punta Arenas, you can board *Cruceros Australis* and motor through the straights and fjords to Ushuaia and Cape Horn.

Chilean Cruise Lines Cruceros Australis.
☎ *800/743–0119 in North America, 2/2840–0100 in Chile* ⊕ *www.australis.com.* **Skorpios.**
☎ *305/285–8416 in U.S., 2/2477–1900 in Chile* ⊕ *www.skorpios.cl.*

Cruise Tour Companies Adventure Associ-ates. ☎ *61/2–6355–2022 Australia* ⊕ *www. adventureassociates.com.* **Victory Adventure Expeditions.** ☎ *61/222–7098 in Chile* ⊕ *www. victory-cruises.com.*

▌ BUS TRAVEL

Long-distance buses are safe and affordable. Luxury bus travel between cities costs about one-third that of plane travel and is more comfortable, with wide reclining seats, movies, drinks, and snacks. The most expensive service offered by most bus companies is called *cama premium* or simply *premium,* which indicates that the seats fold down into an almost horizontal bed. Service billed as *semi-cama, ejectivo,* and *cama* are other comfortable alternatives.

Without a doubt, the low cost of bus travel is its greatest advantage; its greatest drawback is the time you need to cover the distances involved. A trip from Santiago to San Pedro de Atacama, for example, takes about 23 hours. Be sure to get a receipt for any luggage you check beneath the bus and keep a close watch on belongings you take on the bus.

Tickets are sold online, at bus company offices, and at city bus terminals. Note that in larger cities there may be several bus terminals (Santiago has three major terminals, for example), and some small towns may not have a terminal at all: pick-ups and drop-offs are at the bus line's office, invariably in a central location.

Expect to pay with cash, as only the large bus companies such as Pullman Bus and Turbus accept credit cards.

Reservations are recommended all year round, but are essential for holidays and travel during high season. You should arrive at terminals extra early for travel during peak seasons when the terminals can be packed with travelers.

Pullman Bus and Turbus are two of the best-known companies in Chile. Their websites are Spanish-only.

Bus Information Pullman Bus. ☎ *600/320–3200* ⊕ *www.ventapasajes.cl.* **Turbus.**
☎ *600/2822–7500* ⊕ *www.turbus.cl.*

▌ CAR TRAVEL

Certain areas of Chile are most enjoyable when explored on your own in a car, such as the beaches of the Central Coast, the wineries of the Central Valley, the ski areas east of Santiago, and the Lake District in the south.

Drivers in Chile are not particularly aggressive, but neither are they particularly polite. Some common sense rules of the road: Before you set out, establish an itinerary. Be sure to plan your daily driving distance conservatively, as distances are always longer than they appear on maps. Google maps is sufficient but not always faultless, so seek out a CHILETUR guide and map (Spanish only) from a gas station if you are heading off the radar. Bring enough change to pay tolls on highways.

Obey posted speed limits and traffic regulations, and keep your lights on during the day as well as the night. And above all, if you get a traffic ticket, don't argue—and plan to spend longer than you want settling it.

GASOLINE

Most service stations are
attendant and accep
are open 24 ho
American b
ies, b

Attendants will often ask you to glance at the zero reading on the gas pump to show that you are not being cheated. A small tip is expected if attendants clean your windows or check your oil level.

PARKING

You can park on the street, in parking lots, or in parking garages in Santiago and large cities in Chile. Expect to pay anywhere from 500 to 3,000 pesos approximately, depending on the length of time. For street parking, a parking attendant (either official or unofficial) will be there to direct and charge you. You should tip the unofficial parking attendants, called *cuidadores de autos*; 1,000 pesos is a reasonable tip for two to three hours.

ROAD CONDITIONS

Between May and September, roads and underpasses can flood when it rains. It can be dangerous, especially for drivers who don't know their way around. Avoid driving if it has been raining for several hours.

The Pan-American Highway runs from Arica in the far north down to Puerto Montt and Chiloé, in the Lake District. Much of it is now two-lane and bypasses most large cities. The Carretera Austral, a mostly unpaved road that runs for 1,240 km (770 miles) as far as Villa O'Higgins in Patagonia, starts just south of Puerto Montt. A few stretches of the road are broken by water and are linked only by car ferries (check ferry schedules before departing, as schedules may change depending on the time of year). Some parts of the Carretera can be washed away in heavy rain; it is wise to consult local police for details.

Many cyclists ride without lights in rural areas, so be careful when driving at night, particularly on roads without street lighting. This also applies to horse- and bull-drawn carts.

ROADSIDE EMERGENCIES

El Automóvil Club de Chile offers low-cost road service and towing in and around the main cities to members of the Chile Association of America

(AAA). But if you don't speak Spanish, you're probably better off contacting your rental agency, or having your hotel concierge communicate with the automobile club or your rental agency.

Auto Club Information El Automóvil Club de Chile. ☏ *600/464–4040* ⊕ *www.automovilclub.cl.*

RULES OF THE ROAD

Keep in mind that the speed limit is 60 kph (37 mph) in cities and 120 kph (75 mph) on highways unless otherwise posted. The police regularly enforce the speed limit, handing out *partes* (tickets) to speeders.

Right-hand turns are prohibited at red lights unless otherwise posted. Seat belts are mandatory in the front and back of the car, and police give on-the-spot fines for not wearing them. There is a zero tolerance alcohol policy for drivers in Chile. If the police find you with more than 0.3 milligrams of alcohol in your blood, you will be considered to be driving under the influence and arrested.

Plan to rent snow chains for driving on the road up to the ski resorts outside Santiago. Police will stop you and ask if you have them—if you don't, you will be forced to turn back.

It is obligatory to keep your headlights lit during the day and night.

CAR RENTAL

On average it costs 25,000 pesos (about US$50) a day to rent the cheapest type of car with unlimited mileage. Vehicles with automatic transmissions tend to be more luxurious and can cost twice as much as the basic rental with manual transmission. Many companies list higher rates (about 20%) for the high season (December–February). Hertz, Avis, and Budget have locations at Santiago's airport and elsewhere around the country.

To access some of Chile's more remote regions, it may be necessary to rent a four-wheel-drive vehicle, which can cost 80,000 pesos (about US$165) a day. You

can often get a discounted weekly rate. The rate you are quoted usually includes insurance, but make sure to find out exactly what the insurance covers and to ask whether there is a deductible you will have to pay in case of an accident. You can usually pay slightly more and have no deductible. An obligatory extra that all companies charge for rentals out of or returning to Santiago is TAG, an electronic toll-collection system used in that city. This charge is currently about 5,000 pesos (about US$10) per day. If you don't want to drive yourself, consider hiring a car and driver through your hotel concierge, or make a deal with a taxi driver for some extended sightseeing at a longer-term rate.

Major international rental companies (Alamo, Avis, Budget, Hertz, National) operate in Chile, but local companies are sometimes a cheaper option. Rosselot, Bengolea, and Chilean are reputable local companies with offices in Santiago and other cities.

To drive legally in Chile you need an international driver's license as well as your valid national license, although car rental companies and police do not often enforce this regulation. The minimum age for driving is 18, but to rent a car you have to be 22 (or 23 depending on the company).

Local Agencies Bengolea. ✉ *Av. Francisco Bilbao 1047, Providencia* ☎ *2/2790–0200* ⊕ *www.bengolea.cl.* **Chilean Rent-a-Car.** ✉ *Bellavista 0183, Bellavista* ☎ *2/2963–8760* ⊕ *www.chileanrentacar.cl.* **Rosselot.** ✉ *Comodoro Arturo Merino Benítez International Airport, Santiago* ☎ *9/6207–1468* ⊕ *www.rosselot.cl.*

TRAIN TRAVEL

Good train service is a thing of the past in Chile, though there is still limited service from Santiago to cities south of the capital. TrenCentral offers two daily departures between Santiago and Chillán (and points in between), with additional bus service to Concepción. Reservations can be made via the company's website (English version available) or in person.

Train Contacts Tren Central. ✉ *Av. Libertador Bernardo O'Higgins , 3170, Anden 6, Santiago Centro* ⊹ *Estacion Central* ☎ *2/2585–5000* ⊕ *www.trencentral.cl.*

ESSENTIALS

ACCOMMODATIONS

The lodgings that we list are the cream of the crop in each price category. All hotels listed have private bath unless otherwise noted. In Chile, a national rating system is used, classifying hotels on a scale of one to five stars. The rating is determined by SERNATUR, the national tourism agency, and is based on the services offered and the physical attributes of the hotel and its property. The system is somewhat perfunctory, however, and doesn't allow for true qualitative analysis.

It's always good to look at any room before accepting it. Expense is no guarantee of charm or cleanliness, and accommodations can vary dramatically within one hotel. If you ask for a double room, you'll get a room for two people, but you're not guaranteed a double mattress. If you'd like to avoid twin beds, ask for a *cama matrimonial*.

Hotels in Chile do not charge taxes (known as IVA) to foreign tourists. When checking the price, ask for the *precio extranjero, sin impuestos* (foreign rate, without taxes). If you are traveling to Chile from neighboring Peru or Bolivia, expect a significant jump in prices. Also, note that you can always ask for a *descuento* (discount) out of season or sometimes midweek during high season.

HOTELS

Chile's urban areas and resort areas have hotels that come with all of the amenities that are taken for granted in North America and Europe, such as room service, a restaurant, and a swimming pool. Elsewhere you may not have television or a phone in your room, although you will usually find them somewhere in the hotel. Rooms that have a private bath may have only a shower, and in some cases, there will be a shared bath in the hall. In all but the most upscale hotels you may be asked to leave your key at the reception desk whenever you leave.

RESIDENCIALES

Private homes with rooms for rent, *residenciales* (also called *hospedajes*) are a unique way to get to know Chile, especially if you're on a budget. (Many rooms cost less than US$30 per night.) Sometimes residenciales and hospedajes are small, with basic accommodations and not necessarily in private homes. Some will be shabby, but others can be substantially better than hotel rooms. Staying in these types of accommodations allows you to interact with locals (though they are unlikely to speak English). Contact the local tourist office for details on residenciales and hospedajes.

MOTELS

If you spot motels while road tripping in Chile—often recognizable by their palm trees and love hearts signage—you should think twice before heading in for a night cap. Motels in Chile are usually pay-per-hour love hotels and range from seedy or shabby to colorful themed rooms.

COMMUNICATIONS

INTERNET

Chileans are generally savvy about the Internet, and in most cities you'll find Wi-Fi spots and Internet cafés. Connection fees at cybercafés are about 1,000 to 2,000 pesos for an hour, and Wi-Fi is always free for paying customers. In Santiago there are also many free Wi-Fi hubs, particularly in metro stations.

If you're planning to bring a laptop or tablet into the country, check the manual first to see if it requires a converter. Newer laptops and tablets will require only an adapter plug. If you are planning on using your cell phone, check your service providers' roaming charges before leaving. Local pay-as-you-go phone cards are available at phone shops and kiosks in most towns, although they are unlikely

to offer Internet service unless you sign on for a long-term contract.

While most people in Chile walk around the streets with smart phones in hand, carrying anything valuable could make you a target for thieves. Act with caution by concealing your devices in a generic bag and keeping it close to you at all times, especially on public transportation.

PHONES

The good news is that you can now make a direct-dial telephone call from virtually any point on earth. The bad news? You can't always do so cheaply, and good luck getting a signal in Chile's national parks. Calling from a hotel is almost always the most expensive option; hotels usually add surcharges to calls, particularly international ones. Chile has many call centers, and you can also purchase calling cards at street kiosks or phone shops. Mobile phones are usually cheaper than calling from your hotel.

The country code for Chile is 56. When dialing a Chilean number from abroad, drop the initial 0 from the local area code. The area code is 2 for Santiago, 55 for Antofagasta and San Pedro de Atacama, 58 for Arica, 42 for Chillán, 57 for Iquique, 51 for La Serena, 65 for Puerto Montt, 61 for Puerto Natales and Punta Arenas, 45 for Temuco, 63 for Valdivia, and 32 for Valparaíso and Viña del Mar. Mobile phone numbers are preceded by the number 9 (sometimes you'll see it written as 09). Dial the "0" first if you're calling from a landline within Chile; otherwise, drop it if you're calling from abroad or from another cell phone in Chile.

CALLING WITHIN CHILE

A 100-peso coin is required to make a local call in a public phone booth, or 200 pesos to dial a cell phone. It is increasingly difficult to find pay phones in Chile, since most people now use cell phones. *Centros de llamadas* (call centers), small phone shops with individual booths, are common and are priced fairly. Simply step into any available booth and dial the number. The charge will be displayed on a monitor near the phone.

You can reach directory assistance in Chile by calling 103. English-speaking operators are not available.

To call a landline from a cell phone, dial "0" and then the city code and number.

For national long-distance calls, you may need to dial a long-distance carrier code (try 123 or 133—two commonly used codes) then the area code and number.

CALLING OUTSIDE CHILE

The country code is 1 for the United States and Canada, 61 for Australia, 64 for New Zealand, and 44 for the United Kingdom. You must add a zero before these country codes when dialing from Chile, and may also be required to add an international service provider (or "carrier") code before the 0 (try commonly used codes 123 or 133). Using a Telefónica/Movistar phone (the top service provider in Chile), dial 800/207–300 to reach MCI international operator assistance.

MOBILE PHONES

If you have a multiband phone (some countries use frequencies other than those used in the United States), and your service provider uses the world-standard GSM network (as do T-Mobile, AT&T, and Verizon), you can probably use your phone abroad. Roaming fees can be steep, however, and overseas you normally pay the toll charges for incoming calls. It's almost always cheaper to send a text message than to make a call.

If you just want to make local calls, consider buying a new SIM card (note that your provider may have to unlock your phone for you to use a different SIM card) and a prepaid service plan in the destination. You'll then have a local number and can make and receive local calls at local rates. If your trip is extensive, you could also simply buy a new cell phone in your destination, as the initial cost will be offset over time. SIM cards and prepaid service plans can be purchased at offices of

the major cell phone companies in Chile, like Entel and Movistar.

CUSTOMS AND DUTIES

You may bring into Chile up to 400 cigarettes, 500 grams of tobacco, 50 cigars, 2.5 liters of alcoholic beverages, and gifts to the value of US$300. Prohibited items include plants, fruits and vegetables, seeds, meat, and honey. Spot checks take place at airports and border crossings, and fines are common. It's always better to declare all animal and vegetable products you are carrying, rather than risk being fined.

Visitors, although seldom questioned, are prohibited from leaving with handicrafts and souvenirs worth more than US$500. You are generally prohibited from taking antiques out of the country without special permission.

EATING OUT

The restaurants that we list are the cream of the crop in each price category. It is customary to tip 10% in Chile; tipping above this amount is uncommon among locals. Credit cards are generally accepted in big cities (although the tip should preferably be left in cash), but when visiting smaller towns and rural areas, always bring enough cash.

Chileans like to eat three staple meals a day, if not more. You can expect a typically light breakfast to be served between 7 am and 10 am; lunch is usually eaten between 1 pm and 3 pm; and dinner won't usually be served before 8 pm, often running till midnight. Reservations are advisable but generally not necessary unless you are visiting a popular restaurant or are taking a large group.

The dress code for lunch is fairly casual, but eating out in the evening is often a special occasion for locals. You should dress like you care. Chileans can be conservative with dress; if you bare too much flesh you might attract scornful looks or meandering gazes.

ELECTRICITY

Unlike the United States and Canada—which have a 110- to 120-volt standard—the current in Chile is 220 volts, 50 cycles alternating current (AC). The wall sockets accept plugs with two round prongs.

Consider making a small investment in a universal adapter, which has several types of plugs in one lightweight, compact unit. Most laptops and mobile phone chargers are dual voltage (i.e., they operate equally well on 110 and 220 volts) and so require only a plug adapter. These days the same is true of small appliances such as hair dryers. Always check labels and manufacturer instructions to be sure. Don't use 110-volt outlets marked "for shavers only" for high-wattage appliances such as hair dryers.

EMERGENCIES

The numbers to call in case of emergency are the same all over Chile and work from both cell phones and landlines. Operators will generally not speak English, however; your embassy is your best bet for most emergencies.

Foreign Embassies United States. ⊠ *Av. Andrés Bello 2800, Las Condes* ☎ *2/2330–3000* ⊕ *cl.usembassy.gov.*

General Emergency Contacts Ambulance. ☎ *131.* **Fire.** ☎ *132.* **Police.** ☎ *133.*

HEALTH

From a health standpoint, Chile is one of the safer countries in which to travel. To be on the safe side, take the normal precautions you would traveling anywhere in South America.

In Santiago there are several large private *clínicas*, and many doctors speak at least a bit of English. In most other large cities there are one or two private clinics where you can be seen quickly. Generally, *hospitales* (hospitals) or *postas* (centers for emergency first aid) are for those receiving free or heavily subsidized treatment,

and they are often crowded with long lines of patients waiting to be seen.

Altitude sickness—which causes shortness of breath, nausea, and splitting headaches—may be a problem in some areas of the North or hiking in the Andes. The best way to prevent *puna* is to ascend slowly and acclimate, spending at least one night at a lower altitude if possible. If symptoms persist, return to lower elevations. Over-the-counter medications to help prevent altitude sickness are available. If you have high blood pressure and/or a history of heart trouble, you should check with your doctor before traveling to high altitudes.

When it comes to air quality, Santiago ranks as one of the most polluted cities in the world. The reason is that the city is surrounded by two mountain ranges that keep the pollutants from cars and other sources from dissipating. The pollution is worst in winter.

What to do? First, avoid strenuous outdoor exercise and the traffic-clogged streets when air-pollution levels are high. Santiago has a wonderful subway that will whisk you to almost anywhere you want to go. Spend your days in museums and other indoor attractions. And take advantage of the city's many parks.

Visitors seldom encounter problems with drinking the water in Chile. Almost all drinking water receives proper treatment and is unlikely to produce health problems. But its high mineral content—it's born in the Andes—can disagree with some people. In any case, a wide selection of still (*sin gas*) and sparkling (*con gas*) bottled waters is available.

Food preparation is strictly regulated by the government, so outbreaks of food-borne diseases are rare. But use common sense. Don't risk restaurants where the hygiene is suspect or street vendors where the food is allowed to sit around at room temperature.

SHOTS AND MEDICATIONS

Although no vaccinations are required for entry into Chile, all travelers to Chile should get up-to-date tetanus, diphtheria, and measles boosters, and a hepatitis A inoculation is recommended. Children traveling to Chile should have current inoculations against mumps, rubella, and polio. Always check with your doctor before leaving.

If you have traveled to an area at risk for yellow fever transmission within five days before entering Chile, you may be asked to show proof that you have been vaccinated against the disease.

According to the Centers for Disease Control and Prevention (CDC), there's some risk of food-borne diseases such as hepatitis A and typhoid. There's no risk of contracting malaria, but a very limited risk of dengue fever, another insect-borne disease, on Easter Island. The best way to avoid insect-borne diseases is to prevent insect bites by wearing long pants and long-sleeve shirts and by using insect repellents with DEET. If you plan to visit remote regions or stay for more than six weeks, check with the CDC's International Travelers Hot Line.

The Hanta virus, a serious respiratory disease, exists in Chile, particularly in rural areas where rats are found (long-tailed rats are the most common carriers). Pay particular attention to warnings in campgrounds, and make sure to keep camping areas as clean as possible

Chile is one of the few South American countries free of Zika.

OVER-THE-COUNTER REMEDIES

Mild cases of diarrhea may respond to Imodium (known generically as loperamide). Pepto Bismol is not available in Chile (though Maalox is), so pack some chewable tablets. Drink plenty of purified water or tea—chamomile (*manzanilla* in Spanish) is a soothing option. You will need to visit a *farmacia* (pharmacy) to purchase medications such as *aspirina* (aspirin), which are readily available.

▮ HOURS OF OPERATION

Most retail businesses are open weekdays 10–7 and Saturday until 2; most are closed Sunday. Some businesses and shops in regional cities and towns close for lunch between 1 and 3 or 4, though this is becoming less common. Supermarkets often stay open until 10 or 11 pm, as do large malls.

Most banks are open weekdays 9–2. *Casas de cambio* are open weekdays 9–7 and weekends 9–3 for currency exchange.

Gas stations in major cities and along the Pan-American Highway tend to stay open 24 hours. Others follow regular business hours.

Most tourist attractions are open during normal business hours during the week and for at least the morning on Saturday and Sunday. Most museums are closed Monday.

HOLIDAYS

New Year's Day (January 1), Good Friday (April), Labor Day (May 1), Day of Naval Glories, or the Battle of Iquique (May 21), Corpus Christi (June), Feast of St. Peter and St. Paul (June), Feast of the Vírgen de Carmen (July 16), Assumption of the Virgin Mary (August 15), Independence Day (September 18), Army Day (September 19), Discovery of the Americas or Columbus Day (October 12), Day of the Evangelic and Protestant Churches (October 31), All Saints Day (November 1), Immaculate Conception (December 8), and Christmas (December 25).

Many shops and services are open on most of these days, but transportation is always heavily booked up on and around the holidays. The two most important dates in the Chilean calendar are September 18 and New Year's Day. On these days shops close and public transportation is reduced to the bare minimum or is nonexistent. Trying to book a ticket around these dates will be difficult unless you do it well in advance.

▮ MAIL

The postal system (CorreosChile) is efficient and reliable; on average, letters take about 10 days to reach the United States, Europe, Australia, and New Zealand. They will arrive sooner if you send them *prioritario* (priority) post. You can send them *certificado* (registered), in which case the recipient will need to sign for them. Vendors often sell stamps at the entrances to larger post offices, which can save you a potentially long wait in line—the stamps are valid, and selling them this way is legal. There are no mailboxes in Chile. You must mail letters from a post office or through your hotel. Post offices are open from 9 to 6 or 7 on weekdays and from 10 to 2 on Saturday.

Postage on regular letters and postcards to the United States and Europe costs around 700 pesos but depends on the destination and origin.

▮ MONEY

Unlike in some other South American countries, U.S. dollars are rarely accepted in Chile. (The exception is larger hotels, where prices are often quoted only in dollars.) Credit cards and traveler's checks are accepted in most resorts and in many shops and restaurants in major cities, though you should always carry some local currency for minor expenses like taxis and tipping. Once you stray from the beaten path, you can often pay only with pesos.

Typically you will pay 1,000 pesos for a cup of coffee, 1,500 pesos for a glass of beer in a bar, 1,500 pesos for a ham sandwich, and 2,000 pesos for an average museum admission.

Prices throughout this guide are given for adults. Substantially reduced fees are almost always available for children, students, and senior citizens.

▮TIP→ **Banks never have every foreign currency on hand, and it may take as long as a week to order. If you're planning to**

exchange funds before leaving home, don't wait until the last minute.

ATMS AND BANKS

Automatic teller machines, or *cajeros automáticos,* dispense only Chilean pesos. They are ubiquitous but, although most have instructions in English, not all are linked to the Plus and Cirrus systems. Look at the stickers on the machine to find the one you need. Most ATMs in Chile have a special screen—accessed after entering your PIN—for foreign-account withdrawals. In this case, you need to select the "extranjeros/foreign clients" option from the menu. ATMs offer excellent exchange rates because they are based on wholesale rates offered only by major banks.

Your own bank will probably charge a fee for using ATMs abroad; the foreign bank you use may also charge a fee. Nevertheless, you'll usually get a better rate of exchange at an ATM than you will at a currency-exchange office or even when changing money in a bank. And extracting funds as you need them is a safer option than carrying around a large amount of cash.

■ TIP→ PINs with more than four digits are not recognized at ATMs in Chile. If yours has five or more, remember to change it before you leave.

Banco de Chile is probably the largest national bank; its website ⊕ *www. bancochile.cl* lists branches and ATMs by location if you click on the *surcursales* (locations) link, then the *cajeros automáticos* link. Banco Santander (⊕ *www.santander.cl*) is another fairly common option.

CREDIT CARDS

It's a good idea to inform your credit-card company before you travel, especially if you're going abroad and don't travel internationally often. Otherwise, the credit-card company might put a hold on your card owing to unusual activity—not a good thing halfway through your trip. Record all your credit-card numbers—as well as the phone numbers to call if your cards are lost or stolen—in a safe place, so you're prepared should something go wrong. Both MasterCard and Visa have general numbers you can call (collect if you're abroad) if your card is lost, but you're better off calling the number of your issuing bank, since MasterCard and Visa usually just transfer you there.

If you plan to use your credit card for cash advances, you'll need to apply for a PIN at least two weeks before your trip. Although it's usually cheaper (and safer) to use a credit card abroad for large purchases (so you can cancel payments or be reimbursed if there's a problem), note that some credit-card companies *and* the banks that issue them add substantial percentages to all foreign transactions, whether they're in a foreign currency or not. Check on these fees before leaving home, so there won't be any surprises when you get the bill.

Dynamic currency conversion programs are becoming increasingly widespread. Merchants who participate in them are supposed to ask whether you want to be charged in dollars or the local currency, but they don't always do so. And even if they do offer you a choice, they may well avoid mentioning the additional surcharges. The good news is that you *do* have a choice. And if this practice really gets your goat, you can avoid it entirely thanks to American Express; with its cards, DCC simply isn't an option.

Credit cards are widely accepted in hotels, restaurants, and shops in most cities and tourist destinations. Fewer establishments accept credit cards in rural areas. You may get a slightly better deal if you pay with cash (ask about discounts), and some businesses charge an extra fee for paying with a non-Chilean credit card.

Chile has implemented a security system for credit-card transactions called PinPass, which requires you to enter a previously established PIN in a hand-held machine. As a foreigner, you should explain that

you haven't activated your PinPass, and the merchants should be able to process the transaction with your signature.

Credit card receipts in Chile have a line for signatures as well as for national ID numbers, or RUTs. You may be asked to put your passport number on this second line; otherwise, you can leave it blank.

CURRENCY AND EXCHANGE

The peso is the unit of currency in Chile. Note that Chilean currency may be written as $1,000 or CLP$1,000. Chilean bills are issued in 1,000, 2,000, 5,000, 10,000, and 20,000 pesos, and coins come in units of 1, 5, 10, 50, 100, and 500 pesos. Note that getting change for larger bills, especially from small shopkeepers and taxi drivers, can be difficult. Make sure to get smaller bills when you exchange currency. Always check exchange rates in newspapers or online for the most current information; at this writing, the exchange rate was approximately 625 pesos to the U.S. dollar. As long as the U.S. dollar hovers around 500 pesos it's easy to figure out how much you're paying for something in Chile: simply multiply what you're being charged by two and remove three zeros (e.g., a 10,000-peso dinner is about US$20).

Common to Santiago and other mid- to large-size cities are *casas de cambio,* or money-changing stores. Naturally, those at the airport will charge premium rates for convenience's sake. It may be more economical to change a small amount for your transfer to the city, where options are wider and rates more reasonable. Note that exchange houses will not accept damaged dollar notes.

The U.S. State Department warns travelers that Chilean banks, casas de cambio, and businesses may refuse US$100 bills due to past problems with counterfeiting. Chilean banks and police officers have been trained by the U.S. Secret Service to identify counterfeit bills, but some places still won't accept them. If you plan to exchange U.S. currency, bring bills smaller than US$50.

▌PACKING

You'll need to pack for all seasons when visiting Chile, no matter what time of year you're traveling. Outside the cities, especially in the Lake District and Southern Chile, long-sleeve shirts, long pants, socks, sneakers, a hat, a light waterproof jacket, a bathing suit, and insect repellent are all essential. Light colors are best, since mosquitoes avoid them. If you're visiting Patagonia or the Andes, bring a jacket and sweater or a fleece pullover. A high-factor sunscreen is essential at all times, especially in the far south where the ozone layer is much depleted.

▌PASSPORTS AND VISAS

While traveling in Chile you might want to carry a copy of your passport and leave the original in your hotel safe. If you plan on paying by credit card you will often be asked to show identification (the copy of your passport or a driver's license, for example). Citizens of the United States, Canada, Australia, New Zealand, and the United Kingdom need only a passport to enter Chile for up to three months. Keep hold of the customs slip you receive on arrival; you'll need to hand it over when you leave.

▌SAFETY

The vast majority of visitors to Chile never experience a problem with crime. Violent crime is a rarity; far more common is pickpocketing or thefts from purses, backpacks, or rental cars. Be on your guard in crowded places, especially markets and festivals. It's best to avoid wearing flashy jewelry, and handling money in public. Always remain alert for pickpockets, and take particular caution when walking alone at night, especially in the larger cities.

Volcano climbing is a popular pastime in Chile, with Volcán Villarrica, near Pucón, and Volcán Osorno the most popular. But some of these mountains are also among

South America's most active volcanoes. CONAF, the agency in charge of national parks, cuts off access to any volcano at the slightest hint of abnormal activity. Check with CONAF before heading out on any hike in this region.

Many women travel alone or in groups in Chile with no problems. Chilean men are less aggressive in their machismo than men in other South American countries (they will seldom, for example, approach a woman they don't know), but it's still an aspect of the culture (they will make comments when a woman walks by). Single women should take caution when walking alone at night, especially in larger cities.

In the event of an earthquake in Chile, exercise common sense (don't take elevators and move away from heavy objects that may fall, for example) and follow instructions if you are in a public place (metro, museum, etc.). If you are in a coastal location, listen for tsunami sirens, or simply follow the tsunami evacuation route (indicated by signs in the streets) or head to high ground.

Contacts CONAF. ☎ 45/229–8149 in Temuco, 2/2328–0300 in Santiago ⊕ www.conaf.cl.

▍TAXES

A 19% value-added tax (called IVA in Chile) is added to the cost of most goods and services in Chile; often you won't notice because it's included in the price. When it's not, the seller gives you the price plus IVA. At many hotels you may receive an exemption from the IVA if you pay in American dollars or with a credit card in U.S. dollars.

▍TIME

All of Chile is in the same time zone: UTC/GMT minus four hours (or three hours during daylight saving time). Daylight saving time in Chile begins in October and ends in March.

Depending on the time of year, New York is the same time as Santiago or 1 to 2 hours behind, and Los Angeles is 3 to 5 hours behind. London is 3 to 5 hours ahead of Santiago, and New Zealand and Australia are 16 to 17 and 14 to 15 hours ahead respectively.

▍TIPPING

In restaurants and for tour guides, a 10% tip is usual, unless service has been deficient. Taxi drivers don't expect to be tipped. Visitors need to be wary of parking attendants. During the day, they should only charge what's on their portable meters when you collect the car but, at night, they will ask for money—usually 1,000 pesos—in advance. This is a racket but, for your car's safety, it's better to comply.

▍VISITOR INFORMATION

The national tourist office, Servicio Nacional de Turismo, or SERNATUR, with branches in Santiago and major tourist destinations around the country, is often the best source for general information about a region. The SERNATUR office in Santiago is open 9–6 weekdays, and 10–2 on Saturday. The hours of SERNATUR's regional offices vary, but can be found on its website.

Municipal tourist offices, often located near a central square, usually have better information about their town's sights, restaurants, and lodging. Many have shorter hours or close altogether during low season, however.

Contact SERNATUR. ☎ 2/2731–8378 ⊕ www.sernatur.cl.

SPANISH VOCABULARY

ENGLISH	SPANISH	PRONUNCIATION

BASICS

English	Spanish	Pronunciation
Yes/no	Sí/no	see/no
Please	Por favor	pore fah-**vore**
May I?	¿Me permite?	may pair-**mee**-tay
Thank you (very much)	(Muchas) gracias	(**moo**-chas) **grah**-see-as
You're welcome	De nada	day **nah**-dah
Excuse me	Con permiso	con pair-**mee**-so
Pardon me	¿Perdón?	pair-**dohn**
Could you tell me?	¿Podría decirme?	po-dree-ah deh-**seer**-meh
I'm sorry	Lo siento	lo see-**en**-toh
Good morning!	¡Buenos días!	**bway**-nohs **dee**-ahs
Good afternoon!	¡Buenas tardes!	**bway**-nahs **tar**-dess
Good evening!	¡Buenas noches!	**bway**-nahs **no**-chess
Good-bye!	¡Adiós!/¡Hasta -stah luego!	ah-dee-**ohss**/ah **lwe**-go
Mr./Mrs.	Señor/Señora	sen-**yor**/sen-**yohr**-ah
Miss	Señorita	sen-yo-**ree**-tah
Pleased to meet you	Mucho gusto	**moo**-cho **goose**-toh
How are you?	¿Cómo está usted?	**ko**-mo es-**tah** oo-**sted**
Very well, thank you.	Muy bien, gracias.	**moo**-ee bee-**en**, **grah**-see-as
And you?	¿Y usted?	ee oos-**ted**
Hello (on the telephone)	Diga	**dee**-gah

NUMBERS

	Spanish	Pronunciation
1	un, uno	oon, **oo**-no
2	dos	dos
3	tres	tress
4	cuatro	**kwah**-tro
5	cinco	**sink**-oh

6	seis	saice
7	siete	see-**et**-eh
8	ocho	**o**-cho
9	nueve	new-**eh**-vey
10	diez	dee-**es**
11	once	**ohn**-seh
12	doce	**doh**-seh
13	trece	**treh**-seh
14	catorce	ka-**tohr**-seh
15	quince	**keen**-seh
16	dieciséis	dee-es-ee-**saice**
17	diecisiete	dee-**es**-ee-see-**et**-eh
18	dieciocho	dee-**es**-ee-**o**-cho
19	diecinueve	**dee-es**-ee-new-**ev**-eh
20	veinte	**vain**-teh
21	veintiuno	**vain**-te-**oo**-noh
30	treinta	**train**-tah
32	treinta y dos	train-tay-**dohs**
40	cuarenta	kwah-**ren**-tah
43	cuarenta y tres	kwah-**ren**-tay-**tress**
50	cincuenta	seen-**kwen**-tah
54	cincuenta y cuatro	seen-**kwen**-tay **kwah**-tro
60	sesenta	sess-**en**-tah
65	sesenta y cinco	sess-**en**-tay **seen**-ko
70	setenta	se-**ten**-tah
76	setenta y seis	se- t **en**-tay **saice**
80	ochenta	oh-**chen**-tah
87	ochenta y siete	oh-**chen**-tay see-**yet**-eh
90	noventa	no-**ven**-tah
98	noventa y ocho	no-**ven**-tah-**o**-choh
100	cien	see-**en**

101	ciento uno	see-**en**-toh **oo**-noh
200	doscientos	doh-see-**en**-tohss
500	quinientos	keen-**yen**-tohss
700	setecientos	set-eh-see-**en**-tohss
900	novecientos	no-veh-see-**en**-tohss
1,000	mil	meel
2,000	dos mil	dohs meel
1,000,000	un millón	oon meel-**yohn**

COLORS

black	negro	**neh**-groh
blue	azul	ah-**sool**
brown	café	kah-**feh**
green	verde	**ver**-deh
pink	rosa	**ro**-sah
purple	morado	mo-**rah**-doh
orange	naranja	na-**rahn**-hah
red	rojo	**roh**-hoh
white	blanco	**blahn**-koh
yellow	amarillo	ah-mah-**ree**-yoh

DAYS OF THE WEEK

Sunday	domingo	doe-**meen**-goh
Monday	lunes	**loo**-ness
Tuesday	martes	**mahr**-tess
Wednesday	miércoles	me-**air**-koh-less
Thursday	jueves	hoo-**ev**-ess
Friday	viernes	vee-**air**-ness
Saturday	sábado	**sah**-bah-doh

MONTHS

January	enero	eh-**neh**-roh
February	febrero	feh-**breh**-roh
March	marzo	**mahr**-soh

April	abril	ah-**breel**
May	mayo	**my**-oh
June	junio	**hoo**-nee-oh
July	julio	**hoo**-lee-yoh
August	agosto	ah-**ghost**-toh
September	septiembre	sep-tee-**em**-breh
October	octubre	oak-**too**-breh
November	noviembre	no-vee-**em**-breh
December	diciembre	dee-see-**em**-breh

USEFUL PHRASES

Do you speak English?	¿Habla usted inglés?	**ah**-blah oos-**ted** in-**glehs**
I don't speak Spanish	No hablo español	no **ah**-bloh es-pahn-**yol**
I don't understand (you)	No entiendo	no en-tee-**en**-doh
I understand (you)	Entiendo	en-tee-**en**-doh
I don't know	No sé	no seh
I am American/ British	Soy americano (americana)/ inglés(a)	soy ah-meh-ree-**kah**-no (ah-meh-ree-**kah**-nah)/in-**glehs**(ah)
What's your name?	¿Cómo se llama usted?	koh-mo seh **yah**-mah oos-**ted**
My name is . . .	Me llamo . . .	may **yah**-moh
What time is it?	¿Qué hora es?	keh **o**-rah es
It is one, two, three . . . o'clock.	Es la una./Son las dos, tres . . .	es la **oo**-nah/sohn lahs dohs, tress
Yes, please/No, thank you	Sí, por favor/No, gracias	**see** pohr fah-**vor**/no **grah**-see-us
How?	¿Cómo?	**koh**-mo
When?	¿Cuándo?	**kwahn**-doh
This/Next week	Esta semana/ la semana que entra	**es**-teh seh-**mah**-nah/lah seh-**mah**-nah keh **en**-trah
This/Next month	Este mes/el próximo mes	**es**-teh mehs/el **proke**-see-mo mehs

This/Next year	Este año/el año que viene	**es**-teh **ahn**-yo/el **ahn**-yo keh vee-**yen**-ay
Yesterday/today/ tomorrow	Ayer/hoy/mañana	ah-**yehr**/oy/mahn-**yah**-nah
This morning/ afternoon	Esta mañana/ tarde	**es**-tah mahn-**yah**-nah/**tar**-deh
Tonight	Esta noche	**es**-tah **no**-cheh
What?	¿Qué?	keh
What is it?	¿Qué es esto?	keh es **es**-toh
Why?	¿Por qué?	pore **keh**
Who?	¿Quién?	kee-**yen**
Where is . . . ? the train station?	¿Dónde está . . . ? la estación del tren?	**dohn**-deh es-**tah** la es-tah-see-on del trehn
the subway station?	la estación del tren subterráneo?	la es-ta-see-**on** del trehn la es-ta-see-**on** soob-teh-**rrahn**-eh-oh
the bus stop?	la parada del autobus?	la pah-**rah**-dah del ow-toh-**boos**
the post office?	la oficina de correos?	la oh-fee-**see**-nah deh koh-**rreh**-os
the bank?	el banco?	el **bahn**-koh
the hotel?	el hotel?	el oh-**tel**
the store?	la tienda?	la tee-**en**-dah
the cashier?	la caja?	la **kah**-hah
the museum?	el museo?	el moo-**seh**-oh
the hospital?	el hospital?	el ohss-pee-**tal**
the elevator?	el ascensor?	el ah-**sen**-sohr
the bathroom?	el baño?	el **bahn**-yoh
Here/there	Aquí/allá	ah-**key**/ah-**yah**
Open/closed	Abierto/cerrado	ah-bee-**er**-toh/ ser-**ah**-doh
Left/right	Izquierda/derecha	iss-key-**er**-dah/ dare-**eh**-chah
Straight ahead	Derecho	dare-**eh**-choh
Is it near/far?	¿Está cerca/lejos?	es-**tah sehr**-kah/ **leh**-hoss
I'd like . . . a room	Quisiera . . . un cuarto/una habitación	kee-see-ehr-ah oon **kwahr**-toh/ **oo**-nah ah-bee-tah-see-**on**
the key a newspaper	la llave un periódico	lah **yah**-veh oon pehr-ee-**oh**-dee-koh

a stamp	un sello de correo	oon **seh**-yo deh koh-**reh**-oh
I'd like to buy . . .	Quisiera comprar . . .	kee-see-**ehr**-ah kohm-**prahr**
cigarettes	cigarrillos	ce-ga-**ree**-yohs
matches	cerillos	ser-**ee**-ohs
a dictionary	un diccionario	oon deek-see-oh-**nah**-ree-oh
soap	jabón	hah-**bohn**
sunglasses	gafas de sol	**ga**-fahs deh sohl
suntan lotion	loción bronceadora	loh-see-**ohn** brohn-seh-ah-**do**-rah
a map	un mapa	oon **mah**-pah
a magazine	una revista	**oon**-ah reh-**veess**-tah
paper	papel	pah-**pel**
envelopes	sobres	**so**-brehs
a postcard	una tarjeta postal	**oon**-ah tar-**het**-ah post-**ahl**
How much is it?	¿Cuánto cuesta?	**kwahn**-toh **kwes**-tah
It's expensive/ cheap	Está caro/barato	es-**tah kah**-roh/ bah-**rah**-toh
A little/a lot	Un poquito/ mucho	oon poh-**kee**-toh/ **moo**-choh
More/less	Más/menos	mahss/**men**-ohss
Enough/too much/too little	Suficiente/ demasiado/ muy poco	soo-fee-see-**en**-teh/ deh-mah-see-**ah**-doh/**moo**-ee poh-koh
Telephone	Teléfono	tel-**ef**-oh-no
Telegram	Telegrama	teh-leh-**grah**-mah
I am ill	Estoy enfermo(a)	es-**toy** en-**fehr**-moh(mah)
Please call a doctor	Por favor llame a un médico	pohr fah-**vor ya**-meh ah oon **med**-ee-koh
Help!	¡Auxilio! ¡Socorro!	owk-see-lee-oh/ soh-kohr-roh
Fire!	¡Incendio!	en-sen-dee-oo
Caution!/Look out!	¡Cuidado!	kwee-dah-doh

ON THE ROAD

Avenue	Avenida	ah-ven-**ee**-dah
Broad, tree-lined boulevard	Bulevar	boo-leh-**var**
Fertile plain	Vega	**veh**-gah
Highway	Carretera	car-reh-**ter**-ah
Mountain pass	Puerto	poo-**ehr**-toh
Street	Calle	**cah**-yeh
Waterfront promenade	Rambla	**rahm**-blah
Wharf	Embarcadero	em-bar-cah-**deh**-ro

IN TOWN

Cathedral	Catedral	cah-teh-**dral**
Church	Templo/iglesia	**tem**-plo/ee-**glehs**-see-ah
City hall	Casa de gobierno	kah-sah deh go-bee-**ehr**-no
Door, gate	Puerta portón	poo-**ehr**-tah por-**ton**
Entrance/exit	Entrada/salida	en-**trah**-dah/sah-lee-**deh**-dah
Inn, rustic bar, or restaurant	Taverna	tah-**vehr**-nah
Main square	Plaza principal	plah-thah prin-see-**pahl**
Market	Mercado	mer-**kah**-doh
Neighborhood	Barrio	**bahr**-ree-o
Traffic circle	Glorieta	glor-ee-**eh**-tah
Wine cellar, wine bar, or wine shop	Bodega	boh-**deh**-gah

DINING OUT

A bottle of . . .	Una botella de . . .	**oo**-nah bo-**teh**-yah deh
A cup of . . .	Una taza de . . .	**oo**-nah **tah**-thah deh
A glass of . . .	Un vaso de . . .	oon **vah**-so deh
Ashtray	Un cenicero	oon sen-ee-**seh**-roh

Bill/check	La cuenta	lah **kwen**-tah
Bread	El pan	el pahn
Breakfast	El desayuno	el deh-sah-**yoon**-oh
Butter	La mantequilla	lah man-teh-**key**-yah
Cheers!	¡Salud!	sah-**lood**
Cocktail	Un aperitivo	oon ah-pehr-ee-**tee**-voh
Dinner	La cena	lah **seh**-nah
Dish	Un plato	oon **plah**-toh
Menu of the day	Menú del día	meh-**noo** del **dee**-ah
Enjoy!	¡Buen provecho!	bwehn pro-**veh**-cho
Fixed-price menu	Menú fijo o turístico	meh-**noo fee**-hoh oh too-**ree**-stee-coh
Fork	El tenedor	el ten-eh-**dor**
Is the tip included?	¿Está incluida la propina?	es-**tah** in-cloo-**ee**-dah lah pro-**pee**-nah
Knife	El cuchillo	el koo-**chee**-yo
Large portion of savory snacks	Ración	rah-see-**ohn**
Lunch	La comida	lah koh-**mee**-dah
Menu	La carta, el menú	lah **cart**-ah, el meh-**noo**
Napkin	La servilleta	lah sehr-vee-**yet**-ah
Pepper	La pimienta	lah pee-me-**en**-tah
Please give me	Por favor déme	pore fah-**vor deh**-meh
Salt	La sal	lah sahl
Savory snacks	Tapas	**tah**-pahs
Spoon	Una cuchara	**oo**-nah koo-**chah**-rah
Sugar	El azúcar	el ah-**thu**-kar
Waiter!/Waitress!	¡Por favor, señor/señorita!	pohr fah-**vor** sen-**yor**/sen-yor-**ee**-tah

INDEX

PHOTO CREDITS

NOTES

NOTES

Fodor's ESSENTIAL CHILE

Editorial: Douglas Stallings, *Editorial Director*; Margaret Kelly, Jacinta O'Halloran, *Senior Editors*; Kayla Becker, Alexis Kelly, Amanda Sadlowski, *Editors*; Teddy Minford, *Content Editor*; Rachael Roth, *Content Manager*

Design: Tina Malaney, *Design and Production Director*; Jessica Gonzalez, *Production Designer*

Photography: Jennifer Arnow, *Senior Photo Editor*

Maps: Rebecca Baer, *Senior Map Editor*; David Lindroth and Mark Stroud (Moon Street Cartographers), *Cartographers*

Production: Jennifer DePrima, *Editorial Production Manager*; Carrie Parker, *Senior Production Editor*; Elyse Rozelle, *Production Editor*

Business & Operations: Chuck Hoover, *Chief Marketing Officer*; Joy Lai, *Vice President and General Manager*; Stephen Horowitz, *Director of Business Development and Revenue Operations*; Tara McCrillis, *Director of Publishing Operations*; Eliza D. Aceves, *Content Operations Manager and Strategist*

Public Relations and Marketing: Joe Ewaskiw, *Manager*; Esther Su, *Marketing Manager*

Writers: Amanda Barnes, Helen Cordery, Jimmy Langman, Sorrel Moseley-Williams, Margaret Snook

Editor: Amanda Sadlowski, Debbie Harmsen, Alexis Kelly, Jacinta O'Halloran

Production Editor: Jennifer DePrima

1st Edition

ISBN 978-1-64097-038-0

ISSN 2576–0432

All details in this book are based on information supplied to us at press time. Always confirm information when it matters, especially if you're making a detour to visit a specific place. Fodor's expressly disclaims any liability, loss, or risk, personal or otherwise, that is incurred as a consequence of the use of any of the contents of this book.

SPECIAL SALES

This book is available at special discounts for bulk purchases for sales promotions or premiums. For more information, e-mail SpecialMarkets@fodors.com.

PRINTED IN THE UNITED STATES OF AMERICA

10 9 8 7 6 5 4 3 2 1

ABOUT OUR WRITERS

After working as a journalist at British newspapers, **Amanda Barnes** headed to South America in search of sunshine, a real-life Borges fantasy, and mastering the art of a good *asado*. When she isn't trotting around on travel assignments, Amanda is based in Mendoza, Argentina. She is editor of the *Squeeze* magazine and wine guide, and writes for numerous international travel and wine publications. For this edition, she updated the El Norte Grande, The Central Valley, Southern Chilean Patagonia and Tierra del Fuego, and Travel Smart chapters.

Helen Cordery is a former anthropology student and traveler based in Santiago, a city that captured her heart over five years ago. In between raising her two kids, running her own tour company, and writing, she likes to explore Barrio Italia, her favorite area for restaurants and small businesses selling locally made products. You can read about her adventures on her blog, *www.queridarecoleta.com*. She updated the Norte Chico chapter.

Jimmy Langman lives in southern Chile, where he is executive editor of *Patagon Journal*, a magazine about travel, nature, culture, and outdoor sports in the Patagonia region of Chile and Argentina. Since 1998, he has also worked as a freelance journalist, writing regularly for *Newsweek, National Geographic News, Globe and Mail,* the *Independent* (London), and other publications in the United States, Canada, and Britain. Jimmy updated the Lake District, Chiloé, and Southern Coast chapters.

Margaret Snook updated the Central Coast chapter.

Based in Argentina since 2006, award-winning freelance journalist **Sorrel Mosely-Williams** is also a sommelier who writes about luxury and budget travel, food, and wine for an array of publications including *Decanter, Monocle,* the *Guardian,* the *Independent* and *Condé Nast Traveller* among other publications. She updated the Experience, Santiago, and Easter Island chapters this edition.

Santiago Metro Network